WORLD'S COOLEST MOVIE STAR

VOLUME TWO: COMEBACK / PATRIARCH

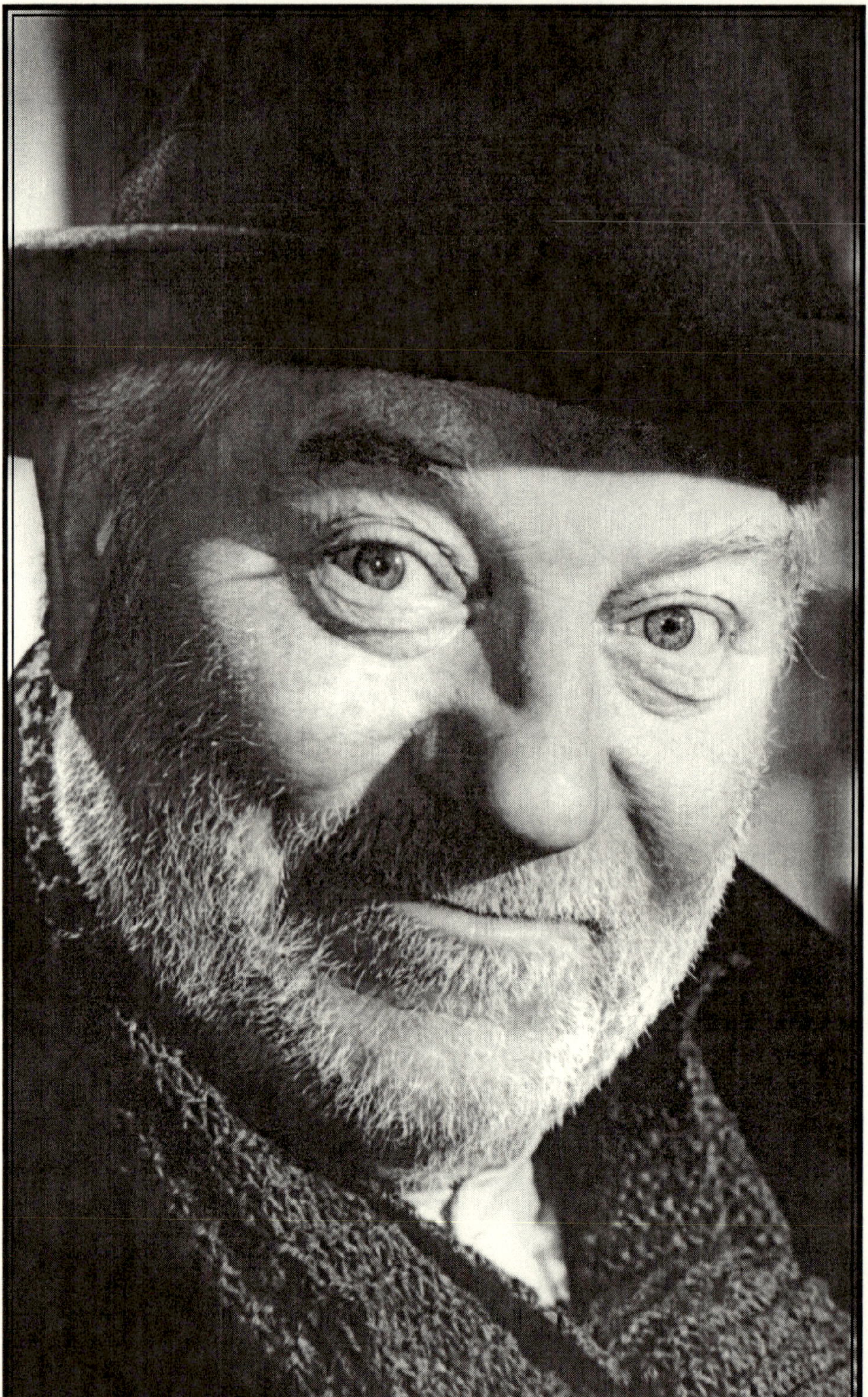

WORLD'S COOLEST MOVIE STAR

THE COMPLETE 95 FILMS (AND LEGEND) OF

Jean Gabin

VOLUME TWO

∽ Charles Zigman ∽

With a Foreword by Brigitte Bardot

ALLENWOOD PRESS

Copyright © 2008 by Charles Zigman
All rights reserved

Printed in the United States of America. No part of this book may be used or reproduced in any manner whatsoever without written permission, except in the case of brief quotations in articles and reviews.

For information contact Allenwood Press
www.allenwoodpress.com
publisher@allenwoodpress.com
www.jeangabinbook.com
author@jeangabinbook.com

ISBN 13: 978-0-9799722-1-8
ISBN 10: 0-9799722-1-5

Library of Congress Control Number: 2007907374
Library of Congress Subject Headings:
Film; Biography; France.

Book design by Michael Kellner

Second Edition (2009)

Published by Allenwood Press
Los Angeles

2.0

This Book is for My Aunt,
Shirley Marilyn Zigman Rothstein
(1927-2004)
Who Introduced Me to the Films of Jean Gabin

WORLD'S COOLEST MOVIE STAR

VOLUME TWO: COMEBACK / PATRIARCH

TABLE OF CONTENTS

Volume Two: Comeback/Patriarch

Foreword by Brigitte Bardot	xv
I On the Set with Jean Gabin	xvii
II Biography, Part Two (1954 to 1976)	xix
III Why I Wrote This Book	xxix

The Films: 'Cycle Five'
1954 — 1976, Film Nos. 47 to 95: The Comeback

More than Half of Jean Gabin's Movies Will Be Made During This Period. After Nine Years of Being Ignored in His Home Country, in 1954, Suddenly, and on the Strength of One Movie, Jean Gabin Will Now Become France's #1 Star Again, for the First Time in Fifteen Years, Since 1941. He Will Remain the Country's Biggest Box-Office Draw for the Remaining Twenty-Two Years of His Career.

Introduction	1
Film Forty Seven: *Touchez pas au grisbi* (1954)	3
Film Forty Eight: *L'Air de Paris* (1954)	11
Film Forty Nine: *Gas-Oil* (1955)	25
Film Fifty: *Napoleon* (1955)	37
Film Fifty One: *Razzia sur la chnouf* (1955)	51
Film Fifty Two: *French Cancan* (1955)	67
Film Fifty Three: *Le Port du desir* (1955)	73
Film Fifty Four: *Chiens perdus sans collier* (1955)	77
Film Fifty Five: *Des gens sans importance* (1955)	85
Film Fifty Six: *Voici le temps des assassins* (1956)	99
Film Fifty Seven: *Le Sang a la tete* (1956)	117
Film Fifty Eight: *La Traversee de Paris* (1956)	127
Film Fifty Nine: *Crime et chatiment* (1956)	137
Film Sixty: *Le Cas du docteur Laurent* (1957)	147
Film Sixty One: *Le Rouge est mis* (1957)	151

Film Sixty Two: *Maigret tend un piege* (1957) — 159
Film Sixty Three: *Les Miserables* (1958) — 165
Film Sixty Four: *Le Desordre et la nuit* (1958) — 171
Film Sixty Five: *En cas de malheur* (1958) — 185
Film Sixty Six: *Les Grandes familles* (1958) — 191
Film Sixty Seven: *Archimede, le clochard* (1959) — 205
Film Sixty Eight: *Maigret et l'affaire Saint-Fiacre* (1959) — 217
Film Sixty Nine: *Rue des Prairies* (1959) — 227
Film Seventy: *Le Baron de l'écluse* (1959) — 241
Film Seventy One: *Les Vieux de la vieille* (1960) — 253
Film Seventy Two: *Le President* (1960) — 267

Bonus Chapter, *"L'Homme qui ralait toujours"* (1960) — 270
—A live, five minute television play, starring Jean Gabin.

Film Seventy Three: *Le Cave se rebiffe* (1961) — 273
Film Seventy Four: *Le Gentleman d'Epsom* (1962) — 289
Film Seventy Five: *Un singe en hiver* (1962) — 293
Film Seventy Six: *Maigret voit rouge* (1963) — 299
Film Seventy Seven: *Melodie en sous-sol* (1963) — 311
Film Seventy Eight: *Monsieur* (1964) — 313
Film Seventy Nine: *L'Age ingrat* (1965) — 323
Film Eighty: *Le Tonnerre de Dieu* (1966) — 337
Film Eighty One: *Du rififi a Paname* (1966) — 351
Film Eighty Two: *Le Jardinier d'Argenteuil* (1967) — 357
Film Eighty Three: *Le Soleil des voyous* (1968) — 367
Film Eighty Four: *Le Pacha* (1968) — 373
Film Eighty Five: *Le Tatoue* (1969) — 377
Film Eighty Six: *Sous le signe du taureau* (1969) — 381
Film Eighty Seven: *Le Clan des Siciliens* (1969) — 387
Film Eighty Eight: *La Horse* (1970) — 393
Film Eighty Nine: *Le Chat* (1971) — 399
Film Ninety: *Le Drapeau noir flotte sur la marmite* (1971) — 403
Film Ninety One: *Le Tueur* (1972) — 423
Film Ninety Two: *L'Affaire Dominici* (1973) — 431
Film Ninety Three: *Deux hommes dans la ville* (1973) — 445
Film Ninety Four: *Verdict* (1974) — 451
Film Ninety Five: *L'Annee sainte* (1976) — 455

Appendix: — 461

IV "Solstice of Mars:" A Poem About Jean Gabin, by Jacques Prevert   463
V "Maintenant je sais" Lyrics to Jean Gabin's 1974 #1 French Song Hit   465
VI Acknowledgements   467
VII How You Can See Jean Gabin Movies on Video (and How I Saw Them)   473
VIII Gabin's Movies, Rated on the Scale of 1 to 10   479
IX Bibliography   483
X Recipe for "Jean Gabin" drink (from *drinksmixer.com*).   491

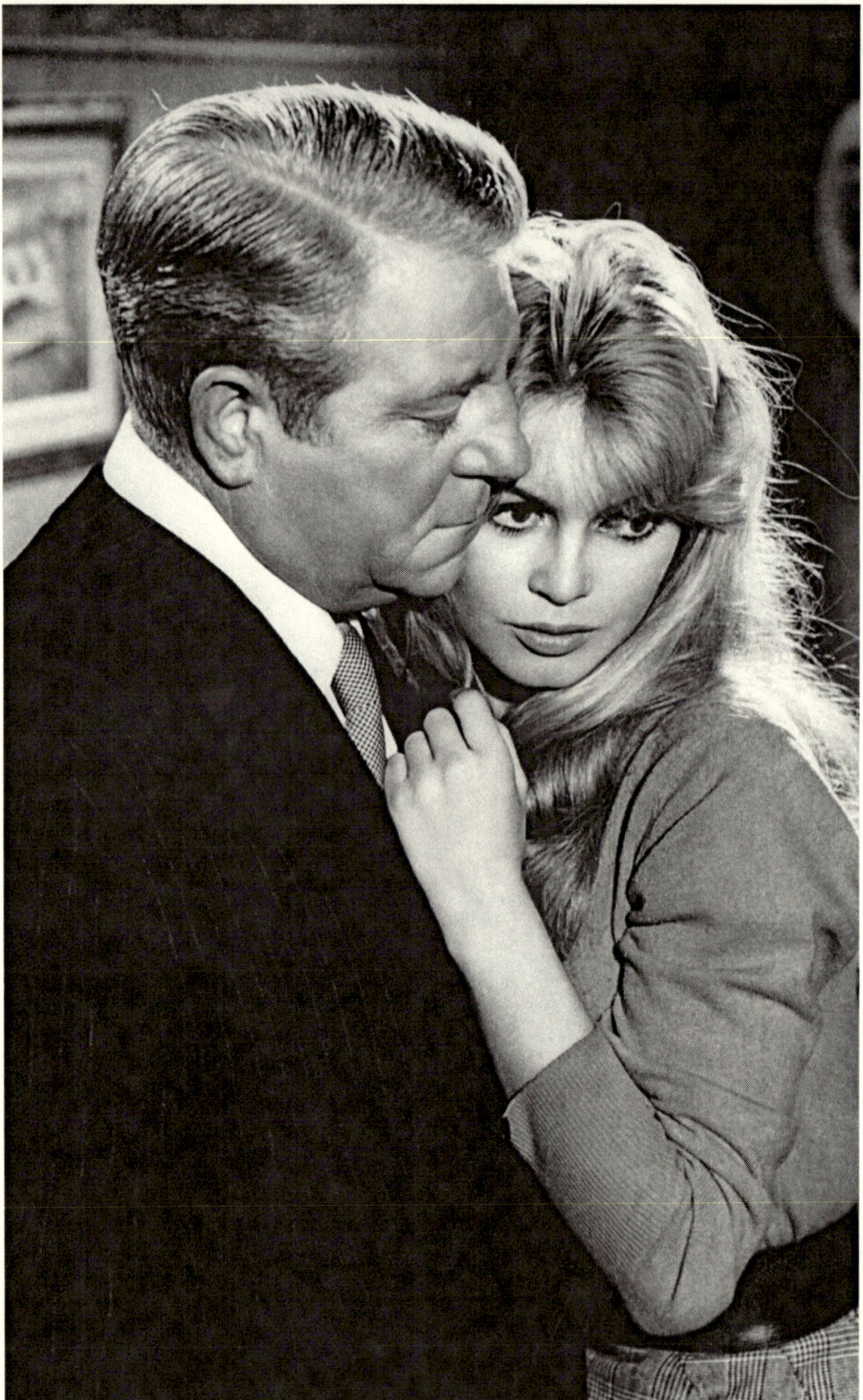

A FOREWORD BY BRIGITTE BARDOT

Co-Star with Jean Gabin in En cas de malheur *(1958)*

Gabin was a man!
A real man —
With his surly side and his tender side, he was such an impressive actor. He played, with brilliance, lovers, fathers, and then grandfathers. Always remaining the same —
— Immutable —
He remains an unforgettable memory for me, a model, an example.
He represents an era, unfortunately, that is gone forever.
He will never be replaced
— And so much the better!

Brigitte Bardot
January, 2006

Gabin with director Marcel Carne on the set of "Le Jour se leve" (1939).

ON THE SET WITH JEAN GABIN

When you read and listen to interviews with the men and women who collaborated with Jean Gabin throughout his career, you'll learn rather quickly that Gabin was pretty much exactly the same on a movie set as he was off of it, which is to say that he was always real (and quiet, and intense), rarely manifesting any signs of pretension. Many directors for whom Gabin worked have always maintained, when they've been interviewed, that Gabin never intellectualized his characters in that way in which 'Method' actors, *a la* Brando, James Dean, and Al Pacino, have often been accused of doing, and yet according to one of the directors of many of Gabin's 1960s' and 1970s' movies, Denys de La Patellière, Gabin would, at the same time, usually stand in front of a mirror for a few moments before the camera rolled, when he thought nobody was looking, to get himself worked-up for a scene, exactly like Robert De Niro's Jake La Motta-character did, at the end of *Raging Bull*.

Gabin, as his collaborators have always maintained, felt that the best way to get people to listen to him, was to speak softly, and the directors who directed him have always spoken about how economical his film acting was—how Gabin seemed to be all about small movements, and about how he was a master of occupying the silent moments, between the dialogue. Gabin became frustrated in the 1960s and 1970s, when young filmmakers, in an effort to try and make their movies appear to be more natural and documentary-like, began physically writing more ellipses ['…'] into the pages of their screenplays, in an effort to make the dialogue trail-off and sound more 'realistic,' but these little written flourishes flustered Gabin because, as he often told anybody who'd listen, he had no idea how to interpret those three little dots! Gabin had always worked with screenwriters who made his dialogue seem natural and never florid to begin with, which is why he only worked with the same handful of writers and directors over and over again throughout his film career, those men who recognized that Gabin always spoke very simply, and very truthfully. In one very sweet television interview which he gave in the early 1960s, Gabin, with a huge smile on his face, told interviewer Leon Zitrone that he loved actors, and when he says it, you can see genuine pride in his eyes. Gabin never would have called acting an art, because that would have been pretentious, and Gabin was always 100%-free of all pretension.

Smooth Criminal. Gabin in his comeback film, "Touchez pas au grisbi."

BIOGRAPHY, PART TWO: 1954 TO 1976

Comeback/Patriarch

THE FILMS, 'CYCLE FIVE'
1954 – 1976, Film Nos. 47 to 95
More than half of Jean Gabin's movies will be made during this period. After nine years of being ignored in his home country, in 1954, suddenly, and on the strength of one movie, Jean Gabin will now become France's No. 1 Star again, for the first time in fifteen years (since 1941). He will remain the country's biggest box-office draw for the remaining twenty-two years of his career.

IN 1954, A YOUNG DIRECTOR NAMED JACQUES BECKER (HE WAS RENOIR'S ASSISTANT DIRECTOR on *Les Bas-fonds* and *La Grande illusion*), who had just directed a very successful film in France, the critically-lauded 1952 drama *Casque d'or* (a 19th-century-set period piece, which starred Simone Signoret) approached an upcoming young actor, the dark-haired and handsome Daniel Gelin, with the idea of Gelin's starring as a super-cool gentleman-gangster in a velvety-smooth *film noir* called *Touchez pas au grisbi* or, in English, *Don't Touch the Loot*. (Gelin, who passed away in 2002, and who had already appeared opposite Jean Gabin in Gabin's two Alcina productions, *Martin Roumagnac* and *Miroir*, is mostly known to American audiences today, for having played 'Louis Bernard,' the *faux*-Arab on the tour-bus who gets Jimmy Stewart and Doris Day into deep trouble, at the beginning of *The Man Who Knew Too Much*, and he was also the real-life father of Maria Schneider, who starred opposite Marlon Brando, in *Last Tango in Paris*.) While Gelin loved *Grisbi's* fast-paced script, he told the film's producer Robert Dorfmann that he felt he was too young to play the film's 'world-weary gentleman-gangster-who's-seen-it-all' and that, in his opinion, a role of that nature could only be played by an older and more seasoned-looking guy. Gelin suggested Gabin and, at first, Dorfmann scoffed, not because Gabin's last twelve movies, which were made between 1946 and 1953, didn't make a red cent in France, but because the producer's second-choice actor, Francois Perier, who was one of France's best-known character actors (he appeared in Fellini's *Nights of Cabiria*, Rene Clement's *Le Samourai*, and Costa Gavras' *Z*) also passed on the role. Jean Gabin (a/k/a, 'the third-choice guy') got the part strictly by default, and the rest, as we say today, is history: Not only is *Touchez pas au grisbi* a terrific gangster picture (it's at least as good as any of America's best *film noir* pictures from the 1950s), but Gabin knew it would be successful because, as he told television interviewer Leon Zitrone in 1959, it represented a continuation of the immensely popular smooth criminal-character whom he had played to the hilt during his late-1930s' heyday, *Pepe Le Moko*. (Yesterday, just like today, people like to see their movie stars doing something familiar, and God help these stars should they ever attempt to play any different kinds of roles!)

With the newfound clout which Jean Gabin received on his home-turf of France, based upon the success of *Touchez pas au grisbi*, producers would now start paying him his asking price of $200,000 per film, and he now found himself, once again, as France's highest paid movie star, just as he had previously been, before the War. He first used his newly reclaimed cache, to hire some of those great Poetic Realist filmmakers who had guided him to the position of 'France's #1 Star,' back in the 1930s: Gabin's *Quai des brumes/Jour se leve* director, Marcel Carne (Gabin had buried the hatchet with Carne, having fought with him eight years before, on *Les Portes de la nuit*) reunited with *The World's Coolest Movie Star* to make the very-well-received-in-France (yet never released in the U.S.) boxing picture, *L'Air de Paris*, although this time, Carne would not be collaborating with his usual writer, Jacques Prevert, because Gabin wanted to use an already-completed script with which he had been very impressed, by a different screenwriter (which, in turn, was based upon an unpublished novel). Even though he would not be associated with this particular picture, Jacques Prevert, too, had ended his feud with Gabin and, in fact, in 1954, inspired by watching Gabin turn-out his masterful performance in *Grisbi*, Prevert even wrote a poem about Jean Gabin, "The Solstice of Mars," which can be found in the appendix of this book.

After *L'Air de Paris*, Gabin hired another old friend from the 1930s to direct him in a picture, as well—Jean Renoir: The two old friends would now team-up for the first time in eighteen years, since *La Bete humaine* back in 1938, to make the wonderful 1955 Technicolor-drama-with-music, *French Cancan* (it's Gabin's only post-World War II movie, besides *Touchez pas au grisbi* and *Le Plaisir* which, at least, at the time of this book's publication, is known to any degree, in the United States), in which Gabin played Henri Danglard, a fictitious version of Joseph Oser, the real-life theater impresario who birthed Paris's famous theatre/nightclub, the *Moulin Rouge*, in 1889. During this same-exact resurgence period, Gabin would additionally re-team, for the first time in fourteen years, with yet another of his great Poetic Realism directors, the stunning visualist Julien Duvivier, for a bizarre murder-melodrama called *Voici le temps des assassins* (*Time of the Assassins*).

Increasingly, as the 1950s evolved into the 1960s, the Gabin pictures which were continuing to achieving theatrical releases in the U.S., and normally only at 'that one art-house in N.Y.C.,' were the ones which had some kind of sexy, exploitable angles. To wit: 1958's *En cas de malheur* (literally, *In Case of Accident*), a picture which would cast Gabin, for the one and only time in his career, opposite another of the screen's great icons, the alluring Brigitte Bardot. In *Malheur*, the now-avuncular-looking Gabin (age 54) played the romantic lead opposite Bardot who, at the age of 24, was more than thirty years his junior, and while these two great actors of different generations enjoyed working together immensely, and while *En cas de malheur* is a very entertaining movie, when Gabin saw the finished product, he was nevertheless embarrassed to watch himself playing the romantic scenes with her, due to their age difference. *En cas de malheur,* then, is an important part of the Gabin movie canon, not just because it's movie history's one and only Gabin-Bardot team-up, but also because it was the last movie, by Jean Gabin's own request, in which he would ever play the romantic lead opposite a much younger woman. (In the movies in which Gabin performed over the next eighteen years—the final eighteen years of his career—he would begin leaving most of *the kissy-face-stuff* to his younger male co-stars; as Gabin once told a friend on that very subject, "Gary Cooper can get away with kissing the young girls—but I can't!") Another exploitable French Jean Gabin production made during this same time period, was 1957's *Le Cas du docteur Laurent* (*The Case of Dr. Laurent*), which was marketed to U.S. art-house audiences very successfully, on the basis of its 'real, live birth scene,' in which actual close-up newsreel footage of a baby's birth was intercut with the face of the film's leading lady (Nicole Courcel), who was merely acting at giving birth. In *Laurent,* Gabin played not a smooth criminal mastermind, but *a new-school gynecologist,* a guy who freaks-out the old and staid residents of a small, provincial town by espousing the relatively new (when the film was made) idea of 'painless childbirth.' (And while *Le Cas du docteur Laurent* was a big art-house hit in America, that picture, too, hasn't seen the light of a projector in the Land of the Free, since it's initial release, more than five decades ago.)

When Gabin teamed-up in 1962 with twenty-nine year-old Jean Paul-Belmondo, in director Henri Verneuil's beautifully-rendered *Un singe en hiver* (*A Monkey in Winter*), these two great movie icons of different generations apparently got along famously, and Gabin even took a paternal attitude toward Belmondo. According to Belmondo, who was interviewed by the French television reporter Philippe Labro in 2004, on the occasion of what would have been Jean Gabin's 100th birthday, Gabin even spent his down-time on the set, grinningly showing the young actor photographs of naked girls! Belmondo told Labro that Gabin always wanted everybody to think that he was 'a regular guy,' adding that Gabin even once told him, "I'm just your average Frenchman," to which Belmondo winkingly replied, "Jean! You have nothing to do with the average Frenchman!"

In the late 1950s, it was already becoming more and more expensive by the year to make movies, and even though French audiences had come to love 'their Gabin' all over again, the producers of these movies also knew realistically that, in order to bolster the box-office take, they would have to start teaming Gabin up with younger talent, and so increasingly, the fatherly-looking Jean Gabin would begin playing all kinds of wise patriarchs and mentors. At first, Gabin reportedly felt threatened by the new generation of younger actors—Brigitte Bardot, Jeanne Moreau, Alain Delon, and Jean Paul Belmondo—but when he worked with them, he discovered that he genuinely liked all of them, that it was mutual (they loved him right back, and wanted to learn from him), and that they were just as dedicated to their craft as he was. But this didn't mean he thought that his own children should become actors: When Gabin's daughter Florence told him once, when she was a teenager, that she was thinking about becoming an actor, he put the immediate kybosh on her idea, telling her that the Gabin name would never help her, and while it seems unnecessarily cruel of him to have told her that, it's no doubt that the sentiment was coming from the right place: Obviously, Gabin didn't want his daughter to get hurt by the sleazy vagaries of the on-again/off-again world of movie fame, a world in which first the public likes you, and then they ignore you: Of course, this is something which Jean Gabin knew about firsthand, after his own French 'public' unceremoniously dumped him for nine years, after the Second World War. Gabin's own wound, although it was now starting to scab-over (*with paper money, for scabs!*) was obviously still pretty fresh.

Not everybody was particularly enamored with Jean Gabin during his big comeback period, however: In 1951, the French critic Andre Bazin (he's the one who, back in the 1930s, had first referred to Gabin as being 'The King of France') co-founded France's most important film journal, *Les Cahiers du cinema* (which literally means, "The Books of Cinema"), the first monthly publication in the world which treated motion pictures as a source of serious study. (In other words, *Cahiers* wasn't just one of those regular old movie magazines which dealt only, and in the most tabloidy manner, with movie stars, *a la* famous American movie magazines of the time, like *Photoplay* and *Movie World*.) In 1953, Bazin's magazine began employing a number of brash, young upstart movie critics, men in their early-to-mid twenties who would all, just a few years later, become film directors in their own right, including Francois Truffaut, Eric Rohmer, and Jean Luc-Godard. (When Rohmer, Truffaut, and Godard began to make movies of their own, beginning in the late '50s, they would very famously become known as France's celebrated New Wave [*nouvelle vague*] of filmmakers, and the movies which they themselves would direct, attempted to 'cinematically overthrow' what they considered to be the tired genre conceits which had been exemplified by the older movies, by presenting a fragmented, proto-MTV style of storytelling, in which their films' narratives very often didn't proceed from 'A to B.'

These younger critics really enjoyed Jean Gabin's Poetic Realist pictures from the 1930s, because those movies were made by directors who, in their collective opinion, really had their own, specific styles: Truffaut and his young colleagues wrote in *Cahiers* that, whenever they watched any old movies which were directed by Jean Renoir, Jean Gremillon, Marcel Carne or Julien Duvivier, they could tell who directed them immediately, just because of each individual picture's distinctive look, tone, and theme. Truffaut and his cohorts felt, however, that many of Gabin's post-War efforts from the '40s and '50, even the ones that were entertaining movies (and that's most of them), were somehow less worthy of serious consideration, because many of them were directed by a brand new group of filmmakers, men who, while they happened to be very good craftsmen, weren't necessarily stylists with their own unique viewpoints, as Renoir, Carne, Duvivier, and Gremillon were. From the 1950s on, while Renoir, Duvivier, and Carne would continue directing occasional movies starring

Gabin and Dominique with their children.

Gabin, the actor would begin working, over and over again, for a brand new small team of 'old-school' (like he was) directors, men in their thirties, forties, and fifties with names like Henri Verneuil (he directed Gabin in five pictures), Denys de La Patelliere (six pictures), Jean Delannoy (six), and Gilles Grangier (twelve films). These men may not have been visual poets as those 'artistes' from the '30s were, but Gabin liked them anyway because, in his view, they knew how to tell good, solid stories and, moreover, they all knew how to present Gabin in the way his audiences liked to see him. (Fortunately however, since regular, workaday movie audiences weren't too apt to pick up *Cahiers du cinema,* this whole academic backlash by the young critics didn't really interfere with Gabin's post-1953 comeback, at all.)

And even though Gabin had always pretended that he didn't care about what these younger critics were saying about him (even his own daughters, Florence and Valerie, supposedly got after him, about the fact that he was always [they felt] playing the same kind of 'quiet, stoic roles,' over and over again, and he reportedly threw up his hands at them, at one point shouting, "I'm not thirty years younger! *What can I do?!*"), as it turns out, he really did care, because even though he was making traditional genre-pictures during this cycle of his career, he would additionally, soon, begin adding a new layer into his film performances, and some really grand movies came out of it: In the late 1950s through the mid-1970s, Gabin gained new respect from France's movie critics, both young and old ones alike (even from those *Cahiers du Cinema* guys), by now, in addition to playing his usual 'serious businessman' and 'gentleman-gangsters,' also appearing in eleven raucously-funny comedies, most of which are fantastic: Gabin's comedies are completely unknown in the United States today, although one of them, 1956's tremendous *La Traversee de Paris*, was presented at the twin Gabin festivals which were held in New York and in Los Angeles in 2002, and it's a crying shame that these films are unknown in the U.S. because, as it turns out, Jean Gabin is a fantastic natural comedian. In his comedies, Jean Gabin is not his usual quiet, moody, and world-weary self, but actually loud, boisterous, and funny-as-hell, particularly in *La Traversee de Paris,* and also in *Archimede, le clochard* (1959, for which Gabin won the Best Actor prize, at 1960's Berlin Film Festival), *Les Vieux de la vieille* (1960), and *Monsieur* (1964). Gabin would even co-star in a 1964 buddy comedy, *L'Age ingrat* (*That Awkward Age*) with his lifelong friend, Fernandel, France's legendarily-likeable, rubber-faced movie-comedy superstar who made more than 150 films, in a career which lasted about as long as his own. Even though the two men had been the best of friends for more than thirty-five years, *L'Age ingrat* represented the first time in which they had appeared on-screen together in over thirty-two years, since a 1932 ensemble comedy in which they had both appeared together in supporting roles, *Le Gaietes de l'escadron*. This time out, Gabin and Fernandel were the headlining co-stars of the picture, and the two stalwarts even started their own production company together, in order to produce it—GAFER Productions ('GA' for 'Gabin' and 'FER' for 'Fernandel'), a company which, between 1964 and 1973, also manufactured five Gabin solo pictures and three Fernandel efforts. (In some very funny behind-the-scenes footage which was shot on the set of *L'Age ingrat*, Gabin and Fernandel, who are clowning for a newsreel camera, take a gentle stab at some of those young, *nouvelle vague* upstarts like Truffaut, Rohmer, and Godard, who didn't approve of some of the older filmmakers, when Gabin gleefully brags to the camera, "Look at us! *We're the New Wave of 1931!*")

Gabin began the 1960s, not just by acting in comedy movies, but also by dabbling in other media: In 1960, when Disney Pictures released its Jules Verne blockbuster *20,000 Leagues Under the Sea,* starring Kirk Douglas, Walt Disney, who was himself a lifelong Jean Gabin fan, personally hand-picked the Gallic actor to narrate Verne's story for the French-language edition of the Disneyland Records soundtrack album, which was distributed in tandem with the movie's French release.

So, while things were going very well for Gabin in the early '60s, suddenly, on July 27th, 1962, everything changed: It was on that date that seven hundred distraught socialist farmers, members of JAC (the *Jeunesse Agricole Catholique* [The Young Catholic Agricultural Society]) surrounded Gabin's farm. The protestors, who were led by Gerard Pottier and Maurice Thorel, were livid with Gabin, even though they didn't know him personally: To them, Gabin was just another example of a wealthy man who owned land, but who didn't 'work it' himself, instead engaging employees to do the grunt-work. Pottier and Thorel demanded that Gabin should immediately give away (for free!) some of his land, to young farmers who were unable to afford to purchase their own, and Pottier even tried to extort Gabin's signature on a contract which would have tied the actor into doing just that. Gabin was reportedly more angered by this than he had ever been by just about anything else in his entire life, and this whole confrontation really hurt his feelings because, in spite of his fame, he still truly believed himself to be 'the everyman.' Gabin, who never took anything sitting down, sued Pottier, Thorel, and the JAC, which he had termed 'the Red Vatican,' for breaking and entering but, at the last minute, before Pottier and Thorel's trial was about to begin, Gabin withdrew his suit. (Still, for the rest of his life, Gabin would never fully recover from the fact that, at different stages of his adult life, there were French people who didn't think he was 'one of them,' even though most French people really did love him, for most of his professional life.)

But enough good things happened to Gabin in the sixties, too, to counteract the bad: Not only did France's general public continue to turn out for all of his movies, but Charles de Gaulle himself, who had been elected as France's President in 1959, sent Gabin a letter, in which he called the actor a National Treasure, and invited him to receive the formal title of *Chevalier* of the Legion of Honor, in 1964. (It's amusing that Gabin was picked to receive such an 'establishment' award, because the actor had always, perhaps identifying himself with the drifter-characters whom he played in the '30s, referred to himself, throughout his life—and even when he was older—as an *anarchist!*) And this isn't the only honor which Gabin would be elected to receive in the 1960s, either: In July of 1969, Gabin was on vacation in Brittany, when he received a call from Dan Gelinet, his old superior from the *Marins Fusiliers*, during World War II. Gelinet who was, at that time, an Admiral, invited Gabin to the French Navy's school ship, the *Jeanne d'Arc*, where Gabin was saluted by the entire Navy. (In fact, in November of 1975, when Gabin's nineteen-year-old son Mathias joined the Navy, Gabin suggested that it might be a good idea for him to perform his service aboard the *Jeanne d'Arc*.)

In the 1970s, while Gabin was continuing to churn out one movie after another (five of his six 1970s titles are uniformly great, and one of them in particular, *L'Affaire Dominici*, is probably one of the very best films of the 1970s, and it's definitely up there—and this is no exaggeration—with *The Godfather* [although, bizarrely, it is almost completely unknown outside of France!]) In 1973, the legendary director of epic spaghetti westerns (*The Good, the Bad, and the Ugly* and *Once Upon a Time in the West*) Sergio Leone even announced, at the

Cannes Film Festival, that his next film, *Once Upon a Time in America*, would star his very favorite actor of all time, Jean Gabin, as the old New York-Jewish gangster, 'Noodles.' Sadly though, Leone was unable to secure financing at that time, and the picture wouldn't appear for another ten years, more than eight years after Jean Gabin's death in 1984, with James Woods playing the role. Sergio Leone movies have always been very popular in the United States, and it's too bad that Gabin didn't get to star in the film, because if he did, everybody in America would know Gabin, today. (But then again, maybe that wouldn't have been such a good idea, because if everybody in America already knew who Jean Gabin was—there wouldn't be any reason for this book to exist!)

A couple of sad things happened to Gabin in the 1970s, too, which surmounted the good things—a couple of milestone events which probably hastened his death: First, Gabin was destroyed, when his great lifelong friend Fernandel passed away, in 1971. In 1971, too, Gabin was disappointed by his own government: France had been experiencing months of draught that year, and the government was, very willingly, handing-out emergency relief to most farmers who had asked for it; but the Minister of Agriculture turned-down Gabin's application for subsidies, on the grounds that, in his opinion, Jean Gabin was a rich movie star, who could afford it. Well, of course, Gabin *couldn't* afford it: It's true that he made a great deal of money for starring in movies, but it's also true that he had dozens of employees to pay on his farm. Ever since Jean Gabin was a little boy, he had always dreamed of being considered a great farmer, and for the rest of his life, he never quite recovered from the fact that the farming world had sometimes treated him like an outsider—and not just in 1971, but before that, too, in 1962, when his farm was attacked by those holier-than-thou members of 'JAC.' (In 1979, three years after Gabin's death, the actor's wife, Dominique, placed the family farm on the market.)

Gabin continued starring in movies right up until his death, even though he had spent the last sixteen years giving interviews to various French newspapers and television programs, in which he was always threatening to retire—*especially,* in 1959, 1969, and 1974! And even though he had continued to make great movies, he just wasn't enjoying the scripts as much as he used to, feeling that it was becoming harder to find good stories.

1976's *L'Annee sainte (The Sainted Year)*, which was filmed in 1975, was Gabin's final film (daughter Florence was the script girl), and you can't really say that the actor ever really slowed down, because he always moved pretty slowly, in the first place! (The Corsicans have a saying, which could apply to Jean Gabin's famously lumbering physicality: "*Slow in the morning, slower in the afternoon.*") He died on November 15, 1976, at the American Hospital in Paris's Neuilly region from a massive heart attack, having already checked himself into the hospital twice, earlier that year, due to heart and pulmonary problems. (Three years earlier, on the set of a gangster movie in which he co-starred with Alain Delon, *Deux hommes dans la ville,* Gabin had checked himself into the hospital, with chest pains.) *Per* Gabin's wishes, his body was cremated at Paris's famous Pere-Lachaise cemetery, the resting place of, among other luminaries, Jim Morrison, Yves Montand, and Simone Signoret, and his ashes were

Gabin becomes an Officer of the Legion of Honor, 1960.

strewn from a military destroyer off of the coast of Ouessant, in Brittany, after a sermon by Dan Gelinet. Gabin's beloved wife Dominique Fournier, the mother of his three children, passed away on October 12, 2002, at the age of eighty-four, having survived her husband by more than twenty-five years.

At the time of his death, Gabin was about to begin production on his ninety-sixth picture, *Le Temoin* (*The Eyewitness*), which would instead get made (and released, in 1978) with the great actor Philippe Noiret replacing him. (Noiret thesped alongside Gabin in the 1964 comedy *Monsieur*, but American audiences know Noiret best, for his role as the drunken old cop, in the great 1983 'neo-noir,' *Coup de torchon*, in which he starred alongside Isabelle

Huppert.) *Le Temoin* is a *policier* in which Noiret's police superintendent is investigating the murder of a seductive teen-aged girl who poses for 'angel paintings,' which are painted (of course!) by a psychopath, and it would have been interesting to see Gabin in this picture, because it was directed by Jean-Pierre Mocky: Mocky, besides being a director, was (and continues to be, today) also an actor, and he and Gabin had shared scenes together twenty years earlier, when they played partners in the same criminal gang, in a 1957 crime thriller, called *Le Rouge est mis*.

Today, the legacy of Jean Gabin reverberates throughout France, where the actor continues to be known as "Le Grand Gabin." Even though his own French people deserted him once, between 1945 and 1953, they have made it up to him since, by loving him more than they have ever loved just about any of their other cultural figures in any artistic medium, and by making him their country's #1 icon of all time. And even when the French people deserted Jean Gabin between 1945 and 1953, he never deserted them—and now, they remember it.

While Jean Gabin has been in that great Casbah in the sky for more than thirty years now, the family legacy which he had 'planted' (so he really was a great farmer, after all!) continues growing, today: On June 7, 2006, *Le Passager de l'été*, the first feature-length film to have been directed by Gabin's daughter, Florence, opened in Paris to stellar reviews, and the film's ensemble cast of young actors even featured an up-and-coming twentysomething actor by the name of Jean-Paul Trem—Jean Gabin's grandson who also happens to be Florence's son, through her marriage to the jockey Christian Asis-Trem. (Florence also has two other adult kids—Christina Trem, her daughter with Asis-Trem, as well as a second son, Hugo Haillet, the product of her second marriage to the former international tennis player, and current cable-television tennis commentator, Jean-Louis Haillet.) Jean Gabin's second daughter, Valerie Moncorge, is a highly-respected filmmaker as well, and his son Mathias, who loves racehorses just as much as his dad did, is a horse breeder who runs the Jean Gabin Hippodrome racetrack. Additionally, Mathias spends much of his time with the charitable organization which was started by Gabin's good friend Lino Ventura, in 1966, *L'Association Perce-Neige* (*The Snowfall Foundation*), which serves the needs of handicapped children (www.perce-neige.org). Mathias' three children are Mary, Cleia, and Alexis.

WHY I WROTE THIS BOOK

If you had come to me even eight or nine years ago and told me that I would be writing a book about France's most beloved movie star of all time, Jean Gabin, or writing any book for that matter, my one-and-only response would have been a medium-polite, "Excuse me?!" As a film school graduate (shake any tree out here in Los Angeles, and twenty zillion of us will fall out), I was much more interested in writing screenplays (typically, producers would put their own names on the byline of my scripts *and* not pay me, and I definitely had enough of that)! Plus, I was never what you would call any kind of an authority on old movies from the 1930s and 1940s: My personal preference had always been for groovy, psychedelic, 'head' movies from the late 1960s—usually, mod freak-outs, starring Peter Sellers.

But everything changed with one phone call, which I received in January of 2001: My father's sister, Shirley Rothstein (at the time, she was 74), called me up. "Hey, you're the family movie buff," Aunt Shirley gently accused. "Just wanted to let you know that *Pepe Le Moko* is playing at the Nuart."

I had no idea what she was talking about.

"*Pepe Le What*? Pepe Le Pew—the cartoon skunk?!"

"No, no! *Pepe Le Moko*. The French gangster movie. With Jean Gabin. I saw it when I was a little girl, and I've always loved it. Anyway, the Nuart Theater [one of L.A.'s most famous retrospective theatres] is showing it for a week. Will you take me?"

Aunt Shirley had never asked me to escort her to a movie before. Granted, she didn't drive, but she was more independent than anybody I've ever met in my entire life, and was used to taking taxis everywhere—especially, to those art-house movie theatres which were forever showing her favorite thing on earth, French movies. Anyway, I was happy to take her: Aunt Shirley was always 'the cool friend-aunt' to all of the (adult) kids in our extended family, and I thought it would be fun to have some bonding-time with her, even if it meant having to sit through what I imagined would probably be some turgid, old subtitled movie; I knew full-well when she called me that, after the movie, she'd ask me to take her for an In-'N-Out Burger. (In-and-Out is one of Southern California's best burger chains, and their burgers were her one other favorite thing in the world, besides French movies. And for me, at that point, it was the burger, and not the movie, which was the big selling-point of the whole evening.)

Cut to that very same night: Aunt Shirley and I were at the Nuart, watching *Pepe Le Moko*. I enjoyed the film (especially, the ultra-cool, maze-like/Dr. Seuss-looking/Algerian-Casbah sets), and I remember thinking that *the star of the show*, Jean Gabin, seemed like *a pretty cool customer*, and to tell you the truth, that night at the Nuart wasn't exactly the first time I had ever seen a Jean Gabin movie: Back in college, as a UCLA undergrad, I had taken a Literature-into-Film (a/k/a, 'English 118') class, in which the professor asked us to read Emile Zola's harrowing 1890 novel of alcohol-related French Family Dysfunction, *La Bete humaine* (*The Human Beast*), and we followed up our reading, by viewing a sixteen-millimeter print of the 1938 film version which starred Jean Gabin although, at that point, I was only nineteen years old, and I don't remember paying too much attention to the film. (I was too busy rubbernecking at the girls in the class.) So, for all intensive purposes, this *Pepe Le Moko* evening, which I shared with my Aunt Shirley in 2001, was my proper introduction to the phenomenon known as Jean Gabin.

What I liked about and responded to immediately in Jean Gabin, is that he reminded me of all of the men on my father's side of the family (my dad and my uncles), all of whom were, and who continue to be, quietly powerful but family-loving men who expressed, and who continue to express, excess emotion only when it is absolutely necessary, each respective man in my family representing his own calm, in the middle of life's many storms. Anyway, while I thought that *Pepe Le Moko* and Jean Gabin were both cool, I didn't think about the film too much after the house lights went up (just as I had also already forgotten all about *La Bete humaine* only seconds after I had seen it, in my UCLA, 'lit-unto-film' class).

A few months later, completely independently of my Aunt, my father informed me that the classic 1937 anti-war picture *La Grande illusion*, or as we call it here in the U.S., 'Grand Illusion' (it continues, today, to be the Jean Gabin picture which is the most known, in the United States), was playing at another L.A. retrospective cinema, the Royal, and he asked me if I would be interested in seeing it with him, having no idea that, only a few months earlier, his own sister had asked me to accompany her to see that other Jean Gabin movie, *Pepe Le Moko!* What I noticed while I was watching *La Grande illusion* was that, even though it was an ensemble picture, and even though Jean Gabin was surrounded in it by other great actors, that no matter how many other people were in any particular shot with him (and you can tell that this was definitely by the director, Jean Renoir's, grand design), Gabin was the guy I was really watching in every frame, even in (especially in) those sequences in which he was positioned in the background, and in which all of the other actors were positioned in the foreground.

It's not coincidental that my father and his sister both asked me to watch Jean Gabin movies with them, because their own father—my paternal grandfather, Fernand Zigman, a Frenchman who passed away when I was two—happened to have been, as I would soon find out, a huge Jean Gabin fan in his own right, and a man who had very specifically conveyed his interest in Gabin, to his own children. A tailor by trade, 'Papa' Fernand, a man who evinced 'the quiet, Gabinian-strength' which is envisaged by all of the other men in my family, was not what you would have ever considered to be a movie fan but, back in the 1940s, whenever a French Jean Gabin movie would find its way over to Fairfax Avenue's Esquire Theater (which, back in the 1930s and 1940s, was Los Angeles's sole foreign-film house, and which is today, the location of the world's famous Canter's Delicatessen), he'd pack his family, including my very young dad and his sister, into the family car—a 1936 Oldsmobile—and bring them to see whatever English-subtitled Jean Gabin movie happened to be playing there, and that included both *Pepe Le Moko* and *La Grande illusion*, as well as the few other Gabin movies from the mid-to-late 1930s which were released in U.S. art-house theatres between the late thirties and the mid-forties. (So, there it is, folks: I wrote this book because, apparently, I have genetic 'Jean Gabin-Appreciating Chromosomes!' [Not 'XX' or 'XY,' but '*XX, avec fromage!*'])

Now, I'm going to jump ahead about six months, to a family gathering— Thanksgiving of 2001—which is when Aunt Shirley confided to me that the best and most hypnotic movie she ever saw when she was a teenager, was yet another Jean Gabin picture, 1942's 20th Century-Fox production of *Moontide*, in which Gabin co-starred with Ida Lupino and which, I would soon find out, was one of only two American-made/English-language movies in which Gabin had ever performed. I had never heard of *Moontide* but, since Aunt Shirley's 74th birthday was coming up, I decided that, for a present, I would get her a video copy of the movie, and this is how I discovered that *Moontide* had been out of circulation in the United States since the early 1980s, which is the last time that it had ever been broadcast on American television. I checked with local television stations all over the U.S. (the ones which used to show movies all night, in the years before TCM began unspooling them all day), and I kept hearing the same speech over and over, from every single program director whom I had contacted—namely, that a lot of local t.v. stations, used to own the broadcast rights to *Moontide* a generation ago, but that when the licenses to show the film came up for renewal, none of them chose to renew. Even eBay sellers, who are notorious for selling bootleg videos of every obscure movie ever made, didn't have *Moontide*, and because *Moontide* wasn't a hit in its own time (not in the U.S., and not in Europe), 20th Century Fox, the studio that made it, didn't even have a projectable copy in its own library.

Remember: Twenty or twenty-five years ago, before the big film restoration boom began, movies which the studios considered to be unimportant were left to decompose and were even *thrown away*—negatives and all! In fact, much of the reason that the film restoration business exists today, is because single-handedly, in 1970, a UCLA film student by the name of Howard Suber, who today is one of UCLA's most respected film professors, founded the University's film archives, and quite by accident: Suber had discovered that a truck which belonged to one of the major studios was about to dump a load of old, obscure (and even not so obscure) Hollywood movies into the Pacific Ocean and worse, that this was apparently a very common practice for all of the studios, whenever they needed to free-up some room in their vaults. Suber and some of his fellow students, as the legend goes (and of course, *per Liberty Vallance*, "you always print the legend") showed-up at the docks and heroically demanded that the dumping be stopped. (The truckdrivers apparently didn't even care: "Sure, kid! You can have 'em. Have fun with 'em!") Soon and rather routinely, instead of trashing their old films, the Hollywood studios would begin handing them over to Suber, and Suber, who was supported by a group of students and alumni, inaugurated the UCLA Film and Television Archives, which today continues to be one of the most respected film archives in the entire world, not to mention one of the great leaders in the field of film restoration and preservation.

But soon—*good news!* After a bit of sleuthing, I discovered that UCLA's extensive, Hollywood-based UCLA Film and T.V. Archives housed one print of almost every movie ever made by Twentieth Century-Fox, so I put in a call to the Archive's coordinator, Mark Quigley, who informed me that UCLA did, in fact, have a 35-millimeter print of *Moontide*, which I was welcome to come and see although, as he also explained to me, the ancient nitrate print, which was extremely fragile and delicate, might not survive the screening without turning into dust. Anyway, whatever the condition of the print was, I was elated: Even if I could just show Aunt Shirley five or ten minutes of *Moontide*, I'm sure she would be happy.

A couple of weeks later, I brought Aunt Shirley down to the UCLA Archives screening facility, where a student-archivist had been commandeered to project *Moontide* for us. He sat us down in front of a small 'upright' editing console, and placed the first, delicate 35mm reel up on the plates, easefully threading the film through the works. He told us how to adjust the focus and the volume knobs, gave us our headsets (we looked like a couple of air-traffic controllers!), and then retreated to the back of the room. This is the moment in which Aunt Shirley and I were transported into the world of *Moontide*.

So we're sitting there, my wonderful Aunt and I, and we're watching *Moontide*. Now, you have to understand that, at this point, even though I had already enjoyed Gabin's performances in both *Pepe Le Moko* and *La Grande illusion*, I still wasn't what anybody in his right mind would have ever considered to be a Jean Gabin fan. (I mean, at this stage of the game, I was still watching these Gabin movies just to placate family members who wanted to see them.) But then suddenly, about five minutes into the film, and without even realizing it—I was hooked.

And by the time *Moontide* was over, and in the space of only ninety-four minutes, I had become North America's #1 Jean Gabin Fan.

Moontide, a film about a French sailor (Gabin) who's drifting aimlessly through a mythical Southern California seaport (getting into fights with brutish men, while brushing up against tempestuous dames) was so mesmerizing that, about twenty minutes into viewing the picture, I forgot I was watching an old movie: *Moontide* was as gripping as any great new movie which I had ever seen, and the glue which held the whole enterprise together, was the great and quietly-powerful performance by Jean Gabin.

When *Moontide* was over (Aunt Shirley and I made it to the end of the film without the celluloid breaking and burning), I felt as though I had just been plugged into the greatest source of electricity in the world: *This cat*, Jean Gabin, was everything that I had always admired about all of the other tough-but-quiet movie heroes who had brightened-up my childhood—Humphrey Bogart, Gary Cooper, Spencer Tracy, Clint Eastwood, Charles Bronson, Lee Marvin, *etc.*—but he was quieter and tougher than all of those guys, combined. I wanted to see more Jean Gabin movies, and I wanted to see them *right now.*

I checked out the web's indefatigable Internet Movie Database (imdb.com), that awe-inspiring listing of nearly every movie ever made, and this is where I learned that Gabin acted in ninety-five feature films over a forty-six year career which spanned the years between 1930 and 1976. I quickly lapped-up the dozen-or-so additional Gabin films which were readily available on American home video, mostly films that had been produced in the mid-to-late 1930s, as well as another three which had been made in the 1950s (the ones with English subtitles or English dubbing), always making sure to share my treasure trove of 'movie booty' with Aunt Shirley. As I began to watch this small but meaningful group of readily-available Gabin films—films with titles like *Le Quai des brumes (Port of Shadows)* and *Touchez pas au grisbi (Don't Touch the Loot),* I was waiting for the 'bad' film, or the 'boring' film (or the 'abstract' film, or the 'pretentious' film), and there wasn't one! So far, all of the Jean Gabin movies which I had seen, had been wonderful. (There are a few—*a very few*—Jean Gabin movies which aren't that great, but I wouldn't be seeing them until much later, and even in his few movies which weren't terrific, Gabin was always great *in* them.)

Now that I was watching all of Jean Gabin's movies, I wanted to learn something about 'the man,' but the internet, as fun as it is, offered only the same half-paged, skeletal outline about his life, which had been evergreened, *ad nauseam,* by literally hundreds of different 'e-zine' scribes. So my next stop, was the movie section of my local public library... and every giant chain bookstore you can think of... and Amazon.com.... and the Library of Congress's search engine—and that's when I found out, to my dual horror and astonishment, that there has never been a single book about Jean Gabin published in the English language, *ever*. Not a one! I mean, here's a guy who, in the late 1930s and early 1940s, was about as popular in the United States as Humphrey Bogart and James Cagney were (even though, post-World War II, he had pretty much fallen off of the American radar), and yet there was nothing at all about him in the King's English, not even an old, out-of-print book. (In Spanish: "*Nada!*" In French: "*Rien!*")

I discovered, at the same time, that even in Jean Gabin's native France, while there are a few excellent published *biographies* about his life (particularly 1987's *Gabin*, by author Andre Brunelin, which is considered to be 'the *sine qua non* of Jean Gabin-related literature'), that there has never been a book in any language, and that includes in French, which concentrated specifically, and in depth, on each of the actor's ninety-five films.

So I decided to write it.

My models for this two-volume *Gabincyclopaedia* which you now own, are those great, overstuffed Citadel Press books which I used to love when I was a kid, growing up in the 1970s—*The Films of Henry Fonda*, *The Films of Spencer Tracy*, *The Films of Barbara Stanwyck*, *The Films of John Wayne*—in which each individual chapter focused on a different film: While I'll probably never see every single one of the movies I read about in those books, I feel, in a way, that I have, because the valiant scribes who wrote them had presented the films' plots and themes so completely.

It took me five years to write this book (2002-2007), and that's mostly because it took me five years to track down, and to watch, all ninety-five of Jean Gabin's feature films (the whole process was really like archaeology, since some of the films I saw in this book came to me from France, Germany, Belgium, and even, in once case, *Serbia!*), and the most satisfying part of the process, is that it was really worth it because, as I've already mentioned in these volumes, and as I will continue to mention many more times, *in my own opinion*, eighty-three out of Gabin's ninety-five films are truly spectacular.

If I were writing about Fonda or Tracy or Stanwyck, finding the films would have been much easier for me: I'm an American writer, and the majority of those other actors' films are available on home video in North America. But with Jean Gabin, I had a very specific problem: His movies were made in France (93 out of 95 of them were made in France, anyway) and, of those ninety-five films, only thirty-three are currently available on American home video and cable television at the time this book is going to print (either dubbed into English, or with English subtitles). Anyway, that left sixty-two films which were not immediately available to me.

It is then that I learned about Francevision, a mail-order video rental house based in Bethesda, Maryland. Francevision specializes in renting-out video copies of French movies which have never been commercially released on DVD in the United States (they make American-format DVD and VHS transfers of the French DVDs, transfers which you can play on your regular old U.S. video machine), and when I called them up, they told me they had forty-nine additional Gabin movies in stock which they would be happy to rent to me. But I had one very specific problem: These movies were without English subtitles or dubbing, and (this is a pretty embarrassing admission for somebody who's just written a book about French movies, to be making), I had, over the last twenty-some years, managed to forget all of the French which I had learned in high school, circa 1982-1984, with the exception of one key phrase from the *French II* textbook, "*On n'a jamais assez des disques*" (translation: "one never has enough records"), which has *never* come up in conversation, even though one of my enduring hopes in life, is that someday, it will. I bought some old, antiquated, "How to Speak French" audio cassettes which were made in the '70s, but at the rate in which the lessons were being delivered on them, it would have taken me seventy years to re-learn French!

Then it dawned on me: I could hire translators, *just like how they do it at the U.N.!* I went to the internet (without which this book would not exist, because the internet and email are exactly how I met a lot of the great people who helped me with it), and placed a want-ad on the invaluable Craigslist.com, advertising for one or two French-to English translators who could sit and watch the videos with me, offering simultaneous translation and, in effect, acting as 'human subtitles.' This turned out to be a capital idea, because I met some truly outstanding people, who will be thanked properly at the end of this book—people who sat with me tirelessly, and translated the majority of those forty-nine English-lacking Francevision titles. My translators were so skilled, that I felt like I was really experiencing the films 'first-hand,' as though I had been watching them in English, and by myself. Before I had settled upon the great translators with whom I wound-up, I auditioned a number of other native French speakers who just couldn't do it as well, but not through any fault of their own: As it turns out, and I didn't know this when I began the project, a lot of Jean Gabin's old movies, not to mention a lot of pre-1970s French genre-pictures in general, feature a great deal of their dialogue spoken in archaic French 'gangster-slang,' an argot which is heavily untranslatable, and not just from French to English, but also from the French of fifty or sixty years ago to the French of today, which is one of the many reasons why Gabin's best movies, all of which are by design 'commercial, audience movies' (cops-n'-robbers dramas, suspense thrillers, and love-triangle melodramas) were never released, or were only barely released, in the U.S.: American distributors probably couldn't figure out just what the hell to write for the subtitles! In fact, in the case of a few of Gabin's movies, even the titles are in near-untranslatable gangster-slang: One picture, a very cool heist movie from the early '60s, is called *Le Cave se rebiffe*, and depending upon who's translating the title for you, it could mean, "*The Cellar is Angry*," "*It Happened in the Cellar*," or even, "*The Nerd is Angry!*" A second Gabin film with a mysterious-sounding title, is the 1957 cops-n'-robbers picture, *Le Rouge est mis:* The title translates literally as, "The Red is Put," but what the hell does that mean? When you watch the movie, you eventually figure out what it means: "*The Red Light is Put On*," is what happens when cops turn on their sirens.

Cut to two years later:

It was now 2004, and I had already seen eighty-one of Jean Gabin's ninety-five movies, including a 1939 effort called *Le Recif de corail* (*The Coral Reef*), which was considered to be a lost film when I started working on this book back in '02, and which was discovered, of all places, in *Serbia,* in 2003, by the prominent French film critic, Lenny Borger, who happened to be at the Kinoteka Film Archives in Serbia, searching for a completely different movie; subsequently, Borger restored the picture, and in '04, it was released on DVD in France, by film curator Serge Bromberg's Lobster Films. There were, at this point, fourteen films left for me to find. Mark Quigley of UCLA's Film Archives had just found that his organization had three more titles and, initially, he didn't even know he had them, because they had been filed away for decades in mislabeled cans, so I was then able to see those three films. (One of the films was hidden away in a can labeled *Fangs of the Undead,* an Italian vampire movie from the 1960s which has nothing to do with Gabin, and everything to do with Anita Ekberg!)

Now, I had only eleven films left to go, and this is where the leg-work, not to mention the frequent flyer miles, really came in: I called, and sent letters and emails, to every film archive-organization in the U.S. and Canada, and found that none of them had even a single one of the eleven remaining Gabin films which I had yet to track down. A good friend of mine in France, Laurence Bardet, who will be thanked properly at the end of this book, recommended that I call the CNC—the French Ministry of Culture—which houses one of France's two largest film archives (the other, of course, pre-eminently being the *Cinematheque Francaise*)—and I was over-the-moon to find that the CNC actually had, in its possession, four of the films which I still needed to see. I asked the CNC's film coordinator, Eric Le Roy, if it would be possible for his organization to loan me some video copies of the film by mail (I assured him that I would return any such videos in a timely manner), but he told me that each of the four prints was unique, and extremely fragile. (In fact, there was only one print in the world of each of these four titles, none of which had ever been available on home video or television, even in France.) He told me that the only way I could ever see these films, would be to come to France, and to see them projected on-site at the CNC's archival screening facilities, as I already done with those other films which I had already screened in my hometown of Los Angeles, at UCLA's Archives; and even though I had never gone halfway around the world to see a movie before (I'm not one of those dilettantes, who hangs out at film festivals. [I'm a dilettante, but not that kind!]), I knew that, in the interest of completeness, and of seeing all of Jean Gabin's movies, that I would have to go. Of course, after I had already booked my ticket to France, Le Roy then called me with some bad news, which was replacing his earlier-offered good news: He told me that, due to unforeseen circumstances beyond his control, he could no longer show me the films which he had promised to screen for me, because the CNC had suddenly received the government funding for which it had applied *years* before, to remodel the building which housed its screening facilities, facilities which, as Le Roy then told me, would now have to be closed, effective immediately. After I panic-wrote Le Roy a few emails (a French friend of mine told me a secret about French bureaucracy: "Don't worry. In France, the first answer is always no, and the second answer is always yes!"), the CNC arranged to screen the films for me at the archive facilities of its archival rival, the *Cinematheque Francaise,* whose screening facilities are located twenty-two miles outside of Paris, in the town of Montigny-les-Bretonneux. In other words, my watching these films became a team-up between the CNC and the *Cinematheque Francaise,* and I will always be extremely grateful to the CNC's Eric Le Roy and the *Cinematheque Francaise's* Gaelle Vidalie, for "coming together as one" and "making it all happen for me." When I went to France, I also made a quick, day-long stop-over at the Royal Cinematheque of Belgium, to view three more ultra-rare Gabin films, which had turned up, in Brussels. So, now (running tote), it was '91 films down, and four more to go!'

Flash-forward, to December of 2005:

Mark Quigley called and informed me that his archive had just received a crate of old films from Paris—a crate which hadn't been opened in more than fifty years!— and that one of the films inside of it was one of the four still-missing Gabin films, the 1932 comedy *La Belle Mariniere* (*The Beautiful Sailor Girl,* which was made by the Paris-based film unit of

WHY I WROTE THIS BOOK | xxxvii

Paramount Pictures). He told me, though, that he could show me only six out of the picture's nine reels, because the other three had decomposed with age. Since this incomplete print was the only surviving print of *La Belle Mariniere* in the entire world, I watched it, bringing a translator with me, due to the film's lack of English subtitles. Luckily, all of the important reels which advanced the story seemed to be present, and even though I was able to see only sixty minutes of the eighty minute film, I mostly felt like I had seen the whole thing.

It was now January of 2006. I had already written about three quarters of this book, and I had already seen 92 Jean Gabin films, which meant that only three more were left. And these three remaining films presented the biggest problem of all for me because, of the ninety-five films which Jean Gabin made, these three (one was made in 1932, and the other two in 1933) no longer exist today: And when I say "do not exist," what I mean, is that they do not exist anywhere in the world, *period*, because, just like a lot of the movies which were made before 1950, they've been lost to the ravages of time. I started to wonder: How can I write a book about "The Complete Films of Jean Gabin," if three of the films don't exist? Should I call my book *The Almost Complete Films of Jean Gabin?* Or, since only two-thirds of *La Belle Mariniere* exist, maybe I could call it, *The Ninety-One and Two-Thirds Surviving Jean Gabin Movies Out of His Ninety-Five!*

But then, as it had already happened so often with this book, 'luck happened' once again, because the three remaining films *did* pop-up… *kind of*…

Today, when filmmakers make their films they, of course film them once, and they then subtitle or dub them into foreign languages, so that the films can be marketed to, and enjoyed by, the rest of the world, and this is a phenomenon which has been in place since around 1934. But during the first seven years of talking pictures—roughly, between the years of 1927 and 1933—nobody had yet dreamed-up the innovative idea of subtitling and dubbing films into different languages: Routinely, and all the way up through 1933, movie producers in the U.S. and in Europe used to film their movies two and three times over in different languages, and with different actors who spoke those languages, for export to different countries. One of the greatest examples of this situation involves movie history's greatest vampire: In 1931, Universal Pictures filmed a Spanish-language version of its English language movie, *Dracula*, which starred not Bela Lugosi as The Great Vampire, but the actor Carlos Villarias (as well as Lupita Tovar replacing the English version's Helen Chandler as 'Mina,' and Barry Norton replacing David Manners, not as 'John' Harker, but as '*Juan*' Harker)! All of the dialogue from the English/Lugosi version was translated into Spanish, and if you watch the Bela Lugosi and Carlos Villarias versions side-by-side, you'll see that the two films are almost identical, scene-for-scene, shot-for-shot, and cut-for-cut: Relatedly, I discovered that those three non-existent Gabin films which I've just mentioned still exist today, in alternate and reportedly identical versions, which were produced in other languages, starring other actors playing the roles which Jean Gabin played in the French versions, each version filmed for use in a different country.

The first of the three missing Jean Gabin movies, *La Foule hurle*, was made twice in 1932:

First, it was made in America and then, secondly, it was re-made from scratch in France: Back in the early 1930s, Warner Bros. studios, just like Paramount, had a fully operational movie studio in Paris, and the job of French-Warner Bros. was to film all-new French-language versions of whatever the studio's current, big American-made/English-language hits happened to be, for consumption in France, utilizing French actors and French directors. In 1932, director Howard Hawks filmed a James Cagney race car picture, *The Crowd Roars*, on the Warners' lot in Los Angeles, and after the shooting was finished, U.S.-Warners sent the script, as well as Hawks' already assembled race car footage, from the completed American version, to Paris, and the French filmed the movie over again, with director Jean Daumery replacing Howard Hawks, and Jean Gabin replacing James Cagney. (Whenever the director of the French/Gabin-version, Daumery, cuts away from Gabin and his French co-stars, to long shots of racing footage, he's actually cutting to Howard Hawks' racing footage from the American/Cagney version.) So, while the French Gabin version of *La Foule hurle* does not exist today, and hasn't been seen anywhere in the world for decades (even though a couple of still photographs from it exist), the reportedly identical James Cagney-version *does* exist, and in the interest of completeness, this is the version which I saw for, and discuss in, this book, and I saw it on Turner Classic Movies, where it screens pretty regularly.

The final two 'missing' Jean Gabin movies, which were likewise re-filmed in identical, alternate versions, were both made in 1933 by what was, at that time, Germany's largest film production company, UFA (Universum Film AG). In the early 1930s, UFA had a co-production pact with France, under which it filmed most of its movies twice—once with German actors speaking their own language, for theatrical showings in Germany, and then for a second time with French actors, for exhibition in France. In the case of Gabin's two UFA pictures, *L'Etoile de Valencia (The Star of Valencia)* and *Adieu les beaux jours (Goodbye, Beautiful Days)*, the French language versions are now gone forever, just like *La Foule hurle* is also gone, but unlike *La Foule hurle*, *L'Etoile de Valencia* and *Adieu les beaux jours* didn't decompose: In 1943, a decade after those two pictures were made, Hitler ordered his Minister of Propaganda, Josef Goebbels, to physically burn the negatives and prints of all of the French films which UFA had made a decade earlier, under its French co-production pact. Thankfully, however, the identical German-language versions of both films, which star other actors replacing Jean Gabin, do survive today, albeit, in the case of both films, in only one thirty-five millimeter print in the entire world. And so it was that, in February of 2006, I saw both of these pictures on-site at the Bundesarchiv Film Archives in Berlin: The German version of *L'Etoile de Valencia* is called *Der Stern von Valencia*, and in it, an actor called Peter Erkelenz assumes the Gabin role. The German version of *Adieu les beaux jours* is called *Die Schonen tage von Aranjuez*, and it stars Gustaf Grundgens. (My original thought was, "Do I want to go all the way to Germany to see 'two Jean Gabin films, which Jean Gabin isn't even in'—two films, in which some other actor is filling in for him?" In the interest of completeness, I decided, YES.)

Anyway:

Now that I've seen all ninety-five of Jean Gabin's movies—or, to be more specific, the ninety-one and two-thirds that exist, plus the alternate versions of the other three, which don't exist!—I don't intend on keeping all of this information to myself, and so, at the end of the book, I'll tell you how *you* can see them or, actually, how you can see *most* of them.

POST-SCRIPT: As I'm finishing this book, two of Jean Gabin's rarest movies, neither of which existed on home video in 2004, which is when I traveled to France and Belgium to see them at archival facilities, have finally been released on DVD, in France: In November of 2006, director George Lacombe's 1947 gangster picture, *Miroir,* which had not been seen in France at all since its initial theatrical release sixty years before, finally 'made the DVD scene,' and in February of 2007, Universal Pictures finally released its ultra-rare, 1944 American-Gabin picture *Impostor* on DVD, but only in France! Both *Miroir* and *Impostor* have now been fully-restored to their original 1940s' luster, and the funny thing about *Impostor* in particular, is that, even though it's an American movie, and even though it was filmed in the English-language, Universal Pictures, at the time this book is going to print anyway, has *zero plans* to release the movie on DVD in America, since, in that studio's opinion, "nobody in America cares about Jean Gabin." That's all about to change. (*I hope...*)

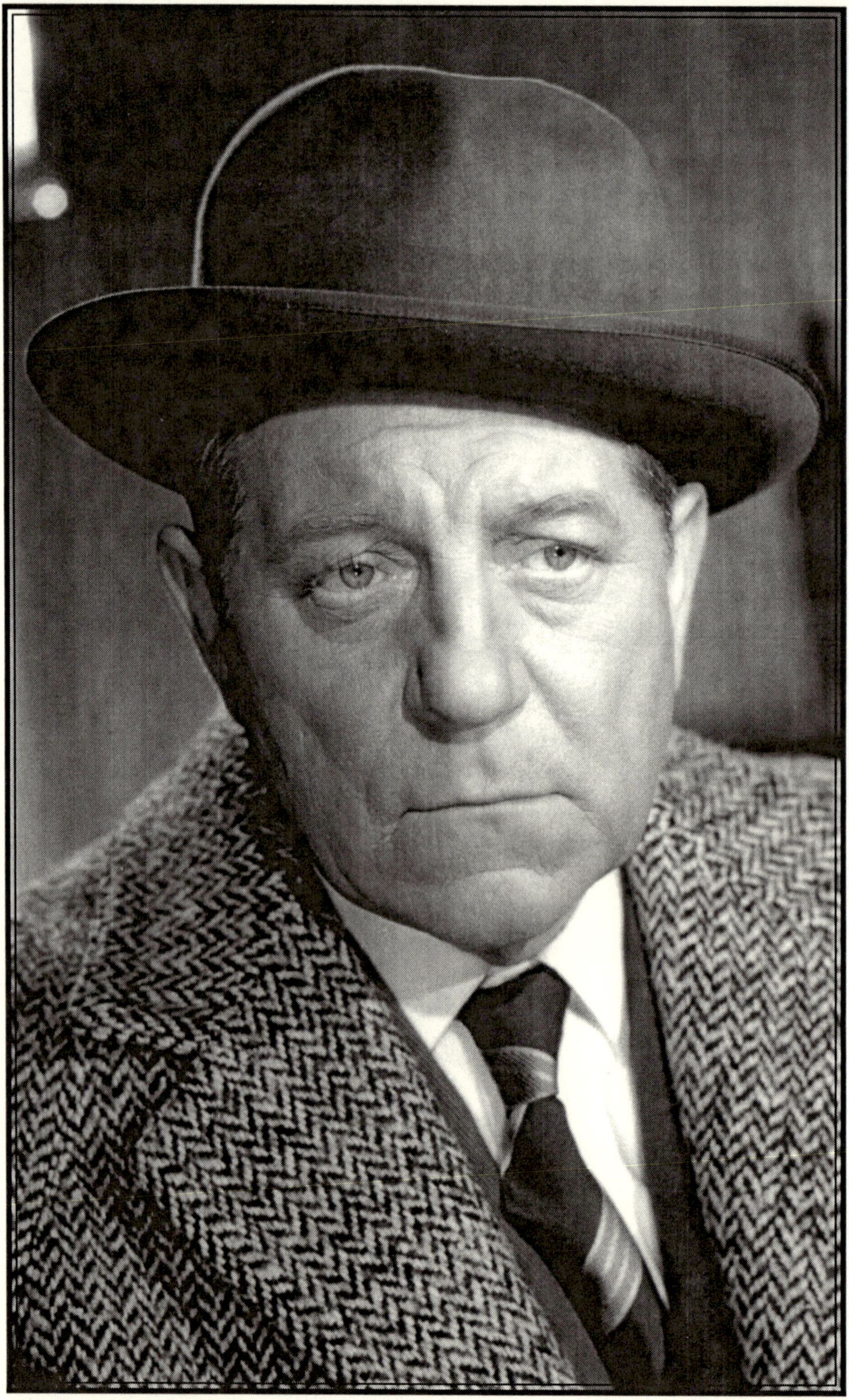

THE FILMS
CYCLE FIVE

The films from this period are known throughout the world, but only a few are known in the United States.

FILM NOS. 47 TO 95, 1954 — 1976

IN 1954, JEAN GABIN WILL MAKE A CRIME MOVIE CALLED *TOUCHEZ PAS AU GRISBI*, a film which will single-handedly propel him to the position of France's #1 star again, for the first time since *Le Jour se leve,* all the way back in 1939. And his fans will remain with him forever even when, on occasion, the critics will not. In these films, Gabin will play a wealthy, *bourgeois* businessman or gentleman gangster who is forced to deal with the problems which come either from within his family, or from within the companies he runs. Gabin's on-screen persona remains as stoic and as quiet as ever, and although sometimes the characters whom he will play are fated for ill, many times (for a change) they are not. Occasionally, during this period, Gabin will also play a working-class character again, usually to remind his audiences from whence he came. He'll also do something completely new during this period: He'll make some great comedies. In the pictures in which Gabin will star during this cycle, instead of being quiet, he will very often be loud, verbose, obnoxious, and talkative; in short, in his comedies, the famed 'Gabin-Outburst' now becomes the entire movie. Gabin made forty-eight of his ninety-five movies during this cycle, and today, as of this printing, only three—1952's *Le Plaisir,* 1954's *Touchez pas au grisbi* and 1955's *French Cancan*—are known to any extent in the United States, although most of the other titles are frequently shown on television and DVD throughout the rest of the world.

Top: With Jeanne Moreau, Dora Doll, Rene Dary, and Denise Clair. Above: With Lino Ventura and Jeanne Moreau.

FILM 47

Touchez pas au grisbi

France/Italy, 1954

(Literal English Translation: "DON'T TOUCH THE LOOT") *Directed by Jacques Becker. Produced by Georges Charlot and Robert Dorfmann. Screenplay by Albert Simonin, Jacques Becker, and Maurice Griffe. From the Novel by Albert Simonin. Music by Jean Wiener. Director of Photography (black and white), Pierre Montazel. Editor, Marguerite Renoir. Production Designer, Jean D'Eaubonne.* (GENRES: CRIME/FILM NOIR) *A Production of Antares Produzione Cinematografica (Italy) and Del Duca Films (France). Running Time, 1 hour 50 minutes. Released in France on March 1, 1954, by Corona. Released in the United States (NYC) with English Subtitles as "GRISBI," on July 10, 1959, by the United Motion Picture Organization (UMPO). Re-Released in United States in 1960, dubbed into English, by Valiant Films. Re-Released Theatrically in the U.S. by Rialto Pictures, in 2003.*

"While you're hoofing it, I'll be snoring."
— *Fifty year old Jean Gabin would rather go to sleep than paint the down red with a twentysomething dish, in "Touchez pas au grisbi"*

While Jean Gabin had made some great (*Au-dela des grilles; La nuit est mon royaume; Le Plaisir; Leur derniere nuit*), some very good (*Martin Roumagnac, Miroir*), some good (*La Minute de verite*), and some 'just o.k.' movies (*La Marie du port, Victor, La Verite sur Bebe Donge, La Vierge du Rhin*) in the nine years since he had returned to France from America, all of those films had something in common: Nobody in France showed up to see them, even the ones which had been so highly regarded in other countries (*Au-dela* won Oscar's Best Foreign-Language Film award, and *Le Plaisir* was nominated for an Oscar for art direction; in addition, Gabin won Best Actor accolades for both *Au-dela des grilles* and *La Nuit est mon royaume*, both at the Venice Film Festival), because the French *still* weren't willing to forgive Gabin for how they felt he had deserted them when he had moved to the U.S. between 1941 and 1943, even though the actor *had* returned to France, fighting for them in the Free French Navy, between 1943 and 1945.

But in 1954, when Jean Gabin starred in director Jacques Becker's film *noir* masterpiece *Touchez pas au grisbi* (*Don't Touch the Loot*), everything changed for the better. This is the movie

4 | **THE FILMS** CYCLE FIVE

With Rene Dary.

in which Jean Gabin 'came back,' as far as the French moviegoing public was concerned, and from this point on, and until the end of his life twenty-two years later in 1976, they'd stay with him, insuring that a great many of his remaining forty-five movies would become huge hits. With *Touchez pas au grisbi*, Jean Gabin would fully regain the status of 'France's #1 Box-Office Star,' for the first time since 1939.

Grisbi, the first of three heist pictures in which Gabin would star, has always been considered to be a great movie in France, and it's one of Gabin's few post-War movies which also happens to be known today in the United States, primarily due to the New York-based distribution company Rialto Pictures, which restored the film in 2003 and bestowed subsequent theatrical and DVD releases upon it. It's also the only picture in which Jean Gabin would ever thesp in the service of director Jacques Becker who, at the time this film was made, had already known Gabin for more than twenty years, because Becker was Jean Renoir's assistant director on two great Renoir/Gabin collaborations from the 1930s - *Les Bas-fonds* and 1937's *La Grande illusion*. (In fact, Becker had even directed a few bits of *La Grande illusion* himself without credit, most notably, part of the sequence in which Jean Gabin's 'Marechal' and Marcel Dalio's 'Rosenthal' characters are escaping from the German prison camp in the snow. Becker also reportedly supervised a few shots which took place in and around Dita Parlo's Bavarian farmhouse.) It's too bad that Becker was only able to

With Dora Doll and Jeanne Moreau.

direct Gabin this one time because, as you'll see when you're watching *Grisbi*, the filmmaker really knew how to 're-present' Gabin to the world, and this is the first film of many, in which Gabin will portray the ultimate smooth, immaculately-dressed gentleman-gangster character which he would be playing a lot during the second half of his film career—an older, patriarchal character who, just like Gabin always did in his older movies, always remained calm in the face of danger, a man who prized friendship and loyalty over anything else.

When the film opens, fifty year old Max (Gabin) and his tough-but-*nebbishy*-looking friend Riton (Rene Dary), two gangsters who have been partners for more than twenty years, have already successfully ripped off fifty million francs worth of gold bullion from Orly Airport, and even better than that—they've gotten away with it! Max is happy, because now that this one last heist is over, he'll be able to retire, which is, of course, the goal of every gangster, in every heist movie ever made.

Max and Riton are dining at Chez Bouche in Montmartre, a restaurant whose owner, Madame Bouche (Denise Clair) favors gangsters over regular clients, and they're accompanied by two younger showgirls, Josy (a stunning twenty-six year-old Jeanne Moreau, in her eighth film) and Lola (Dora Doll, the French answer to Jayne Mansfield). Max and mustachioed Riton are such good friends, that Max is even willing to overlook Riton's big weakness: Riton's a guy who lets women walk all over him, not even caring that they're just into him for what he's got in his wallet. Also *au table,* is Marco (Michel Jourdan), a young member of Max's gang, to whom Max always acts very paternally.

After dinner, it is decided that our diners will continue their evening at a local nightclub, the Mystific, where Josy and Lola are expected anyway, because they're part of the floorshow, and at first, a tired Max is resistant to it ("While you're hoofing it, I'll be snoring!") The Mystific is co-owned by Pierrot (Paul Frankeur), Max's loyal friend who, for obvious reasons, goes by the name of "Fats," and Marinette, who's played by Gaby Basset, Jean Gabin's real-life first wife who divorced him in 1931 but with whom he would always be friends. While the Mystific is a legitimate club, it's also a front for drug operations which are spearheaded by Fats and Fats' scheming #2 Man, Angelo Frasier, a guy whom Fats plainly just employs out of fear. Angelo is played by a French movie icon who is almost as beloved in France as Jean Gabin is—thirty-five year old Lino Ventura.

Soon to be a major French star in his own right, *Grisbi* was former wrestler Lino Ventura's very first film as an actor, and Ventura would also become one of Jean Gabin's real-life best friends, even joining Gabin, eventually, in five additional pictures which would be made throughout the '50s and '60s. In fact, Gabin and Ventura were so identical, both physically as well as temperamentally (both men fashioned careers out of playing 'stoically-quiet tough guys'), that whenever Gabin turned down movie roles, they were usually offered to Ventura and *vice-versa,* and the two men always helped each other out in real life, as well: On August 19, 1975, when Gabin's daughter Florence married the well-known jockey Christian de Asis-Trem with whom she had already been living for several years, Gabin was vehemently opposed to the union: He didn't want his daughter to be with a jockey because, in his belief system, jockeys were 'rogues' (read: *players*), so Gabin didn't attend Florence and Christian's wedding in Deauville, instead sending Ventura, in his place, to give his daughter away!

After the floorshow is over, Max decides to head home and catch some *zzzz*'s. He opens the door to Josy and Lola's dressing room to say goodbye to them, and this is where he catches a glimpse of Riton's girl, Josy, who's enmeshed in a hot make-out session with the much more virile-looking Angelo. When Angelo leave the room, Josy, who looks flustered because she's just been caught, tells Max to please tell Riton that she doesn't love him anymore, and that she now loves Angelo.

Not wanting anything to do with this (Gabin doesn't mix in with other people's soap operas), Max has a driver bring him home, and he's followed by some of Angelo's thugs who, very menacingly, drive around in an ambulance. The thugs confess to Max that Angelo wants to see Riton. Confused, Max phones Riton and asks him why Angelo's thugs are looking for him, and Riton confesses that he told Josy that it was he and Max who stole the gold bars because he wanted to impress her, and that Josy, in turn, mentioned it to Angelo, and now, of course, Angelo wants Max's gold. After all, why should Angelo settle for being Fats' #2 Man, when fifty million worth of bullion will make him #1 on his own? (RITON [to Max]: "Josy told me she was going to leave me for Angelo, and that I'd never be big time, like other guys. So I told her that I'm the one who took the gold, and that I'm set for life!")

While Max is upset with his friend, he still feels protective of him anyway, and he remains Gabin-Calm. He knows that Angelo will probably come try and kidnap him and/or Riton to find out where they're stashing the bullion, so he escorts Riton to a secret apartment he owns in the city, a safehouse where the two men will be able to spend the night, without fear.

The reason why *Touchez pas au grisbi* really connects with audiences, is because of the subsequent scene which takes place in Max's secret apartment, and this is the sequence in which we get to see the essence of what makes the Max/Riton friendship so durable. Co-screenwriters Jacques Becker, Albert Simonin, and Maurice Griffe very wisely stop the plot-driven narrative for five minutes, to present us with a great, character-revealing scene between the two men, a scene which makes them seem very real to us: Max sits down beside Riton at a tiny table, shares a Gabin-Silent meal of crackers and paté (Max even spreads some paté on Riton's bread), prepares a bed for him, and hands him a pair of vertically-striped pajamas which are identical to his own. This is one of the most moving scenes about unspoken friendship in movie history, because it touches on a universal truth, which is that our true friends, even for all of their faults, are all we've got in the world, and we should treasure them and protect them whenever we can. Some of the next Gabin movies, particularly a 1956 drama called *Gas-Oil* in which Gabin will play a trucker, will also slow their own narratives down in order to give us similar small moments which make the characters seem real, and when you have moments like these in any movie, it's definitely the difference between a film that's 'just okay' and a great film, because whenever we can see a movie character's vulnerabilities, we always like him all the more.

The following morning, while Riton sleeps, Max dashes off to his elderly Uncle Oscar (Paul Oettly's) office. Distinguished-looking Uncle Oscar is a high-end fence, and Max wants Oscar to sell the gold bars for him. Oscar replies that he'll try his best, although it will be difficult, since everybody will know these are the gold bars which were snatched from Orly. In Oscar's momentary absence, Max even takes the opportunity share a hot kiss with his Uncle's young, hot-chippy secretary (who is played by Delia Scala): Jean Gabin may have been a little bit older now—in fact, he was fifty when he made this picture, but he was still Jean Gabin!)

When Max arrives back at his secret pad, he can't find Riton, and Riton's not even at the hotel where he lives, so he next heads over to the Mystific. In retaliation for Angelo's kidnapping of Riton, Max and Fats nab a young gangster from Angelo's outfit, baby-faced Fifi (Paul Crauchy), drag him into the basement under the club, and begin torturing him, asking him where Angelo has taken Riton. Marinette comes down into the basement and tells Max that the phone is for him, and of course, the caller is Angelo, and he's very threatening: "If you want your friend Riton back, you'd better meet me and my men tonight, and we'll exchange your gold for Riton." Max telephones his Uncle Oscar in the middle of the night, and tells him he needs the gold back, and right now.

THE FILMS CYCLE FIVE

EXT. DESERTED ROAD, OUTSIDE OF PARIS—3:00 A.M.:

Angelo and his gangsters show up in one car, and they've brought a second car along, which contains three "back-up gangsters," just in case anything should go awry. Angelo instructs the three back-up hoods that they should make themselves and their vehicle scarce, and that they should hide a few yards away in the brush, where they won't be seen by Max, when he arrives. A moment later, Max, Pierrot, and Marco pull up in their own vehicle, and Angelo, true to his word, exchanges a blindfolded Riton for Max's gold.

After Angelo and his men drive away in their own car, the second gangster-car—the one with Angelo's three 'auxiliary gangsters'—screeches up, and these gangsters immediately blow up Max's car, so that Max, Pierrot, Riton, and Marco now have no way of getting back to Paris. Max and his guys, and Angelo's reinforcement gangsters, begin shooting at each other, and in the hail of bullets, Marco is killed. Max, Riton, and Fats, who no longer have a car of their own, commandeer the *suddenly-available* 'secondary gangster car,' and Max, Riton, and Fats jump in. They're going to have to floor it, if they want to catch up with Angelo's car, so that they can retrieve the gold and hopefully shoot Angelo, thereby avenging Marco's death. In the not-too-lengthy-but-truly-exciting car chase which ensues, Max shoots out the tires of Angelo's car, and Max's car and Angelo's car both screech to a halt. Angelo bolts from his own car looking demonic, and just when he's about to lob a grenade at at Max, Max shoots him dead. The grenade in Angelo's hand explodes, blowing up not only Angelo's car, but also Max's gold, which is now gone forever. In this movie, just like in every other heist movie, the gangsters fatalistically lose the loot which they've worked so hard to attain, and just like in every other Jean Gabin movie, our (anti)-hero accepts his fate fatalistically, without even breaking a sweat.

The following morning, we see that Riton is in the hospital recovering from his gunshot wounds, and the Doctor informs Riton's visitors, Max, Fats, and Marinette, that Riton is strong, and that he will certainly recover. Max and Riton share a joke, and we can tell that Max is happier to have his friend back than the gold. (In Gabin movies, not only is the friendship of men the most important thing in the world, but it's even more valuable than millions of dollars worth of gold bars.) Max promises that he will return to the hospital and visit Riton again, after lunch.

The film ends where it began: Max is back in Montmartre at Chez Bouche, and he's about to share a meal with a young girlfriend, Betty (Marilyn Buferd). As they're about to sit down, Fats telephones Max, and informs him that Riton has just expired. While Max looks momentarily shaken, he also looks more than a little relieved, because not only is the whole Gold Affair over now, but he's even been cleared of any possible involvement: The day's newspaper features a fake headline stating that it was, in fact, Angelo who stole the gold bars from Orly airport, and from Max's satifsfied smile, we can tell that it was he who planted the fake story. Anyway, now Max can finally retire, and in spite of everything that's happened, Jacques Becker is now providing us with a medium-happy (and certainly, wistful) ending.

Touchez pas au grisbi was photographed, quite beautifully, by one of French cinema's most masterful practitioner of light and shade, Pierre Montazel, whose striking blacks and whites bring to mind the American cinematographer James Wong Howe's best work, and the picture also features a very memorable harmonica score by Jean Weiner. *Grisbi's* producer, Robert Dorfmann, almost didn't cast Gabin in the film, at all: Jean Gabin was considered 'cold' at the French box-office when the movie was first being prepared, and Dorfmann wanted Daniel Gelin, the young actor who had played both Gabin's rival in *Martin Roumagnac* and Gabin's son in *Miroir*, to appear in *Grisbi*, as Max. Gelin, who was seventeen years younger than Gabin, felt that because he was only thirty-seven, he was too young to play the 'seasoned' Max-character, so he recommended his fifty-year-old friend and real-life mentor Jean Gabin, for the job. And the rest, as they say, is history.

What a Critic Says Today: "A wonderful treasure... a major work by the underappreciated Jacques Becker... Unbeatable as a gripping story of loyalty, betrayal and the price of friendship in the Parisian underworld... What stays with you most, however, is the poetry of Gabin's face. He's an actor who actually looks like he's lived the life he plays on screen, and by the closing scenes there's so much of the past in his face—regrets, memories, despair, even a kind of love—that a glance from him is worth an entire performance from lesser actors." (Kenneth Turan, Los Angeles *Times*, 9-5-2003 issue.)

What Another Critic Says Today: "A few years [after *Touchez pas au grisbi*], in Godard's *Breathless* (1960), Belmondo would be deliberately channeling Bogart, but here Gabin is channeling only himself. He is the original, so there is no need to look for inspiration." (Roger Ebert, Chicago *Sun-Times*, February 2, 2004 issue.)

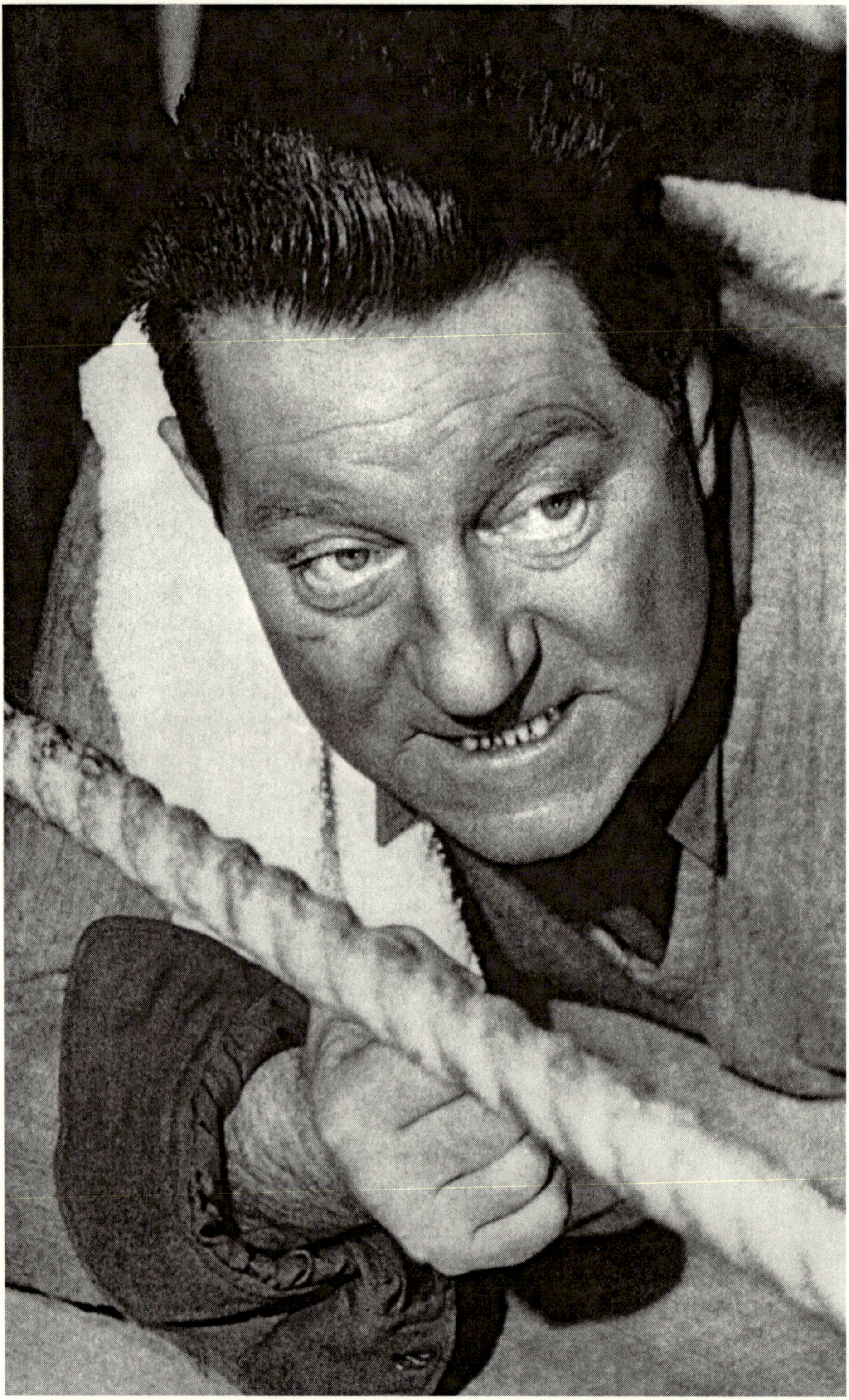

FILM 48

L'Air de Paris

France/Italy, 1954

(Literal English Translation: "THE AIR OF PARIS") Directed by Marcel Carne. Produced by Cino Del Duca and Robert Dorfmann. Screenplay by Marcel Carne and Jacques Sigurd. Based Upon the Novel, "La Choute," by Jacques Viot. Director of Photography (black and white), Roger Hubert. Editor, Henri Rust. Music by Maurice Thiriet. Production Designer, Paul Bertrand. (GENRE: DRAMA) A Production of Del Duca Films (Italy) and Galatea Film (France). Running Time, 1 hour 50 minutes. Released in France by Corona, on September 24, 1954. Never Released Theatrically in the United States.

—boxing-trainer Gabin's wife hates that he spends more time in the gym 'with the guys,'
than he does with her:
GABIN (to his Wife): "So, friendship—it really bugs you women, huh?"
WIFE: "It makes you guys all idiots!"
GABIN: "I'm going to give you a big kick in the butt!"
from "L'Air de Paris"

With the same year's previous Gabin effort, *Touchez pas au grisbi*, Jean Gabin had become France's number one star again for the second time, his first big fame since his initial Big French Fame of 1935 to 1941, and since *Grisbi* was such a big hit in his native France, he was now, just like fifteen years before, allowed to call the shots, and to pick his future projects. And so it was that he chose, as his *Grisbi* follow-up, his first and only boxing picture, which he made as a tribute to his beloved Jean Poesy, his sister Madeleine's husband. (More importantly, Poesy was the man who taught Gabin how to box when he was a teenager.) *L'Air de Paris* is a one-two punch-of-a-picture, literally, not to mention, it's a picture which represented Gabin's first team-up in fifteen years with director Marcel Carne, who had supplied him with two of his biggest pre-war hits, *Le Quai des brumes* and *Le Jour se leve*; as I have mentioned elsewhere in this book, Gabin and Carne began working together on another motion picture back in 1946, *Les Portes de la nuit* [*Doors of the Night*], but Gabin had a number of problems with the script which caused a temporary rift in the Gabin-Carne partnership. Carne made *Portes de la nuit* in 1946 with Yves Montand starring in lieu of Gabin, and in 1954, Gabin finally ended his rift with the director, when he hired Carne to helm this original boxing story, which was based upon a novel that Gabin had enjoyed by the author Jacques Viot. Carne's usual screenwriter, Jacques Prevert, did not work on *L'Air de Paris*.

As *L'Air de Paris* begins, we meet forty-something Blanche, played by Arletty who, in this film, would be reuniting with Gabin and Carne for the first time since the three of them first teamed up together in 1939's *Le Jour se leve*. Blanche is arriving in the city of the film's title, and she's departing from the train, fresh from visiting a rich, maiden-aunt on the Riviera who has left her a house in Nice. Concomitantly, on another train which is arriving on a separate platform, the beautiful actress/model Corinne (Marie Daems) is also arriving home to Paris, fresh from visiting her older suitor Pierre in Monte Carlo; basically, she's the 'kept' woman of a much-older man. Corinne's older friend Chantal (Simone Paris) picks her up, and Corinne's arrival is duly noted by a ruggedly handsome young blonde man, Andre Menard (Roland Lesaffre), who's working on the tracks. Andre even manages to pick up, and to pocket, a small pendant which Corinne drops, a pendant which is in the shape of a human hand, and he is unable to attract her attention so that he can return it.

Next, we're in a boxing studio in Paris, and we get to meet Blanche's husband Victor Le Garrec, played by Jean Gabin, whose white hair has been dyed black in this film. And while Blanche is delicate and refined—well, at least in her own mind she is—her husband Victor is a typically-Gabanian salt of the earth-type, a middle-aged boxing trainer who paternally mentors Paris's lost street teens in much the same way as Clint Eastwood's crusty old boxing trainer Frankie Dunn manages Hilary Swank's Maggie Fitzgerald character in 2004's *Million Dollar Baby*. Both Gabin's and Eastwood's characters, in their respective pictures, have already experienced their own careers-in-pugilism when they were younger men, in fact, Gabin's Victor-character was France's heavyweight champion decades ago when Blanche married him, which is no doubt why she probably deigned to do it—and both Gabin and Eastwood are now happy to help young people get their starts in return for the residual appreciation which the discovery of talented young people always brings. Blanche genuinely loves rough-hewn Victor, but it's obvious from how she looks at him, somewhat condescendingly sometimes, she might feel, in some way, that she's married-down, and maybe, although it's not mentioned in the picture, she also might feel that she's just married Victor to mess with her own family, a family which no doubt would have been happier had she married a doctor or a lawyer, in lieu of a boxer. Blanche's foremost wish is that Victor should give up the fight game and retire with her to the Riviera where she's inherited that house, and where, as she tells him, they'll be able to "just sit back and look at the sunflowers," but working-man Victor is 100% Urban, and he needs buildings and noise and gray skies just as much as Woody Allen needs the Upper East Side of NYC. ("I need Paris," Victor tells Blanche matter-of-factly, at one point early in the picture.) Victor likes the small apartment which he and Blanche share over his boxing studio, and whenever Blanche goes away to visit her relatives, which she does quite often in order to gulp-down quick tastes of the good life, he always boards some of the more transient young men whom he trains, and every time Blanche returns from the Riviera, the first thing she always has to do, is to get rid of the young boxers he's taken in, a recurring tableaux in this movie which is endlessly amusing to us, the audience, but not to her. On the occasion of Blanche's current return to Paris, she even chides Victor about how messy the apartment always becomes in her absence: "Instead of training these kids to fight, you should train them do to the dishes! Did you have the whole French army staying here?" But Victor needs his work just as much as he needs Blanche, and he tells her that, for him, it's most definitely worth living in poverty, comparative to what Blanche was used to when she grew up or what she was used to when she first married Victor, because he knows that eventually, he'll discover a new, up-and-coming, young fighter who will make his life worthwhile. While Blanche is conflicted when it comes to the lifestyle which she leads as Victor's wife, Victor is not. Blanche tells Victor that, as much as she loves him, she'll "... never be able to fully get used to this life. Maybe it's the smell." Well, they've already been married for ten years, and when Victor was young and famous, the smell didn't bother her so much; we, the film's viewers, feel like she shouldn't be complaining at all, because she's chosen to stay with him of her own free will and accord, and so if she doesn't like where they are, well, that's just her own fault.

Now if Blanche were only snooty we wouldn't like her, but it's to Carne and co-scenarist Jacques Sigurd's credit that we do, because they have invested her with good qualities which counterbalance her occasional shrewishness—ultimately, why else would the eternally real Victor ever have consented to married her? So, even though Blanche talks a pretentious game, a surprise which we will now be getting at this point in the narrative, is that she actually spends her days working in the small grocery store which belongs to their close friends, portly Angelo Posi (Folco Lulli) and Angelo's wife, Angela Posi (Ave Ninchi), and that she actually has a lot of fun working there. In spite of the brisk business that his store is doing, however, Angelo can't afford to see a Doctor, and because of his girth, he's a guy who's beset by a whole range of small but meaningful medical problems.

Meanwhile, we're going to be finding out that one of Victor's brightest young protégé/ shining-stars, Roger, a man who Victor felt was about to become boxing's Next Big Thing, was killed on the job before the movie started, because he was a part-time factory-machinist by day, while spending his nights in-training. "Roger made a mistake," Victor mumbles to himself at one point in the narrative, "He forgot that machines don't like people to get too close."

Victor lopes over to a local hospital where the clerk (Lucien Rambourg) asks him if he's related to Roger, and Victor replies that Roger didn't have any family, but that he is "a friend" and would like to pay for the boy's funeral. The clerk reminds Victor, however, that the government will be footing the bill for the burial, because twentysomething Roger, besides being a machinist and a boxer-in-training, also happened to have been a military man.

At the funeral home, Victor meets Andre Menard (Roland Lesaffre), whom we have already glimpsed at the train tracks at the beginning of the film, during that scene in which Andre had found that fallen pendant. Andre, it turns out, was Roger's best friend, and the two now bond over the fact that they both knew Roger. Victor invites Andre for a coffee at the local bar, and it is important to mention here that *L'Air de Paris* is the only movie in which Gabin will co-star with the French star Roland Lesaffre, who happened to be the real life much-younger lover of the film's openly gay director, Marcel Carne. (Gabin and Lesaffre both served in the Marine Fusiliers during World War II, so it is probable that Gabin may have introduced Lesaffre to Carne. Carne had previously awarded Lesaffre a bit part in Gabin's 1950 effort *La Marie du port* and Lesaffre would appear in a number of Carne's future pictures, as well.)

Andre Menard, as Lesaffre plays him, reminds us a lot of the younger Gabin movie-persona from those old 1930s pictures—so much so, in fact, that when Victor is meeting Andre, he's also, in a way, meeting his old, younger self, face-to-face. Andre's a consummate drifter, a man who works, and only when he chooses to, in the trainyards, and from watching some of the older Gabin pictures, and particularly *La Bete humaine*, we already know that working on the railroad is the perfect job for a tragic drifter, because if you're a trainsman, you can never be in one place for long enough for other people to injure you emotionally.

Victor, who's now needing a new #1 Protégé, notices that Andre's in good shape, and he sees that the young man could probably be in excellent, and even fighting, shape, if 'somebody' were to train him properly. Andre tells Victor that he used to box a little in the army, which is where he met the now-deceased Roger, who also boxed, but that he gave it up because he felt like he wasn't good enough, and Victor now tells Andre that Andre could definitely be a great pugilist, if only he'd spend some time training with him. Of course, Andre, a depressive master of self-sabotage who is ashamed of his own, natural gifts, demonstrates little interest in this.

But sure enough, it won't be long before Andre's venturing (cautiously) over to Victor's boxing studio. Andre has come to inform Victor, coolly, that he hasn't come to train (and we already know that this is a lie; we know that Andre's really come to sound Victor out a bit more, and to make sure that Victor is serious about his offer of training him) but to pick up Roger's clothes which, as he's now telling Victor, he's been asked to return to Roger's grieving parents, and Victor immediately, and very skillfully, gets Andre into the training spirit, by pointing out Andre's shortcomings: "By the way, kid, as long as you're here, your stomach is a little flabby, and you're short of breath. And when you start boxing professionally, it's not going to be a good idea for you to show your opponents how tired you are. So what do you say we start training right now?"

Andre tells Victor that he doesn't like people judging him—after all, that's why drifters drift, so they can't be judged—and at this point in the narrative, we're beginning to wonder: Who is it exactly that hurt Andre so much in the past that he's become so defensive? (A girl? Roger?) It's a question which is never answered in this movie, but it's possible that Andre and Roger may have, at one point, been lovers: Why else would he be picking up another man's clothing? Anyway, before Andre can make a clean getaway, Victor grabs a second young man, and asks him to go a few rounds with Andre.

When Andre and the young boxer begin throwing punches at each other, Andre really seems to like it, because people who have been hurt by life have lots of rage hidden under the surface, and a few good punches are always the best way to bring that rage out, so that it can be examined properly. Andre agrees to train with Victor, and during the course of the next few sequences, and we knew this would happen even if Andre didn't, Andre quickly becomes Victor's new 'Great White Hope,' and the two men, one old and the other young, quickly become quite the team.

Weeks pass. Victor spends all of his free time training Andre, and Blanche starts growing jealous of the two guys' ever-solidifying relationship, because she knows that now, she's never going to be able to get Victor to move to the Riviera with her, not that she would have ever been able to do this, anyway. The whole 'Blanche-Victor-Andre' relationship in this movie is a definite love triangle, and if you don't believe it, director Carne is now going to be giving us a scene in which Victor is massaging Andre sensuously in a locker room, while Andre's laying on his stomach on a long table, wearing tiny, little bikini underwear, actually purring like a kitty under the touch of Gabin's hands. (Yes, there's some heavy-duty man-mewling going on in *L'Air de Paris*.) In fact, during Andre's first big fight, which we'll be seeing later in the picture, Corner-Man Victor will even be seen to be rubbing Andre's stomach in between rounds, actually digging his fingers beneath the waistband of Andre's trunks. Gabin's getting a little too 'handsy,' and what Carne is doing in this film, and you'll never see a scene like this in any American picture made at the same time, is going beneath the surface (so to speak) and showing us the not-so-underlying homoeroticism which is part of a sport in which sparsely-dressed men in shorts, punch, grab, and rub each other all day long, and all of it is about as subtle as a Tom of Finland catalog.

When Andre wins his first match effortlessly, a small one in which his opponent is a swarthy Algerian, he gets so put-off by the adulation of the crowd—a very shy sort, he gets embarrassed when anybody pays any attention to him—he rents a small, dark, hotel room over a Moroccan restaurant, and sits alone, just like how Jean Gabin himself sat alone fifteen years earlier, in his previous collaboration with director Marcel Carne, Le Jour se leve.

Later that night, Victor appears in Andre's hotel room and confronts him: "So, you win a match and you leave without saying goodbye to me? I came to look for you, and you're in this type of a place?" Andre tells Victor that he has no intention of leaving with him or, for that matter, with anybody else: "I didn't ask you to come here, Victor. And if you want me to keep fighting for you, well, you can just forget about it, okay?" Now, Victor's primed for a Gabin-Outburst: "So, they're right about you: You're mean! You're cocky and sensitive, like a woman. You can't stand losing a match, can you? Are you going to go away, each time you lose?" Andre tells Victor that he's thinking about re-enlisting: "I was eating every day, in the army. The food wasn't great, but at least it was three squares. And, besides, the railroad's just paying me minimum, and even if it wasn't, I'm too tired to box."

Victor tells Andre, doing his best Svengali bit, that the kid has no choice in the matter: "Well, I'm taking you back home with me, whether you like it or not. You're a gift to me and to the boxing world. You're a champion but you don't know it, and you're going to be listening to me from now on, you got it? We're going to be doing a lot of hard work together, and that's the end of the story!" It's going to take a lot of work to bring Andre up-to-speed, and not just as a boxer, but also as a man: Andre has a serious inferiority complex which is in direct opposition to his very pronounced musculature, and he now begins crying and telling Victor that everything in his life has always failed, so what's the point of trying anything? When they arrive back at Victor's apartment, Victor insists that the scowling Blanche should make-up a bed for Andre, which she does, and only under complete duress.

Enter Angelo Posi's comely eighteen-year-old daughter, Maria (Maria-Pia Casilio), whose crush on Andre is instantaneous, so now, if you're keeping track, we've got not a love triangle, but a love quadrangle, consisting of Blanche, Victor, Andre, and Maria, a polysexual love-soufflé which only French filmmakers and American pornographers can ever hope to cook up with such abandon. "I'm not into boxers," Maria tells Andre, but her drooling eyes belie her phonily-disinterested mien.

Of course, it won't be long before Victor and Andre are running together in the woods, and young Andre's exhausted out of his mind—but hearty old Victor is just getting started. "I'm never going to make it, and I don't even want to try anymore," Andre huffs, and Victor heads into immediate supportive mode, to buoy the boy up: "You're progressing very well. Keep going!" Andre asks Victor when he'll be a professional, and Victor answers, "Maybe in a couple of years. It depends on you. Also, if I didn't say it before, you're going to have to keep working at a day job, whether it's at the trainyard or somewhere else, because boxing alone, no matter how big you get, will never bring you enough money to live on." (Gabin is saying this, of course, forty years before the now-common mega-million dollar paydays which every famous sports figure pulls down as a matter of routine.) When Andre's asleep that night, Victor tells Blanche, "The kid acts tough, but I know he's a softy," and of course, this same quality always applied to Jean Gabin himself, both in his movies and in real life. (You already know the drill: Gabin was, to parapharase Marlene Dietrich, "… tough on the outside, but tender on the inside…")

That night, Victor sits at Andre's bedside, like any father might do with his high school-aged kid, except Andre's not Victor's son, and Victor's sitting a little too-close-for-comfort, so the whole thing is verging on creepiness. "What's in all of this, for you?" Andre asks Victor, since Victor's leering at him like he probably also leers at the tasty rabbits which hang in any Parisian outdoor marketplace. Victor tells him, "When I was your age, I wasn't working. I had no career. I met somebody older than me—a mentor—and he took me away from the gutters." "I have nothing in life," Andre replies, "except for my strength," and Victor next eyes Andre's supple body, moaning, "When you have an opponent, he is as naked as you are!" Victor massages Andre again, and tells him that he's going to get him a job at his friends,' the Posis,' grocery store.

That night, Blanche is getting a little ultra-rare face-time with Victor. She tells Victor she thinks that he's made the wrong decision in bringing Andre home to live with them: "You think you've found that rare bird, haven't you—but that kid is lost. Why are you getting so excited about him? I wish he'd lose. I wish you'd take care of me, for once!" Hilariously, Victor just Gabin-Shrugs, telling her, "I would love to spend more time with you, dear, but you're never going to be a famous boxer," and he proceeds to chuck her under the chin (he does this twice in the movie)—What a pal!

Before long, Victor's training program, which consists alternately of damning Andre with faint praise and pretty continually rubbing Andre's groin, is really starting to work, and we now see Victor smiling, which Gabin atypically does a lot in this picture, because *L'Air de Paris* gives us a rare, 'hopeful' Gabin instead of the traditional world-weary one. Andre tells Victor, "Guess what. I think it would be good for me to have a win in the ring as a present to myself, for my twenty-fifth birthday." In fact, Victor already knows that Andre's victory in his forthcoming fight is assured, so he's already started planning a surprise, post-match birthday bash for the boy.

Now, it's time for a scene set in a fancy restaurant in Les Halles (in the first arrondissement), home of Paris's major outdoor market, a restaurant in which the well-heeled are chowing-down in style, and these 'heels' include upwardly-mobile dater Corinne, the pendant-dropper whom we met at the beginning of the picture. Corinne is seated at a table with a group of too-trendy fashion business friends, who include the flamboyant dress designer Jean-Marc, as well as Chantal, and an old haute-couture-wearing lady (Marcelle Praince) whose weird headdress makes her look, to one of the diners, like a "Sioux." At this point, Andre and two of his surly/unwashed trainyard pals enter the restaurant. While Chantal and the Sioux are horrified that these lowlife vagabonds have dared to corrupt the rarified air of such a fancy establishment, Jean-Marc is delighted by the sight of 'rough trade,' and this scene is very reminiscent of those restaurant scenes in older Gabin pictures like *Gueule d'amour*, *Martin Roumagnac* and *Gloria*, in which rich people wigged-out whenever poor people made their fetid way into their stodge-lodges. Jean-Marc even decides that he'd like to take a photograph of Corinne with Andre, for an American magazine in which she'll soon be appearing. Andre, of course, likes Corinne immediately and it's mutual, in spite of the fact that they are from different classes, and he now tells her that he saw her once on a train, but she is unable to recall him. Corinne and Andre, who are now seeing each other for the first time in the movie, look at each other with instant love, and Corinne whispers, "It's so painful to have a lot of money," trying to score points with him by making an excuse for her gauche, and way-too-loud, friends.

After dinner, Corinne leaves the restaurant with Andre, and she lets him take her home to the most opulent apartment you've ever seen which she shares with Chantal, an apartment which doubles as a high-end trinket shop from whence Corinne and Chantal sell expensive looking kitsch items to rich people—and most of the items, as Corinne confesses to Andre, are fake. On their first night together, Corinne is definitely ready for Andre to take her in his arms and engage her in a heavyweight 'round' of petting, but he tells her he can't because he's in training, and she's saddened when, very suddenly, he leaves. And just when he starts walking down the street, and heading back to Victor and Blanche's place, he suddenly has a change of heart, but it's too late because, at that same moment, Chantal pulls up in her fancy car, quashing any potential quashing.

Back at the Posis' grocery store, we see that Victor's bought Andre a pretty great birthday present: It's a real boxer's robe, which Victor has had tailored especially for Andre, and the robe even happens to have Andre's initials sewn into it. Yes, today is both Andre's birthday and the night of his big fight, and Victor, Blanche, and the Posi family are busily setting up the grocery store for the party which will commemorate what they know will most certainly be Andre's incipient victory, and Blanche is the only one among them who harbors some doubt that Andre will win; she even asks Victor, somewhat coldly, "Is this a party to celebrate the death of your illusions?"

> BLANCHE: What the hell is it with you and Andre, anyway? You didn't do this much for all the other ones! You're totally into him!
> VICTOR (mutters/eyes, narrow slits): The other ones weren't champions.
> BLANCHE: I hope he loses.

While Andre is a complainer by nature, he's also man enough to have shown up for his big fight. At the outset of the event, Victor is worried, because he knows the specific judges personally, and he knows that they are notoriously difficult. He's also aware that Andre's opponent, Pietro Mancini, looks like he could wipe the floor with him. As the fight begins, we get to see how French spectator sports attract hecklers, just like any other sporting event around the world, and one smartass in the crowd even baits Andre with a cry of, "Hey, Popeye, you forgot your spinach!" Director Carne is now giving us a tres-solide, Raging Bull/Champion-esque fight scene, and one great thing about watching *L'Air de Paris* for an American, is that it's an opportunity to see French Boxing, which is seemingly free of all of those crazy regulations which tie the hands, almost literally, of American boxing. In the French version of the sport, or at least in this movie's version of French boxing, moves which are considered verboten in the U.S., such as grabbing, holding, strangling and, per Alduous Huxley, everything, are totally permitted. Mancini has already won the first few rounds, and Andre looks like he's not going to make it. In between rounds, Victor starts massaging Andre's stomach again, and while he does, he simultaneously offers-up some confidence-boosting platitudes, along the lines of, "Mancini is down today! You can win him!" and, with his hand down Andre's pants, "You're almost there!"

Just when Andre's almost down-for-the-count, Corinne enters with her fashion-forward friend Jean-Marc, and when Andre sees her, he becomes revivified with a burst of newfound energy and confidence, and now he's suddenly winning! Hilariously, grocerman Angelo Posi

With Roland Lesaffre.

is so caught up in the thrill of the moment, he accidentally starts cheering for Mancini by mistake, and his whole family stares daggers at him. Corinne and Jean-Marc are happy: Now that Andre is winning, he is no longer too low class for her. When Andre wins the fight (although he can't really enjoy it, because he's been punched in the liver), the only person who's visibly not happy about Andre's win is Blanche because—and we can tell this just by looking at her face—she knows it means that, for as long as Victor's managing Andre—a/k/a, 'The Boxing World's New King'—she and Victor will have to remain in Paris indefinitely. Conversely, however, Blanche's moment of anger is also proving how much she loves Victor because, if she didn't, she would have up-and-quit him a long time ago.

Post-fight, Andre's all gussied-up ('Joe Success'), and is busily canoodling with Corinne in Chantal's swanky apartment, having rather smugly blown-off the victory party which Victor is currently throwing in his honor, back at the Posi family's grocery store; while only a few sequences ago, Andre had no interest in prizefighting for a living, he's now bragging to Corinne that boxing is 'his big love,' even in spite of the fact that he's not showing up for his own victory celebration. And just as Blanche is jealous of Victor's beyond paternal love for Andre, so too are we finding out, during this scene, that Corinne is jealous of 'Andre's new mistress,' boxing, even though she is also ecstatic about his newfound success. Corinne asks Andre if he plans on attending his birthday party, but he just brushes off her suggestion, telling her, "I don't want to be with people who don't really love me, people who are just using me." Corinne asks Andre if he's afraid of Victor's wrath and, simultaneously, across town at the party, where the guest of honor is nowhere to be seen, Blanche is pulling a whole 'I-told-you-so'-number on her husband: "Why are you complaining about how that ingrate didn't show up? You knew what he was like when you dug him up!" Victor is so mad—at Andre, for not showing up; at Blanche for yelling at him—that he now starts defending his friendship with Andre, in spite of the fact that he's mad at Andre, on account of Andre's rude no-show.

>VICTOR: Friendship: It really bugs you women, huh?
>BLANCHE: It makes all you guys idiots.
>VICTOR: I'm going to give you a big kick in the butt!

The next morning, at Chantal's apartment, Andre has just stepped out of the shower and, obviously, the two have spent the night making love. Andre kisses Corinne and tells her, "You're the only one who could love me, but I just wish you weren't part of such a [high-toned] lifestyle." He tells her she's so down-to-earth and real, that she really doesn't fit into this grandiosely-garish apartment, and this is where she hints around (he doesn't get it) that even though both love each other, ultimately, it can't last, because she's part of the world of wealthy and he's working-class and, in France, never the twain shall meet. At that moment, the phone rings: It's Corinne's unseen-in-the-film suitor, Pierre, who happens to be calling from Monte Carlo. Andre asks her who's on the phone, and she replies, "Somebody who loves me, but whom I don't love." (Corinne clearly loves Andre more than she loves Pierre, but because Pierre is rich, he's the clear winner—at least, at the moment, anyway.)

Andre shows up at the boxing club the following morning, having missed the entirety of his own birthday party, and Victor begins paternally reprimanding him for his selfishness: "Where were you last night? You seem healthy. Were you in the country? Are you tired? Well, you can do what you want. You're old enough. But listen, I have to tell you that you're not polite." Andre looks very healthy from his previous night's lovefest with Corinne, something which is not lost on Victor: "Enough with women, Andre, okay? You have to preserve yourself for other guys!" (Okay, now the homosexuality in *L'Air de Paris* isn't just implied; Victor has just uttered that exact line. It's no wonder boxing is called 'the sweet science!')

But Victor can't stay mad at Andre, his son-slash-unrequited gay crush. Andre has dinner with Blanche and Victor that night in the couple's kitchen, and Andre is now mostly reconciled with Victor, who continues to be so taken with Andre that he's already forgotten about how angry he is with him. As far as this dinner sequence's visual composition goes, it's right out of a Saturday Evening Post/Norman Rockwell-style painting of a husband and wife having dinner in a cozy kitchen, except that, in this case, we've got a big, lumbering boxer sitting between the couple, scarfing down their bread and paté with all the precision of a lumberjack. Anyway, these few moments of almost-domestic bliss are now interrupted by Andre, who tells the couple that he's going to be leaving Paris, and for good.

The big surprise, here, is that the first person to react in horror to that statement is not Victor, but Blanche (we didn't see this coming!) who has actually grown, without even realizing it, to love Andre, almost as a son, and this is one of many nice moments which make this movie seem so real. When Andre storms out of the room, Blanche asks her husband about why the boy is leaving them, and Victor replies that Andre's in love with someone; in fact, Victor believes that the reason Victor is leaving Paris, is that he wants to run away with Corinne. And just as Andre's heading out the door, Victor stops him and tries to manipulate him into staying: "You'd better be careful with that girl, that Corinne. She's different than you are." (Yes, here's another old French movie, in which one of the main themes is class-difference.) Andre tells Victor that this is a matter between himself and Corinne only, but Victor begs to differ: "It's between us, too, Andre, because you're using the girl as an excuse to give up fighting. Did you know that an evening out with a girl is a week of training wasted?" This new bout of cold, Gabinian logic works again, and Andre suddenly looks like a little kid who's been caught with his hand in the cookie jar. Andre pleads with Victor not to be mad at him, and Victor tells him, as Blanche listens from behind a closed door, "When I met you, Andre, I was at a point where I was just about to give up on management. I bet everything on you and, thanks to me, you can become somebody. But it's really up to you, and ultimately, you can do whatever you want." Victor now sulks away, rejoining his wife at the table.

Soon after Andre has left Blanche and Victor's apartment, and he's walking down the street, he runs into cute, eighteen-year-old Maria Posi, whose crush on him has continued, unabated. He asks Maria if she can relate a message to Victor, for him, some sentiments which he hasn't been able to utter himself: "Maria, could you do me a favor? The next time you see Victor, can you tell him that I'm not a bastard… and that I love him?" Andre knows that Maria has come to see him to confess her love to him and, because he's dating Corinne, he knows that he's going to have to let her down easily: "And there's someone else I love, too, Maria: It's Corinne. You're a good girl, and I'm glad that you like me. But, believe me, all of you will be happy without me around."

Andre next arrives at Corinne's house, believing that he will be going away with her, but he shouldn't have put all of his eggs in one basket, because Chantal is there, and she gives him an unexpected surprise. She tells him that Corinne has left Paris suddenly, because she wants to 'start her life over, fresh' by herself, and without any men—not Andre and not Pierre (ni l'un, ni l'autre). She also recounts to Andre that Corinne felt like she was keeping Andre back from becoming mega-successful, by occupying too much of his time. Chantal hands Andre the pendant which he had earlier returned to Corinne, and Andre asks her if she knows where Corinne has gone, to which her reply is simple: "She told me not to tell you. She doesn't want to see Pierre or you."

In the next scene, Andre is alone, down by the Seine. He's unsure of where to go next, knowing only that now, he can return neither to Corinne, nor to Victor. Suddenly, Victor, who's been able to track Andre down (before Corinne left town, she called Victor and tipped him off that Andre was leaving) barrels-up to the kid and gives him a paternal pat on the shoulder—because a 'father/lover' always forgives—and he seems ready to take him back into the fold immediately. Andre asks Victor if he knows where Corinne is, but the older guy has no idea. They walk away together, and Carne superimposes the sound of Andre winning a fight sometime in the future, and based on this, we know that Victor will resume his training of Andre, and that Andre will, and soon no doubt, be enjoying a legendary career as a famous, championship boxer—that is that is, if he doesn't keep running away!

L'Air de Paris is not only a very entertaining movie, but it's also a very sumptuous love-letter to Paris, a city which the picture's cinematographer, Roger Hubert, shows-off to great effect, in the same idyllic manner in which Woody Allen and his own director of photography, Gordon Willis, depicted their own city of *Manhattan*, in the eponymous 1979 film-comedy. This picture's title, *L'Air de Paris*, refers not only to Paris's sweet, fresh air, but also to the pretentious, rich people, like Blanche, and like Corinne's fashion industry friends who are always 'putting on airs,' thereby freaking out all of the 'real,' working people, who include Jean Gabin's Victor character. A number of times in the movie, co-screenwriters Marcel Carne and Jacques Sigurd even work in references to "air"—when Victor visits Andre at his Algerian hotel room, he tells him the air outside is clean, and Blanche tells Victor at one point, that whenever Andre makes one of his sudden disappearances, that he always leaves a powerful draft of air behind him.

Since *L'Air de Paris* is one of Jean Gabin's warmest and sweetest 1950s' movies, and also because it's a definite crowd pleaser—after all, it's a boxing movie—why was it never released in the United States? Probably, it's because of the film's homosexual undertones which, as I've already mentioned, become slightly more than implied as the narrative progresses, moments which bring that whole, 'Gabin Movie: Friendship-of-Men-Trope' to a new and completely different level. Still, *L'Air de Paris* is just as engaging as those more famous American boxing pictures, *Champion*, *Body and Soul*, *Rocky*, and *Raging Bull* (which are mostly pretty gay anyway, what with all of those shirtless men pounding away at each other... and come to think of it, all sports are gay). And while *L'Air de Paris* may have been a hard-sell for Americans, it wasn't too potent a brew for Europeans to swallow: At the 1954 Venice Film Festival, Jean Gabin won the Best Actor prize for his performance as Victor.

L'Air de Paris is a very good film for the same reason that *Touchez pas au grisbi* is a very good film, which is that Carne and Sigurd have taken the time to make all of the film's characters real, humble, and sweet-natured, and therefore recognizable to, and likable for, audiences. While Victor and Blanche are always exchanging harsh words with each other, we really feel like they love each other more than anything in the world, and that their true love overrides all of the day-to-day bickering in which they are always engaging. Blanche says she wants Victor to retire to the Riviera with her, but when push comes to shove, we can tell that what really makes her happy, is when her husband is happy, and she knows that he'd never be happy living in the frou-frou Riviera, and that the mean streets of Paris, and the city's sweaty boxing rings, are where Victor really belongs. In the film's very best moment, Blanche and Victor are in bed together, and she tells him that she's always going to be with him, no matter what he decides to do with "the rest of his life." It's a small moment which nevertheless conveys big feelings, and it is also a moment which neutralizes all of the vindictiveness which Blanche is always throwing at Victor; it's a moment which proves to us, the film's audience, that love is stronger than anything else in the whole world... and it might even be stronger than a smartly-delivered right-hook.

Pierre Granier-Deferre, the film's young assistant director was also First A.D. on Gabin's 1951 drama *La Nuit est mon royaume*, and he will one day direct two Jean Gabin films on his own—1970's *La Horse* and 1971's *Le Chat*.

What a Critic Said at the Time: "Gabin is as wonderful as ever, with his relaxed strength. He is sensitive and vulnerable." (*Telerama Magazine*, 10-3-54 issue. Critic: Andre Bazin.)
What Another Critic Said at the Time: "Gabin is remarkable, with his power. His emotions are calm and controlled." (*Le Monde, Paris*. 5-8-54 issue. Critic: Jean de Baroncelli.)
What a Third Critic Said at the Time: "Arletty and Jean Gabin are sympathetic. They bring out tears and make us feel emotional. Their simple story is written tenderly." (*Le Figaro, Paris*. 10-2-54 issue. Critic: Claude Mauriac.)

Top: With Roger Hanin. Above: He drives by night…

1954 — 1976 | 25

FILM 49

Gas-Oil

France, 1955

Directed by Gilles Grangier and (uncredited) Henri Verneuil. Produced by Jean-Paul Guibert. Written by Michel Audiard and Gilles Grangier. Based Upon the novel Du raisin dans le gas-oil by Georges Bayle. Director of Photography (black and white), Pierre Montazel. Editor, Jacqueline Thiedot. Production Designer, Jacques Colombier. Music by Henri Crolla. Assistant Directors Jacques Deray and Michel Ayats. (GENRE: DRAMA) Running Time 1 hour 32 minutes. A Production of Intermondia Films. Released in France on November 9, 1955 by the J. Arthur Rank Organization and Victory Films. Never Released Theatrically in the United States.

"If I get fired from my job, I'll still wake up at five in the morning, anyway!"
– defiant trucker Jean Gabin rebels by waking up early when he doesn't even have to,
in *"Gas-Oil"*

In the 1950s, the burgeoning American car culture, which was typified by the '57 Chevy, the convertible, and Elvis, began its spread to Europe, because Europeans were hot for American cars, and if you don't believe me, skip a few chapters ahead and check out the chapter on Gabin's 1961 picture *Le Cave se rebiffe*, in which one of the main characters pines away for a big American sedan of his own, because he knows that if he has one he'll be, as the French love to say—at least, this is what they say in this author's mind—"*soopaire*-cool." The 1950s' car culture, both in America and abroad, would breed all manner of racecar and hot rod flicks, and not just B-movies like 1956's Chuck Connors/Frank Gorshin non-classic *Hot Rod Girl*, but also A-pictures, none of which is more famous than Nicholas Ray's James Dean classic *Rebel without a Cause* which, like the Gabin picture you're about to read about, was also made in 1955. And car movies, both in the U.S. and Europe, begat trucker movies, because as we already know, the 1950s would also give the world Robert Mitchum as a trucker/moon-shiner in '55's *Thunder Road*, which Mitchum also produced, and for which he also warbled the theme song (Jean Gabin's not the only tough-guy who can sing, ya know), and Jules '*Rififi*' Dassin's exciting 1957 film *Thieves' Highway*, in which Lee J. Cobb played a psychotic fruit-industry kingpin who made life hell on wheels, quite literally, for the trucker who moved his sweet-n'-pulpy merchandise, Richard Conte.

The Jean Gabin picture, *Gas-Oil,* is pretty pedigreed: It was directed by Gilles Grangier, and it's a much more assured piece than the first one which Grangier and Gabin made together, *La Vierge du Rhin.* It also features the crisply beautiful cinematography of Pierre Montazel who, just one year before, had added his trademark zest to *Touchez pas au grisbi.*

Gas-Oil also has the distinction of being Gabin's first of nineteen movies to have been penned by one of France's premiere screenwriters, not to mention one of the actor's dearest friends, Michel Audiard, a man who continues to be so popular in France, (Audiard wrote 107 produced screenplays in his lifetime, and many more which weren't filmed), that today, about twenty-five years after his 1985 passing, he happens to have his very own popular on-line fan club, 'michelaudiard.com,' and all over the world today, filmmakers continue to spin out remakes of his old movies. In 2000, for example, Gene Hackman and Morgan Freeman co-starred in director Stephen Hopkins' *Under Suspicion,* a remake of Audiard's Lino Ventura-starring thriller from 1972, *Gard a vue.*

In *Gas-Oil,* Gabin plays a surly, fiftysomething truck driver, and who better to "keep on truckin'" than tough, silent Jean Gabin, a/k/a, 'the Original Rebel without a Cause.' After all, what do truck drivers do? They're drifters-on-wheels who are never too long for one place. They sit alone; they think; they stare pensively out of the window. And who's better suited to sitting, thinking, and being alone than Our Man from Meriel?

Michel Audiard adapted his screenplay from the novel *Du raisin dans le Gas-Oil* (*Grapes in the Gas-Oil*) by Georges Bayle and, of course, its title is a play on Steinbeck's *Grapes of Wrath,* a dramatic work which itself involved the travails of the working-classes. The languid French countryside of Clermont-Ferrand, which is eight hours south of France by car (today, of course, it is home to the popular Clermont-Ferrand Short Film Festival) which Gilles Grangier depicts in this movie, is not so different than the languid Oklahoma dust bowl which Steinbeck painted for us, in *Grapes of Wrath.*

As the film begins, Jean Chape—Gabin is 'The Everyman' so, naturally, his character is going to get the Anglified surname of 'Chape,' or in English, 'Man' (which, in effect, means that J.G.'s character's name, is 'Jean the Man')—is waking up at home at his usual 5:00 am, and upon awakening this particular morning, he plods over to the gas stove (Quick! Let's get the film's 'gas motif' started, ASAP!) to brew up, per Dolly Parton, a 'cup of ambition,' and he next heads outside to prepare his newly-purchased truck, of which he's very proud, for the day's runs. A couple of his driver buddies, Lucien Rangondin (Camille Guerini) and Lucien's son Pierrot (Marcel Bozzuffi, a handsome young guy whom we'll be seeing in five different Gabin pictures, and also in William Friedkin's Academy Award-winning 1971 monster hit, *The French Connection* in which Bozzuffi is the hit-man who hesitates, open-mouthed, before falling backwards when Gene Hackman shoots him off of the staircase), turn up in Chape's kitchen, and the three men start discussing their movements for the day. Chape and *les Rangodin* have an eight-hour drive to Paris ahead of them, in fact they're due

1954 — 1976 | 27

in the City of Lights by 5:00 p.m., and even though they're not looking forward to the long haul, the guys love their job, anyway.

Chape hasn't yet finished paying off his sleek new truck, which he treats with kid gloves, in the same way that Gabin treats the trains under his care delicately, in *La Bete humaine* and *La Nuit est mon royaume*. Pierrot rides shotgun with Chape, and before they make their run, they first visit the local butcher, because they're delivering a huge meat order to him. Next, they stop over at their favorite trucker bar, Serin's, for an early-morning pick-me-up.

Twentysomething Mauricette (Lisette Lebon) is the savory barmaid whom all of the truckers crave, and the bar's owner, Emile Serin (Albert Dinan), is the go-between for Chape and the other drivers, all of whom are employed by Mr. Felix (Robert Dalban), the proprietor of the Felix Trucking Company. So whenever Chape stops by the bar, he's showing up not just for a booze-up, but mainly, to secure from Serin an updated list of his daily runs and, of course, to flirt with the able-bodied Mauricette. *Gas-Oil* shows us how tightly-knit the truckers are, and how truckers comprise just as much of a community as the Freemasons or Yale University's Skull and Bones Society. If you mess with one of them, you've messed with them all.

After Serin gives Chape an updated list of the day's runs, Chape laughs heartily, and accepts the flirtation of an older waitress, Lucienne (Simone Berthier) who today, and probably just like every other day, is making him a sandwich to take on the road, and also just like every day, she's using old bread and sausage. This, of course, is a joke between Chape and Mauricette: Here Lucienne is comically impugning Chape's masculinity, because he won't return her (frequent) advances; if he's not hot for her, maybe, in her opinion, he's old, dried up and impotent. As we're going to be seeing, *Gas-Oil*, besides being a film about friendship, is also a film about ageism and aging and, of course, impotency is the most mortifying part of aging.

Just as Chape and Pierrot have now, finally, steeled themselves—and boozed themselves, and sandwiched themselves—for the day's runs, director Grangier next cuts to the highway, where two cars which, together, contain a total of four gangsters—Scoppo (Francois Darbon), Schwob (Roger Hanin), Paulo (Bob Ingarao), and the panama-hatted 'Driver' (Jean Le Fevbre)—pull up alongside a payroll truck. The gangsters shoot the two payroll workers to death in broad daylight and take their money, but one of the four gangsters, Scoppo, suddenly double-crosses the other three: He takes the money—fifty million francs—and burns rubber outta there, in the second vehicle.

That night, oblivious to the headline, as well as to the existence of the payroll worker-snuffing gangsters, Chape That night, Chape arrives alone in the small town of Retournac, which is not far from Clermont-Ferrand. He pulls his truck up in front of the local schoolhouse, and it's now time for him to be making a very special delivery, the kind of a delivery which only mega-smooth Jean Gabin can make: Chape is involved with Alice, the town's fetching school-teacher, who's played by Jeanne Moreau, in fact, *Gas-Oil* represents the second film in a period of one year in which Jean Gabin would appear with Moreau, because the two of them were also in 1954's *Touchez pas au grisbi*, although Moreau was only featured in a supporting role in that picture. Alice loves Chape, but she also feels a bit stigmatized, because she's been having an affair with him for years, and he's never asked her to marry him. Chape often, and not-so-secretly, stays overnight in Alice's room which happens to be right above the schoolhouse, and while she truly loves him, she also feels uncomfortable at times because, even though the people in her town truly like her, they all also feel scandalized by her illicit relationship. (French movies which were made at the time of *Gas-Oil* were very often among the sexiest in the world, as far as what filmmakers could present visually on the screen, but—and God Bless French-Catholic Morality—at the same time, quite hypocritically, the characters would always have to get punished for their dalliances, just like how, in the American crime pictures of the 1930s and 1940s, on-screen violence could be depicted, as long as the message at the end of the movie involved that austere admonishment, "Crime Does Not Pay.") "When you're on the road, you should see how the other women look at me," Alice tells Chape. Her dream, of course, is that Chape will give up the trucking life and marry her, good-n'-proper, but of course, Jean Gabin's a peripatetic fellow, and his movie characters always eschew being, per Gabin's dialogue in a Jean Renoir picture which he'll make in 1955, *French Can-Can*, "tethered like cows." Chape tells Alice that, now that he's 'older'—Gabin, in real life, was fifty-one years old when he made this movie, which isn't *that* old—no employers are going to be lining up to get him started on a brand new, and completely different, career should he decide to quit this one, and that she should be careful about what she wishes for.

Today's Alice's birthday, and he's bought her a very sheer dress which, as she's now telling him, reminds her of "what angels probably wear," and when she tries it on for him, she loves it so much, that she suddenly feels compelled to read him a couple of verses by the 17th century poet, Jean de la Fontaine. (Chiffon dresses, just like fish, are probably 'brain food.') "You don't give me gifts very often," she teases him, "but when you do, they're nice!" Chape, as we're seeing now, makes up for his frequent absences, by buying Alice a lot of sexy and frilly clothes, and even though she sees through his gestures, she loves his gifts anyway, in fact, she'll even admit that she is turned-on by the fact that he's so frequently absent, because his absences just make him even more desirable, and even more 'Gabin-Mysterious,' than he already is.

Then, Chape, unexpectedly and shyly, proposes an idea, because he wants to upgrade their relationship to something that's more than dating but which, at the same time, is less than marriage. (You know: "More than kith, but less than kind… with benefits.") "You know, Alice, you don't have to live here at the school. I mean, the kids don't need you all the time. So why don't you come and live with me?" He adds that if she comes to shack up with him, maybe, in two-to-three years, he'll think about retiring from his trucking career, but that is, only if she'll give up her teaching career, as well. The best teachers are always eloquent though, and so Alice is now very level-headed when she makes her response: "If I give up teaching in two or three years, you'll reproach me for it." He tells her that, in his opinion, "women

With Ginette Leclerc.

should stay home and do the ironing," and when he says this, she can't even get mad at him, because he says it with a mischievous, and rarely-seen, Gabin-Grin. She next summarizes 'their relationship, so far:' "When I took you as a lover instead of a husband, Jean, maybe I made a mistake. Sin never pays. I mean, when you visit me here, you always have to wake up early, so that nobody will see you leave, and you're always impolite and grumpy in the morning, and I only get the best of you for one or two hours, at night… I wonder why I love you so much." Of course, Chape's got the perfect answer, which he proceeds to download, just as easily as he downloads crates from his truck: "I guess you must think I'm really cute. Even when it's dark, I'm cute!"

The next morning, just before dawn, Chape wakes up in Alice's bed, heads out to his truck which is parked in front of the school, and drives away through some heavy morning rain and extra-thick fog. And just when he's only been on the road for a few seconds, an arm (whose arm?) pushes a dead body out of the car. It's the body of Antoine Scoppo, the gangster whom we saw ripping off his three cohorts at the beginning of the picture, but we don't see who's pushing him out. Chape, who hasn't yet been properly caffeinated, is so tired, that he doesn't hit the brakes in time, and accidentally, he plows right over the corpse. (What's French for 'human speed bump?') He gets a little flustered, believing that he's killed the guy, since he doesn't know that Scoppo was already dead when 'the mystery arm' pitched out of the car, but he doesn't get too flustered—remember, we're talking about masculine Jean Gabin, not one of today's young, chinless, pretty-boy actors—and he runs back to the school, waking Alice and pontificating loudly about what he thinks he's just done, and Alice proceeds to console him, in language which nobody will ever construe as being true 'legalese:' "If the man was already lying down, you're not responsible!" (Wow! You've got to love those French driving laws!) She asks him if he's already phoned the accident in, to the police, and he tells her that he can't: "The cops will ask where I'm coming from. They'll know I was leaving from your house!" In the puritanical France of 1955, much worse than murder, at least according to the logic of this film, is the horrible stigma which Chape knows will attach itself to him, should the cops, followed by the newspapers, ever get wind of the fact that Alice has been sleeping with a man who doesn't 'belong to her,' legally.

Chape thinks that Scoppo wasn't dead, but merely dead-drunk, and that his truck changed the guy's fate from 'dead-drunk' to 'dead-dead.' Not wanting to think about it anymore, he solemnly drives himself down to the police station to tell the police what happened, just as resigned to his fate as any of Jean Gabin's characters used to be in any of those old, mid-to-late 1930s' pictures. The local cops are a little bewildered since, not only is Chape not intimidated by them, but he's actually yawning as they question him, and the Inspector in charge (Jean Lanier) now fires off a couple of questions. "Were you drinking? Are you coming from Paris? Most truck drivers are carrying too much cargo in their trucks. You guys can't steer well, and your trucks never have good breaks. You were driving over the speed limit and ignoring the fact that the roads are bad." This unwanted evaluation of his driving skills wakes Chape up, just enough for the first of two Gabin-Outbursts which he'll spew-out during the course of the picture, and we'll actually see him, just like his truck, going from zero-to-sixty in the space of about two seconds: "You're pushing me to my limits! You're treating me like an assassin! *J'EN AI MARRE!*" ("I've had enough!") The Inspector tells Chape that he'll have to stay in jail until it can be proven that he's not guilty, also letting him know that his truck will be impounded, as well. Now, of course, Chape doesn't give a damn about doing jail time, but he does worry about the fact that he's going to be losing his new rig, because his truck is his only source of livelihood and, to further the film's unspoken truck-as-phallus metaphor, his potency. Chape, who's tired of cops, is thrown in jail for forty-eight hours and is then released, when the cops can't find any evidence against him.

When Chape leaves the police station, Alice is waiting outside for him with the Mayor of Clermont-Ferrand (Albert Montigny) by her side. She's just been telling the Mayor that she's resigned from her teaching post, and she's also confessed to him—and he already knew this anyway, just like everybody else in town already knew it, as well—that she's been sleeping with Chape. The Mayor is her friend, so she doesn't feel too uncomfortable telling him about her 'immorality:' She knows that scandals, such as 'sleeping with somebody to whom you're not married,' can taint a whole town, so she's taken the pre-emptive strike, and she's told the Mayor about her relationship with Chape herself, before the press can grab ahold of it—which, in a small town, it probably would, and sooner, rather than later.

Chape is now at the offices of the Felix Trucking Company, and he's asking his boss, Mr. Felix (Robert Dalban), for a little help in rescuing his truck from the police impound, and even though Felix is nice to his friend Chape, he is unable to help: "Because of you, Chape, this company is going to start having problems with our clients in Paris. Since we don't have your truck, a lot of folks won't be getting their deliveries today. Our [client-companies] are going to sue us!" Chape, with his tail-between-his-legs, decides to make-nice: "I really need my truck back, and today, okay? If I can't drive long distances, I have nothing in life." At this point, Felix brings up the real reason he can't help—"It's not my fault you've been with a girl, Chape."—and by this, Felix means that his trucking company would be just as scandalized by Chape's illicit affair with Alice as it would by Chape's highway 'misfortune.' He tells Chape he can loan him a small truck and that Chape can deliver coal for him, but Chape, who usually drives luxury items around, feels that this would be beneath him. Driving is a part of Chape, and ten days without driving for him, is unheard of. As he'll tell Lucien and Pierre Rangondin in an ensuing scene, "I don't know what to do. If I can't drive my truck, I'll still get up every morning at five o'clock, anyway!"

When Chape sees Alice that night, he tells her, somewhat deflatedly, that Felix won't let him drive for ten days, and that for the next week-and-a-half, he might have to be—horror-of-horrors—riding a bus to visit her; and when he says this, we can tell, from his pouty-mouthed Gabin-Grimace, that not having his truck around is definitely the worst punishment he's ever received in his entire life. Chape is envious of his sometimes co-drivers, Lucien and Pierrot Rangondin, because he knows that the next morning, Lucien and Pierrot are going to be making a big run down south to Marseilles, and he had counted on being able to go along with them. Chape tells Alice, as he's already told Felix and the Rangodins, that he's not sure what he's going to do without work for the next ten days.

Alice has a bit of good news for Chape, as well: She tells him that, since the town's new teacher—the lady who's going to be replacing her—will be starting work at the school the following Monday, and since she (Alice) won't be needed there anymore, she'll now be able to move into Chape's place. Now, Chape's got a woman *and* a truck, and it's just like that great line in the French director Barbet Schroeder's 1991 American movie *Barfly*, where Mickey Rourke's Charles Bukowski-clone, Henry Chinaski, happily chimes to Faye Dunaway, "Yesterday, I had nothing: Now I've got a woman and a radio!"

That night, Chape and Alice dine with Lucien and Pierrot Rangodin as well as Lucien's wife Maria (Germaine Michel), and Chape offers-up a smattering of wine-soaked, working class wisdom: "Friendship and Beaujolais are the most important things in the world!" After this toast, director Grangier and screenwriter Audiard relax the narrative a bit, and give us a great little slice-of-life moment, in which the three truckers, Lucien, Jean, and Pierrot, are relaxing at the table, as Alice and Maria are wiping-down the dishes, and Maria, an older woman who seems like the type whose specialty is dispensing good advice, tells Alice that it's time for her to "strike when the iron is hot," and that Alice should, in her opinion, marry Chape as soon as she can. Post-*ciesta,* Lucien takes Chape down into his wine cellar, where the two men examine wines, while musing about what their futures will hold. Chape tells Lucien that he feels he's been devalued in the marketplace, not just because, in his own words, he's "over fifty," but also because of his non-married relationship with Alice and, tertiarilly, because of the 'accident' he has endured, involving the body of Antoine Scoppo. Lucien commiserates with Chape, telling him that he, too, just like everybody else on earth, is going to have to deal with getting phased-out one day, and that time marches on for all of us, and much faster than we'd like it to.

It's not long before Chape is happy because his big-rig now back in his possession. He's in the truckyard with Alice, helping her load her belongings onto it for her move over to his place and, as they're doing it, the gangster-sedan cruises sneakily past the truckyard, just like the shark in *Jaws*. Although Chape doesn't see the bad guys, the not-so-smooth criminals do manage to have learned his name which, very handily, happens to be printed on the back of one of his truck's mudflaps. Chape tells Alice that her he'll pick her up later, after the day's runs, and they tenderly kiss goodbye for the day.

Next, Chape hops into the driver's seat and begins his run, and after a few moments—and this is no big surprise to us—he sees the gangster sedan in his rearview mirror: The hoods are following him! Far from looking upset, because Jean Gabin is always in control, he waves them around, and they drive away. Apparently, he's more upset by their presence than he looks because, when we next see Chape, he's heading into Serin's bar, now suddenly in need of a stiff drink. He asks a good-natured driver friend, Jojo (Guy Henry), if Jojo's ever seen the sedan-in-question, but Jojo replies that he has not. Emile Serin's wife Camille (Gaby Basset, Jean Gabin's real-life ex-wife from the early 1930s) gives Chape a sausage sandwich, but he's too pre-occupied by the gangsters' recent presence to be properly cheered-up by it.

The next day, the gangsters pull up in front of Alice's school. They've been spying on Chape—they know he's there, sometimes—because apparently, Scoppo, the gangster who was tossed out of their car, had a bankroll on him that could choke a chicken, and they believe, quite erroneously, that Chape absconded with the cash after his truck 'did its little dance' over him. The gangsters, not knowing that Alice is just in the process of leaving the school, and that she isn't teaching there any longer, have decided that the best way to get their money back from Chape might be to kidnap one of Alice's students: These guys are good movie-gangsters so, in their estimation, if they do this, Chape will most certainly come to the rescue, and then they'll have him—and, they think, their cash—right where they want him. (The gangsters won't kidnap a kid, although humorously, one of Alice's students is named 'Deray,' probably a nod to the film's young assistant director Jacques Deray, who would one day become a prominent film director in his own right.)

At the end of the day, Chape's back at the truckyard, and he's now accosted by Antoine Scoppo's bursting-with-sex widow, Madame Scoppo, who's played by the fetching Ginette Leclerc. She tells him that she's the wife of the man whom Chape ran over, and he makes it

With Jeanne Moreau.

known to her immediately that he didn't kill her husband. He adds, truthfully, that the man was already deceased when he drove over him, and that the police have already dismissed him as a suspect. She starts laughing, and even flirting with him, telling him that she actually knows that he wasn't the killer, but that she does think Chape walked away from the mishap with her husband's cache of cash, and her tone now becomes serious. "I know you took my husband's money after you drove over him. Now, give it to me right now!"

So now, we've got the three gangsters who worked with Scoppo, and we've also got Scoppo's widow, and they're both, independently of each other, shaking Chape down for money which he doesn't even have, and next, director Gilles Grangier gives us the not-so-surprising twist which we knew was coming: When we see Madame Scoppo next, she's in the gangsters' hotel room with them: She's actually working in collusion with the gangsters, and all of them take turns hitting on her, even though we're not sure she ever returns their advances, although she does flirt with them, and she even tells them that in life, she enjoys "variety." As we'll learn now, this 'black widow' even gave the go-ahead for the gangsters to 'off' her hubby and, not only that, but the mystery arm which threw her husband out of the car, happened to have been her own! She tells Schwob and his men, "If we want the money, we're going to have to kill this trucker—this Jean Chape—and if you don't get rid of him, I will! I'm tougher than all of you put together! You're all just big bags of wind!"

The next day, the gangster sedan cuts Chape's truck off on the road just to screw with him and to let him know that they're still there, and this whole scene is kind of a reversal on Spielberg's 1971 television movie *Duel*, except in *Gas-Oil*, it's the truck that's menacing the car, and not *vice-versa*. The gangsters don't stop at that, though: When Chape and Alice arrive home to Chape's house, which is now, of course, also Alice's house, Chape discovers that the gangsters have already paid them a visit. The hoods have really turned the place over, tearing the whole joint up in their search for the 'pimpernel-elusive' cash. Now Alice is, and very rightly so, afraid to move herself officially into Chape's place, because she thinks that it's probably, to say the very least, unsafe. Chape, although he continues to act calmly, is a bit worried that the gangsters will come back to kill him and Alice, and he suggests to her that she should stay in a safe hotel which is occupied by his trucker pals (the hotel over Emile Serin's bar), so that Emile and Camille Serin will be able to stand watch over her. The gangsters phone Chape and tell him to meet them over at a different truck-stop, because they want to have a conference with him, face-to-face.

The three gangsters and Madame Scoppo are present, and they tell him that they know Chape has the money, and that they want it. Of course, Chape, as he was during his interrogation at the police station, is completely unafraid of them (even though they're armed and he isn't), and he tells them, in the film's 'Mighty Gabin-Outburst #2,' "I have never seen this money that you're talking about. First the cops are harassing me, and now, you! You've messed up my house! I don't want this anymore! Now get out of here and leave me alone!"

After that previous plot twist, in which we found out that Madame Scoppo was working with the gangsters, we now get a better one: As it turns out, Madame Scoppo has actually been in possession of her dead husband's money for the entire time, and not only has she always had it, but she's the one who threw the gangsters onto Chape's track, as a way of deviating the focus away from herself. When we next see her, she's at the train station, removing the briefcase full of her dead husband's money from a locker which she's rented - and, suddenly, a police inspector, Baudier, shows up, nabbing both her and the money.

Now that Madame Scoppo is out of the picture, it's time for the bad guys to get their just desserts, and the cops are going to be aided and abetted by Chape and his brotherhood of tough truckers, *a la* that scene in Sam Peckinpah's overlooked 1978 gem *Convoy*. Chape's trucker friends mean to take a little sweet revenge out on the gangsters screwed with their good buddy, Chape, and it is in this way that *Gas-Oil* is another Jean Gabin movie in which the power of male friendship not only triumphs over everything, but it also saves the day. The truckers know the gangsters are still hanging around in Clermont-Ferrand, so they block-off all of the roads which lead out of town with their trucks; the truckers—who include Chape, Lucien, Pierrot, Jojo, Emile Serin, and a couple of other guys—Lulu and 'Big Robert'—are there, and even the town's butcher Marcel (Jacques Ferrier) has come along to help the truckers out, because he's as pissed-off at the gangsters as they are since, when Chape was on suspension, a large meat order which he had placed hadn't been delivered. Local farmers have shown up, too, and they're even using their own cows, as barriers. (The French certainly loved their barriers in 1789, in 1830 and in 1848 and—well, let's just say—"It was still alive in '55.")

Right on target, the gangsters show up at the truck/cow roadblock, and the cops arrest them. The gangsters even shoot Lucien Rangodin, but he survives. Alice, who's been right there, standing alongside Chape, sighs relievedly: "Now it's all over!"

Presumably, even though we're not going to be seeing it in the film, Alice will get her old teaching job back, and everybody will stop looking down their noses at Chape and Alice, because the loving couple will probably be, although we won't be seeing it in the film, getting married... maybe. The last shot of the film is a poignant one, because we see Chape doing something that he's never done before: We see him in bed, sleeping late, and Alice kisses his cheek.

Gas-Oil never merited a theatrical release in the United States, although the film's production company, Intermondia, thought that might be a possibility, and they and even decided on a U.S. release title, *Hi-Jack Highway*. But throughout Europe, admirers of great genre cinema have always considered *Gas-Oil* to be a very invigorating day at the movies, in fact, the film performed so well at the French box-office, that a different set of producers would, in the following year of 1956, star Gabin in the actor's second trucker movie, and one which happens to be just as good as this one: It's *Des gens sans importance* (*People of No Importance*), and it will be directed, with style to spare, by *Gas-Oil's* talented, young assistant director (not to mention uncredited director of the film's several scenes) Henri Verneuil who, himself, will soon begin directing a number of movies starring Jean Gabin.

What a Critic Said at the Time: "An original idea, very well written and developed. It is a film which the public will enjoy. Gabin seems to have driven trucks all his life." (*France-Soir*, Paris. 11-13-1955 issue. Critic: Unknown.)
What Another Critic Said at the Time: "This film is... natural and truthful." (*L'Information universitaire*, Paris. 11-12-1955 issue. Critic: Rene Guyonnet.)

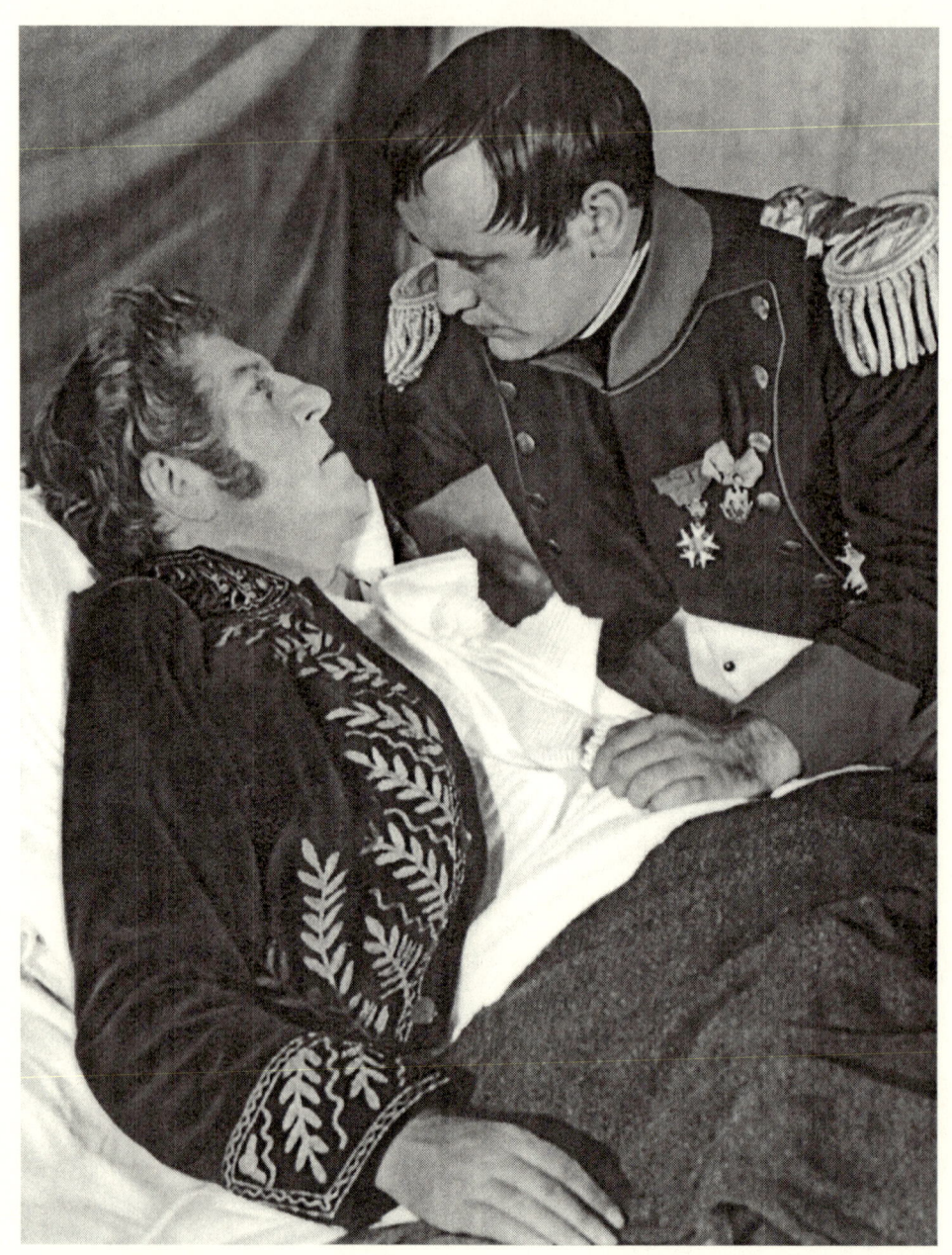

With Raymond Pellegrin.

FILM 50

Napoleon

France/Italy, 1955

Directed and Written by Sacha Guitry. Produced by Clement Duhour. Director of Photography (color), Pierre Montazel. Editor, Raymond Lamy. Music by Jean Franciax. Production Designer, Rene Renoux. (GENRES: DRAMA, HISTORY) A Production of Filmsonor S.A. and Les Films CLM (France) and Francinex (France/Italy). Running Time: 3 hours in France, 2 Hours in United States. (Gabin's one scene does not appear in the short, U.S. Release Version.) Released in France on March 25, 1955, by Cinedis. Released Theatrically in the United States by United Artists, in 1956.

"Once, there was an extraordinary being who, nevertheless, resembled a man."
— French Foreign Minister Talleyrand, telling houseguests the story of his one-time best friend, in "Napoleon"

Note to any of today's movie producers who happen to be reading this (although I'm sure there aren't any; today's movie producers are too busy, making movies about teenagers): "Hey, you guys, how about making a contemporary movie about Napoleon? What's great about Napoleon's story, is that his whole take-over-the-world imperialism-bent, just by its very nature, resonates with what certain leaders-of-the-free-world may, or may not, be doing today. (Stanley Kubrick was about to start shooting his own version of *Napoleon*, starring Jack Nicholson, back in the seventies, but Warner Bros. shut the whole thing down, because the film's projected cost would have been staggering.)

Unfortunately, director Sacha Guitry's 1955 French-language version of *Napoleon* doesn't 'resonate' at all, because it's not a very good movie. It was France's contribution to that great 1950s' movie phenomenon—the giant, historical epic.

Starting in about 1952, the American studios had started churning out gigantic Cinemascope/Technicolor historical epics, in an effort to draw audiences away from the movies' brash and physically diminutive (by comparison) new competitor, television. Hollywood's first Cinemascope epic was Fox's production of *The Robe*, starring Richard Burton, and other epics followed, some of them amazing (1959's *Ben-Hur*), and others, less so (Mankiewicz's 1963 *Cleopatra*). *Napoleon* falls more on the side of the disastrous *Cleopatra*, which is to say that it's a big, expensive, 'spot-the-star' folly that looks more like a bunch of fine actors 'playing 19th-century dress-up,' than it resembles an actual motion picture.

I understood, going in, that Jean Gabin had only a small role in the film, as one of Napoleon's innumerable right-hand-men, Marshal Lannes, but I was excited about seeing the picture anyway, because I knew I'd be seeing Gabin pulling the rug out, acting-wise, from under All Those Other Big Stars. (Plus, *Napoleon* was photographed in color, which made it Gabin's first 'polychromatic' film appearance.) Anyway: I watched the whole movie. And I waited. And waited. And waited.

And I didn't see Jean Gabin.

And here's why:

Jean Gabin's role has been excised completely from the two-hour American release-version of the film, which is the version that is currently available on the public domain, dubbed-into-English DVD which is available in America, although the company distributing it *does* proclaim, on the video's box cover, that Jean Gabin appears in the film. Well, you can toggle your remote control backwards and forwards until your DVD player is blue in the face, and you won't be seeing Jean Gabin.

Months later, I tracked down a video copy of the uncut, three-hour French-language print, from 'French Amazon.com' (www.amazon.fr), and I learned that, while Jean Gabin truly *does* appear in the longer, three-hour version of Napoleon that, even in the long version, he only appears on-screen in one scene, and for less than two minutes. Plus: When Gabin finally shows up in the picture, he's wearing a powdered wig and two tons of Kabuki-like pancake make-up, and so you're going to have to blink a couple of times, if you want to see him. (This is the only movie, out of ninety-five, in which Gabin is caked in goofy-looking make-up!)

Guitry's version of the Napoleon saga will never be confused with Abel Gance's landmark 1926 silent version, which was also produced in France, a motion picture that was truly revolutionary in its dual explorations of Napoleon and of cinema's evolving visual language. Sacha Guitry's Napoleon, by contrast, is strictly 'by-the-numbers,' one of those 'been-there, done-that' biopics, in which the filmmakers seem like they're trying to touch on every important moment in the main character's life, as though they're going down a checklist, and trying to hit on everything important that happened. Of course, this kind of approach to biographical storytelling, in which none of the sequences builds on another dramatically, still occurs today, in pictures like Richard Attenborough's soporific *Chaplin;* Taylor Hackford's 'too-t.v.' *Ray,* Kevin Spacey's bizarre, James Darren mish-mosh *Beyond the Sea,* and James Mangold's spray-on nostalgia/Johnny Cash-snoozefest, *Walk the Line.* All of these pictures, from Guitry's to Mangold's, play like outlines of stories, rather than actual stories, and these film all try to cram so much random ephemera into their films' two-to-three hour narratives, that we don't come out of watching any of these films having gleaned any information at all, so we zone out. (And let's not forget about Michael Mann's heinous *Ali,* a film which, weirdly, wasn't really even all that much about Muhammad Ali!)

One can't find too much fault with Jean Gabin for appearing in this big, bloated mess, however, because lots of other Big International Movie Stars are in it too, and so, by all rights, if you wanted to blame Gabin, you'd also have to blame everyone else who turns up, including Orson Welles, Yves Montand (like Gabin, his sequences appear only in the film's longer, European cut), Silvana Pampanini and Serge Reggiani (the circus couple who double-crossed Gabin in *Fille dangereuse* [although in this film they appear separately from Gabin]), *La Grande illusion's* Erich von Stroheim (in a very brief, and majorly unrecognizable turn as *Beethoven,* complete with a powdered wig!), Danielle Darrieux (*Bebe Donge,* herself), Michele Morgan, and more, more, more! The weirdest thing about the movie (even weirder than the cast), is that Sacha Guitry chose not one, but two actors, to play Napoleon: In the first half of the picture, boyish-faced Daniel Gelin plays Bonaparte (from the ages of about eighteen to thirty-five), and from Napoleon's mid-thirties on, history's famous Little Corporal is played by a more mature-looking actor, Raymond Pellegrin. In other words, this film is giving us two Napoleons for the price of one.

I vacillated on whether or not I should present a whole chapter about this long and uninteresting film in this book; after all, of Jean Gabin's ninety-five full-length feature films, this is the only one in which he briefly cameos, instead of stars or co-stars. But in the interest of completeness: Ladies and gentlemen, this is Sacha Guitry's *Napoleon!*

The film, in both its long and short versions, begins in the same way: An onscreen title card alerts us that the film which we're about to see takes place in the actual locations in which Napoleon lived his life—that is, at his homes at Malmaison, Fontainebleu, and Versailles, as well as at a few of the actual battlefields in which he waged war against the nations of Europe.

In the first scene, a sequence to which Guitry will return throughout the movie (it's the film's wraparound segment), a group of four aristocratic-types are sitting around the parlor of Napoleon's great one-time friend/associate, and France's former Foreign Minister, under Napoleon), Charles Maurice de Talleyrand, who's played by Guitry, himself. Talleyrand is recounting, for his guests, the story of his old friend's life, in fact, he's actually cued to begin telling the story, because one of his guests inquires of him, "So, what was your opinion of Emperor Napoleon?" Talleyrand thoughtfully replies that he never much liked Napoleon: "He is known as one of the greatest men who ever lived, but he had need of nobody, and nobody could ever catch him. For twenty years, he got on my nerves!" As Talleyrand continues his storytelling, 'Guitry the Director' now dissolves to flashback footage (which comprises ninety-eight-percent of the film), of Napoleon's childhood:

Talleyrand begins his tale colorfully, and we get to hear all of what he's saying, in voice-over, "Once, there was an extraordinary being who, nevertheless, resembled a man. Born on an island, he was raised on an island, and he even dreamed, all his life, of conquering an island [Europe]. In fact, he would even die on an island. His story starts in Ajaccio, on the Italian island of Corsica, on August 15th, 1769, at his family home. And, my friends, you might be interested in knowing that, if Napoleon had only been born forty-five days later, when Corsica had already been conquered [for France] by Louis XV, he may have been known as an Italian, instead of as a Frenchman."

April 23rd 1779: Napoleon, age ten, starts school, and we get an early glimpse of his future fearlessness, when he stares-down a group of much bigger bullies, and they run away in tears, and at this point in his young life, he has only one friend, a boy named Bourras. Guitry now returns to the film's wraparound sequence, in which Talleyrand is telling his parlor guests that the reason the two boys got along so well, was because of the old, 'opposites attract' maxim: "He [Bourras] was as taciturn as Napoleon was surly and quarrelsome."

With one cut, director Guitry now jumps ahead six years in Napoleon's story, and we see the future Emperor leaving military school at the age of sixteen, and joining the army. He attains the rank of Second Lieutenant very quickly, but carries some resentment, because he'd much rather be a First Lieutenant; anyway, he won't have to fret too much about the perceived slight because, in 1796, at the age of twenty-seven, he'll become a Corporal. (In fact, as you know, he'll eventually be nicknamed, among other monikers that he didn't really like, 'The Little Corporal,' after his brave attack on France's long-time arch-enemy Austria, in which he'd win Austrian lands for France, after fourteen pitched battles.) Talleyrand tells his parlor guests in the wraparound that, in his estimation, it's amazing Napoleon was so successful at such a young age, because he had a routine mind, and never really sported what Talleyrand terms to be 'the kind of genius' which one readily associates with 'true leaders.'

Shortly after his Austrian victory, Napoleon visits Marseilles and, along with his brother Joseph (Robert Manuel), he attends a fancy-dress ball, where he meets Desiree Clary (Dany Robin), heiress to her wealthy *daddy-o's* mega-ultra-swank silk fortune. Desiree's interested in Joseph, and not Napoleon, whom she finds to be clownish-looking, self-important and, even worse, *short*. Of course, *'What Nappy Wants, Nappy Gets.'* Without having to expend too much effort, he's able, ultimately, to wrest Desiree from his brother's vice-grip, and after a brief period of courtship which lasts only about one month, he leaves her, and the end result is that now, neither brother has Desiree. (An equally soppy movie about the whole short-lived, but meaningful, Napoleon-Desiree relationship, is director Henry Koster's 1954 American picture *Desiree,* a 'Napoleon Chick-Flick' which starred Jean Simmons as Desiree and Marlon Brando as Napoleon.) Subsequent to the big Marseilles shindig, Desiree's sister Julie (Michele Cordoue) will start boinking Napoleon for a few months, but their relationship will, according to Talleyrand, "last no longer than the life of a rose," because in her opinion, Napoleon "looks like Puss-in-Boots."

But Napoleon's a real partier, and he's basically, at least, in the world of this film, the 'Hef' of 1800. And at the next fancy ball he attends, he'll meet the love of his life, Josephine de Beauharnais (Michele Morgan), a woman whose husband, Alexandre de Beauharnais, a general in the French army, was recently killed in battle. Josephine, like Desiree, thinks Napoleon is a major-league goofball when she first meets him, especially because he bursts into her bedroom, uninvited (she's receiving visitors while splayed across her bed, *a la* Mata-Hari)! He starts staring at her like a crazed wolverine, and asking her if she's afraid of him, and this just makes her giggle uncomfortably; it's not just his weird behavior that's creeping her out, but also the fact that he's wearing *the super-humongous codpiece of all time*. Screw the conquest of nations: Napoleon wants to conquer Josephine!

When morning comes, the party guests are still *throwing-down,* and the celebration has spilled out of the house and onto the front lawn, and everybody's dancing the too-chaste, 18th-century line-dance, the 'Monaco.'

Eventually of course, as history will bear out, Napoleon is able to wear Josephine down: Finally, now, he's able to 'get with' the sister he really likes (and don't think that he hasn't put in the hours)! Josephine is not only a brand-new widow, but she's also got two teen-aged kids to contend with—daughter Hortense, who is 16 (she is played by Micheline Presle, who was in her thirties) and son Eugene (Jacques Fayet), 12. Napoleon knows that, when it comes to 'dating a single mom,' you've got to make points with the kids first, so he tries to get in a little face-time with Eugene, telling the boy that he knew his dad: "Your father and I fought together. I would like to present you with this sword, which belonged to your father." Josephine's a little older than Napoleon—in fact, she's six years older—and the age-difference bothers her (remember, this is two-hundred years *pre-Demi and Ashton*); so knowing this, he tries to assuage her by telling her, in one of the film's more treacly lines of dialogue, "You take off six years, I'll put on three more, and we'll meet along the way!" Talleyrand tells his parlor guests, in the wraparound segment, that Napoleon had lied to Josephine previously, telling her not only that they were the same age, but also that he was born in Paris, since there was no better status-symbol, in 18th-century France, than claiming you were born in Gay Paree. (Yes, Napoleon is the ultimate 'fake it 'til you make it' guy!) Even when Napoleon and his hot 'cougar' Josephine eventually do become an item, she continues to think that he's patently weird, but she is also, nevertheless, genuinely impressed by his mad scientist-y meanderings, concerning how he intends to take over all of Europe, and place his relations on the thrones of every country, so that not only will all of Europe be under France's yoke, but all of Europe will actually be French. Even though Josephine was reportedly a very smart woman, she buys into Napoleon's dreams wholecloth, in the same way in which we all buy into those silly idealized illusions which we harbor about other people who don't really merit them—those 'grand illusions' which get us all through our boringly-joyless and routine lives.

We next get a battle scene which takes place in Toulon, in southern France—birthplace of Pepe Le Moko!—in which Napoleon fights off British invaders (the Brits will be a thorn in Napoleon's side throughout his military career), and is, resultantly, promoted to the position of Commanding General of the Army. It is there, that he will meet Paul Barras (Pierre Brasseur), a bright young officer who, like Talleyrand, will become one of his great friends and advisors. Talleyrand, in the wraparound, tells his parlor guests next that, for Napoleon, it was now "… off to the Bridge at Arcole, in Italy, where he would write the first chapter of his legend in the Italian sky," when he took Italy back from the Austrians, who had previously conquered it. Napoleon's now a hero, both in France and in Italy (Italy, at the time, was France's Big Ally), and Talleyrand tells him, "I know you will seduce all of France!" Napoleon asks Talleyrand to pledge a lifetime of support to him, to which Talleyrand humorously retorts, "I promise to never betray you… unless I give you notice the day before!"

1798-1799: Napoleon now decides that, as part-and-parcel of his wacky *world conquest-jones,* that he's going after Egypt next because if he captures Egypt, he'll then be able to attack the all-important British trade routes to India. (Anything that makes life hard for the British is just *a-ok,* with 'Big Daddy Nappy-B!') On the ship to Egypt, Napoleon tries to strengthen the resolve of his troops by telling them that they all "lack courage." (Yeah! *Reverse psychology!* That'll work!) He plays cards with them too, and a young soldier who's got intestinal-fortitude to spare accuses him of mishandling the cards: "General! You're cheating!" He answers the young man in a very calm way: "I know. I cheat. It's my way. But when this war is over, I will give you back everything which you lost to me, and more—and I'll do it with complete honesty." In the next scene, Napoleon and his men are in Egypt, duking-it-out with the *wogs,* first at the Battle of the Pyramids (successful), and secondly at the Battle of the Nile (unsuccessful; the British, who showed up in support of the Egyptians, sink most of Napoleon's ships).

Back in France, Napoleon starts double-timing Josephine with Madame Foures (Eleonora Rossi Drago), who is doing the whole '*Diane Keaton-dressing-like-a-man-thing,*' two hundred years pre-Keaton. Napoleon's other right hand man, beside Talleyrand, General Barras (Pierre Brasseur) next illuminates Napoleon on a subject which everybody in Paris knows about except, it seems, for Napoleon himself, which is basically, that Josephine's been cheating on him with various men, for the entire length of their marriage. (Basically, every time *Nappy* steps out the door, *she's banging!*) "She's deceiving you. You're a great man, and she's making you ridiculous," Barras tells his friend, and it's funny that this is coming from him because, while it's not brought up in this film, Josephine was engaging in relations with Barras, while she was married to Napoleon, as well! Barras is one of the few people in the world, like Talleyrand, who can say this kind of shit to Napoleon, without risking a knuckle sandwich on whole wheat. Alone in the small hotel room, where he sometimes takes his meetings, Napoleon next asks Barras about why he thinks Josephine has been cheating on him. (Talleyrand tells his guests, in the wraparound segment that, while Josephine was cheating on Napoleon, that "…'Lady France' was always faithful to him," and the cinematography, in this pension scene, is really amateurish, because it looks a whole lot like somebody's uncle's bad super-8 millimeter home movies, circa-1972, replete with major shadows on the wall behind Napoleon, which emanate from an improperly-placed key light, with no secondary lights around to fill-in the shadows; this is very weird indeed, considering that *Napoleon's* cinematographer, Pierre Montazel, was one of France's best; indeed, he was the man who gave many of Jean Gabin's black and white movies from the 1950s, including *Touchez pas au grisbi, L'Air de Paris, Gas-Oil,* and *Razzia sur la chnouf* their stunning looks.)

When we see Josephine next, she's returning home from one of her assignations, and she gets briefed by a servant that Napoleon's already there waiting for her, and that he's, in the Terry Southern-penned words of Peter Sellers' President Muffley Merkin-character in

Dr. Strangelove, "hopping mad!" Napoleon's ready to *chew her a new a-hole,* but she's just as strong a character as he is, and she takes the pre-emptive strike, by cooing at him that he's the only man for her. (For a brilliant tactician, he's as *whipped* as they come.)

At this point, after winning-big in both Austria and Egypt, Napoleon is seen as being France's Great Hope. We're now 'post-Monarchy' (the general public's hated Louis XVI and Marie-Antoinette have already been beheaded), and we're also 'post-General Robespierre's reactionary/citizen-killing Reign of Terror,' and the country, which is now being run by the five-member Directoire, the executive branch which is supposed to be acting in the interests of the people but just isn't, is in complete disarray. The foppish Count of Provence, played by Lucien Baroux (who happens to be Louis XVI's little brother), wants to rule France himself, christening himself anew, as 'Louis XVIII,' in the bargain, and returning a system of Monarchy to the currently kingless France, but Talleyrand thinks that Napoleon should govern the country instead, since Napoleon, in spite of the fact that he's a major hard-ass, truly loves the Common Man, but only in the most abstract way possible: It doesn't seem, in this film anyway, like he actually gives *two shits* about the Common Man, and Talleyrand is even seen to worry out loud that, unchecked, Napoleon could be a really scary dictator.

The morning after one of Napoleon and Josephine's fights, one of the film's rather constant *contretemps,* in which, as per usual, he's yelling at her for cheating on him, Barras walks into Napoleon's bedroom (this guy has *carte-blanche* to go anywhere he wants!), and sees that Napoleon and Josephine have just enjoyed a nice post-fight reconciliatory fuckfest, and are in bed together, blissfully post-coital. As a housekeeper, a black woman whom he's brought back from his Egyptian campaigns, serves the couple some *nice hot brekkie,* Barras tells the freshly-fucked General that he'd better drop his cock and grab his socks, because Talleyrand's waiting out in the anteroom to see him, and that he has an intriguing proposition. (Talleyrand tells Napoleon, "You have honored yourself in France and in Italy, and I am here to inform you that the people of France would like very much to place the French Republic in your capable hands.") The next day, Napoleon is named First Consul of the Consulate, which is the name he's just given to the country's newest governing body, which he establishes shortly after personally handing the astounded Directoire members their walking papers. Napoleon tells the people of France that his new government, which will be replacing the oppressive Directoire, will base itself on freedom and equality, without the attendant elitism which had characterized France's previous governing bodies. He appoints a lot of trusted Generals from his most successful battles to keep an eye on France's various acquired territories.

Next, director Guitry gives us a sequence in which Napoleon is getting a haircut. The Barber throws a sheet over his head during the haircut, and Barras is present as well, reading Napoleon some letters: One letter has come from the Count of Provence, who still wishes to become 'Louis XVIII.' In his letter, the Count tells Napoleon that, if only Napoleon and his two fellow Consul members will abdicate, and let him take over, that he'll pay them all very handsomely, and Napoleon does his great, 'dictated-but-not-read'-best to reply: "Sir, thank you for your letters—but, no thank you!" When the haircut is over, something really bizarre happens: The Barber removes the sheet from Napoleon's face, and we see that, post-haircut, Napoleon isn't played by the Buster Brown-coiffed Daniel Gelin anymore, but that he is now played by the more mature-looking and shorter-haired Raymond Pellegrin. According to Talleyrand's wraparound V.O., "When the deft hands of the barber were done, Napoleon was changed. Unrecognizable." The haircut is a visual motif for the fact that Napoleon is now going to 'change a nation' (or *some shit like that*; anyway, it's patently weird to see a movie in which somebody new comes in halfway, and starts playing the main character just when we were getting used to 'the old guy').

On December 12, 1804, Napoleon crowns himself as France's new Emperor, and even though he's always been anti-Monarchy, he's made an exception—for himself! He's got Pope Pius VII (Gino Antonini) on-hand, allegedly to crown him, but of course, as we all know from the David painting, he grabs the crown away from the surprised-looking Pontiff, and crowns himself instead, and since he's in 'crowning mode,' he also takes this opportunity, at the same time, to crown Josephine as Empress. He makes an announcement to all assembled that, as Emperor, he'll be creating the authentically-democratic Civil Code (a/k/a, the 'Code Napoleon') which will consist of one set of laws for all of France, under which all Frenchmen (and women) will be equal; prior to the inauguration of the Code, each region of France had its own rules, and not necessarily rules which anybody was so hip to follow.

What's interesting about Napoleon, as an historical figure is that, during the time in which he was a sitting Emperor, and he really didn't have to do anything outside the house if he didn't want to, he genuinely loved the stench of the battlefield and would, whenever he felt like it (and very frequently) replace his crown with his general's cap, joining his men in combat, although usually, only in a supervisory position, and from a nearby hilltop. Talleyrand tells his parlor guests that, at this point in Napoleon's life, it had been a long time since the Emperor/General had been to war, and that it was on December 12, 1805, one year and ten days after he had crowned himself as Emperor, that he fought his old arch-enemies, the Austrians, as well as the Austrians' buddies the Russians, at the Battle of Austerlitz. (Today, the formerly-Austrian town of 'Austerlitz' still exists, and it's now called Slavkov u Brna, and is part of the Czech Republic.) There, he conquered the combined Austrian and Russian armies, both roundly and soundly. The Commander of Austria, Karl Mack, has even given up thirty-three thousand of his troops to Napoleon, and the French army is now bigger and stronger than ever before. The night after the Battle, Napoleon's men all congregate on the battlefield, singing under the night sky, and they sound a whole hell of a lot like the singing skeletons in that old Max Fleischer/Cab Calloway/Betty Boop cartoon, "Minnie the Moocher." "From this day forward, all of Europe was his," Talleyrand tells his Parlor Pals, in the wraparound segment.

In both the French and the American cuts of the film, we now get a title credit which reads, "End of Part One." (At this point in the film, there was an intermission in the theater, and I'll bet you dollars-to-donuts that nobody came back, for the second half.) As "Part Two" begins, we now see a group-meeting, consisting of all of Napoleon's family members—

1954 — 1976 | 45

brothers, sisters, and spouses—whom Napoleon has placed in charge of the various countries which he has conquered in the name of France. He tells his brother Jerome, who is currently King of Westphalia (Germany), that he won't be able to hand him the Crown of Spain, as he originally thought he would do, since Jerome has just married an American girl, Elizabeth Patterson, a marriage of which 'big bro' Napoleon has never approved. Jerome bitches about how unfair this is, and Napoleon tells him that he'd be willing to put the offer back on the table, provided that Jerome will divorce E.P., and A.S.A.P.! Jerome says no can do, though (apparently, this younger Bonaparte brother is on a whole archaic 'getting-married-for-love'-trip), and Napoleon replies, "Well, in that case, I will send your passport, and hers, to America. Neither of you are needed here, any longer." (How about that for a dysfunctional family? When Napoleon doesn't need you anymore, he just exiles you to another country. Well, don't worry too much, my friends, because the Karmic Exile Gods will be riding up Napoleon's own ass, soon enough.) At the end of this meeting, all of the women in the room—the ones who are married to Napoleon's brothers, as well as a few hangers-on (*'Napoleon Groupies!'*)—all start whispering seductively to him, one at a time: Obviously, each wants to be the one in his bed tonight, and he's now acting very coy about the whole thing, telling each girl, "Maybe, maybe, maybe. We'll see. Yes, we'll see about that!" (At one point in the film, he even tells his little brothers to abstain from the sex act, which he calls a detriment to the heart, but meanwhile, he wants to boff all of his brother's babes, himself! What a hypocrite!)

Next, we're going to get a very funny sequence, in which one of Napoleon's servant girls, Josephine's lady-in-waiting Eleonore Denuelle (Danielle Darrieux: She played *Bebe Donge*, and she also played 'Rosa,' one of the prostitutes, in Ophuls' *Le Plaisir*), hits on him: This *hot lady* just sits in the Emperor's lap and tries to make out with him, not even caring that he's, like, fifty thousand social classes above her: "My scoundrel husband is in prison," she pouts, "and I am lonely." She bats her eyelashes at the *Emp*, asking him, "Am I pretty," and she then continues, "I heard you're impatient [about getting into girls' pants]. You're a funny man who gives orders—but you'll take them from me!" Napoleon digs it when a woman takes charge, just like today's monstrously mean business executives who berate their administrative assistants all day, and then call escort services by night, and have hookers defecate on them, while they (the executives) are all dressed-up in swaddling clothes! Anyway, needless to say, Napoleon and Eleanor fuck immediately, and nine months later, it's baby-time: Eleanor has given birth to a boy, Leo, a seven-pounder who, she says, looks just like Big Daddy-o. Napoleon can't officially recognize the whelp as being his own, because he's still married to Josephine, so he gives the boy an honorary position of nobility, making him a Count.

So, here's Napoleon's Love Scorecard: While Napoleon is still married to Josephine, and pounding out the puppies with Eleanor, he's also having an affair with Madame Foures (the woman who dresses like Diane Keaton), as well as an Italian songstress by the name of Brazini, while also 'having carnal knowledge' (or, as Benny Hill once famously quipped, 'carnival knowledge') of the Contessa Marie Walewska (Lana Marconi) of Poland, a country which has been taken over by Russia. Marie's husband, the Count Waleska, actually pushes his wife into Napoleon's arms, because he thinks that if she screws the Emperor, just maybe, the Emperor will see fit to help Poland to regain her independence. Napoleon wins Poland back for her, by marching into Poland in the winter of '06, and kicking the *Russkies* out. Turns out, Marie's such a hellion in the sack (implied not by the film, but by 'your author's fertile imagination'), that Napoleon's ready, immediately, to divorce Josephine for her.

Josephine approaches her philandering husband and advises him that, while she's tired of his infidelities (Yeah, like, she should talk: Her round-heels are all over the map, too!), she's not going to be divorcing him anytime soon, and that if divorce is what he's thinking about, it's just not going to happen. Instead of fighting back (Napoleon's the greatest military strategist the world, and he and Kenny Rogers both know 'when to hold 'em and when to fold 'em'), he simply looks the subject of 'divorce' up, in a law book, and finds that in France, a man can divorce his wife, if his wife can bear him no children—which is something that Josephine can't, bodily, do, and which he now claims, ridiculously, has been the main reason for all of his incessant philandering.

Of course, since *everything has to be a spectacle with this guy,* Napoleon gets Josephine, as well as all of his siblings and their spouses around his conference table, for his bizarre, public-divorce ceremony. First, he reads a written dissolution-of-marriage statement (which he's written, himself!) out-loud: "Josephine, since you are unable to bear children, our marriage is now officially dissolved." He then, actually, makes Josephine read out a statement of her own (obviously, he wrote hers, too), which reads, "Because I, Josephine, am barren, I must hereby resign from my marriage." She's so humiliated by what she's just been forced to read that, after she finishes, she passes out cold, but we don't have to worry about her too much: Josephine will make out very well in their divorce, and Napoleon will even 'give her the house' (Malmaison).

Now, it's time for Napoleon to start thinking about his long-time arch-enemy, Austria, again: He knows that the Austrians are just going to keep popping out of the woodwork to challenge him every few years, especially after the good trouncing he gave them, back at Austerlitz, so he realizes that he's really just going to have to *beat their Teutonic asses* once and for all, by taking the country over for France. He decides that the best way to do it, now that he's divorced Josephine, will be to marry yet another New Squeeze, the Austrian Duchess Marie-Louise (Maria Schell), a girl with whom he's obsessed (he's seen paintings of her, but that's it), even though they've never actually met before in person. He knows that if he marries her and makes a son, and then places that son on Austria's throne as a French ruler of Austria, that the rest of his life will be a whole lot more peaceful than it is right now.

Of course, Napoleon's going to have to actually *meet* Marie-Christine before he marries her (not that it's a prerequisite!), so he plans a big party for her in Paris, and not only does Marie-Louise turn up in the flesh, but the party band for the evening is *Beethoven,* himself (!), and not just Beethoven, but Beethoven as played by chrome-domed Erich von Stroheim

(*La Grande illusion's* aristocratic Colonel von Rauffenstein), who is almost unrecognizable in this movie, in a powdered wig. The numerous hot women at the party swoon over '*Beethoven Lee Lewis*,' as he kicks out the jams, pounding-out a mean *Eroica Symphony*, a piece which he's composed in Napoleon's honor, on the piano. And while he's tickling the ivories, Napoleon's off in a corner hitting-on Marie-Louise, who hates *Eroica*, which she finds to be completely ear-splitting, although she's definitely vibing on the guy whom the song is about. After he finishes playing his piece, Beethoven himself makes a speech (in the uncut French version of the film, only) about Napoleon's great glories and, no doubt, Napoleon wrote this hagiographic speech himself, and gave it to Beethoven to read, just like he also made Josephine read the dissolution of marriage statement which he had written. It's a big chunk of dialogue in untranslated German and, basically, the whole point of the speech, and of the music, is to get Marie-Louise *Betty Crocker-moist* for *Big Nappy*.

March 20th, 1811: We see Napoleon waiting for the birth of the child he is about to have by Marie-Louise, and he's more than a little concerned, because Marie-Louise's labor is a difficult one. The Doctor tells Napoleon that, due to difficulties, they'll either be losing the mother or the child and, amazingly, Napoleon picks the child to lose, even though he knows it's a boy, the all-important male heir which he needs to rule Austria. He needn't have worried, though, because, as it will turn out, "both mother and baby are fine."

Now that Napoleon has conquered most of his longtime enemies and placed his own people on the various European thrones, he's saved the biggest enemy for last: He's now ready to invade, and for the very first time, that Mighty Lion itself, Russia, which happens to be under the rule of the nice, torture-hating Czar Alexander. On September 7th, 1812, Napoleon wins a brilliant victory at Moscow, a victory which is pretty easy to come by, especially because when Napoleon and his troops show up in Moscow, the city is completely deserted, and there's no Russian army there for him to fight. (We don't even get to see a single, solitary *dust-bunny* roll by: I mean, it's a friggin' ghost town.) Alexander, who's a larger-than-life character in his own right (he's 'the Napoleon of the East'), knowing full-well that Napoleon would wipe him out, has evacuated his city, and has also placed timed explosive charges everywhere, including one at his own palace at St. Petersburg! But Napoleon and his men are able to escape from the many simultaneous conflagrations, without a problem. Napoleon next learns that the 'mole' who told Alexander about his incipient invasion was Talleyrand, himself (*et tu, Brutae?*), and on Napoleon's return to Paris, he calls his old friend a traitor right to his face, and it's the last in-person meeting which the two men will ever have. Talleyrand tells the Emperor, very truthfully, "Sire, I did not conspire against you. You are the biggest enemy, only to yourself. I only worked against you, during those times when I had the majority of France with me, and I only did it for the good of France. You're a great man, sire, but you're too coarse." With the friendship between Napoleon and Talleyrand now, effectively, ending, Napoleon's new *#1 Man*, next to General Barras, is going to be another of his generals, General Caulaincourt (Roger Pigaut), in fact, Caulaincourt will now take over the film's voice-over narration-duties from Talleyrand for the film's next forty-or-so minutes.

(For the next forty minutes, we won't be getting any scenes of Talleyrand telling his guests about Napoleon, from his parlor room.)

When Napoleon returns to Paris from Russia, the people aren't that into him anymore, feeling that he ignored them when he was away in Russia, and that he should have been taking care of them, instead of living the high life in other countries. (Of course, that's exactly how the French felt about Jean Gabin after World War II, when he returned home from North Africa where he was fighting for them, but they just weren't interested in him anymore.) Worse, in Napoleon's absence, Louis XVIII finally took over, with the full support of the people, and Napoleon, even though he was a tough *hombre*, never fought against the will of the people. (Remember: He was the 'Code Napoleon Guy' and so, when he returns to France, he formally reads an abdication letter to his public.) Louis XVIII, as a consolation prize, makes Napoleon the Governor of the small Italian island of Elba (at this point in history, the Italians and the French were as thick as thieves), and he provides Napoleon with a small two-room house, and even a tiny little army for him to ride roughshod over, during those periods in which the mood strikes him.

Of course, Napoleon's not one to be nattering around the garden for too long. (He didn't like all of that 'Elba room.' [*Get it? 'Elba room?' 'Elbow room?' Okay, forget I said it!*]) After a few months, his *Austro-hot* wife, Marie-Christine, comes to visit him, and although they're still married, she doesn't live with him. (Elba's too far from 'where the good after-parties are.') She tells him that the French people have changed their minds, and that they now want him back, especially because the Prussians and British are ready to invade France, and Louis XVIII has no earthly idea how to fight them. Well, needless to say, Napoleon is no slouch in the 'fighting back' department and, on the 18th and 19th of June, 1815, he and his vast armies fight against the combined forces of the Prussians, who are led, by General Blucher (remember Cloris Leachman's 'Frau Blucher'-character, from Mel Brooks' *Young Frankenstein*, that not-too-attractive lady who makes the horses whinny, whenever anybody says her name? Well, she's named, after this famous Prussian General!) and the British, under General Wellington, at the Battle of Waterloo, which is about nine miles south of where Brussels stands, today. (In Woody Allen's hilarious 1975 comedy, *Love and Death*, Napoleon tells Woody that if Wellington and his British troops conquer France, everybody in France will be forced to eat unhealthy Beef Wellington, instead of that belovedly-delicious cake, 'the napoleon!')

The Battle of Waterloo is the first big defeat of Napoleon's life, unless you count the time that his battleships got sunk, by the Egyptians; in fact, it's so massive (the British, alongside the Austrians and Prussians, totally decimate Napoleon's army), that it's the beginning of the end, for our hero: Many of the generals under Napoleon are even shot, by British firing squads. Talleyrand, who's now resumed narrating the film, tells us that the battlefield was a raging inferno. Having lost their shirts, the French people again have no place for Napoleon, nor are they all that interested in that useless figurehead Louis XVIII, either. (Louis XVIII died in 1821, and Charles X took over, forming yet another provisional government for

France [in Paris, in 1824].)

Not wanted in France anymore, Napoleon is now exiled for a second time, and this time out, to the British-owned island of St. Helena, where his guardian becomes the English General Sir Hudson Lowe. Yes, the British won their biggest 'spoil' ever at Waterloo—Napoleon, himself!—and, surprise: Lowe is played by Orson Welles, although Welles is hardly recognizable under forty-thousand inches of pancake makeup, a giant pompadour, and massive press-on eyebrows. ("I am placing myself under the guard of an idiot," Napoleon mutters under his breath, as he stares daggers at the buffoonish-looking guy.) Welleses' largely-incomprehensible few lines of dialogue have been completely excised from the short version of the film, and exist only in the long version.

Napoleon grows old in Lowe's home, hating that Lowe refers to him as a General, and not as 'the Emperor.' (Napoleon finds it insulting, even though *really*, he is no longer a general, nor is he even the Emperor, anymore.) In a scene which is meant to be haunting, but which really comes across as being utterly ridiculous, Lowe tears a piece of paper with Napoleon's initials on it ('NB') in half, and when he tears it (the 'N' is one side and the 'B' is on the other), Napoleon dies in the very next scene, a victim, at least, according to the way in which the film has been edited, of *some kind of exotic voodoo paper-tearing ritual!* It is December 15th, 1821.

Oh, yes, and before I forget—What about Jean Gabin? Well:

The uncut three hour version of *Napoleon* restores Jean Gabin's one scene, which comprises less than two minutes of the entire movie: It's May 22, 1809, and Marshal Lannes (Gabin) is dying in a tent, having gotten his stomach blasted by a cannonball (this moment is unseen, in any version of this film) at the Battle of Aspern-Essling, during Napoleon's never-ending Austria campaign. Napoleon leans by his friend's cot, and Lannes whispers a few lines to him—something along the lines of how he loves Napoleon as a friend, but wishes that "all of this senseless killing would stop." (Gabin's character serves, narratively, as this long-winded movie's only 'pacifist voice-of-reason.') After whispering to Napoleon that he thinks war is hell, Lannes yells out, a bit too dramatically, "Assez!" ("Enough!"), and drops dead. This scene represents Jean Gabin's shortest movie appearance and, like Orson Welles and Eric von Stroheim, you really have to squint to see him.

The longer cut of the film gives us more footage, too, but none of it is actually that interesting, nor is it even of any importance: There are a few 'value-added' sequences, which include: A sequence in which the boy Napoleon is lying in the grass; a scene in which twentysomething Napoleon has been jailed after an early battle; some lovey-dovey stuff with Josephine before Napoleon marries her; a brief bit, in which a lady singer is performing for Josephine at the party where she first meets Napoleon; a scene in which Napoleon is bidding goodnight to Josephine for a second time, upon their first meeting; more festive dancing scenes; and 'a between-wars visit' in which long-distance marrieds Napoleon and Josephine question whether or not they still have the hots for each other.

The longer version of the film also restores: An opera sequence, in which a male tenor sings to the newly elected Napoleon while everyone in the audience stands and salutes the new Emperor; Yves Montand, appearing in a few sequences as another of Napoleon's top men, Marshal Lefebvre; Napoleon sitting on a bench at his Fontainebleu home, tearing his hat after a loss in battle; a scene taking place at the Arc de Triomphe in which Talleyrand tells Napoleon, of Napoleon's son, by Maria-Louise, "Your son resembles you, marvelously;" and a Russian Winter scene in which Napoleon's troops carry him on a fancy rickshaw.

Sacha Guitry's *Napoleon* is basically just *Cliff's Notes* on everything that ever happened to Napoleon, so if you actually want to learn about the Emperor, do yourself a favor and get the *Cliff's Notes*, instead. And if you want to watch a more interesting version of Napoleon's story, try either director Abel Gance's landmark 1927 version, or even director Yves Simoneau's French/Canadian/American "*Napoleon*" miniseries, an international co-production from 2002. And if you want to see this film's Raymond Pellegrin playing Napoleon in a second movie, try director Jean Delannoy's 1963 Italian-French co-production, *Venere imperiale* (*Imperial Venus*), in which Pellegrin plays the Emperor opposite the picture's first-billed Gina Lollobrigida, who plays his sister, Paulette.

What a Critic Said at the Time: "This may tire many. An axe, not scissors, would have to be taken to this long-winded expose of the Emperor's life, which dwells in [uninteresting] anecdotage…Jean Gabin [is seen, briefly] dying and shrieking, as he points at some wounded men." (*Variety*, 4-13-55 issue. Critic: "Mosk. [George Moskowitz.]" Reviewed in Paris.)

FILM 51

Razzia sur la chnouf

France, 1955

(Approximate English Translation of French 'Slang' Title: "RAID ON THE SNIFF" or "RAID ON THE SNUFF") Directed by Henri Decoin. Produced by Paul Wagner. Screenplay by Henri Deloin and Maurice Griffe. Based Upon the Novel by August Le Breton. Director of Photography (black and white), Pierre Montazel. Music by Marc Lanjean and Michel Legrand. Editor, Denise Reiss. Production Designer, Raymond Gabutti. (GENRES: POLICIER/NOIR THRILLER) A Production of JAD Films. Running Time, 1 hour 45 minutes. Released in France by Gaumont, on April 7, 1955. Released in the U.S. with English subtitles as "RAZZIA," by Kassler Films, Inc., on November 18, 1957.

"Kenavo!"
—Breton slang for 'goodbye,' as spoken by Gabin, in "Razzia sur la chnouf"

In 1967, America's maverick B-movie producer Roger Corman unleashed *The Trip*, his hypnotic LSD flick which, in its telling, was neither 'pro' nor 'con' the ingestment of psychedelic substances. The independently-produced film's distributor, American International Pictures, prior to the film's release, asked Corman to tack a disclaimer onto the opening of the film, which he did, in which a voice-over narrator inveighed against 'the evils of psychotropic drugs.'

But *The Trip* wasn't the first time such a disclaimer was utilized. In fact, if we go back twelve years to 1955, and travel across the Atlantic to France, we see that director Henri Decoin had already utilized this device in his supersonic Gabin-*noir*, *Razzia sur la chnouf*, and that he had probably cribbed the device from American, 1930s'-cautionary tale-pictures like *Reefer Madness*. The word '*chnouf*,' in the title, is onomatopoeic French slang, and is meant to replicate a drug-snorting sound; there's no direct translation of the word in English, except maybe to say 'sniff,' which isn't exactly right.

The film's ultra-serious opening credit crawl informs us that "This film shows the brutal truth, presenting drugs in their true light. Drugs can exist only in a violent environment, an environment with no room for pity. The following images will serve to prevent people who,

With Magali Noel.

by weakness or ignorance, may be the victims of an epidemic called *LA DROGUE* (drugs)."

Razzia sur la chnouf is the first of five Gabin crime flicks, made between 1955 and 1970, which were based upon novels by Auguste Le Breton (1913—1999), who was born Auguste Monforte in Brittany. 1955 was a banner year for the wine, woman, and song-loving Le Breton because, besides *Razzia*, four of his other novels were made into films, and two in particular—Jules Dassin's *Rififi* and Jean-Pierre Melville's *Bob Le Flambeur*, neither of which features Jean Gabin—are recognized universally today as being two of the greatest international *film noir* thrillers. *Razzia* is directed by Henri Decoin, who had put Gabin through the paces three years earlier, in the marital drama *La Verite sur Bebe Donge.*

As *Razzia* begins, an Air France jet arrives at Paris-Orly Airport, and two cops, Inspectors Lecharme (Alain Nobis) and Dupont (Jacques Morlaine) are lying in wait for a man who's about to disembark, and they've even got a picture of the fellow for whom they're waiting: It's none other than opium-syndicate underboss Henri Ferre (Gabin), better known as 'Le Nantais:' In France, lots of criminals, not to mention lots of characters in crime fiction, are nicknamed after the regions where they were born—so, for example, the film's author, Auguste Monfort, took the pen-name 'Le Breton' because he's from Breton (Brittany), Jean Gabin is called 'Le Nantais' because he is from Nantes, a major seaport town near the Loire River in northwestern France, and another gangster-character in the picture, played by Lino Ventura, is called 'Le Catalan,' because he is from the Catalan region of Spain. (Similarly,

With Lino Ventura and Albert Remy.

in director Jules Dassin's Gabinless Le Breton adaptation *Rififi*, actor Jean Servais plays a gangster called 'Le Stephanois,' because his character is supposed to have been born in the 'Stephanois' region of eastern France.)

Instead of arresting Henri, Lecharme and Dupont just watch him as he disembarks from the plane, crawls into a taxi, and makes for the Hotel Napoleon, in Paris's Eighth District. Lecharme and Dupont follow him there in their own unmarked vehicle, keeping a safe distance behind his cab, so that he won't see them.

Henri's first stop, pre-hotel, is the office of a man who 'might' be one of France's biggest opium czars/*capos*, his boss, Paul Liski, who is played by Gabin's *La Grande illusion* co-star, Marcel Dalio: Yes, this time out, the man who played Gabin's 'little buddy' Rosenthal is now, eighteen years later, playing Gabin's mega-tough boss, and in between the making of *La Grande illusion* and the making of *Razzia sur la chnouf*, Dalio had faced true life horror—members of his immediate family were slaughtered in the Holocaust. Henri Le Nantais is one of the Organization's top international underbosses, and he's just returned to France for the first time in ten years: Over the last decade, Henri's been all over the world, supervising many of the Liski Organization's foreign operations. Liski is excited to see Henri, clearly one of his favorite operatives, and immediately after welcoming Henri back, he issues him new marching orders: "Henri, I need a specialist here in Paris to put some order back into this organization. Some of our people have become lax. You're going to be replacing [another underboss], Le Bosco, who screwed up a lot, and even worse than that—he was weak. [And not only was Le Bosco weak: According to a newspaper headline which we see at the beginning of the film, he was just killed in a shoot-out with police.] You're going to be taking care of all of the Organization's European-based drug businesses, making sure that everything is happening in just the right way. For your troubles, I will pay you one hundred thousand francs up front, and I will establish you in an apartment which I know you will find to your liking."

And Liski's not lying when he says that the Organization has really fallen into disrepute, during Henri's time overseas: Liski oversees certain distributors who are supposed to have been selling the company's opium—most of which is reconstituted as opium—throughout Paris, and many of these distributors have been skimming, or else they've been selling the Organization's merchandise on their own, without handing over their profits.

Liski tells Henri that, principally, he'll be working out of a restaurant called Le Troquet. ('Le Troquet' means 'The Exchange,' and this is Auguste Le Breton's wry joke: By operating out of a venue with that name, the bad guys are practically telling the cops what they're *really* doing at the place—they're 'exchanging' drugs for money!—but none of the cops in the picture is going to be figuring that out—at least, for awhile, anyway.) Liski gives Henri *carte blanche* to hire anybody he wants to work at the restaurant, although he does issue Henri a stern warning, which is that none of the employees is to be made aware of his (Liski's) existence: "As you know, Henri, I like to move my people around. Today, I will have you in this restaurant, and tomorrow, maybe, you'll be somewhere else." He also advises Henri—and, no doubt, the tough-looking Henri already knows this, and only too well—that Henri should "…always be ruthless to the employees who are screwing us." Not only in *Razzia sur la chnuouf,* but also in a lot of other French crime pictures as well, Gabin's characters are always having to deal with the crimes which are committed by those 'bad eggs' who exist within the crime organizations for which they work, and sometimes even more so than they're having to deal with the problems which exist between the criminal organizations and the police.

Henri must begin working immediately, because it's now time for him to bust the Organization's 'Dirty, Skimming Employee #1,' and the film's director, Henri Decoin, now cuts to a trainyard, where we meet a wimpy trainsman, Emile (Francois Joux), who is boarding a passenger car. When he's sure that nobody is around, Emile sneaks into a train car, opens a panel, and extricates massive packets of opium, which he's supposed to have been selling for the Liski Organization, and which the Organization regularly receives from the Balkans. Emile's been keeping the stuff himself, for his own 'clients' and his own profit.

In the ensuing sequence, Emile enters a local bar and plunks down at a table. Henri comes in, sits down next to Emile, and Emile nervously makes a speech which we can tell he's been rehearsing: "I don't want to work for the company anymore, Mr. Henri. What I want, is to be able to retire. I want to be a simple farmer with the money I've saved up. I want to cut myself free from this life." Henri is gentle with Emile, a guy whom he immediately pegs as being "as

1954 — 1976 | 55

weak as they come," and he asks Emile how much he's been putting aside for retirement (read: how much he's been skimming), and Emile, who is far too dim to understand what Henri really means, admits that he hasn't really been able to save-up as much as he's wanted to.

Henri now arrives at his new restaurant/crime-front, Le Trouquet, which is a pretty fancy place, and for him, the best thing there is the cute, young cashier-girl, Lisette, who's played by the fetching Magali Noel (Americans might know Noel from Costa Gavras' 1969 thriller Z, in which she plays the distraught sister of the film's hospital-bound character). At this point, two thugs, Roger Le Catalan (Lino Ventura) and Bibi (Albert Remy), enter: They're the Organization's two toughest enforcers, and they'll now work directly under Henri, although from what we'll be seeing throughout the film, it seems like their main job is just going to be sitting in the restaurant, eating everything on the menu, day and night, as they await Henri's orders to beat the hell out of anybody who might be screwing with The Organization. Le Catalan knows Henri from long ago, and is excited to have him back in Paris, and Henri agrees that it's good to be home: "I'm done with traveling. I was away for ten years, in America, China, and South America. But Paris is the best."

Henri takes Le Catalan and Bibi upstairs to his private office, and hands them a picture of Emile, the wimpy trainsman whom Henri had met at the diner. "So this is the one who wants to stop working for us?" Le Catalan asks, as he studies the photo. "What's his address?" Just like in *The Godfather*, or innumerable episodes of American television's "The Soprano's," it is impolitic to 'leave the family,' and now, just as we've been expecting, it's time for Emile to pay his exit tax. Henri tells his two thugs, "Take care of him. I'll pay you after."

Emile, meanwhile, is playing pool at a local pool-hall near the Paris-Strasbourg line and, when a train passes that he recognizes—because he can differentiate between the sounds made by individual trains—he's happy. He then takes a phone call: It's a voice, which is telling him that he's got intruders at his house, and that it is far too dangerous for him to go home. He knows that the intruders are probably men who have been sent by Henri and, rather than staying-put in the bar, he runs home to meet his miserable fate, without putting up a fight. (Wow: Those French movie characters with their 'existential resignedness;' well, sure, they call it 'resignedness,' but we real Americans know it by its true name—sadomasochism. You know the drill: "I've been bad! Whip me! Hurt me! Kill me!")

Emile arrives on his property, not entering his house, but remaining in the backyard, which he now starts digging up with a shovel, as the yard is where he's been hiding all of his cash profits. Suddenly, he is face-to-face with Le Catalan and Bibi. Le Catalan holds a gun at Emile's chest, and while Emile is concentrating on it, Paul stands behind him and whacks him over the head—mercifully, off-screen—with an axe, at exactly the same moment during which the Paris-Strasbourg line is again passing, the piercing scream of its smokestack replicating and obfuscating Emile's own screams.

While this is happening, Henri is dining alone, as Gabin's characters are wont to do, at Le Trouqet: In the 1950s, which is the decade when Gabin will start playing smooth gentleman-criminals like Henri Le Nantais, or like his Max character in *Touchez pas au grisbi*, we're always going to be getting sequences in which his characters are dining alone, just minding their own business. Henri asks his waiter, Julien (Robert Le Fort), who's leaving for the night, what's he's hiding in the suitcase he's lofting and, upon further inspection, it turns out to be a ham. Julien, embarrassed, tells Henri that he lost 14,000 francs betting on horses, and that because of his actions, his wife and children will have no food. Henri, a good boss, slaps his face, hands him 10,0000 francs, and tells him never to steal from him again. (These Liski Underlings are so corrupt, that they're not only pocketing dope, but meat, as well!) In *Razzia sur la chnouf,* we learn that it is human nature is to steal, and that the whole world is basically just one big store, which exists only for our looting pleasure.

It's now the end of the evening, and pretty cashier Lisette is going home, so when Henri offers to give her a lift, she naturally takes him up on his offer. ("Good! Now I don't have to take a taxi!") When the two of them are up in Henri's apartment, he helps her out of her clothes quite easily, although she does tell him she feels slightly uneasy about the whole thing, especially because, as she told him on the car-ride over, she's twenty-two (and he's in his fifties). She has already told him that she has no family and that her father has recently died and, as we all know, vulnerable gals 'lose their laundry' faster than anybody else!

The next day, Henri shows up at a country house, in an ultra-cool white trenchcoat. He asks the young blonde woman who answers the door, Solange Birot (Jacqueline Porel), where her husband is, and she proceeds to lead the way, taking Henri into her husband's secret basement laboratory. Solange's husband, Birot (Roland Armantel) is a mild-mannered old chemist who cuts most of the Organization's Balkan-raised opium. The rumpled Birot informs Henri that he has 're-imagined' twenty-five kilos of opium, with the help of baking soda, into fifty kilos of heroin, per Henri's orders, and Henri now tells him that he wants to change the system a bit: "I don't want your chemists to work on more than one kilo at a time, because I don't want them [to leave with it, and possibly to resell it] without my knowing about it." Henri next asks Birot to cut him an extra forty kees: "For our operations in England. And mind your own business..."

Enter one of the Organization's prime skimmers, a young, motorcycle-driving, leather jacketed, cauliflower-nosed punk, Marcel (Michel Jourdan) who, like the trainsman Emile, is one of the Organization's corrupt pushers. This brash James Dean-wannabe pats Birot's wife's ass as he enters the house, and damn if she doesn't love it, especially because her husband looks so ancient. After the ass-grabbing is done, Birot and Marcel carry bags of newly-cut 'H' out of the house, and into Henri's car.

Henri drives north of Paris to Le Havre and, as he parks along a deserted stretch of road, a British Chauffeur (Rene Alie) pulls up in a car and asks Henri for the forty kilos which he knows Henri has brought along, and this particular foot-soldier is the underling who will be transporting the stuff from France to the Organization's U.K. operations. Henri and the Chauffeur converse briefly in English as they load-up the Chauffeur's trunk. The gist of their conversation, is that some rival drug kingpin in London has killed the Organization's British underboss, and that the new UK underboss is not English, but Italian-American, a guy named 'Big Rossillio' whom we will hear about, but not see, in this movie.

That night, Lisette's prepared dinner for Henri, and she informs him that Le Catalan came by earlier that evening, before he got home, to meet with him. She serves her much-older lover his meal, but doesn't sit down with him, telling him that it will probably be smarter for her to take her meals with the rest of the restaurant's staff, so that nobody will know that she's dating the boss—that he is, in other words, playing favorites.

Le Catalan and Bibi now return to Henri's apartment. (Everybody always bugs you during dinner time. Hit-men are more impertinent than telemarketers!) Le Catalan tells Henri that Marcel, the James Dean-ish messenger with the motorbike, and Birot, the Organization's trusted chemist, are in cahoots, processing extra drugs, which they've been selling on their own, without feeding the Organization's till. Henri, who is very 'Gabin-Level-Headed' when he hears this, replies, "Well, we'll have to kill Marcel, then. But we can't do anything really bad to Birot, because he's smart, and we need him. I'll take care of him myself."

Le Catalan and Bibi make it over to elderly Birot's home, letting him know, in no uncertain terms, that the jig is up, and while Henri has instructed his two henchmen not to use too much force with Birot, it is in their nature to do so, so they give him a good thrashing anyway, and right in front of the scientist's weirdly non-horrified wife, who's actually getting turned-on by seeing her ancient hubby getting sucker-punched by hoods. After the two henchmen beat the crust out of Birot, Le Catalan gives Birot's horrified wife a deep soul-kiss, which she lovingly accepts.

Now, it's time for Henri to bust Marcel: He enters the Café du Coin, a Parisian corner coffeehouse, where underground crap games are held, and the games happen to be run by one 'Auguste Le Breton,' a character in his own film (but not the real Breton: the 'movie Breton' is played by an actor). Henri descends into the Café's smoke-filled underground card parlor, and walks right up to cocky, young Marcel, sneaking up behind him, and ordering him to walk outside. He marches the young guy out onto the street and, as Marcel starts shaking like a little girl, Henri coolly informs him, "You're going to take me to the five kilos you've stolen from me. You and Birot are in big trouble."

Henri, with Le Catalan and Bibi now in tow (they've joined him on the street, outside of the Café du Coin), enter Marcel's apartment together, and Marcel nervously hands over four of the purloined kilos (he's already sold one). Henri asks Marcel where he's hiding the fifth kee, and Marcel confesses that he's already sold it. As a way of thanking Marcel for the information which he's just given them, the three men take him outside, and Le Catalan—and this is extremely proto-Tarantino—stoically pumps eight shots into him, point-blank.

Later that night, Henri's in bed, having just made love to Lisette. Even though she believes Le Troquet to be 'just a restaurant,' and he's never told her about what really goes on there, she's smart, and she's already figured out that this place doubles as something else, and so she asks him if he might be in on anything dangerous; but as he leaves for the night, he tells her that she needn't worry for his safety. ("You're weird sometimes, Henri," she grins at him, in the parlance of 'The Not-Always-Articulate-Young.')

58 | **THE FILMS** CYCLE FIVE

Looking for clues.

Now it's time for Henri to go and bust another Dirty Skimmer, and and he and an operative head over to an ornate opium den owned by Lichian (Andre Weber), a place that's scattered with a few stoned-out-of-their gourds businessmen and elderly Chinese. (When Sergio Leone directed *Once Upon a Time in America*, you know he must have been familiar with *Razzia*, and not just because Jean Gabin was Leone's very favorite movie actor of all time, but also because the opium den in which Robert De Niro is seen 'smoking-out' at the beginning of Leone's picture, is a direct lift, visually, from *Razzia sur la chnouf*.) Henri tells Lichian he knows that he's been selling the Organization's merchandise without offering the Organization its rightful cut, and he tells Lichian that it's fine if he sells Liski opium, as long as he pays up *and* orders twice as much as he's already ordering.

When Henri arrives back at Le Troquet, Le Catalan and Bibi are there, and the evening's newspaper is spread out in front of them: The headline proclaims that the British police have just arrested Big Rossillio for possessing forty kilos of heroin, when Henri gets wind of this, he decides to take a pow-wow with his elusive boss, Liski. Henri asks Liski if he thinks the cops will find any connection between their Organization and Big Rossillio's, and Liski tells him that as long as they are careful, there shouldn't be any problems.

Next, in one of French Gangster Cinema's most noteworthy scenes—and this surreal bit is right out of Jacques Tati—a bunch of cops raid Le Troquet during the busiest part of dinnertime and, hilariously, they start busting all of the patrons—probably about a hundred

With Magali Noel.

people, including scores dining couples who are involved with the organization, not to mention an elderly couple who isn't involved in any crimes, and who just manage to look completely bewildered by the whole *mishegoss*. The bulldog-looking Commissioner Fernand (Paul Frankeur) and handsome Inspector Leroux (Pierre Louis) of the Vice Squad ask Henri who the owner of the restaurant is, and Henri exasperatedly replies, "You know it's me. Look, my papers are in the cash register, so you can stop questioning me, okay?" One of the dining patrons, who happens to be another one of the Organization's lieutenants, is played by Marcel Bozzuffi, the actor whom we saw already as trucker Gabin's partner, Pierre, in *Gas-Oil*. (Like Magali Noel, Bozzuffi will also appear in Costa-Gavras' Z.) Bozzuffi's character's name is 'Man with Revolver,' and it's an apt moniker, since the beautiful woman with whom he's been dining is safekeeping his revolver for him, in one of her stockings. Bozzuffi's character doesn't have any drugs or weapons on him, but the cops take him away anyway because, as one cop points out, "He might know someone who knows someone," and, as the cops leave, this funny 'gag' scene has a great payoff: The restaurant is now completely free of patrons, and a befuddled old janitor sweeps up all of the hundreds of guns which the diners have ditched on the floor: The place's one remaining patron, is a befuddled British diner who's still munching-out on his soup (he's played by a French actor, Paul Azais); weirdly oblivious to the gargantuan purge which has just gone on in his presence, he cheerfully holds up a gun which he's just discovered under his table, and proudly lisps—with a raised pinky, yet—"I found another one!"

Fernand and Leroux, who don't like Henri's insolence, bring him down to the station and begin interrogating him, and we're now going to get Another Great Gabin Interrogation Scene, one of those sequences in which our hero is tougher than all of the cops who are working him over, and he's not feeling threatened by them at all. When they ask him again if he owns Le Troquet, he suddenly gives in to a great, and mega-cathartic, Gabin-Outburst:

> HENRI: Are you guys nuts? Shut the hell up! I don't know anything about it!
> FERNAND: Come on, Henri. Give us something! We know you've been in America and Yugoslavia. Why are you so stubborn that you won't tell us? Is this your operation, or do you work for somebody else?
> HENRI: I'm from Brittany!

Meaning, that he's just not going to talk: Brittany, from whence Henri Le Nantais and Henri's creator, Auguste Le Breton, both hail, is a regional of tough/stoic individuals who never say or do anything that they don't want to (as we already remember from Jean Gremillon's weepie *Remorques*, in which tugboat captain Gabin congratulates one of his young swabbies, for possessing "a fine Breton head"). Instead of losing his cool, Henri just shuts the lamp above his head off—it's the room's sole source of light—and the room goes dark. Suddenly, Henri begins kicking some serious cop ass. When the lights come up again, all three of the cops in the room are blood-spattered, and Henri quietly walks out, dusting off the shoulders of his suit. When he walks out of the interrogation room, we see that all of the people whom we had met earlier, when they were dining at Henri's restaurant, are lined up *en masse* in the hallway and, from the sour looks on each of their faces, we can tell that they just want to go home, but Henri just slinks by them, trying to avoid their hot glances, and not too successfully: What are you all looking at me like that for? Do I look weird?" Le Catlalan and Bibi, who were interrogated simultaneously in another room, were also 'keeping mum' about what they know, and we see them as they tell the cops, "All we do at Le Troquet is eat. They have good food! Maybe if you're nice, we'll invite you one day!"

Henri, whose face is bruised and broken from his interrogation-altercation, next sulks up to Lisette's place, plops down on her bed, and asks for a mirror, and when he sees his own messed-up face, he smiles. "I don't look so good!" he grins, wearing his battle-scars like badges of honor. Le Catalan and Bibi visit him, not just to see how he's doing, but also to tell him, truthfully, that they didn't give him, or the Organization, away to the cops during their own interrogation, and Henri knows that they're telling him the truth, because they're both very loyal. Because the film's director, Henri Decoin, cast Jean Gabin's 'real-life loyal friend' Lino Ventura as Le Catalan, on a not-entirely-subconscious level, we, the film's audience, already know that Le Catalan will always be loyal to Henri.

The next night, Henri ventures out to another Paris nightspot, because he wants to meet

Leah, another of the Organization's corrupt distributors. She's a hopped-up beatnik, and she's played by none other than the legendary actress, Lila Kedrova.

A stand-out in the cast of *Razzia sur la chnouf* is the great, Russian-born, Canadian-reared actress Lila Kedrova (1918-2000). In the 1960s, '70s, and '80s, Kedrova's name was known internationally, especially after she won the Best Supporting Actress Oscar at America's 1964 Academy Awards, for her role as Madame Hortense in director Michael Cacoyannis' classic film, *Zorba the Greek,* in which she played opposite Anthony Quinn. Kedrova continued to make movies all over the world—she spoke Russian, English, French and Italian—right up through her death in 1994.

Leah, as Lila Kedrova plays her, is a gaunt, twitchy, vibrating proto-Goth, and if she's not certifiably insane from 'getting high on her own supply,' she's definitely on her way. He sits down next to her, and she immediately starts screaming at him, not even realizing that he outranks her in the Organization: "What the hell are you looking at, creep? I'm over 18!" Henri tells Leah that he'd like her to take him to meet some of the Organization's pushers with whom he's not familiar.

First, they meet Jo Cingalet (Francois Patrice) a young, well-dressed gay pusher who is attracted to Henri (Henri kind of plays into it, by grinningly telling the guy that when he was young, everybody used to call him "Sweet Henri"). Cingalet shows Henri how he hides packets of heroin, sealing them into the back of a Paris phone book, and he then takes Henri and Leah down into the Varennes subway station and shows him one of his typical transactions: We get to see Jo hiding the drugs in a vending machine.

Next, Henri and Leah head into a dark underground bar in the rue Vercingeroix, a street which is named after the Gallic chieftain Vercingeroix, who led a revolt against Julius Caesar, in 53-52 B.C., and this isn't just any club: It's a black/gay club where marijuana is smoked out in the open, and where a shirtless, well-muscled African is shaking his stuff in front of the place's besotted regulars. This club, too, is a place where people sell the Organization's drugs, without giving the Organization its rightful cut of the profits.

The next day, Henri's over at Liski's office, and he lets Liski know that he's warned Leah to stop selling to 'sub-dealers' he doesn't know (such as Jo Cingalet and the bartender at the black club), and Liski tells Henri (he knows Henri's 'style') that he hopes he's not acting too kind with the girl-skimmers. As we've already seen, Henri doesn't reprimand the crooked women in the Organization in quite the same way in which he handles the men.

Back at La Troquet that night, the Maitre'd (Jean Olivier) informs Henri that Lisette has just been arrested. Clearly, even though it's not stated in the film, the police now know that Le Trouquet and Henri are both tied to the Liski Organization, that Lisette is dating Henri, and that grabbing Henri's main-squeeze is a good way to get to Henri.

Night falls, and we're now outside of a bar called Chez Nanard:

Two gussied-up prostitutes emerge from this American-style watering hole, adorned in fur coats. Le Catalan and Henri, who are hiding around the corner, have planted the hookers there as a 'ruse,' so that local cops will concentrate on them, instead of on Henri, but as long as Henri and Le Catalan are there anyway, they shoot a few of the cops who have just walked by, just for chuckles-'n-grins. Le Catalan tells Henri that, because of what they've just done in this scene, it will probably be best for them to hide-out somewhere; in every country, cop-killing is not what you would ever call a 'thought-out idea.' He asks Henri if Liski has a place where they, along with Bibi, can hide, but Henri tells him 'no dice,' that they're going to have to come up with a hiding place on their own.

Henri thinks that he, Le Catalan, and Bibi should hide out at the chemist Birot's house, and why not? That hot wife, Solange, is there! Lisette, who has already been interrogated and released, has learned from Henri—no doubt off-screen, because we don't see it in the movie—that Henri (and, in fact, she herself, as well as everybody else at Le Troquet), actually works for the ultra-secret Liski, so she telephones Liski and asks him to help Henri. (Henri left Lisette Liski's phone number to use in case of an emergency—in case anything should happen to him—without telling her who, exactly, Liski is.) And it's not just Lisette who is now learning about Liski's existence, either: Even though he's been told not to, but because he has no choice, considering the dire circumstances they are in, Henri takes Le Catalan and Bibi to see Liski (neither of Henri's two thugs have met Liski before) and it is here that we get a big, surprise twist: Liski's the one who's set Le Catalan, Bibi, and Henri up, to get plugged by the cops, so that nobody will be able to trace all of the Organization's current problems back to him.

When Henri, Le Catalan, and Bibi arrive at Liski's office, Liski looks super nervous, because he knows that *they* know he's set them up, and he also knows that they've definitely come to kill him: One look from that tough old bird Henri, and Liski, one of Europe's biggest drug czars, turns to jelly.

While it's true that Liski has set them all up, they can't kill him, because he's a *capo,* and they realize that if they did kill him, they'd be rubbed-out in about two seconds by other Liski's lieutenants. Flustered anyway, Liski now begs for his life: "Look, guys: Don't shoot me. You can have anything you want. I'll even let you hide out in my [secret] hunting lodge!" That night, Henri, Le Catalan, and Bibi get lost, driving to Liski's lodge, and Henri tells Le Catalan, who's behind the wheel, not to take the main roads because, if they do, the cops might find them.

Eventually, these three refugees-from-the-law arrive at Liski's, and it's sweltering in there—probably, the windows haven't been opened in ages. Henri tells the other two that he doesn't mind the heat, and that it would probably be best for their "health" if they left the windows closed. Le Catalan wonders aloud about **whether Liski is really the #1 Man in the Organization,** and Henri responds, "Maybe he's not '**Number One.**' Maybe our real boss is an Italian, or maybe he's even a German. It might even **be Big Rossillio, but it might not be. Nobody knows.**" (It's just like 'the drug-problem' today or, **for that** matter, it's a lot like international terrorism: Where does it start? Where's 'the head **of the** snake?' Nobody knows.)

1954 — 1976 | 63

In the next sequence, cops cruisers start converging upon the hunting lodge and, of course, the cops have shut down their headlights so that they won't be seen, just like in the famous finale of De Palma's *Scarface*. Liski—talk about a 'toxic boss'—has, of course, tipped-off the cops that Henri, Le Catalan, and Bibi are there (it's a good way to deflect attention away from himself), and Henri, at this point, asks Le Catalan and Bibi if, possibly, the two of them have been setting *him* up as well, and both of them immediately freak-out on him: "How can we be setting you up, boss? We're here, too!"

Next, we get the obligatory, and beautifully shot, 'major shootout-scene,' which features Henri, Le Catalan, and Bibi, *versus* the fuzz. Henri turns all of the lights in the house off, so that they can't be seen, and the cops start firing into the windows and, of course, Henri and the other two guys, shoot back. "Someone sold us out!" Henri exclaims. "We're caught!"

Director Decoin next intercuts this massive shootout sequence with another event which is occurring simultaneously, in Paris: Exactly at the same time as Henri and the guys are holed up in the country house, a giant *Kristallnacht*-like purge/sweep by Paris P.D. of every single drug criminal in Paris is in progress off-screen, and it's a massive arrest of just about every snaky-looking person we've seen in the movie so far, from the bartenders at Leah's little underground clubs, to everybody else who seems to be part of the 'food-chain,' and even of the most seemingly 'minor' characters, whom we've already forgotten about. Henri now decides, paranoiacally, that Le Catalan is the one who sold him out, and he orders Le Catalan at gunpoint, to put his hands up. And just as this is happening, the cops plug Bibi through the window, killing him instantly. Now, Henri and Le Catalan are all alone in the house, shooting at each other, while the cops are outside continuing to fire at both of them.

Finally, the *flics*, who include Commissioner Fernand and Inspector Leroux, bust down the door, and grab Henri and Le Catalan - and now, in the film's weirdest surprise twist, Henri reveals that he's really a cop, and that he's been infiltrating Paul Liski's crime organization to help rid Paris of drugs. (O.K.: So, this is a great plot twist, but it also presents a weird inconsistency in the film's storytelling and logic: If the cops knew Henri was 'one of them,' why did they beat the hell out of him and blacken his eye during the interrogation scene?)

Back at Paris P.D., the cops (Fernand, Leroux, Decharme and many others) have now managed to assemble a massive line-up/cattle round-up of every criminal character we've seen in the movie so far, and not only is it hilarious, but it looks, for all the world, like that endless line of stalled-out cars we see on the highway in Jean-Luc Godard's socialist car-stravaganza from 1966, *Weekend*.) Beatnik Leah who is, of course, part of the line-up, tells a police officer that she guessed Henri was a cop when she first met him, and right after she says this, she starts screaming and going through a major drug withdrawal ("Somebody kill me! Throw stones at me!"), so a couple of helpful cops quickly find her a syringeful of 'H,' and 'fix' her—it's a good thing cops always have some extra dope, on hand.

In the final shot of the film, Paul Liski is now in the interrogation room, himself, and Henri joins a group of other cops who are interrogating him, and because of this scene, *Razzia sur la chnouf* winds up being the second movie in French cinema history—*La Grande illusion* being the first—which ends with a scene of Jean Gabin and Dalio, better known as *La Grande illusion's* Marechal and Rosenthal, together. Obviously, this was done by design, to remind people of that earlier, 1937 film, and lest you think that Dalio only had small, supporting roles in French films, serious cineastes know that he is actually the lead in Jean Renoir's legendary 1939 comedy *La Regle du jeu* (*The Rules of the Game*), which is the film which Renoir made directly after *La Grande illusion,* and that he is spectacular in it.

Razzia sur la chnouf is right up there with any of the best *noir* thrillers ever made on either side of the Atlantic, and it's a shame that, today, it is unknown in the U.S. (although, at the time of this book's printing, a very good quality bootleg, with English subtitles, has surfaced, and can be purchased from an internet seller called notavailableondvd.com), because 'noir-heads' would love it to death. The picture was released in the U.S. in 1957, at a couple of art-house theaters, by the now-defunct Kassler Pictures, but hasn't been seen in America since that year, although in France, it is still considered, today, to be one of the classic gangster films of all time. It is very much a piece, stylistically and as far as its tone, with another Gabin picture from the previous year in which the actor also portrayed a classy, level-headed gentleman gangster who's dealing with problems within his own crime organization, director Jacques Becker's *Touchez pas au grisbi,* although to this author's mind, *Chnouf* kind of edges *Grisbi* out a bit, because *Chnouf* has some pretty wild scenes to which Americans, at the time, may have been unaccustomed. In particular, I'm talking about the 'trippy,' almost psychedelic scene in the black/gay bar, in which customers writhe on drugs, a scene which seems to be right out of Orson Welles' *Touch of Evil,* except for the fact that *Razzia sur la chnouf* lensed two years before the Welles picture. In spite of a couple of 'weird-o' scenes like this, though, the movie is almost as politically conservative as any episode of t.v.'s "Dragnet," and not just because of the 'anti-drug' credit crawl at the beginning of the film, but also in a very striking way: In *Razzia sur la chnouf,* heroin is a 'sophisticated' drug which is used only by smart, upscale white characters, while marijuana, which we see only once in the film, at the nightclub on the rue Vercingeroix, is a 'degenerate' drug used only by blacks and gays, similar to how the Nancy Reagan Brigade portrayed crack-cocaine as being a 'degenerate' drug to be ingested only at crack-houses, in the 1980s and 1990s. (In this movie, heroin is the relatively harmless drug which leads to that much harder drug—marijuana!)

One of the neatest things about *Razzia,* is that, at the end of the film, when you learn that Gabin's character was really a cop the whole time, you can go back and watch the movie a second time, and see if he was doing anything to give his true identity away, just like how, more recently, movie audiences went back for a second helping of director M. Night Shamalyan's 1999 Bruce Willis thriller *The Sixth Sense,* once they realized that Willis' character had been dead throughout the entirety of the picture. In fact, you'd be hard-pressed to find anything wrong in *Razzia,* because it's just such an entertaining and well-structured movie on every possible level.

An extended version of the New York *Times* review of the film by Bosley Crowther, which appears below in expurgated form, quotes from the film's press kit: According to the picture's American distributor, Kassler, U.S. drug enforcement agencies were actually screening *Razzia sur la chnouf* for their operatives, as a training film, so that agents could learn about 'the underground drug world' in a sophisticated and complete way.

What a Critic Said at the Time: "Gabin is appealing as a sleuth impersonating a gangster. A hardboiled opus [that] dips deeply into the drug racket of France, to come up with some excitingly-detailed aspects of the trade [although the film does get bogged down in some] draggy, prolonged detail." (*Variety*, 6-15-55 issue. Critic: "Mosk. [George Moskowitz.]" Reviewed in Paris.)

What Another Critic Said at the Time: "Just as starkly real and sordid as [American director Jules Dassin's French heist picture, the all-time classic] *Rififi* [which was released in France earlier in the same year of 1955], if not as polished, [*Razzia*] is an excursion through the Parisian lower depths that is chillingly revelatory. Jean Gabin, an experienced strong and laconic type, adds another portrait to the gallery for which he has become justifiably well-known. He is forceful in action, and sparing with his words. Lino Ventura and Albert Remy [who play the hoods 'Le Catalan' and 'Bibi'] leave the impression that they never saw a casting director's office, [like they] just stepped right out of a police line-up." (New York Times, 11-18-57 issue. Critic: Bosley Crowther.)

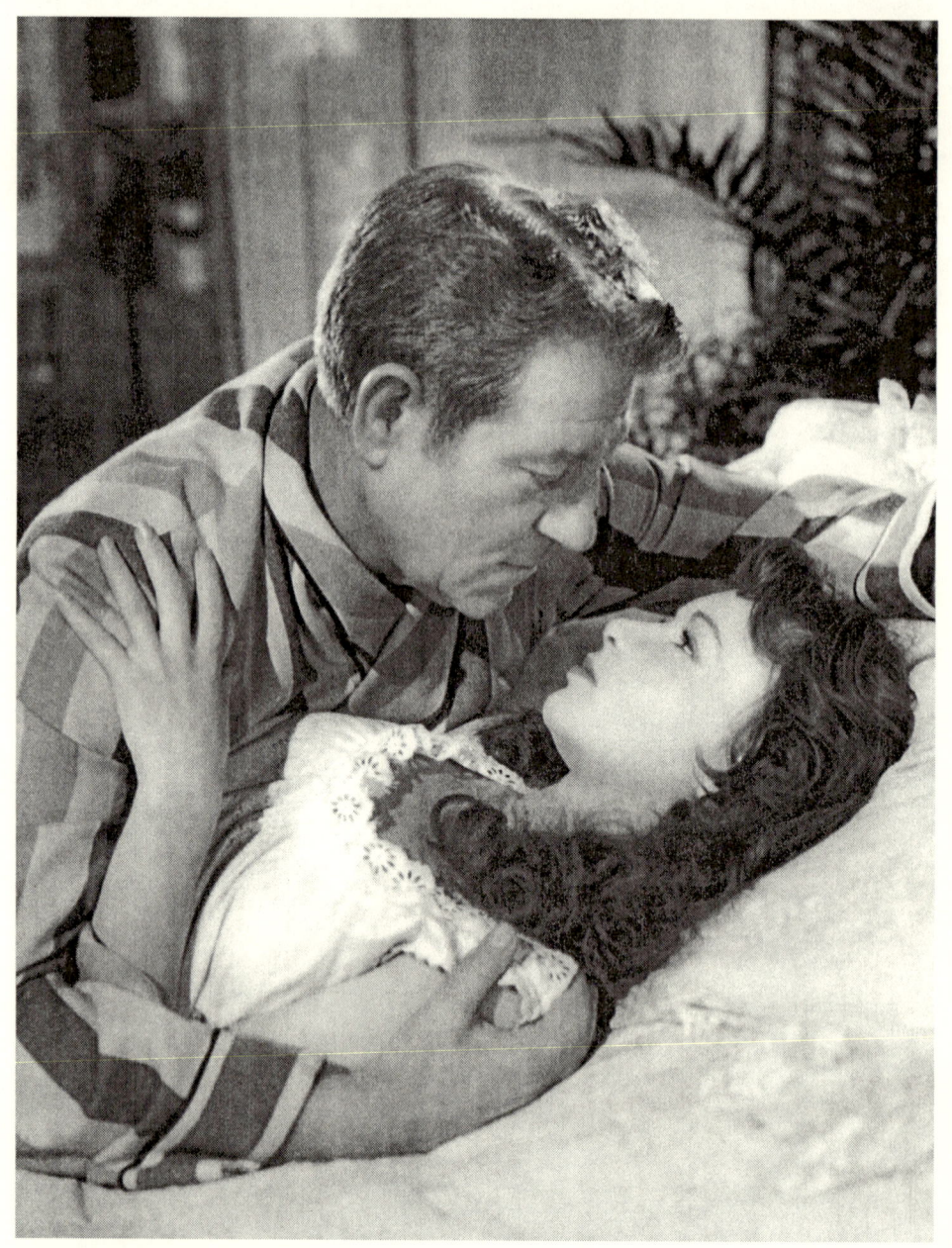

With Francoise Arnoul.

FILM 52

French Cancan

France/Italy, 1955

Directed and Written by Jean Renoir. Based Upon a Story Idea by Andre-Paul Antoine. Produced by Louis Wipf. Director of Photography (color), Michel Kelber. Editor, Borys Lewin. Music by Georges Van Parys. Production Designer, Max Douy. (GENRE: DRAMA, WITH MUSIC) A Production of London Films (France) and Jolly Film (Italy). Released in France by Franco-London Films, on April 27, 1955, with a Running Time of 1 Hour 42 Minutes. Released in United States on April 16, 1956 with English Subtitles, in a truncated (1 hour 33 minutes) version, by United Motion Picture Organization (UMPO), as "ONLY THE FRENCH CAN."

"You think I want to be caged like a canary? I will not wear slippers! You'll never have me alone. I like a lot of women!"
— Jean Gabin explains to his girlfriend that he is not a one-woman man, in *"French Cancan"*

Also in 1955 (Gabin made eight movies that year), Gabin would return to his music hall-roots for the first time in more than twenty years, joining director Jean Renoir for the fourth time (after *Les Bas-fonds, La Grande illusion,* and *La Bete humaine*), and for the first time in eighteen years, in the tremendously entertaining Technicolor extravaganza (Gabin's first starring role in a color film) *French Cancan,* which alleges to be the story of the origins of Paris's most famous 19th-century show-place, the Moulin Rouge. But because *Cancan* is a Jean Gabin movie, it will, by its very nature, be edgier and more substantive than were the fluffy MGM musicals of the day. (It is the second Moulin Rouge film, after John Huston's 1952 *Moulin Rouge;* the American-made Huston picture involved the diminutive painter Toulouse Lautrec [Jose Ferrer]'s 'whoring-adventures,' at the famous nightspot.)

The year is 1889: Gabin's Henri Danglard is a jaunty, fiftysomething theater impresario, whose vaudeville club, The Chinese Wall, is patronized by the rich and beautiful of Paris, and features such *multo-impressivo* acts as a whistling clown and a sexually-charged belly dancer, who also happens to be his girlfriend, Lola (Maria Felix), a woman who's billed, at the Chinese Wall, as *'La Belle abbesse.'* While Lola is Danglard's main-squeeze, he enjoys secondary (and even tertiary) flings with many of his dancers, in spite of Lola's more-than-frequent protestations that he should be comporting himself as 'a one-woman guy.' (*She's so full of shit!* Doesn't she know that men aren't built for that!)

Just like Jean Gabin is "the most famous movie star all over the world, everywhere except the United States," the same can be said for the Mexican film actress Maria Felix, who appeared in more than forty feature films throughout her career, in France, Argentina, Spain, and Italy. Throughout the 1940s and 1950s, American studio heads tried to get her to come to America and make English-language films, trying to position her as a 'new Rita Hayworth,' because both Hayworth and Felix were of Mexican extraction, but she turned them down every time, because she wasn't interested in learning to speak English. As a result, she was forever blacklisted from working in Hollywood, which goes a long way toward explaining why today, Maria Felix continues to be admired all over the world, everywhere *except* for in the United States. (*Exactly* like Jean Gabin!)

At the end of each evening's performance, customers are permitted to get up from their tables and dance with the stage performers who descend into the crowd, and this is where Henri first takes notice of the beautiful young laundress, Nini (Francoise Arnoul), a good-hearted, 'latter-day Zou Zou.' Henri dances with Nini, and becomes so captivated by her gossamer beauty and by her dancing abilities, that he immediately sets out on a constitutional to her impoverished home, where he asks her mother's permission (the mom is played by Valentine Tessier), to put her in his show.

Nini, who's been told by her naïve girlfriends that part of the job of being a dancing girl involves sleeping with the show's impresario, quickly goes to her fiancé, Paulo (Franco Pastorino), a jealous young baker with whom she has not yet enjoyed fleshly desires, and asks him to introduce her to the world of sex. At first Paulo is thrilled, because she's finally going to be 'giving it up' to him; but when he learns that she's really just doing it because she wants to 'learn sex' in order to please another man, he forbids her to join the show, telling her that if she does, their marriage will be off. Increasingly more intrigued by the inviting world of showbiz than she is with Paulo, Nini roundly ignores her hot-headed fiancé, setting up a 'Paulo *vs.* Danglard' rivalry, which will take us through the rest of the picture.

Danglard gives Nini dancing lessons at the studio, which is owned by crusty old Madame Guibolle (Lydia Johnson), and it is here we'll learn that the Cancan, an amazing (and, not to mention, gynecologically-revealing) dance, in which women throw their legs up as far over their heads as they can possibly go, is quickly becoming all the rage. Also, in this sequence, very amusingly, assembled characters try to come up with catchier names for the racy, new dance. (A male dancer cleverly opines, "Maybe we can give the dance an interesting American name—like 'lavatory!'")

But, suddenly, just like in the fickle movie business of today, the money behind Henri's popular burlesque house dries up. The owner of the property, Baron Walter (Jean-Roger Caussimon), tells Danglard that it is his unfortunate duty (he really likes Henri, as well as all of Henri's performers) to throw everyone in the show out on their asses. Not dissuaded by this sudden bad news, because he knows that his luck will turn around again (this is one of only a handful of Gabin's films in which he believes that Fate will be kind to him), Henri moves himself, his loyal performers, and Lola into a hotel, and all on his own dime. Henri, like most of the 'bosses' whom Gabin had played in his 1950s' movies, treats all of his good employees like family, even during those hard times during which he isn't making any money at all.

Soon, 'flush with francs' again, Baron Walter decides to back a new, Danglard-run club, which will be bigger and better than the Chinese Wall, and he even gives the place a flashy, new name, the *Moulin Rouge* (in English: The Red Woods). The mission statement of the new club seems to be: 'Entertainment for Everybody'—*not* just for the well-heeled.

Opening day of the Moulin Rouge is a major event in Paris, but Lady Fate gets everything Tangled Up in Blue, once again: Everyone in Paris is rioting to get inside. (Renoir shoots this sequence just like it's 'French Revolution No. 2') and, in the middle of the mayhem, Nini's jealous fiancé Paulo shows up, pushing Henri down a manhole, and fracturing Henri's leg, which is any hoofer's worst nightmare. Police shut the Moulin Rouge down immediately and, again, in spite of broken leg and shut-down-club, Henri remains upbeat. ("You'll come out all right," a homeless woman living in a doorway who we'll learn, eventually, used to be one of Henri's dancers a generation ago, tells him. [Her character is called 'Mimi Prunelle,' and she's played by an actress who's billed in the film's opening credits as 'Paquerette.']) Henri's sidekick, Casimir, who is played by a popular music hall and film comedian of the time named Philippe Clay, a goofily-likable seven-foot-tall singer, even entertains his boss with a jaunty song about the company's communal poverty, and his song is actually about eating rats and how delicious rodents taste! And during this whole setback, Nini has returned to work as a laundress, just like Josephine Baker's singer-character did, twenty-one years earlier, in *Zou Zou*.

Lola informs Henri that she will personally back a new Moulin Rouge (it will be the club's third incarnation, in just under a year), provided that only the rich will be able to gain admittance, just like how it used to be, back in the days of the Chinese Wall, and also provided that the performers will offer something classier than what she terms as being, "that vulgar Cancan." But Henri tells her 'no dice:' Remember, Henri is being played by Jean Gabin, the ultimate man-of-the-people, and the characters he plays always love populist entertainment, whether it's the extravagance of music hall, or even just a simple accordion.

Henri finally beds Nini and, for spite, Lola beds the Russian officer, Paulus (Jean Raymond), but because Henri's Gabin-ian motto, as we already know, is 'live and let live,' he doesn't care a whit about her grudgefuck, which frustrates her even more; Henri even calls the often Cruella DeVille-like Lola, "a queen bitch," and he does so, right to her face!

Meanwhile, bakerboy Paulo, who's not satisfied enough at having pushed Henri down a hole, next returns, horror movie psychopath-style, to kill him but, just as in that other Jean Gabin/Jean Renoir collaboration, 1936's *Les Bas-fonds*, the townspeople, who love Gabin, all congregate around him, protecting him from the scary interloper.

At this juncture, a new suitor emerges onto the scene, for Nini: He's a Russian Prince, by the name of Alexander, and he's played by Giani Esposito, who plays the part like a naively-sheltered trust-fund kid, and Nini is instantly smitten with her. Nini doesn't reciprocate the Prince's attentions (she digs much-older Henri, instead) and so, to woo her, Alexander puts up the money to build a *neo-neo* Moulin Rouge (this will be the dance hall's third incarnation, in the film). When the place is rebuilt again, Nini is now the main star, but she still has no love for Prince A. Frustrated, by the fact that she can't love him as he loves her, *the whipped-prince* shoots himself, getting injured, but remaining firmly in the land of the living. (Naturally, all of the Moulin Rouge's other *super-hot* dancing girls would love to be the object of Prince Alex's desires, but he's single-minded in his love for Nini, and has zero interest in any of them.)

In the next scene, Prince Alexander presents Henri with the deed to the new Moulin Rouge, which will now, effectively, make Henri the place's full owner, for the very first time. When opening night comes, Henri has promised the public the biggest and splashiest show ever, but star Nini won't come out of her dressing room, unless Henri can promise her that, from now on, he will make love only to her. Nini's Mom appears on the scene, too, and tries to coax her daughter out of the dressing room, by talking some sense into her. What's set off Nini's jealousy, specifically, is that Danglard has now betrayed her with the show's new singer, Esther Georges (Anna Amendola). Henri gives Nini an apportionment of his *"there's enough of me to go around"*-mantra which he had previously made to Lola, which gives rise to Gabin's one angry outburst, of the film: "You think I want to be caged like a canary? I will not wear slippers! You'll never have me, alone! I like a lot of women!" Nini comes to understand that Gabin's Henri, like all men, needs a variety of women, and once she understands this basic fact of life, she instantly loves him again. Nini makes egress from her dressing room, to dance on the stage and, happily, to share Jean Gabin with all womankind!

Needless to say, opening night is magnificent, and the last fifteen minutes of the film are given over to some of the most eye-poppingly energetic dance numbers ever captured on celluloid. (In fact, these production numbers are much more dazzlingly-impressive than anything in Baz Luhrmann's 2001 CGI video game-disguised-as-a-movie, *Moulin Rouge*.)

As Jean Renoir's stunning look at late-19th century Paris comes to a close, the entire Moulin Rouge audience, and this even includes a group of long-in-the-tooth-looking investors in the front row who look like they've all got one foot in the grave, gets up from its chairs and energetically dances the Mighty Cancan!

French Cancan isn't a musical, but a great drama with music, and if you don't like musicals, there's still much to dig in this picture, which is as entertaining as any of Jean Gabin's other best movies. While the film is fifty-some years old, it remains intensely-watchable today, especially because the tribulations which it depicts, in which an entertainment organization alternately acquires, and then loses, and then reacquires its financing, has obvious parallels to the fickle entertainment world of today, in which deals fall apart faster than Pontiacs.

French Cancan was a big hit in France when it was released there in 1955, and it was also a major art-house hit in the U.S., when it was shortened by nine minutes and released in N.Y. and L.A. as *Only the French Can*. 20th Century-Fox's house producer Jack Cummings took notice, and decided to make his own, American-made/French-set cancan movie: The result, 1960's *Can-Can,* which was directed by Walter Lang, is as excruciating as any of the *non-great* MGM musicals (and MGM made just as many bad musicals, as they made good ones). In the Lang picture, Frank Sinatra and Maurice Chevalier play two 19th-century bachelors who try to pick up all the cancan dancers they can—especially, one who's played by Shirley MacLaine. Needless to say, the songs in *Can-Can* are truly horrendous, the movie is a car crash, and these great and charismatic actors can't save it, so if you want to see a real cancan movie, you've got to 'go the Gabin/Renoir way.' Fortunately, you can do this quite easily, because Jean Renoir's fully-uncut version of *French Cancan* is currently available on North American DVD, in a beautifully-restored and English-subtitled print, courtesy of the Criterion Collection.

What a Critic Said at the Time: "[*French Cancan*] is a pic that glows with love, charm, and eye-filling movement. A stirring personal affair. Might be just the thing for U.S. art-houses. Gabin is perfect as the showman whose life only reacts to the boards, and [to] audiences. All comes to a head in a vibrant cascade of color, energy, and sheer elegance." (*Variety*, 6-8-55 issue. Critic, "Mosk. [George Moskowitz.]" Reviewed in Paris.)
What Another Critic Said at the Time: "A bright and lively show with such taste and fine design in Technicolor that [director Jean Renoir's] famous father [Auguste Renoir] might have been proud of him. [The film simply] makes the head spin. Not since Jean Huston's splendid [1952 film] *Moulin-Rouge* have we had such a rash of splashy color and spinning dancing girls. Jean Gabin is a bit on the bored and blasé side, but Maria Felix plays a grandly-formed cooch-dancer." (New York *Times*, 4-21-56 issue. Critic: Bosley Crowther.)

With Andree Debar.

FILM 53

Le Port du desir

France, 1955

(Literal English Translation: "THE PORT OF DESIRE.") Directed by Edmond T. Greville. Underwater Sequence Directed by Louis Malle. Produced by Eugene Tucherer. Written by Jacques Viot. Director of Photography (black and white), Henri Alekan. Editor, Jean Ravel. Music by Joseph Kosma. Production Designer, Lucien Aguettand. (GENRE: DRAMA) A Production of Elysee Films. Running Time: 1 hour 34 minutes. Released in France on April 15, 1955, by Corona Films. Released in United States with English Subtitles as "HOUSE BY THE WATERFRONT" by Union Film Distributors, Inc. on February 20, 1959. Released in Great Britain as "HARBOR OF DESIRE."

"You've never put a down-payment on my beaver!"
— *A gold-digging stripper is angry that her boyfriend hasn't laid any money out for the beaver-skin coat of her dreams, in "Le Port du desir"*

1955 finds humanity far-too-involved in Le Hula Hoop, Le Korean War and, in France, director Edmond T. Greville's moody *film noir*, *Le Port du desir* (*House on the Waterfront*), a velvety-smooth French *Casbalanca* for the Elvis Age, in which Gabin's distinguished, black shirt-garbed Captain LeQuevic serves as our 'Rick.' We first meet LeQuevic when he's ensconced in his own quiet, privileged booth, in the oceanfront bar he owns, in the seaside port town of Brest, the 'Port of Desire' of the film's French title, in which a rogues' gallery of assorted international riff-raff are embroiled in shady deals all around him.

Besides owning the bar, LeQuevic is also an aging diver, who's paid to salvage and rescue wrecked ships, which makes his character similar to the tugboat captain whom Gabin had already played fourteen years earlier, in *Remorques*. Immediately, a hot brunette, Martine (Andrée Debar), enters the bar, and she looks very familiar to LeQuevic, because she's the spitting-image of her identical twin sister Suzanne, who used to dance—*and so much more*— for the bar's patrons. Martine has come to 'Le Port du desir' to find out what has happened to Suzanne, who has disappeared under mysterious circumstances. Jean Gabin was now older (he was fifty-one, when he made this movie), and with this movie, we notice immediately that he's starting to play the romantic lead less frequently. (About half of the time, he's now going to start leaving *the lovey stuff* to his younger co-stars). LeQuevic takes the same paternal interest in Martine, which he had shown earlier for Suzanne.

While Martine is sleuthing around, she discovers that Suzanne didn't *just* dance at the Port of Desire, but that she also labored for the wealthy gentleman-pimp, Mr. Black (Jean-Roger Caussimon, who played Baron Walter, the old theater impresario, in *French Cancan*). Angered because Suzanne did not report her earnings to him, Black has had Suzanne killed, and he's placed her body aboard a ship called the *Venus*, which he's sunk, so that nobody will ever be able to find her.

Fearing that LeQuevic and Martine have figured out that he's the one who was responsible for the murder, Black hires young punk/unemployed layabout, Michel (Henri Vidal) to blow up the ship, including all evidence of Suzanne's inert body. Michel lives with, and off of, his hot blonde girlfriend, Lola (Edith Georges), who occasionally dances at the club, performing what is billed (it's a nod to the *nuke-happy* fifties) as her 'atomic striptease,' although there's nothing particularly 'atomic' about her dancing. (The number which she dances in the film is no different than the burlesque numbers which appear in any number of other French movies.) Lola's stated goal in life, is for Michel to buy her a new beaver-skin coat, and in the film's moronically-translated English subtitles, she actually chides him, for not "… *putting a down-payment on my beaver.*" (!)

LeQuevic has no way of knowing that Black has hired Michel to blow up the ship, and he, too, hires Michel—to dive with him, and to bring-up Suzanne's body. Fearing that LeQuevic will incriminate him, Black sends surly thugs into the bar to kill Our Hero but, still agile at mid-life, Gabin's LeQuevic summarily beats the crap out of them with punches, kicks, and even a carefully placed fire extinguisher. (It's all very Adam West/"Batman"-esque, and all that's missing, are signs that read, 'WHAM!' and [this author's personal favorite], 'BOFF!')

The high-point of the film is a breathtaking sequence in which LeQuevic sits on the edge of a diving boat, wearing a bulky heavy-metal 1950s'-style diving suit, waiting to submerge himself. His face is an expressionless mask, and he's got *a cigarette dangling right out of the helmet!* When LeQuevic dives down, finding the Venus and discovering Suzanne's inert body, her hair is splayed out wavelike, an image which would be copied very expressly by director Charles Laughton the following year, in his landmark American *noir* feature, *Night of the Hunter*, which starred Robert Mitchum and Shelly Winters. The breathtaking underwater sequence in *Port du desir* was directed by a young Louis Malle, who would later become one of France's premiere directors (*Lacombe, Lucien; Atlantic City; Au revoir, les enfants; Black Moon*; etc., etc., etc.).

Desir is a well-paced *noir*, notable for its atmosphere, as well as for the fact that one of the principal roles, a character called Baba (Leopoldo Frances), is a good-hearted black cop from the Ivory Coast: In Baba's sub-plot, director Greville shows us how hard it is for a person of color to get along in 1950s' France, in spite of the erroneous illusion, which was mostly propagated by dilettantish white, American jazz fanatics, that the French have always been accepting of blacks, and of black culture.

Port du desir is another fine Jean Gabin picture from the '50s which, like many of the others which he made during that decade, was quickly released, only to one or two arthouse theatres in America, and then never heard from in the U.S., again. The film's director, Edmond T. Greville, who was equally-comfortable making both French and English-language pictures, directed Josephine Baker in her Jean Gabin-less *Zou Zou* follow-up, *Princess Tam-Tam* (1935), and today, he is mostly known to U.S. film buffs for having helmed one of the coolest British 'angry young man' pictures of the early sixties, *Beat Girl* (1960), a satisfying Saturday night at the movies which features a very cool rockabilly score by Adam Faith. If you like Jean Gabin, and if you also like your *film noir* as smooth and as dry as twelve-year-old scotch—*Le Port du desir* is for you!

What a Critic Said at the Time: "Gabin etches one of his usually fine performances." (*Variety*, 7-6-55 issue. Critic: "Mosk. [George Moskowitz.]" Reviewed in Paris.)

What Another Critic Said at the Time: "… as smugglers close in on the sweethearts, *Mr. Gabin begins to scowl!*" (New York *Times*, 2-23-59 issue. Critic: Bosley Crowther.)

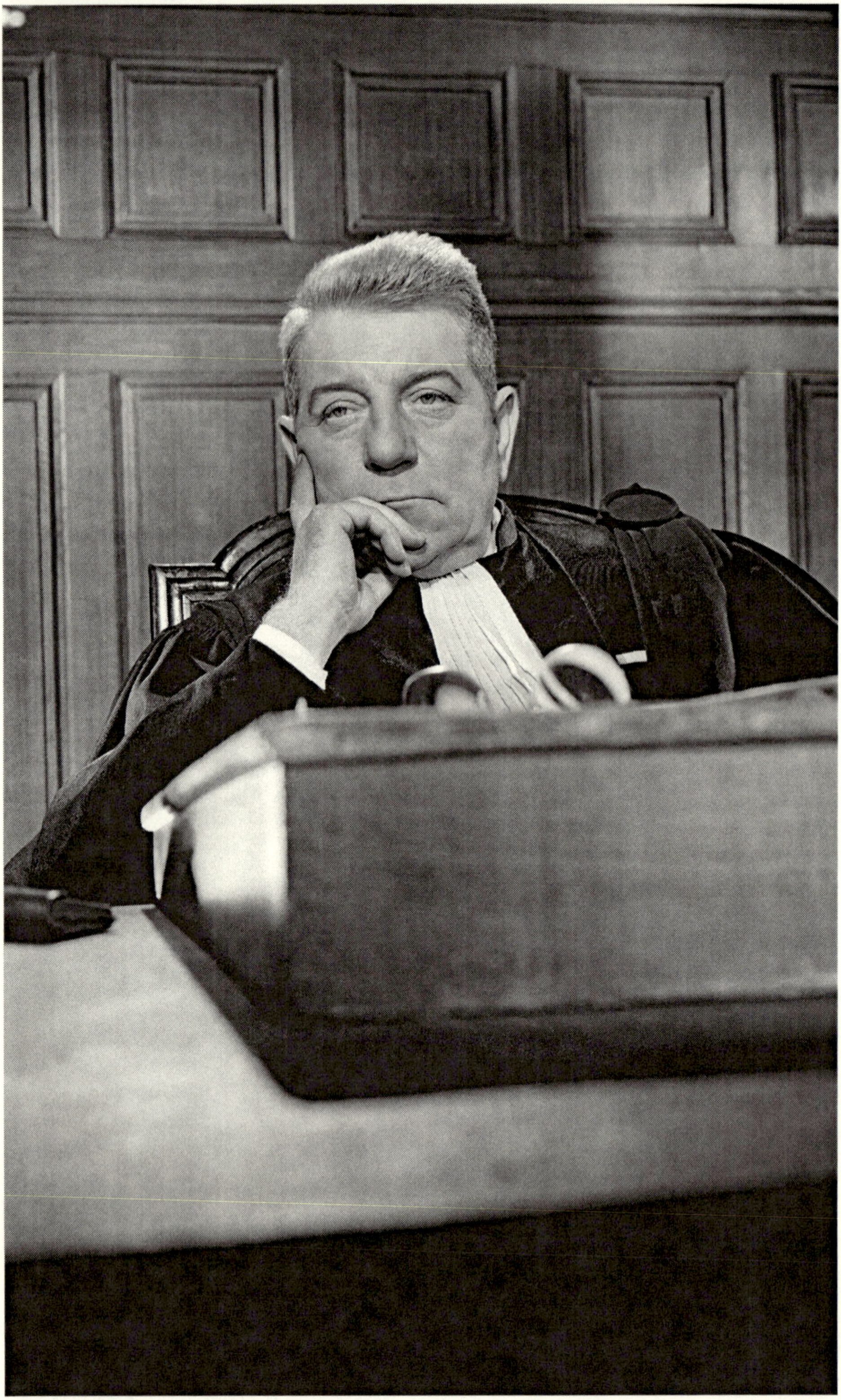

FILM 54

CHIENS PERDUS SANS COLLIER

France, 1955

(Literal English Translation: "LOST DOGS WITHOUT COLLARS") Directed by Jean Delannoy. Produced by Joseph Bercholz, Henry Deustchmeister, and Louis Wipf. Screenplay by Jean Aurenche, Pierre Bost, Francois Boyer, and Jean Delannoy. Based Upon the Novel by Gilbert Cesbron. Director of Photography (black and white), Pierre Montazel. Editor, Borys Lewin. Music by Paul Misraki. Production Designer, Rene Renoux. (GENRE: COMEDY-DRAMA) A Production of Continental Produzione (Italy) and Franco London Films/Les Films Gibe (France). Running Time, 1 hour 33 minutes. Released in France by Cocinor, on October 21, 1955. Released in the U.S. in 1958, as "THE LITTLE REBELS" by Continental Film Distributors.

"In every court, we need one Judge who sleeps. And that's me!"
—Judge Gabin's response to the other judges, who hate when he sleeps during the boring trials over which he presides, in "Chiens perdus sans collier"

Chiens perdus sans collier is based upon a novel by Gilbert Cesbron, a book which traditionally gets read by every high school kid in France, when that special time comes for every teen-ager (those teen-agers who still read, that is) to pick up that obligatory book about teen-aged angst and anomie. (The equivalent in the United States, might be S.E. Hinton's *The Outsiders*, or maybe even J.D. Salinger's *Catcher in the Rye*.) The title-phrase, 'Lost Dogs without Collars' is slang, and it means, roughly, 'lost kids, who just don't know what to do with themselves,' but this French colloquialism can also mean 'someone (such as a bad guy) who will shortly be put to death.' The picture, which was directed by Gabin-regular Jean Delannoy (this was their second picture together, after 1952's *La Minute de verite*, and four more films would follow), is kind of like the French version of Spencer Tracy's 1940 classic, *Boys' Town*, but instead of Spencer Tracy (who, of course, played a Priest who helped-out all of the disenfranchised kids), here, we're getting 'the French Spencer Tracy,' Jean Gabin, as kindly Julien Lamy, a Children's Court Judge (the kids call him *'Monsieur Juge'*—'Mr. Judge') who sentences boys from impoverished families to Juvenile Hall, and who is always respected by the boys who are under his care. ('Good-old *Monsieur Juge*' instinctively understands kids, in a way in which parents just can't.) In this film, we get a very paternal and warm Jean Gabin, who gets personally involved in the lives of three boys of different ages, really making a difference with all of them:

Gerard: About seven years old, Gerard (Jacques Moulieres) is a member of a poor circus family, but he's been taken away from them by the courts, because *his hotpants mom is a* prostitute.

Alain: About ten years old, tow-headed Alain (Jimmy Urbain) lives alone in a barn, having run away from a family that *beats the living shit out of him* on a regular basis. Alain's fashioned his barn into the ideal little boy's room and, when we first see him, he's swaggering around, wearing a crown and looking very commanding, a King of His Own World *(a la* the little boy in Maurice Sendak's classic American children's book, *Where the Wild Things Are)*—a world which, admittedly, isn't all that much. He also happens to be a firebug with a match-lighting fetish, and when he accidentally sets the barn on fire, and the place burns to the ground (and he's seen wandering around in the middle of the night, almost naked), the court remands him into Judge Lamy's care.

Francis: The oldest of the three boys, Francis (Serge Lacointe), 17, has knocked-up his girlfriend, Sylvette (Anne Doat), and has been sentenced to juvey, for stealing the little soaps and towels out of a public restroom. (Yeah, they don't call this kid 'badass,' for nothing!) Anyway: Gerard. Alain. Francis: These are our film's three 'Dead-End Kids.'

When we first meet Judge Lamy, in his office at Children's Court, he's surrounded by a huge number of noisy kids, and he's questioning them, one-by-one, about why they're here, and he even gets amused, and not angered, when he finds out that a fifteen-year-old prostitute (Josette Arno) has pulled all of the nails out of his chair, while he was walking around the room, interrogating her. (Fortunately, he catches the problem, before he sits down.) But, as in so many other Jean Gabin pictures, Our Hero doesn't get riled up: He just tells her, calmly, to "put the nails back in," and even gets a good look at her posterior, while she's doing it! (The way in which director Jean Delannoy films this bit doesn't seem exploitative and titillating, but only real and natural.) "If you [prostituted yourself] as an adult," Lamy informs the girl, "that would mean ten years in jail. Anyway, you're not eighteen yet, and since it seems like you can't handle your own life too well, I'll handle you." (Lamy utters this sentiment, very innocently... we hope!)

Next, bathroom rip-off artist Francis bolts into Judge Lamy's office with his crazy-looking, and obviously alcoholic, grandparents in tow, and the Grandfather is played by the good-naturedly-slovenly French character actor Jean Y'd, who played Marlene Dietrich's Uncle Ferrand, in *Martin Roumagnac*. Besides stealing bathroom supplies, young Francis also happens to be deaf in his right ear, so Lamy has to yell directly into the dead appendage: "So, kid: What do I do about you?" Francis' Grandmother (Rene Passeur) has a solution, but it's not the one we've been looking for, because she now tells Judge Lamy, that she reads Francis' tarot cards a lot, and that she's always known that her grandson will, one of these days, be dying a violent death. (This lady is not what we would today call a 'supportive family member.') Lamy just rolls his eyes, used to the crazy people who cross his door, and when these bizarro-world grandparents leave, a chortling Lamy chucks the boy under the chin: "Now that I've met your grandparents," he tells Francis, "I understand you!" A really nice thing about *Chiens perdus sans collier,* is that Judge Lamy always takes the kids' sides, no matter what they did, because he understands, and even respects, that they are not yet mature. Lamy now tells Francis, "I'm going to be sending you somewhere for observation for a few days, and to a place you'll like: You'll be able to play sports in the courtyard… instead of in the men's room!"

Alain comes in next, with an elderly lady of his own, and she's some sort of a guardian to him, although we don't know the exact nature of their relationship (and she's played by Helene Tossy). "I don't want to go back to the farm!" Alain screams at her, "I don't want to be a peasant! I want to be an auto mechanic!" (*It's nice to have goals!*) It is explained to Lamy, by a cop, that firebug Alain burned down the barn which he lived in, and Lamy next explains to the boy, and to the boy's guardian, that he can't take him under his protective wing, "… because you didn't do anything that bad. If you had stolen something, I could take care of you, but because you just burned something down, there's nothing I can do." Alain immediately takes to the Judge, whom he recognizes immediately, as being way cooler than his guardian, so he clutches at straws for anything which will allow him to remain in gentle Lamy's care; and after thinking for a few moments, he admits, truthfully, that he really *did* steal something, recently—some chocolate, from a store! Lamy, who looks apprehensive about the fact that he might have to send the boy back to live with an old lady who looks like she can't take care of herself, much less of a little kid, is relieved: "There you go! Stealing candy is bad! Now, I can take you!"

While Judge Lamy investigates kids to see if they belong in juvenile facilities, and while he really enjoys the part of the job in which he's dealing with kids, he gets bored as hell doing the second part of his job—judging adult trials, which he finds to be extremely uninteresting. (He likes helping kids much more than he likes sentencing grown-ups.) He even meets the enmity of some of his fellow Judges when, bored out of his skull during one trial in particular, he actually falls asleep, and then, when he's caught, hilariously defends his God-given right to nap to another Judge, a guy who's eyeing him very suspiciously: "In every court, we need one Judge who sleeps. And that's me!"

When Lamy is back at his office, he hands Alain, the little firebug, over to one of his juvenile facility's preferred directors, sharp-eyed Joseph (Robert Dalban), who lifts the boy's shirt up, to reveal whip marks, and it is here that we learn that someone at home has been thrashing him, and very brutally. Lamy and Joseph turn the shower on, and Alain gets frightened, because he's never seen one before! And once the kid is clean, Joseph and Lamy send him in the direction of a lady Psychiatrist, played by Veronique Deschamps, who asks Alain to draw pictures and, of course, the first thing he draws, is a woman in a bikini! The film pokes sly fun at the whole concept of psychiatry, because when the shrink tells Lamy that the drawing obviously means that Alain is thinking about his mother's breasts, Lamy rolls his eyes at her, but he then smiles at the kid, because you know that he's thinking, "Anybody who's thinking about breasts is okay with me, my inventive little friend!" Then, the Psychiatrix shows Lamy a second picture which Alain has drawn: It's a very innocuous representation of an apple tree and, of course, this lady, who's obviously crazier than her patients, believes that the apples, too, represent boobs! Lamy, who wants to end this goofy discourse and *stat*, throws his shoulders up in a Mighty Gabin-Shrug, and sasses-back, "Well, he didn't draw any pictures of fire, so at least we know he's not crazy!"

Lamy next visits the seventeen-year-old bathroom-thief Francis, who's been remanded into the facility's care, and he tells the teen-ager, that he (Francis) hasn't brought enough clothes with him from home, and that he's going to have to accompany him back to his family's house, to get some more. When Lamy and Francis arrive back at Francis' family's clapboard shack, the first thing we see, is that his parents are dead-asleep in the middle of the day, surrounded by bottles of alcohol, and that his crazy grandparents (including Jean Y'd), who've been raising him (kind of!), are nowhere to be seen. Lamy instructs Francis to take as many clothes as he can, and not to forget a sweater, and he next places Francis on the bus, by himself, back to the juvenile facility.

When he boards the bus, Francis just so happens to run into his girlfriend (the one he's knocked-up) Silvet, who's also 16, and we can tell that the two are very much in (puppy) love. She looks very 'preggers' and, as she's suggesting to Francis, in this, their tender reunion scene, "Maybe you can talk to your new Judge-friend. Maybe he can perform a marriage ceremony for us!"

Judge Lamy finally tracks-down Francis' grandparents, and tells them that Francis will be staying at a juvenile facility until his eighteenth birthday, since they are too poor to take care of him themselves and, as it's now turning out, not just the boy's mother, but his elderly grandmother, is a prostitute, as well!

Next, it's a few weeks later. By this point in our narrative, seventeen-year-old Francis has become almost like a big brother to Alain. As they lay in their bunks that night, all of the boys are bragging to each other, just as though they're 'cons' in the most hard-boiled of American prison movies, about all the people they've killed to get sentenced here! Francis, who is one of the oldest boys in the facility, is boasting to the other kids that he's here because he wanted to marry his girlfriend, Silvet, but that her father said no, and so he beat the guy to a pulp—which is probably true. Young Alain, who's trying to keep up with the older boy's cool brags, then boasts that, in his own (short) lifetime, he's "set many destructive fires" and "torched many, many acres!"

While all of this has been happening, little Gerard has run away from the institution into which Lamy has sentenced him and, in the next scene, Lamy goes to Gerard's family's home, to see if that's where he's gone, and when he arrives at Gerard's family's meager shack, he discovers (horror-of-horrors!) that the boy is part of a sleazy circus family! Creepy-looking

With Serge Lecointe and Jane Marken.

carnies are sitting around playing cards, and Gerard's cheerful Mom (Dora Doll, the French Marilyn Monroe/Jayne Mansfield-clone, who had already appeared with Gabin the previous year, as the blonde stripper, in *Touchez pas au grisbi*) brags to Lamy (she has no idea that that he's 'the guy from Juvey,' and merely believes that he's just a guy who happens to have been walking by), that she is offering herself as the 'prize' to whomever wins the card game. Meanwhile, little Gerard kneels by the stream, fishing-out bottles of water-cooled wine, which he then serves to the appreciative men. (Only in a French movie, will we ever see a tiny little *sommelier!*) When Lamy sees Gerard interacting with his mom, he can't understand why the little boy ran back home to be with her because, as we're seeing right now, she's very cold and unemotional toward him. (Or maybe, it's not too hard to understand: Gerard's a very young boy and so naturally, he'd have some attachment to his mom, just by virtue of the fact that she's his mom.) Gerard, knowing that Lamy's there and is looking for him, hides under his mom's bed but, thankfully, it's never too hard to find a small boy's hiding place: Lamy peeks under the boy's army-cot and, smilingly, tries to cajole Gerard out, but the boy cries that he doesn't want to go back to the juvenile facility, and that he'd rather remain here with his own 'family.' Lamy asks the boy who his mother's friends are, and Gerard replies, excitedly, that one of the guys is an acrobat. As usual, Lamy is amused by the whole set-up: "Well, I can't leave you in a home where people are playing cards to win your mother," he grins, and he's finally able to get Gerard out from under the bed, by telling the little boy a story about himself: "During World War II, I was a prisoner, and I escaped. You're a prisoner, too [of your unsavory home-life], Gerard, and now it's your job, just as it was mine, to escape. I was captured many times, so don't feel too badly that I've come to capture you!"

Back at juvey, the boys are now having a contest: They're digging up worms and trying to make Alain eat the biggest one, promising him that if he swallows it, he'll win the big stack of delicious cigarettes which they've all thrown in to the pot! Badass Alain chows-down on what the Spanish call *'el gusano,'* in full view of all the (other) young dudes, but he then, very promptly, runs over to the stream, and upchucks the slippery little creature. (So: No smokes for him!) Francis threatens the boys for insisting that his best little buddy Alain should munch-out on that freaky-deaky old worm.

Soon, it's mail-call time, and all of the boys are getting letters from home—everybody, that is, except for Francis, who's lachrymose, because his girlfriend, Silvet, never writes to him, even though in an attempt to save face, he's now bragging to the other boys that she writes to him all the time. Anyway, little does Francis know but, that very same night, Silvet locates and goes over to Judge Lamy's house, and she tells Lamy that she's Francis' girlfriend (he's heard of her, of course, during his conversations with the boy), and that she's waiting for Alain to be released from the juvenile center. "Well, you do know that your boyfriend will be under my care until he's eighteen, don't you?" Lamy asks her. She asks the Judge if it's possible that he might be able to perform a wedding ceremony for herself and Francis, and she also picks this moment to indirectly reference her own, ever-burgeoning pregnancy: She points to her own stomach and innocently smiles, "In a way, sir, you might say that we're already married." Lamy asks Silvet about her own parents, and she replies that she's left home, just like Alain has, because her parents wanted her to have an abortion, and also because her father beat her up a lot which, as we're now finding out, is the justifiable reason that Francis 'K.O.'d' her dad. Lamy, feeling sympathetic toward the girl, hands her a sheet of stationery, and asks her to write a letter to her *baby-daddy*, which he next promises her he'll hand-deliver to Francis, himself. He even gives Silvet a glass of wine since, in France, *mercifully*, one can drink at any age. Lamy asks Silvet if she thinks that Francis really wants the baby at such an early stage in both of their lives, and she optimistically gloats, "Yes! Alain adores our baby already," a sentiment which is as sweet as it is true: Even though Alain is a 'young tough,' what makes his character great and real, is that director Delannoy has taken great pains to show us that he's also very loving, and not just toward Silvet, but also toward all of his friends.

Francois Truffaut, who would become internationally famous as a film director in the 1960s, couldn't stand Jean Delannoy's films, feeling that they were too sentimental, but in 1976, Truffaut borrowed a lot of elements from Delannoy's *Chiens perdus sans collier*, when he made his own rough-and-tumble street urchin-picture *L'Argent de poche* (released in the U.S. as *Small Change*), which, even though it's a very good movie in its own right, definitely copied its tone from Delannoy's 1955 movie.

Meanwhile, back at juvey, Francis and Alain are escaping, just like a kid version of Marechal and Rosenthal, from *La Grande illusion*. Joseph, the facility's director, catches them sneaking out, and also stealing cans of food and milk from the pantry, and so crazy-brave little Francis actually knocks Joseph flat on his ass with a broom handle. Alain and Francis, who have become as thick as thieves (literally), next hide out in a not-yet-open-for-business bar/tavern, and Francis has some not-so-great news to break to the little guy, which he'll now do, and very gently: "Look, kid. You can't stay around me. I have a wife now!" Alain falls asleep at the table, and Francis tells the bar's owner that he's going to split, but that he's leaving the kid there, and that when Alain wakes up, the guy should give him a glass of milk. Of course, Alain immediately wakes up, and starts chasing after Francis, and Francis tells him to shove off: "Didn't you hear me, kid? I have a wife! So I can't have anything to do with you anymore, get it? Now beat it, okay!" Alain screams out, like the little kid he is: "You can't leave without me! I want to go with you!" Francis tells Alain that he should go and find his own parents, knowing full-well that the younger boy doesn't have any, but he's unable to think of anything else to say which might possibly serve to get rid of him.

Francis leaves, and little Alain, who is now wandering the city streets alone, decides to take himself on a top-secret mission in search of his parents. First, he heads into the local post office: Somebody has been mailing him *Tintin* comic strips, *c/o juvey*, from a Paris address, and he thinks that it must be his own long-lost parents, so he asks the postal clerk if he can look at a phonebook. While Alain is, *per* that old American t.v. commercial from the '70s, 'letting his fingers do the walking,' a creepy child molester sees him and starts licking his chops. The guy offers to help Alain find his parents and Alain, too-trustingly, goes off with him. Fortunately for all of us though, the next scene takes place at the police station: The Cops, having seen Alain with the guy (who, as we're now learning, is a frequent kid-stealer), have rescued him and brought him back to juvey, where Lamy is happy to see his young charge, and one of the nice young cops calms Lamy: "The old guy didn't do anything. He just bought the kid ice cream." Lamy asks Alain, "So, I heard Francis dumped you like a dirty sock, huh?"

Alain shows Lamy the *Tintin* cartoons, and tells him that he thinks that it is his parents who are sending the cartoons to him, but Lamy sets him straight: "Kid, I'm the one who sent you the cartoons. You don't have any parents." Alain cries-out that he wants to go back to be with Francis, and it's a genuinely heart-breaking moment.

Lamy tells Alain, gently, that there are two other juvenile facilities besides this one that he can go to, and that he'll let him choose the one which sounds the best: "Do you want one near the mountains, or one near the ocean?" Alain immediately chooses the ocean, and Lamy gives him a bar of chocolate, the foodstuff which, as we already know, the kid prizes more than anything else on earth. He tells the boy, very paternally, to visit him whenever he can: "I want to keep track of you." Boy and man share a tender hug.

Meanwhile, Francis is now being reunited with Silvet down by the Seine, and he asks her if she's mentioned her pregnancy to anybody, but she lies, telling him that she hasn't. Meanwhile, Lamy happens to be walking by with the police (it's not too big of a dramatic stretch that he might be there, since the Seine extends through the length of Paris) looking for Francis, and when Silvet sees the cops, she jumps into the water and tries to drown herself, but Lamy jumps right in and saves her life, just like how Gabin saved a drowning Ida Lupino, thirteen years previously, in *Moontide*.

Now, Lamy heads back to little circus-boy Gerard's house, because the boy has run away from the facility (now, for the second time) and this time, he even compliments the boy's 'easy' Mom: "Look, even though I can't see it, obviously you must be a good mother, otherwise your son wouldn't keep coming back to you." Lamy looks up and sees Gerard on a tightrope, high above the city: The boy is actually standing atop the head of the acrobat who won his mom in the card game, and both Gerard and the acrobat are wearing Devil costumes! Lamy is at first scared that something might happen to his little charge, but he's then impressed by Gerard's amazing acrobatic feats. Lamy decides that Gerard will be happier with his unconventional family than he might be back at juvey, and that, ultimately, the little nipper really belongs with his mother. (With a smile and a Gabin-Shrug, Lamy then admits to himself, "Well… at least, the kid is working!") After performing his amazing feats, 'little Devil' Gerard next runs through the crowd with a tin cup, scoring boat-loads of change, and even Lamy is compelled to make with the coinage. "Thanks, *Monsieur Juge*," Gerard grins. "Not Monsieur Juge," Lamy smiles, tousling the boy's head. "Just *Monsieur*."

Chiens perdus sans collier is a really wonderful film about disenfranchised kids, and it's even better, in its own way, than two more recent, and both Brazilian, street-urchin classics, Henri Babenco's *Pixote* (1979) and Fernando Mereilles' *City of God* (2004). The kids in *Chiens perdus sans collier*, although they're very often 'as crude as they wanna be,' are never less than 100%-likable because, just as in those two Brazilian pictures, they're also completely unprecocious, and none of them ever comes across as being anything less than 100%-real. This is a credit to the kids themselves, and especially, it's a credit to director Jean Delannoy who, in spite of Francois Truffaut's opinion, didn't make treacly movies. While Jean Gabin is always likeable in his movies (it's the whole reason for this book), in this movie, he's definitely at his warmest. When American teen-agers get tired of *Catcher in the Rye* and *The Outsiders,* and all of those Judy Blume novels which introduce teen-aged girls to *cock* for the first time, maybe U.S. high schools can adopt the novel and film of *Chiens perdus sans collier,* as a just-as-effective replacement.

What a Critic Said at the Time: "Juvenile delinquency is the theme of this film, and Gabin [is] off-the-cuff as the Judge, a tender man who is interested more in children than adults." (*Variety*, 11-9-55 issue. Critic: "Mosk. [George Moskowitz.]" Reviewed at Venice Film Festival.)

FILM 55

Des gens sans importance

France, 1956

Literal English Translation: "People of No Importance") Directed by Henri Verneuil. Produced by Rene Lafuite and Georges Charlot. Screenplay by Henri Vernuil and Francis Boyer. Based Upon the Novel by Serge Groussard. Director of Photography (black and white), Louis Page. Music by Joseph Kosma. Editor, Christian Gaudin. (GENRE: DRAMA) Running Time, 1 hour 51 minutes. A Production of Ardennes Films/Chaillot Films/Cocinor. Released in France by Cocinor on February 15, 1956. Never Released Theatrically in the United States.

"I'm not married, because I don't want anybody to bother me."
— *Gabin's co-driver shares 'The Jean Gabin Ethos,' in "Des gens sans importance"*

Gabin Trucker Movie #2, which was made one year after the first one, *Gas-Oil*, is the first Jean Gabin movie credited to director Henri Verneuil, a real stylist who also happened to be Gilles Grangier's assistant director on *Gas-Oil*, and who would star Gabin in movies of many genres over the next fifteen years. The film's opening music, which we get to hear over panoramic shots of a sweepingly-lonely, existential desert, is a sad, *proto-Zamfir* pan-flute dirge, composed and performed by Joseph Kosma. This same exact shot of the desert, and the pan-flute music which accompanies it, will both open and close the film, and it will even 'cameo' once in the middle of the film, to remind of us its very cool existence.

Verneuil sets his scene sixty kilometers from Bayonne, in northern France, at a lonely desert-outpost trucker bar called *La Caravanne*, where the first time we see the movie's truckers, they're doing what truckers do best—they're driving around the parking lot and *honking their big-ass horns at a hot lady!* Jean Gabin (this time, his character is 'Jean Viard' instead of 'Jean Chape' [which is what his character was called, in *Gas-Oil*]) enters the place, which is owned by peg-legged Emile (Paul Frankeur, who'll be playing a bartender in innumerable Jean Gabin movies from the 1950s and 1960s). Emile is complaining to Viard that, every time he gets a new barmaid/waitress, some customer comes in and sweeps her off her feet, taking her away forever, to a better life; in fact, just today, as he's now telling Viard, his newest *drink-a-trix* has been co-opted: "Someone kidnapped another of my waitresses. And if that's not bad enough, it was some bastard in an American car!" Emile, who smiles as he's revealing this, is actually more amused than he is, bitter. Meanwhile, another trucker (a

86 | **THE FILMS** CYCLE FIVE

guy in the background) can be heard complaining that he has to drive all the way down to Biarritz, in the southwestern part of the country (eleven miles north of Spain), today.

Viard, in between runs, sleeps in the hotel over Emile's bar and, as he lies on his bed, completely worn out from a hard day of work, we get our first dose of the gravelly Jean Gabin voice-over, which we're going to be hearing throughout the film. (J.G.'s voiceover worked to such a great effect in *Touchez pas au grisbi*, it's no wonder that director Verneuil will re-use the device in this, his newest Gabin picture.) "That poor Emile," Viard tells 'us,' "he has no luck with with barmaids—even though he pays and feeds them well. Although, I guess it's not really fair to the girls to get stuck here, in the middle of nowhere. Here at Emile's place, we give all the waitresses the same name, 'Marie,' since none of them is really around long enough for any of us to get too attached to them. Anyway, the story I'm about to tell you happened two years ago. It was the day before Christmas, and I had been driving for sixty hours in a row..."

Right on cue, director Verneuil dissolves to two years ago: Viard's in mid-run, driving through a small town with his co-driver pal Bertil (Pierre Mondy) by his side, and Bertil is catching some shut-eye, while Viard's at the wheel. When Bertil wakes up, he opens the passenger-side door to invigorate himself with the brisk, night air, and he then takes the wheel from Viard, whose Gabin visage has been staring-out into space, deep-in-thought, onto the lonesome highway. Now, it's Viard's turn to sleep and Bertil's turn to drive, but Bertil's still so sleepy, that he almost crashes into a furniture shop window—but thankfully, he's able to stop, just before his twin dates with both death... and hideous sofas. A few minutes later, a refreshingly not-dead Viard and Bertil pull up in front of *La Caravanne*, but Bertil's not interested in going inside to sleep: He prefers snoozing in the truck, in close proximity to the warmth of the radiator.

When Viard enters the place, he finds that, in the space of only one day, Emile has already hired a new waitress (a 'new Marie'), Clotilde Brachet (Francoise Arnoul, 'Nini' from *French Cancan*, in the first of five films in which Henri Verneuil will direct her). He asks her to serve all of his customers a complimentary Xmas-Eve duck dinner, but Viard decides to bypass the canard, not to mention all of the other Xmas frolicking (such as it is) to go up to his usual room, and doze. Clotilde, who is very clearly enchanted by the much older Viard, unmakes the bed for him, and asks him if he's going to be attending midnight mass, and he replies that, at this point, he's more interested in sleeping, but that if she feels like she wants to bring some of that tasty duck up to him, he won't be declining it.

While *Gas-Oil*, Gabin's previous trucker movie, is a picture about a guy who just wants to be free, to drift along life's open—and more than occasionally, closed—roads, *Des gens sans importance* is a movie about being tired. We feel it in the film's languorous rhythms, rhythms which actually replicate the feeling you might have if you were lucky enough to actually be riding in a truck with Jean Gabin.

Downstairs, at the same time, Emile is telling his patrons that Christmas represents "the birthday of the day I lost my leg, ten years ago. It happened in a church. Something electrical burst, and I went flying, but I didn't land properly." Some of the truckers start muttering to themselves: Obviously, they hear Emile telling this same-exact story every Christmas and, very clearly, they're beyond tired of it. (This film, like lots of French pictures in general, and like a lot of Gabin pictures specifically, features the usual 'Greek Chorus' of bar patrons, who continually sit-around, commenting on the story's main action.) "If you idiots can't handle my story, just go to bed," Emile yells at the ungrateful lot, shaking his fist at everybody, but also, very clearly, enjoying himself. "You're just a bunch of weaklings!" In this movie, all of the characters, from the leads to the most minor of the supporting characters, are the eponymous 'people of no importance' of the film's title—simple men and women who silently wish that they could somehow make their marks in a world that just doesn't care.

Bertil, who's younger than Viard, and who is definitely a young guy on-the-make, follows Clotilde around incessantly, like a puppy in heat. "Why do you always call me Marie?" she asks him, hating the appellation that gets apportioned to all of the bar's waitresses. "Marie is like Mary—it's a virgin's name! My name happens to be Clotilde!" Here, she's proudly admitting that she's 'been around the block', and judging by her mega-hot sexiness, she's probably also been around most of the city, as well!

Clotilde pads up to Viard's room again, this time to bring him a sandwich (guess they're out of duck), and since Viard is already on the verge of sleep, she leaves him with an alarm clock instead, and lets him know that if he wants Santa to bring him something, he's going to have to hang his shoes up on the room's hearth. Viard, a man who's 'seen it all, and more,' resignedly moans, lending a little Christmasy-spin to Jean Gabin's usual 'resigned/ Existentialist-*shtick*.' "I don't believe in Santa Claus anymore." He then falls soundly asleep.

Christmas morning arrives, but it's not a day off for Viard and Bertil, who show up to work at the trucking company, where the dispatcher, Gillier (Robert Dalban, who played one of the cops in *Razzia sur la chnouf*, not to mention the main juvey-hall administrator in *Chiens perdus sans collier*), tells them where the day's runs will be taking them. Gillier asks Bertil if he's ever going to settle down and get married, to which Bertil replies, "I'm not married, because I don't want anybody to bother me." (Clearly, this man has been hanging around with Jean Gabin for far too long!)

So far, we thought that Viard, himself, was unmarried—an unattached drifter, no different than any number of other Gabin characters; but when this particular day ends, he goes home, and *not* to his hotel room, but to his real home, which is a small apartment, and to his wife and kids (he's got a seventeen-year-old daughter and two little boys, who are probably around six and seven). Even before she greets him, Viard's wife, Solange (Yvette Etievant) hands her incredibly-exhausted husband a Santa Claus costume, which she just so happens to have fashioned for him out of his red pajamas, without having asked his permission, and a face mask, and demands that he put them on: "The boys tried waiting up for you, but they fell asleep. You've got to put this costume on for them, so that when they wake up, you'll be Santa. You've got to do it!" The sight of Gabin—fiftysomething, dour, haggard, dog-tired, and middle-agedly-paunchy—standing there, uncomfortably eyeing the goofiest makeshift

Santa suit you've ever seen is, all by itself, worth the price of admission to this movie.

He tries to get out of doing this 'quick change,' telling Solange, "Yesterday, I had to drive all the way down south, to Bordeaux. So cut me some slack, okay?!" He also tries to change the subject, by fixing himself a sandwich and, while he's smothering on the Best Foods, we notice that director Vernuil has designed Viard's apartment to look like a prison, replete with barred windows and latticework shadows, which are thrown over every wall.

While honking down his tasty sandwich (or, as they pronounce it in French, '*sond-weeeesh*'), Viard looks out of the window, where he immediately sees his pretty, seventeen-year-old daughter Jacqueline (Dany Carrel) with a suitor and, apparently, she's just arriving home from a hot date. He looks disgusted by the fact that she's been out so late but, as Solange informs her husband, "Your daughter has the right to go out on Christmas Eve! She doesn't have to be housebound, like I am. She doesn't deserve that fate. Plus, you're not around enough to determine what she can and cannot do!" When Jacqueline enters, we see that she gets along famously with her mom, and completely ignores her dad, whom she brushes by uncomfortably, without even acknowledging his presence.

We can tell that Viard resents his daughter's freedom: Even though he, like the Gabin movie-characters of twenty years before, aches for freedom, and tries to 'live free' by being a perennially-peripatetic truckdriver, ultimately he's not free because, at the end of most days, he's got a wife and kids to support. He tiptoes into his twin sons' bedroom to say hi, but the two little kids are already dreaming of sugarplums, or whatever it is, that little seven-year-old French kids dream of (maybe, cigarettes and stinky cheese)?!

As if Jacqueline isn't rebellious enough (actually, 'rebellious' isn't the right word; she just really loves yanking daddy-o's chain), she then picks this exact moment to announce to her father that her goal in life is to become a movie star, and if this film were a comedy, and Gabin were drinking a glass of water, this is the part in which he'd now be doing a gy-normous spit-take! At this moment, the two little boys (they're played by Charles Humbert and Christian Loiseau, both of whom are making their only on-screen appearance in this film), are awakened by the sound of their dad and their big sister, who are fighting: Viard is totally Gabin-Outbursting at his daughter, and all while wearing his Santa Mask! "Oh," one of the boys mutters calmly, noticing that it's just 'that dad guy' making one of his infrequent cameo appearances in the house, "so I guess there is no Santa Claus." (A junior Gabin-in-the-Making, this kid is already world-weary, silently accepting of life's cruel revelations.) Just as it happened in Jean Gabin's real-life boyhood, the Viard family lives next to a trainyard, and the shrill, piercing screams of a train, which is now passing by at this very moment, gives voice to the family's constant, and constantly agonizing, pain.

The next day, Viard's back at Emile's, playing foosball with his buddies. Emile tells Viard that his newest 'Marie,' Clotilde (the one who was warm-for-Gabin's-form) is upstairs, packing her bags to return to her hometown of Bordeaux in the SW, and that she's not coming back. Just as she's about to leave, she sees Viard and asks him if he'd like to join her for a goodbye drink.

90 | **THE FILMS** CYCLE FIVE

Post-booze-up, Viard walks Clotilde over to the bus stop and while, very clearly, he likes her just as much as she likes him, he's trying to keep it professional—after all, he *is* thirty years older than she is. She admits to him now, that the only thing that stopped her from hitting on him on Christmas Eve, was the fact that she saw his wedding ring, and even though it's obvious that he likes her as much as she likes him, he tells her that she's probably made the right decision: "*Tant mieux* [so much the better], because I'm 50 [Gabin was 52 when he made this movie], and you're 22." He offers to drive her to Bordeaux and, naturally, she accepts his offer.

When the pair arrives in Bordeaux, he drops her off in front of a novelty shop, which is the storefront where, as she has told him, she's already got a job all lined-up. As he shakes her hand, bidding her goodbye, Clotilde's mom, Mrs. Brachet (she's played by Nane Germon) approaches, welcoming her daughter home. As Viard drives away, Clotilde shrinks down to microscopic size, in his sideview mirror.

Clotilde and her Mom, when next we see them, are sitting in the park, watching a group of musicians who are delighting a small crowd with an outdoor concert. Mrs. Brachet asks her daughter how her dating situation has been going lately, and Clotilde replies that she recently dumped her old boyfriend Armand, because he left her for one of her friends. Her mom tells her that nothing in her own life has changed since she (Clotilde) left which, apparently, as we're now finding out, was several months ago.

As it turns out, after Viard dropped Clotilde off, he never left Bordeaux: His truck broke down, and now he's got his pal Bertil there with him, helping him to fix it. As the two men slave over their repairs, Clotilde now comes walking down the street, directly toward Viard, just as we expected her to do; in the one day in which she's been home, she's already become depressed. So far in the pic, she's been pretty placid-looking, although we can see that if something bad were to happen to her, she'd freak out in a second, and that she's a raw nerve, who's just waiting to explode: Apparently, the novelty shop job which she was promised—or maybe she just imagined she had this job, because she never really did—no longer exists. (This movie was made fifty years before outsourcing, so that can't be the problem!) She tells Viard, which is a cry for help, not to mention a cry for sex with him, that she thinks she might kill herself and, as she's now telling him, she's even formulated a method by which she means to do it: "I can jump out of your truck while you're driving! People will think it's a suicide, and they won't ask you about it." He offers to give her a ride back to Bayonne, along with himself and Bertil. ('Jean Gabin: Helping One Person at a Time.')

As the three start *choogling* down the highway, a second truck, in the next lane, starts careening toward them, because its driver is falling asleep. Viard yells out the window at the guy, shaking a fist at him at the same time: "Hey, pal! Are you on automatic?! If you continue driving that way, you're going to be in Heaven!" In a great stunt, Viard, while driving, yanks open the passenger door and lets Bertil out, and Bertil jumps heroically into the other guy's truck! But instead of driving the thing like we expected him to, he just goes right into the back seat of the other guy's truck and, hilariously, falls asleep within about two seconds—but only after slapping the other sleepy driver's face, to wake the guy up!

Now, Gabin's alone in his own truck, with Clotilde. Obviously, they're getting warmer for each other by the minute but, instead of making a move on her, he tries to cool her ardor, telling her, "You know—I could be your father;" still, she's happy that he finally seems to be taking an interest in her, no matter how obliquely. ("There's progress!" she coos, suddenly not as depressed as she was a few moments ago. "You're looking at me now!") Unable to cage his mighty desire any longer, Viard next pulls over to the side of the road and dips Clotilde out of frame, as Verneuil dissolves to that same shot of that huge dust storm which he had already given us at the beginning of the picture: At the beginning of the pic, the dust storm represented 'boredom,' but now, the same exact shot, with the same exact wind blowing, seems to indicate 'the wild freneticism of a burgeoning love' (or some such *happy-crappy*)!

Cut to what must probably be a few months later—Clotilde and Viard have been enmeshed in an affair for quite awhile now, and it seems that their 'honeymoon period' is over, and that she's become needy. She asks him, as she sits shotgun in his truck, about why he can't stay in Bordeaux with her full-time, and he responds, pragmatically, by telling her that he can't leave his three children, but this answer is unacceptable to her, and she's also angry because, in her opinion, Viard talks about his wife too much. Clotilde next asks Viard, "Why don't you just work non-stop, so your boss can give you two full days off—two full days with me, here in Bordeaux?"

Clotilde feels badly about having just tried to order Viard around (you can't tell Jean Gabin what to do, anyway), and so she then lightens the mood—"This is the first time that we're fighting. I'm so sorry"—but we can tell that Viard's too old to engage in petty relationship fights. (He's not some high school kid who's newly-invested in the world of Adult Emotions.) So he just Gabin-Shrugs and dumps her mouthy ass off on a Bordeaux street corner. By doing so, he's showing her that 'she's not the boss of him,' without even having to utter a single syllable.

That night, he's back in Bayonne, trapped in life's worst prison of all—the prison of family life. Solange is smart, and knows her husband's been out, diddling someone, and while we're not sure about this, we can guess that this is probably the first time she's ever called him on it (or, for that matter, on any of his infidelities), to his face: "To leave me and the children, you are always right on time," she chastises him, asking him, as well, why he's just been in Bordeaux for two straight days without coming home, to which his answer is a mere Gabin-Shrug. Meanwhile, big-mouth daughter Jacqueline is gloating to her dad that she's just been hired to be a photographic model, and that she's going to be posing for a photographer named Francis; she adds that soon, people throughout France are going to be seeing her picture all over the place (and this is going to turn out to be very true, especially in ways which we cannot yet anticipate). Her admission, of course, leads to a fiery Gabin-Outburst: "I will not have a girl who models in my home!" He's obviously not mad at his daughter, but is only feeling guilty about his own recent illicitness, and is clearly projecting his own 'sins' onto his daughter, who's not really bad—she's just young. Viard thinks that posing for pictures, even if they're only for commercial advertisements, is dirty, and she tells her dad that, no matter what he wants her to do, she's going to be France's new 'Camembert Cheese Girl,' anyway!

Needless to say, all of this tension at home is putting Viard in the mood for a new, two-day tryst with Clotilde, in Bordeaux. He shows up at his trucking company's office, hoping that dispatcher Gillier will give him a run to Bordeaux and, surprise—Gillier *cock-blocks* his efforts: "I've decided that you are spending too much time in Bordeaux, Viard. So instead of going there, your new line will be Strasbourg!"

Now he won't be able to see Clotilde! What excuse will he ever be able to make to her? 'Clo,' as Viard calls her, during their 'sweet' moments, is more sensitive than anybody you've ever met in your whole life. (She's one person with whom you don't want to share your bad news.) Well, what Viard does next, is that he tells-off Gillier, who won't give him the 'run' which he wants—hell, the run which he's entitled to! (Jean Gabin doesn't take shit from anybody, and that includes not just police officers who interrogate him, but also, all of the assholes who employ him!) In our film's incredibly primordial 'Gabin Outburst No. 2,' he now proceeds to chew his boss a new one: "Listen, you! You just do your job and put me back on my line to Bordeaux, and right now!" The guy's answer is, *per* the twenty-years-later-world of CB radios, something along the lines of 'negatory, good buddy,' so Viard tells him that, in that case, he just won't be getting into his truck today, at all; but after thinking about it for a few moments, and level-headedly realizing that he's got a family to take care of (no matter how ungrateful they are to him), he apologizes to Gillier, telling him that, on second thought, he actually believes Strasbourg to be really cool. Then, he phones-up Clotilde, in Bordeaux: "Hello, honey? I can't come to see you, tonight. The company's sending me someplace else. It's not my fault, though, so I'll try to come tomorrow." Then, in a great tough-guy movie moment, he punches Gillier out, and it's a real roundhouse, straight to the kisser!

That night, Viard takes his dressed-up family to the Annual Truckdriver's Ball, a fancy dress-do which happens to be bursting at the seams with dashing, dancing truckers and the wives who love them—an event which finds all attendees duded-up to the nines. Jacqueline, the errant daughter, is embarrassed to be seen at a lowly trucker party, which, as we can tell by the smug expression on her face, she finds to be completely *declassé*. Viard, as it is now being revealed at the party, has been fired by his company for having punched Gillier out, and so, more or less, he's just shown up at the party tonight, to try and feel-out acquaintances for jobs with other companies. One such acquaintance, Philippe (Max Megy) buoys Viard up with news that maybe, his own boss will hire him; but a few minutes later, Philippe returns with some bad news, which replaces the good: As it turns out, Philippe's boss said no to hiring Viard because, in his opinion, Viard is too old. (Viard, like other Gabin characters, is stoically-resigned to his Fate, and he just shrugs and sighs when he receives this verbal slap-in-the-face, realizing that there's nothing he can do about it, anyway. Just like in *Gas-Oil*, this movie, too, touches on the delicate subject of ageism: None of us can ever truly be free, from its vice-like grip.)

Bertil arrives at the ball too, solo (single guy on the make!), and guess who else shows up? It's Clotilde, who just couldn't be away from her precious old lover, Viard, for a moment longer. Will she have a confrontation with Viard's wife? Her dramatic entrance into the party has given us a set-up for what will potentially be a real throw-down of a 'wife-*vs.*-mistress confrontation scene.' Seeing Clotilde entering, Viard coolly grabs Bertil, and asks him to pretend to be Clotilde's escort. "Be careful," Bertil tells Clotilde dumbly, of Viard, "Jean's family is here, too!"

A bit later in the evening, Clotilde is able to steal Viard away from his family, and she complains that he never answers the hundreds of letters she's been writing him, in care of his family's house. (Stalking is no way to 'keep love alive!') He tells her that he's not trying to defend himself, but that he's truthfully never seen any of the letters, and that he's more than uncomfortable with the fact that she's been sending them to his home address. She turns off the waterworks when Max approaches them, telling Viard that he's just talked to another trucking-world bigwig, a guy who has been able to secure Viard a one-time run if he wants it, delivering cattle to Paris's Montparnasse district. When Max walks away, Viard introduces Clotilde to his family, under the guise that she's dating Bertil, but he isn't fooling anybody. Viard's daughter Jacqueline more than suspects that there's something up between her father and this much-younger woman.

Clotilde, next, takes a job in Bayonne, not too far from Viard's family home, at a sleazy, pay-by-the-hour sex motel, where she toils away, not as a prostitute, but as a cleaning lady. Illicit couples, who comedically shade their faces, parade up and down the hotel's dark stairway, and the most important part of her job, as her new boss Mrs. Vacopoulos (the future star Lila Kedrova who, of course, had already played 'Leah' the beatnik in *Razzia sur la chnouf*), is now telling her, is basically the 1956 version of 'what happens in Vegas, stays in Vegas:' "The customers will reward you for your discretion, by tipping you very well."

The next night, Viard takes Clotilde out to dinner: "I just saw your family and all of your problems," she tells him, referencing the trucker party of the other night, "and I really think we should separate." (Now suddenly reversing herself, she's the one who wants to cool it!) Viard knows this relationship with Clotilde will probably be his last chance in his *ever-dwindling-down* life of his ever being with a much younger woman, so he now asks her to reconsider: "My wife Solange is used to not seeing me so much, because I spend most of my life away from her, driving. So, really, it will be of no consequence to her if I leave her for you." He's not really begging her to stay, because Gabin's movie characters usually won't allow themselves to be that vulnerable; he's just making her a firm offer, and he's doing so in a very calm, and even businesslike, manner.

We now learn that the reason Viard never saw the love letters which Clotilde was sending to him, in care of his home address, is because daughter Jacqueline's been opening them, and in an incredible sequence, Jacqueline confronts her philandering father, personally, about the letters, blackmailing him (in effect) into giving his approval for her to be France's new 'Ms. Camembert,' on the billboards: "Daddy, I'm the only one earning money around here right now—so you're going to have to shut up!" While Jacqueline might seem to have the upper-hand over her dad for a few seconds, it won't last! She starts reading the letter from Clotilde out-loud, mostly so that her mom can hear it: "Hey, mom! Listen to this! Dad really is with another lady, like we thought he was! And her name is 'Clo!' And this letter she wrote to daddy says she's pregnant! Oh, wow, this is so fantastic! I'm going to have a little brother!" Even though the movie is in black and white, we swear we can see Viard's face reddening, and the resulting Gabin-Outburst is not dialogue-based: He just slaps his daughter's mouth really, really hard, and storms out of the house, both angry and embarrassed, telling Solange, resolutely, that he's now going to be leaving her, and for good. (Even though Viard's mad at what his daughter just did, he's also relieved, because her actions gave him the opening he needed to get the hell out, and to be with Clotilde.) In a very bittersweet moment, one of Viard's little twin sons, a youngster who is too little to understand what's going on, takes this moment to proudly announce to his dad that he's been voted 'third in his class,' but Viard's so hopping-mad, he isn't even hearing the little boy. Viard's a cheater, but he's not an asshole… well, he's not a huge asshole (he's just a medium one), and we can tell that, if he were calmer, and was able to listen to his little boy, he'd be fairly *kvelling* with pride over what his son is telling him right now. (It's just that the little shaver has picked a rather inopportune time to share his good news.)

Viard calls up his friend Max's trucking company to see if that one-off delivering-cattle-to-Montparnasse-job is still available, and he finds out that it is, but Max tells him that he's going to have to be getting on the road, immediately. Jacqueline, who's newly a woman, but who is still immature, feels badly that she has broken up her parents' marriage, so she next apologizes to her dad, even telling him that, if he wants, she'll tell her mother, that she "made the whole thing up." He smiles, and lovingly tells her, "Forget it, kid."

Back in Clotilde's love motel, meanwhile, a blonde hooker is asking her *nebbishy* old john to tip her, and the old creep responds nerdily, by pitching a bunch of coins right at her face! Clotilde, who's been sweeping-up outside the room while this was happening, grimaces, now clearly hating this job more than ever before. She doesn't say it, because she doesn't have to, but we know, based upon how badly things seem to be going in her own life, that she's probably about an inch away from having to turn tricks, herself. Amusingly, she starts making the room up, for another couple, and a creepy guy-customer tells her, "Don't worry about cleaning this room! I only need it for a few seconds." Mrs. Vacopolous thinks Clotilde is frightening the customers away, by doling-out judgmental looks and rolling her eyes at them, and she knows something about Clotilde from looking at the young woman's newly-distended stomach, which is (as we already found out, when Jacqueline read the letter), that Clotilde's got a Little Gabin-bun in the oven! Vacopolous tries to console the girl: "You could have told me, honey. I'm not a monster!" (This lady, who looked so intimidating at first, has turned out to be super-nice, and very maternal.) She tells Clotilde that she can't figure out why the girl has gone and gotten herself preggers, since she doesn't have the money to care for a child, and she next gives her the address of a discreet, back-alley abortionist, along with a stern admonishment: "You'd better have this procedure done right away, otherwise in a few more months, you won't be able to work anymore." (She's right, too! When you're pregnant, you don't have the energy to mop up '*pervert-spooge*.') At this point in our narrative, Clotilde is about three-months pregnant.

In the next sequence, Clotilde nervously enters the dark, dank, abortion clinic which Vacopolous told her about, and it's a place which looks like it could be right out of a Universal horror movie, circa 1931. (Outside of the facility, at the same time, and very atmospherically, a phalanx of little Dead-End Kid-urchins are exploding fireworks, which she can hear from inside, and the noise really sets her on edge, and even more so than she already is; it's similar to that great scene in P.T. Anderson's 1997 porn-biz epic, *Boogie Nights,* in which the teen-aged hustler explodes cherry bombs all over the slimy drug dealer's house.) Clotilde clearly wishes she could be anywhere, but here. (The movie takes place in 'Present-Day 1956,' and she should consider herself lucky because, in France, up through 1944, women could actually be executed for enduring abortions, and there's even a 1988 film, *Une affaire des femmes*—or, in English, *The Story of Women*—starring Isabelle Huppert, which is a stunning movie on that very same subject, if you're ever interested in seeing it.) Meanwhile, Viard, not knowing that he's two trimesters away from being a *daddy-o* again, has dispatched his major-domo, Bertil, to the love-hotel, to find Clotilde. Mrs. Vacopolous tells Bertil that Clotilde's sick with the flu, not wanting him to know that she's really out *getting wire-hangered,* but Bertil knows that this is all B.S.: "Tell me where she is! I'll kick down all the doors of this hotel, until I find her!"

He finds Clotilde, and not in the hotel, but wandering around Bordeaux, *post-fetus-kill,* and tells her that he's taking her back to Viard. He brings her back to him directly, and it's definitely a happy reunion between the illicit May-September lovers—and very literally so, because Jean Gabin, in real life, was born in May! Clotilde even accompanies Viard on his cattle run to Montparnasse, and now everything is a-okay, at least, for the moment, and Viard and Clotilde are now free to be *2gether4ever.* As the truck pulls away, we get an earful of Joseph Kosma's mournful pan flute theme, which we've been hearing throughout the movie.

As they drive, Clotilde checks out the signs which Viard has plastered all over the cab of his truck, all of which humorously reference Jean Gabin's legendary silently-stoic movie personality. (The funniest sign even reads, "Don't talk to the driver," and the runner-up signs, are: "Don't forget to flush;" "not drinkable water;" and "wipe your feet!") *The V-Man's* also got a little plastic devil head bouncing around on the dashboard, which predates today's fun bobble head phenomenon, by fifty years!

While Viard always enjoys silence, he'd actually like to hear Clotilde talk a little, since he likes her, and he now tells her, "If you're not going to talk, it's going to be tough, especially because we're going to be living together now." She wants to tell him that she was pregnant with his child, and that she's aborted it, but she can't bring herself to do it, and after a few seconds, she carefully opens up, albeit only very obliquely. ("I've done something wrong...") She doesn't want to devastate him with the news, because she knows he's a good man, in spite of the fact that he's not all that interested in having anything to do with his wife and kids, and besides, he's already left his wife, expressly to be with her.

A road-sign alerts us to the fact that we're now one hundred and thirty miles away from Montparnasse, and Clotilde is starting to become violently ill. (Obviously, the abortion clinic wasn't 'sanitized, for her protection.') As Viard navigates his truck through thick fog, the vehicle's headlights make it look exactly like the vehicle is a monster with satanic eyes; in fact, it's so foggy, that Viard can't even see the "Danger! Roadblock!" sign, which we can see. Moments later, visibility is one hundred-percent non-existent, and Viard is unable to drive any further. He now sees, for the first time, just how sick Clotilde is, and tells her that he's going to now head out into the night by himself, to try and find her some medical attention, and that she should just try to rest during his absence. Off-screen, she's already told him what the problem really is—that she was pregnant, and that she went through an abortion—and far from being mad, he now, very sweetly, holds her hand; he knows he was responsible for what happened, and he also now looks like he's carrying the weight of the world.

After walking for an hour, Viard comes upon a farmhouse, and asks the man-of-the-house (Marcel Rouze) if he can borrow the phone, because someone in his truck is feeling ill, but the guy tells Viard to get lost. Viard counters, "It's not somebody who's wounded! It's a woman, and she's really sick," and the guy relents, after hearing that the *sickie* is a woman. Viard grabs the phone and asks the Operator to send an ambulance out to the countryside, *stat*, and she tells him she'll do the best that she can, but that the nearest hospital is one hundred and twenty-five miles away, and most of the ambulances have been grounded for the night, due to the heavy fog.

When Verneuil returns to the truck, we see that Clotilde, who is alone, is now sweating, screaming, and hallucinating, and the director now, very moodily, starts pumping-up the off-screen sounds of scary-sounding cows, which low all around her. (It's a very scary and very stylized moment, one that's as relentlessly nightmarish as any scary moment in any of the better flicks directed by that great Italian horror movie *maestro,* Dario Argento.)

The ambulance doesn't show up until the morning though, and as we can now see, Viard's been in his truck with Clotilde, holding her hand, all night. The arriving Doctor apologizes for how long it's taken him to get to the scene, and Clotilde's carried into the ambulance on a gurney, as the cows continue to low.

And only moments after the ambulance gets rolling, it suddenly comes to a complete stop. There's no reason for the vehicle to continue making its trek to the hospital anymore, because Clotilde has just died from the infections which she has sustained from her abortion. Viard, a guy who always looks exhausted to begin with, looks like this might really be the thing that finishes him off. But it doesn't.

TWO YEARS LATER:

We're back now, and for the last time in the picture, in our favorite trucker bar, *La Caravanne:* Loud American MP's are holding court in the movie's famous tavern, and the establishment's

French clientele are all circulating a joke, because somebody in the bar thinks that somebody else in the bar has just said, "Americans go home" but, as it turns out, the guy really just said something else. Emile tells the MPs that his newest 'Marie' has been kidnapped, by yet another American, a guy who was driving yet another humongous American car, and Bertil's present, in the bar, as well. The two men haven't seen each other in a long while, because Viard's been retired for two years, and he now updates Bertil on his recent life, telling his younger friend that his daughter Jacqueline is still working at being a star, and that his little boys have both just recovered from some minor children's disease (unspoken in the film, but probably mumps or chicken pox). The film ends with Joseph Kosma's haunting pan flute theme, and it's here we're figuring out that, while the movie we've just been watching has been really great, and really cool, that the method of its storytelling was a bit odd because, just as in the case of a lot of other French movies which were made between the '30s and the '50s, the screenwriters were trying to have it both ways: In a lot of older French movies, characters are punished or even killed for having sex out of wedlock while, at the same time, these same exact films are visually, in terms of how they portray the topic of sexuality, way more frank than were the American movies which were produced at the same time; in old French movies, it seems, you can show whatever you want, as long as the characters pay for it, either with their sanity, or else, with their very lives. (See! 'We Americans' didn't invent hypocrisy! The whole world did!)

Director Henri Verneuil's *Des gens sans importance* is a great companion piece to Grangier's *Gas-Oil:* These are two great Gabin Trucker Movies from the 1950s, and both of them definitely deserve to be known in the U.S., and maybe (pay attention, North American DVD distributors who are looking for 'new-old' material to release), on a double-feature DVD.

What a Critic Said at the Time: "A grim, plodding film. Never gets to the true spark of the drama. Gabin is competent, as usual, but plays it too off-the-cuff to give much credence to the truck-driver's attitudes. Director Henri Verneuil gives it careful mounting, but has been unable to overcome the pedestrian story." (*Variety*, 2-29-56 issue. Critic: "Mosk. [George Moskowitz.]" Reviewed in Paris.)

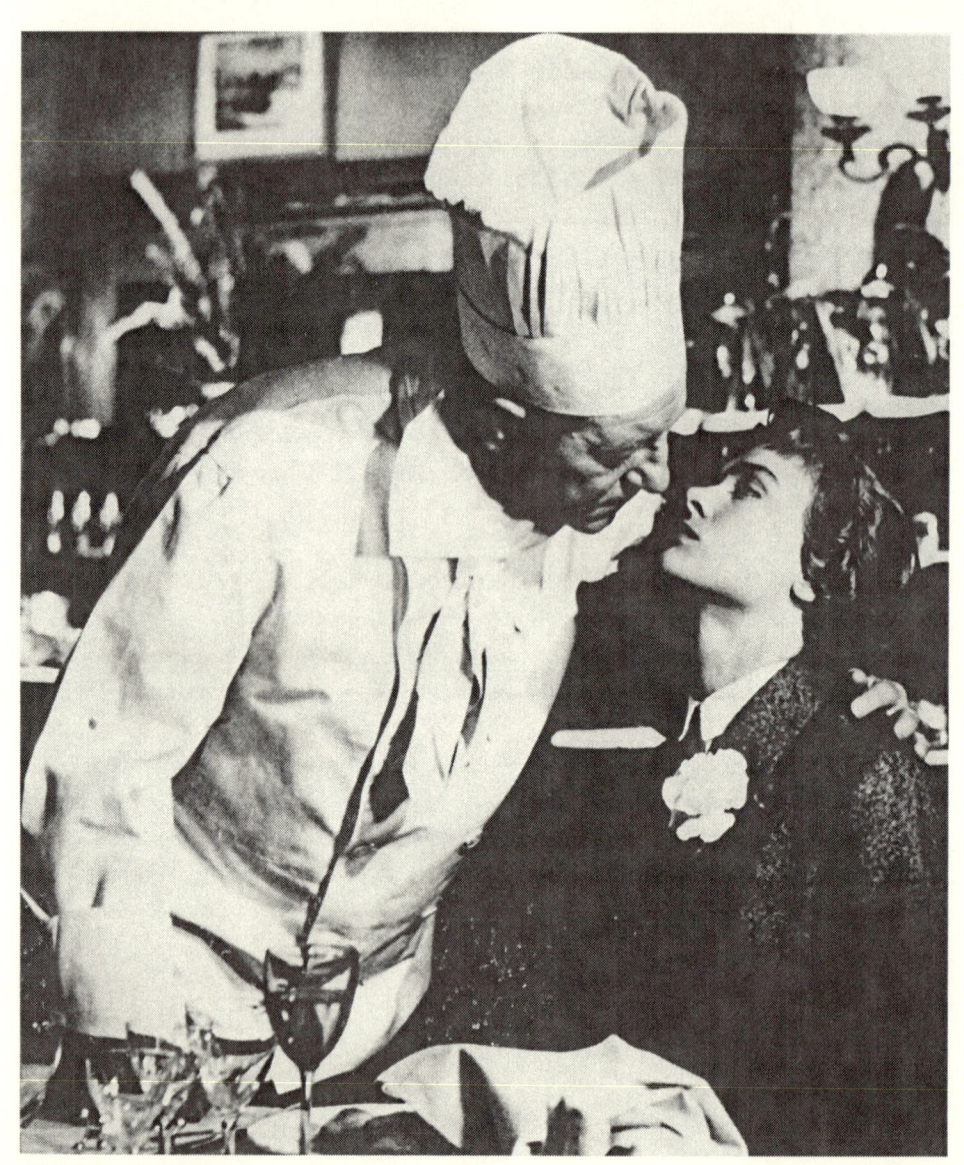

With Daniele Delorme.

FILM 56

VOICI LE TEMPS DES ASSASSINS

France, 1956

Literal English Translation: "TIME OF THE ASSASSINS" Directed by Julien Duvivier. Produced by Georges Agiman, Rene Bezard, Raymond Borderie, and Pierre Cabaud. Screenplay by Charles Dorat, P.A. Breal, and Julien Duvivier. Story by Maurice Bessy and Charles Dorat. Director of Photography (black and white), Armand Thirard. Editor, Marthe Poncin. Music by Jean Weiner. Production Designer, Robert Gys. (GENRE: DRAMA) A Production of CICC/Films Borderie/Les Films Agiman/Societe Nouvelle Pathe Cinema. Running Time, 1 hour 53 minutes. Released in France on April 13, 1956, by Pathe Consortium Cinema. Released in the United States (NYC), Dubbed Into English, on October 8, 1957, as "DEADLIER THAN THE MALE," by Continental Distributing, Inc. Released in Great Britain as "TWELVE HOURS TO LIVE."

"When these guys turn fifty, they really lose it!"
—*a waitress who works in Chef Gabin's restaurant knows the score, in*
"Voici le temps des assassins"

Like many American films of the 1950s, Julien Duvivier's *Voici le temps des assassins*, the first movie the director made with his friend Jean Gabin since the 1944 effort they made together in America, *The Impostor*, begins with a musical overture which is heard over a jet-black, imageless screen. In American movies made at the same time, a big, booming, orchestral overture always suggested that the audience was about to be subjected to a huge epic, grand in scope and breadth—*Ben-Hur, Fall of the Roman Empire, How the West Was Won*, etc.—but in France, and even since the beginning of talkies, even small, personal—or, what we today call 'character-driven'—movies have always made use of overtures, as well. French filmmakers utilize their overture sequences not to suggest stampeding cattle or wanton, imperialistic empire-plundering, but instead, to guide us into the usually wistful mood of their films' sad/unfulfilled/working-class characters. French movie overtures, further, often make use of the musical instruments preferred by the working class, instead of the big, orchestral overture-music familiar to us from American movies, and of course, that mostly means the accordion, because in the world of French working-class cinema, when language is insufficient, the mournful or joyful accordion always explains what mere verbiage cannot. The lyrics which are sung in this particular film's overture—it's a song called "The Assassins' Lament," and it's performed by Germaine Montero, and features lyrics by Julien Duvivier—accompanied by a mournful accordion, immediately clue us in that we are not in for happy times:

"This is the time of the ass.
A time of poison and the rope.
You're miserable in your existence.
Time of the 11:00 drink…
A wife makes her husband's drink.
They may be drunk, but happy.
But she's happier still, in the arms
of her new *cherie*."

Don't you love movies in which some jezebel plays two guys, who are usually friends, against each other? It happens in real life, and it happens in this movie: Yes, *Voici le temps des assassins* is another one of those later-period Gabin movies in which our hero is 'a well-off guy,' a woman takes advantage of him, and he doesn't fight back as much as we want him to, although this particular movie is a million times better than those other ones, which of course include *La Marie du port, Victor, La Verite sur Bebe Donge,* and *La Minute de verite,* just because it's weird, trippy, and the closest thing you'll ever see to Greek tragedy in any Jean Gabin movie; in fact, it happens to be one of the all-time favorite movies of the contemporary director Bertrand Tavernier, who's mostly known in the United States for his films *'Round Midnight* (1986), *Coup de Torchon* (1981), and *Death Watch* (1980).

It's morning in the Les Halles section of Paris in the first *arrondissement,* home of the city's largest outdoor markets (but not the real Les Halles—Les Halles was re-created on the set, by the film's production designer Robert Gys). Catherine (Daniel Delorme) steps out of the subway, canters through a crowded market, and enters a restaurant, *Le Rendez-vous,* where the owner/chef is Jean Gabin's Andre Chatelin, not to be confused with the Henri Chatelin character whom Gabin played in 1949's *La Marie du port*. When we first see Andre, it is through the restaurant's front window, which his hand wipes clean. Just like the demanding chefs we see today on t.v., Andre orders his huge staff of employees to produce twelve eggs and some cream and *plus vite,* so that he'll be able to get started on creating one of his much-prized soufflés. Much of the staff consists of Andre's relatives—most of his extended family works there—and as far as atmosphere goes, this restaurant's got it to spare. While Jean Gabin is his usual stoic self in the film, he also, this time out, has several moments in which he looks sublimely happy and even smiley. But since Duvivier, who made many of Gabin's greatest 'tragic, ill-fated drifter movies' of the mid-to-late 1930s *(Pepe Le Moko, La Bandera, etc.)* is at the helm, we already know that the smiles won't last for too long.

Amedee (Jean-Paul Roussillon), a young chef who works in the restaurant, excitedly thrusts the morning newspaper right into Andre's face, showing Andre that he's made the front page: Recently, according to the article, Andre Chatelin made a journey to the United States, where he participated in a cooking contest and won the First Place medal over forty-nine other chefs from all over the world; so now with this film, Jean Gabin, besides playing drifters, *bourgeois* guys, and criminals, can now add 'world-class chef' to the litany of characters he's played (and I'll bet that everybody in the U.S. really loved Chef Gabin's Mule-Kickin' Chili). Elderly Madame Jules (Gabrielle Fontan), who's also present in the restaurant, is especially excited to see him in the newspaper, because she's known Andre longer than anybody else there who's not family, in fact, more than fifty years ago, this tiny, eighty-something lady started out as Baby Andre's governess, and in this scene, she proudly tells everyone present, that when Andre was little, she used to wipe his nose. In fact, Madame Jules also lives with eternal bachelor Andre, who was married only once and long ago, because she keeps his house for him.

Andre doesn't have any children of his own, although there is a handsome, young early-twentysomething, Gerard (Gerard Blain), whom he treats as such. Andre calls Gerard 'Fiston,' which is the equivalent of saying 'Sonny' in English and, per Andre's wish, Fiston will someday stand to inherit the restaurant if he's so inclined—which, so far, he is not. Fiston's a hard-working medical student who works at Les Halles' outdoor market on a part-time basis, to put himself through school. Andre respects the younger man's work ethic, which reminds him of his own, and he brags to everyone who works for him that he wants to "help Fiston to get along in the world." Andre thinks that a career as restaurateur would be way more rewarding for Fiston than one as a medical doctor will be, and he's probably right, because most Doctors in France have never been paid all that much.

Catherine (Daniel Delorme), whom we earlier saw when she was rising up out of the subway station, now enters the restaurant, and tells one of the employees that she needs to talk to Mr. Chatelin, and that it's personal. Amedee lyingly tells her that he's "Mr. Chatelin's right-hand man," but we know he's not, because that position has already been occupied by Fiston, whether Fiston likes it or not. Also entering Chatelin's restaurant at about the same time as Catherine, is Bouvier (Robert Arnoux), the restaurant's vegetable broker, who supplies the place with The Fruits of Our Good Earth. Bouvier always orders way more veggies than Andre needs on purpose, and he then sells the rest on his own, making a tidy profit, and in that respect, he's just like those skimming drug pushers who pilfer the drugs from Gabin's criminal organization, in *Razzia sur la chnouf*.

Catherine now meets Andre and, very clearly, he's intrigued by the beautiful young woman. "I've come to see you about your ex-wife, Gabrielle," she reports, as he half-listens to her while getting the kitchen up-to-speed for the day, and this is where we find out that Andre was married to the as yet unseen Gabrielle twenty years ago. Andre—like all Gabin characters, he's seen it all—smells a grift coming, and he now lets her know, in so many words, that he's not interested in being held-up, if that indeed is why she's come: "You're my ex-wife's friend? She wants money?" Catherine has, in fact, come to tell Andre that Gabrielle passed away six days ago, but Andre doesn't react to the news at all: "Oh. So… what can I do for you?" Truly, this is the most incredible non-reaction to a family death in all of movie history.

Andre gently tells Catherine, who's clearly been very affected by the death, to sit down, and he immediately offers to fix her something to eat. As it turns out, Andre knows very well who this young lady is, but he didn't want to let on about it, at first: Catherine, we're now learning, is Andre's ex-wife Gabrielle's daughter by the man whom Gabrielle married after Gabrielle and Andre were divorced. "When Gabrielle told me you were born," Andre tells Catherine, "I didn't think it was true. I thought she was blackmailing me again." It is through this simple, linguistic device of the old Anglo-Saxonsim 'again,' we're now learning that Gabrielle was probably a very frequent-blackmailer. "You look like your mother," Andre continues. "Your eyes are hazel, like hers were."

Andre lets Catherine stick around the restaurant all day, and that night, he drives his newfound stepdaughter to his own home: He's invited her to stay, and he now asks her to fill him in a bit more about the circumstances which surrounded her mother's death. Catherine tells him that, for the last few months of her life, her mom, Gabrielle, was in the hospital, and she also tells him that she has never really been all that close with her mother; she even tells Andre about how mean and vicious her mom has always been to her, as well as the fact that Gabrielle's mom—Catherine's mother's mother—was apparently a pretty mean lady as well, back in her own time. (*Voici le temps des assassins* really traffics in the issue of 'hereditary meanness,' a mental condition with which we're already familiar from a much-earlier Gabin picture, 1938's Zola adaptation—or, 'zoladaptation'—*La Bete humaine*.) Catherine starts crying, so Andre now rubs her shoulders, and he then, soothingly, carries her up to the guest bedroom. "This will be your room," he tells her gently, continuing, "Someone else stays here sometimes." Here, he's referring to his own, on-again/off-again girlfriend, whom he says is 'away' right now, but since we'll never meet Andre's alleged girlfriend in the film, we don't even know if she really exists: Maybe Andre's just telling Catherine that he's got a girlfriend, because he's interested in her and wants to prove to her that he's potent. Catherine shows Andre a recent picture of her mom which was, as she's now telling him, the last one ever taken of her, and Andre is starting to like Catherine a lot, in spite of the Evil Womb from whence she's sprung. He tells her, supportively, "If you want to, you can be my daughter for awhile," and it doesn't even sound creepy when he says it, in fact, it actually manages to sound quite paternal. At this point, Andre's likeably-smart-mouthed housekeeper, Madame Jules, whom we've already met in Andre's restaurant, and who's overheard the whole conversation, laughingly calls him 'Papa;' Andre has already taken Fiston under his wing, and now he's going to be doing the same thing with Catherine. Jean Gabin, it would seem, is all the world's father, although in Catherine's case, it's clear, from the glances he's sending her, that he's also beginning to think of her as 'more' than just a daughter.

Back in Andre's restaurant the following evening, an uproar has ensued, because Andre's figured out that Bouvier, the vegetable broker, has just ordered three tons of asparagus after Andre had only asked him for two, sold the surplus, and pocketed all of the excess green stuff—the money, not *'les haricots verts'*—for himself. Like all good Gabin Movie Characters, Andre doesn't look agitated: He just tells the guy to gird his loins, because the two of them will be having a talk later.

Andre next strikes up a conversation with his surrogate son Fiston, who eats dinner all by himself at a small table while scrutinizing his medical textbook, while his sheepdog, Caesar, lies admiringly by his side under the table, since Andre allows animals to roam frequently through the restaurant, in fact one particularly eccentric character called The Duchess (Olga Valery) frequently brings her dachshund, whom she calls 'The Group Captain,' and she orders her dog a brandy-soaked dessert, and we even get to see the dog staggering away drunkenly after he consumes it! (Today, PETA frowns on directors who get animals too liquored-up on the set.) Andre greets his 'almost-son' with a firm, "How are you, my best friend?" and he takes this very same moment to introduce Fiston to Catherine, who's also present, thinking he can make a match between the two. Fiston, whereupon first meeting Catherine, starts immediately extolling Andre's virtues to her: "I don't have a family of my own, and if I didn't have Mr. Chatelin to help me, I would really be messed up. He's kind-of adopted me." Catherine tells Fiston that she's an orphan, too, having lost her own mother only six days ago, and while they talk, Andre sneaks away, giving the two a little 'getting-to-know-you/getting-to-know-all-about-you' time. Fiston tells Catherine that he lives in the Latin Quarter, and he then asks her, in the same breath, if she has a boyfriend, but she replies demurely that her friends are "…my books and Paris," a statement which, of course, really means, "Come and get me, Sailor!" Grinning, he cries out, "Me, too. My friends are the little chimneys!" The two share a laugh about their shared, lonely condition, and right after this, he invites her out for a T.B.A. evening-of-fun in the future.

After Catherine leaves, Andre susses Fiston out about what he thought of her, and Andre offers up a few of his own opinions about the girl, most of which seem to be favorable. ("She's a very nice girl. I wish her mother had been more like her!") Andre next elaborates to Fiston on his feelings about his now-deceased ex-wife: "Gabrielle wasn't all bad, I guess. She had some nice qualities. We had some good days." 'Glass-Half-Full Andre' has a much more positive outlook on life than other, more world-weary Jean Gabin movie characters, although he still knows that other people don't always have the most sterling of motives in mind, and that most people, most of the time, act only in their own selfish interests.

Later that night, Fiston's outside the restaurant, repairing a flat tire on his bike, when Catherine approaches him. He's happy to see her, and now they're both singing Andre's praises (Fiston: "He's cool… he's a MAN!") and what they're really describing, of course, is the much-vaunted Jean Gabin Movie Persona. Catherine seconds Fiston's opinion: "He's unusual, isn't he? He's different—he's not too intimate. He's 'friendly, but not friends.'"

That night, Andre acts as chauffeur on the couple's first evening-out together. (Fiston's got a big exam coming up on Monday, but Andre's persuaded him to take a few hours off, for a little light socializing.) While the date is starting out pretty cheerfully, Andre happens to drive past a cemetery, and this is where Julien Duvivier now gives us an ominous shot of a huge, monolithic crucifix, an image which he'll be repeating a few times, and which suggests that, even though everything is going 'great-guns' now, Lady Tragedy will be making her standard Gabin film appearance, later.

Andre brings the couple to the edge of town to the very popular *guinguette* (dance hall) which is owned by his elderly mother, Madame Chatelin (Germaine Kerjean, a great stage actress, who was also a member of the prestigious Comedie Francaise actor's studio) and, as we remember, *a guinguette* was also the main setting of another great Gabin/Duvivier picture, 1935's *La Belle equipe*. Andre's mother is a spry old coot who, antithetically to her son, sees the absolute worst in everybody. While Andre, as played by Jean Gabin, is certainly no 'momma's boy,' it's clear that his mother still makes the rules, and there's definitely some Oedipial competition going on whenever Andre meets a woman, and mom never approves of most of them, and for someone who runs a joyful establishment, she's a major crab. We see immediately how much mother and son really love each other, and Andre's mother now brags to him about how excited she was to read about him in the newspaper during the past week. He tells her he's just learned that his ex-wife Gabrielle died and she curtly replies, "Nobody will miss her." Andre next introduces his mom to Catherine. ("*Maman*, this is Gabrielle's daughter from the man she married after me: I'd like you to meet Catherine!") Madame Chatelin is cordial with the girl, but also tells her son that it wasn't fair of Gabrielle to leave him with her. Andre's Mom is a tough old bird and, in fact, she's a good deal tougher than anybody else in this movie, and that includes Andre. In fact, we'll soon see just how tough she can be, not just because of how she treats her son, but because of the way in which she slaughters the chickens she cooks for her *guinguette's* restaurant: She goes out to their pen and whips them to death with a huge whip, which she knows how to use because her own father was a lion-tamer.

There's a jukebox in the bar, and Fiston steps aside, a bit less than willingly, so that Andre can dance with his step-daughter, and now, in an amazing End-of-the-First-Act-Plot Twist, we're going to learn that there's both more, and a whole lot less, to Catherine than meets the eye, and that she's actually the kind of person whom we would today call a 'toxic personality' or, to borrow the title of an American suspense movie from 1994, a *Hand that Rocks the Cradle*.

The next day, Fiston is mooning away again to Catherine, about "how cool Mr. Chatelin is" (hero-worship to the nth -degree) and Catherine next starts in with some deviousness, laying a big whopper of a lie on him: "I overheard Mr. Chatelin say that he regrets all of the help he's ever given you!" After she plays Fiston against Andre, it's now time, of course, for her to start playing Andre against Fiston: Obviously, Catherine's a con-artist, just like her mom is, and just as obviously, she wants someday—or even now, if she can swing it—to be the recipient of the Andre Chatelin fortune, instead of Fiston, for whom she's pretending to have the hots, just so she can get at step-daddy's *moolah*.

Three days later: Andre notices that Catherine hasn't seen Fiston for a few days, and he asks her if something's wrong. ("I thought you kids really liked each other. I thought you two would be a really fantastic match.") She replies, tartly, "I already told you: I don't like young people. They're selfish and ungrateful. He [Fiston] is just like the others. He doesn't interest me." Andre thinks Catherine's anger is sexy, and we can tell from the way he's looking at her that he's now feeling more *sex*ternal toward Catherine than he is paternal, even in spite of the fact that Catherine's just maligned his surrogate son, directly to the young man's face. (That's right, friends: Andre's thinking with his 'other brain.') "Once, your mother was sitting where you're sitting right now. You look like her!" And now that Catherine's reeled Andre in, it's time to move in for the kill: "It feels good to find a nice man like you!" she coos, grabbing Andre's arm, lasciviously: Earlier in the film, Andre told another character that, at this point in his life, he's "done with women," and at least at the time he said it, he meant it. Is this going to be another one of those movies, like *La Marie du port, Des gens sans importance,* and *Razzia sur la chnouf,* in which a fifty-something Gabin will overcome his reticency to fall in love with an early-twenties girl who's hot for him? We shall see…

At Andre's restaurant that same night, a delivery man is now dropping off some clothes which Andre has just bought for Catherine, and one of the place's young waitresses just shakes her head and mumbles, "When these guys hit fifty, they really lose it!" So far, Andre still isn't hitting on Catherine directly, though.

What superficially separates *Voici le temps* from the other melodramas which Gabin made in the 1950s, and here I'm referring to both the family melodramas and the love triangles, is that director Duvivier has wisely included some fun, comedic moments to lighten the whole thing up, moments which are provided by the litany of ridiculous secondary characters who dine in the restaurant, a group of slap-happy regulars who always make Andre roll his eyes, but whom, we also know, he just couldn't live without; Andre's really in his element when he's in his restaurant—he's a much-calmer version of John Cleese's irrepressible Basil Fawlty, and he really seems to get a kick out of dealing with all of the problems that can happen during the average workday. And speaking of crazy customers, we now get to see a Moronic American Tourist (Eugene Stuber) who has no idea how to order properly in a French restaurant, because old French movies always manage to throw in a couple of crass 'Ugly American-types' who are too uncouth to know what to order in a 'proper' restaurant: In *Voici le temps des assassins,* the Moronic Tourist, who's dining alone at one table, asks Andre to bring him "… one radish, one egg, and a bottle of expensive champagne," and Andre shakes his head, amusedly; similarly in an earlier Jean Gabin movie, Marcel Carne's 1954 *L'Air de Paris,* there's a scene, also set in a fancy Les Halles restaurant, in which a completely different Moronic American Tourist goofily orders "oysters and chocolate" together, on the same plate, and the waiter just shakes his head.

Another amusing customer in Andre Chatelin's *Voici le temps des assassins* restaurant, is elderly Mr. Prevost (Aime Clariond), a comically-pathetic seventy-something stockbroker, who shows up at the restaurant with the much younger woman he's dating, and he's about

With Daniel Delorme and Gerard Blain.

fifty years older than she is. When Prevost's current jail-bait date heads for the restroom, Prevost asks Andre what he thinks of her. ("Isn't she nice? I told her I'd enroll her in art school!") Andre, who still won't cop to the fact that he's interested in his own step-daughter, asks the guy if he doesn't feel ashamed to be hanging out with young girls, and Prevost just thinks about it for a few moments, before replying, "Of course not. Youth is great!" Another 'crazy' comes into the restaurant now as well, and this one is a bearded, homeless man, Gegene (Camille Guerini, Gabin's trucker friend, Lucien, from *Gas-Oil*) who's clutching a fake, 'novelty' five thousand-franc bill, of which there is no such thing, and he asks Andre if he can redeem it for a piece of cheese. Andre, who's tickled by the humorous situation, lets the fellow know, in no uncertain terms, that "the kitchen is closed."

Andre's restaurant has one client, though, who's seriously not funny: It's a nerdy mustached guy who reminds Catherine that he knows her from Marseilles, that he has never been able to forget her, and that he can't live without her, but she cuts him off quick: "There's nothing between us, so leave." He screams, "You'll never forget me! If you don't leave here and come back with me, I'll run head-first into a truck and kill myself! I mean it!"

Bouvier is also present at our restaurant; he's at a back table, eating dinner—and we notice that he keeps a strong-box under his chair, which contains some money which Andre has given him to buy vegetables for the restaurant. We also notice that Catherine's eyeing the box lasciviously, even offering to carry it for Bouvier, but he declines. We think she might abscond with the money box, but she doesn't. Since Julien Duvivier lingers on this strongbox, we think that the item might have some kind of a dramatic pay-off later in the picture, but we'll never actually see the box again, outside of this one sequence. (So maybe there *was* a subplot involving Catherine's taking the money from the box, which Duvivier cut out, or perhaps, the moment was never even filmed.)

New Plot Twist Time: Catherine's mother, Gabrielle, isn't really dead! Gabrielle's played by Lucienne Bogaert, who will also appear in another Gabin picture, 1958's *Maigret tend un piege*, and she's the second of the film's mean-old-ladies (the first, being Andre's mother, played by Germaine Kerjean). Yes, *Voici le temps des assassins* is giving us a pair of mother-daughter con-artists who seem to have jumped right out of a Jim Thompson novella, and when the two women meet, which they're doing right now in Mom's room at a transient hotel, both of their true personalities are definitively coming to light. Gabrielle asks her daughter where she's been, but Catherine clearly wears the pants in this mother-daughter relationship, and she even advises her Mom (so much for filial piety), "Dead people can't talk… so shut up!" (Old junkie Gabrielle lives in solitary, sending her daughter out to grift for her, since she's obviously too whacked-out on smack to be able to con anybody on her own, anymore.) Gabrielle asks her daughter if she showed Andre the fake obituary which the two of them planted in the newspaper regarding her alleged 'death,' and she also asks her if he cried when he read it. (Of course, Andre didn't cry; he might cook food for a living, but he's still Jean Gabin!)

> GABRIELLE: He didn't cry? What a bastard! Is he remarried?
> CATHERINE: No.
> GABRIELLE: How has he been treating you?
> CATHERINE: [disappointed] Mostly like a daughter.
> GABRIELLE [eyes lighting up like cash registers]: Hmmm…
> CATHERINE: It's hard to really get to him, though. He's a hard man to read. Anyway, I'm going to have to get rid of that 'son' of his, this Gerard, if you and I are going to be getting any money out of him.
> GABRIELLE [gets a great idea]: You know what you should do: You should marry Andre! Anyway, you can, because he's not your real father… So, just try to do it, okay?

Catherine doesn't like that idea—what a dirty thing for her mom to ask her to do, even for such a dirty old lady, but she then says that she'll give it The Old College Try anyway, because like all good grifters worth their salt, we already know that Catherine will do whatever it takes to get her lunch-hooks on Andre's money. She gives her mom a few francs which, we're not sure but we can guess, she may have stolen out of the Vegetable-Guy's strong-box, then telling her, "You'll get a lot more money when I become the New Mrs. Chatelin!" Gabrielle helps her daughter to strategize: "But don't agree to marry him, right off the bat. You have to make him want you. If he's still on the fence about liking you romantically, you should fake leaving his house, so that he'll like you more. It's only when you leave that they start running after you."

Just like Gabrielle said (Momma Knows Best), Andre *does* start chasing after Catherine, when she tells him that she's thinking about moving out of his house and, while we know already that Jean Gabin's movie characters don't wear their emotions on their sleeves that much, his characters do draw the line at women leaving him, even when, as in this film, his Andre character has already remarked that he's done with women. In this movie, just like in Jean Gabin's movies from the 1930s, his character is a loner, mostly because he doesn't want to open himself up to the possibility of getting hurt by a woman.

At this point, Fiston hasn't been into the restaurant in days, and Andre is now beside himself with happiness, when finally, the younger man makes his triumphant return. He tries to hug Fiston, but the boy backs off. "We used to see you around here, Fiston, but now we don't," Andre says. (If Andre were a Jewish dad, he'd be grumbling, "*Oy!* You don't write, you don't call…") Andre tells Fiston that he hopes he didn't stop coming around, just because Catherine turned Fiston down for a date, and this remark causes Fiston to suddenly blow up at the older man: "Why, Chatelin, do you think I'm jealous because she likes you?" This is the first time in the film that we're getting some good old Electra Complex-inspired ('dad likes his daughter') fighting, because the fruits of Catherine's larceny—the fruits of the fact that she's been playing one man against the other—have already began paying off: Both men are now mad as hell at each other.

Andre's elderly mother tells him that, even though she's only met Catherine once, she's already figured out that the young woman is trouble, but Andre is still unable to see it, even with Gerard now acting so strangely toward him. *Or*, maybe he does know it, on a subconscious level, but prefers living in 'that special Egyptian river called Denial,' just like another character Jean Gabin will be playing in a soaper which he'll make directly after this picture, *Le Sang a la tete* (*Blood to the Head*), in which Gabin's wife's-character will repeatedly run out on their marriage, and yet he'll still refuse to believe that there's a problem in their relationship.

Catherine, who said she was leaving, comes home to Andre anyway, and he tucks her into bed, after first helping her out of her dress, and trying his hardest not look at her, sexually. Such close-quarters, naturally, start elevating the feelings, and she now begs him, "Don't leave me, darling!" She next pushes Andre down, onto the bed, and kisses him, full-flush on the mouth. Andre's mother, who's been staying at her son's apartment, in another bedroom (she lives above her *guinguette* on the edge of town, but stays with son Andre whenever she's visiting him in Les Halles), comes in, right in time to see the kiss, and it freaks her out, majorly. ("Get out of that bed, young lady! You're not my son's happiness!") In a Gabin-Outburst, Andre now lets his mom know that she should mind her own business: "You think I'm a child!" (As strong as Jean Gabin's Andre Chatelin is, his mom is stronger, and if Norman Bates' mother in *Psycho* were actually alive, she'd be Madame Chatelin; between

Andre's elderly mother and Catherine's elderly mother, this movie isn't exactly an ode to mothers.) Next, Madame Chatelin gives her son a guilt-trip: "Oh, go ahead. Do what you want. Marry your step-daughter. You don't need me anymore." (Great, now we've got some Oedipus Complex to go with the Electra Complex.) Catherine's now out in the hallway crying, having just been chewed-out by Andre's mom, and Andre is consoling her in a way which is a little wimpier than what we might ordinarily expect from *The World's Coolest Movie Star:* "You can marry me, but you have to be nice to my mom." Andre wants to make love to Catherine, and it's taken that big chew-out from his castrating mother to make him see The Whole May-September Truth which has been right there in front of him, for as long as Catherine's been around his house and restaurant. Not surprisingly, Andre and Catherine are soon married, but the wedding is off-screen and private, with no guests in attendance.

When we next see Andre in his restaurant, it's closed for a private wedding night dinner, and he's wearing a giant, elongated chef's toque which limps at the top, and it looks, and no doubt this was intentional on the part of director Duvivier, like the erection of a sad middle-aged man. Catherine enters, and he tells her that he has invited Fiston to join them for coffee. ("He's practically my son. I want the three of us to get along, so I want to break it to him gently that we were married.") Andre begins flambéing her a nice dinner: "As your chef tonight, I am at your service. Tonight, I'm going to be cooking you some fattening food, made with rooster blood!"

As expected, Fiston shows up at the restaurant, as Andre's in the kitchen, supervising the preparation of the post-prandial cocktails, and outside, Catherine is having a private moment with Fiston, and she lyingly whispers to him, "I was forced to marry Andre. I love only you, Gerard!" Fiston knows she's lying, but he's so angry, he's not even able to respond. Then, Catherine bee-lines over to Andre, in the kitchen, and starts lying to him, as well: "That Gerard is such a dirty boy. In fact, did you know that he's just insulted me!" She's very obviously setting the two men up to throw-down with each other like two welterweight fighters.

Andre, who is enraged and repulsed by what Catherine's just told him, bursts through the kitchen doors, physically grabs the confused-looking Fiston, and throws him bodily out of the restaurant, telling him never to return. That night, in their honeymoon bed, Catherine sleeps, and Andre's staring at her; hopefully, it's finally dawning on him that something's rotten in Denmark.

The next day, it's business as usual at the restaurant, with more goofball customers showing up for lunch: First, it's That Crazy American, and he's ready for his radish again. ("Your radishes are coming," Andre assures him with Gabinian-Calm. "Relax!") Plus, to add insult to injury, today, the guy also wants one egg and a glass of water! ("And a little butter for my radish, if you don't mind.")

Another customer today, is wild-eyed, balding Mario Bonnacorsi (Robert Manuel, who played Joseph Bonaparte in Sacha Guitry's *Napoleon* and who will, in 1958, play a pimp in another Gabin thriller, *Desordre et la nuit*). Mario's another man who knows Catherine from Marseilles, which is where not only she, but also her mom, used to sell their bodies. Bonnacorsi informs Andre that Catherine and her mother were both prostitutes at a local whorehouse, and he also tells Andre, shyly, that he'd like to say hi to Catherine, if it's okay. Andre is mad at the guy for suggesting that Catherine might be a hooker, but when Mario leaves the restaurant, a concerned Andre actually wants to know more, and Bonnacorsi wryly sings "Here Comes the Regiment," which was apparently a favorite melody of soldiers who were on their way to the whorehouse. Simultaneously, a bitter old-lady-customer at the next table, who happens to be dining on sheep testicles, starts frantically screaming out for more; literally, this lady now begins crying-out, "Where are my balls?" and, at this point in the picture, we feel like Andre should be asking himself that same exact question. When Catherine next visits her mother in her mother's flophouse bedroom, she looks a bit worried: "So, mom, do you remember Mario Bonnacorsi? He came to Andre's restaurant today, and he recognized me."

That night, Fiston visits Catherine: She's crying and telling him how she's now ashamed that she's married Andre, but he sees right through her crocodile tears, and it's finally dawning on him that everything that comes out of her mouth is a lie, calculated to play him against Andre, and that includes what she is about to tell him next: "You've got to help me, Gerard. I can't stand Andre. He's violent toward me! I thought I knew him! You've got to beat him up for me!" Fiston knows Andre would never hit a woman, and that's exactly what he tells her: "Even if Andre and I aren't friends right now, he was my friend and he will be my friend again, and I will not betray him." Then, the double-dealing Catherine returns to Andre and tells him, "I went to see Gerard today, because I wanted to make you two be friends again, but he told me awful things about you. He cannot accept that a girl my age is in love with you!"

Of all of Jean Gabin's 1950s' love-triangle melodramas, *Voici le temps des assassins* is the one which can most be described as being a crowd-pleaser because we, the audience, are now really wanting to see Catherine get her comeuppance. She even picks this moment to tell Andre what definitely has to be her Greatest Lie of All Time: "Sometimes, Gerard rapes me!" She would love it if the two men could kill each other right now, so that she'd get— she thinks—Andre's inheritance, instead of Fiston's getting it; but since neither Fiston nor Catherine is Andre's real, flesh-and-blood kid, who's to say that either one of them would be entitled to it? I mean, we know that Andre wants to give Fiston the restaurant one day, but we don't know if he has willed the boy any money.

On fire from what Catherine's just revealed to him, because Andre still believes a lot of Catherine's lies, even if Fiston doesn't, Andre now pays a visit to Fiston and, even without so much as a 'hello,' Andre starts pummeling the stuffing out of the younger man: "You little bastard rapist! I'm going to break your neck!"

Meanwhile, back at Gabrielle's flophouse-hotel, the old lady's in bed, strung-out on heroin, and screaming like Martin Landau's Bela Lugosi-character(ization) in Tim Burton's *Ed Wood*. The Landlord (Eugene Stuber) hears her scream and, when he opens the door to her room, he and we now see her, and she's flailing about in her bed. ("I'm dying! I want to see my daughter!") He phones Andre, and the way he introduces himself is very funny and deadpan: "Hello, Mr. Chatelin. I'm sorry to bother you, sir. Listen, can you tell your wife that her mother is asking for her?" The Landlord gives Andre the flop-house's address.

Now, having finally figured out that Catherine's been lying to him—and he figured it out about an hour later than the audience, but that's fine; we'll give Our Friend Gabin the benefit of the doubt—Andre finally decides to pay his crazy ex-wife a visit: When Andre arrives in Gabrielle's room, we finally get the scene we've been waiting for, the one scene in the film in which we'll see Andre and his ex-wife together, and she's so out of it, she doesn't even know he's there. Andre sees the newspaper—the one with the article about his winning the cooking competition—crumpled up next to Gabrielle's spazzing feet.

The next day, when Gabrielle is no longer 'high,' she's sitting upright, opposite Catherine, and mother and daughter are now strategizing about good ways to kill Andre: "His car could fall into a lake… Somebody could push him in… but it's got to be an accident." Gabrielle tells Catherine that her daughter should think about drugging him with ether.

Catherine goes to see Fiston and fills him with more lies about how Andre has abused her. Genuinely worried, he asks her if she's hurt. "Andre beat me up again," she cries, and she now lets-fly with her Murder Plan: "I had a dream about us, Gerard. We were in the country, holding hands. We were watching Andre sleep. Then, a black fly was on his nose. I called to him and he was dead. You and I laughed like children. I wish we could really kill him! Sometimes I wish he could have an accident. I know I can count on you to make my dream come true. Oh, and by the way, if we want to kill him, we have to act now. Don't you see how much I love you!" While Fiston no longer believes anything Catherine says, she's so convincing in this scene that, once again, and against his better judgment, he starts believing that Andre is actually, per the lingo of any random American country-and-western singer, 'doing her dirt.'

Back at Andre's restaurant, it's business as usual: Moronic 'Radish-Eating American-guy' is there, but this time, he's (over)-ordering a proper meal, which makes Andre happy. Andre's on the phone with his mother, telling her that he's going to be seeing her today at four o'clock. He's making this call, knowing that Catherine can hear it; she's present at the restaurant in another room, and is eavesdropping on another receiver. Andre who, thankfully, seems to be recovering his intestinal fortitude, is about to start 'playing' Catherine, just as she's been playing him.

After Andre hangs up from talking to his mother, he tells Catherine, sweetly, that he's going to take her for a nice drive to his mother's *guinguette,* and immediately, she begins worrying, because this is going to interfere with the carefully-laid plans which she's made for herself and Fiston, to kill him today. "But, Andre, dearest: I thought we were going to go and visit your mom tomorrow, not today!" He tells her that he's changed his mind and, reluctantly, she climbs into his car beside him. Now on the roads outside of Paris, Andre and Catherine drive right by that graveyard which we saw at the beginning of the film, the one with the big, scary-looking cross which we're now seeing for a second time, and we can feel that something really bad is about to happen. And now that Catherine's locked in the car with Andre—he's got a captive audience—he finally starts calling her to the mat about all of the sociopathic mayhem she's been up to: "Now: Tell me again about your mother's funeral!" Catherine confesses that her mom is actually still kicking—and very literally, too: We saw Gabrielle's feet actually kicking, while she was jonesing. Catherine has no idea that Andre's already been to visit Gabrielle, and that he already knows she's still alive.

He drags Catherine up to the *guinguette*, where his own tough, old mother is waiting in silence, and in front of his mother—and for her benefit—he runs down the list of all of Catherine's trespasses: "So! You and your mother were going to kill me, hmm?" Catherine, defensively now, begins spouting-out a whole pack of new untruths: "It's mother who made me fool you! She started taking drugs, back when we lived in Marseilles." But Andre neither knows about that, nor does he care, and next, in an incredible scene which would make Quentin Tarantino cream his Wranglers, Andre exits, leaving Catherine alone with his elderly mother, who stands in the middle of her large, empty dining room, and Big Momma now starts brandishing her giant whip, and since, we previously saw her whipping her chickens to death, this isn't entirely far-fetched. Mom now starts whipping the holy-hell out of Catherine, berating her with all the acumen of a waterboarding Guantanamo guard: "Your mother is a drugged-out whore! When you pick your sleeves up, of course it means that you pick your dress up, too!" Tough old Mom-Chatelin hates women who mess with her Gabinian sonny-boy, and we're getting the idea now, from seeing how great and professional she is with the lash, that she's probably whipped a few of his son's other errant women in the past. This is definitely the most off-the-charts-weird Oedipian jealousy sequence we've ever seen in any movie made anywhere in the world at any time, and it's a very Bunuelian moment (here, I'm thinking about the scene in Luis Bunuel's 1951 film *Susana*, in which Rosita Quintana gets whipped for her indiscretions), and it's also kind of a Russ Meyer-like moment—a moment which is way kinkier than any other moment in any other Gabin movie (however, it's definitely not too weird of a scene for a Julien Duvivier picture). Duvivier's movies, like Quentin Tarantino's movies three decades later, will often burst-free from their tightly-fitting genre-corsets, to incorporate and explore moments of extreme ultra-weirdness. To wit:

In the Duvivier/Gabin collaboration *Pepe Le Moko*, there's that spaced-out montage sequence, in which all of the characters in the Casbah start singing and gesticulating wildly about how happy Pepe is, that moment in which Duvivier starts cutting hyper-kinetically around the Casbah, like some kind of early, proto-MTV experiment gone amuck.

In Duvivier/Gabin's *Golgotha*, the camera speeds dizzily around the marketplace, as Robert LeVigan's Jesus begins horse-whipping the holy hell out of the moneylenders. (It's another great 'Duvivier Whip-Moment.' Wonder if Duvivier was a tad kinky in his private life?)

1954 — 1976 | 113

And let's not forget the harrowing conclusion of Duvivier/Gabin's *Maria Chapdelaine*, in which the character of the fur-trapper rides up to Maria's cabin on a sled which, upon closer inspection, we find out isn't a sled at all, but actually a frozen-stiff Jean Gabin carcass.

Lastly, there's that manically-charged voodoo wedding sequence between Gabin's Pierre Gilieth and Annabella's Aischa, in Duvivier's *La Bandera*.

Back at the *guinguette*, in *Voici le temps des assassins*, Madame Chatelin locks the newly-whipped Catherine into a bedroom, promising the girl that the two of them will definitely be having more fun with the lash later that evening, and this is where we're finding out that they're not alone. There's one more person in the house, and it's one of the *guinguette's* waitresses, who's played by the real-life 'ex-Mrs. Jean Gabin' from the 1930s, Gaby Basset, and it is this nice lady who helps Catherine to escape, since she doesn't like Madame Chatelin's methods all that much, either. (Madame Chatelin probably whips this waitress, too, but it's not personal because, as we all know, *when the lash is hungry, it needs meat!*)

That night, Andre is surprised to find that Catherine has escaped from his mother's *guinguette*/home, and that she's back in town, and in his restaurant, and even though Andre hates her evil pettiness, and the fact that she's completely free of all morality, he's obviously been having some misgivings about the fact that he's just left her alone with his whip-loving Mom, and he asks Catherine for forgiveness. (No, Gabin! Don't leave yourself open like that! Don't wimp out!) She says that she'll forgive him, if he'll agree to meet her tonight at ten o'clock in the graveyard, and he probably realizes, like all of the other good, fate-bound Jean Gabin Movie Characters, that if somebody's going to kill you, there's no way you can stop it from happening. So he steels himself, and agrees to the meeting.

Back at Gabrielle's transient hotel, Catherine phones Fiston and tells him to meet her five hundred meters from the restaurant, just before ten o' clock p.m. Meanwhile, in Fiston's apartment, Fiston's asking his roommate (Jacques Fayet), another young medical student, if he can borrow his car. After the phone call, Catherine fills a syringe with ether.

A few minutes before 10:00 pm, as Fiston and Catherine are driving into the cemetery, with Fiston's beloved sheepdog Caesar in tow, Duvivier gives us a glimpse of that scary graveyard crucifix for the third time, and she lyingly tells Fiston that it wasn't just Andre's mother who whipped her, but that Andre himself was able to get a few lashes in. After a few moments, some headlights are seen, but they're not Andre's—the lights just belong to somebody else who's driving by. When the coast is clear, Catherine leans her head into Fiston's driver's-side window, and she now fills Fiston's head with more lies about Andre which, she hopes, will make Fiston more eager to kill the older man:

> CATHERINE: He wants to kill me, you know. That's why he sent me to see his Mom. When we kill him, we have to make sure we push his car into the river. Then we'll be together, at last.
> GERARD: Did he force you to marry him?

CATHERINE: My Mom made me do it. I never wanted to.
GERARD: But your Mom is dead!
CATHERINE: Well… not exactly…
GERARD [epiphany]: You mean… you lied to me?! You want me to kill Andre, and you've been lying to me! So that means you've probably been lying to me about everything else, haven't you! Wait a minute… Andre's never been mad at me at all, has he!
CATHERINE [the jig is up]: I can explain!
GERARD: I'm not a killer. You made a mistake, lady. I'm taking you to Andre right now, and I'm going to tell him about all these things you do.

Freaking, she pulls out the syringe and 'etherizes' Fiston, so that he's now out-cold. Laughing like a lunatic, she next pushes him, and his car, into the cemetery's little lake, like Norman Bates sinking Janet Leigh's car in *Psycho,* and since Caesar the dog is in the back seat of the vehicle, he's going down with the ship, too!

Andre, it turns out—and let's give him some credit—never planned on meeting Catherine at the graveyard, after all. While this whole event has been transpiring, he's been at his restaurant, hosting a show of his cooking for local dignitaries. One of Andre's very-impressed guests even toasts, "To the stomach and the heart …in that order!"

The next morning, the car which houses Fiston's inert body is being dragged-up by the cops, although Caesar the dog is still alive, but soaking wet. Andre shows up, finally, at the graveyard—he's only twelve hours late (one of the film's international release titles was *Twelve Hours to Live*)—and, truthfully, he doesn't know anything about what's happened there. Especially, he doesn't know that Fiston, his beloved surrogate son and almost-heir, is dead.

Catherine, as an alibi, has returned to the *guinguette* after the murder, so that she will not be associated with the crime. Andre makes his way into the *guinguette* and sees Catherine and Caesar. When Caesar starts barking at Catherine, Andre figures out that the dog "knows something," and surmises that Catherine killed Fiston and sank the car. Pissed-off, he makes Catherine write her mother a letter which reads, "Dear Mother, please come and visit me, I'm in terrible trouble." Madame Jules takes the letter over to the transient hotel and then returns to say that Gabrielle is her worst shape yet, and will not be able to visit. Catherine escapes from the room and runs through Paris, to her mother's aide, followed rather closely, on foot, by Andre and Cesar. When we see the flophouse, in the next scene, the landlord is in the middle of throwing Gabrielle out into the cold, and Gabrielle is hiding in the staircase. Catherine runs past her mother into her mother's room, and slams the door, and Cesar runs in just before she is able to close it. Next, we hear, but do not see, Cesar the dog growling and Catherine screaming: Cesar, the angriest sheepdog you've ever seen, is killing Catherine, for having murdered his master! When Andre opens the door, he sees that Catherine is dead, and Gabrielle just sits in the stairwell, watching this shocking moment, her mouth forming a wide silent-scream. Andre walks away, 'Gabin-Alone' as the film comes to its unbelievably bizarre conclusion.

Voici le temps des assassins, which is widely considered in France to be director Julien Duvivier's final masterpiece, is the only Greek tragedy you'll ever see that's set in a French restaurant, which, I suppose, makes it both *Oedipal* and *edible* at the same time. The picture had a very brief art-house release in the U.S. under the lurid title *Deadlier Than the Male,* a title which would be re-used ten years later in a British, James Bond movie knock-off from 1967, starring Elke Sommer and Richard Johnson, and the English-dubbed version of this Gabin picture definitely loses something in the translation: The actor who's dubbing Jean Gabin's voice in English sounds nothing like Jean Gabin, the story has been re-written, over-simplified, and 'cleaned up' for more puritanical American tastes, more than fifteen minutes have been trimmed, and the "Assassin's Lament" overture song which is sung at the beginning of the uncut French-language print, even though it is credited in the opening credits of both versions, has actually been replaced by an instrumental tune in the English-dubbed version. It was recently announced that director Tonie Howard will remake the film, starring Gerard Depardieu in the Jean Gabin role, and hopefully this 21st-century redux will lead to a new awareness of the original film, here in America.

The title of the film, *Voici le temps des assassins* (literally, in English, it means, "Here is the Time of the Assassins") is actually the last line of Jean-Nicholas Arthur Rimbaud's 1872 poem, "*Matinee d'ivresse*" ("Morning of Drunkeness"). It's always a beautiful thing, when 'a poem about madness' inspires a great, S&M-infused melodrama.

What a Critic Said at the Time: "[Director Julien] Duvivier has served up a grim slice-of-life. Though well-mounted, the lack of deeper character analysis makes this only mild melodrama. Gabin displays his usual good acting..." (*Variety*, 7-18-56 issue. Critic: "Mosk. [George Moskowitz.]" Reviewed in Paris.)

What Another Critic Said at the Time: "A taught, and compelling, drama, even though it is never explained why the girl [has such] an utterly ruthless aggression against the whole race of males. [The director, Julien] Duvivier has plainly made it as candid as the censors will allow [and, in the role of the restaurateur], Mr. Gabin displays a sense of epicurean enjoyment, presiding over his restaurant in his white high-bonnet. The film is a top level combination of actor Jean Gabin and director Julien Duvivier." (New York *Times*, 10-8-57 issue. Critic: Bosley Crowther.)

Top: With Monique Melinand. Above: With Jean-Louis Bras.

FILM 57

LE SANG A LA TETE

France, 1956

(Literal English Translation: "BLOOD TO THE HEAD") Directed by Gilles Grangier. Produced by Fernand Rivers. Screenplay by Michel Audiard and Gilles Grangier. Based Upon the Novel, Le Fils Cardinaud (The Carniauds' Son), by Georges Simenon. Director of Photography (black and white), Andre Thomas. Editor, Paul Cayatte. Music by Henri Verdun. Production Designer, Robert Bouladoux. (GENRE: DRAMA) A Production of/Distributed by Les Films Fernand Rivers, S.A. Running Time: 1 hour 23 minutes. Released in France on August 10, 1956. Never Released Theatrically in the United States.

"I am a bourgeois. And the role of a bourgeois, is to be able to take a lot of shit in style."
— *Captain-of-Industry Gabin, explaining his role in life to a friend, in "Le Sang a la tete"*

Le Sang a la tete (*Blood to the Head*) is the final forgettable Gabin soaper from the 1950s, the last of that mini-series of movies in which a woman takes advantage of Gabin, and we lose interest in his character because he doesn't fight back, like we want him to. (The other movies which are guilty of the same crime, to refresh your memory, include *La Marie du port*, *Fille dangereuse*, and *La Verite sur Bebe Donge*—and *Sang a la tete* is the slightest of the lot.) Story-wise, it's *so onion-skin paper thin* (not to mention, *so cirrus cloud-wispy*), that it's almost not even there, and it's a shame, too, because the screenplay was adapted by the great Michel Audiard, who was working from a novel by the august George Simenon. This picture represents the second of nineteen screenplays which Audiard will write specifically for Gabin, as well as Gabin's third of ten Simenon-book adaptations.

Gabin, here, assays another of those wealthy, *bourgeois* captain-of-industry-types whom he plays in the other pictures I've just mentioned, a guy called Francois Cardinaud who 'started from nothing' as a working-class guy, made it to the top, and then seemed (it's what the idle rich do, in the movies which Gabin made during this period) to become completely bored by everything. Francois owns all of the businesses by the banks of Port Rochelle in western France, which makes him Waterfront Kingpin, just like Gabin had already played other waterfront kingpins in *La Marie du port*, *Port du desir*, and *La Vierge du Rhin*. In fact,

Francois is so amazingly wealthy, that one of the minor characters kisses his ass, thusly: "Ahh, Monsieur Francois! Only the water doesn't belong to you!" Director Gilles Grangier who, here, is making his third of twelve Gabin pictures (the first two, being *La Vierge du Rhin* and *Gas-Oil*), gets the movie started with a scene which takes place down at the local customs office: Francois' ten-year-old son, Jean (Jean-Louis Bras) has come to visit him at work, and the kid is so excited, when he recognizes one of his dad's company-boats bobbing up and down in the water, that he cries out with delight. ("That's one of my dad's boats! *Yeahhhh!*")

Francois' business partner, mustachioed Charles (Leonce Corne), gives Francois the skinny on a current upheaval at work and, just like in *Razzia sur la chnouf*, Gabin's going to be spending a lot of this movie putting out the fires that come from within his organization, both literally and figuratively, except in this movie, the 'screw-ups' won't be criminals, but only dunderheaded morons who don't know how to do their jobs. Charles tells Francois that Mr. Drouin (Paul Frankeur), a captain of one of the fishing boats which Francois owns, has damaged one of the company's best seagoing vessels, and to the tune of three hundred and twenty thousand francs (whoopsie!), but Francois doesn't feel like hearing about any problems today, and he waves Charles off. Today, Francois is more interested in hanging out with his little boy. (Francois is a great father to Jean—a cool and always-present *buddy-dad*, in the best possible sense.)

That night, Francois and little Jean arrive home to the family mansion, and Jean immediately asks the family's comely maid, who's known in the film only as 'Mademoiselle' (Renee Faure), if he can see his mom (Francois' wife), whose name is Marthe. Mademoiselle tells the little boy, matter-of-factly, that his mom "isn't home," and the youngster doesn't react at all: Apparently, 'Mama Bear'-Marthe, a total head-case, disappears from the homestead quite a lot—sometimes, even, for days-at-a-time!—and her small boy is already (he's stoic, 'just like dad!') used to her frequent absences; Marthe Cardinaud, whom we won't even see until very late in the picture, is racked with mental problems, and it almost seems, sometimes, like she's the human incarnation of one of those dogs that runs away every time the door is open, and her inappropriately un-reactive hubby, Francois, is so used to it, he never even tries to stop her. In fact, Francois has become so inured to Marthe's constant running away that today, when Mademoiselle mentions it to him, he barely even reacts to the news. We understand, without his ever having to say so (which is what makes Jean Gabin such a great actor, since we can see it all, in his expressive eyes), that he'd probably like her to come home, mostly for his son's sake, although we can see that even little Jean, outside of asking where she is, doesn't really even seem to care about her all that much. Francois and Jean have a quiet Father-and-Son dinner, and it's the first of many silent dinner scenes which we're going to start getting in the movies Gabin will make in the late 1950s through the 1970s: Jean Gabin's a friendly guy, but during dinner time, do him a favor: SHHH! He's had a hard day, and he just wants a little quiet, okay? (Thank you!)

The next day, Francois makes his usual rounds, to all of the places Marthe may have gone: First, it's a visit to Marthe's crazy old mom, Sidonie Vauquier (Odette Florelle), who lives in an apartment building which Francois owns. She's a really bitter, vicious (not to mention *viscous—she's one of those lifetime smokers, who coughs up phlegm, for a living!*) and dirty-looking old lady, a virago who's cut from the same ragged cloth as Danielle Delorme's ('Catherine's') heroin-addicted mom, in the same year's Gabin epic, *Voici le temps des assassins*. We can tell that Francois is really repulsed by the old bag but that, because she's his wife's mom, he's 'thrown her a bone,' and appointed her as concierge of this modest apartment building. Sidonie tells Francois that she hasn't seen her daughter in a long while, and that she's worried—not over Marthe's health, but because Marthe was supposed to bring her some money, so that she could pay this month's the electricity bill! Sidonie tells Francois, also, that her other grown child beside Marthe, her son, is in the doghouse with her as well, because he too hasn't brought her any money this week. ("He's supposed to be working, but instead, he's out gambling!") Francois stone-facedly gives his mother-in-law a handful of electricity bill-money. (With a whack-job of a mom like this, it's no wonder Marthe's turned out to be a little bit 'off.')

To take the bitter taste of Sidonie's bad parenting off of his lips, Francois next pays a visit to his own aged parents (played by Paul Faivre and Julienne Paroli), who are happy to see him, and who live very well. (Francois obviously takes care of them a whole lot better than he takes care of his wife's mom.)

"Your wife… here?" Francois' Mom asks. "Mightn't she be at her own mother's house?" Francois tells her that he's just come from Marthe's mother's place, and that there was no Marthe in sight. Francois' Mom now lectures him, and he's heard this all before, no doubt, about how his wife should be with him; and while Francois is about three decades too old for a parental lecture, he's a good son, so he listens attentively, and he's then saved, very literally, by the (door)bell: It's Francois' brother Arthur (played by Gabriel Gobin), and Arthur's wife Mauricette (France Asselin), who are now showing up with their own little boy. Arthur and Mauricette ask Francois what he's doing here, but their own smart little kid already knows: "I'll bet Uncle Francois' wife forgot to come home again!" (Even a little kid knows that his Auntie has a *pathological disappearing problem*.) Francois' family starts gossiping, rather archly, about Marthe's uncouth family, but Francois remains Gabin-Cool. Mauricette offers to care for little Jean, until such time as Marthe should design to come home, but Francois— a/k/a, 'Joe Self-Reliance'—gives her a polite 'no thank you,' telling her that his governess is perfectly able to take care of the boy. Francois' brother, Arthur, is the one in the family who didn't get the breaks, and while he's content enough working as an iron smelter at one of his brother's companies, he's also (naturally) super-jealous of his brother's wealth, and when Francois leaves, Arthur feels compelled to apologize to his parents and wife for his status in life as a non-earner; he even tries to placate them, by adding, "I could have been a bureaucrat, if I had set my mind to it!" (*Woulda-coulda-shoulda! Woulda-coulda-shoulda!*)

Next, Francois goes to his business partner Charles' house, to see if (possibly) Marthe has stopped off there, but of course Charles, like everybody else in the film, has to start the conversation off by reminding Francois that Marthe's not good enough for him, which

Francois is already hearing fifty-five thousand times a day anyway, from everybody he knows. Not finding her at Charles' place, he next heads over to the police station. The Desk Sergeant (Jacques Marin) tells Francois that a young woman was brought in today—a woman who has just endured a car accident—but that it wasn't Marthe. (The film takes place in one of those small towns, in which everybody knows everybody else.) Finally, Francois (he's 'a detective without clues') goes to the nightclub where he and Marthe sometimes go during their rare happy moments, but she's not there, either.

Back in her filthy apartment, meanwhile, we're now finding out that Sidonie, Marthe's old mom, doesn't live alone and that, in fact, she's got an old bum-of-a-husband, Julien (Paul Oettly), with whom she fights, and rather incessantly. Even though Francois gave his monster-in-law Sidonie money to pay her electricity bill, she's pretending, in front of her husband, that she doesn't have any, trying to cadge some extra bread out of him, and not willing to part with *une centime rouge* ('one red cent'), Julien suddenly shows some balls: "Your mother and father died in a mental hospital—and you're on you way there too, you bitch!" (Oh! Well, that explains a lot of things: Sidonie and Mauricette must be one of those hereditarily-crazy families, like the family we already met in 1938's *La Bete humaine,* or the family we met in the Gabin film which came right before this one, *Voici le temps des assassins.*)

When Francois arrives home that night, Mademoiselle, his housekeeper, asks him if he's been able to find Marthe, and he replies, simply, that no news is good news.

Charles calls, too, and asks Francois if Marthe's returned yet, and he then asks his 'Gabinian' partner if he can go down to the fish market and bid on his behalf, on a new fishing boat, since their other one is D.O.A. Francois can't attend the auctions himself, because he wins everything he ever bids on, so there's a lot of animosity toward him from all of the town's smaller businessmen (namely: everybody in town), who are unable to compete with him, so he always sends Charles to bid, on his behalf. (As one independent fish-biz guy muses to another, "You can't even complain to anybody about Francois Cardinaud, because *Francois Cardinaud is everybody!*")

In time, Francois learns that Marthe's been hanging out, not at her crazy mother's house but, supposedly, at her nicer godmother's house: Marthe's left word with Mademoiselle that she won't be coming home for dinner, because she's with her sick godmother, in Noire (it's in western France, not far from the country's sixth largest city, Nantes), because she's "taking care of her." If this all sounds too good to be true, it is (as you'll be discovering, a few paragraphs down).

Back at Francois' office the next day, we see that not only did Francois and Charles not win the big boat which Charles was bidding on, but that Cardinaud Industries has even more heavy-duty problems which we don't know about. *Francois is one weird dude:* He doesn't like to deal with problems at home *or* at work, and maybe the 'blood to the head' of the movie's title represents the pounding sensation which he must get in his noggin from sitting around and not taking any direct action, at home or at work. The bills are piling up, and Francois suggests to Charles that cashing-in on some of the company's insurance policies might help to allay some of their present financial straits, but Charles tells him that he thinks that would be a bad idea. Drouin, the sailor who wrecked Francois' best fishing boat, is present too, and he's a perennially worried-looking guy, but the always calm Francois tells him not to worry about the damage he's caused, and Drouin lightens up immediately, happy that Francois isn't firing his ass!

It's no surprise at all that Marthe's not really with her godmother: She's really in a hotel room, *diddling* her early thirtysomething boytoy-lothario, dark-haired Mimile Babin (Jose Quaglio, who's best known to serious American movie fans for playing the role of 'Italo' in Bernardo Bertolucci's 1970 classic, *Il Conformista* [*The Conformist*]). Mimile loves Marthe, but he's got a cruel streak too, and he uses the fact that she's *The Most Insecure Person on Earth* to post-coitally taunt her, in a creepy sing-song voice: "*Heeeeey, baaaaaby!* It's not very responsible of you to leeeeave your family! Baby, I *haaaate* that you married a guy with such a *biiiig* house. It really hurts me a lot, that the woman I *looooove* is with a guy who's *maaaade* it in *liiiife*." (This guy loves his *looong* vowel sounds.)

Mimile's been fooling around with Marthe behind Francois' back for more than ten years, waiting (wimpily) for her to leave her husband, and what we're basically looking at plot-wise, in *Le Sang a la tete,* is a re-hash of Jean Delannoy's 1952 *La Minute de verite,* in which Michele Morgan fooled around on her husband Jean Gabin for ten years, with the younger Daniel Gelin, before Gabin's bored/self-absorbed doctor-character discovered the infidelity. And Mimile's not just a gigolo either, but he's also a real, dyed-in-the-wool Norman Bates-freakshow-of-a-wimp and, as we're now seeing, he's even more insecure than she is: After he berates her, for being a "rich bitch" (it's their standard foreplay), he routinely begins crying (wimpy 'baby-men' are a regular occurrence in Georges Simenon works [as we'll also be seeing the following year, in another Gabin-Simenon collaboration, *Maigret tend un piege*]), and Marthe hugs him like a baby, cradling his head into her bosom. Marthe's clearly the boss of their decade-long illicit relationship, and she tells Mimile that she's never really loved Francois, and only married him for his money. (Somehow, when she says it, it's not coming as too much of a shock to us.)

Unlike Gabin's character 'Dr. Pierre Richard' in *La Minute de verite,* though, his character Francois, in this picture, has always known that his wife is cheating on him, but he's just in heavy-duty denial about it: "If my wife says she's with her godmother in Noire, then she's with her godmother in Noire," he Gabin-Outbursts at hot Mademoiselle. Francois isn't a very likeable guy to people other than his small son, and not just because he doesn't do anything to fix, or end, his 'non-marriage,' but also because he doesn't want to face any problems, at all. He apologizes to Mademoiselle for freaking-out on her, and next tells her that he's just been mad lately, because people keep telling him that he's being cuckolded, and he can't stand it!

The next morning, Francois has breakfast with Mademoiselle, and we now see (not that we haven't seen it already) that she's completely *ga-ga* for him, and that their relationship clearly has the makings of more than 'master-servant' (at least it will if she has anything to say about it). She's happy that Marthe never comes home, because it leaves her more time to flirt with the man-of-the-house and, when she leaves to clear the breakfast dishes, Francois next has a *pow-wow/confab/tete-a-tete* with his little son Jean, who asks him that question which we all want to see answered: "When's mamma coming home?" The answer is just a standard-issue Gabin-Shrug, but it satisfies the boy. When little Jean heads off for school, Mademoiselle is elated, because it means that she gets some more flirting time with Francois.

Gossip along the waterfront has it that, in fact, it's Francois' own fault that his wife keeps running away, and not just because he looks so bored by life, either: In this scene, we'll find out that Francois, too, is having an affair, and with none other than his business partner, Charles,' wife, Isabelle, who's played by the actress Yolande Laffon. (No wonder Francois doesn't ever seem to be worrying about the possibility that Marthe's cheating on him: He's been busy screwing-around on her, too!) Mademoiselle asks Francois what he's going to do the next time his wife comes back, and he just Gabin-Shrugs. (J.G.'s shoulders must get a major workout, what with all of the constant shrugging he always seems to be doing in his pictures.)

In the next scene, Marthe returns home for the first time in the movie, *via l'autobus*, while Francois is at work, and it's the first time in the movie where we're getting to see her in person, as opposed to just hearing other characters talk about her, and she's played by an actress called Monique Melland. It should go without saying that, while Mademoiselle is warm toward Francois, she's ice-cold toward Francois' wife (B-R-R-R-R! Feel the chill!), whom she regards as being competition. After Marthe leaves again, after only the briefest of visits home (she's just come to pick up some extra clothing, and isn't even interested in waiting around until her little boy comes home from school), Mademoiselle phones Francois at his office: "Your wife was here, but she stayed only for a few minutes." This hot governess obviously didn't want to tell Francois about his wife's return, at the time when Marthe was bodily in the house, because she doesn't want them to reconcile; Mademoiselle definitely wants Francois all to herself, and why shouldn't she? She's the one who cooks for Francois, and she's the one who properly cares for him, just like a wife should be doing.

The next day, Francois visits his old friend Vittorio (Rudy Palmer), on Vittorio's fishing boat. Vittorio's an old friend whom Francois hasn't seen for eight years, and the two fiftysomething guys now start reminiscing about a mutual friend who passed away, eight years ago. Before Francois became La Rochelle's super-wealthy King of the Sea, he and Vittorio were longshoremen together. Vittorio's own wife, as he's telling Francois now, left him years ago for another man and, unlike Francois' wife, as Vittorio is telling him, "she never even came back to pick up a change of underwear!" Vittorio tells Francois that he, too, knows, as does everybody in town, about Marthe's relationship with the young stud, Mimile: "Everybody's laughing at you but me, Francois!" (Francois doesn't get mad at Vittorio, though; he knows the guy is right and besides, they're old friends.) Vittorio knows Mimile as well, since Mimile used to work, for a time, on Vittorio's boat, as a deckhand: "Mimile's a crook, and he owes me: When he worked on my boat, he stole a lot of money. And now it's your wife who's taking care of him, financially." (Great! So, not only is Marthe having an affair with Mimile, but Francois is learning, in this scene, that he's been subsidizing it! Forget the fact that Gabin's character, in this movie, is called 'Cardinaud'—this guy is more like a '*corniaud,*' which is the French word for 'sucker.') Vittorio has an idea: "Look, Francois, since we both of us hate this little bastard, let's go and find him. We can beat him up together!" These two older men don't actually know where the hell Mimile is, but they do know that it sure would be fun to crack a few of his teeth.

Vittorio and Francois head into a local boat bar, and beat a path upstairs, against the express wishes of bartender/owner Pionsard (Bruno Balp), next coming upon an ineffective old man who's in bed with Raymonde (Claude Sylvain), a prostitute who also happens to be Mimile's sister. After the client amscrays, Francois hands Raymonde some money for *les informations sur son frere,* asking her if she knows where her brother might be hiding out, but she doesn't want to hear about Mimile, and tells Francois that her brother, in her opinion, is a no-good thief; she even throws a *Mimile Fun-Fact* into her speech free-of-charge, which is that Mimile's and her father abandoned them when they were small. She tells Francois that not only has Mimile stolen money from stores, but that he's even stolen from his own family. Not only does she have no idea that Mimile is screwing Francois' wife, but she actually thinks, because this is what he's told her, that he's away in Gabon, West Africa, with friends, trying to strike it rich. She also tells Francois and Vittorio that her brother served a long stretch in jail about a year ago, for robbery. Suddenly, though, after running her 'bro' down so completely, she starts feeling badly about talking shit about him. (Mimile might be an asshole, but he's family!): "Are you going to hurt him? Please don't hurt him!" Francois tells her that it's not his style to kill anybody, but that if she hears anything about where he might be, that she should definitely let him know, because "it's very important."

That night, Mademoiselle is having dinner with Francois again, and she has dressed-up sexily, to entice him. (We're learning, in this scene, that she went to school to become an artist, before real life dictated that she become a servant. [*It happens to the best of us!*]) She tells Francois that she likes how he sometimes (including right now) looks at her, and asks him if he noticed that she changed her hair-style (for him), today.

Now, we get to meet this movie's 'Old Hag #2:' Old Hag #1 was Marthe's mother, the revolting Sidonie, and Old Hag #2 is Mimile's equally phlegmatic-looking fish-merchant mom, Titine Babin. Francois asks her where her son is, and all she does, is cackle at him like a crow: "He's on his honeymoon... With your wife!! *Hahahahah!!*" This old bat is laughing at Francois in public, but he remains Gabin-Calm, and Vittorio can't believe how Zen-like his pal is acting, and as the two men walk away, Francois tells him how he always remains so even-tempered: "I am a *bourgeois* now, Vittorio, and the role of a *bourgeois,* is to be able to take a lot of shit, in style." (This is the one great line in an otherwise not-so-great movie, and it also happens to be true: *When you're independently wealthy, jealous creeps give you a lot of shit, and you just have to learn how to take it in stride.*) Vittorio wants to brag a little bit too, so he smiles and tells his pal that he, himself, has done time in jail over the years, and that "doing time in jail, is just as honorable as being a *bourgeois* like you!"

Vittorio, with Francois still in tow next beats up a friend of Mimile's, a character called 'The Expert' (he's played by Hugues Wanner), as a way of trying to ascertain where Mimile is, and the lead which this beaten guy gives them, is to the Hotel Robinson in Sette, a town in the south. (Vittorio is like Thomas Mitchell's 'Tiny' character in *Moontide:* He's a good-naturedly oafish friend-to-Gabin, but he's also got a definite psychotic streak a mile high. Even though he's a cool pal to have, you wouldn't want to cross him!) Vittorio and Francois hustle the bruised-up Expert into the back of Francois' car, needing to keep him there so that they'll be able to beat him up again, should it turn out he's lying. "If we're lucky, we'll catch them in bed," Vittorio tells Francois, gleefully salivating over the thought of seeing a live sex show starring Francois's wife. 'V and F,' next, arrive at the Sette hotel, and Francois tells Vittorio to wait in the car, because he's going in himself, and he tells the Don Rickles-looking hotelier (Rivers Cadet) that he's looking for Mimile Babin. (Does the name 'Babin' = 'Gabin' + 'Buffoon?' [Maybe the name is an in-joke, from the writers?!]) The guy tells Francois that Mimile already left his hotel, the evening before, and with a woman: "They left last night without paying. She left her suitcase, though." Francois takes possession of his wife's suitcase and dutifully pays the bill for his wife's tryst, because he knows that the *hotelier* is a good working man, and he doesn't want him to lose any money. (Plus, no doubt, he wouldn't like it if word got around that Francois Cardinaud doesn't pay his bills.)

Back in the car, Vittorio's gushing about how much fun it's going to be when they finally find Mimile and start clocking him like it's eight-thirty, and Francois tells him to knock it off with the tough guy 'tude: "Keep it up, and you won't be long with me!"

Now, it's time for another surprise: Marthe hasn't just been having sex with Mimile: *Au contraire, mes freres (et mes soeurs)*, she actually used to be married to Mimile, before she was married to Francois, and she just kept right on doing him, even after she married Francois! She'll never love Mimile, just as she'll never love Francois either, but she loves the idea that Mimile needs her, as opposed to self-sufficient Francois, a guy who doesn't look like he needs anything at all, except for people to just leave him alone!

Francois goes back to see Mimile's mom, Titine, who still won't tell Francois exactly where her boy is, and she taunts him as she did before, with cries of, "Ha Ha! No more wife!" (Coolly, Francois tears up her license to sell fish on his docks and, with a rare smile, shrugs, "Ha Ha! No more license!") Of course, she becomes nice to him after he tears it up since, as we all know from the real world, people respond better to brutishness than they do to niceness, in spite of what your mommy told you, and she even starts to cry, the tears now flowing down her hairy, pustulating face-moles: "If I tell you where my son is, will you tell him that I told you?" She confesses to Francois that the police are after her little sonny-boy for a laundry list of crimes which he has perpetrated in the past (we already know that he was involved in a robbery, but there were other crimes, as well), and that she'd rather Francois find her son than the cops, since, in her mind, and whether this is true or not, Francois is the genteel sort, a guy who will probably go easier on him, than will the psychotic, Rodney

King-beating police. Babba gives Francois her son's current address, and not jut because she thinks Francois will go easier on him than the cops, either: She's actually doing it because she, just like every other woman in every other Gabin movie, is hot for Francois (*yuck!*) and she even asks him, through her few-toothed smile, "Do I disgust you?" to which Francois's ultra-dry reply is, "Does that surprise you?" She tells Francois that her son and Marthe are now at a different hotel, the 'Charentes' in Lille, a town in the north.

Francois and Vittorio make it to Lille, and Vittorio's now acting like a pouty woman, because Francois once again insists that he should remain in the car. As Francois begins walking toward the hotel, Vittorio, whose rage is building inside of him because he's no longer being included, jumps Francois and starts punching him! The two old men are now rolling around in the dirt, in a comical *mano-a-mano* which seems like it could have emerged wholecloth, right out of *The Good, the Bad, and the Ugly*. Both men really like each other, but neither guy is the most vocally-demonstrative person in the world and so, not just to Vittorio, but really to both of them, the only way to properly blow off steam is to knock each other the hell out! Even though Francois is older and richer now, we see him reminding his friend Vittorio (with his fists) that he can still clean up in a fight. What's really great, though, is that after the fight, and even during it, the two guys are laughing hysterically, and really having fun with it. They're the best-of-buddies but they're also bored, and sometimes in life, when you don't know who to beat up first—just start with whoever's closest!

Francois arrives at the Charentes Hotel, where he finally confronts Mimile, who looks shit-scared to see his lady's husband standing right there, in his face. Mimile not only owes Vittorio money, but he also owes Francois *bukku* cash, from years ago. (As I've already mentioned, Mimile worked for Francois more than ten years ago, and now, Francois is starting to put the pieces together: That's where Mimile first met Marthe.) It's a tribute to director Grangier and screenwriter Audiard that, during this expected Mimile-*vs.*-Francois confrontation, there is no physical violence (which is the reason that Francoise wanted Vittorio to stay in the car). Francois is (and we, too, are) now surprised, because when he's finally face-to-face with Mimile, he discovers that he's not really mad enough at the younger guy to take a swing at him. "You'd better run away," Francois warns Mimile, "because my sailor friend Vittorio is out in my car, and he's looking for you, and he's not nice like I am!" (One icy look from Jean Gabin cuts deeper than the serrated edge of the sharpest Ginsu knife.)

At the end of the movie, Francois is returning home to Port Rochelle, not by car, but on the ferry (in real-life, the Port Rochelle Ferry, which is shown in the film, no longer exists), and guess who he runs into: It's Marthe, who's also coming home (returning from Lille), and this 'accidental' meeting between them represents the first and only time in the whole film in which we'll actually see husband and wife together. Marthe tells Francois, truly and apologetically, that she is now coming back to him and, this time, for good, and after she says this, *very weirdly*, Francois now apologizes to her for not being a good husband, since (he doesn't have to tell her this, but we know this is what he's thinking) he was cheating on her as well, and he must now be realizing (or maybe he always knew it) that this is the reason she's always been running away from him, and from their son. (This is the one Gabin love-triangle movie from the 1950s in which the husband-character will take responsibility for the failure of his marriage, instead of its being 'the wife's fault.') The ferry pulls away and, as the picture ends, we hope that both Francois and Marthe Carniaud will stop their philandering, talk out their issues with each other, and settle the hell down.

Le Sang a la tete was presented to the public, by its distributors, as a mystery, but the only criminal act in the picture seems to be the main character's ambivalence to all people, and to all things on earth. Worse, this only minimally-involving movie doesn't wrap-up Mademoiselle's crush on Francois.

What a Critic Said at the Time: "Pic [is] about small town Gallic pettiness... Main attribute is the solid performance by Jean Gabin, who walks through this with a resoluteness and understatement that gives the film its few dramatic moments. In fact, he gives it more than director Gilles Grangier has been able to [because the film is] somewhat inconclusive in characterization, and lacks depth." (*Variety*, 11-14-56 issue. Critic: "Mosk. [George Moskowitz.]" Reviewed in Paris.)

With Bourvil in "La Traversee de Paris" (Film 58, at right).

FILM 58

La Traversee de Paris

France/Italy, 1956

(Literal English Translation: "CROSSING PARIS") Directed by Claude Autant-Lara. Produced by Henry Deustchmeister. Screenplay by Jean Aurenche and Pierre Bost. Based Upon the Novel Four Bags Full, by Marcel Ayme. Director of Photography (black and white), Jacques Natteau. Editor, Madeleine Gug. Music by Rene Cloerec. Production Designer, Max Douy. (GENRE: COMEDY) Running Time, 1 hour 20 minutes. A Production of Franco London Films (France) and Continental Produzione (Italy). Released in France by Gaumont, on October 26, 1956. Released in the United States with English Subtitles on September 4, 1957 (in NYC) by Trans-Lux, Inc., as "FOUR BAGS FULL." (Also known internationally, as "PIGS ACROSS PARIS.")

"If you don't give me a glass of wine, I'm going to tell the authorities that you're using a Jewess as a drudge!"
— *Gabin calls elderly bar proprietors on the fact that they're not paying their serving girl, in "La Traversee de Paris"*

Fall, 2002. Los Angeles County Museum of Art. Twelve-film, five-evening tribute to Jean Gabin. Tonight's program: *Sold out.* Glancing through the crowd, there's the American movie actor Robert Forster, the terrific actor who played bailbondsman Max Cherry in Tarantino's *Jackie Brown*. (In fact, Forster was in attendance for almost every night of the Gabin Festival.)

Starting in the 1950s, Jean Gabin will do something new, and something which he never did before in movies: He'll start making *raucous comedies*. Gabin, of course, had already dipped his toe into comedy in two of his earliest movies, 1930's *Chacun sa chance* and 1932's *Les Gaietes de l'escadron*, and again in 1950's *Heaven Can Wait*-clone *Pour l'amour du ciel*, but now, here he is, Gabin the Comedian, in *Traversee de Paris* (*Crossing Paris*), a wonderful confection which the French consider, to this day, to be one of their country's very best comedy movies ever. What we Americans think of Billy Wilder's *Some Like it Hot*—well, that's exactly what the French think of *Traversee de Paris,* and if anybody would know how great this movie is, it would be the late, great American movie critic, Pauline Kael:

Pauline Kael (from her book, *5001 Nights at the Movies*): "... this explosively funny movie, directed by Claude Autant-Lara, was known in England as *Pigs Across Paris;* in the U.S., it was called *Four Bags Full*, but [today, it remains mostly] unknown under any title. Somehow it never caught on here. (It had won the award for best film of the year, in France)... The star of the film is Gabin, lusty and powerful as the man enjoys life so much, he can play games with it."

Although *Traversee de Paris* was released only briefly in the United States, at one NYC art theater back in the 1950s, it was so popular with the crowd when it was shown at the Los Angeles County Museum of Art's Gabin Series in 2002, that the Museum repeated the film in the Spring of 2006, as part of a series of films which were set during the German Occupation, which the film, the winner of France's *Prix Melies* award for Best Picture, in 1957 (it's the award which is given by the critics), is.

Jean Gabin will appear in nine comedies in all, throughout his career, and not only is he great in all of them, but he's different in his comedies, than he is in his dramas: In his nine comedy films, the whole 'quiet, stoic' Jean Gabin is nowhere to be seen: In his comedies, Jean Gabin is loud and boisterous throughout—*he's a non-stop talking machine* and, in effect, the entirety of each movie becomes a Gabin-Outburst. He's still the consummate everyman, but his characters inveigh, non-stop, against the pretensions of society, by calling everybody (rich people, poor people, and hypocrites of every stripe) to the mat, on all of their falsities.

On your next trip to Paris, walk along the Seine, and check out the literary selections which are being proffered by the used paperback book dealers; every dealer has at least one dog-eared copy of the novella upon which the film was based—Marcel Ayme's long-short story, which was first published in France, in Ayme's story collection, *Le Vin de Paris,* in 1947. When you look at the front cover of the novella—even the recent editions, which were published in the 1980s and 1990s—Gabin's photograph, from the movie, is still featured prominently on the cover.

In 1956, *La Traversee de Paris* was released in the United States, at one New York City art house, by distributor Trans-Lux (yes, *that* Trans-Lux, the company that imported not only Japanese television cartoons to the U.S.—"Speed Racer," "Gigantor," and "Kimba, the White Lion"—but also, some very cool European theatrical features).

La Traversee de Paris takes place in the German-occupied Paris of 1943, a city which is fueled by both fear and rationing. France, at this point in history, was totally bereft of such necessities as food, soap, coal, and booze, and one of the first things we see in the film's opening montage, which is mostly culled from actual documentary footage of Paris in '43, is a shot in which housewives are lining up outside of a market, only to be turned away, because there's nothing left for the vendors to sell them. (Plus, as all of the women wait in line, we see German tanks rolling through the streets—*which definitely makes shopping way less fun than it already is!*)

1954 — 1976 | 129

As the opening credits complete themselves, a blind violinist plays *"Le Marseillaise"* on the steps outside of a subway station, as Marcel Martin, who's played by the great actor and comedian Bourvil (a guy who looks a great deal like the American actor James Cromwell) and his wife, Mariette (Jeannette Batti), emerge from its hoary depths. They see him playing the tune and tell him to watch out, because the Gestapo are coming, and if they hear him playing the French National Anthem—well, needless to say, *his ass will be grass.*

Marcel used to be a taxi driver before the Germans invaded, but now, during the Occupation, there are few taxis left on the streets of Paris—only German military vehicles, which are busily picking up anybody who looks even remotely suspicious or rebellious. So Marcel does what a lot of unemployed French did during that period: He sells illegal goods on the black market, a crime which is punishable by death, should one get caught. Mariette is angry with him for doing this, and often threatens to leave him, as indeed we're going to be seeing her doing in this scene, because she knows that he's probably going to get caught one day, and she loves him too much to be there when it happens.

Marcel and Mariette enter the home of a character called Jambier (in English it means, 'leg'), a fast-talking neurotic who's played to the hilt by France's great mega-star/comedian, Louis de Funes—the French Jerry Lewis—an actor who's trademark is 'the comically nervous tic,' and who's known in the United States, mostly on the strengths of his only movie which was a big hit here, director Gerard Oury's 1974 classic, *Les Aventures de Rabbi Jacob* (*The Mad Adventures of Rabbi Jacob*). De Funes appears in only two sequences in *La Traversee de Paris*, and he'll also appear in another Gabin effort, 1961's *Le Gentleman d'Epsom* (*The Gentleman of Epsom*/American release title: *Duke of the Derby*). In 1968, Gabin and De Funes will even co-star together as a comedy-team, in another picture, *Le Tatoue* (*The Tattooed One*).

Jambier takes Marcel and Mariette into his basement, and shows them a big, fat, juicy, two-hundred-plus-pound pig which he's been hiding away: In war-torn Paris, pork is the rarest commodity of all, and Marcel often freelances for Jambier, transporting the guy's ill-gotten gains across Paris, where they're sold at a premium by a broker called Marchandot. Typically, Marchandot pays Marcel, Marcel takes the money back to Jambier, and Jambier gives Marcel his cut which is, in most cases, a few hundred francs. Tonight, Jambier wants Marcel to take all two hundred pounds of pork, and to deliver it in secrecy across Paris, to Marchandot, in four large suitcases—the 'Four Bags Full' of the film's American release title.

Right in front of their eyes (but thankfully, not ours) Jambier next slaughters the pig, cheered-on by his wife, who's played by Monette Dinay, while Marcel plays accordion to mask the sound of the pig's screams. (We don't see the pig being slaughtered, but we *do* see Marcel's reaction to it and, needless to say, he's horrified even though, no doubt, since he's always transporting meat for Jambier, he's seen all kinds of pigs being slaughtered in the past.)

Jambier tells Marcel, that the four suitcases are going to be too heavy for him to carry by himself, and that he's definitely going to need a second man to help him out. Marcel mentions here, that he used to use a guy to help him, 'Altamont,' who is unseen in the film, but that Altamont was recently arrested for selling black market soap. (Soap was another rarity in 1940s' France, and as Jambier tells Marcel comically, "I haven't washed since France was occupied!")

Jambier asks Marcel if he knows anybody else who would be available to help him out, and neither man can think of anybody immediately, so Marcel tells Jambier that he'll get back to him within the hour. Marcel and Mariette then hit a local bar, to celebrate Marcel's (very) temporary new pig-transporting job, and since it was illegal for French bars to sell hard liquor during WWII, they have to settle for some really bad homemade beer, which is all that the bar's proprietors have to offer them.

Just as Marcel continues to puzzle-over trying to find somebody who can help him carry the pork, a very serious-looking guy comes in, and it is here that we're going to be meeting Grandgil, who is definitely one of Jean Gabin's very best creations.

Marcel notices that Grandgil, who's now off in the corner, minding his own business (as usual, for Gabin), is a pretty *hearty-looking cat*, and that Marcel would probably be a good person to help him carry the heavy pork-luggage across town, on foot. Marcel introduces himself to Grandgil, and asks him if he's interested in the job, thusly: "Listen, Mister, I'm sorry to bug you—it looks like you're really enjoying your solitude [Author's Note: *That's our*

Gabin!], but I have a little business proposition for you: I've got one night to transport two hundred pounds of pork across Paris. We'd have to walk six kilometers, and my boss will be paying us six hundred francs each, for our troubles." Grandgil looks like he could use a job, because he's wearing a shabby jumpsuit (which was probably crisp and white, a very long time ago), but Grandgil just Gabin-Shrugs, telling Marcel, "I don't do dirty work. *I paint.*"

Marcel, not wanting to take no for an answer, takes Grandgil into the men's room, so that they can continue the conversation without being heard ("Let's go wash our hands!"), and once inside *le crapper,* Marcel produces, from the crusty recesses of his jacket pocket, a bar of impossible-to-find soap, and Grandgil is very impressed with the fact that the guy has it. Changing his mind, Grandgil now tells Marcel that he'll help him out, but for no less than one thousand francs, and not a *sous* less. (So: Grandgil is interested [kind of!], but only, as with all other Jean Gabin characters, on his own terms.) Marcel says he doesn't know if this new amount, this one thousand francs, will 'fly' with his superiors, Jambier and Marchandot, but that he'll bring Grandgil over to Jambier's house anyway, so that Grandgil can discuss the matter with Jambier, personally. When Grandgil meets Jambier, Jambier is immediately suspicious of Grandgil, a man upon whom he's never laid eyes before in his entire life, and Marcel now talks Grandgil up to the pig-man: "My new friend here, Mr. Grandgil, says he will help me to transport the pork, but only for one thousand francs—one thousand for him and another thousand for me."

As soon as Grandgil sees the huge stockpile of purloined goods (alcohol, expensive foods) all around Jambier's basement, he immediately and boisterously ups his price, even more than he already has and, very regally, he cries out, "I will absolutely transport the pork for you, Mr. Jambier… for only *two* thousand francs!" Jambier knows that if he doesn't give this guy, whom he doesn't know from Adam, whatever he wants, the guy might narc him out to the Gestapo (these are 'the times that try men's souls,' so you can't trust anybody), and he then proceeds to *freak-out* (the 'well-timed freak-out' is comedian De Funes' métier): "Mr. Grandgil, sir, I will not be grifted by you!" While you can't fight city hall, you sure can blackmail it, though: Grandgil now gets a sweetly malicious glint in his eye and says, "Okay, well, then, in that case, I guess I'll have to tell the cops about all the stuff you've got down here—all of this booze, soap, coal, and meat. Did you know that you're not supposed to have this?" Mrs. Jambier takes her husband aside, and tells him not to worry, because this Grandgil character—she thinks!—doesn't know any personal information about him, nor about the clandestine operations which they've got going down in their basement, but the punchline to the scene is that, of course, Grandgil already knows everything there is to know, and more: "I know that you are Jambier of Poiveau Street, and I will tell the police everything that I have just seen down here, unless you will agree to pay me the sum of *five* thousand francs!" (When Grandgil utters the number 'five,' Jambier almost has a coronary, right there on the spot!)

Jambier next agrees to pay Grandgil and Marcel whatever they want, at such time as the two men should deliver the pork to Marchandot, and obviously, he's saying it just to get this con-artist off his back. Marcel and Grandgil then pick up the four suitcases—two, each—and begin hefting them across the streets of Paris, which are lit only by streetlamps: Three-quarters of the film involves Gabin's and Bourvil's characters, as they drag the suitcases-full-of-pork, by night, and the picture's director of photography, Jacques Natteau, does a stellar job of making the streets look great: In *Traversee de Paris,* the city streets are shrouded in jet-black darkness, and are lit only by the tiniest pinpoints of light which emanate from rows of carefully-placed street lamps and, needless to say, it looks very cool. Every once in awhile, some Gestapo officers march by, and Grandgil and Marcel are forced to duck into alleyways, to hide.

After they've been walking only for a few blocks, Grandgil and Marcel are already thirsty, so they head into a local bar, plopping their suitcases down loudly. Because it's cold outside, Grandgil loudly orders the owners to bring him a glass of hot wine, and the few assembled customers start to wonder aloud about the contents of the two guys' suitcases, one lady-customer even mumbling that she "smells pork." The bar's elderly husband-and-wife proprietors, Lucienne and Alfred Couronne, who are played by Georgette Anys and Jean Dunot, start freaking, because they know that if the cops come in and see pork, they're going to be the ones who get arrested (not Marcel and Grandgil), and Lucienne whispers to her husband that they should take the pre-emptive strike, and call the cops. When Grandgil hears her say this, though, he flies into one of the mightiest and most hilarious Gabin-Outbursts in the entire history of Gabin movies, raging at the proprietors that they are "scum," and that if they're thinking about ratting him and Marcel out to the Gestapo, that he will tell the cops that they are "using a Jewess as a drudge:" Grandgil, because 'Jean Gabin sees all,' has already lifted back the simple curtain which separates the bar from the kitchen, revealing an emaciated young Jewish woman, who is washing glasses for the bar-owners as *an unpaid slave* (and she's even wearing a yellow star on her tunic). "You people are filthy," Grandgil yells at the Couronnes. "I hate you both, and I obliterate you from my memory!" Grandgil and Marcel leave, without having consumed the hot wine which Grandgil wanted, and only after having freaked out all of the customers. Grandgil is so scary, that the Couronnes were too frightened to call the Gestapo on them, obviously worried that, if they did, fiery Grandgil might come back and trash the place!

As Grandgil and Marcel continue walking across Paris, a pack of dogs starts following them, because the mutts have gotten a scent of the pork which is coming from the suitcases. Thinking on-the-fly, Grandgil throws a little piece of pork into the gated courtyard of an apartment building, the dogs run in, and he slams the gate shut, behind them. Marcel doesn't like the fact that Grandgil's wasting the profits like that but, of course, he doesn't say anything about it, because it's readily clear to him that Grandgil wears the pants in this ad-hoc—or should I say, '*ad ham-hock!*'—relationship. As they continue to walk, Marcel now informs Grandgil that they are passing his own apartment building, and Grandgil asks him if he wants to stop in and see if his 'lobster' is home, and here, he's referencing Marcel's wife: Yes, Grandgil is so cool, he actually calls women *lobsters!*

And just as the two men are about to enter Marcel's apartment building, air-raid sirens blast, and they now hide in the courtyard of another building, along with a Hooker (Anne Carrere), a young woman who believes our two friends to be *parachutists,* because she thinks that they've got parachutes in their suitcases. When the air-raid is over, the two men head over, not to Marcel's house, but to Grandgil's, and the surprise that director Autant-Lara is giving us here, is that Grandgil really isn't an impoverished con artist at all, but that he's actually a fabulously wealthy artist, a painter who, judging from his ritzy digs which are covered from floor-to-wall with his own artwork (his paintings and his sculptures), doesn't need the money which he's going to be getting from transporting the pigmeat, at all. Marcel is confused, and asks Grandgil why he would accept a job which he doesn't really need, and Grandgil just Gabin-Shrugs, responding that he accepted the job to alleviate his *ennui,* and Marcel is flabbergasted: "Gee, Grandgil, when you said you were a painter, I thought you meant that you were a housepainter." Grandgil fixes his new friend, with whom he genuinely gets along (and we sense that there aren't many), a cup of coffee.

After their coffee break, the two men continue their overnight constitutional, finally arriving at the apartment of the 'pig-fence' Marchandot, who's played by Robert Arnoux, and just as Grandgil and Marcel are about to ring Marchandot's doorbell, two officers of the Gestapo are immediately upon them, arresting not only them, but also Marchandot, and even Mrs. Marchandot (Myno Burney).

The Gestapo-guys take Marcel, Grandgil, and the Marchandots over to the temporary police station which they've organized in an ornate, Louis XV-style mansion, and they're all suddenly thrown into a room with a lot of other Frenchmen (and French women) who have also been arrested, and probably for no good reason.

The Commandant of the Gestapo, who's played by Harald Wolf, recognizes Grandgil and, not only that, he's excited that Grandgil has just turned up in his makeshift police station: "I'm a great fan of your work, Mr. Grandgil. It's a great honor to have you with us tonight! My cousin in Cologne has one of your paintings. But I wonder: What is it that would inspire a wealthy guy like you to get into black marketing?" Sucking up to the Commandant, Grandgil, who's a master of self-preservation, self-deprecatingly chuckles, "Well, I guess, inside every Frenchman is a *pig* waiting to get out!" The Commandant allows Grandgil to go free, but Marcel will not be so lucky: Marcel gets thrown onto a Nazi transport truck with some of the other accused-criminals, all of whom are now, right in front of our eyes, being carted away to a concentration camp. Grandgil looks really angry when he sees his new friend Marcel being dragged away, and he now appeals to the Commandant to set Marcel free, but sadly, it's *no-go,* and as the truck vanishes into the darkness, director Autant-Lara lingers on the truck's license plate for a full two minutes: We think that the license plate number is going to have some significance to the story, since it's on the screen for such a long time, but weirdly, it does not.

Cut to 1952 (nine years later): WWII has now been over for seven years, and the formerly-Occupying Germans are now mostly just an unpleasant memory, in Paris. Grandgil is at the

Gare du Nord, running to catch a train, with his suitcase in hand, and there's no pork in this suitcase—only a few changes of clothes—because, presumably, he's going on vacation. Just after he's boarded the train out of Paris, he's shocked, when he looks out of the window and sees Marcel, upon whom he hasn't laid eyes in nine years. Marcel's now a porter at the train station, and Grandgil asks him, "Do you remember me?" But Marcel is different now: Whereas he used to be sharp and intelligent when Grandgil used to know him nine years earlier, he is now hollow-eyed: Obviously, even though the film doesn't state this directly, something horrible has happened to him (either physically, emotionally, or both) in the German concentration camp. Marcel just smiles at Grandgil, and this comedy ends, surprisingly, with a supremely poignant, and quietly powerful, moment.

> GRANDGIL: Hello, my friend! Do you remember me?
> MARCEL: [Not remembering Grandgil, but wanting to make him feel good]: No… oh… yeah… I think so. Uh… hi!

The film's final sequence is sad, but the film as a whole is fun and uplifting, and we come out of the experience of having seen it, knowing that we have just seen one of Jean Gabin's very best movies, not to mention one of the best filmed comedies ever made, anywhere in the world. After a six year period in the 1950s, during which Jean Gabin seemed to be making the same '*bourgeois* relationship drama' over and over, it's great to see him rejuvenate himself here, with such high-quality material. Not only did the film win the *Prix Melies* in 1957, but additionally, Gabin took home the Best Actor award at the British Academy Awards (the BAFTA's), and he even won it over Henry Fonda, who was nominated for *Twelve Angry Men*. Gabin's *Traversee de Paris* co-star, the great Bourvil (his full name was Andre Bourvil but, like a lot of the other French actors and film technicians from decades ago, he was billed only by his last name) won the Best Actor Prize at that year's Venice Film Festival for his funny and ultimately heart breaking role of Marcel.

Author Marcel Ayme, who wrote the novel upon which this film was based, controlled the film rights, and initially, he scoffed at director Autant-Lara's offering Bourvil the role, because he knew that the role of 'Marcel' called for an actor who could really carry off that important dramatic bit at the end, and up to that time, Bourvil had been known to moviegoers only as a broad comedian; but when Ayme saw the finished film, he knew (as we, the audience know, when we're watching this movie today) that the director had made the correct decision. After *La Traversee de Paris,* Bourvil would appear in both comedies and dramas, and when he died in 1970, at the age of 53 (of Kahn's Disease, an especially pernicious form of bone-marrow cancer), he would be recognized in his obituaries, not just as one of France's finest comedians, but also, as one of the nation's best serious actors, as well.

After *La Traversee de Paris,* Jean Gabin would have six more great comedies to come, comedies in which, just like in this one, he'll be deflating people's pretensions, by being loud, instead of being his usual, 'quiet and reserved.' These comedies, are *Archimede, le clochard*

(1959), *Les vieux de la vieille* (1959), *Le Baron de l'ecluse* (1960), *Le Gentleman d'Epsom* (1963), *Monsieur* (1964), and *Le Drapeau noir flotte sur la marmite* (1971). These are all wonderful pictures, and each one continues to be unknown, at least at the time of this book's printing, in the United States.

Fun-Fact #1: Today, in France, when people of a certain age get mad at each other (or, should I say, 'mock-mad'), they shake their fists at each other and yell-out, "Jambier!" which is a direct reference to what Jean Gabin's character often screams-out, in this movie. In France, Gabin's catch-phrase from this movie has passed into the lexicon, just as Clint Eastwood's famous "Go ahead, make my day" has done, in America.

Fun-Fact #2: A street is named after author Marcel Ayme in Paris, and you can tell you're in the right place, because the wall has a giant Ayme head/bust, sculpted by Jean Marais, jutting out of it. Marais, additionally, crafted the sculpture of Jean Gabin which, today, guards the Gabin Museum, in Meriel.

Fun-Fact #3: In 1960, Bourvil (but not Jean Gabin) would re-team with *Traversee de Paris's* director Claude Autant-Lara and co-scenarist Jean Aurenche, for the film *Le Jument verte (The Green Mare)*, a film set in the mid 1700s, which was apparently the inspiration for the better-known film, *Tom Jones*. *Jument* reportedly shocked French audiences, because there's a scene in the picture in which a woman lifts up her skirts to take a pee, and France's version of the American Catholic Legion of Decency tried, unsuccessfully, to ban the whole picture. *Traversee de Paris's* credited screenwriters, Jean Aurenche and Pierre Bost, will also write the script for another Jean Gabin movie, 1958's *En cas de malheur*, which will co-star Gabin along with Brigitte Bardot.

Fun-Fact #4: Among the other awards which it received, this film was also nominated for the Golden Lion (the Best Picture Award) at the Venice Film Festival. Additionally, it won France's Syndicated Critics Award, in 1956.

What a Critic Said at the Time: "Offbeat! Garners enough yocks to make this 'in' for pop-value [but] the tacked-on ending could be dispensed with, to tighten up the film. Jean Gabin turns in some good scenes when he is venting his spleen at crassness and stupidity." (*Variety*, 9-19-56. Critic: "Mosk. [George Moskowitz.]" Reviewed at the Venice Film Festival.)

What Another Critic Said at the Time: "Jean Gabin seems to be enjoying every minute of it. The film moves at a fast clip… Unusual and interesting." (New York *Times*, 9-5-57 issue. Critic: A.H. Weiler.)

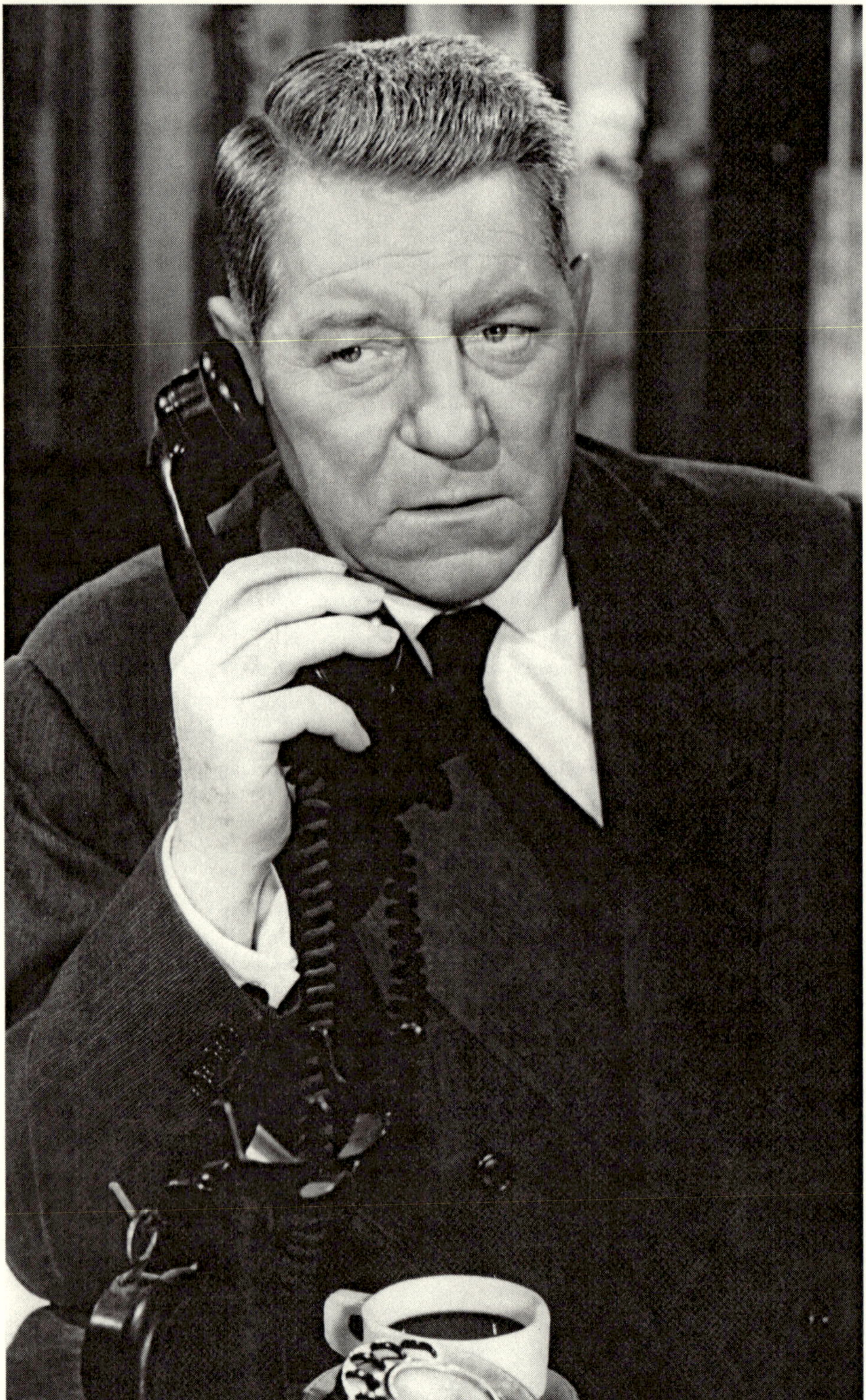

FILM 59

CRIME ET CHATIMENT

France, 1956

(Literal English Translation: "CRIME AND PUNISHMENT") Directed by Georges Lampin. Produced by Jules Borkon. Screenplay by Charles Spaak. Based Upon the Novel by Fyodor Dostoyevsky. Director of Photography (black and white), Claude Renoir. Editor, Emma Le Chanois. Music by Maruice Thiriet. Production Designer, Paul Bertrand. (GENRE: SUSPENSE) Running Time, 1 hour 47 minutes. A Champs-Elysees Production. Released in France on December 4, 1956, by Pathe-Consortium Cinema. Released in the United States with English subtitles as "THE MOST DANGEROUS SIN" on September 15, 1958, by Kingsley International Pictures, Inc.

> "Two things are for certain in this life. One, is that I'm disgusting.
> Two, is that I love you!"
> — *An old, fat nebbish crassly hits on young flesh, in "Crime et chatiment"*

Just when we thought *Le Sang a la tete*, *Fille dangereuse*, *Bebe Donge*, and *Victor* were the most uninvolving Gabin efforts of the 1950s, we're now going to get one that even manages to be slower, and even more ponderous and tedious, than those films: Here's another film in which we're not sure what the characters want, or even if they want anything at all, and a film which offers very little in the way of drama. It's screenwriter Charles Spaak's strange, slow-moving, contemporarily-set redux of Dostoevsky's legendary 1866 novel, *Crime and Punishment* (or, if you speak Russian: *Prestuplenie I Nakazanie*), directed by George Lampin who, with this film, will be directing Jean Gabin for the one-and-only time in both of their careers—and it's not too hard to see why. (Here's a hint: ZZZZZ!)

Rene Poinel, who's played by the handsome, dark-haired, French-Iraqi leading man Robert Hossein, who continues to make movies to this very day, is our film's version of Dostoevsky's Raskolnikov, the guy who, as we all remember from 12th grade Literature class, kills an old lady-pawnbroker, and then sits around, acting paranoid and waiting to get caught. As the film opens, Rene's angry, because his beautiful sister Nicole (Ulla Jacobson), who's otherwise a very smart girl, is about to get married—and for money only—to a rich, balding *nebbish* by the name of Antoine, who's played by Bernard Blier (who, in this film, is making his first featured role in a Jean Gabin picture, although he can be glimpsed briefly as 'a guy in the crowd who yells up to the attic apartment-bound killer Jean Gabin,' in 1939's *Le Jour se leve*, and he also turned up as a chauffeur, in 1937's *Le Messager*). Bernard Blier's son, Bertrand Blier, is more known in the United States than is his father, principally because Blier, the Younger directed a 1978 flick called *Preparez vos mouchoirs*—or in English, *Get Out Your Handkerchiefs*—which was a major hit, in U.S. art houses). The Poinel family is dirt-poor (they *wish* they could afford dirt), so Nicole and Rene's mom, Mrs. Poinel (Gaby Morlay), is happy to allow her daughter's wedding to the rich man, even though, decidedly, he's no Tom Cruise. Rene even confronts Antoine about how unsavory he finds the whole arrangement to be: "Look, I know you gave my mother twenty-thousand francs to enter our family. Well, I'm returning it to you. You are not welcome in our family, and I never want to see you again. So get lost!"

It's hard for Rene to have given back that much money, especially since he, his mom, and his sister are so poor, so to make it up to them, he goes to the apartment of an elderly loan shark, Mrs. Orvet (Gabrielle Fontan), and borrows one hundred-eighty francs, to tide his mom and his sister over until one of them can get a job. As collateral, Rene leaves his watch, and Mrs. Orvet tells him that if he doesn't pay the loan back in ninety days, the watch, which happens to be an old Poinel family heirloom, will belong to her. During this scene, humorously, it's hard for Rene and Mrs. Orvet to communicate, because she's filled her apartment up with some really noisy songbirds, who trill like the dickens, non-stop.

Frustrated about how shitty life is, Rene next heads over to a bar, where the bartender Gustave (Lino Ventura, *Razzia sur la chnouf*'s own 'Le Catalan') is holding-court. An aged barfly, Pierre Marcellin, who's played by Julien Carette (he played 'Cartier,' the singing P.O.W. in *La Grande illusion*, and he was also Gabin's co-engineer in *La Bete humaine*, and the 'toxic' Santini in *Pour l'amour du ciel*), is on-site, and he's regaling Rene with a sob story about how his consumptive wife ("she coughs up blood") and his two young daughters have just tossed him out on his ass, for being a drunken n'er-do-well. Pierre is really pathetic and, when we meet him, he's going around the bar, asking everybody to pour some of their wine into his glass, and he's promising all of the bar's patrons that God will smile on them, if they give him a taste of whatever it is that they're sucking down. Rene takes pity on Pierre, whose life is even worse than his own, and when Pierre asks Rene to escort him home, to explain to Pierre's wife, from his position as an objective innocent-bystander, that her husband is actually a good man, but one who has a disease (alcoholism), Rene is only too happy to oblige him. As the two men traverse the staircase-of-broken-dreams which leads up to Pierre's decrepit old flat, Pierre tells Rene that he not only has two small daughters by his physically-sick wife, but that he also has a seventeen-year-old daughter by his previous marriage, Lillie (Marina Vlady), who sells her body down by the harbor. (Talk about dysfunctional families!) Pierre confesses to Rene, "Not only am I a bad husband to my current wife, and a terrible father to my little daughters, but I did a terrible thing to my older daughter, Lillie: She came home with three thousand francs [from turning a trick], and I took her money away. Then,

1954 — 1976 | 139

when it happened again, I took the money again—and all because I am always thirsty! Do you think God will forgive a drunkard?"

As soon as Rene and Pierre enter the house, Pierre's wife Therese (Yvette Etievant, who played 'trucker-Gabin's' long-suffering wife, in *Des gens sans importance*) starts screaming at her tanked-up hubby: "Did you bring us something home to eat, or were you out drinking our money away again?" She keeps yelling at him too, and right in front of their two young kids: "Look at your lush-of-a-father," Therese cries, "he's a piece of trash! He'll be the cause of my death! He's a monster, a grub. One day, he'll come home and we'll all be dead!" Therese, prior to marrying Pierre, as we're now going to be finding out, was previously married to a military man who abandoned her—and not just because she's such a shrew, either: Her first husband, as she's now telling Rene (who hasn't even asked) was actually gay; and after Therese gets all of this information off of her voluminous chest, her rage dissipates, and she apologizes to her husband for the fact that she's just chewed him out: "Look, just don't leave us again, okay?!"

Rene sees the wretched family, a family which is even poorer than his own, and feels so badly for how they live that, on his way out, he leaves the one hundred and eighty francs which he's just borrowed from Mrs. Orvet on the table for them. Pierre walks Rene outside, to thank him for bringing him home ("See how my wife talks about me? I told you!"), and leans over the banister to say goodbye to the younger man: In fact, he leans over so far, that he plummets to the ground, dying instantly. Remember how, only moments ago, Pierre asked Rene if God could ever forgive a drunk? Well, the Good Lord has just given Rene His very decisive answer!

Before Rene goes home, he decides to make a stop down by the waterway, to find Pierre's hooker-daughter, Lillie. Obviously, his stated goal is to tell her that he's a friend of her father's and, more importantly, to tell her that her *daddy-o's* just kicked the bucket, but he's also obviously intrigued by the fact that she sells her ass—and apparently, at competitive rates! When Rene meets Lillie, he likes what he sees, but he reigns it in, and gives her the news which he's shown up to make known to her: "Miss Lillie? My name is Rene. I met your father tonight. He just died. I met his wife, too, as well as your little sister and brother." Lillie, who has become estranged from her parents only recently (after her dad grabbed her earnings) thanks him for the news, and not only is she not emotional about losing her father, but we can tell, from the way she's checking Rene out, that she thinks that he's as hot as he thinks *she* is!

When Rene arrives home to his own home, he thinks he's already endured enough drama for one day, but he's just going to have to go through a little more: *Nebbishy* Antoine, his sister's goofy suitor is, even in spite of the warning which Rene has given him to "never show his face again," present again, and Rene gives him the good verbal going-over that the guy truly deserves. ("Stay away from my sister! You're pathetic! And worse—you're ancient!") Meanwhile, of course, Rene and Nicole's mother, Mrs. Poinel, is furious with her son, for having returned Antoine's gift money back to him. (While it's not said in the film, Mrs. Poinel is no better than drunken old Mr. Marcellin. [The role of parents, this pessimistic movie seems to say, is *to sell their kids!*])

About a week later, Rene goes back to Mrs. Orvet's apartment to get his watch, and then, for absolutely no reason given in the film, he stabs her to death, even though personally, she never did anything to merit it, nor did he have any antipathy toward her. (She was just "in the wrong place, at the wrong time.")

This 'murder of an old-lady pawnbroker' is what happens in Dostoevsky's novel, and here it is in this film, as well. And even though the Old Lady Murder is the cornerstone upon which the novel is built, it doesn't work in this particular film adaptation: Back in '12th grade lit,' which is when most of us were exposed to the novel, we believed that the main character, Raskolnikov, had been sufficiently beaten down by life, to the point where he could kill somebody just to alleviate the boredom of his life. But in the movie, when Rene (a/k/a, 'the 20th-century Raskolnikov) kills an old lady-pawnbroker, it doesn't work, because the film hasn't shown Rene as being angry enough to have killed anybody at all. (Yes, Rene is frustrated because his family is poor, and because his sister might have to marry a creep to pull them out of their financial straits, but the film doesn't present him as being angry enough to have killed anybody; in fact, the screenwriters really screwed up, because they should have figured out that, 'how it happened in the Dostoevsky novel' notwithstanding, it would have made more sense, as far as this film is concerned, for Rene to have killed Antoine instead of Mrs. Orvet, since Antoine is the one that Rene doesn't like.)

Rene can't find any money in Mrs. Orvet's house, so he just steals some cheap costume jewelry of hers which he knows is worthless, so that the cops will think that the bad guy was some robber who had a motive for the murder—in other words, that the murder wasn't committed arbitrarily. (Woody Allen copied this conceit of Dostoevesky's in his 2005 drama, *Match Point*.) He leaves from the rooms without being seen, and the building's Landlord (Jacques Hilling) enters the room, shortly after he's left, and just in time to see the puddle of the old lady's blood which happens to be spilling out of the doorway, and flooding the hallway. Shortly thereafter, Rene, who feels guilty about what he did today, and who doesn't want anybody to see him, runs to the pier where he is immediately accosted by Lillie, Pierre-the-Drunk's prostitute daughter. She thanks him, because she knows he's the one who gave her family the one hundred and eighty francs.

So now, we've got a murderer (Rene) and a crime (murder), and forty-five minutes into the movie, we're finally going to be meeting, for the very first time, the police inspector who's job it will be, to try and solve the case—Jean Gabin's Inspector Gaillet; Gabin, who was now once again France's #1 box office draw, due to the recent success of Becker's *Touchez pas au grisbi*, was obviously added into the cast to bolster the film's French box-office appeal, since he has what only amounts to a supporting part.

Gaillet enters Gustave's (Lino Ventura's) bar for a Pastis, and mentions that he's in this part of town to investigate Mrs. Orvet's murder, and as good-fortune—or bad-fortune—has it, Rene, the old lady's killer, happens to be in the bar, as well: He's dining at a table alone, and reading about the murder which he himself has committed, in the evening's newspaper, and something which he's now reading, gives him a shock: While he had been unable to find anything of true value in her apartment when he was killing her, he looks suddenly flustered, because he's now discovering for the first time, through the article, that the old lady actually had ten million francs hidden beneath her mattress, which he didn't find!

Rene is relieved to see Gaillet—a real, live policeman: He looks incredibly guilty, and it's obvious that he wants to turn himself in to free his conscience although, at the same time, he also looks really freaked-out about doing it. So he starts, in a very roundabout way, talking (to another customer, *loudly,* so that Gaillet can hear) about some very specific details of the murder which weren't in the newspaper, details of which only Mrs. Orvet's true killer would have been apprised. In this not-so-indirect way, Rene's trying to let Gaillet know that he's the guilty party, but Gaillet is, by dint of his profession, a very intuitive guy, and whispers to barman Gustave that he knows what Rene is up to: Gaillet tells Gustave that he thinks Rene is one of those crazy people (*oh, yeah, we've still got 'em!*) who want to turn themselves in for crimes which other people have committed because, on some weird psychological level, they feel inadequate, and want to take on the whole world's guilt as their own. Amused by Rene's weird behavior, Gaillet corners him: "Young man, why are you trying to incriminate yourself, when you're not a murderer?" Suddenly though, their conversation is interrupted by a phone call for Gaillet: It's Gaillet's colleague, Inspector Renaud (Rene Havard), who's letting Gaillet know that Mrs. Orvet's real killer has just been arrested. We, the audience, having actually witnessed Rene in the act of killing the old lady, already know that the cops have the wrong guy, even if the Inspector, at this point, does not.

When Gaillet arrives at the police station, a bunch of cops are interrogating the guy whom they have arrested, erroneously, for the murder: It's Mrs. Orvet's Landlord, the guy who saw the blood seeping out of her apartment, and who reported it to the cops. "You were seen leaving the building, and talking to the concierge," Detective Renaud offers accusingly, and we know this is true, because we saw it. Gaillet tells the Landlord and Havard that, just now, on the way over to the station, he stopped over at the Orvet crime scene and did a little reconnaissance mission, checking things out for himself, and that one thing he did while he was there, was to remove the old lady's songbirds. ("If they could talk, instead of just singing," Gaillet 'Gabin-Shrugs,' his thoughts trailing-off into the ether.)

The next day, both Inspector Gaillet and Rene are back in Gustave's bar, and Rene is once again trying to incriminate himself, telling Gaillet that he knew Mrs. Orvet personally, and Gaillet tries to sympathize: "Look, kid. I know you weren't there when the old lady was killed, and that the killer was that Landlord. But I'm glad you're here, just the same, because I wanted to ask you about something: When I was in the old lady's apartment yesterday, I found this invoice, stating that she had acquired a wristwatch which belongs to you. But I couldn't find any watches there at all, and I believe that when the landlord killed the lady, he also stole your watch." (Wait: Gaillet's a smart cop. Does he really know that Rene did it, and he's just telling Rene all of this crazy stuff in order to get Rene to confess? [Yeah! That must be what he's doing!])

That night in private, *nebbishy* old Antoine, who both is and *isn't* as dumb as he looks, asks Rene, off the record, if it was he who killed the old lady since, from prior conversations which the two men have had together, Antoine knows that Rene sometimes goes over to Orvet's apartment to pawn things whenever he needs extra money, and he knows that Rene is always pretty volatile, and even more so than most other angry young men. Rene's excited that somebody wants to hear him confess, even if it is the *uber-creepy nerd* who's drooling away for his sister, and so, 'confess, he does:' "Yes, I did it! I killed Mrs. Orvet! I'm sick!" While Antoine believes what Rene's just told him, we also know, just the same, that he won't be turning Rene in, because Antoine really feels like he needs Rene to give his okay, so that he can marry Nicole. (Since Nicole and Rene's father is dead, big brother Rene has taken on the father mantle, as far as raising Nicole is concerned.) What follows Rene's sudden confession to Antoine, is one of the film's few really interesting moments: Antoine incorrectly interprets the confession which Rene has just made to him as Rene's way of trying to bond with him, and so, in return, he tells Rene a secret about himself, and one which Rene didn't even ask for: "You know Rene, it's not just you who is in trouble. I have a problem, too. I love young girls—like, for example, your sister. And with each passing year, I need them to be younger and younger! I'm proud of being disgusting!" (Rene's horrified expression says it all, but mostly, it says, "*Check, please!*" [In 1939's *Crime and Punishment*-like *Le Jour se leve*, Jules Berry's Valentin character makes pretty much the same exact speech in praise of young girls, exclaiming, "I love youth!"]) Antoine tells Rene that he should probably think about leaving for Switzerland, because it's a great and neutral place to go, whenever one thinks that the cops are coming to apprehend 'one.'

In a plot twist which was not found in the Dostoevsky novel, Antoine now tells Rene a second secret about himself, and this one is a little more disturbing than the fact that he digs teens: "I helped with my first wife's suicide so that I would be free to marry your sister!" (In this movie, everybody has something that he wants to confess and, in that way, it's just like life. *Don't you, 'my esteemed Reader,' have stuff that you wish you could tell your friends and family about yourself, but that you just can't, because it would mean a one way ticket to the sexual-addiction clinic… I mean, 'the funny farm…!'* [I do! Or: Do I…?!])

While Nicole isn't into Antoine romantically, there *is* a guy in the movie whom she does like: It's her brother Rene's handsome friend Jean (Gerard Blain), an up-and-coming (definition: *currently starving*) young crime novelist. If anything, though, Nicole's a realist, and she realizes that to keep her family from starving, ultimately (and although it is going to make her totally nauseous), she might have to suck it up, and marry the creepily-persistent Antoine.

That night, Nicole, Rene, and Rene's handsome novelist pal Jean all attend a fancy outdoor dance together, and when they get there, they see that Antoine's there as well, and that he's dancing with an eighteen-year-old girl (a girl whose character, in the movie's credits, is billed very economically as, 'Girl at the Dance'), and she's played by Marie-Jose Nat. Antoine leaves the girl for a minute, takes Nicole off into a corner, and tells her that Rene is the one who killed Orvet: "I'm telling you this, because I'm scared for you and your mother. If the police come, I don't want them to put you through anything." She doesn't believe him though, and not getting flustered at all by what he's just told her, she goes off to dance with Jean, right in front of him, and obviously she's doing this to hurt Antoine—but of course, it just makes him want her all the more, since we all want what we can't have.

Later that night, Rene meets Marcellin's (the drunk who died in the first act) prostitute-daughter Lillie by the harbor, and confesses to her, just as he had earlier also confessed to Gaillet and to Antoine, that he's the guy who killed Mrs. Orvet. He tells her he's scared, because he knows that the police will probably be looking for him soon, and that he doesn't know where to go; so naturally, she invites him up to her place.

The next day, Nicole is horrified when Antoine visits her at the Poinel house, and tells her what Rene has just told him, which is that Rene was Mrs. Orvet's murderer: *In Andre's bizarre mind*, he feels that sharing this private information with her will make them closer, although really, it just makes her even more creeped-out by Antoine than she already is. She tells Antoine to get out and to never see her again, and even though this is the wrong moment, he now makes another plea for her to marry him. She tells him that she would never consent to be with him, even if he was the last man on earth, and then, melodramatically, he asks her to kill him, or else just to leave the room, so that he can do it, himself; but she just kicks him out, more tired than ever of all of his bullshit.

A few hours later, though, Antoine now decides that, even more fun than killing himself, would be killing Rene, since Rene has been *cock-blocking* all of his attempts to get Nicole, since day-one. Antoine heads up to Rene's apartment (he doesn't live at home with his mom and sister [he just hangs out there, a lot]), and the note taped to his front door cryptically reads, "You are too late." Antoine thinks, as we do as well, that Rene's killed himself, and his idea that this may have happened is confirmed when he busts the door down and sees a straight razor lying out, on top of the dresser, but Rene, as it turns out, is just lying on his bed awake, and looking like he's feeling more guilty than ever about his murder of Mrs. Orvet. (Obviously, he wanted to cut his own throat, or slit his wrists, but was unable to go through with it.) Anyway, Rene and Antoine are now on a 'level playing-field,' because Rene and Antoine, each of whom murdered a different woman, are now both completely without hope. (Rene mutters, "We kill for nothing," and Antoine next mutters that, now that he's never going to have Nicole, his life is worthless.) Both men, it seems, are doomed (as we all are!) to loneliness and death.

Rene goes to see Gaillet, down at Gaillet's office at police headquarters, and tells him that he'd like to confess fully to the crime, and this is the moment that Gaillet, and we, have been waiting for, because this is the scene in which Gaillet will confirm that he's really known for the whole time that it really was Rene who was the killer, and not the Landlord. At this point, Gaillet poses a question to Rene, and one which we would probably ask Rene too, if we were cops: "There were other old ladies, Poinel. Why did you kill that one?" Rene can't answer the question though, and he leaves. He's come to sign the confession paper, but just isn't able to do it, and Gaillet can't take him in without the signed confession because, in the world of this movie, a cop can't arrest a criminal without a written confession, even if the cop has hard evidence that the person has committed the crime. (But here, screenwriter Charles Spaak is taking liberties, because that's not how it happens in actual French law: In France, as in the United States, a police officer can arrest a suspect, as long as the arresting officer has a reasonable suspicion that the 'arrest-ee' is the criminal; also in France, just as in the U.S., a suspect can be held for only forty-eight hours, at the end of which he must be arraigned before a Judge. If a French Judge can't find any hard evidence upon which to convict the suspect during that two-day period, the Judge alone, must make the decision to let the suspect go for good since, in France, juries always acquit whenever there isn't any hard evidence, and once the Judge lets the guy go, he can never be tried or re-arrested, even when new evidence presents itself, unlike how it's always been done in the Good Old U.S. of A.)

Meanwhile, Antoine, who's feeling dejected because he knows for sure that he'll never have Nicole, goes for a walk down by the harbor. He runs into Lillie (this meeting is just happening by sheer happenstance) whom he has never met, and tells her that he is the last person she will ever see: "I am going to end it all tonight. I am going to kill myself, because a woman I love doesn't love me back." He hands Lillie a big wad of cash—the five thousand francs which were rejected by Rene—and then runs out of frame and shoots himself. (We hear it, but don't see it.)

Lillie goes to the Poinel house to tell Rene about the money which Antoine has given her, having no idea that Rene already knows Antoine. Lillie says to Rene, "Look, if you're not willing to save the man who is in prison in your place (the Landlord), then at least save yourself. Come with me, and we'll get out of France!" He tells her, "No, I'll just stay here in my cage." (P.S: 'cage' = 'life.') Lillie tells him that he's going to have to choose between 'a lifetime of guilt over the murder of the old lady OR 'loving her.' (Rene is very obviously falling in love with her.) He goes and sees his Mom, telling her he's leaving France. She asks him if she's leaving for a job, and he's cryptic: "Some people might say that I did something, and I won't say whether I did or not. Anyway, don't listen to what people will say about me, even if it you read about it in the newspapers." We know that his guilt is now too much to bear, and that he's not really leaving the country with Lillie, but is actually on his way, finally, to see inspector Gaillet, to sign the written confession for which Gaillet had asked him. He says goodbye to his Mom, and is now ready to meet his fate, whatever it may bring.

Rene sulks into Gaillet's office, and tells him, "I've come here for two reasons. First, I've come to tell you that I hate cops, because they just exist to keep rich people happy, and to keep poor people without money. I've also come to sign the [written confession, stating] that I am the killer of Mrs. Orvet." After signing the confession, Rene looks like a great burden has been lifted, and Gaillet cuffs him, and Lillie's waiting outside for him in the anteroom, while he does it. (Confession to a policeman is almost, in the world of this film, like confession to a priest.) She's happy, knowing that his confession is complete, and crosses herself, with a little smile. Lillie really loves Rene—in fact, more than ever now—and the audience finally likes him, too (but only at the tail-end of the movie), because he's the only character in the entire movie who's not only done something honorable, but he's actually, *actively,* done something! While Doestoevsky's *Crime and Punishment* is one of the greatest novels ever written, the whole idea of 'somebody killing somebody, just because he feels unfulfilled or empty' doesn't really fly in most movies, unless they're really outstanding movies, because it's too abstract of an idea: Relatedly, Columbia Pictures took another stab (pun intended), at a contemporary version of Dostoevsky's story, twenty-one years before this one, back in 1935; it starred Peter Lorre who, in that picture, was making his first starring role in an American movie, and even that version wasn't too great. Jean Gabin is very good (and solid, and Gabinian) in his supporting role as the Inspector, but he's really just the film's voice of reason: He's not a main character, nor does he drive the engine of the plot; he just shows up, periodically, to try to get Rene to sign the confession, and you can see why Gabin would want to involve himself with a Dostoevsky adaptation (answer: for the prestige)—but why this one? In Gabin's 1939 Dostoevsky-like *Le Jour se leve,* which is more like Dostoevesky's novel of *Crime and Punishment* than is this actual *Crime and Punishment* adaptation, Gabin's character kills a guy and waits up in his attic bedroom for the authorities to come and get him, but Marcel Carne's *Le Jour se leve* is a great movie, whereas Georges Lampin's *Crime et chatiment* is not because, in the Carne movie, Gabin's character actually hates the person whose life he has taken whereas, in this picture, there is no bad blood at all between the killer and the 'kill-ee.' And so, in a way, *Le Jour se leve,* which is not a direct adaptation of Dostoevsky's *Crime and Punishment* and is only inspired by the novel's basic themes, is more *Crime and Punishment-*esque than is this movie, *Crime et chaitment,* which is a direct adaptation of the novel. So if you're aching to see a really great film adaptation of *Crime and Punishment* with Jean Gabin in it, see *Le Jour se leve,* instead.

Crime et chatiment was the eighth and final film which screenwriter Charles Spaak would write, which involved the participation of Jean Gabin, and it's the only one that's not great. (Spaak's seven great Gabin entries were *La Bandera; La Belle equipe, Les Bas-fonds, La Grande illusion, Le Recif de corail,* and *La Nuit est mon royaume.*)

What a Critic Said at the Time: "[This film] lacks deep character analysis, never invoking the suspense [it needs] to make it jell, filmically... Plods through its grim tale. Gabin is the policeman who breaks down the murderer's morale, doing it in his usual laconic manner." (*Variety,* 1-30-57 issue. Critic, "Mosk. [George Moskowitz.]" Reviewed in Paris.)
What Another Critic Said at the Time: [While Director Georges] Lampin and his cameraman, Claude Renoir, have done themselves proud, pictorially, this drama [is] beautifully photographed, but not stirring. [A] hero wrestling with his conscience doesn't constitute a very exciting sight, when his adversary is [only an abstract] 'sense of justice,' [as] symbolized by the laconic detective, played by Jean Gabin." (New York *Times,* 9-18-58 issue. Critic: Bosley Crowther.)

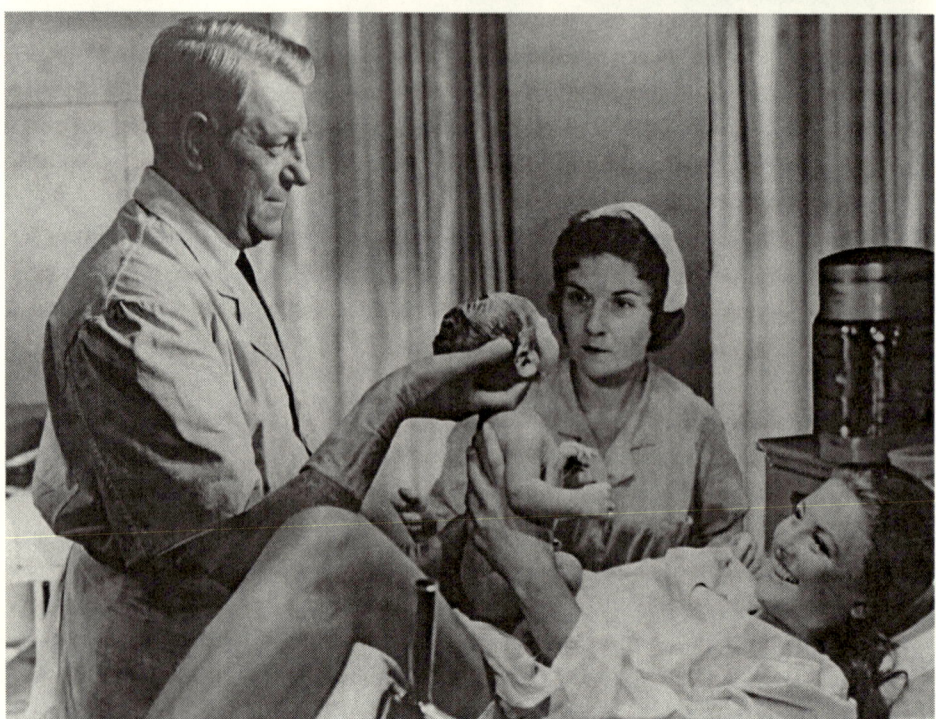

Top: Tragic drifter-as-small town gynecologist. Above: Nicole Courcel gives birth.

1954 — 1976 | 147

FILM 60

Le Cas du docteur Laurent

France/Spain, 1957

(Literal English Title/U.S. Release Title: "THE CASE OF DR. LAURENT") Directed by Jean-Paul Le Chanois. Written by Rene Barjavel and Jean-Paul Le Chanois. Produced by Ignace Morgenstern. Music by Joseph Kosma. Director of Photography, Henri Alekan. Editor, Emma Le Chanois. Production Designer, Serge Pimenoff. (GENRES: DRAMA/COMEDY) A Production of Cocinex S.L. (Spain) and Cocinor (France). Running Time, 1 hour 50 minutes. Released in France on April 3, 1957, by Cocinor. Released in U.S. with English Subtitles by Trans-Lux, on June 25, 1958.

> "The people in our town have no idea how to make love without having children. Please—you've got to help us!"
> — *Elderly rural doctor asks big city gynecologist Gabin for help in stopping an out-of-control childbirth epidemic, in "Le Cas du docteur Laurent"*

In 1957, Gabin will interrupt his spate of 'just o.k.' 1950s' melodramas, which he mixed with first-rate triumphs like *La Nuit est mon royaume, Le Plaisir, French Cancan*, and *La Traversee de Paris*, to star as big city M.D. Jean Laurent, in Jean Paul Le Chanois' beautifully-rendered 'dramedy' *Le Cas du docteur Laurent*, a film which would be released in a few U.S. art-house theatres as *The Case of Dr. Laurent*. There is much to like in it.

In *Laurent*, Gabin's middle-aged Paris obstetrician has come to the provincial mountain village of Martinet, in southern Brittany, having survived a scandal which will only be hinted-at one time in the picture, a scandal which has involved his own medical skills somehow being related to his wife's death, as well as his own nagging liver trouble, an infirmity which, although minor, will necessitate, as his own doctors have told him, "mountain air.")

The farming citizens of Martinet are cheerful people, although they're as backwards, and as back*woods*, as anybody in any of Al Capp's *L'il Abner* comic strips from the 1930s and '40s. The town's septuagenarian Doctor, elderly Dr. Bastid (Henri Arius), who fixes both the people of the town, as well as their animals, has summoned Dr. Laurent to the village, because of what he has actually termed to be the town's "epidemic of childbirth," which he has no idea how to contain! The simple townsfolk, who are completely unconversant in the ways of birth control, are churning out five and six kids per family and, as Bastid now tells Dr. Laurent, "The people in our town have no idea how to make love without having children. You've got to help us!" (It's very probable that the character name, 'Bastid,' is a play on 'bastard'—and God knows, lots of little bastards are being churned out, over in IUD-free Martinet.)

Laurent will now serve alongside Dr. Bastid in Bastid's suite of offices and, while at first, much of the citizenry is resistant to being treated by this 'new guy,' he soon begins the slow process of winning them all over with his warm, Gabinian charm—charm which works well on some people, and less well on others.

Even though Laurent has been summoned to the town to inform the masses about birth control, he takes his real pleasure in espousing an idea which was pretty new and revolutionary for the whole world, at the time this film was made, that of 'painless childbirth,' an idea which is in direct opposition to what many of the town's bitter and simple-minded old women have told the town's young women about how "pain in childbirth is a woman's duty."

Laurent's first patient is Catherine Loubet (Silvia Monfort, a waif-like blonde *doppelganger* of the great Swedish actress Ingrid Thulin, who starred in those Ingmar Bergman movies), whose builder husband, Andre (Michel Barbey), won't touch her, because he feels that her pregnancy (she's now on their second baby) has made her unclean. ("You repulse me now!" the cro-magnon-like Andre screams at Catherine, charging away from her, as fast as he can.) Dr. Laurent becomes an avuncular Dear Abby-figure to Catherine, advising her, in no uncertain terms, on how to deal with her squeamish mate.

Laurent also meets Francine (Nicole Courcel), a sweet-natured young Audrey Hepburn-clone who is, nevertheless, considered to be a pariah of the community, because she'll soon be dropping a whelp of her own, and (horror-of-horrors!) she's going to be having her baby out of wedlock! Laurent sees Francine's inherent goodness, and, as we notice from how he's checking her out, *her inherent hotness*, and so he takes her under his (estimable) wing.

The Good Doctor sets up a 'Painless Childbirth Lecture' at the small city hall, for the following evening, and invites everyone in town to come. His presentation is extremely underattended however, because most of the town's citizenry (and this is a very funny sequence) is ensconced at a local watering hole, salivating over a t.v. boxing match. The few who attend the conference—mostly elderly women, as well as some bored young guys-on-the-make, who think they're going to be hearing something *good-and-perverted*—are instantly intrigued by Laurent's idea that childbirth is not, in fact, a painful ordeal which women are meant to suffer alone, but that it's a joyous event which is to be shared, and even savored, by husbands and wives together. He tells the amazed crowd, which is starting to grow, now that the boxing match has ended that, with proper pre-natal care and breathing exercises, the experience can be a great one. While, at the beginning of the evening, many of the townspeople had regarded Laurent with suspicion, by the end of the night, almost everybody in the room has been won over, respecting him, and even welcoming his brave new ways.

While Laurent's fan base in the town is ever-growing, there is still a sizable contingent of people, led mostly by a group of the town's crotchety old drinkers, as well as jealous old Dr. Bastid, who remain strongly opposed to Laurent's newfangled medical ideas: "Sometimes, the old ideas are best," a mean old biddy barks at Laurent, storming out on his presentation. Bastid jealously decides to have Laurent investigated by the French Medical Association, with an eye toward having Laurent's medical license suspended.

Dr. Laurent is present at his own investigation, which takes place in the conference room of a nearby big-city hospital, and it's a terribly austere affair, in which he sits silently and expressionlessly, while ancient physicians from all over France are complaining about how horrible he is, for having introduced his 'weird' new methods to the world of medicine.

But then fate, as it only is in about five-to-ten percent of Jean Gabin's movies, decides to be kind, for a change: Young, unmarried Francine, parallel to Laurent's inquisition, is about to give birth, and she decides that, in lieu of giving birth at home, surrounded by cross old viragoes who would seem to take near-orgasmic delight in the physical pain of expectant mothers, she would rather have the baby right there, in the middle of Laurent's investigation proceedings, so that Laurent can physically demonstrate his new methods and prove to the assembled doctors (a/k/a, his inquisitors) what she already knows very well, which is that Laurent is a great doctor, not to mention a wonderful man.

To that end, Francine and a group of other young townswomen steal a bus (it belongs to one of their husbands) and high-tail it over to Laurent's hearing, and the women even sing a joyous song of female empowerment on the way to the hospital (it's one of this great film's many charming moments).

The picture has a cheerful wrap-up: Dr. Laurent helps Francine to give birth during his hearing (the Doctors retreat to an adjoining O.R., to watch it happen), everyone is impressed by his delivery of the baby, and Laurent remains in Martinet, where he'll now be the town's #1 Beloved Doctor, and the best news of all, is that the other doctor, creepy old Bastid, gets the axe.

Trans-Lux pictures, which also distributed Jean Gabin's picture *La Traversee de Paris* in the States, marketed *Docteur Laurent* in the U.S. very successfully, and it would become one of the few Gabin films from his later period which, by art-house standards, would turn a sizeable American profit, because Trans-Lux advertised the film in American newspaper ads on the merits of its live-birth scene, which occurs at the end of the picture. Because of this sequence (actress Nicole Courcel's head is intercut with the nether-regions of a real-life new mother who's popping-out a kid), Laurent was shown, in America, in skeevy 'adults-only theaters,' and mostly, in various big cities' skeezy tenderloin districts, although when you watch this movie now, fifty-some years after it was made, you immediately notice that the sequence is much less clinical than the scene in which Patricia Arquette gives birth in Sean Penn's excellent 1991 flick *The Indian Runner*, or even the sequence in which Katherine Heigl delivers, in the 2007 Judd Apatow comedy *Knocked Up* (or, for that matter, the 'that-was-way-waaay-more-info-than-I-wanted-to-know' birth scene, in experimental filmmaker Stan

150 | **THE FILMS** CYCLE FIVE

Brakhage's notorious 1975 documentary, *Window Water Baby Moving*, in which Brakhage's wife pops out 'a little Baby Brakhage' right on-screen, and the audience gets to see an opened-up placenta which looks, for all the world, like a wokful of meaty stir fry)!

What a Critic Said at the Time: "A courageous, controversial film that will profit, by word-of-mouth. Gabin makes a perfect doctor, what with his patient air of understanding, and his unruffled demeanor." (*Variety*, 7-2-58 issue. Critic: George Gilbert. Reviewed in New York.)

What Another Critic Said at the Time: "Boldly, intelligently, and tastefully, a new French film dramatizes an adamant plea for natural childbirth. [This is] a candid, commonsensical film which should absorb any adult spectator. It's a happy picture, and Jean Gabin performs with utter credibility, but [director] Jean-Paul Le Chanois rates the longest applause. The dialogue is consistently realistic and effective. A sensibly-wrought film." (New York *Times*, 6-3-58 issue. Critic: Howard Thompson.)

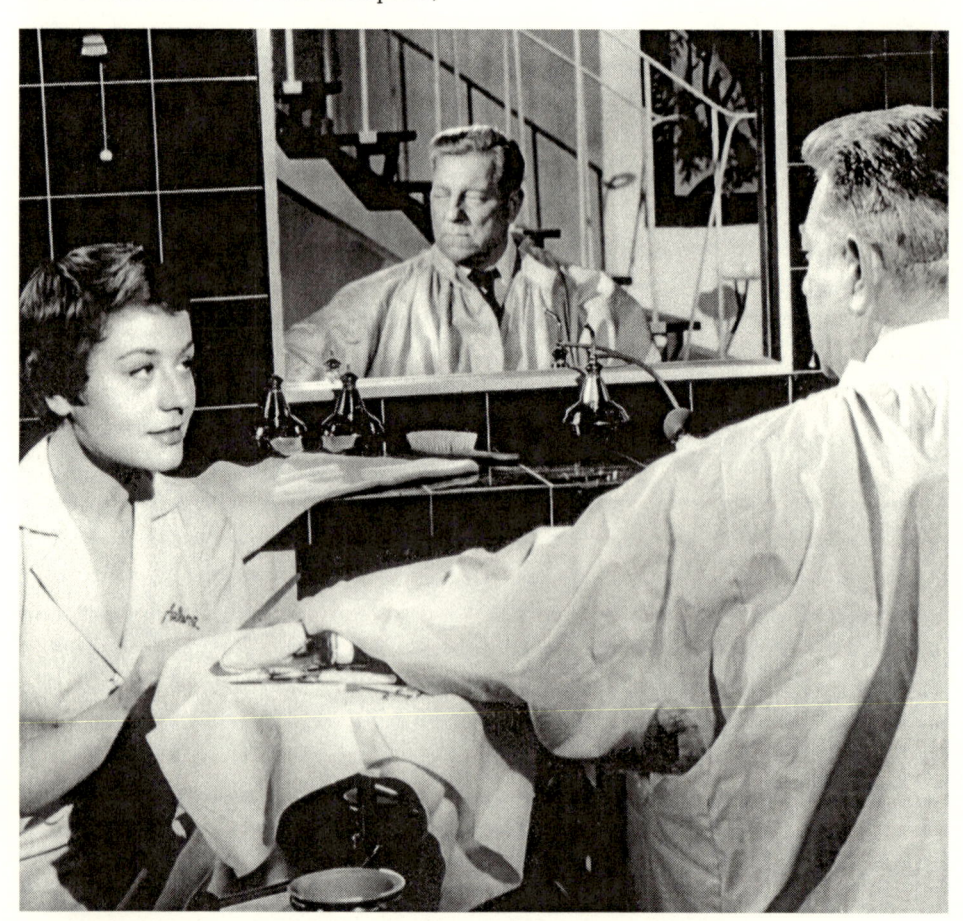

A manicure from Annie Girardot, in "La Rouge est mis" (Film 61, at right).

FILM 61

LE ROUGE EST MIS

France, 1957

(Approximate English Translation: "THE RED [LIGHT] IS PUT ON") Directed by Gilles Grangier. Produced by Jacques Bar and Alain Poire. Screenplay by Michel Audiard and Gilles Grangier. From the Novel by Auguste le Breton. Director of Photography (black and white), Louis Page. Editor, Christian Gaudin and Jacqueline Sadoul. Music by Denis Kiefer. Production Designed by Robert Clavel. First Assistant Director, Jacques Deray. (GENRE: SUSPENSE) A Production of Cite Films and Societe Nouvelle des Etablissements Gaumont. Running Time, 1 hour 35 minutes. Released in France by Gaumont, on April 12, 1957. Released in the United States on October 10, 1959, by UMPO (United Motion Picture Organization) with English Subtitles, as "SPEAKING OF MURDER."

"I don't know anything! Stop interrogating me!"
— *Gabin hates when cops give him the third degree, in "Le Rouge est mis"*

This extremely watchable crime pic, which was based, like *Razzia sur la chnouf*, on a novel by Auguste Le Breton, opens with a well-shot bank robbery: Pepito (Lino Ventura) and his two cohorts, elderly Joe, a/k/a 'Pops' (Lucien Raimbourg) and twentysomething Pierre (Jean-Pierre Mocky), rob a Paris bank and beat the crap out of everybody inside. Jean Gabin's *Louis le Blonde* (or, 'Louis the Blonde:' Gabin's white hair has been dyed blonde for the picture, which is the color that it actually *used* to be, when he was younger, in the 1930s) waits outside in the getaway car and, on the way out of the bank, Pops and Pierre quickly change the license plates, so that they won't get caught. Jo, Pierre, and driver Louis will each make two million francs (a few thousand dollars, in 1950s' old-francs) from the take, but Louis knows they can do much better: Clearly, he's more than just their driver.

Alfredo (Paul Frankeur) is the underboss of one of France's biggest criminal organizations, which means, of course, that there's a 'big boss' superceding him, whom we'll be meeting later in the film, and he's the guy who's commissioned Louis, 'Pops,' Pepito, and Pierre, who are freelance 'thieves-for-hire,' to perpetrate this job. (Louis and Pepito have nicknamed Pierre, '*Qu'est-ce qu'il Dit?*'—which in English means, 'What'd he Say?'—because that's the character's oft-repeated little catch-phrase in the movie: Apparently, Pierre earned this ridiculous nickname on a 'job' a long time ago, in which he, Pepito, Louis, and Pops were dealing with Americans, and Pierre didn't understand Word #1 of what they were saying.) Louis and Pepito visit Alfredo in his office and hand him the entirety of the day's take, expecting that he'll now be parceling-out their cuts from it, but Alfredo tells them that before he can do it, he'll first have to show the whole shebang to his own boss, Mimile, the company's #1 man/*capo-di-tutti-cappi*. Alfredo promises Louis and Pepito that, after Mimile's had the chance to examine the *grisbi*, and to liberate his own chunk out of it, that everybody else will get his rightfully-owed percentage; but the guys don't believe him, because this is the first time they've worked for Fredo and Mimile.

"How can you prove your boss is going to pay us?" the volatile Pepito asks Alfredo. "Of all of us, you're the only one who knows him personally." Pepito and Alfredo now have what can only be described as being a French variation on the classic Mexican Stand-Off: Alfredo, who's *a tough hombre* in his own right, as well as being a guy who never takes any shit off of his hired hands, points a gun at Pepito, and Pepito, who is completely unthreatened, points a knife right back at him: And of course, it's now up to Gabin's level-headed Louis to diffuse this tense situation. A few moments later, when Louis, Pepito, Pierre, and Pops leave Alfredo's office, Louis whispers to his assembled cohorts that it's time they acted as their own bosses, and he mentions to them that there's a huge, new bank in Provence that definitely deserves some robbing. Louis says that he's been scoping the place out, and that robbing it, probably around Christmastime, will take them about two hours, should everything go ahead, as planned. Pepito, Pierre, and Pops are as sick of working for other people, as Louis is as well, and they're all excited about the prospect which *Big Louie* has just offered them. Alfredo is listening to them through his closed office door, and since we've already seen a lot of gangster pictures, we can figure out already that Alfredo and Mimile are probably going to try to get in on Louis' new idea and, no doubt, forcibly.

Even though Gabin's Louis character is in his early fifties, he still lives with his mother (but you'd better not call him a mama's boy), just like Gabin's blind train conductor-character lived with his mom, too, in 1951's *La Nuit est mon royaume*. Mom (Gina Nicloz) alerts her fiftysomething Gabinian son that his little brother, Pierrot (Marcel Bozzuffi, not to be confused with 'Pierre,' who is Jean-Paul Mocky's character) is in jail again, and this time, for driving without a license, and that he'll be remaining behind bars until such time as Louis, the only person in the family who ever brings home any cash, should design to spring him. (Over the last thirteen months, as we're going to be learning in this scene, Pierrot's been in and out of jail for having committed petty crimes several times.) Pierrot wants to be a big-time gangster, just like his big-brother, Louis (instead of being a small time crook, which is what he is right now), but Louis isn't interested in bringing family members along for the ride, especially family members with big mouths who can't be depended on to keep secrets. (Pierrot is one of those great, weak-willed movie brothers, like John Cazale's 'Fredo,' in *Godfather I* and *II:* He's a guy who can't be trusted with any information at all. Like Fredo, Pierrot is likable, but oh-so-dumb!) Louis, who is paternal to his moronic little brother, just as Michael Corleone is to his little brother Fredo in *Godfather*, tells his mother that he wants to keep Pierrot pure, even though the skeevy (and oily)-looking Pierrot is already about as far from pure as one can possibly get. (In Jean Gabin movies, 'Our Hero' always idealizes family, placing everything else in life second to it although, paradoxically, his characters are always drifting away from the families which overwhelm them.) Louis promises his mom, "When Pierrot gets out, I'll see to it that he gets an honest job." Louis owns an auto mechanic's garage, which is his 'legitimate' work (a/k/a, 'his cover'), and that's where he intends for his little brother to work.

Simultaneously, Alfredo is already over at the jailhouse, leaning on Pierrot: "So: What do you know about that robbery your brother Louis is planning in Provence? He's not including me and *my boss*, and I want to know everything about it. If you tell me what you know, I'll get you out of here, *and* I'll let you join my outfit." Pierrot, surprisingly, doesn't cop to anything though, telling Alfredo truthfully that he doesn't know anything about any job in Provence, or anywhere else for that matter, and since Alfredo is unable to glean any info out of him, he leaves Pierrot behind bars.

Shortly after Alfredo leaves the jailhouse, Louis arrives there, finally springing his little brother. "I know Alfredo was just here," he tells Pierrot, matter-of-factly. "What did he ask you about?" Pierrot tells Louis that Alfredo wanted to know about some future robbery in Provence which Louis is engineering, but that he didn't tell him anything, because he doesn't know anything about it, which is the truth. Louis looks a little steamed that his brother has just learned about the Provence job from Alfredo (Louis was trying to keep Pierrot in the dark about it) but, per Dick Van Dyke's song in *Bye, Bye Birdie*, he "puts on a happy face," anyway, inasmuch as Gabin can ever do that, and going against his better judgment, he now decides to make Pierrot part of the gang. In fact, Louis decides that Pierrot will be his gang's new driver.

As the two brothers leave the jailhouse, Louis lets Pierrot know that if he's going to be driving for them, he's going to need a driver's license which, as we already know, he doesn't have. (Even cars don't trust Pierrot!) Louis now commissions a forger whom he knows to make some fake identity cards for Pierrot, including a driver's license; Louis, Pepito, Pops, and *Qu'est-ce qu'il Dit* already carry similar fake i.d.'s so that, if they're ever caught, the cops won't know who the Sam Hill they're arresting!

That night, Louis puts his little brother up in his own apartment, and Louis walks around, wearing striped pajamas just like 'that moronic porcupine,' Riton, in *Touchez pas au grisbi*, the stripes portending 'jail' or 'the bad fate' which we know will be befalling one or more of Louis' gang, by the end of the picture. While Pierrot's going to be driving for them in Provence, he will not otherwise be involved in the bank job.

Now, of course, when any man gets out of jail, the first thing on his agenda is always women. The first thing he does, when brother Louis gets him freed from jail, is to head over to the apartment of his girlfriend, Madeleine (Annie Girardot, one of France's finest actresses), a woman who's a manicurist in a fancy Parisian salon by day, and a hooker by night. She's mad at Pierrot because he was in jail again, but he diffuses her anger by telling her that he's been saving up his money to buy her the mink coat which she desires so completely. He even lies to her modestly, telling her that his big brother Louis has just asked him to be his right-hand man.

Louis knows all about Madeleine, although the two of them have never met, and he doesn't want Pierrot to date her anymore since, in his opinion, hooker-dating is not the image which a 'classy' gang of gentleman gangsters should be projecting and, correspondingly, Big Brother's got a doozy of a plan to break the two of them up: Louis goes to the salon where Madeleine works and gets a manicure from her, not letting her know that he's Pierrot's older brother; he suavely invites her to lunch and, as they leave the salon together, two young guys who know her (probably, they're her johns) accost her (nicely), bringing her candy, and offering up their own 'lunch' invitations, but Louis, rather intimidatingly, swats them off with a major Gabin-Scowl. Madeleine and Louis walk through the park, and she tells him she has a handsome boyfriend named Pierrot, whom she "sees, every Wednesday." This is the moment when Louis admits to her who he really is and, not only that, but he slaps her face too, for good measure, after which he issues this simple Gabinian command: "*Bitch!* Never see my brother again!" After she scampers away in fear, he spends a few moments casually watching some bicycle riders. (Louis has a violent nature, but he also enjoys every Frenchman's favorite pastime—looking at bicycles.)

A few days later, Louis brings Pierrot to a preferred local bar to surprise their Mom, and their Mom, a lady who enjoys a good stiff drink, is ecstatic when she sees that the younger of her two sons, Pierrot, is out of the joint. Pierrot asks his mom if she's had any news from Madeleine, since she hasn't been answering his phone calls for a few days (she has no idea that his big brother told her to screw off) and she tells him, truthfully, that she hasn't heard anything. Pierrot, who's eager to see Madeleine, next struts-over to her apartment, and asks her, through the locked door, why she won't let him in, and her ultra-brief response is, "You'd better ask your brother about that." Now, not only do we have a potential double-cross coming to the gang *via* Alfredo, but screenwriter Michel Audiard, whose third of nineteen Gabin movies this is (after *Gas-Oil* and *Sang a la tete*) is also setting up some rather heady brother-*vs.*-brother conflict.

Pierrot is pissed beyond belief that his big brother went and talked to his girlfriend, telling her not to see him anymore, and to make matters worse, Pierrot, who is now standing behind yet another locked door at Louis' garage (he has a habit of doing that), is overhearing a meeting between Louis and Pepito, who are whispering some specifics to each other pursuant to the upcoming Provence caper. Pepito, however, has Super-Sensitive Lino Ventura-Hearing, and can hear Pierrot lingering outside, so he throws the door open and holds a gun squarely at Pierrot's head. ("What did you hear, jerk?") "Don't shoot him," Louis freaks, running to Pierrot's rescue. "He's my brother!"

Now that Pierrot's heard everything, Louis fills his little brother in on the rest of the details, which Pierrot's already heard most of, anyway: Louis tells Pepito, with Pierrot present, that banks, including the Provence bank, never keep much money on-hand during the holiday season, instead keeping their cash ever-moving in armored trucks (just like Saddam Hussein's alleged 'mobile WMD-vans' of the 21st century!) so that now, their new updated goal will be *not* to heist the bank-proper, but only to hijack one or more of the trucks which will be hefting the bank's currency-supply. Pepito's worried about the fact that Pierrot knows (and talks) too much, but Louis reassures him that he'll make sure Pierrot doesn't utter a word. Getting Pierrot alone, after Pepito goes home for the day, Louis immediately Gabin-Outbursts at him: "Okay! So now you know exactly what we're going to do. And now that you know everything—you'd better not screw up! And, while we're discussing it, *also*, I forbid you to see that girl! And not just now, but always! Got it?!"

Robbery Day in Provence is now at hand and somehow, between the last sequence and this one (although we don't know it for sure), Louis has come to his senses, and has decided against Pierrot's participation in the operation: Pierrot's not with the gang, driving the car (Louis, himself, is piloting the sedan), and Pepito, Pops, and *Qu-est-ce qu'il Dit* are all together in the back seat. Louis and the guys cautiously follow the bank's main armored truck, but not close enough wherein they might be seen by the truck's drivers. (The truck, additionally, has two motorcycle cops accompanying it.) Without breaking a sweat, Louis and his boys suddenly whip out their heaters, and Louis blasts one of the motorcycle cops, *Easy Rider*-style, and then, in short order, he also blasts the other one. (A huge technical gaffe in this scene, is: How come this robbery is happening in broad daylight, with a group of onlookers standing around and looking excited, like they're watching a movie being filmed? And how come, too, when Louis shoots the first cop, the second cop doesn't call for back-up? It's definitely a cool and action-packed scene, but it does have these problems.) Needless to say, the robbery is successful: Our Team was able to get the armored truck drivers out of the way, without killing them, as they had killed the motorcycle cops, and they've grabbed all of the money sacks.

Night falls now, and Louis and the gang take their sedan and head for the country; and after blowing-up their car, so that (to use the subjunctive tense) "there shouldn't be any evidence," they next hijack a farmer and commandeer his farm-truck, which happens to have a live cow hitched to the back, at gunpoint. They then shoot the farmer to death (dead men tell no tales), and dump his inert body down a hill. The sight of this team of leathery-countenanced crooks driving back into Paris with a farm-truck and cow in tow, not making eye-contact with any of the Parisian pedestrians who gawk at them, is priceless.

The gang now descends into its underground lair under Louis' garage, where Louis keeps a large safe. The guys have successfully stolen *the big bucks* from the armored truck and, of course, they mean to keep it all for themselves, although Pepito, even though he's a tough guy, expresses some momentary concerns to Louis, on the subject: "Shouldn't we give Alfredo and Mimile a piece of the action, just as a precaution, so that they won't come after us?" Louis' response is eloquent: "Screw Alfredo and his boss!" Louis now divvies-up the money evenly between himself, Pepito, Pops, and *Qu'est-ce-qu'il Dit*, telling them all that this Provence robbery has been his very last job, and that they should all go now, and find some other criminal enterprise to work for. (As we all know from watching other gangster pictures, any time any career-criminal utters the magical phrase, "this is going to be my last job before retirement," we know his death is lurking right around the corner.) In this film, as we can also guess, Louis' demise will probably come at the hands of his little brother Pierrot, who is now enraged on two counts: First, he's mad because his brother cut him out of the Provence action at the last minute, and secondly, he's also *p.o.'d*, because Louis made Madeleine cease her affair with him (with Pierrot).

Later that same day, when Louis and his guys walk out of his garage, some cops who've been hiding out there beat the crap out of them, and arrest them all, because Pierrot told Madeleine that Louis was The Provence Bank Robber, and Madeleine then told the cops. 'Pops,' who is too old and tired to demonstrate any kind of resistance during his interrogation (each man in the gang is being interrogated in a separate room), confesses that "what the hooker said was true," and that it was he and his gang who ripped off the armored truck.

And now, ladies and gentlemen, here comes another one of those great 'Gabin Interrogation Scenes' in which Our (Anti-)Hero is (as usual!) interrogated by the cops, and doesn't *blow his cool*. "Your brother and your cohort Jo ['Pops'] both told me that it was you," Inspector Pluvier (Albert Dinan) threatens, "so don't try and deny it!" Louis, smiling, doesn't deny it—he just tells the cop to go screw himself! Pluvier informs Louis also, that the police have already have taken possession of part of the money: "We found your share at your mother's house, and I want you to tell me where the rest of it is—and right now!" Louis bolts up out his chair, unleashing a torrent of Mighty Gabin Fury on the shocked, surprised, and frightened-looking Inspector: "Look, you! Stop interrogating me! I'm not telling you anything!"

Simultaneously, another Inspector, Bouvard (Gabriel Gobin), is giving Louis' old crime (under)boss Alfredo the third-degree in a nearby room, and Louis passes by, having successfully walked out on his own interrogation without having been restrained. "Don't you want to see your friend," Bouvard asks Louis, *re:* Alfredo, but Louis just Gabin-Shrugs, "I don't know him," and Bouvard, of course, believes him. The police let Alfredo go, since he wasn't part of this Provence crime, and the next thing Alfredo does, is to go over to the bistro, where his own boss, Mimile (Jo Peignot)—a/k/a, 'The Big Capo,'—keeps an office, to let him know that everything's cool, and that the cops weren't able to connect them to the Provence Job, which is accurate, because Alfredo and Mimile weren't involved in it. (While Alfredo's a tough bruiser when he's with other people, he cowers in fright whenever he's around his own boss.)

So, while there are three different people who gave Louis' gang up to the police, the only one whom Lino Ventura's hard-ass Pepito-character is pissed-off at is Pierrot, and Pepito even makes a threatening phone call to Louis: "Hello, Louis? I just want to tell you that I'm coming to kill your stoolie brother, today. Tell him that he can run, but he can't hide!" Louis, who's scared for his dimwitted younger brother, now makes for a local bar in which Pierrot likes to hang out, and he tells a young neighborhood gangster who's befriended Pierrot (a character who's called 'Le Grenouille,' because he's from Grenoble, in the French Alps [and he's played by the actor Rene Hell]), "You've got to find my brother! And when you find him, tell him not to open the door to anybody. Pepito's coming to kill him!" Le Grenouille tells Louis that he knows what Louis is now telling him has to be the truth, "… because I already saw Pepito earlier today, and he told me that he was looking for your brother."

Louis next storms into the 'movie-large' cavernous lobby of his own apartment building (it's obviously a film set), and finds Pepito standing on the second floor balcony, staring down at him menacingly. "My brother didn't give us up to the cops," Louis lies to Pepito, "*Alfredo* did!" Louis walks up to the second floor, and he and Pepito are now suddenly engaged in major fisticuffs. Pepito knocks Louis off the balcony, and very coolly, in the same moment in which Louis is falling to his death, he fires three shots into Pepito—POP, POP, POP! (Yes, Jean Gabin is so cool, he can even unload while falling!) Within nanoseconds (or is that: Gabin-o-seconds?!), the two tough guys have killed each other.

Le Rouge est mis, a 'just-o.k. actioner,' would be released in the United States by a small, mom-and-pop art-house distributor called United Motion Picture Organization (UMPO) in 1959, but the picture hasn't been seen in the U.S. since that year. For the movie's American art-house release, the original (and lackluster) French title, *Le Rouge est mis* (in English, it means, '*The Red [Light] is Put-On,*' which is a slang reference to the red light which police cars flash when giving chase), was ditched in favor of an even more lackluster title, *Speaking of Murder,* but even with its snazzy new title, the film made nary a ripple in the U.S. The flick is neither bad nor good (or, as the French say, it's '*ni l'un ni l'autre*'). One purpose of this book, is to help Gabin movies get re-discovered in countries in which they're not as well known as they are in France, but if this particular movie doesn't want to be re-discovered— well, I guess it's okay…

What a Critic Said at the Time: "[This] film has some excitement, but is generally plodding. The main asset is the presence of Jean Gabin, who gives the pic some weight as the gang-leader. The film is well-played and has a rugged, crude aspect in the earthy dialogue of Auguste Le Breton, who wrote *Rififi* (although this lacks the verve of the former). Gabin displays his usual vigorous assurance." (*Variety,* 7-24-57 issue. Critic: "Mosk. [George Moskowitz.]" Reviewed in Paris.)

What Another Critic Said at the Time: "It is Mr. Gabin who sets the pace and tone, ambling about with his deceptive deadpan casualness, like a relaxed and aging cobra. [Gilles] Grangier's direction is impersonal, but the climax—a bloody staircase duel—is a pip. Taking their cues from Mr. Gabin, the other performers are first rate… The film [also features] a parade of svelte, hungry-eyed girls…" (New York *Times,* 10-12-59 issue. Critic: Richard Nascio.)

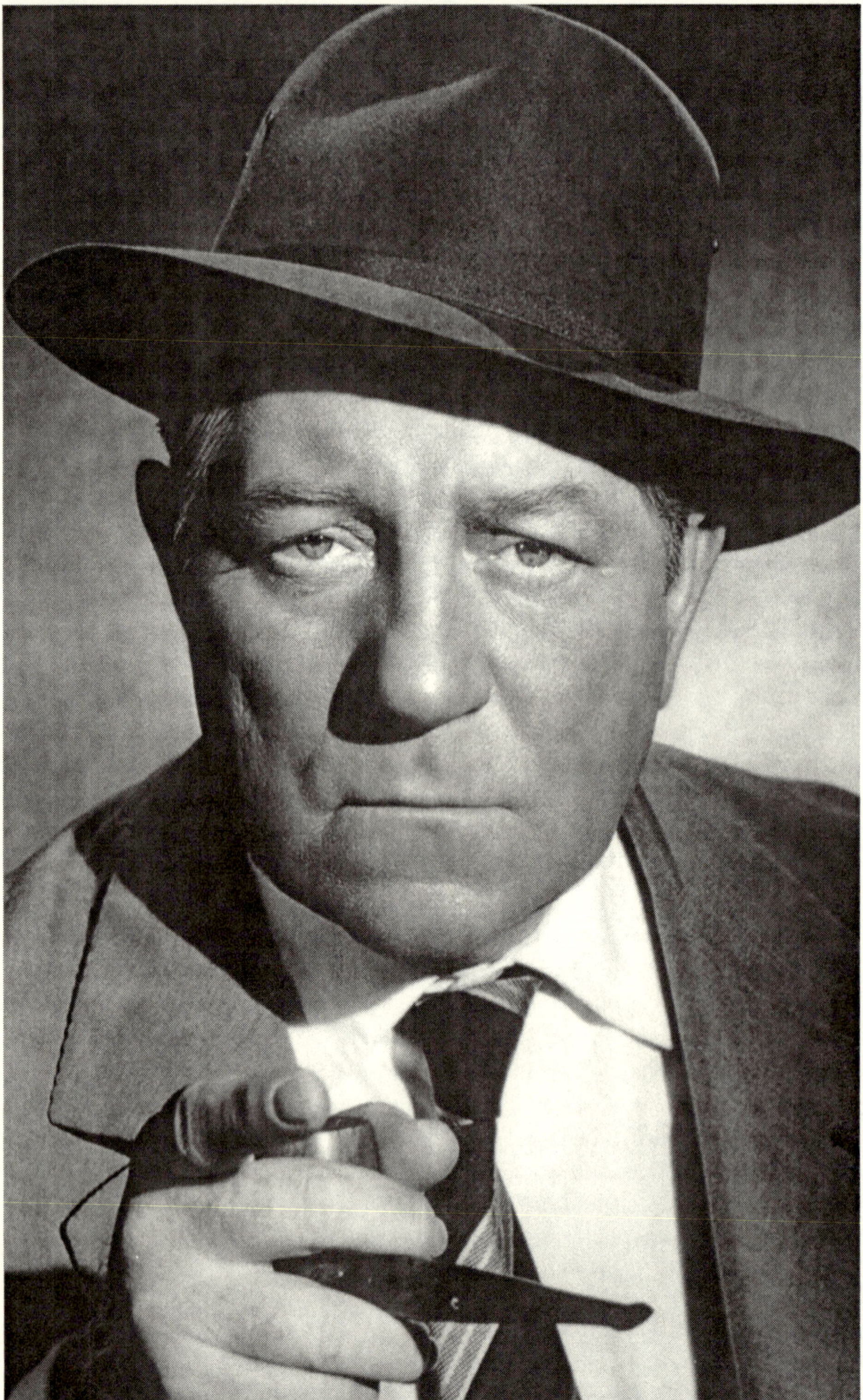

FILM 62

Maigret tend un piege

France/Italy, 1958

(Literal English Translation: "MAIGRET SETS A TRAP") Directed by Jean Delannoy. Produced by Jean-Paul Guibert. Screenplay by Jean Delannoy, Rodolphe-Maurice Arlaud, and Michel Audiard. Based Upon the Novel by Georges Simenon. Director of Photography (black and white), Louis Page. Editor, Henri Taverna. Music by Paul Misraki. Production Designer, Rene Renoux. (GENRES: DRAMA/POLICIER-THRILLER) A Production of Intermondia (France) and Jolly Film (Italy). Running Time, 1 hour 59 minutes. Released in France on January 29, 1958, by Intermondia. Released in United States by Lopert Films, Inc. with English Subtitles as "INSPECTOR MAIGRET," in April, 1958 (NYC only). Re-Released in United States by United Artists in the Winter of 1958, as "WOMAN BAIT."

"All those lowlife apes! You just love rough trade! Admit it, slut!"
— *A husband berates his hooker wife, in "Maigret tend un piege"*

Jean Gabin, at this point in his career, had already starred in three film adaptations of novels which had been written by his Belgian-born/French-living friend, Georges Simenon—*La Marie du port, La Verite sur Bebe Donge*, and *Le Sang a la tete*, and all three were tepid relationship dramas, with practically the same-exact plot in each film. ('Gabin = wealthy, bored *bourgeois*-guy who gets used by women and doesn't fight back.') But Simenon was always at his best when he wrote detective fiction, and many film adaptations of the author's detective stuff, both with and without Gabin, are pretty strong, including this very good and entertaining effort.

If you know Agatha Christie's famous detectives Hercule Poirot and Mrs. Marple, there's a good chance that you're also already familiar with Simenon's ultra-cool, pipe-smoking Inspector Jules Maigret, a character who's been portrayed (beginning in 1932, and continuing right up through today) in nearly 150 feature films and television episodes, and not only by Jean Gabin (as in this film, and in two others which would follow it, in ensuing years), but also by some other great French actors, including Harry Baur (Herod, from Duvivier's *Golgotha*), Louis Arbessier, Bruno Cremer, and Albert Prejean. Some great *Brits* have played

Maigret too, including Richard Harris, Charles Laughton, and (most recently in 1992, on a popular BBC-TV series) Michael Gambon. There's also been an Italian Maigret (Gino Cervi) and even—if you can believe it—a *Russian* Maigret, in 1974's *Megre [Maigret] I Staraya Dama* (a/k/a, *Maigret and the Old Lady*).

As Jean Gabin's first of three Maigret movies, *Maigret tend un piege*, directed by Jean Delannoy (who had already directed Gabin in *La Minute de verite* and 1955's *Chiens perdus sans collier*), was entering production at the end of 1956, Georges Simenon was ecstatic that Gabin, one of the few actors whom he *truly* admired, was going to be playing Maigret. In the French magazine *Cine-Revue* (No. 21, May 24, 1957), Simenon would even give this first Gabin-Maigret movie some very good advanced publicity, when he stated:

"My old friend Jean Gabin, who has already starred in some of my movies, is going to be interpreting the character of Maigret. He has signed on for three Maigret flims, and I believe that he will be nearest to the idea that the public has of Maigret, and the idea that I, myself, have of him."

After the beginning credits of *Maigret tend un piege* (all we see over the credits, is a shadow of the character's iconic pipe), four women, all of whom wear their hair in the same short hairstyle, have turned up dead throughout Paris, and Jean Gabin's crafty Inspector Maigret gets a great idea: He and his colleague Inspector Torrence (Lino Ventura again) are going to be requiring all of the young women in Paris who have short hair, to fan out throughout the city, as decoys for the killer: In a very amusing sequence, Maigret and Torrence get a large group of women together in one room, and one particularly strong gal karate-flips a stunned Torrence over her own head!

As it's going to be turning out, Maigret's idea, in which short-haired women are used as bait (one of the film's two American release titles, was the lurid-sounding *Woman-Bait*), is a good one, because more murders are being committed, although the good news, is that there *has* been a breakthrough in the investigation: At the site of the most current murder, the killer, whoever he may be, has left a butcher's knife, and this rare-old knife's unique serrated edges have been found scratched across the faces of each victim. Maigret is able to trace the instrument, quite speedily, to a well-known butcher shop, and the meat-cutter who belongs to the notorious blade is Barberot (Alfred Adam), a big happy lug who's not even a suspect, because he's so beloved by his community. Barberot is horrified that his prized knife, which went missing weeks ago, has been used to slice-and-dice all of these women.

Taking Barberot's advice, Maigret decides to interrogate the constantly-bickering and rather dicey (pun intended) couple whose apartment is located right over this butcher's shop and, as it turns out, that's a good idea, because this is the apartment in which one of Barberot's most frequent customers, the wimpy interior decorator Marcel Maurin (Jean Desailly) lives with his hotpants/roundheels wife, Yvonne (Annie Girardot, who played Madeleine the hot manicurist, in *Le rouge est mis*). Not only does Yvonne cheat on Maurin regularly, and right in front of her husband's weak, no-chinned face (with every guy she can

1954 — 1976 | 161

With Annie Girardot and Olivier Hussenot.

get her hands on, and he's too much of as simp to stop her, but she also happens to have that same exact short haircut which all of the women who've been turning up dead also have had. Maigret's beginning to figure out that Maurin hates his wife so much for screwing-around on him, that he's taking it out on all of the women who resemble his wife, by murdering them. (The Maurin character is, very definitely, a three-years-earlier precursor to moviedom's very favorite wimpy child/man, Norman Bates, from Hitchcock's *Psycho*). The film never addresses the issue of why Yvonne would stay with such a doormat like Maurin, and the nearest we can figure, is that he must have some money socked away.

After investigating everybody whom the couple knows, including all of the men with whom Yvonne has been running around, including a goofily-mustached gigolo named 'Jojo' who's played by Gerard Sety, a man whom she pays in the expensive jewelry which her husband is always giving her, Inspector Maigret finally solves the crime, learning that it *was* in fact Maurin who committed the murders, and he is immediately arrested. While he is prison, however one additional murder of a woman takes place. Maigret understands that someone has killed this new woman to make Maurin appear innocent, so he summons Maurin's mother (Lucienne Bogaert, who played the drug-addicted old prostitute in *Voici le temps des assassins*) and Yvonne, because he's certain that one of the two is guilty. He questions both of them, because he's trying to ascertain which of the two of them loves

Maurin enough to the point that she would have killed a woman to clear his name. Maurin's mother gives herself up, because she wants to appear to be the one who loves Maurin better than anybody else, but when Maigret asks her how the woman who had been killed was dressed, she is unable to answer. Yvonne then calmly depicts how the woman was dressed and, based on this, we understand that it was Yvonne who has killed this woman.

Just when we think the film is over and Maigret is walking home, he passes the butcher shop, accidentally stumbling upon Maurin who is, himself, about to stab a brand new woman to death with a different knife, and the pipe-wielding detective gently talks him out of it, just like how fathers talk, when they're trying to calm their eighty-year-old boys.

Maigret tend un piege was so popular in France, and continues to be popular in its regular runs today on French television, that Gabin would reprise the role in two additional films— 1959's *Maigret et l'affaire Saint-Fiacre* (*Maigret and the Saint-Fiacre Affair*) and 1963's *Maigret voit rouge* (*Maigret Sees Red*)—two fairly good sequels (although the first one, *Piege*, is definitely the best 'Gabin-*Maigret*' of the three) which would, unlike *Maigret tend un piege*, never achieve North American theatrical release. *Maigret tend un piege* was released in the U.S. by United Artists as *Inspector Maigret*, a few months after its French release, and it was then re-released by UA later that year, under the more lurid (and more *noir*-ish) title, *Woman-Bait*. The picture is occasionally broadcast over American cable television in an English-subtitled version, and the current best place to find it if you're an American, is on America's French-language cable television station, TV5.

Does Maigret = Magritte? Just like Agatha Christie's Hercule Poirot character is always identified by his rather prominent mustache, so, too, is Georges Simenon's Inspector Maigret-character always identified by his pipe, which he always happens to be holding or smoking during his pensive, clue-gathering moments. In fact, the very first image we see in *Maigret tend un piege*, even before we see Jean Gabin, is the shadow of the famous Inspector's pipe, which casts itself ominously over a wall during the beginning credits. How did Simenon come up with the name 'Maigret,' and with the Maigret character's omnipresent pipe? Well, while a specific Maigret/Magritte connection has never been substantiated, Simenon's first Maigret novel, *Pietr-Le-Leton* (*The Case of Peter the Lett*) was published in 1931, and two years before that, in 1929, France's legendary surrealist painter Rene *Magritte* (sounds like '*Maigret*'), a man who, just like Simenon, was Belgian-born, painted his celebrated giant canvas, "*La Trahison des images*" ("*Treachery of Images*"), a painting which, of course, depicts a giant pipe, accompanied by the written inscription, "*Ceci n'est pas une pipe.*" ("This is not a pipe.") More recently, in 1968, the British playwright Tom Stoppard played on the two words, 'Maigret' and 'Magritte,' in his short play, "The Inspector Hound."

Does Maigret = Magritte? This question must, by necessity, be left unanswered.

Does Gabin = A Fun, 'Surprise T.V. Guest?': On April 8, 1958, *Maigret tend un piege*'s director Jean Delannoy popped up on a popular French t.v. show called, "*La Joie de vivre*" ("What Makes You Happy"), a series in which each week, a different guest would talk about things in life which gave him great joy. While Delannoy is interacting with the show's host Jacqueline Joubert, and telling Joubert how he loves working with Jean Gabin, the two suddenly receive a 'surprise' visit from Jean Gabin, who rarely appeared on television. Delannoy feigns astonishment at the arrival of the great star: "Jean! It's amazing that you're here! You don't do television!" Gabin tells Delannoy, "We already made three movies together" [*Minute de verite, Chiens perdus sans collier,* and *Maigret tend un piege*], and we're about to start two more [*Maigret et l'affaire Saint-Fiacre* and *Le Baron d'ecluse*]. I know I'm famous for having a bad, 'complaining' personality, but I'd go anywhere for you, my friend. You're always nice to me, and you always wrap everything up in shiny paper. [That's 'Gabin-Slang,' for 'You always make people feel happy.'] So how I can refuse your offer to appear on television with you?"

Delannoy asks Gabin what he thinks about the relatively new medium of television, and Gabin actually lights up: "I love television! I never go anywhere when I'm not working; usually, I'm just at home, watching t.v. in my slippers, with a glass of wine. I have two televisions at home—one in my bedroom and one in the living room—and there's nothing I like better than watching other people working [since most t.v. was "live," at the this time], while I'm at home, relaxing!"

What a Critic Said at the Time: "The cast [members] are all competent, but Jean Gabin's presence overshadows everything. It is Gabin who gives this whodunit some form and semblance, because otherwise, it [might] lack the drive and suspense of [its] Yank counterparts. (*Variety*, 3-26-58 issue. Critic: "Mosk. [George Moskowitz.]" Reviewed in Paris.)

What Another Critic Said at the Time: "A don't-miss picture for the mystery fans. An exciting example of [writer Georges] Simenon's sophisticated work, and a beautifully clear and catchy portrait of the gumshoe, performed by Jean Gabin. This is the first time that Mr. Gabin has played [the legendary Inspector Maigret] and he plays it to perfection. He has the cool, dry, frank, insistent air of the distinguished veteran of the *surete* [French police force], and uses his bewitchingly inscrutable [Gabinian] deadpan. He gives a fetching impression of a man who has experienced almost everything, and knows all the necessary angles [about] those things [which] he hasn't." (New York *Times*, 9-9-58 issue. Critic: Bosley Crowther.)

Top: With Bourvil. Above: Superhuman strength.

FILM 63

LES MISERABLES

France/Italy/East Germany, 1958

Directed by Jean-Paul Le Chanois. Produced by Paul Cadeac. Screenplay by Michel Audiard, Jean-Paul Le Chanois and R. Barjavel. Based Upon the Novel by Victor Hugo. Produced by Paul Cadeac. Director of Photography (color), Jacques Natteau. Editor, Emma Le Chanois. Music by Georges Van Parys. Production Designer, Serge Pimenoff. (GENRE: HISTORICAL DRAMA) A Production of DEFA-Studiofur Spielfilme (East Germany)/Serena (Italy)/and Societe Nouvelle Pathe Cinema (France). Running Time, 3 hours 42 minutes. Released in France (in two parts, each part presented separately) on March 12, 1958, by Societe Nouvelle Pathe Cinema. Released in United States in November 1958, dubbed into English, by Continental Distributors, as one long film with an intermission.

> *"You should kill me now when you have the chance, because if you don't, I'm never going to stop bothering you! Hahahahaha!"*
> *—In Victor Hugo's immortal story, the villainous Inspector Javert lets Gabin's Jean Valjean know that he's going to be spending the rest of his life making Valjean's life a living hell, in "Les Miserables"*

In 1958, *Le Cas du docteur Laurent's* director, Jean-Paul Le Chanois, would reunite with Gabin, who was now, in real life, both old enough (56), and authoritative enough, to play the legendary Jean Valjean, in a mega-budgeted, grand-scale, three-and-a-half hour, Eastmancolor re-telling of Victor Hugo's immortal epic-*bouillabaisse*, *Les Miserables* which, after *French Can-Can*, represents Gabin's second starring role in a feature that was filmed in color. This version of *Les Miserables* was France's second epic 'sound' version of Hugo's story, the first being director Raymond Bernard's four hour-and-five minute 1934 version, which starred Harry Baur (who played King Herod, in the Gabin/Duvivier *Golgotha*), as Jean Valjean. As anyone who suffered through the unendurable 1980s' musical version knows (remember sitting next to your mom during the musical, and listening to her emote, "Isn't the staging *won-dah-ful?!*"), Jean Valjean has just been released from prison, after a nineteen-year sentence, for stealing a loaf of bread. (That's why they call him '*badass!*') He *drags-ass* over to a church, where the caring Monsignor (Fernand Ledoux) takes him in, feeds him, and puts him up for the night, and of course, Valjean repays the Monsignor's generosity by making off with the church's fine silverware, and by escaping during the night. (Once a convict, always a convict.)

The next morning, the cops return Valjean to the church, telling the Monsignor they have arrested him for stealing the forks and knives. The Monsignor lies to protect Valjean, in whom he recognizes inherent goodness, telling the cops that not only did he *give* Valjean the silverware as a present, but that Valjean forgot to take *the other gift* which he was *also* given— *a pair of expensive silver candlesticks!* When the police leave, the Monsignor tells Valjean that, because he's just saved Valjean's hide from the police that he must, in return, promise to spend the rest of his life being a good, upstanding citizen.

Cut to a few years later: Jean Valjean is now a solid citizen, thriving in the southern town of Vigo (today, it's part of northern Spain) under a new identity—just like Gabin used to do in his old Foreign Legion Pictures—and he's now such an upstanding citizen, that he's actually become the town's Mayor, his carbohydrate-pilfering past firmly behind him, and this is very funny: It's basically Victor Hugo telling us that, in his view, politicians are really just criminals! Valjean has turned his life around and, in addition to being the Mayor, he now also owns a factory, in which he has very progressively placed the means of production into the *oh-so-supple* hands of his lady workers, one of whom, Fantine (Daniele Delorme, who played Gabin's scheming step-daughter, Catherine, in *Voici le temps des assassins*), is a prostitute to whom he ministers paternally, as she lays around in bed, dying of syphilis. Valjean has taken a shine to Fantine because, like him, she's been trying to turn her life around and, especially, she's laboring hard to send money to her eight-year-old daughter Cosette (Martine Havet), who's boarding in a small town with a family of con-artists, the Thenardier family. (If Fagin from *Oliver Twist* 'spawned,' his heirs would be the Thenardiers!) And just when it seems that things are going copacetically for Valjean, Cruel Fate rears its ugly head, and it's a head which happens to belong to the devious Inspector Javert (Bernard Blier, who played the wimpy balding suitor to Ulla Jacobsson's 'Nicole' character, in Gabin's 1956 Dostoevesky-adaptation, *Crime et chatiment*). Javert is Jean Valjean's old jailer, a man whose one stated goal in life, is to remind the citizens of Vigo, on a daily basis, that their beloved Mayor is a fraud, and that he is really that *arch-criminal bread-thief,* Jean Valjean. Even though Valjean is no longer a scofflaw, and lives his life as an upstanding citizen (as *'Hizzoner, the Mayor'* no less), creepy Javert, for those who never took 11th Grade World-Lit, is basically just a *huge, fascistic asshole,* a character who represents 'France's oppressive monarchy, and a man who believes that no man can ever truly be reformed.' (Javert can also be seen, if you will, as being Victor Hugo's living embodiment of *that one nasty freak in your workplace who makes your life a living hell, for no other reason than the fact that he [or she] is just a jealous fucking prick!*)

One morning, the newspaper headlines inform the 'Vigo-ites' (*'Vigo-ians?* [*Vegans?*']) that someone claiming to be Jean Valjean has just been apprehended, in Paris. The real Valjean (Gabin) makes haste to the trial, where he finds out that the guy who's been tried, is

With Bourvil, Beatrice Altariba, and Silvia Monfort.

just a helpless, mentally-challenged man who's been goaded into taking credit for being the thief, by a bunch of drunken street bullies. Valjean becomes so angry that this oafish innocent is being persecuted for erroneously admitting to be him, that he admits finally, in front of the court, to being the real Jean Valjean. Both the real Valjean and the moronic fake Valjean are played by Jean Gabin, and the 'two Gabins' even appear together in few shots, thanks to some pretty high-end-looking optical photography. And just when you already knew that Gabin was the coolest guy in the world, here comes something better—two Jean Gabins standing side-by-side in one movie-frame, just like the two little twin Hayley Millses, in *The Parent Trap!*

At this point in the narrative, now that his true identity has become common knowledge, Valjean knows that he's going to have to escape from Vigo, to avoid the wrath of a general public which would otherwise become enraged about having elected a thief to office, but before Valjean leaves, he heads over to the decrepit house in which gross Thenardier, who's played by the great Bourvil (who helped Gabin *wield his pork* [get your mind out of the gutter!], in *La Traversee de Paris*), and his wife (Elfriede Florin), are raising eight-year-old Cosette, treating the little girl like crap, and even (it is more-than-implied) pimping her out, to old men. Valjean informs *The Nasty Thenardiers* that he was appointed by Cosette's mother (it was Fantine's dying wish) to care for the little girl, and he takes her away: Thenardier, an actor who's never been able to get any work (probably, he just needs to update his headshots!) happily trades Cosette to Valjean, for the paltry sum of only one hundred francs, and Valjean and Cosette then run away together, father and new surrogate daughter, far from the evil forces (Javert and his men) which are now moving in on Valjean, at an alarming pace.

Ten years later: Cosette has grown into a graceful young gazelle of about eighteen years old and, as an adult, she'll now be played by Beatrice Altariba. She and Valjean have been hidden away in the church for years (Gabin, just like in all of his 1930s movies, is sequestered away in a safe-haven, where authorities are not free to tread), under the alias of 'Lafitte.' As it turns out, Valjean was able to get himself and Cosette taken in by the church, under the guise that, when Cosette is of age—which she now is—she will become a nun. (Since we never actually see Cosette nunning in the film, we'll assume that she never became one.)

Meanwhile, outside of the church, a Republican insurrection is taking place, and a huge crowd of disenfranchised Frenchies are out in the town square, listening to the dashing young student rabble-rouser, Marius (Giani Esposito, who had already appeared with Jean Gabin in 1955's *French Can-Can,* in which he played Prince Alexander, the young dope who fell in love with Francois Arnouls' laundress-cum-showgirl, Nini [and not to be confused with today's great actor Giancarlo Esposito, who appeared in Spike Lee's *Do the Right Thing*]), with whom Cosette is, of course, falling madly in love. Javert, having given up hope of ever tracking down Valjean, has transferred his anger to a new enemy—that revolutionary riff-raff! He's now in Paris, keeping his (evil) eye firmly on Marius.

Javert sees Marius walking with Cosette a few days later, and is able, quite easily, to trace them back to the church, where he learns that the father of the woman whom Marius is dating, 'Lafitte,' is really his old arch-enemy, Jean Valjean, in the flesh! Javert visits the church in Valjean's absence, instructing Cosette to tell her father that Marius is a dangerous revolutionary. Cruelly, Javert also takes this moment to lyingly reveal to Cosette, "Did Valjean tell you you're a bastard child? The daughter of a whore?"

Valjean now realizes that, since Javert is once again onto him, he must now escape—and probably to England—and Cosette is torn between staying with Valjean, who raised her, and who rescued her from abuse at the hands of Thenardier and Marius. While Valjean is afraid of Javert, young Marius, clearly, is not, and the young revolutionary angrily drags the evil Javert bodily to face the people, actually hog-tying him. Valjean escapes.

And as this film version of *Les Miz* comes to an end, Javert finally catches up to Valjean who, mad as a bull after years of being tormented by Javert, asks him, "Why couldn't you have just left me alone," and Javert starts hooting and cackling like the evil villains at the end of any animated Disney feature: "You should kill me now, when you have the chance, because I'm never going to stop making your life hell! Hahahahaha!" Valjean tries to shoot Javert, and even though he really wants to do it, he's a good man (as are almost all of Jean Gabin's characters), and so instead, he just tells Javert that he's going to set him free. Recognizing that there's no way he'd ever be able to win against Valjean (Javert, as it turns out, has a grudgingly-jealous respect for Valjean, which is what their whole rivalry has always been about, anyway), Javert next throws himself into the Seine, drowning himself instantly.

Valjean, Cosette and Marius escape, and live happily ever after.

Director Chanois' big, bold, and sumptuously-entertaining color version of *Les Miserables* was exhibited in France in two separate halves, so that if you were interested in seeing the whole thing, you had to go to the movie theater on two different days. In America, however, the film was released—and sadly, only in the usual one-or-two art-houses—as a single, three hour and forty-two minute epic. This U.S. release version was dubbed into English, and it is this version which is today readily available in America, on DVD.

You'd think that the Gabin/Chanois *Les Miserables* would be better known in the U.S. today, not only because it's extremely entertaining, but also because Americans love every other version of Victor Hugo's timeless story that they're given the chance to see, and that includes the 1980 musical version, as well as 1988's non-musical film which starred Liam Neeson as Valjean and Uma Thurman as Cossette. In this author's opinion (and we all know what opinions are like!) Chanois' French-produced *Les Miserables* is just as great as any of those other great adaptations of *Les Miserables,* and it even compares very favorably to some of the more critically-acclaimed epic movies which were made in the 1950s and 1960s, like *Lawrence of Arabia* and *Ben-Hur* (and if you ever see the Gabin version of *Les Miserables,* you'll believe me). And speaking of *Ben-Hur:* The only thing that the Gabin/Chanois version of *Les Miserables* is missing, is a scene which we *do* get to see in the American-made, 1935 film version of the story (it starred Frederic March, and was directed by Richard Boleslawski), in which March's Jean Valjean is sent to the Galley—just like another great movie character, Judah Ben-Hur—where he gets tortured, for stealing that famous loaf of bread.

What a Critic Said at the Time: "The French, on the surface, have their first blockbuster in this pic. The film's main strength is Jean Gabin's thesping. [It's a] good reconstruction of the 19th century. It's [a bit overdrawn and sometimes] plodding, and [some] pruning [might be] in order, but the main burden rests in the capable hands of Gabin. The directing is academic, if competent. It should be a smash grosser, in France." (*Variety*, 4-9-58 issue. Critic: "Mosk. [George Moskowitz.]" Reviewed in Paris.)

With Nadja Tiller.

FILM 64

Le Desordre et la nuit

France/Italy, 1958

(Literal English Translation: "DISORDER AND THE NIGHT") Directed by Gilles Grangier. Produced by Lucien Viard. Screenplay by Michel Audiard and Gilles Grangier. Based Upon the Novel by Jacques Robert. Director of Photography (black and white), Louis Page. Editor, Jacqueline Sadoul. Music by Henri Contet and Jean Yatove. Production Designer, Robert Bouladoux. (GENRES: DRAMA/THRILLER) A Production of Orex Films (France) and Cine del Duca (Italy). Running Time, 1 hour 33 minutes. Released in France on May 14, 1958, by Corona. Released in the United States with English Subtitles as "DISORDER AND THE NIGHT" (press materials)/"NIGHT AFFAIR" (on-screen title) by President Films, on October 12, 1961.

"Just look at her! She's half-woman and half-heroin!"
—*Inspector Gabin checks out a cute girl who O.D.'d on heroin, in "Le Desordre et la nuit"*

The detective thriller *Desordre et la nuit* (*Disorder in the Night*), Gilles Grangier's fourth Gabin picture after *La Vierge du Rhin, Gas-Oil, Le Sang a la tete,* and *Le Rouge est mis,* is watchable, because Jean Gabin is so good in it, and because technically, it's very well-made, although it also happens to be one of the most baffling, confusing, and overly-complicated crime movies you've ever seen, especially in its last half-hour; the picture actually makes even less sense ('disorder,' is right!) than the ten-years-earlier suspense classic which many consider to be the most confusing narrative feature film ever made, Howard Hawks' 1945 Raymond Chandler adaptation *The Big Sleep,* and that's really saying something (and if you don't believe me, check out the excerpt from critic Howard Thompson's New York *Times* review, from which I'll quote at the end of this chapter). I'll spend this chapter filling you in on everything that I saw happening in the movie—or, should I say, everything that *I think* happened—although, I'm also admitting freely, at the same time, that I'm probably just guessing, and that in the end, I have no idea what some of the characters' relationships really were to each other, and repeated viewings didn't clear the confusion up for me, either.

Le Desordre et la nuit opens with a jazz-infused bang, as an ex-pat African-American jazz drummer pounds out his 'reet' beat in an American-themed Paris Jazz club called *Ville d'oeste*

(*'Western Town'*), and it's a very cool movie-opening—one which will, in fact, be copied, in not one, but two, first-rate American *noir* pictures—director/star Allen Baron's recently re-discovered *Blast of Silence* (1961), and Ralph Nelson's French/U.S. 1965 co-production, *Once a Thief*. In fact, since *Desordre et la nuit* wouldn't make it to American cinemas until 1961, it's easy to see that Allen Baron lifted the opening of his own film, wholecloth, from this Gabin/Grangier picture.

Desordre is set in Boulogne, in northern France: We first meet jazz club *chanteuse*/prostitute Lucky (Nadja Tiller), when she's negotiating with a john, and this guy must be some kind of an accountant or banker (or talent agent), because he tells her that he wants to pay her "ten percent less" than her usual hooking fee. ("It's too exorbitant," the guy yells out.) Instead, she dances with a balding nebbish, Blasco (Robert Manuel), who tells her, while they're dancing, that he's tired of life. (That's no way to 'get to third-base' unless you're trying to get to third-base, with Sylvia Plath!) In spite of his pessimistic outlook, she likes him better than that other guy—the one who was trying to cadge a discount.

But Blasco isn't half as nerdy as he seems to be: He is, in fact, a big-time drug lord, and the club's owner Albert Simoni (Roger Hanin) wants Lucky to cozy up to Blasco, so that he (Albert) will be able to rip Blasco off. She tells Albert that she doesn't want to be involved in his schemes anymore, and that she just wants to sing (and presumably, fuck), however, he's not interested in any of her backtalk: "It's my club, and I'll give you orders if I want to, okay?!" (End of Sermon!)

At this point, a jazz songstress, Valentine Horse, emerges down the staircase, and this movie's nicest surprise, is that she's played by a true legend—Hazel Scott:

Born in 1920, the legendary singer and pianist Hazel Scott deserves to be remembered: She was the very first African-American woman to ever star in her own t.v. show, the eponymously-named 1950s' variety program, "The Hazel Scott Show." When Scott was accused of being a Communist-sympathizer by HUAC, and when she also refused to appear in racially segregated nightclubs, her show was cancelled, only months after it began. Unable, subsequently, to glean any work in the United States, she divorced her husband, the Congressman (and Reverend) Adam Clayton Powell, Jr., and in 1957, she moved to France, where she began performing on stage to great acclaim, even acting in a couple of films (including 1958's *Desordre et la nuit*), before returning to America in the mid-'60s. A 2002 telefilm, *Keep the Faith, Baby*, is a great introduction to the Hazel Scott/Adam Clayton Powell marriage, and in that picture, Vanessa L. Williams portrays Hazel Scott, and Harry J. Lennix plays Adam Clayton Powell.

The tune which Scott's 'Valentine' character trills in her first scene, features those typically-weepy kind of 'lost-love lyrics' which always seem to find their way into the cabaret scenes of any number of 1930s-through-1950s' French movies. SAMPLE LYRICS: "Locked up all alone... I adore only you... Will he come back?" (You know the drill...)

1954 — 1976 | 173

Driving home that night, and taking a detour through the *Bois de Boulogne* (the Boulogne Woods), Lucky (talk about 'shit luck!') comes upon her boss, Albert Simoni, right as he's in the process of getting plugged like a nickel, but we can't see who the gunman is. We, the film's audience, immediately suspect that it was Blasco—but maybe it wasn't...

Down at the precinct house, Commissioner Janin (Francois Chaumette) and Inspector Chaville (Paul Frankeur) are checking out Simoni's mug shot because, as we're finding out now, not only has he been arrested before, but he's been arrested more than once. The cops discuss how Simoni, before he became the owner of the *Ville d'oeste,* had already been jailed three times and that, in fact, his rap sheet stretches back to WWII, which is when he made his living selling drugs to American G.I.'s who were stationed in France. Simoni, as the two cops are now telling each other, and us, took over the bar when its original owner was killed, and there have always been unsubstantiated rumors that Simoni had the guy rubbed-out. The cops know that there is currently prostitution and drug-peddling going on inside the club, so they decide to put in a phone call to Jean Gabin's level-headed/white-trenchcoated Inspector Vallois, a guy who's basically Inspector Maigret, only without the pipe and the name. The Commissioner and the Inspector are sure that always dependable Vallois will find Simoni's killer—and quickly, too: "Vallois found the killer (a strangler) in another case, a case which was impossible for us to solve," Janin tells Chaville. "He'll really be put to the test, to see who killed Albert Simoni." Chaville replies, "I'll phone Vallois and see if he wants to work on the case, but it'll be tricky to get him, because he doesn't like to speak too much (that's Our Gabin!), and he doesn't like the phone." At this point, the two cops' hot Secretary, who's played by Lisa Jouvet (daughter of Louis Jouvet, who played the Baron in *Les Bas-fonds*), is very amusingly, walking around the office with a little tin can, trying to raise money for a cause that she supports, but Chaville and Janin are busy, and they ignore her.

We first see Gabin's Inspector Vallois as he's interrogating a gangly, pencil-mustached guy in a bar, a crazy who wants to take the credit for having murdered Simoni even though he was nowhere near the Boulogne Woods when the murder happened, because he longs for the comfort and three square meals which only jail can provide. (Remember the Landlord who had a 'jones' for getting arrested, in *Crime et chatiment?* Well: *Same kinda dude, different flick.*) "You're not asking me *why* I killed Simoni," the guy grins, continuing, "I wouldn't tell you, anyway. But I *will* tell you, that I still have the gun I used." Vallois, amused, plays along with this loser, who's now, in addition to his other horseshit, telling Vallois that he planned on taking over Simoni's club (which is funny, because this is a guy who looks like he doesn't have two nickels to rub together).

Vallois next heads over to the *Ville d'oeste*, where he interrogates hooker-with-a-heart-of-gold Lucky who, of course, is instantly fascinated by this older man, and so much so, that she even invites him up to her pad: "Want to come over to my place?" she coos, in sultry hookerspeak. "You're all alone, Inspector... and I have all night." She follows him into a phone booth and continues hitting on him, but Vallois just tells her that he'd rather go home, to his *own* home, and go to sleep. (Jean Gabin no longer has to prove his masculinity in his

174 | **THE FILMS** CYCLE FIVE

With Nadja Tiller.

films—it's just 'a given.') She keeps trying to seduce him anyway, and just when it seems that she's not getting anywhere, *finally*, she's able to wear him down.

Up at her place, in the next sequence, Lucky's now changing into a sexy negligee, and telling Vallois that she's German, but that she's been in Paris for three years: "I'm from Munich," she informs him, "but I wanted to come to Paris to learn French." Weirdly, even though Vallois knows what Lucky's line of work is (that's why he's there!), he persists in asking her about what she does to make a living, anyway. (Maybe he just wants to hear her say it herself, so that he can do some kind of tough-love/intervention-act on her.) She tells him, guardedly, that she always "finds money," and we see that she genuinely likes gruff old Vallois, and we can also tell that, most probably, she won't be hitting him up for any bread, for the sex which we know they're probably going to start having over the next few minutes.

Vallois tells Lucky that he already knows she was Albert Simoni's mistress, and he asks her, next, how long she was with Simoni for. She admits only that she had an affair with Simoni for a year, and that right now, she's interested only in present company: "I'm 23," she moons at gruff-faced Vallois, "and tonight, I want to be in your arms." Then, weirdly (and this is pretty unexpected), instead of moving in for a little kiss, Vallois slaps her face! And the slap just makes her hot, and they next start mashing their faces together, in complete and utter abandon.

Simultaneously, back at the *Ville d'oeste*, the Creole Combo (it's how this real-life musical act is billed in the opening titles of this film), is serving-up some griddle-hot licks. Janin and Chaville are on the premises and, as they stare down at the revelry over the railing of the club's second storey, they continue their seemingly ongoing discussion of Simoni's killing: "Simoni had a private life," Chaville remarks to Janin, which is something that we already knew. "I don't know if it was *that* private," Janin returns. "His friends always knew what he was doing [dealing drugs]." As the two lawmen continue talking, director Grangier now cuts to the stage, where a pair of Afro-Cuban dancers (a muscle-bound male and a hot, sinewy female) are performing a steamy, 'proto-dirty dancing'-act, and both the man and the woman are adorned only in musculature-and-sinew-revealing undies. (This same dance duo will replicate its fiery act on film two years later, in director Michelangelo Antonioni's hypnotic 1961 classic, *La Notte:* Marcello Mastroianni and Jeanne Moreau are front-and-center at a trendy Rome supper club, watching the exact-same duo, who are putting on the exact-same performance.) "This show is dirty," Chaville smiles, clearly relishing every second of it. "Well, that's what the clientele wants," Janin winkingly reminds him, continuing, "That's how they dance in Cuba. It brings out passion. It's primitive!"

At this point, the very striking Therese (Danielle Darrieux—Bebe Donge, herself) enters the club, looking for Simoni and not knowing that he's been killed, and while we're not exactly sure who Therese is right now, we're going to find out later, that she's the shady pharmacist who supplied Simoni with many of the illegal narcotics which he had sold at his club.

Back in Lucky's apartment, concurrently, we see that Vallois and Lucky have just consummated their new relationship, and are lying in bed together. Post-coitally, and now that her defenses are down, he tells her that he'd like to know more about her relationship with Simoni, but even though she's just been 'Gabined' (!), she still won't say very much more than she already has, and he can't even get mad at her for not wanting to talk because, right after she says that she has nothing to add to the subject, she begins convulsing like a Looney Tunes Tasmanian Devil, her body absent of the strong heroin to which it is very clearly addicted. Cruelly, instead of helping her, Vallois continues trying to interrogate her, even while she's writhing-away, which makes Vallois kind of a fucker, even though we still like him: "Ahhh," he opines, watching her spin like a top, "So, you were going out with Simoni because he gave you drugs! Aren't you ashamed? Can you go without heroin? Speak! Did he give it to you two or three times? Tell me everything!"

The next morning, when Lucky is 'back on planet Earth,' Vallois heads back into the *Ville d'oeste* with her and, as they enter the place, another prostitute (this one is wearing a fur coat) is getting chased into the building, by cops. This 'new whore' hides behind Vallois' estimable frame (she's probably slept with him, just like Lucky has), and begs him, "Tell them I'm with you!" Vallois grabs one of the entering cops by the scruff of the neck: "You look nervous. What are you guys looking for—more girls who knew Simoni?" Vallois drops Lucky back at her apartment.

The next day, Vallois is at his office typewriter, when Commissioner Janin drags himself in, and asks him if he'll be going back to the *Ville d'oeste,* tonight. Vallois just Gabin-shrugs: "Naaahhh. I'm only off one night a week." And of course, we already know what he's going to be doing with his night off: He'll be going back up to Lucky's usual hotel room, to 'get lucky with Lucky!'

When Vallois arrives in Lucky's room, he sees an older man who he thinks is one of her johns, arguing with her in German, and he's s ready to lay the guy out, but as it turns out, he's not a customer at all: It's Lucky's very sympathetic father, Friedel (Harald Wolff, *La Traversee de Paris's* gestapo-guy), who's pleading with her to come back home to Germany with him so that he can take care of her, and Friedel looks totally miserable when his daughter sends him away, alerting him that she's just not interested in family life. After Friedel has left the room, Lucky explains the situation to Vallois: "My father has been trying to get me to come home for the last three months." Vallois tells her that maybe, her dad has the right idea.

Vallois next tells Lucky that he wants her to give him some more information about the lounge-singer, Valentine (Hazel Scott's character), but she tries to evade the subject matter: "What do you want to know about her, for? I'm a singer, too, you know. But not at the *Ville d'oeste.* Somewhere else—a place where a lot of the girls go, to pick up some extra money."

What Lucky's just been referencing, is a private apartment in which Valentine, Lucky, and some of the other lady 'singers' from the club entertain generous gentlemen, and not just Frenchmen either, but international (especially, American) businessmen. Vallois insists that Lucky should take him there, so he can see the whole set-up for himself, and when Lucky and Vallois arrive at the secret apartment, Blasco (that volatile-looking *nebbish*) is there, so Lucky introduces them. Blasco tells Vallois that he's seen him before, hanging around the club, and when Blasco leaves the room, Lucky tells Vallois that Blasco has just taken over ownership of the *Ville d'oeste.* (Vallois is now wondering, just as we the audience are now wondering, as well: Did Blasco kill Simoni? And if he did, did he do it expressly for the purpose of taking over the club?) Vallois, now somewhat jealously, asks Lucky if she's ever slept with Blasco, and her great and extremely uncomfortable reply is, "The least amount possible!"

Hazel Scott's Valentine-character is present in this secret apartment as well, and she introduces herself to Vallois, by telling him that she, too, has seen him around the *Ville d'Oeste,* and that she's happy that he's now, finally, putting in an appearance here, at this other, more private 'party.' She asks him if he's eaten, and hands him a chicken leg, informing him that Mr. Blasco, whom he's just met, has some pretty unusual eating habits. ("He only eats chicken *with caviar.*")

More women (and men) are luxuriating in the adjoining room, including a drunken, James Dean-looking American playboy, Peter (Edward Fleming), who's getting a bit rough with the ladies. While Vallois munches-out on his chicken leg, Lucky's now belting out a torchy standard for the customers, which is exactly what she told Vallois she did—so she wasn't lying to him. While she sings, Peter starts insulting her singing-skills to her face (he's another of French Cinema's much-vaunted 'Ugly American'-characters), telling her that her singing is "reminiscent of a dying duck." Vallois, without a moment's hesitation, knocks the guy on his ass, and Lucky calls Vallois, "my hero." He tells her that it will probably be hard for her to land a good singing job in the 'real-world' because, as he explains it to her, "… you're a white girl who sings like the blacks" (and of course, what the filmmakers didn't anticipate fifty years ago, when this movie was made, is that today, every white-girl diva-songstress on MTV makes her living by 'sounding black')! Peter, who's too drunk at this point to be feeling any pain, next goes after somebody who he thinks will be an easier target for his whiskey-soaked criticisms, Blasco who, as we already know, is a tough-guy himself, in spite of his outwardly-goony-looking appearance. The American whacks Blasco over the head with a broken bottle, and Vallois slaps the shit out of the American guy for a second time, just because in 'French Wish Fulfillment/Dreamland,' French guys can actually beat up American guys!

Since the bottle has cut Blasco's head open, Vallois now takes him to the local pharmacy. (As we're going to be seeing in another Gabin picture, 1965's *Le Tonnerre de Dieu*, 'Our Gabin' always nurses the people whom he beats up, back to health. [He's a fighter and, per "Saturday Night Live's" Al Franken character, Stuart Smalley, he's also 'a healing nurturer.']) There's a reason that Vallois has picked this particular pharmacy, too: It's pharmacist Therese Marken's (Danielle Darrieux's) apothecary.

Therese asks Blasco how his head got cut, and he cryptically replies, "I fell," which must be the 1950s' version of our contemporary 21st-century battered housewives, who are prone to proclaiming that they've 'fallen down the stairs.' As Therese sews 'Blotto Blasco' back up, she reveals to Vallois that she knew Simoni personally, but only for six months. Her 'Rx' for Blasco, is that he's going to have to stay in the hospital overnight (which, of course, he starts whining about).

Vallois and Lucky proceed *au bar* for a late night coffee, and she tells him that she's feeling extra-tired lately, and also that she 'feels ugly.' (If it were the present day, she'd be asking him, "Am I fat?") Feeling safe around Vallois, she also confesses to him, for a second time, that she dreams of singing to bigger crowds, and maybe even international crowds, and she also tells him that she knows, whether he wants to admit it or not, that he's falling in love with her. Probably though, she's just projecting her own feelings onto him because, in this movie, Gabin, who is even more stone-faced than he's ever been in any other movie made up to this time, isn't showing any emotions at all: "You're drinking with me right now, because you love me. I don't care about your investigation—only about you." After getting all *mushy and lovey-dovey* on him, the obviously bipolar Lucky next, in the same exact two-second period, throws Vallois a big, hairy contradiction curveball, telling him that she's going to be leaving Paris, and for good. (To paraphrase the great 20th-century American bard Charles M. Shulz, women are so "wishy-washy!")

Lucky's combination come hither/go away, 'I-Love-You-But-I'm-Leaving'–salvo sends Vallois, who likes things to be entirely black or white (and never both) into this film's one-

and-only Gabin-Outburst: "You think you're a big singer, and you think you're a black girl?! Well, I've got news for you: You're not! I'm done with you! And I'm going home!" (And he does, too!) She thought he would be mesmerized by her mixed messages (<u>Author's Note</u>: Why do chicks think always think that?), but Jean Gabin doesn't go in for that! Frustrated that her mind-games didn't work on him, she now exclaims, *"Merde!"* and hides her head in her hands.

The next day at the precinct house, Commissioner Janin informs Vallois that Albert Simoni has a step-brother whom were now hearing about for the first time, Henri Marken (Louis Ducreux), and that Henri has just become the newest suspect (besides Blasco) in Albert's murder. Henri is president of France's biggest government-run pharmaceutical house, the Laboratory of France, and—surprise!—he's also married to Therese, the pharmacist. The cops are now learning, as well, that Therese Marken had been cheating on her husband with Albert, which also explains how she's been able to get all of the *medicaments* which Henri's step-brother Albert sold at the *Ville d'oeste*. "It's not a game to sell morphine in clubs," Vallois now informs a group of his fellow cops, looking right into the camera as he says this (just like Jack Webb on any episode of *Dragnet*).

When we first meet Henri Marken (Louis Ducreux) in the film's next sequence, a bunch of cops are visiting him at his wife's pharmacy, and he's trying to deflect them away from the fact that they consider him to be a suspect in his step-brother's murder, by pressing them to investigate the murder even more than they already are—but he's not fooling anybody, because this highly-strung guy looks completely guilty! Down at the precinct, meanwhile, Vallois is promising his cop brethren that he's going to start working doubly hard on this investigation: "And it's not because I might be 'getting along' with that girl, Lucky, that I'm so fascinated by this whole affair—I mean, if that's what you guys are thinking."

Next, Lucky's dad, Friedel, appears again: He's returned to Paris, and is pleading with Vallois to intercede on his behalf, in trying to get Lucky to come home to Germany with him. Maybe Friedel feels that, because Vallois is similar in age to him, Vallois would understand 'a father's feelings:' "My daughter is leading a dangerous life. Inspector, I will pay you, if only you will just bring her back to me, and to Munich!"

Jean Gabin, as we know from the characters which we've already seen him playing in other 1950s' pictures, is a devout family man, but only when it comes to his own movie families: "I can't take your money," he tells Friedel… and then Friedel actually starts crying! "Please, Inspector! Have mercy on an old man! I want my daughter back!" Vallois tells Friedel that he'll try to help him, but that he can't promise anything.

Vallois heads back to Therese's Pharmacy, and since Therese doesn't want people who might be lurking around to think that she and the Inspector are talking police business, she pretends that Vallois has come here for a medical checkup, and she weighs him on her medical scale. (That's right: In France, or at least in the France of this movie, a pharmacist has the power of an actual doctor.) But Vallois comes right to the point: "I know that you and your husband Henri were, and probably still are, supplying narcotics to the *Ville d'oeste*.

Lucky's my friend, and she already told me it's true—we have no secrets from each other." But Therese doesn't want to hear this, and she now introduces a new *fun-fact* which we didn't know about: "That bitch was sleeping with Albert when I was sleeping with him, so don't trust anything that comes out of her mouth." Next, not wanting to invite any problems her way, she changes her tone, and starts appealing to Vallois more gently: "Listen, Inspector, instead of all of this accusing, maybe we can help each other." She then pretends to be vulnerable (strong-looking Therese has probably never had a vulnerable moment in her whole life), telling Vallois that her marriage to Henri hasn't been all peaches and cream, and that Henri beat her on more than one occasion, when he found out that she was 'seeing' his step-brother.

Back at the *Ville d'oeste* that same evening, Valentine Horse is belting out another of her torchy tunes (LYRICS: "My friend… I love to love you… My heart is crazy… Love forever," [*etc.*]) and, after this brief musical interlude, it's plot-twist time: Vallois, as we'll now learn, is 'getting played' by his police-force 'brethren,' Commissioner Janin and Inspector Chaville, two guys who are always perfectly nice to him when they're in front of his face, but who are, in all actuality, total backstabbers when he's not around: Even thought it was their idea to bring Gabin's Inspector Vallois onto the case, they are both intensely competitive with Vallois, since Vallois always solves every case which he's made a part of, and he's the one cop who always gets all of the *kudos* from the top brass. We're learning, in this scene, that Chaville and Janin are actually competing with Vallois to find out who Simoni's killer was, and Janin now confronts Vallois, and in an angry tone: "I don't care about you, Vallois, and it was a mistake for me to assign you to the case. I am personally going to close up that nightclub in three days, because of all of the drug trafficking that's going on there, and I want you to stay out of my way when I'm doing it. Is that clear?! And guess what: I'm going to bust your girlfriend Lucky tomorrow, as one of the prime suspects, and now that I think about it, I could probably haul *your* ass in too, for personal negligence [read: for 'sexing-up' one of the murder suspects!], if I really wanted to. And don't try to stop me because, if you do, everything you do in your life will just be gardening after that!" (Jean Gabin Movie-Rule #1: Do Not Threaten Jean Gabin!)

A big problem with this movie, besides the fact that the story is too convoluted, is a problem with which we're already familiar from *La Marie du port, Fille Dangereuse, La Verite sur Bebe Donge, La Vierge du Rhin,* and *Le Sang a la tete,* namely: None of the characters really knows what he or she wants: Janin wants Vallois on the Albert Simoni case and yet, at the same time, he doesn't want him on it; Lucky tells Vallois that she loves him, and that she wants them to be together, but in the same breath, she also tells him that she's thinking about leaving Paris for good. Now, I know what you're thinking, 'Reader:' You're thinking, "Well, in real-life, everybody is wishy-washy, and sometimes none of us knows what we want, and every single one of us is a walking contradiction." Okay, granted. But, dig: A movie isn't real life! In a movie, we need our main characters to want something specific, because the narrative of every good movie is always driven by the character's need to overcome obstacles, and to attain the thing that he or she really and truly wants. In any movie, our characters must want something, or else we can't root for them, and we lose interest. Ambiguity in a movie (when the audience doesn't know what's going to happen to a character) is good, because it keeps a film's viewers interested. Apathy, on the other hand (which is when a movie character doesn't want anything at all) is a cardinal sin.

Vallois now leaves the precinct house, and Lucky is waiting outside for him in the passenger seat of his car. She tells him that if the other cops are feeling any animosity toward him, that she knows it's all her fault: "I told the other officers that I slept with you. I'm sorry." When Vallois hears this, he becomes a little mad at her, as he knows he should, and tells her she's going to be "sleeping alone tonight," but really, he's unable to get too mad, because she's so beautiful; and so he now, more soothingly, adds, "Look, Lucky: I think you know exactly who Simoni's killer is, and if you want me to get you out of this, you'd better give me the person's name, so I can lock him up before [the other cops come and] lock you up." (*A-ha!* Now, it becomes clear! Janin wants to bust Lucky for Simoni's murder, not because he has any proof that she murdered him, but because he's jealous that his arch-enemy Vallois gets to be with her, and he doesn't!) Lucky next confesses to Vallois truthfully that, in fact, she *does* know the identity of Simoni's killer, but that she can't tell him, because the killer is a friend of hers. (It's got to be someone who gives Lucky drugs, since her drug connections are the only friends she hangs around with outside of work, which means that we're probably talking Therese, and/or Henri.)

Then we get another cool plot twist: It's not just the cops and the killers who are 'playing' Vallois:

It's Lucky, too!

As Lucky and Vallois motor through town in Vallois' car, with Lucky behind the wheel and Vallois in the passenger seat, Vallois pumps Lucky for any information she might have about Therese. (He's figured out, as we all have, that Therese is the one who's 'fixing' Lucky, whenever she needs 'H.') Lucky, who suddenly feels more of an allegiance toward her (probable) supplier Therese than she does to Vallois, suddenly jams her foot on the brakes and stops-short on purpose, and Vallois' head smashes against the windshield! (Obviously, Lucky doesn't want Therese and Henry arrested for Simoni's murder, because then, the drug train will stop.)

The next time we see Vallois, he's in a hospital bed. (He can't catch the bad guys if he's laid-up: Maybe Henri [or Therese, or Blasco] put Lucky up to the whole 'stopping short'-bit, or else maybe some of Vallois' enemies on the force, like Janin, put her up to it, since Janin knows that Vallois can't solve the crime from a hospital bed.)

Just who you don't want to see when you're immobile and helpless in a hospital bed, is a guy who hates your guts—and so it is that, at that exact moment, Janin enters Vallois' room, bearing a box of cigars and wearing an ear-to-ear grin because, now that Vallois is in the hospital, he can investigate the Simoni murder, and maybe even solve it, by himself! Janin opines, "I'll bet it was that freak Blasco who forced Lucky to stop short on purpose, so that you wouldn't be able to investigate," and Vallois tells him that he doesn't know who told her to do it. Janin, who's happy because he's now holding the reins in the investigation, now brags to Vallois that, when Vallois gets out of the hospital, he won't be on the case anymore: "I'm going to assign you to something else. Oh, and as long as I'm here, how about telling me where Lucky is hiding?" Vallois, who's as steamed as a cracked-crab, now starts lying through his teeth, plaintively stating, "I don't remember anything." Janin doesn't like it when people don't tell him what he wants to know, and now that tough-guy Vallois is prone, he can fuck with him all he wants to: "Look, if you don't tell me everything you know about the case, I'll see to it that you're off the force for good, okay!" As soon as Janin leaves the hospital room, Vallois, having had more than enough of this shit, gets dressed, and sneaks out of the hospital. (Maybe he was bluffing everybody, including Lucky and Janin, and maybe he was never hurt in the car, but wants them all to think he was, so that he can leave the hospital and continue his investigation, unmonitored by Janin, Chaville, Blasco, and everybody else.) When Vallois arrives back at his precinct house, and to the horror of all of the other backstabbing cops on-site (which is basically, as we're now finding out, all of them), there's only one young Cop (Jacques Muller) who's happy to have him back, and this kid is excited about being in the presence of the legendary Inspector Vallois. He pledges to help Vallois in any way he can.

Vallois arrives at Therese's house, surprising her at two-in-the-morning, and tells her, point-blank, that he thinks she might be the one who killed Albert Simonin in a moment of extreme-mega-anger, because he once slapped her in front of other people, and this slap-heard-'round-the-world has apparently become a thing of legend down at the *Ville d'oeste*. Therese can't make any response though because, at this moment, Lucky and Henri both enter the room. (Henri and Therese have been hiding Lucky out at their house for the last few days.)

Since Therese won't admit to anything, even though Vallois thinks that she's the most likely murder-suspect, he must now ask Lucky again if she killed Albert Simoni, since Lucky is Vallois' 'second-choice.' She tells him that she didn't do it, and we know that she's telling the truth, because her face is radiating nothing but total honesty.

Henri now says (and he looks very truthful as he's saying it) that he didn't kill Albert Simoni either, although he *does* admit to Vallois that he's always hated his step-brother. (For sleeping with his wife? The movie doesn't say, but probably, that's why.) Henri, who's no longer required in the questioning, storms out into the street to buy some cigarettes.

Therese takes the opportunity of her husband's absence to tell Vallois that her husband Henri was (long ago, and 'once upon a time') a nice guy, which is why she married him, but that he's not so nice anymore, and that Albert (who, in her opinion, was an 'idiot') was "no good," either. Vallois doesn't know if it is Therese or Lucky who was Simoni's killer, but suddenly, he is unable to question Lucky any further, because she now starts having another one of her famous seizures, due to the lack of drugs in her system. As she falls down and starts shaking, Vallois makes a diagnosis of her present medical condition: "Right now, she's 'half-lucky' and 'half-heroin…'"

Unable to take any more of this interrogation by Vallois, and rattled by Lucky's *conniption* fit, Therese next denies what she's just said about how she *didn't* kill Albert: She now admits to Vallois that she killed Albert herself, and she even gives him the long version: Lucky knew Therese was screwing her husband's brother, Albert, who Lucky was also screwing, and Therese admits that she thought if she supplied Lucky with drugs, maybe Lucky wouldn't *narc* on Henri about the affair.

Therese continues: "One time, Albert asked Henri and me for some morphine, which he needed for a friend at the club, a guy who (he told us, anyway) was a cancer patient. I gave him the morphine, but he kept asking me for more. I knew it was for something else, but I kept giving it to him, anyway. Then, Albert kept wanting greater and greater amounts.

"Then, I met Lucky, and I understood that at least part of the drugs he was asking me for, was for her, and I was hurt, because Lucky is somebody whom I trusted as a friend." (So: Both Lucky and Therese were sleeping with Albert!) "Albert blackmailed me, telling me that if I didn't give him drugs, he would tell Henri that I was sleeping with Albert. So to keep my husband safe—I killed my lover."

"So it was a crime of passion?" Vallois asks, non-plussed. He tells her that he's "taking her in," adding that after he brings her down to the station and books her, that he's done with police-work for good, and that he's retiring because, in his opinion, "the police are just as corrupt as the criminals."

Therese continues her confession, now admitting to Vallois that it wasn't just because of the slap that she killed Simonin, either: "Albert was going to leave me, for Lucky."

At this point, Lucky has finally stopped convulsing, and becomes lucid once again: "I took too much heroin," the scared-out-of-her-wits girl meekly pouts to Vallois and Therese, then asking, "Am I going to die?"

Henri returns to the pharmacy now, and tells Vallois that he knows Therese was cheating on him, but also that they both were truly in love with each other when they were first married. (We can tell that this Caspar Milquetoast-type character didn't get a lot of action before he was married, and that he just took whatever he could get. [And what he got, was very good!]) Vallois calls Commissioner Janin in, and gloatingly informs him that he's solved the crime, and that Lucky wasn't the murderer.

The nice Young Cop (Jacques Muller) now arrives at the pharmacy, and Vallois hands the wrap-up work on the case over to him, telling the younger man that he's going to be going away to the country for two or three weeks, so that he can be "surrounded by palm trees." Lucky asks him if he'll be coming back to Paris, and he replies, in ultra-suave Bogart-Gary Cooper-(Jean Gabin!) fashion, "Don't I always?" Lucky tells Vallois that she loves him, and that she'd like to go to the country with him, since she adores seeing cherries bloom in the spring. He agrees to her proposition, and she gets in his car with him (this time, he's driving!), and she's got a big smile plastered across her face. And surprise: Instead of taking Lucky to the country, he now drives her to a *rehab clinic!* The shingle over the door reads, '*La Maison de repos,*' and it's a very funny ending to a very confusing movie. And it's not just the film that was so confusing: The picture's American title is pretty confusing, as well:

The IMDB (Internet Movie Database) mentions that the film's American release title was *Night Affair,* and while it's possible that this may have been the on-screen title, the film's small North American distributor (New York City-based President Films) gave it a different title in its pressbook, *Disorder and the Night,* which is the exact English translation of the film's French title. In this American pressbook, Max Ophuls, who had previously directed *Desordre et la nuit's* co-stars, Jean Gabin and Danielle Darrieux together in his own picture, the much better *Le Plaisir,* is quoted:

"There are two people in the film world for whom the camera does not exist: Jean Gabin and Danielle Darrieux. They are not playing their parts to the camera when they act in films. They simply enter into their characters, and live their characters with disconcerting ease.'"

What a Critic Said at the Time: "By now, no Gallic actor should feel so much at home in the Paris underworld as the burly, cobra-eyed Jean Gabin [but the film is] weak… and lacks the cold, pounding drive of *Grisbi* and *Inspector Maigret.* The middle-third dangles too many details for the sake of suspense, and this film may try some viewers' patience—some of it is indeed meaningless, [and] you will wonder, we guarantee, exactly what this picture is up to!" (New York *Times,* 10-16-56 issue. Critic: Howard Thompson.)

What Another Critic Said at the Time: "Jean Gabin's solid filmic presence gives this film its main trump, but [it] has a telegraphed plot and plodding pace. The film tends to drag, without any penetration into character." (*Variety,* 7-23-58 issue. Critic: George Moskowitz. Reviewed in Paris.)

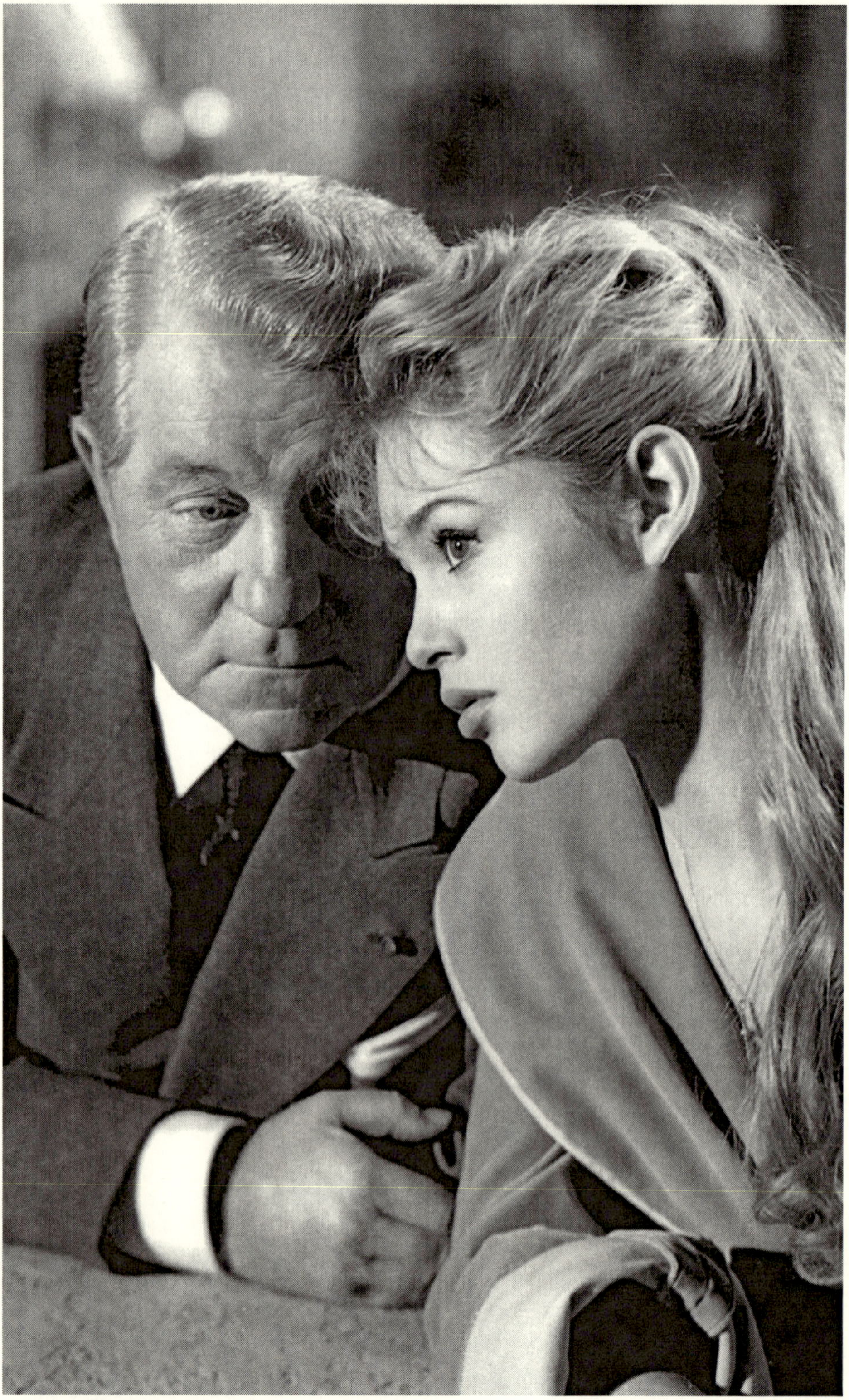

FILM 65

EN CAS DE MALHEUR

France/Italy, 1958

*(Literal English Translation/Release Title in Great Britain: "IN CASE OF ADVERSITY")
Directed by Claude Autant-Lara. Produced by Raoul Levy. Screenplay by Jean Aurenche and
Pierre Bost. Based Upon the Novel by Georges Simenon. Director of Photography (black and
white), Jacques Natteau. Editor, Madeline Gug. Music by Rene Cloerec. Production Designer,
Max Douy. (GENRE: DRAMA) Running Time, 1 hour 45 minutes. A Production of Incom/Iena
Productions/Union Cinematographique Lyonnaise. Released in France on September 17, 1958, by
Union Cinematographique Lyonnaise. Released in United States (in both English-Subtitled and
English-Dubbed Versions) on April 27, 1959 by Kingsley International Pictures, as "LOVE IS MY
PROFESSION."*

> "Well, here we all are! Now: What's next?"
> *— Gabin gets ready to have a ménage-a-trois with his girlfriend and his chambermaid, in "En cas de malheur"*

Now that snowy-haired Jean Gabin was turning the corner on 60, French production companies were still interested in starring him in their movies but, in an effort to bolster the box-office (read: to attract younger moviegoers, many of whom were not even alive during Gabin's 1930s' heyday), they'd begin teaming him with young 'up-and-comers,' including Jean-Paul Belmondo and Alain Delon—the latter with whom Gabin would make three films. But the most exciting team-up (from this author's prurient perspective, anyway) would definitely be the one between Gabin and the world's newest (at the time the movie was made) and *smokin'est* new sex bomb, Brigitte Bardot, in *En cas de malheur*, a film which would reteam Gabin with his *Traversee de Paris* director Claude-Autant Lara, a filmmaker who had always managed to make good and entertaining pictures. Brigitte Bardot (a/k/a, "BB") had just become well-known in America, based upon the successful North American 1957 art-house release of her 1956 Roger Vadim-directed classic, *Et Dieu... crea la femme* (*...And God Created Woman*).

In *Malheur*, Bardot's Yvette is a prostitute who, along with her friend Janine (Nicole

186 | **THE FILMS** CYCLE FIVE

Bardot in the foreground: She makes the rules.

Berger), has just robbed a store with a toy gun. She endeavors to hire Gobillot (a more-silent-than-ever J.G.) to be her lawyer, but he's not interested: He's already got a serious backlog of cases to work on, and besides, he's 'this close' to retirement. But when she flashes him some leg, she breaks through his steely resistance, landing herself the best mouthpiece in the Republic of France, and the name of Gabin's character in this picture, 'Gobillot,' is pretty wonderful: When Gabin meets Bardot, the look on his face says it all—he's ready to 'go below!'

Besides possessing hot legs (the kind that writers like Dashiel Hammett like to write, 'go all the way up'), Yvette's also got a young, layabout boyfriend, Mazzetti, who's played by Franco Interlenghi, an Italian actor who is best known in America, for two films: He's one of the swingin' bachelors who turns Rome on her ear in Federico Fellini's *I Vitelloni* (1953), and even before that, he played everybody's favorite heart-tugging shoeshine boy, in Vittorio De Sica's neo-realist 1946 masterwork, *Sciuscia* (*Shoeshine*). Mazzetti is freaked-out by Yvette's newfound May-September attraction to the much-older Gobillot. Gobillot even puts Yvette up in her own swanky apartment (on his own dime) which he visits nightly, telling his wife of more than thirty years, Vivianne, very solemnly, that he's "going out." (Mrs. Gobillot is played by Edwige Feuillere, who had already played Jean Gabin's wife once before: Twenty-three years before *En cas de malheur*, in 1935, she played Claudia—a/k/a, 'Mrs. Pontius Pilate'—to Gabin's Pilate, in Duvivier's *Golgotha*.) Mrs. Gobillot is pretty upset that her

Morning eye-opener.

husband is gallivanting around with another woman, but she also understands, instinctively, that a husband's natural right (ah! the good old days!) is to take a mistress, or two (or even *three*…).

Within days, Yvette and Gobillot are shacking up at Yvette's place, while he's working on Yvette's case (he gets her 'off the hook,' and she's getting him 'just plain off')! Gobillot's even hired a hot young maid, Noemie (Annick Allieres) to serve Yvette, and in one extraordinary sequence, Yvette and her lady-in-waiting switch roles: Yvette puts on the maid's outfit, while Noemi pretends to be 'the lady of the house.' The two hot twentysomething vixens sit opposite stony-faced old Gobillot and, as they start edging sensuously toward him, director Autant-Lara next fades slowly to black, and we understand that a *menage-a-trois* is now about to ensue. The following morning, when Yvette gets out of bed, we're treated to a notorious, 'blink-and-you'll-miss-it' tableau, which you can 'freeze-frame,' on the DVD, in which Bardot scampers across the room, displaying her five-star posterior. (The film's American theatrical distributor excised the famous 'ass' shot, although it's back today, on most of the film's various home video versions.)

As the film comes to its conclusion, Gobillot, who is aware that Yvette is also seeing Mazzetti besides him, finally asks her to make the choice between them. Yvette decides to remain with Gobillot, who buys an apartment for her, thus, Yvette leaves the old apartment (the address of which was known to Mazzetti) and moves into the new one. Mazzetti tries to locate Yvette's new place, but is unsuccessful. Yvette tells Gobillot that she is pregnant with his child, and Gobillot seems happy at the prospect of becoming a father, since his marriage to his wife Vivianne has been childless. Gobillot and Yvette go into a clothing shop to purchase a few articles for the winter holiday which they intend on taking together, and when Gobillot leaves the shop, Yvette remains inside, and purchases a sweater for Mazzetti, since she's continuing to see him, as well. She then goes to Mazzetti's place and they make love. Later, Gobillot phones the maid at the apartment and learns that Yvette never returned home. Gobillot goes to the police and is told that Yvette has been murdered. He goes to Mazzetti's where Yvette's body is on the bed. A cop tells him that they have arrested Mazzetti, and that Mazzetti told them that he has killed her because she didn't want to stay with him. She genuinely loved both men, in her own way.

If you have only a limited time left to live, and you can only see one of Jean Gabin's films from his later period, this is the one which I would recommend—not because it's his greatest film (although, to quote Peter Sellers, from the 1969 film, *The Magic Christian*, "it is very, very good, indeed"), and not because of the powerfully-moving Bardot Ass-Moment, but because *En cas de malheur* is the one Gabin movie in which, in one beautifully-edited sequence, director Autant-Lara shows us visually, *exactly* what it is that makes Jean Gabin's movie persona so unique:

Near the beginning of the picture, Bardot comes to Gabin's home, to enlist his lawyer-character, Gobillot, to represent her. First, we get a close-up of Bardot, in which she asks him, politely and demurely, to take on her case. Autant-Lara next cuts to a close-up Gabin's face, which is completely expressionless. (He's *totally* doing the whole 'Gabin-Scowl,' in which the actor gives us a shining example of his much-vaunted 'upside-down/parabola mouth.') The next shot, involves Bardot's trying to captivate Gabin by showing him some leg and after this, Autant-Lara returns to the exact same close-up of Gabin's expressionless scowl, which he had already shown us before (Autant-Lara duplicated the shot in the lab). In the shot which follows, Bardot changes her tactic: Instead of acting calm, she's now acting completely crazy, screaming and yelling for him to represent her and, after this, Lara returns, for the third time, to his reprint of that same exact close-up of Gabin's expressionless mug, which we've already seen twice before. Something amazingly cinematic has just happened during this sequence, and it's something so subtle, you might not even notice it the first time you see the picture: Lara uses one shot of Gabin's expressionless face, which he repeats three separate times, and each time we see the identical shot of his face, we believe that he's thinking something different about Bardot: When she asks him politely if he'll represent her, and we first see his face, we guess that he's thinking, "Not interested." When, next, she shows him some leg, Autant-Lara repeats the same shot of Gabin's expressionless face, and we now guess that he's thinking, "Hmm… Sounds pretty interesting! Maybe I *could* represent her, at that!" Finally, she begins acting *totally off-the-wall-nuts*, and Lara then cuts back to that same exact shot of Gabin. And even though his Gobillot character isn't saying anything, we now believe that he's thinking, "Okay, she's obviously a nut-ball, so I'm going to get her out of my house, and as fast as I can." In this one sequence, which has involved three different shots of Bardot, intercut with only one shot of Gabin which is repeated three times, Claude Autant-Lara has boiled down the essence of what makes Jean Gabin great: Each time Autant-Lara returns to that one shot of Gabin, we think that *Our Favorite Movie Star* is thinking something different, but he's not! We're creating his reactions to the different (and seductive) ploys which Bardot is trying out on him, in our minds, because he's not actually 'doing' anything at all. The great early Russian filmmakers who codified the grammar and syntax of movie editing back at the turn of the 20th century, including Dziga Vertov and Sergei Eisenstein, knew that any individual camera shot makes sense not by itself, but only in relation to the other shots which are placed both before and after it (just like how, when you write a sentence, none of the individual words make any contextual sense without the other words which come before and after it), and Gabin gets more out of doing 'less' in this film than he does in any other picture which he ever made. Gabin's whole minimalism-bag definitely reminds this author of that famous Billy Wilder story, in which Wilder was directing Jack Lemmon on the set of *Some Like It Hot:* Apparently, after the end of each take, Wilder told the usually histrionic Lemmon to "do less," and Lemmon apparently complained to Wilder, "But Billy, if I do any less, I won't be doing anything," to which Wilder, with a sly grin, replied, "Exactly!"

En cas de malheur, which is currently available in the U.S. on a bootleg DVD, is a great flick, and Bardot is really great in it. It was remade in 1999 by director Pierre Jolivet, as *En plein coeur* (*The Plain Heart*), and in this remake, Gerard Lanvin and Carole Bouquet (the 'Bond girl' from 1979's *Moonraker*) are 'Mr. and Mrs. Lawyer,' while Virgine Ledoyen plays the hooker role.

What a Critic Said at the Time: "Claude Autant-Lara is one of the best directors [working presently] in France. Jean Gabin is remarkably self-possessed, as a man obsessed with secret passions." (New York *Times*, 4-30-59 issue. Critic: Bosley Crowther.)

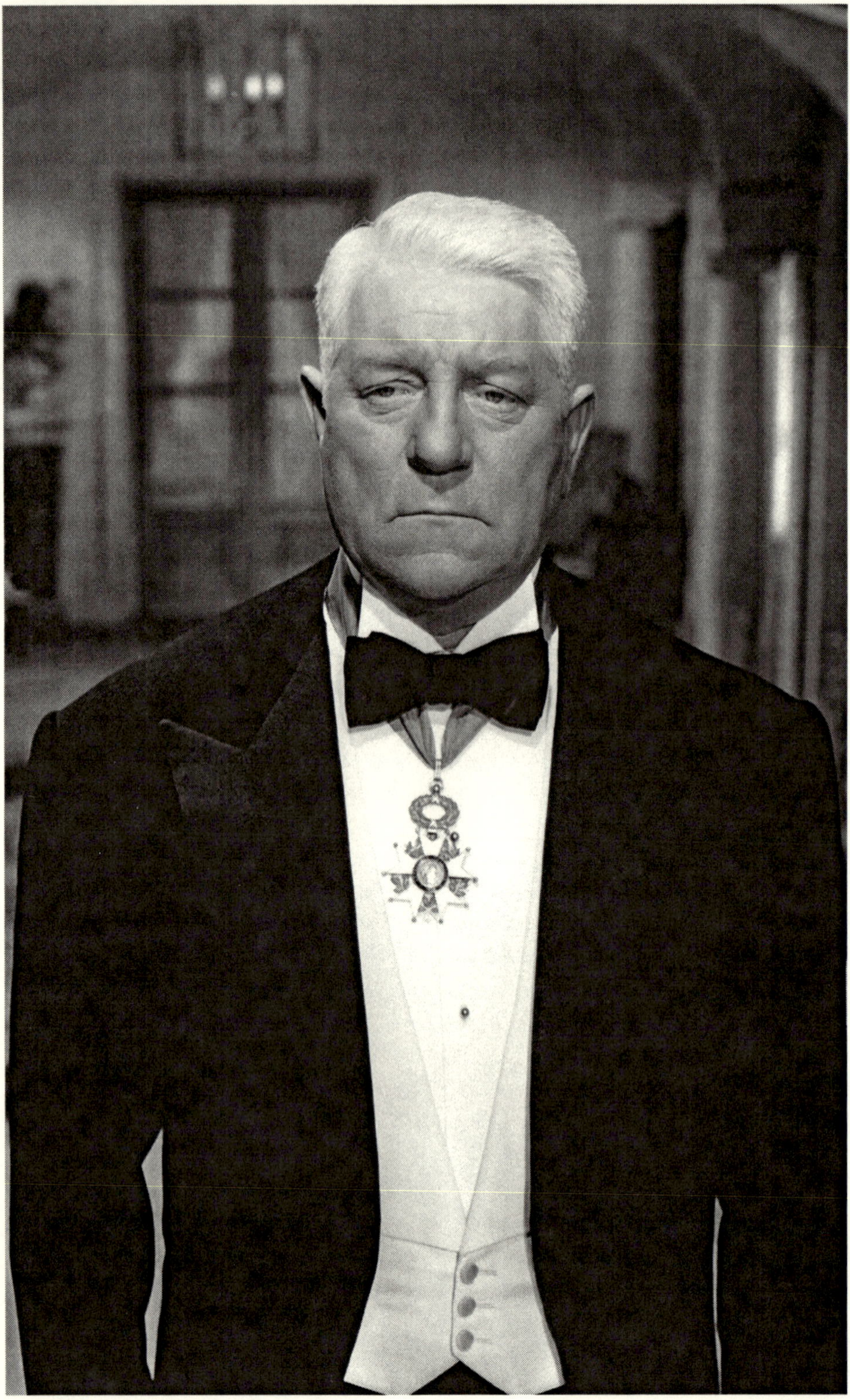

FILM 66

LES GRANDES FAMILLES

France, 1958

(Literal Translation: "THE GRAND FAMILIES") Directed by Denys de La Patelliere. Produced by Jean-Paul Guibert and Claude Hauser. Screenplay by Denys de La Patelliere. Based Upon the Novel by Maurice Druon. Director of Photography (black and white), Louis Page. Editor, Jacqueline Thiedot. Music by Maurice Thriet. Production Designer, Rene Renoux. (GENRE: DRAMA) A Production of Filmsonor S.A. and Intermondia Films. Running Time, 1 hour 32 minutes. Released in France on November 19, 1958, by Cinedis. Released in U.S. (in New York City) by Lopert Films Inc. with English subtitles on July 20, 1959, as "THE POSSESSORS."

"You're a nice moron!"
— *Multi-zillionaire industrialist Gabin tells-off a freeloading relative, in "Les Grandes familles"*

Les *Grandes familles*, which was released in the U.S. under the lurid, Harold Robbinsy-sounding-title *The Possessors*, is anything but lurid; in fact, it's very regal and staid (and cold, and uninvolving, and slow-paced), although like all Gabin movies, it's also exceedingly well-made (a special nod, here, to the film's great cinematographer Louis Page, who photographed eighteen Gabin movies, during the 1950s and 1960s). Like a lot of French movies, it's a very dry ensemble comedy—one which deals, very subtly, with the pretensions of 'the idle rich' *bourgeoisie*; in fact, in its own pompous way, this film is France's perversely-non-sexy answer to Tennessee Williams' *Cat on a Hot Tin Roof*, the film version of which was made earlier in 1958, right before *Les Grandes familles*. In *Grandes familles*, just like in *Hot Tin Roof*, we've got the requisite big, wealthy patriarch (Gabin) who's surrounded by a boatload of shifty/crafty family members, all of whom are trying to get their meathooks on his *bling-bling*; except where *Hot Tin Roof* traded in sex, *Les Grandes familles* substitutes a bunch of boring stiffs who prattle on (and on, and on), particularly during the film's final half-hour, about the intricacies of a stock market, which might be interesting if you've got twelve MBA degrees, but which will send you on *a one-way trip to Snooze-City* (first class!), if you don't. Gabin, as usual, comes across as cool, delivering one of his smooth/bored rich guy-characters with aplomb, and in fact, he comes off well, even when the movie itself does not. (To be honest, this movie is very well-regarded in France, which means, maybe, that it just wasn't lowbrow enough for this author!)

Like many of Gabin's other 1950s'-made pictures, *Les Grandes familles* is based upon a novel (this one, by author Maurice Druon), and part of the problem with the film, is that it seems like it was trying to incorporate every single plot complication and intrigue from the book, and so relatedly, about three-quarters of the way in, it becomes hard to follow, if you're not using a scorecard. What limited interest that *Les Grandes familles* might hold for American audiences today, in the 21st century, is solely related to the fact that it's a movie about 'the corrupting influences of nepotism:' In this movie, just like in real life, lots of people aren't getting their rightful breaks, because *some moron who's related to some other moron* is getting those breaks instead of *you*, and while Gabin's character is decidedly not a moron in this film (that would be impossible, anyway), his character *does* have a rather moronic son, and I wouldn't even say 'moronic:' What this manchild really is, is just naïve, spoiled, dilettantish, and marshmallow-soft.

Director Denys de La Patellière who, with this film, would be making his first of six Gabin films, starts us out with a voice-over narrator (*Bad Sign! Red Flag!* It means that the film has too much information, which the filmmakers weren't sure how to incorporate into the fabric of the drama), who starts the film off, by introducing us to about seven thousand members of an extended clan, the Schoudlers, who are presented to us as being "one of France's wealthiest families." The Schoudlers are on their way to a family funeral, and they happen to be arriving there *via* a long limousine wagon-train, so we're going to be meeting all of them at roughly the same time, one right after another. First, let's say *bonjour* to the white-haired family patriarch, Noel Schoudler (Gabin). Noel, our film's '*Big Daddy*,' is, as the film's Narrator is now informing us, a Commander of the Legion of Honor, not to mention the CEO of France's most popular newspaper, and as if that's not already more than enough, he also owns the country's largest sugar company. Noel's wife Adele (Annie Ducaux), who's sitting beside him in the limo, is described to us as being the President of the French Red Cross (wives of the privileged—yesterday, just like today—have always been enmeshed in their goofy, charitable causes), and Noel and Adele's dilettantish son Francois (Jean Desailly, who played Annie Girardot's wimpy manchild-hubby in *Maigret tend un piege*, and who is traveling in the next limo in line), used to be a student at the local polytechnical school, before he figured out that a young guy in his position would do better to just sit back and let the family wealth-spigot trickle-down in his general direction. Francois and his young wife, Jacqueline (Francoise Christophe), have a little son, Jean-Noel (Patrick Millow), as well as the requisite cute Governess (Michele Naidal), who spends much of her day teaching the little boy English—this, in spite of the fact that the boy is too young even to speak French!

Other limos contain, or should I say, CONtain, a gaggle of shifty Schoudler cousins: Eightysomething Robert de La Monnerie (Jean Murat) is a decorated (World Wars I *and* II) French General, who's about to be retired from the military, and when we first see him, in his own limo, he's telling his wife that, even though he realizes he's ancient, he feels that he's not, as we say here in the U.S., 'ready for Miami;' the next limo in line is transporting Isabelle de La Monnerie (Francoise Delbart), Noel's cute, twentysomething niece, who's riding with Simon (balding, nebbishy Bernard Blier, whom we already know from Gabin's *Crime et chatiment* and *Les Miserables*), Noel's dutiful executive assistant/right-hand man, whose role in life is to 'clean up' Schoudler family, and Schoudler organization, messes; just like in Gabin's 1955 gangster flick, *Razzia sur la chnouf,* this film too is more concerned with the double-dealings which come from within the company and the family, than with the problems which emanate from without.

To break up this chain of stodgy relatives, the film now introduces us to a funny/grotesque one, the Schoudlers' creepy/bearded/fat/perennial-schemer/gastronomme (most of what he eats winds up on his comically-wide ties), Lucien Maublanc (Pierre Brasseur, who twenty years and seventy-five pounds ago played the gangster who was also called 'Lucien,' in 1938's *Quai des brumes,* the picture in which he was Gabin's rival for Michele Morgan's affections. [Brasseur killed Jean Gabin at the end of *Quai des brumes,* and he'll practically kill Gabin again in this picture, only not with a gun this time out, but with his character's raging obnoxiousness.]) Lucien is Noel's cousin by marriage (he's Noel's wife's brother) and he is, in every sense of the word, *the 'anti-Noel:'* Independently-wealthy, because he inherited millions when his parents died, Lucien is every fat/effete/layabout/never-had-a-job/trust fund-leech you ever met in grad school, filtered through a semi-permeable membrane of every unsavory Disney movie villain you've ever seen and, as we'll find out, he's going to be a great complement to the movie's other dilettante-character, Noel's son Francois.

Whose funeral are all of these family members attending? Well, it's the big send-off for Jean de La Monteuil, Noel Schoudler's Grandfather. (Even though Monteuil is dead, we're going to be 'meeting' him, too, in a manner of speaking, since, during the church service, a huge painting of Grandpa Monteuil happens to be propped-up, right over his coffin!) At the church, all of the Schoudlers, and their kin, sit in sections under signs which indicate their fancy titles in life—'Parliament;' 'Government;' 'Military;' *etc.* The Reverend who's leading the funeral (Julien Bertheau) is heavily invested in his speech about how "death is glorious," and he also uses his speech to inveigh sarcastically against what he calls, "the horrible power of riches," as the Schoudlers try unsuccessfully to conceal their laughter! He's talking about how "God has protected this great family, the Schoudlers," and of course, at this point in the service, Fat Lucien enters; he has arrived a bit late (because, no doubt, he stopped off at a Quiznos, for a Cabo Chicken Sub on Rosemary Bread).

According to the Reverend, Dead Grandpa Monteuil, in addition to his other accomplishments, also "wrote beautiful verses," one of which the Reverend is now reading out-loud, and this poem is more corny than it is actually 'good.' (As the Reverend continues to speechify, director Patelliere next, hilariously, shows us a close-up of the church's collection plate: As it gets passed through the aisles, Schoudler family members casually toss *huge, thousand-franc notes* into it!) Then, *it's Noel's turn up at the bimah,* and he's Gabin-Eloquent: "First, I'd like to thank the Reverend for the wonderful job that he's doing with this service. But Reverend, you haven't mentioned my Grandfather's last words!" At this point, Noel whips a tiny slip of paper out from inside of his jacket pocket: It's a note which his grandfather, apparently (at least, according to what Noel is now telling the crowd) wrote to him shortly before his demise, and Noel reads it to the stunned mourners: "My dear Noel, when I am gone, I want you to succeed me as the President of the *Academie Francaise.*" (For non-French readers, the *Academie* is, to quote that great bastion of knowledge, Wikipedia, "France's learned body on all matters concerning the French language.") When Noel has finished reading the letter, he 'takes the temperature of the crowd,' and sees that the family members are all shooting each other, and him, all manner of mean, 'how dare he'-glances. (Apparently, lots of family members in this crowd thought that they would be the ones who would be inheriting the *Academie Francaise* gig.) Noel Schoudler, differently than most of the other movie characters who have been played by Jean Gabin in Gabin's past movies, is a popularity-loving egomaniac, a guy who 'can't get no satisfaction' until, just like Al Pacino in *Scarface,* 'the world is his;' and so what this film, and what novelist Rene Druon's 'lefty-oriented' book upon which the film was based, is really about then, is 'the Evils of Capitalism,' and it's also, relatedly, about 'how absolute power corrupts, absolutely.' (You know the drill!) Noel Schoudler is definitely David Bowie's "Man who Sold the World," come to (dynamic/silver-haired/Type-A Personality) life.

At the end of the funeral, it's back to the Schoudler family mansion, where both generations—Noel and his wife, and Noel's son Francois, and Francois' own wife, Jacqueline—live together, and not exactly, in peace: The family had been trying to keep up appearances at the funeral, but apparently, Francois, who's a wimp (but a wimp with a violent temper), had, on the way home, in the limo, beaten the shit out of his wife because, apparently, she had recently spent too much money on a huge (and in his view, unnecessary) purchase, and with all of their fighting (and punching!), Francois and Jacqueline have forgotten that that their little boy, Jean-Noel, has had an important doctor's appointment set up for today—an appointment which the boy has now, effectively, missed.

The next morning, in his magisterially-appointed office (Noel works out of his home, and you would too, if you had a nice pad like this), he calls in his *nebbishy* right-hand-man Simon, for 'The Daily Report on the State of the Schoulder Group of Companies.' Noel reveals his dissatisfaction with his lazy offspring, Francois, to Simon, telling Simon, who's closer to his own age than he is to that of his son, "We will soon be led by children! I wounded myself in this world to make my son happy, and my son doesn't even care!" Noel then mentions a family problem to Simon, telling Noel he knows that someone has knocked-up Noel's niece Isabelle, but that he has been unable to ascertain who exactly it was. (But of course, Noel knows *exactly* who did it: Weren't Simon and Isabelle traveling to the funeral together in the same limousine? [Yes, yes, and yes!] But Noel wants Simon to confess to the sperm delivery of his own free will and accord, just like Gabin's Inspector-character wanted Robert Hossein's 'Raskolnikv-esque' character to confess in that same manner, in 1956's *Crime et chatiment.*)

With Annie Ducaux.

Next, Francois enters his dad Noel's office for a meeting with Noel and Simon. On Francois' behalf, Simon now broaches a subject with Noel, which Francois wanted to ask him about, but he has been unable to do it himself, because he's deathly afraid of his own intimidating father: "Noel, Francois says that you should get rid of our brokers, because they're not picking the right stocks; also, he wants to make some architectural changes to the Schoudler Bank's main offices." Now, it's time for Noel to show his son that he's still the boss, even though he's getting older: "I didn't ask you to come and talk about any of this son, so why would you think I'm interested?" Francois next tries to make a stinging rebuttal, by letting his dad know that he is part of the 'new wave' (and, by comparison, that his dad is 'old school').

That comment about the 'New Wave' was meant to be ironic: In 1958, when *Les Grandes familles* was being made, the new generation of French directors—the proto-MTV stylists of France's non-linear New Wave (*nouvelle vague*) cinema, which was led by young men such as Francois Truffaut, Jean Luc-Godard, and Alain Resnais, famously dismissed Jean Gabin's genre pictures as being 'stodgy' and 'out-of-date.' (Well, certainly, a few of Gabin's 1950s movies, including this one, are a tad stodgy, but most of them are good!) In fact, it seems very probable that director/screenwriter Patelliere named the character of Noel's nasty son 'Francois,' after Francois Truffaut...

Francois also wants to change the Schoudler Family newspaper, and not just its physical layout, but also the style of its writing, telling his dad that he feels like they're going to need to start jazzing the articles up a bit. Astute dad Noel, however, recognizes that his son just wants to turn the newspaper into a lurid tabloid. He thinks that his son's ideas are *beyond-moronic*, and isn't afraid to tell him so: "Everyone wants to take over my newspaper—not just you, but everybody! I have to think about it, but I'm telling you right now that the answer will probably be no." In the next scene, father and son step across the hall into the family's newspaper offices, where editors are busily completing the obituary for Noel's grandfather, while Noel is telling Francois that changing the paper's layout, and its writing-style, won't increase sales, but Francois counters lamely, that if they keep the newspaper going 'the way it is now' (stodgy, dense), that they'll lose readers. ("Dad, I'm telling you: The readers of today want fast articles and shocking pictures!") But then, Francois lightens up a bit (he wants to advance his cause, not screw it up!), and so he now starts speaking a bit more carefully: "Dad, you know, it's not just me: Everyone in the family has ideas about how some of your companies should be run, but we're all afraid of you, so we can't tell you!" This comment gives Noel pause, and Francois now continues running his dad down, blissfully unaware (ignorance is bliss) that he's hurting the older man's feelings: "You do too much, dad. Your sugar company, the newspaper, the bank—you take care of too many things. The newspaper needs punch! Let me concentrate on it myself, and you can keep running all of your other businesses. If you listen to me, dad, I guarantee you a hundred-thousand new readers." Noel sharply retorts, "Well, if we make the changes you're talking about, we'll lose two hundred thousand old readers!" Francois leaves, frustrated now because, like all dads in the world (past, present, and future), this one's never going to listen to him. Back in his office, alone with his *aide-de-camp* Simon, Noel now issues a decree: "When I'm dead, and my son becomes boss, you can listen to him. But until then, only listen to me, okay?!"

Just as Simon is leaving the room, grotesque Lucien Maublanc, Noel's goofily-porcine brother-in-law, pays Noel a visit. (It's like that long sequence in 1947's *Miroir*, in which all of Gabin's casino employees filtered into his office one at a time, to tell him about their problems.) Lucien asks Noel (he only tolerates Lucien because he has to, since Lucien is his wife's brother), if Noel can run an article in the newspaper about a young up-and-coming actress, Sylvaine, whom Lucien's been trying to *bang*—and in fact, Lucien's already promised the piece to this woman without first consulting with Noel. "I told this girl we'd do a story about her," Lucien grins idiotically, and Noel immediately starts giving him hell: "I'm going to say no to you Lucien, because newspapers don't need that fluff. For thirty years, since I married your sister, I have been withstanding your eccentricities. But now, you've gone too far. Promising a layout to some whore?!" Noel's also pissed, as he's now telling Lucien, because Lucien brought the aforesaid whore to Grandpa Schoudler's funeral, when she wasn't even a member of the family.

"Lucien, you're a nice moron," Noel cautions the big fatso, "but don't get me involved in your schemes." Lucien, like all guys who've never worked for the money they have, instantly turns into a giant, whining crybaby: "Everybody gets favors from you but me, Noel. *It's not faaaairrrrr!* We both have money. [Noel made his, but Lucien's just came by association.] But you, Noel: You also have power. You're the one that protects the family! The bottom line, is that you hate me because I spend my life having fun! But guess what, Noel: I'm going to bug you about running this photo-spread, until you feel like killing me!" (If Noel doesn't kill this obnoxious freak then, needless to say, the audience certainly will!)

Out in the front yard of Schoudler mansion a few minutes later, Francois and Lucien are now getting hammered together, and they're both livid, because neither man has been able to bend steely Noel to his will and, at this point, Francois starts talking trash about his dad, not knowing that Noel is lurking behind a tree, listening to the whole diatribe. After eavesdropping for a few moments, Noel pops out from behind the *baobob*—inasmuch as the slow-moving, older, Jean Gabin can ever, actually, 'pop out' from anywhere—and before you know it, it's time for this movie's great Gabin-Outburst: "Son, I listened to you this afternoon, and I'm going to tell you for the last time that it's my newspaper. I'm the boss! Everything you are in life—I paid for!" Jacqueline, Francois' wife, is nearby, and she's watching her husband as he gets dressed-down by his Big Daddy, and Noel doesn't spare his daughter-in-law from his torrent of abuse, either: "And you, young lady: You stay out of this, all right? You are not representative of this family! I know my son loves you, and that you love him, but would you have married the son of a janitor? I think not!" (She looks down at her shoes. [For some moments in life, there are no words.])

Now, it's back to the family's 'current personal problem,' the one about Noel's niece Isabelle being *preggers*. Again, Noel believes that Simon is the father, but nobody else in the family has figured it out, yet. Noel calls Simon (who, incidentally, is married, and to somebody else) into his office and, pretending he doesn't know that Simon is the guilty party, he smiles (he's really having a lot of fun with the moment), growling that he's going to "kill the guy" who knocked-up his niece. ("Find this bastard for me, so I can break his neck!") Simon, who's ashamed of himself now, finally admits that it was he who was 'the mystery pollinator,' and Noel is happy that his longtime pal has just told him the unvarnished truth: Simon has always been one of Noel's best and most trusted friends, and 'in The Gabin World,' as we already know, the friendship between males, is blah, blah, *etc., etc.* So Noel doesn't really even get mad at him. Besides, Noel has some pressing business for Simon to take care of on his behalf, today: "Simon, I have just suspended my son from his job at my newspaper [Francois has been one of the paper's associate editors], so you have to break the news to him about it, for me—I don't have the energy. Also, there's a problem with my wife's stupid brother: Please remind Lucien for me, that I will not be printing a puff piece about this girl he wants to [date] in my family newspaper!" Simon still can't believe that Noel isn't reacting harshly to the fact that Simon is the one who's impregnated Isabelle, and Noel now tells his friend why he's not mad at him: "What's saved you just now, Simon, is your honesty and your intelligence." Like any rich businessman, Noel knows that people are going to spend their whole lives trying to screw him, so at least he wants the people who are screwing him to be honest and truthful, which is a very mature way for a person to think. Since Isabelle can't marry Simon, because Simon is already married to someone else, Noel tries to think of a suitable man who *could* marry her. (Noel is such a controlling patriarch that, naturally, Isabelle isn't even going to get a choice about whom she marries.) Noel opines, "If we don't find her a husband, she will keep sinning and sinning, with one guy after another," and he first considers, for Isabelle's husband, a guy named Oliver, a wealthy family friend whom we will never see in the film.

Noel then sends Simon on a mission to see Sylvaine (Nadine Tailler), the actress to whom Lucien has promised the article, and when he meets her, she's modeling a way-too-sheer dress, for a photographer: "I have been sent here on behalf of Mr. Noel Schoudler," Simon tells Sylvaine. "I am returning these photographs which your boyfriend has recently dropped off at Mr. Schoulder's office. Anything that comes to us from Lucien Maublanc is refusable." He then advises her, *per* Noel's request, that she must now cut off all relations with Lucien: "If you sleep with Lucien, it will just put the paparazzi out on our family, and you won't become a famous actress, at all—you will appear in our newspaper, but only in an article which states that you are the mistress of a maniac!" Sylvaine admits to Simon that she knows, just like everybody else does, that Lucien is a big fat slob, and she now apologizes for trying to hook up with him, for publicity's sake. (Sylvaine must be a good actress, because now, she's also trying to seduce Simon, a man who, it seems, is just as easy a mark as Lucien is.): Simon is deciding now, just as Lucien had already decided before him, that this girl is *niiiice*—and now, he wants to get into her pants, too! He leeringly tells her, "Look, my dear: Just between you and me—maybe we *will* put out a nice little article about you, after all. What do you think about that?"

That same day, Lucien and Francois perambulate the Schoudler mansion's grounds, rehashing old arguments which each man has had individually with Noel. The two men are now officially conspiring together, because Noel has just removed Francois off-screen, and not just from the young man's Associate Editor position, but also from all of the family businesses, and he's mostly done this because he can't abide the fact that his son has been hanging around with treacherous old Lucien. Lucien and Francois are now hatching a plan to drive Noel out of the newspaper forcibly, and Lucien tells Francois that, since Francois is Noel's only legal heir, he would probably be within his right to do it, and that Francois should definitely be spending his time in researching how to go about it.

At that moment, Noel drives up to the house with Simon, and Noel (again!) sees Lucien and Francois conspiring together. Noel is great at nipping potential problems in the bud before they start (it's how he got where he is today), and he now decides to teach his son a lesson in 'why not to mess with daddy!'

Noel takes Francois aside, and puts on a total act, acting completely friendly toward his unfriendly progeny, for probably the first time in his entire life: "Son, there is truth to what you told me yesterday. I think you would be a very good company president. I will not allow you to head up my newspaper but, effective right now, I would like to offer you the Presidency of my sugar company!" Noel's got it all planned out: He's going to make Francois the President of the family's sugar enterprise, which is called Sonchelles Sugar, because Sonchelles is the one Schoudler-owned company which is not doing well—in fact, Sonchelles Sugar has been going under for quite some time now and, unbeknownst to Francois, Noel was thinking about dumping it, anyway. Noel's doing this, not only to get Francois away from Lucien (because once Francois is running a company, he most-assuredly won't want creepy Lucien riding on his coat-tails), but also because if Francois thinks he's responsible for the sugar operation's downfall, he'll think twice about wanting to run a business again. Francois isn't smart enough to see that his dad is giving him the sugar company just to mess with him!

In the next scene, Francois and Jacqueline show up at the docks, where Sonchelles Sugar's offices are located, and Noel smilingly hands the company over to his son: "It's all yours, Francois. My grandfather's grandfather started the family sugar business, and now I give it to you. Good luck with it!"

When Noel goes home that night and turns on the t.v., he's horrified, when he sees his cousin, Professor Emile Lartois (Jean Ozenne) on a local talk show, announcing, with great pride, that he has succeeded Noel's grandfather, Robert de La Monnerie, as *President of the Academie Francaise*, a position which Noel took for granted would be his. (He thought he had it 'in the bag.') Now royally-p.o.'d, Noel shuts off the t.v., and squinches his face into the tightest, most closed-eyed Gabin-Grimace you've ever seen, and without his having to say anything, we can tell that, among the other feelings which he's now harboring, that he must also be super-embarrassed since, when he was at his grandfather's funeral, he had read the crowd that note, stating that grandpappy himself had named Noel to be his successor.

When we see Francois next (we know already that he isn't the sharpest tool in the shed), it seems like he's already forgotten about his new sugar company presidency, because he's still completely obsessed with taking over the family's newspaper. (In movies, as in life, one always wants only what one cannot have.) With the smile of one who's not too bright, he cheerfully waddles into his dad's office to tell him that he's been working with architects, and planning an eight hundred million-franc remodeling of the newspaper building's h.q., even in spite of the fact that his dad's cut him off already from the journalism world. Noel asks Francois how he thinks such expensive construction would get paid for, and Francois hesitantly replies, "Ummm… won't you help me?"—which, of course, leads Noel right into another great Gabin-Outburst: "Daddy doesn't have a lot of money for your eccentricities. Go and find eight hundred million francs by yourself!" Francois, who suddenly looks more like a three-year-old than the late-twentysomething he is, now whines, "But you *haaaave* to help me! [Long beat:] And I also need some more money for the sugar company!"

Noel next goes to visit Lucien, who's lunching-out at a fancy restaurant with a *new hotty*—another girl who's obviously just using him for the free meal—because he wants to mess with Lucien, as well: Lucien, I would like to bring you in with my son on the family sugar business—that is, if you're able to come to the table with some of your own capital." (So now, Lucien is going to pour his own money into the sugar company, and both Noel's son and Lucien will go downhill together!) Noel continues, "Schoudler Organization stock has suddenly plummeted from an all-time high to an all-time low, and I'm on the verge of bankruptcy. In fact, I hate to ask, but—do you have eight hundred million francs you could loan me?!" Idiotic Lucien, who's been suddenly manipulated into thinking that he actually has the upper-hand over Noel (and Noel, of course, in this film, is meant to be the smartest businessman in the world), now turns up his nose: "No can do, Noel. Wish I could help. But I'm not a philanthropic enterprise!"

Noel wants Lucien to spread the misinformation which he's just given him, which is that all of the Schoudler Group's companies are going under, because he wants the shareholders to sell all of their stocks, so that he can buy them all back personally—which means that for the first time in his life, he will own one hundred percent of his own enterprises, thereby becoming even richer than ever. Noel knows that if all of the stockholders sell, Francois will think it was his fault, because he wasn't able to run the sugar business properly, and he'll then have to then apologize to his father for entrusting him with it. Noel continues to 'play' Lucien and Francois, as though they're two not-so finely-tuned Stradivariuses.

Needless to say, it's not long before Lucien is walking around like a Big Shot, telling a friend, "This bastard came over, and told me a bunch of garbage to try and get eight hundred million francs out of me, just because he wants to get his sugar business out of hock. But I didn't accept, because I don't give a damn about the sugar industry." (It's hilarious that Lucien says he doesn't care about sugar, because he's grossly fat, and looks like he probably spends most of his day actually quaffing sugar, straight out of the 'C&H' bag!)

Francois knows that his father won't give him any money to save the sugar company, so he instead goes to Lucien, to beg for the money which he needs to bail the company out: "I want to say yes to you, Francois, because I said no to your dad," Lucien grins smugly. Francois is so embarrassed to ask Lucien to borrow money (he's never embarrassed to ask for money from his dad, but he definitely has a hard time asking other people), that he asks for a lesser amount: "Well, how about if you just loan me one-third or one-half of what I need? For right now, three hundred million would probably get the sugar business up on its feet again."

Lucien and Francois are now both exactly where Noel wants them. Francois is learning his lesson, which is that he can't run a company himself, and Lucien thinks that when all of the Schoudler shareholders sell their stocks, he'll be able to buy them all up himself, and turn the company from 'Schoudler Industries' into 'Lucien Maublanc Industries.'

Director Patelliere next cuts to a hilarious trading floor sequence (which would be xeroxed in John Landis' 1983 comedy, *Trading Places*), in which Noel (who's wearing a jaunty bowler-hat) and Lucien are both on the trading floor (along with dozens of Schoudler family stockbrokers and hundreds of Schoudler investors), and they're both waiting for the Schoudler stocks to plummet, so that each can buy them all back at bargain-basement prices. Meanwhile, Noel's *major-domo* Simon is running around the floor, secretly paying off the Schoudler Organization's brokers to go around lying to all of the investors, by telling them that the Schoudler companies are on their way down, so that they'll all consent to sell.

Francois is present too, and Simon whispers to him conspiratorially, "I think I should tell

Reunited with his "Quai des brumes" co-star, Pierre Brasseur.

you, Francois: Lucien Maublanc is playing you against your father. Lucien's not really your partner at all—he's just in it for himself." Francois finds out that his dad is telling the truth about this, and that in fact, he is really being duped by Lucien.

Within the space of a few minutes, all of the Schoudler Industries stocks are valueless, and Noel's ready to buy them all back at a price which is low, but with which Lucien who, comparatively to Noel, is cash poor, still can't compete. Lucien begs him: "Noel, have a heart! If you don't let me buy the stocks, I don't know what I'll do." With a huge grin (and this is a great Jean Gabin Moment), Noel just Gabin-Shrugs and grins, "Well, then, Lucien—I guess you're just going to have to kill yourself!" Noel buys all of his own company's stocks up by himself, and now, for the first time in his life, he owns the Schoudler Group of Companies outright.

But now, this droll comedy-of-manners suddenly takes a sudden turn for the morose: While the entire extended Schoudler clan is eating dinner in Noel and Adele's fancily-appointed dining room that same night, a gunshot report issues noisily from the next room: Francois, thinking that he's ruined his own father, has just shot himself to death! When Noel enters the room and sees his son's inert body, he shows no emotion, in the typical Gabin-Stonefaced Fashion.

After the requisite family-freak out, and all of the obligatory crying, Adele now starts screaming at her husband: "You made your son kill himself, to teach him a lesson about how he should never go against you—like his life was some kind of a game! Well, now you can play with his death too, just like how you play with everything else. You're a monster!" Francois has left a suicide note, which reads, "You were right, dad. I could never be a success." Jean Gabin is such a fantastic actor that now, as he continues staring at his son's dead body, we get the sense that a huge volcano of sadness is erupting inside of him, but he's doing all of the scene's 'emotional heavy-lifting' only with his famously demonstrative Gabinian eyes. Even now, during what must probably be the saddest moment in his life, Noel displays no outward emotions which might make him seem weak.

Simon, apologizing to his boss (because he knows that now isn't exactly the appropriate time to be discussing business), worriedly nudges him: "Noel, the bank has just taken control of your sugar company. I know that this isn't the right time, but you must fight now, if you want to get it back." Noel, who's upset about what's just happened to his son (upset, in other words, at what he's made happen, personally) now mutters, and what he says is barely audible: "Fight for what? I can't lose anything else now." He next walks away, 'Gabin-Alone,' accompanied by the Reverend's voice, which is now being reprised from the funeral scene at the beginning of the movie—that scene in which the Reverend was inveighing against "the horrible power of wealth." When we heard the speech the first time, Noel and his family were laughing about it, but this time, only we, the film's audience, are hearing it. And this time, nobody's laughing.

Les Grandes familles, although it is slow-paced and dry (and confusing, what with all of its boring stock market-talk) was, nevertheless, a major theatrical hit in France, and on its first theatrical release, in 1959, it sold five hundred thousand tickets in its first eight days, at only one Paris movie theater. While unknown in the U.S. today (the picture played, very briefly, in one NYC art theater [accompanied by a cartoon called "Truth, Love, and Beauty," directed by the noted British animator Richard Williams], as *The Possessors*), it remains popular on French television today, and it also happens to be the only Jean Gabin movie which you might even find today, in French phone booths: If you go to France today, and you don't have a cellphone, you're probably going to have to use a greasy old payphone and, of course, in Europe, the payphones operate on those little plastic credit-card-looking 'phone cards.' Included on a recent crop of cards is Gabin, who's pictured, in his bowler hat, from the trading floor sequence of *Les Grandes familles*.

In 1989, *Les Grandes familles* was remade for French television, as a mini-series, by director Eduardo Molinaro, the man who 'made the world laugh' with his internationally-successful French-Italian 1979 film comedy, *La Cage aux folles*. But going to back to the original 1959 Gabin version, for a moment: The film's assistant director was a young man named Pierre Granier-Deferre, who would himself, a decade later, direct Gabin in two very good movies, both of which, incidentally, shared animal names: 1970's *La Horse* and 1971's *Le Chat* (*The Cat*).

What a Critic Said at the Time: "Somewhat talky, and its fine points of observation on the French business, social, and governmental scenes might be elusive in foreign markets. Jean

Gabin's extraordinary presence lends weight and credulity to the pic, in his portrait of a strong, rugged individualist." (*Variety*, 12-24-58 issue. Critic: "Mosk. [George Moskowitz.]" Reviewed in Paris.)

What Another Critic Said at the Time: "Perfunctory. Unfortunately, the script is an anemic presentation of the thesis that 'it is hellish to be rich.' There are three or four scenes that have some tension… but it's too static, and there's too much dialogue." (New York *Times*, 7-21-59 issue. Critic: Bosley Crowther.)

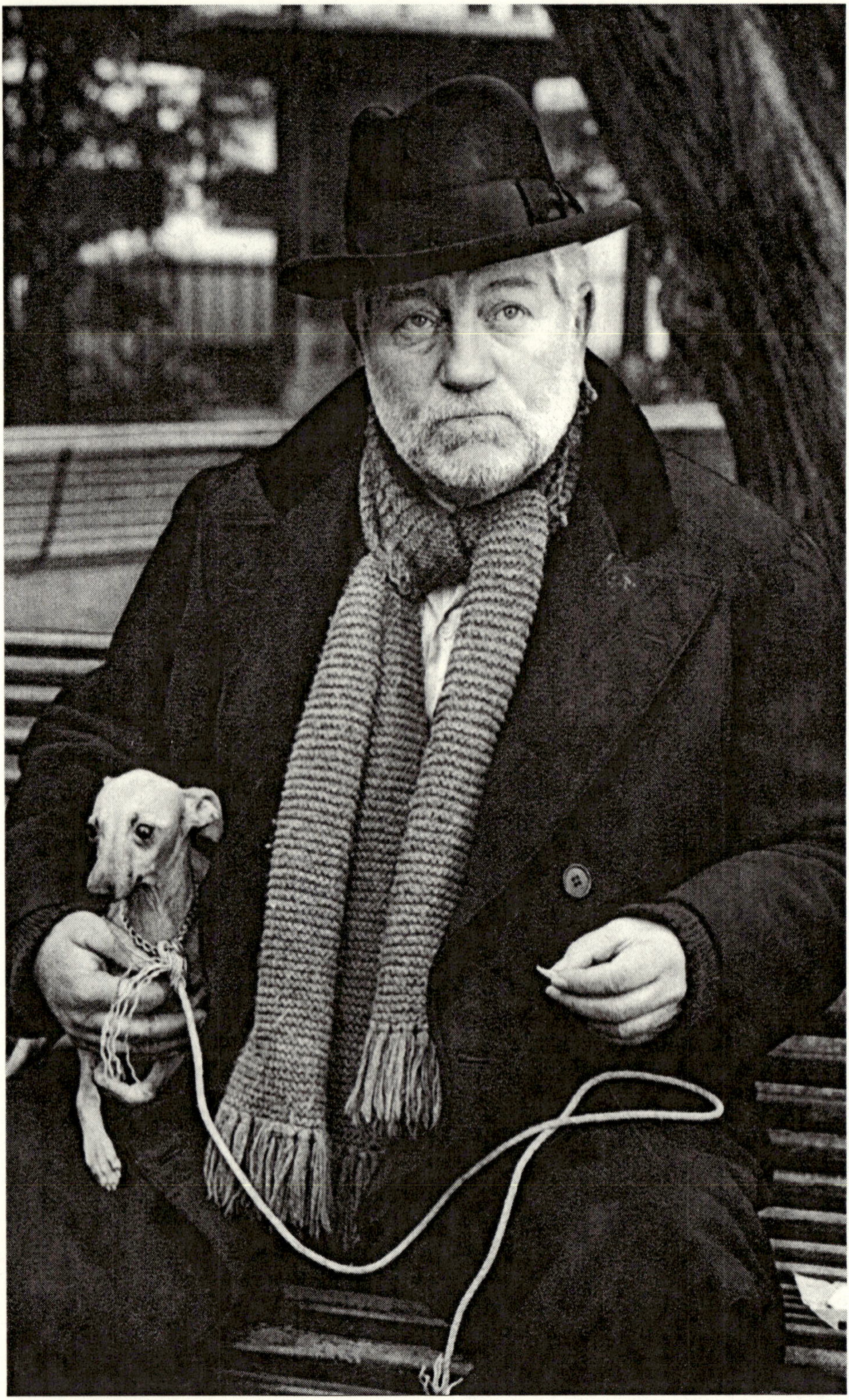

FILM 67

Archimede, le clochard

France/Italy 1959

(Literal English Translation: "ARCHIMEDE, THE BUM") Directed by Gilles Grangier. Produced by Jean-Paul Guibert. Screenplay by Michel Audiard, Gilles Grangier, and Albert Valentin. Based Upon an Idea by Jean Moncorge (Jean Gabin). Director of Photography (black and white), Louis Page. Music by Jean Prodromides. Editor, Jacqueline Thiedot. Production Designer, Jacques Colombier. (GENRE: COMEDY) Running Time, 1 hour 16 minutes. (Cut from its original running time, as presented at the Berlin Film Festival, of 1 hour 31 minutes.) A Production of Filmsonor SA and Intermondia Films (France) and Pretoria Films (Italy). Released in France by Cinedis, on April 8, 1959. Released in the U.S. with English subtitles as "THE MAGNIFICENT TRAMP" on April 24th, 1962, by Cameo International Pictures.

"Going to work is like getting syphilis."
— *Ebullient homeless-guy Gabin, in "Archimede, le clochard"*

The whole point of this book, is that many of the Jean Gabin films which were either barely released, or never released at all, in the United States, deserve to be seen because they're so insanely wonderful, and there's no better example of this, than Gabin's tremendously entertaining 1959 comedy, *Archimede, le clochard (Archimede, the Bum)*, a robustly-entertaining movie which is just as much fun to write about as it is to watch: It's one of those very few movies you'll ever see in your whole life where, after you've seen it, you won't be able to wait to start singing its praises to everybody you've ever met. *Archimede* is a joyful, enthusiastically-made, upbeat (but never syrupy), sharp Gabin comedy—a comedy which definitely can hold its own next to *the second greatest comedy of 1959*, Billy Wilder's *Some Like It Hot*. (After you see *Archimede*, you won't make fun of me for suggesting this; granted, *you might even take me to dinner, on your next visit to L.A.!*) The fact that this film, like many of the others in this book, was released in the U.S. only briefly, at one New York City art theater, by a tiny distributor of foreign films, is *beyond tragic*.

Three years had passed since the world had seen Gabin tearing his way through an uproarious comedy (*La Traversee de Paris*), and French audiences were ready for more. In

Archimede, le clochard, as in *La Traversee de Paris,* and as in the other comedies which Gabin would make throughout the 1950s, 1960s, and 1970s, Gabin *isn't* quiet, calm, and reserved: He's still *the everyman,* but instead of being a quiet everyman, he has, in his comedies, been re-born as 'the everyman-as-loudmouth,' a Freudian *id* who has no filter between his thoughts and what comes out of his mouth, a guy who says what everybody's thinking but what nobody else has the guts to say, and a guy (to boot) who uses his wits to screw with the pretensions of the holier-than-thou. Gabin even came up with the idea for the movie himself, because according to the opening credits, the film is "Based Upon an Idea by Jean Alexis-Moncorge" (*Gabin*)! Gabin knew that audiences and critics loved him whenever he played working-class guys, but he was also savvy enough to know that he had already made two zillion serious, 'working class-guy *dramas,*' and that they might like to see a comedy version of that character which, with this film, he would definitely be giving them, *and in grand style.*

While Archimede (Gabin) is a bum, he's a *noble bum:* He's very opinionated, charming, and loud—a guy who dresses in long coat and scarf, and who always tries to look sartorially-splendid, even though he has nothing. (He's a guy who turns his lemons, *not* into lemonade but, let's just say, into *nice, dressed-up lemons.*) When we first see Archimede, he's sitting on a bench opposite a factory, lunching-out with a younger (and bespectacled) fellow bum, his young friend, Arsene Gerricault (Darry Cowl), and the two are busily laughing, proto-Beavis and Butthead-style, at the unfortunate people across the street who have to actually go to work. (In Archimede's not-so-humbly-offered opinion, "*Going to work is like getting syphilis.*") Archimede's such a charming guy, in fact, that he's able to live on the handouts which people freely give him, because all of the people he makes fun of, really love him. (He makes fun of working people because they have to go to work, and he also makes fun of rich people, because they *don't* have to go to work!) He's very charismatic, and is *just plain fun to be around.*

Archimede lives alone, in the rotted-out penthouse of a condemned building (where else?) which is about to be torn down by construction workers who are toiling, noisily, all around him. Even though Archimede's just a squatter on this property, he actually has the temerity to lean out of the window and tell the drilling construction workers that they need to be quiet, because he's sleeping (it's three o' clock in the afternoon!), and further, that they should go and do their noisy construction work somewhere else, "Stop with the earthquake," he commands, to which one of the construction workers shakes a defiant fist, yelling back, "I throw shit at you, old man!" Archimede dryly retorts, "Ehhhh, today drills, tomorrow, the bulldozer," since he's a guy who always gets the last word in, even if nobody's listening to it. As he'll tell his pal Arsene later that same day, "That time they decided to put plumbing in the building, I was out a place to live, for three months!"

Archimede hobbles over to the local bar, La Maison Gregoire, where the patrons are never happy to see him, since he's always trying to cadge free drinks out of them. He orders a glass of Muscadet, France's favorite fancy, dry white wine and, rather effusively, starts bellowing out his opinions about *everything under the sun*, which stops patrons from being able to enjoy their own conversations. He tells the bar's proprietor, Gregoire (Paul Frankeur), stories about how he (Archimede) is more appreciated by the *hoi polloi* on the fancy beaches of the Cote d'Azur, and that he might just pack up and go there, right now! There's nothing anybody on earth can do to ruin the always-happy Archimede's day (he's not a tragic figure at all; he's a drifter, but he has more life in one of his little pinky-fingers than anybody you've ever met in your whole life); nobody can even threaten him with being arrested (on being 'drunk and disorderly'), because Archimede loves getting arrested and going to jail, since jailers always give their charges nice, hot coffee and three square meals, and jail is the one place in the world, in which he always gets his meals served to him. (The only thing Archimede doesn't like about jailhouse cuisine, as he informs the bar's patrons, who just wish that he would *shut the hell up*, is that they don't use olive oil, and that there's no caviar!) The only thing in this life which Archimede flatly refuses to do besides going to work, as he's now telling Gregoire, is "… to live under the bridge" which, in any country, is the lowest thing you can do, if you're a bum. (It's tantamount, in the U.S., to living beneath a freeway underpass.) "Freedom," Archimede tells the Maison Gregoire's customers, "means being able to choose to do whatever you want, even if it means choosing to go to jail." Whenever Gregoire sees Archimede entering the bar in the movie, he always mutters, "Here we go again!" because he knows that Archimede, without being asked, is going to start automatically inveighing noisily against everything which he believes to be false in contemporary society. Today, in particular, a couple of patrons make the mistake of telling Archimede to "keep it down," and he doesn't like it one bit: "If you piss me off," he announces to all assembled, "I'll break everything in this bar!"—and, by golly, no sooner does he say it, than he actually does it! It's a tribute to Jean Gabin that, while Archimede is loud and blustery, he manages to remain charming, funny, and likeable at the same time.

Archimede starts busting up the bar, pissed because Gregoire just told him that he's full of shit. Obviously, Archimede is just busting the place up on purpose, so that he can get arrested and (right on cue, and just like he wanted) the cops take him away, and he 'goes quietly.' (It's just like in those old Gabin pictures from the '30s, in which Gabin's characters knew that they had to go to jail, and didn't try to fight it. [But in this picture, at least, he's excited about it!]) Before jail though, the first stop is night court, and he gets angered when the exhausted-looking Judge, who's played by Jean Degrave, only hands him an eight-day sentence! ("Eight days?! I want more! This is a scandal!")

Back at the bar, Gregoire is busy assessing the damage with a bearded insurance investigator, Seraphin (Leonce Corne, who played Gabin's double-dealing business partner Charles, in *Le Sang a la tete*), a clownish-looking guy who looks like he could be a missing Marx Brother. Seraphin, knowing who caused the damage, wants to sell Gregoire "fire insurance, water insurance, and [he actually says this, and *he's not kidding, either*] Archimede Insurance." We've already figured out though, that even though Archimede keeps busting up Gregorie's bar, which always necessitates a lot of pricey remodeling, Gregoire genuinely has a soft spot

With Noel Roquevert.

for good old Archimede—and, in fact, so do most of the customers, even though none of them would probably ever cop to it—because he's Maison Gregoire's biggest attraction. (If some people in life provide us with local color, then let's just say that Archimede is 'the whole palette.') Truth be told, Gregoire's not even mad that Archimede has just destroyed his whole bar (again), and he's only upset, because Archimede busted his brand new, and very expensive, espresso machine. (ESPRESSO JOKE: Or should I say, "He's *steamed* that Archimede has busted his espresso machine! [Get it?!])

Director Gilles Grangier now flashes-forward to eight days later: Archimede is being released from jail, and doesn't want to leave! He threatens the Warden (Henri Coutet) that he'll be back and, if not through the front door, then through the back, and furthermore, that if the cops won't arrest him again (which is all he wants out of life), he'll become an exhibitionist, and walk the streets naked! The Warden tells him to get lost, but he grasps at straws—at anything, in other words, which will help him to stay: "Hey, wait! You didn't search my clothes well enough. Look closer! Maybe you can find more stuff that will incriminate me!"

Bummed that he can't stay in jail anymore, Archimede next hobbles over to a wine shop. The Owner (Pierre Leproux) watches Archimede shoplift three liters of vino in his coat, and Archimede even swigs down a fourth bottle, right in front of the guy. The terrific punchline to this scene, is that instead of being mad at Archimede, the Owner instead looks thrilled,

Everybody loves crepes.

and even awed: "That's amazing! You're a guzzler! Wow, terrific!"

Archimede tries, immediately afterwards, to get arrested again, and this time, by running into the middle of a parade and disturbing it. His little buddy Arsene watches from the sidewalk, as Archimede starts singing at the top of his lungs, but his plan backfires, because the crowd loves him. ("Who's going to get a cop and arrest me?" he begs the crowd. "Somebody arrest me! Please!") Instead, the cops arrest Arsene, his friend, who's just been standing quietly on the sidelines, minding his own beeswax. "Why are you taking him, instead of me?" Archimede shouts, at one of the cops. "I'm the one who always calls you cops, 'idiots'—not him!" As he watches the cops drag Arsene away, Archimede mumbles to himself incredulously, that he did everything to get arrested, but that unfortunately, it just didn't work out the way he wanted it to. "I guess they're tired of arresting me," he mopes. (He looks like he might even start crying!)

At the end of another hard day of trying to get free stuff, and *bugging the shit out of people,* Archimede heads back to his little room at the construction site, a room which is accessible only by ladder. While the noisy workers have (mercifully) gone home for the night, he's suddenly surprised, when he discovers a mustached bum in his bed—*and it isn't himself!* It's Felix (Julien Carette, the toxic *shnorrer* who made *bourgeois* Gabin buy him a house, in *Pour l'amour du ciel* [and, of course, years before that, Carette, more famously, played Cartier *in La Grande illusion,* Pecqueux in *La Bete humaine,* Santini in *Pour l'amour du ciel,* and Havelock the cook, in *Le Recif de corail*]), who's got a bunch of stray dogs with him, and to make matters worse, the guy's quaffing Archimede's wine. "Who the hell are you?" Archimede demands. "And why the hell are you drinking that wine? It's mine! And get those stinking dogs the hell out of here!" Felix fights back: "People like you who don't like animals—it's a sign of meanness!" Archimede's reply is, "I don't know anything about dogs, but I know about thieves. So get the hell out!" He grabs the guy and starts trying to push him out, when suddenly, Felix falls and breaks a leg. Now, Archimede suddenly feels very sorry for the guy, so he carries him back up, and nurses him back to health. ("Just be careful," Archimede, who's now carrying on like a sweet-natured *Florence Nightingale-on-wine*, tells him. "You might give your dog fleas!")

The next day, Archimede heads back to Gregoire's newly refurbished bar, but Gregoire is gone: A new owner, Pichion (Bernard Blier, whose character is named after Gabin's real-life Normandy farm) and his wife (she's played by Dora Doll) have just bought the place. Some old men, who are sitting at one of the bar's tables playing cards, and who can't hear very well, see Archimede, and one guy nudges another, winking, "Here comes the squatter," but the second guy thinks that the first guy said 'scooter,' instead of 'squatter.' Pichion (he's nervous, highly-strung, and all-business) is upset, because his wife is being too nice to the customers, and insurance-guy Seraphin is present too, and he's actually trying to sell Pichion some 'Archimede Insurance,' on top of all of the other insurances which he's sold him already!

Pichion orders Archimede to leave, but Archimede's a guy who can pick out anybody's Achilles heel after looking at him for only two seconds, and he figures out immediately that the guy seems like a total hypochondriac. So he looks into Pichion's eyes, and makes with a little hypnotic suggestion: "Your *liiiiiver!* It is in *baaaad shaaaape!!!*" Pichion, unlike Gregoire, won't put up with Archimedes' crap, though, and what he does now is, he goes into the back room, pours some bleach into a bottle of wine, and serves Archimede a huge glassful of the mixture. Archimede wolfs down the whole glass, and tells Pichion that the drink is delicious (!), and that the only problem with it, is that it's too weak and too watered-down. (He even asks for a second glassful!) Pichion is flabbergasted that Archimede didn't get sick from the concoction, and meanwhile, Seraphin, who's turned out to be quite the lush in his own right, now ambles up to the bar, and Archimede, not knowing that the yummy aperitif which he's been drinking is a bleach cocktail, offers him a sip! Of course, Seraphin's eyeballs roll-up into his head, and—KLUNK!—he immediately passes out cold. But tough-old Archimede is still going strong: "Let's all have some," he cheers, as the patrons just look on in abject, open-mouthed horror. (When the French filmmaker Barbet Schroeder directed Mickey Rourke as the happy drunk in his American-made 1987 film adaptation of Charles Bukowski's *Barfly*, he had to be thinking of *Archimede, le clochard*.)

After a few tasty glasses of Ajax, Archimede is bored, and he now brags to the patrons that, for his encore, he will bust-up the newly remodeled bar, even promising, "When I'm finished, this place will look like Picasso's *Guernica!*" Archimede does what he says, turning the place into a great copy of what Dresden looked like after the Americans fire-bombed it, and he then starts dancing with Pichion's wife (who loves every minute of it!), and hurling glass bottles at the walls. Pichion looks like this is the worst moment of his whole life... and it probably is!

After reducing the bar to near-rubble, Archimede heads back to his construction site-home, which he's now sharing with Felix, the broken-legged bum, on a full-time basis. (Archimede feels fraternal toward the other bum, now that the guy can't move!) Felix's dogs like Archimede, but Archimede tells Felix that he can't keep them there. ("We can't keep your mutts here, because they are getting too attached to me.") In his older, 1930s pictures, Jean Gabin rarely gets attached to people for too long, because the act of attaching himself interferes with his freedom—and now, almost lampooning his earlier movie image, he's extending his 'no-attachment clause' even to everybody's favorite four-legged-friends! He tells Felix that, if the other man is going to be staying with him until his leg heals that, at the very least, the two of them are going to have to sell the dogs—and he next starts lecturing Felix's dogs, and very seriously: "To be real dogs, I no longer want you to sit up, look cute, and beg for food, is that clear? Just go grab it! That's the way of a dog!" (And this is sage advice for everybody: All this horseshit about 'being nice,' and about 'good things, coming to those who wait,' is all a load of puke, created by people who want to steal your future opportunities for themselves!)

Archimede next heads over to a local outdoor market, with the one dog out of the bunch to whom he's become attached—a tiny, little basset hound. (It's funny to see tough, surly, paunchy, Jean Gabin lumbering around with a tiny little lapdog!) As he walks, he comes across some other bums, who inform him that they just took part-time factory jobs yesterday and, hilariously, after only one day back on the job, they all start bragging to him that they've already decided to go on strike, and one homeless guy, who's played by Jacques Couturier, is even carrying a sandwich board! Archimede chastises the striking bums, telling them in so many words that real men don't work: "What kicks me in the balls, is that you guys are working like prostitutes. You're a bunch of hypocrites!" After chewing them all out, he talks sweetly to the little basset hound, and discovers that his favorite little doggy has a tag around her neck, which has a fancy Neuilly address on it (Neuilly is 'the Beverly Hills of Paris'). The dog, whose name, according to the tag, is 'Patricia,' is apparently owned by a wealthy family ('*patricians,*' get it?) from whom Felix had clearly pinched him. Probably, lots of Felix's dogs have been stolen from rich people and, more probably, he always tries to extort those rich people, although we won't be seeing him do that in this movie.

Archimede, with Patricia in tow, makes his way, now, to the dog-owner's fancy apartment, where a high-toned/high-society party is in full effect, and where the tuxedo-and-gown-swathed guests are busy, preparing crepes on an indoor skillet, and gleefully tossing the dough into the air, as though they're making pizzas. The lady-of-the-house, Mrs. Marjorie (Jacqueline Maillan), is so excited that Archimede has returned her prized doggy to her, that she invites him to stay, and to *party-down* with them. At first, obnoxious Archimede feels self-conscious about being around rich people: For the very first time in his whole life, this blustery loudmouth who always talks a good game can't speak, because he feels inferior, and this is definitely the film's most poignant moment. After the jubilant and wealthy partiers have fed him a few drinks though, he warms up like a George Foreman Grill, and begins charming them all with an incredible (impromptu, joyful, vibrant) *Zorba the Greek*-like dance, as the guests all surround him, making a circle, and clapping along! (The song to which he dances would even become a momentary hit single in France, when the movie was released: It's an instrumental called "The Archimede Charleston," and the movie's composer, Jean Prodromides, wrote it.) Gradually, everyone in the place joins Archimede in his mirthful, life-loving dance, and within minutes, Archimede's got more friends than he's ever had in his whole life! (I'd never say that *Zorba the Greek's* director, Michael Cacoyannis, plagiarized *Archimede, le clochard* [No, I'd never do that! Far be it from me!] for his own film, but you might be interested in knowing that *Archimede* was made one year before *Zorba the Greek*, and that the two films share many striking similarities: In both pictures, 'simple, and lovably-effusive poor guys' [Jean Gabin, in *Archimede* and Anthony Quinn, in *Zorba*] teach rich and disaffected people about the simple pleasures of life, all of which can be attained through 'the power of ecstatic dance.')

As the party winds down, all of the guests want to thank Archimede for having given them such a great day. Mrs. Marjorie feels so comfortable around the noble-acting Archimede that she now accidentally blows it, by making a wildly inappropriate drunken *faux-pas* (just when Archimede was starting to think that some rich people can be cool), confiding to him that she believes all of her servants to be "… idiots: In fact, that's why I hired them!" (She liked Archimede so much, that she forgot he was poor [as if 'liking somebody,' and 'their being poor,' are mutually exclusive]!) Archimede feels so badly about the fact that the Butler has heard her make this pronouncement, that he befriends the guy, and says nice things to him, just to make him feel better, and it's a great scene, because it reminds us that Archimede is not just obnoxious (we already knew that, anyway), but that he also, like most of Jean Gabin's movie characters, has a very big heart, and never wants other people to feel hurt. (Whenever somebody hurts a working-man, Jean Gabin feels hurt! [*If you cut a working-man, Jean Gabin is the one who bleeds!*])

One of the society ladies at the party, who's played by Helene Tossy, now starts boasting to everybody that she's taking "a college class in sociology," because she's interested in, as she's now putting it, "… learning about real people. "Let's present *Monsieur* Archimede to her," a nose-in-the-air British guest, who's played by Sacha Briquet, grins. *"She's writing a paper about bums!"* Archimede starts messing with the society lady-in-question (she, of course, is too dim to know that he's joking around at her expense), telling her he knows that this one particular painting which the two of them are now staring at, a massive eyesore which hangs in the living room, isn't an original, because the signature is fake, and she's impressed by his knowledge of the painting, even though we can tell that he's making it all up, just to mess with her. He tells her, since he knows she's taking a class in, as he puts it, *"how to be a bum,"* that it's not bad to be a derelict, and she actually believes him when he tells her, "We bums all have fancy bank accounts in Switzerland!" Archimede next starts reciting a poem about Napoleon's death—"Napoleon's Dream," by Mary Russell Mitford—and the other guests, who overhear him doing it, are impressed, each of them knowing that having committed this particular poem to memory, happens to be the mark of a private school-educated person (which Archimede, no doubt, really is! The film doesn't traffic in too much of Archimede's backstory, although we will become privy to a fascinating revelation about his past near the end of the movie, which is that it's very probable that, before he was a bum, he was *something more*)! The guests tell Archimede that he has great taste in poetry and music, and he replies that the only piece of music in the whole world which he's never been able to abide is, "Yes, Sir, That's My Baby," which he characterizes as being a 'vulgar American song.' (In this picture, he'll brag constantly that he "only like[s] things which are distinctively French in nature," and so, it's no wonder that this cool movie only garnered a token U.S. theatrical release, and in only one or two art-house theaters.)

Before he leaves, the partiers all ask Archimede to dance for them one more time, and they giddily follow his lead, just like in the most opulent of MGM musicals. "You're not dancing well enough," he shouts at them, "You've got to feel the rhythm in your legs!" The partiers all mimic everything he does, as if he's some kind of an enlightened being (which, very probably, he is). In movies, as all of us already know, wealthy characters always proscribe special mystical powers to the poor characters; it's just like how, in today's American movies, the white, Yuppie characters always have that one, enlightened, mystical black friend who usually speaks in maxims—and, most of the time, he's played by Morgan Freeman!

All partied-out, Archimede now bids his new friends goodbye, and heads over to the fish market. A Fishmonger (Bernard la Jarrige) friend of Archimede's, who also happens to be an 'ex-bum,' invites Archimede to work there with him, but 'Big Arch' waves the guy off, with a mighty cry of, "Work?! No way!" He then picks up his pal Arsene, whom he sees hanging out on a nearby bench, and the two of them head into a fancy restaurant. The Restaurateur (Albert Dinan) is enraged at an Italian couple (Phillipe Mareuil and Gisele Grimm), because the couple has had the nerve to come into his French restaurant, and to order Italian pasta; the Restaurateur hates Italians and, as we now find out, he also *loves Archimede!* "Why don't they go somewhere else and eat noodles?" he asks Our Favorite Bum, continuing, "Some clients really piss me off! I feel like poisoning their soup!" Cued by the Restaurateur, who wants the couple out of his establishment (and as quickly as possible), Archimede and Arsene now start dancing around wildly, exactly like Belushi and Aykroyd will do in the very similar 'fancy restaurant-scene' in John Landis' 1980 classic *The Blues Brothers,* and the horrified Italians run out of the establishment, as fast as their little angel-hair pasta-legs can carry them. To thank Archimede and Arsene for getting rid of them, the Restaurateur, who is a true man-of-the-people (just as Archimede and Arsene are also men-of-the-people), invites them to sit down, and to finish the couple's meal, and he even offers Archimede and Arsene a standing invitation to eat in his restaurant anytime they want to.

In a very funny sequence which is set later that same day, Arsene now takes two of

Felix's dogs out for a walk, having piled them into an old baby carriage which he's found somewhere (don't ask!), and he walks alongside a nanny, who happens to be pushing two babies, in the exact same pram. (*Everyone's 'pounding out the pups:'* That seems to be the film's comedic criticism of Roman-Catholic France's *bulk childbirth* situation—at least, as it used to be, back when this film was made. In the unstated but obvious opinion of the filmmakers, there are just too many babies in France, and not enough work for anybody to support the little *cracker-munchers*. [In this film, there are definitely more bums in France than there are rich people.])

Back at Maison Gregoire, Pichon, the new owner, having taken Archimede's diagnosis of his 'liver problems' to heart, is now sipping a teaspoon of liver medication, Archimede's *faux-diagnosis* of his alleged problem, having actually manifested itself for real, through some kind of self-fulfilling prophecy. ("Don't be stingy with my medicine," a flustered Pichon yells at his wife, convinced that he's ready for the grave!) At this point in the narrative, Arsene enters the bar and, as soon as he does, the cops burst in, accusing him of trying to sell the two dogs he was wheeling around, because they've figured out that the dogs weren't his to sell.

Meanwhile, back in Archimede's room (he finally threw Felix the hell out), other cops are engaged in carrying Archimede out of his room, and when they do, he's sitting majestically atop his old, tattered mattress, and it looks, for all the world, like the cops are his servants, and that they're carrying an Emperor out on a sedan-chair! As the cops forcibly remove Archimede from the premises, he again gets in the last word, bellowing-out, "I never should have camped here, in such an expensive place!"

Earlier in the picture, when Archimede was busting up the parade and making a nuisance of himself, a photographer had taken a picture of him—a picture which has now, amazingly, found its way onto the cover of *Paris France* magazine (which still exists today, as *Paris Match*). The magazine describes Archimede as being a great French patriot, and his face is plastered all over the newsstands! On the beach, an old military man, Captain Brossard, who's played by Noel Roquevert (one of France's all-time acting giants), buys copies of the magazine for each of his children, who are with him, informing them, "Do you see this man on the cover? He is a real patriot!" Archimede just so happens to walk by in the flesh, at this very same moment, and Brossard, who's excited to see him, introduces his children to him proudly. (So! That's why Archimede is always so proud, and why he feels such a sense of entitlement and respect: *He was a genuine hero, during World War II* and, as it continues to happen today with a lot of returning vets, no matter which war they fought in, when he returned home, he wasn't given the recognition and respect, and more importantly the good, well-paying job which he so richly deserved, for having put his life at risk to defend his country, and this part of the story was, no doubt, Gabin's dig at how the French didn't welcome him back, after he fought so valiantly for them, during World War II). As the two men talk, it turns out that Archimede was actually Captain Brossard's superior officer, which means that Archimede was either a corporal, or else a major! Knowing this, makes us like Archimede even more than we already do (which is almost impossible, because we already like him *a whole helluva lot,* since he's one of the most purely fun of all of Gabin's movie characters). Archimede, with a huge smile on his face, starts commanding Brossard to march up and down the beach, which the guy does, seriously and dutifully, right in front of his own kids, while his kids giggle about how their father has just turned into a total moron in the presence of this bizarre old homeless guy, whom none of them has ever seen before.

Archimede, le clochard, one of world cinema's greatest, yet least known (in the U.S., anyway) screen comedies (it's definitely, without any equivocation, 'up there,' with any of movie history's best and funniest comedies), clocks in at a brisk 76 minutes, and it's one of those rare movies which is so much fun, you never want it to end; you could *totally* hang-out with Jean Gabin's gruff-but-amiable Archimede for days, without ever getting bored. (The film premiered at 1959's Berlin Film Festival at 90 minutes, and those extra fourteen minutes are now, sadly, gone forever. [Or… are they? *Come on, archivists!* Archimede will come and kick your asses, if you don't find his missing footage! *Now, get to work!*])

What a Critic Said at the Time: "Primarily, a vehicle for Jean Gabin, held together by his exuberant antics." (*Variety*, 5-13-39 issue. Critic: "Mosk. [George Moskowitz.]" Reviewed in Paris.)

What Another Critic Said at the Time: "An uninhibited Gabin towers high [in this film]. Mr. Gabin has been assaulting the movie barricades for more than thirty years with impressive results, and he has not failed his public this time. He gives the viewer joy because, unlike the rest of us, he can make a mockery of conformity and the pressure of everyday life. His experience and artistry shine here. It is all Gabin's show. Since tramps are disenfranchised [in our world], it is a minor pleasure to note that at least one of them gives that unsettled group a charming, and wonderful aura." (New York *Times*, 4-24-62 issue. Critic: Bosley Crowther.)

Top: With Serge Rousseau. Above: With Paul Frankeur and Michel Auclair.

FILM 68

MAIGRET ET L'AFFAIRE SAINT-FIACRE

France/Italy, 1959

(Literal English Translation: "MAIGRET AND THE ST. FIACRE AFFAIR") Directed by Jean Delannoy. Produced by Jean-Paul Guibert and Robert Gascuel. Screenplay by Jean Delannnoy, Maurice Arlaud, and Michel Audiard. Based Upon the Novel by Georges Simenon. Director of Photography (black and white), Louis Page. Editor, Henri Taverna. Music by Jean Prodromides. Production Designer, Rene Renoux. (GENRES: POLICIER/THRILLER) A Production of Cinetel and Intermondia (France), Pretoria Film and Titanus (Italy). Running Time, 1 hour 41 minutes. Released in France by Cinedis, on September 2, 1959. Never Released Theatrically in the United States.

"Only one of you is the murderer... which doesn't mean that the other six of you aren't the murderer!"
— *Inspector Maigret solves the case, in "Maigret et l'affaire Saint-Fiacre"*

Two years after playing Georges Simenon's famous pipe-smoking Inspector, Jules Maigret, in *Maigret tend un piege*, Gabin would now return as Maigret for the second of three films, in *Maigret et l'affaire Saint-Fiacre*, a 'pretty good' picture which begins with a close-up on a hastily-scribbled kidnap note: "The hour of judgment has arrived. You will die in front of the Office of Ashes."

We're in the small village of Saint-Fiacre, in Brittany, which is fifteen minutes away from Nantes, and in the picture's establishing shot, we see children laughing and playing. Maigret (like every Jean Gabin character must invariably do) enters a neighborhood bar, where he's meeting, at the appointed time, a woman of about his age, and the first thing she says to him is, "You haven't changed in forty-one years, Jules!" Apparently, Maigret and this woman knew each other when they were younger, but they never dated, although she tells him that she admired both him and his father greatly. (Apparently, the pipe doesn't fall far from the tree!)

This woman carries herself a bit differently now than she used to forty years ago, and mostly, it's because she married rich—she's now, through marriage, the Contessa of Saint-Fiacre, and she's played by Valentine Tessier. The Contessa tells Maigret that she received a crazy/threatening note, four days ago. She gives it to him and, after he reads it, he asks her if it's a joke; he's trying, obviously, to soothe her jangled nerves, and he also asks her if she has any enemies. She replies, a bit sarcastically, that she's not even sure if she has any friends.

Maigret now questions her, further: "You don't know anybody who wants to scare you? What about your son, Maurice, the one you mentioned when you called me yesterday and asked me to meet you. Is there an inheritance that's going to be coming to him one day?" She's *freaked-out* by the idea that Maigret thinks the letter's sender might be her own flesh and blood: "How could you think that, Inspector? My son and I haven't talked for awhile, because he lives all over the world—in fact, at the moment, he's traveling in Tahiti. But he'd never write me a letter like that one. Anyway, he's returning to France: He's coming home tomorrow, if you'd like to talk to him, but be gentle with him—he's very delicate." We can tell, even before meeting Maurice that, no doubt, he's going to be another one of those great 'Mama's Boy'/child-man characters that Georges Simenon loves to write about. (Remember Jean Desailly's mama's-boy character in the first Gabin/Maigret picture, *Maigret tend un piege?*)

Maigret agrees to stay at the Contessa's stately chateau for a few days, because he wants to question her servants about the letter, and so as not to raise suspicion, he tells her that, since nobody in Saint-Fiacre knows him, he'll pretend to be her antique-dealer friend who's coming to the house to appraise some of her rare artifacts.

When Maigret arrives at the Chateau Saint-Fiacre, he meets a young, Anthony Perkins-esque man whom he believes to be Maurice (if anybody looks like a mama's boy, it's this guy)! But it's not Maurice: It's another young man, Lucien (Robert Hirsch), and he's the thirtysomething houseboy who takes care of the Contessa, in her son Maurice's absence. "So, you've come to look at our furniture?" the guy sniffs queenily at Maigret, obviously threatened by the presence of another male in the house. "Well, okay, then. Very well. Look, if you must." Lucien, who's a conniving sort, then tries to sell Maigret some paintings right off of the wall (!), but when the Contessa enters the room, Lucien conveniently forgets about his little, under-the-table operation. The Contessa instructs Lucien to show Maigret up to the guest room, and then immediately afterwards, to bring her 'medicine' to her, in her own room.

Maigret stays that night in a lushly-appointed guest room—it's one of those cobweb-festooned, Agatha Christie-esque rooms that, in prime Christie fashion, probably hasn't been opened since the original inhabitant (in this case, the Contessa's dear/departed hubby, the Count) passed on. And just as we always get in every Christie novel, here, too, in *Maigret et l'affaire Saint-Fiacre*, we're going to be getting 'the obligatory shaving bowl with the black widow spider crawling around inside of it'-scene, and of course, calm, cool Maigret dispatches the arachnid, without breaking a sweat. The presence of the spider bodes badly for the future, and here, perhaps a bit too obviously, director Jean Delannoy, novelist Georges Simenon, and screenwriter Michel Audiard are pointing out, in their not-too-veiled manner, that the Contessa of Saint-Fiacre, too, is (no doubt) a 'black widow,' although the filmmakers never tell us if her husband is dead because she killed him, or just because he died of natural causes.

Lucien heads up to the Contessa's room with her medicine, which doesn't appear to be Geritol: He's got a huge syringe in his grip, and he injects her with something which we've already figured out (because we've seen these kinda pictures before) isn't what she thinks it is: Obviously, he's trying to get her health to deterioriate on purpose, so that he'll be able to get at her money; and in fact, when she tells him that the medicine he's brought her tonight isn't her usual tonic (he tells her that it's just a 'vitamin shot'), she believes it, and doesn't even question him about it.

The grounds of the Contessa's manor house an ornate church and, the next morning, the Contessa heads over there, to attend her usual morning services. And maybe she shouldn't have bothered showing up at all, because while the cathedral's white-haired priest, Father Jodet (Michel Vittold), is delivering his sermon, the Contessa suddenly dies of a massive coronary!

The township's old Doctor (Paul Frankeur, and for a change, here's one Jean Gabin movie, in which he's not playing a bartender) checks out the Contessa's inert body, and declares that he's been treating her for years, and that she's always had a heart condition. (But is that true? Is this Doctor in on some kind of a scam with Lucien and Father Jodet, wherein all three men mean to bilk the Contessa's son, Maurice, out of his rightful inheritance, thereby taking it for themselves?) Maigret tells Father Jodet that the church's twelve-year-old altar boy, Ernest Boufard (Marcel Peres), who is present, 'looks like he knows something'—something which he's not telling, because either one of the film's insidious characters is threatening him off-screen, or else, *maybe*, he's just too young to know how to articulate what it is that he knows.

Back at the Contessa's place later that day, Lucien is now crying, and a bit too theatrically (this is duly noted by eagle-eyed, and eared, Maigret), and he actually seems to be implicating himself in the Contessa's death (even though he doesn't know he's doing that) just by virtue of his ridiculous overacting: "Oh, the poor dear! She died without seeing her son, Maurice! He would go a month without calling her, and I always stood in for him, in his absence. She trusted me to take care of all of this [and here, he indicates the whole manor, with a sweeping arm gesture] for her." Even through his alligator tears, Lucien now asks Maigret, whom he still reckons to be an antique dealer, if he thinks that he might be able "to get a good price for the furniture;" Lucien, at this moment, has no idea if the Contessa has even willed any of the furniture to him, but he's definitely not letting anything as corny as a legal document stand in his way!

The Doctor, who knows Maigret's true identity, even if Lucien still does not, now gives Maigret the final results of the Contessa's autopsy: He tells Maigret that her heart attack was brought on by 'her tiredness,' and by 'her emotions.' (Is this guy in on the con, as well?) Maigret knows *horseshit* when he smells it, but doesn't say anything. He investigates around the house, where he comes upon the Contessa's locket. Inside, there's a picture of Maurice, when he was a little boy.

At this point, *the prodigal, twentysomething son,* dilettantish Maurice (Michel Auclair) finally arrives home, spiriting up to the manor in his *fancy-shmancy* new Citroen. Maigret introduces himself to Maurice as being an old friend of his mom's, and he also admits that he happens to be a cop (it's the first time he's told anybody in the household what he really does for a living), and he also (gently) breaks the news to Maurice, that Maurice's mother has just died. Maurice, who happens to be a Count in his own right (because he inherited the title from his late father), doesn't seem appropriately unhinged by the news, and the question which we, the audience, are now asking ourselves as we watch the movie, is—could Maurice be in on some kind of 'group, Contessa-bilking scheme' along with Lucien and/or the Doctor, and/or Father Jodet? Since Maurice, apparently, hasn't been home for many months, this is the first time that he's meeting Lucien in-person, and Maigret and Maurice are both asking Lucien, in this scene, if it was normal for Lucien to give the Contessa injections, but Lucien doesn't immediately answer.

That night, Maigret assembles the entire household staff, including the Doctor, Father Jodet, Lucien, and Maurice, into the drawing room—*Hercule Poirot/Miss Marple-style*—and tells anybody who still doesn't know it yet, that he's Inspector Maigret from the Paris Bureau, and he also tells the uneasy crowd that he believes the Contessa's sudden death was caused by a newspaper article which somebody had hidden inside of her Bible, expressly for her to see. (Each parishioner who attends this Church, it seems, has his or her own personal copy of the Bible.) "According to this phony, completely-made-up article, which was dated the day before the Contessa's fatal heart attack, Maurice was killed overseas, and proof that this article is a fake, is that Maurice is alive and standing here in front of us, right now!"

"So," Maigret continues, "somebody wrote the article, and I don't know who, because there is no byline on the piece, and when that person wrote it, he knew full well that the Contessa had a weak heart, and that if she read about her son's death, she would have an immediate heart attack and die. And that 'somebody,' whose identity—and don't you worry, my friends, I'll figure out—was clearly somebody who would stand to inherit the Contessa's fortune, in the event of Maurice's death. So my question to all of you now, is: Who would go to the trouble of planting an article, stating that the Contessa's still-living son has just died? Obviously, it's somebody who lives or works here—somebody who, as we say, is, 'on the inside.'" Maigret reads the article to the crowd, and each person present remains poker-faced. According to the article, Maurice committed suicide after "something bad happened in the family"—something in which he was involved directly. (The article doesn't reveal what that 'something' was, nor will we ever find out.)

Maigret now makes an assumption: He tells the crowd that clearly, the article, and the Contessa's perusal of it, had been planned-out far in advance. Maurice tells Maigret that he just can't understand why anybody would write an article claiming that he was dead, in order to give his mom a fatal heart attack. Maigret asks Father Jodet if the Contessa had any enemies, and the Holy Man beatifically replies, "Only God knows!"

That night, Maigret stops in at a local bar, and the old proprietress, Marie Tatin (Gabrielle

Fontan) knows him, too. ("Jules Maigret!" she screams out, excitedly.) And guess who else is in the bar: It's Lucien himself who's there, enjoying a coffee at a corner table. Maigret goes to the bar's payphone, calls up the editorial offices of Saint-Fiacre's tiny local newspaper (right in front of Lucien) and asks the night editor if he knows who wrote the article about Maurice's suicide, since the piece had no byline. The Editor (Jean-Pierre Granval) says he has no idea who wrote it, and Maigret tells the guy that next time he publishes an article, he should probably try to remember who it is that wrote it (!): "The Count, Maurice, is very-much alive, my friend, and your 'invisible writer' is going to be in hot water, for faking this story." Maigret has found out recently, off-screen, that Lucien, when he's not busy drugging old ladies, sometimes writes occasional articles for the newspaper on a freelance basis (besides being a nurse, he writes the occasional puff piece about art), so Maigret is really making this phone call, in Lucien's presence, just to see if he can make the young guy squirm. Maigret knows that Lucien spends all of his nights, not at the chateau, but in another nearby town, Moulin, where the newspaper's offices are located, and Our Favorite Inspector has also learned that Moulin is exactly where the story was phoned in from—and don't ask about how he found out, because the film won't tell us! 'Cutting to the chase,' and dispensing with his normal politeness, Maigret then asks Lucien, point-blank, if it was he who phoned-in the article, and the wigging-out Lucien tells Maigret that he's not going to answer any questions, unless his attorney is present.

While Maigret thinks that Lucien might be the killer, he's also crafty enough to know that, even in spite of Lucien's crazy behavior, he'd better not rule out everybody else who also knew the Contessa. His next investigative stop, is the tiny Saint-Fiacre home of elderly Mr. and Mrs. Gaulthier (Camille Guerini and Helen Tossy), the Contessa's groundskeepers. Maigret informs the couple that somebody in the Contessa's household, in the few days since her demise, has been selling her paintings. He then asks them politely, if it was perhaps they who sold them—maybe, to pay for her funeral, which was very opulent—but they assure him that they did not.

Maigret asks the Gaulthiers, too, a few questions about the young Count Maurice, since the old couple has been the Contessa's groundskeepers at the estate, since Maurice was a small boy. They tell Maigret that it was always a dream of Maurice's to bring industry into this countrified area, and he asks the couple if they knew where the constantly-traveling Maurice had been recently, since he's been unable to get a straight answer out of Maurice himself, and they tell him that, as far as they know, Maurice was off in Tahiti, buying himself a boat and a race horse. The Gaulthiers have a son, Emile (Serge Rousseau), who works in the local bank, in the Department of Titles (Emile was thirteen when he and his parents settled in Saint-Fiacre) and, at that moment, friendly Emile comes in, and meets Maigret for the first time.

That night, back at the Contessa's house, Maigret is asking Maurice why he returned home yesterday, right after his mother's death, and Maurice replies that, when he got home, he had no idea that she was dead: "I came home to see her, and to help her to strategize a plan for paying-off some of her debts. Didn't my mom tell you that everybody in our family is an alcoholic, and that all of our relatives have been bleeding her dry, to feed their addictions?" Maigret tells Maurice that he's going to go and interrogate Father Jodet a bit more: "If he took your mother's confessions, maybe she confessed to him, on one occasion or another, about other people who may have had problems with her."

Maurice next heads over to the Church with Maigret, and Maurice (and this is no way to behave in church!) starts, suddenly and violently, accusing Father Jodet of being complicit in his mother's demise: "You were trying to get my mom to give all her money to the Church, weren't you, Father? You abused her trust, during her confessions to you!" Then, Maurice turns around, and makes a new and different accusation, and this one is lobbed right in the general direction of Inspector Maigret, himself: "Inspector, maybe you're the murderer! Did you come here to have an affair with my mother?" Maigret tells the young man to calm down, but once Maurice starts pointing fingers, he just can't stop! He tells Maigret that he hates, and doesn't trust, this "bastard nurse," Lucien, whom he's just met.

In the next sequence, Maigret sulks into the Moulin newspaper offices, where he meets the Writer of the falsified newspaper article, who's played by Christian Brocard. The Writer tells Maigret that he got the story about Maurice's suicide from Paris—or, at least, he *thought* it came from Paris: "Somebody called me and told me the story, but I don't know who it was." Maigret has a problem believing him, though: "So, what you're telling me, is that anyone can call you and tell you anything, and you'll print it?" The Writer tries to save face: "It was a different source than the guy who usually 'leaks stuff' to us. We believed the guy—he sounded convincing. And I had to publish the story, because if the information turned out to be correct, and I missed out on it, I would have been fired." This admission causes the film's one, long-awaited Gabin-Outburst: "Did you know that this false news which you printed caused the death of a woman? You are an accomplice, my friend. And you are in a lot of trouble!"

That night, Maigret heads into a local café. The Writer, whom he's just reamed out, is there, and Maurice (coincidentally?) is present as well, but he's alone, ensconced at another table. (Do Maurice and the Writer know each other?) Maigret asks the Writer what he's doing there at the same time as Maurice, and the guy replies, not too convincingly, that he's an acquaintance of Maurice's: "He's just come to give me gas money. I'm his driver, sometimes." (It's easy to figure out that the Writer's obviously come to this place where he knows Maurice hangs out whenever he's in town, to give Maurice the skinny about the Inspector's recent appearance, down at the newspaper's office.) Interestingly, in this scene, we now get a young, twentysomething brunette, Arlette (Micheline Luccioni) who's drinking at the bar, and checking Inspector Maigret out. (Even though Arlette's not a part of the story-proper, the filmmakers don't want us to forget that, while Jean Gabin is getting older, *he's still got it!*) Maigret sits down next to the rubbernecking lassie, and asks her if she knows anything about the late Contessa and her family, and he gives her his usual *spiel* (that he's a family friend, and that he's just in town for a few days). She tells him that she, herself, just met Maurice the previous night, and that she went with him to 'his place,' at 3:00 a.m. So: Maurice has his own secret apartment in town where he can bring girls, a place that even his own family knows nothing about.

So, not only is Maurice straight (he seemed *a l'il fruity*), but so, too, as we're going to be discovering in the next scene, is the equally *light-loafered-looking Lucien* (how's that for alliteration?) who, when we next see him, is sitting center-stage at an American-style strip club, which is actually called *Le Hula Hoop*. He's pissed that Maigret has shown up there ("You're following me now, Inspector?"), and so he leaves immediately. At that moment, Maigret gets sidetracked by a blonde Stripper (she's played by Andree Tainsy), who takes an instant shine to him, and Maigret tells her that he's "a visiting antique dealer." (He's telling all the ladies that "he's just visiting." [Yes: Once a drifter, always a drifter!])

Maigret follows Lucien back to the chateau and, when he gets there, Lucien's in his room, and is frenetically packing his suitcases: "Moving, Lucien? Trying to get away?" At this point, Lucien doesn't really feel like talking: "I don't have any reason to obey you, cop!" Maigret blocks him from leaving the room: "Instead of leaving town, son, you'd just better call that attorney you mentioned! He's going to become very important to all of our lives, during the next few days!"

Next, Maigret's interrogating Father Jodet again, at the property's church: "I need your help again, Father. I'm just not making any headway, in this case." The Priest replies that he doesn't know anything either, although he does tell Maigret that, when the Contessa suffered her fatal heart attack, "… she was sitting in that seat. And the expression of agony she had when she read the article—well, even after she had 'passed,' Inspector, that expression just stayed frozen on her face."

Maigret now decides to reconstruct the moment of the Contessa's death, with Father Jodet helping him out: "Father, if you could indulge me for a moment: If you would, could you please position yourself where you were yesterday, during your sermon? All right, now—you were here, and the altar boy was there. The Contessa, as you've already told me, had just expired. Now what happened next, hmm?" Father Jobet replies that, after he phoned the Doctor, he next took the Contessa's Bible and placed it back in the cupboard, but that today, it's not in the cubby-hole where he had left it: He shows Maigret the cupboard, and the little empty space where it's supposed to be.

Maigret next asks the little altar boy, Ernest, who's just entered the chapel, if he knows where the missing Bible has gone. At first, the boy is a little scared of the bulldog-faced Inspector, but Maigret makes the kid feel more comfortable by telling him (whether this is true or not) that he too used to be an altar boy!

"Let's play a game," Maigret winks playfully at little Ernest: Man and Boy now play a game of 'hot and cold' in which, when Maigret gets closer to where the Bible is (wherever that may be) Ernest has to say, "hot," and when Maigret gets further away, the boy is supposed to blurt-out, "cold." The game is successful, and Maigret finds the Bible on top of the cupboard, instead of inside of it where it usually is; even though the book wasn't in its proper place, it remains intact, with the article still inside of it.

Maigret next heads into the *Depot des Titres* (the local bank's Title Department), where Emile Gaulthier, the son of the Contessa's groundskeepers, works. Maigret means to ask Emile a few penetrating questions, to see what Emile knows, if anything, and it is here that Emile will reveal something which is pretty surprising: "Maurice came here, to the bank, the day before his mother's death." (Aha! So: Maurice was already home, in Saint-Fiacre, for the last several weeks, at his own secret apartment, and not in Tahiti, where he had claimed to be, which means that Emile's parents might be in on the murder, because maybe they were covering it up. Emile tells Maigret that Maurice had visited the bank to evaluate the title to his mother's land, and to see how much it was worth, and that Maurice also wanted to borrow eight hundred thousand francs from the bank, to help his mom pay off some lingering debts which she had accrued.

In the movie's final, Agatha Christie-like scene, Maigret now invites all of the accused to the manor for dinner, during which time he means (the guests don't know this yet) to announce the name of the one among them who caused the Contessa's death: Yes, friends, sharp-witted Inspector Maigret has finally figured it all out (we knew he would), and the cherriest part of this interrogation scene is that, while it's happening, the Contessa's body lies directly overhead, in her bedroom.

The guests arrive, and Maurice has unexpectedly brought his no-nonsense lawyer Mauleon (Jacques Morel) along, having determined that it will be difficult for Maigret to accuse him of anything with his attorney present. Mauleon immediately dispenses with the formalities, informing Maigret that he has neither the right nor the jurisdiction to investigate Lucien, nor for that matter is he within his rights to investigate anybody else in the room. Emile and his father are present as well, as is the town's old Doctor (Paul Frankeur).

Now, even before the *foie-gras* is served, it's time for Maigret to begin his round of questioning: "Why did you invite all your friends?" Maigret asks Maurice. Lucien's beginning to look really nervous, and he tells Maigret that he's leaving. ("Nobody is leaving this room!" the pipe-smoking Inspector shouts, authoritatively.)

Maigret now addresses what Mauleon said to him, only moments before: "I know I'm not supposed to be investigating, but I spoke to local authorities already, and they have given me permission, and are ready to back me up. First, I want to tell all of you that this murder was a coward's crime." He turns to the assembled guests: "There are a number of you here, and even if only one of you is guilty, it doesn't necessarily mean that the others *aren't* guilty." In other words, everybody in the room, at least to the cunning Inspector's way of thinking, has had something to gain out of the Contessa's death, and Maigret tells all-assembled that he knows Maurice had sent his mother a telegram several days before her death, asking her for eight hundred-thousand francs. Maurice blanches, and then Maigret turns the spotlight onto the old Doctor: "Sir, you knew the Contessa was sick. So why did you not call in a specialist?" The Doc replies, "People in small towns are known to gossip. So sometimes, calling in a specialist isn't such a good idea."

Maigret now turns his attentions toward Lucien: "The Contessa thought about you, Lucien, as her son. You and Maurice are basically the same age, and Maurice, more often than not, is always out, gallivanting around the world. You were in the Contessa's will as well, Lucien, but you tried to get even more money than she had promised you, by trying to sell her paintings. You wanted her to consider you as her son, even though you're not related to her." Lucien looks freaked, because he's getting busted: "So, you're saying I killed her? Why would I do that, if I was in her will to begin with? Murderers don't get inheritances!"

Maigret next throws the room a curveball, using some extra information of which he's just gotten wind over the last couple of days: He tells everyone in the room that he knows Lucien isn't just a surrogate son to the Contessa, but that he was also sleeping with her, as well! Maurice looks like he's going to throw up.

But Maigret hopes Maurice won't vomit, because it's time to turn the questioning onto him, and we can really see Maigret's wheels turning: "So, Maurice, you wanted money to buy the manor from the bank, not because your mother had debts, but because she didn't leave the place to you. And you, Lucien: You needed money right now as well, because you also recently purchased some land [elsewhere in France], and you had a debt of eight million francs to pay off."

Maurice, not wanting to hear anymore, and just wanting this whole fiasco to end, throws up his hands: "Okay, I did it! I killed my mother! I'm the guilty one!" Maigret, the world's greatest detective, sees through this ploy quite easily, however: "Oh, you've killed your mother several times throughout her life, Maurice. But her actual death didn't come at your hands, at all. And it is only her actual, physical death, of which you were not the cause, which really interests me right now."

"Lucien is an idiot," Maigret chirps gleefully, looking right at Lucien as he says this. "He couldn't have done it. The actual murderer is the one who placed the article inside the Bible. The newspaper was stolen from the publisher's offices the night before it came out, so, I already know that the murderer is someone who had a connection to the newspaper office. And Maurice was in the café at 2:15 in the morning the night before the newspaper came out, which means that somebody in this room met him in the newspaper offices and handed it over to him. And there was somebody else in that café, too: Maurice was there, and so was the person who wrote the article, and there was a young lady, there, as well. [Here, he's referencing Arlette, the young woman who thought Maigret was cute.] And there was also somebody else! But who? WHO?!"

Emile's father, Mr. Gaulthier, has a copy of the false article crumpled up in his hands, and now, Maigret turns his attention to him: "For ten years, you have been buying the land all around Moulin, haven't you? And you wanted to buy the Contessa's manor, as well! You had to see Maurice because, even though he's not that bright, he wouldn't sell his mother's land to you. Your son, Emile, was the killer. He planted the article. And you, the father, told him to do it, so you are his accomplice." In the amazing scene which follows, Maigret takes Emile upstairs and makes him beg forgiveness in front of the Contessa's corpse! Maigret takes Emile to jail, and so unfortunately, we don't get to find out if anybody actually got to eat dinner that night.

The second of Jean Gabin's three Inspector Maigret mysteries, one which is merely 'pretty good,' has now come to an end, and audiences would now have to wait four more years for Jean Gabin's third and final Maigret picture, 1963's *Maigret voit rouge* (*Maigret Sees Red.*) *Maigret et l'affaire Saint-Fiacre* is not as good as *Maigret tend un piege,* Gabin's first Maigret movie, but it's better than the one which will follow, four years later.

What a Critic Said at the Time: "This [one...] is short on suspense, but long on solid characterization, atmosphere, and talk... It insists on psychology over action and tension. The supporting players are good, but are subordinated to Gabin's quizzical figure of the plodding but shrewd Detective." (*Variety*, 9-23-59 issue. Critic: "Mosk. [George Moskowitz.]" Reviewed in Paris.)

1954 — 1976 | 227

FILM 69

Rue des Prairies

France, 1959

(Literal English Translation, "MEADOW STREET") Directed by Denys de La Patelliere. Produced by Georges Danagers, Jean-Paul Guibert, and Alexandre Mnouchkine. Written by Michel Audiard and Denys de La Patelliere. Based Upon the Novel by Rene Lefevre. Music by Georges Van Parys. Director of Photography (black and white), Louis Page. Editor, Jacqueline Thiedot. Production Designer, Rene Renoux. (GENRE: DRAMATIC COMEDY) A Production of Intermondia Films and Les Films Ariane. Running Time: 1 hour 27 minutes. Released in France by Cinedis, on October 21, 1959. Released in the United States (NYC) with English Subtitles on December 22, 1960 by Lopert Pictures Corporation, as "RUE DE PARIS."

> "If you ever bring home a child by that guy, I'm going to have it stuffed and show it off to the public!"
> — *Gabin doesn't approve of his daughter's choice of boyfriends, in "Rue des Prairies"*

Now that Jean Gabin was getting older (he was 55 when he made this movie), he was starting to make a lot of movies in which his patriarchal characters seemed to be spending the entire movies 'extinguishing the fires within' (the fires within his own criminal organizations in *Miroir, Razzia sur la chnouf,* and *Le Sang a la tete,* as well as the conflagrations found within his characters' own nuclear and extended families). We saw this happening previously in *Les Grandes familles* and now, we're going to be getting it again here, in director Denys de La Patelliere's superbly-enjoyable comedy/drama, *Rue des Prairies [Meadow Street].* When you're watching this picture, it becomes obvious very quickly that the French were doing 'dramedies' twenty-five years before American critics coined the term in the '80s (which is when America started making movies like *Terms of Endearment* and t.v. shows like "Thirtysomething"). Patelliere and Gabin made *Les Grandes familles* and *Rue des Prairies* the same year, and *Prairies'* light, frothy fun more than makes up for *Grandes familles'* stodgy monotony.

The picture opens with two pre-opening credit flashback-sequences: In the first one, a battalion of French soldiers is fighting a pitched WWII battle, and one of them is Jacques

Neveux (Jean Gabin: And because Gabin's hair was now, in real-life, a snowy white, in this flashback sequence the filmmakers have loaded him up with the requisite *black* hair-dye even though, in real-life, when Gabin was younger, his hair was *blonde,* and not black!) Then, in the second pre-credit flashback, we see Jacques arriving home from battle, and for what must be the first time in a couple of years: Jacques kisses his wife and two little kids, who look to be about four or five years old (a boy and a girl) and his kids aren't too excited to see him (just like the kids in 'Trucker-Gabin's' *Des gens sans importance* weren't so happy to see him, either) but you can't really find too much fault with them, because he's been away fighting for most of their larval lives. There also happens to be a new kid in the household, as well: Seems that, while Jacques was away shelling the Krauts, his wife was busy shelling-out a baby, a tot which she made with one of Jacques '4F' friends. When Jacques sees the infant (it's the first time he's ever seen or heard of the kid), who happens to be asleep in the back bedroom, he doesn't get mad, nor does he even react. In the customary Gabin-Manner, he fatalistically understands and accepts that it was only human nature that his wife should have been lonely while he was away, and so he reticently accepts this new 'little bundle'—in fact, he puts the whole subject to bed, so to speak, by sighing, and Gabin-Shrugging, "Well, I guess after two years… everything has changed."

Now, director Patelliere flashes forward to the story-proper: It's now 'Present Day, 1959' and we get to see a group of Parisian locals who are guzzling away at the local corner-bar, and we're introduced, one-by-one, to the film's main characters and the actors who play them, with the help of printed titles which are superimposed over each performer, just like Patelliere did also, in *Les Grandes familles*. Twenty-two year old Claude Brasseur (the real-life son of Pierre Brasseur, who had just played Gabin's grotesque brother-in-law, Lucien Maublanc, in Patelliere's *Les Grandes familles*) plays Louis, Jacques' extremely popular, bike-racer son. (In the film, Louis is meant to be nineteen or twenty years old.) Handsome Louis wins every race he ever enters, big or small, and there's no sign that his luck will ever abate. In fact, the whole Neveux clan is busy at the bar, partying, and celebrating Louis' most recent win of a big race in Amsterdam. A hilariously-loopy Jacques is mentioning, to some other guys in the bar who are around his own age, that the Tour de France will be coming up this summer, and that he knows Louis is more than ready for it. Gabin's Jacques, post-War, is a construction worker who builds those giant, boxy high-rise apartment buildings which had begun popping-up all over France and the Eastern Bloc nations after WWII, and he also finds time to be his son's dutiful manager: French audiences turned out in droves to see Gabin as a trainer of young boxers in Marcel Carne's 1954 effort *L'Air de Paris,* so the producers of *Rue de Prairies* felt, no doubt, that they would be 'making bank,' by putting Gabin back into a similar, mentoring-of-young-men-type of role. (*Jean Gabin is the original 'Mr. Miyagi!'*) Jacques' two-timing wife has died, somewhere between the World War II flashback and now, which means that Jacques now has three teen-agers, whom he's raising all by himself. (You'd better not call Gabin "Mr. Mom," or he'll slap the shit out of you!)

The regulars at the bar, all of whom are good friends of *la famille Neveux* now start

With Roger Dumas.

jokingly 'taking the piss' out of their old friend Jacques, just because they think it's funny to 'get his Irish' (or, more accurately, '*get his French*') up: "Look, Jacques: We're not saying that your Louis didn't win in Amsterdam. All we're saying, is that it's quite possible there was a tie between him and the Dutch cyclist!" Hilariously, Jacques leaps on a barstool, as if it's a bicycle, and starts re-enacting exactly how and why his son won, and it's a terribly funny moment, in which Jean Gabin is as loud, and as boisterous (and as funny, and as full-of-life), as he was in *Archimede* and *La Traversee de Paris*.

That's right: Just like in director Jean Gremillon's 1941 Gabin flick, *Remorques*, here comes more of France's much-vaunted 'Dutch-bashing:' In the opening moments of *Remorques*, the French characters loathed the Dutch characters because they felt like the Dutch sailors were taking away their shipping businesses in the French port of Brest; but *Rue des Prairies* takes place 'up north,' in Paris, and not in Brest, and this whole anti-Dutchness in some French cinema got me (a/k/a, '*this author*') wondering: Do (or *did*, in the past) the French hate the Dutch, and if so, why? I asked Seattle-based historian Andrew J. Williamson, who had this to say on the subject:

"Some Dutch fought side-by-side with the British at Waterloo, against Napoleon. One hundred years previously, the Dutch and British were also united against the French, during the War of the Spanish Succession. There may be less historically arcane reasons but, as we know—'*Old Worlders' have long memories*."

Next, we're at a local high school: While Louis is Jacques' famous and well-respected son (the one who gets the lion's share of attention and approval from 'daddy,' and from the public), the same can't be said for Jacques' other son, fifteen-year-old Fernand (Roger Dumas), who's actually the stepson whom we last saw, when he was a baby, fourteen years ago. In fact, Fernand (maybe, Jacques never gave the boy any attention, since Fernand wasn't Jacques' own, natural son) has become quite the school bully, taking expensive thousand-franc bets on his brother Louis' bike race wins, and then beating the shit out of the kids who won't pay up, when they've bet against Louis!

While Jacques is excited that Louis is famous, he's apprehensive too, about Louis' fame, because he's afraid that if Louis gets too well-known, people will bother him (Jacques) more—and Jean Gabin, as we already know from watching his previous forty films, prizes his moments, and even whole days, of uninterrupted quietude, more than anything else on earth.

Jacques knows (Jean Gabin's characters are smart) that the reason Fernand has turned into bully, is because he (Jacques) never pays as much attention to him as he does to his own, real kids: As Jacques now tells his brother-in-law, Ernest (Paul Frankeur), who works with him on the construction site of one of those boxy, new apartments (Ernest's the construction company's Chief of Security), "My other two kids—I made them, so I know what they want in life. But Fernand is something else. Maybe his real dad was cool... although probably, he was just a jerk!" When he's at home, Jacques is always pushing the rebellious Fernand to finish high school, but incorrigible Fernand just wants to drop out and take a menial job. Meanwhile, the third kid in the Neveux brood, Jacques' daughter, Odette (Marie Jose-Nat, the girl whom we saw dancing at the fancy trucker party *in Crime et chatiment*) has grown up into *quite the little hotty*, and she's keeping a huge secret from her dad: She makes pocket money getting photographed—in sexy poses, and by lecherous men!

One afternoon, Jacques gets called into the Principal's office to talk about Fernand, who is, as usual, in trouble, for beating the stuffing out of another boy:

> PRINCIPAL: Your son is anti-social. He hit our best student.
> JACQUES: Is it true? Did you beat a kid up?
> FERNAND (tough-guy smirk): Yeah.
> PRINCIPAL: And then, after beating the young man up, [your son] then tried to extort money from him.
> JACQUES: Is that true?
> FERNAND (arms crossed [don't fuck with me]): No.
> PRINCIPAL: My normal policy, is to expel kids who steal and fight. But I'm willing to give your son one more chance.

Fernand, who's acting surly even in front of his own principal, makes no apologies for his behavior and, at the end of the meeting, as Jacques leaves the office with Fernand, Fernand scolds Jacques: "You took a thousand francs off of a kid? Do you know what my dad would

With Marie-Jose Nat.

have done if I'd been caught doing something like that? He'd have kicked my ass out the door! Not only are you anti-social, but worse: *You're annoying!*"

Next, Jacques is at a family luncheon, and every Neveux relative in the history of the human race is present and accounted for. Even though Jacques works construction, he must have some money squired away somewhere, because his working-class family can afford membership at a seaside country club, the outside of which happens to be festooned with a hot line-up of staggering yachts. (Or: Young Louis is keeping the family in [relative] luxury, with the proceeds from his race winnings.) One of Jacques' friends asks him if his daughter is still single, and Jacques gives the guy the major Gabin-Grimace of all time.

At the luncheon, Louis (he's not perfect, either; he's arrogant, and he's also a braggart) dances with a woman, and tells her that he's just won a big race in Amsterdam, but she doesn't seem all that impressed, and it's just like in 1932's *Du haut en bas*, when Gabin's soccer playing Charles Boulla-character tried to impress the girl with the fact that he had just won the big match for France, and she just didn't care.

Back at work on Monday, Jacques is at the construction site with Ernest, and Ernest is boring the *holy hell* out of him, discussing the government's new helmet laws for construction sites, and it's hard for Jacques to pay attention, because he's still hung-over from the three glasses of wine which he drank at the big family get-together the previous night. Then, to stave-off boredom, the two men start hilariously debating which of the two of them can get the drunkest at family functions, and clearly, Ernest is ready to concede to Jacques: "You're definitely a bigger drinker than me. Remember your son's communion, when I had to stop you from taking your pants off?" Jacques and Ernest, now visualizing this, both start giggling like little girls, and it's another one of those great moments which the best French movies seem to do really well, in which the narrative relaxes for a few moments, and we get to see the characters just 'being themselves' (which is what makes them so real, and so memorable, and so likeable).

At the Country Club that same evening (real men can party two nights in a row, even when they're fifty-five years old!), Jacques is now 'going *Scared Straight*' on bad seed Fernand's ass, telling him that he's tired of having to get him out of trouble all of the time: He even rubs Fernand's face in the fact that Fernand's not his real son. ("Where did you get manufactured, anyway?") But hot-tempered Fernand, who's famous for his ability to overreact, remains calm in the face of his dad's cruel diatribe: The young man has known, ever since he was small, that he's not Jacques' natural son, and he's grown used to Jacques' taunting him about it. But Jean Gabin can never really play a mean guy and, ultimately, he realizes that he's just said something which he didn't mean to say, and so, to make it up to Fernand, he now rents out a paddle-boat for the two of them. (Paddle boats are those little two-man boats, popular in France, in which two people can sit side-by-side, both of them steering with their *footsies*.) Jacques, for all of his Gabinian-bluster, is also an intuitive and introspective guy, as are most of Gabin's characters, and he realizes that perhaps some of the trouble which he endures with Fernand regularly, has to do with the fact that he and Fernand don't spend enough father-and-son time together. Jacques and Fernand have a great time in the boat, paddling away together, and Fernand, for the very first time in the film, looks happy, because he's finally getting a little face time with 'Big (Step-) Daddy.'

After fixing things at least temporarily with Fernand, Jacques now has to deal with his daughter, Odette. Odette's told her father that she wants to move out, so that, as she's now putting it, she can be closer to her job. (Posing nude, for perverts!) Jacques tells her that he's not too excited about the idea (he's a family man, and likes his family to be together, even when he's not paying attention to them!), but that if she wants to move out, she's fully within her right to do so. Turns out, her wanting to move has nothing to do with her job, and everything to do with the fact that she wants to shack-up with her rich older boyfriend, a real suede shoe-type called Pedrell (Roger Treville).

The next morning, Jacques breakfasts with his 'favorite' son Louis, and Jacques is absolutely *kvelling*, because he's just found an article in the morning's newspaper about Louis: "Look! They wrote an article about you. It's good, I guess, although what troubles me, is that half of this stuff about your life—well, it seems kind of made-up." Louis tells his father that he sometimes has to invent facts when he's interviewed because, in his opinion, "nobody wants to read about happy people." Jacques laughs heartily, now questioning Louis on one of the made-up fun-facts from the article: "Hey, kid: Since when are you a vegetarian?!"

Now that Fernand's on good terms with Jacques again, ever since their 'father-and-son paddle-boat excursion,' Fernand's embarrassed to tell his dad about what's just happened at

With Claude Brasseur.

school: After running one scam too many, he's finally been expelled! While Fernand puts himself across as being a tough kid, he's shit-scared of his dad, and tells Odette, his hot halfsister, that he couldn't sleep all night, thinking about how his dad would take the news, and that she'd better not mention the expulsion to him. And as Fernand and Odette are talking about this in Odette's room, Odette's undressing, right in front of him. (In France, when brothers and sisters aren't related by blood, I guess, all systems are go!)

Concurrently, Louis has been accepted into a major race in Bordeaux, a match in which the winner will get to represent his country in the following summer's Tour de France. Louis' amusingly out-of-shape coach, Alfred Adam (who played the butcher, Barberot, in *Maigret tend un piege*), seems worried that Louis might not win, but of course, when the day of the Bordeaux race comes (and we're going to be seeing the race, in the next scene), 'win, he does!' And this victory, of course, means more raucous, and wine-soaked, family celebration:

That night, Jacques, Louis, and Odette are at their favorite neighborhood bar, and are all playing pool together. Jacques is complaining to the Owner, who's played by Albert Dinan (Dinan played cops who tried to bust Gabin in both *La Vierge du Rhin* and *Le Rouge est mis*, and he also 'trucked' with Gabin in *Gas-Oil*), about the freshness of the alcohol, and the guy smilingly retorts, "Maybe I'll make my doorway bigger, so you can fit through it!" Jacques is now more proud of Louis than he's ever been before, and this is definitely a happier moment for the father, than it is even for the son. "When I see you out there winning, I feel like I should have had a sports career, myself," Jacques tells Louis admiringly, next going off on a drunken tangent (on the subject of his own 'cool years,' long ago).

Then, 'Buzzkill Fernand' enters the bar and, somewhat passive-aggressively, he's picked this happy family-moment to inform his dad that he's been kicked out of school: This is the moment in which he hands Jacques the sealed envelope from the school's Director. Perceptive Jacques, though, doesn't get mad at Fernand, because he can already guess what's coming: "I don't open envelopes, anymore," Jacques Gabin-Shrugs decisively at Fernand, sick of the boy's ongoing *proto-podcasts* of bad news.

So, while Jacques will be able to get through the night without hearing about Fernand's expulsion, he won't be leaving the bar completely unscathed, because he now overhears the bar's Owner talking to some patrons about Pedrell, the rich guy who's been having a torrid affair with Odette: "He likes to get his women from the working class," the Owner tells them, and when Jacques overhears the guy talking shit about his own daughter, although the bartender, too, is 'working-class,' it's time for *Mega-Gabin Outburst, 1959:* "I know that you people are saying my Odette is a roundheels! But she's not!" He storms out of the bar, completely infuriated.

Jacques confronts Odette about her May-September relationship with the as-yet-unseen-in-the-film Pedrell, and father-and-daughter next have a balls-out *contretemps:* "It's true. Pedrell is my lover! We sleep together. And I'm proud of it!" Jacques understands everything there is to know about this infatuation which she's feeling for this older guy and, calming himself, he proceeds to set her straight about what he *thinks* she feels. ("You just love his car and his wallet!") Jacques simmers down, though, because in spite of what he's just said, he truly loves his daughter, and doesn't want her to hate him, so he now switches-over to a much-gentler tone: "You're my daughter. I love you. But you're still young, and I want to help you understand the things that you don't. Of course, I know you are in love. I can see it in your eyes. But your boyfriend—he's not in love. He's just using you for your youth. You know, I always thought that you would fall in love with someone your own age. So, please, come home, okay?" But Odette, as confrontational as is any other teen-age girl in the throes of her hormones, now ruins the nice mood which her dad's just tried to set: "I'm not coming home, dad. I'm tired of being your maid!" Jacques gets *all outbursty* again, and tells her he doesn't care about her philosophy, and he then ruins any goodwill which he's just engendered with the movie's audience, by slapping her face! ("I've been hearing this shit from you for twenty years, Odette! Now, knock it off, and come home with me, right now!") Instead, Odette just storms out of the bar, returning to the comforts which only her boyfriend can provide. (But what did Jacques expect? He never gave Odette enough love, and now she's trying to get it from another older man.)

Now, it's time to check back in with step-son Fernand: The boy is packing his suitcase and leaving for his new school (which is, of course, a reform school), and he tells Jacques that he's tired of all schools, and that he hates studying; so now Jacques has to set him straight about how nobody gets a fair shake in this life: "You think that what I'm doing—working construction—is glamorous? I have four people living in two tiny rooms. Just go to school for one more semester, and then I'll let you decide what you want to do, okay?" Fernand asks dad Jacques why it was okay for him to leave school at fourteen and, of course, Jacques tells him that it's because times were very hard when he was a kid, and that he had to take care of his own parents.

The next day, Odette meets Jacques at his construction site, and tells him that not only is she not coming home, but that she's actually going to marry Pedrell, although there *is* a bit of a rub: Pedrell is already married! (He's told Odette that he'll be divorcing 'his current wife' for her, but that hasn't happened, yet.) After making the veins in her dad's forehead fairly pop, she apologizes to him for her behavior, but it's too late. Jacques stalks off. And we know just where he's going!

Now, it's time for Jacques to pay a visit to Pedrell (Roger Treville) at Pedrell's ultra-swanky townhouse. Wearing overalls, and looking extra-stone-faced (even for Jean Gabin), Jacques definitely looks out of place in Pedrell's opulent *stabbin'-cabin,* and it's very reminiscent of how Gabin's working-class characters also felt out of place in 'ritzy' joints in other pictures, like 1931's *Gloria,* 1946's *Martin Roumagnac* and 1959's *Archimede, le clochard.* Since Pedrell is fabulously wealthy, and since Jacques can't compete with that, when Jacques arrives at Pedrell's apartment, he uses the only 'wealth' he has—*his 'Gabinian' intimidation factor*—first, telling the guy, who happens to be cowering in Jacques' presence, to turn off his loud record player, so that they can talk. (Pedrell, who was tipped off by Odette about Jacques' incipient arrival, has turned an opera record on at full-blast, hoping to drown-out the drubbing which he knows he's going to be taking from *his girly's angry pops.*) Pedrell looks down his nose at Jacques, telling him, *re:* the opera selection which he's just been playing, "I'm sorry I don't have any accordion records for you," and here, Pedrell is, of course, pejoratively referencing the accordion, because in France, the accordion is an instrument which is preferred (at least in 'the old days,' when this movie was made) by the working-class. "I didn't spend an hour on the train to get a music lesson," Jacques growls at the wimpy little freak, continuing, "You have no intention of marrying my Odette—you're just using her [for sex]. Well, you'd better be careful my friend, because she likes you. And she's a smart girl, so you can't buy her like you buy everything else." This is a great moment in the film, because it's confirming for us just how much Jacques really loves his daughter, *which is one helluva lot,* and so we can now *almost* forgive him for slapping her in that previous scene. (In fact, here's how much Jacques loves his daughter: He defends her, even when she spends most of her life acting mouthy to him!) Jacques next, and rather surprisingly, switches gears, *not* exactly becoming more kind and gentle, but bringing the volume down a bit: "You know, I'd rather you continue to be my daughter's occasional lover than her husband. Oh, and by the way, did you know she's already cheating on you?" (Of course, Jacques has just made this up, since he doesn't really want Pedrell near his daughter at all.)

When Jacques arrives home that night, Odette is freaked: "You went to see my boyfriend?" Humorously, Jacques tells her—and this is one of the all-time-great Jean Gabin Movie Lines—"If you ever bring home a child by that guy, I'm going to have it stuffed, and show it off to the public!" Louis is happy about the fact that his sister is with a rich guy, though, because, while the money which he's been able to pocket from winning small-ish bicycle races throughout France and Holland is nice, he realizes, also, that the money which the family would be near, if Odette were to marry Pedrell, would be even a thousand times better. Louis tells Jacques, "Dad, that Pedrell-guy is more loaded than you even think he is. If Odette marries him, we'll really be able to go places!" (Jacques, however, isn't all that convinced.)

Now, we're going to find out that Fernand has been missing from reform school for two solid days, and when we next see him, he's in a fancy café, sitting with a *hoity-toity* late-thirtyish-looking blonde woman named Josette (Dominique Page), a woman who, of late, has been paying for his meals and sleeping with him. (Fernand's become a glorified gigolo! [Nice job, if you can get it!]) When she discovers that he's only seventeen, though (because she truthfully believed him to be eighteen or nineteen), she very honorably calls the cops, and tells them to bring Fernand back to his dad; Josette's 'easy,' but she has a conscience (at least, after her 'little conscience' has been sated!), and feels post-coitally weirded-out by the fact that she's been getting her cookies off of a minor. "Don't hurt him," she pleads with the cops, as they drag Fernand home, and back to Jacques.

Concurrently, Jacques is back at the construction site and, as usual, he's bitching to Ernest: "I put Fernand in reform school for his own good, and he's had the nerve to escape!" Jacques doesn't know about the whole Josette situation yet, but at this moment, a police inspector (Pierre Vernier) arrives at the site and gives him the rundown: "Sir, we've just found your son—at a prostitute's apartment! [So: Fernand's not the whore! *Josette is!*] He beat up a cop, so the Judge has decided to keep him." Not-so-incredibly, Jacques (Jean Gabin, in all of his movies, is famously anti-authority, even in the cases when he's playing an authority figure!) now starts defending his son, telling the officer, "Hitting a cop is doing a service! I know my son: He gets into trouble, but I know he didn't hit the cop first. So you just get the hell out of my face now, okay?" Even though Jacques is mad at Fernand for being a bully, he is also, in this moment, more proud of him than he's ever been in his whole life, but that just makes sense: If you were a father, who would you rather have representing you out in the world—a fighter or a hairdresser?

The next morning, Jacques heads over to the Judge's chambers (*Le Juge* is played by Jacques Monod), and the scene plays out like any of those other great 'Jean Gabin Interrogation Scenes,' in which his characters are always setting the pace of their questioning, over the authority figures who are supposed to be in charge. He tells the Judge, "Look, I didn't come here to argue with you. I just came to get my kid out of your cell." The Judge says *no-can-do*—at least, not until Fernand's trial, which won't be for another week. So Jacques is forced to go home without his incarcerated sonny-boy, and that night, when we see him next, he's drinking in his favorite bar with an older lady-barfly, Madame Gildas (Gaby Basset, J.G.'s real-life first wife [circa 1925-1931]). Like most Jean Gabin characters, Jacques isn't one to easily divulge his feelings, but after a few drinks, he loosens up to her, and not just about

Fernand either, but also about everything else which has been bothering him lately: "I've got a son who might be locked up until he's twenty one. My daughter is with a rich guy, and she won't come home. All of my girlfriends always dump me. And now, my kids are dumping me because they're adults. Hell, I don't care if they're adults—they're still my kids!" This is a very moving speech about ageism, and what we today call 'empty-nest syndrome:' Accepting that his kids have grown up also means that Jacques is also going to have to accept the fact that he's getting older—and he just ain't ready for that, Jack.

The week passes quickly, and now it's time for Fernand's trial. (Jacques is there, and he's seated in the front row.) The Judge asks Jacques why he thinks his son, Fernand, escaped from reform school: "Why is your son 'bad?' Is there anything you ever did to him to make him that way?" Jacques keeps his cool though, when he delivers his reply: "I never hit him, if that's what you mean." While Fernand is the one who's having sentence passed on him, it looks to us like it's really Big Daddy Gabin who's on trial: *Rue des Prairies* is a film in which parents are getting called to task for having messed-up their kids psychologically, and Jacques definitely messed Fernand up, always treating him like a leper, just because Fernand wasn't his own, natural offspring. Looking guilty, Jacques tells the Judge that maybe the reason his kids are always in trouble, is because he "overprotected them too much," but it's really just the opposite: As we've been seeing throughout the picture, Jacques isn't at home all that much: When he was younger, he was away fighting in the War; right at this moment, he's in a bar; and when he *is* home, he's not what anybody would ever call the most supportive guy in the world. Granted, he's supportive of Louis, his first-born male ('his champion'), but he hardly puts in any time at all with Odette and Fernand.

Now, finally, it's time for Fernand to take the stand, himself. "Everyone thinks you're anti-social," the Judge tells Fernand directly, addressing the teen-ager, "but I think it's something else. Why did you leave the reform school?" Odette decides to intercede, and to answer on her brother's behalf, now telling the Judge, "We all leave home in our family, because our father will never forgive us for doing better than he has." (Ahhh! So, that's the problem the characters are having! Now it makes sense! Jacques is jealous of his kids, because they're good-looking, young, and successful. Even Fernand is 'successful,' from Jacques' point of view [he's a superstar, when it comes to grifting and bullying other kids], and all three of Jacques' kids seem to have an easier time of it than he had, when he grew up.)

Next, it's brother Louis' turn at the podium and, for the first time, we see that this 'good' son has a few unresolved issues of his own with his dad: "My sister is right about what she's just told you, Your Honor, and I know, because I started feeling weird about my dad when I started winning bicycle races: My father became jealous of me. My brother Fernand has run away from home a lot, over the years, because it's always been very hard for him, just like it's also always been hard for Odette and me to live with our father." The Judge, who is a sympathetic sort, is starting to figure it all out, and he now pronounces judgment: "Fernand doesn't need to be punished. Just redirected." Throughout the trial, Gabin's Jacques has just been sitting there, head down, trying to keep his cool, but looking like he's about to blow a

With Marie-Jose Nat and Roger Dumas.

gasket. He shoots angry glances at anybody in the courtroom who dares to make eye-contact with him, and the Judge whispers to his Baliff, *re:* Jacques, "It wouldn't surprise me if this guy insults our whole panel, when he leaves!"

Fernand, perhaps not unexpectedly (since we already saw him being friendly toward Jacques, when the two of them were on the paddle boats together), next says something nice about Jacques—something which Jacques never expected him to say—and Jacques looks genuinely touched by it: "Even though my dad and I have a lot of problems, if I had a choice, I would have chosen him to be my father anyway, over anybody else. Because even though he's not really nice or fun—he's really cool!" When Jacques hears this, he lights up just like the White House Christmas tree. Of course, Jean Gabin is cool! And now, he looks extra-proud, because his son has finally figured it out for himself.

At the end of the movie, Jacques walks away, not with his champion-son Louis, but with Fernand, the son for whom he has just gained newfound respect. Jacques asks Fernand what kind of job he thinks he'd like to get, and Fernand surprises him again, by telling him that he's decided that he'd rather go back to school! Jacques walks away, not downcast and alone as Jean Gabin does in so many other movies, but happily, and with his son in tow.

Rue des Prairies is another really great/criminally-unknown-in-the-U.S. Gabin comedy, which definitely leaves its viewers smiling, although the picture *does* forget to answer a couple of key questions which it has set up:

1.) Did Louis ever make it into the Tour de France? We know that he qualified for it, based upon his win at Bordeaux, but did he ever participate? There's no Tour de France sequence in this movie.

2.) Does Odette stay with Pedrell, or does he dump her (or she, him)? Maybe director Patelliere didn't feel the need to wrap-up every single plot point, and maybe that's a good thing: After all, the film is meant to be a funny-poignant slice-of-(real) life, and in real-life, most of our problems don't get resolved. (Life loves to leave us hanging…)

One thing which this superb film does do, though, is to introduce us to the fine young actors who play Gabin's young-adult children—Marie-Jose Nat ("Odette"), Roger Dumas ("Fernand"), and Claude Brasseur ("Louis"). In 1964, five years after playing Gabin's bicycle champ-son Louis, in *Rue des Prairies,* Claude will become known internationally, for playing the young male lead in New Wave director Jean-Luc Godard's 1964 classic, *Bande a part* (which happens to be Quentin Tarantino's favorite movie). In fact, at the time of this book's publication, Claude Brasseur, who is today in his seventies, remains a very popular movie star/box-office draw in France, and Claude's son, Alexandre Brasseur, the third generation of 'the acting Brasseurs,' is currently making his own mark on French cinema, as well.

Rue des Prairies is based upon a novel by the actor/author Rene Lefevre; Gabin already knew Lefevre personally, because before Lefevre was a novelist, he was a movie actor, and Gabin and Lefevre acted together twenty-four years earlier, in Jean Gremillon's Foreign Legion picture, *Gueule d'amour.*

What a Critic Said at the Time: "This is a Jean Gabin vehicle. In it, he gets a chance to play drunk, noble, and angry—his well-oiled gamut. He's always helped by his expert timing, sincerity, and pro aplomb. Director de La Patelliere has wisely let [the film] rest on Gabin, and [the picture] averts being sudsy, because of his knowing thesping." (*Variety*, 12-16-59 issue. Critic, "Mosk. [George Moskowitz.]" Reviewed in Paris.)

What Another Critic Said at the Time: "The acting is consistently good on all sides (was Mr. Gabin ever otherwise?), and Gabin gives poor, suffering *Stella Dallas* some portly competition." (New York *Times*, 12-24-60 issue. Critic: Howard Thompson.)

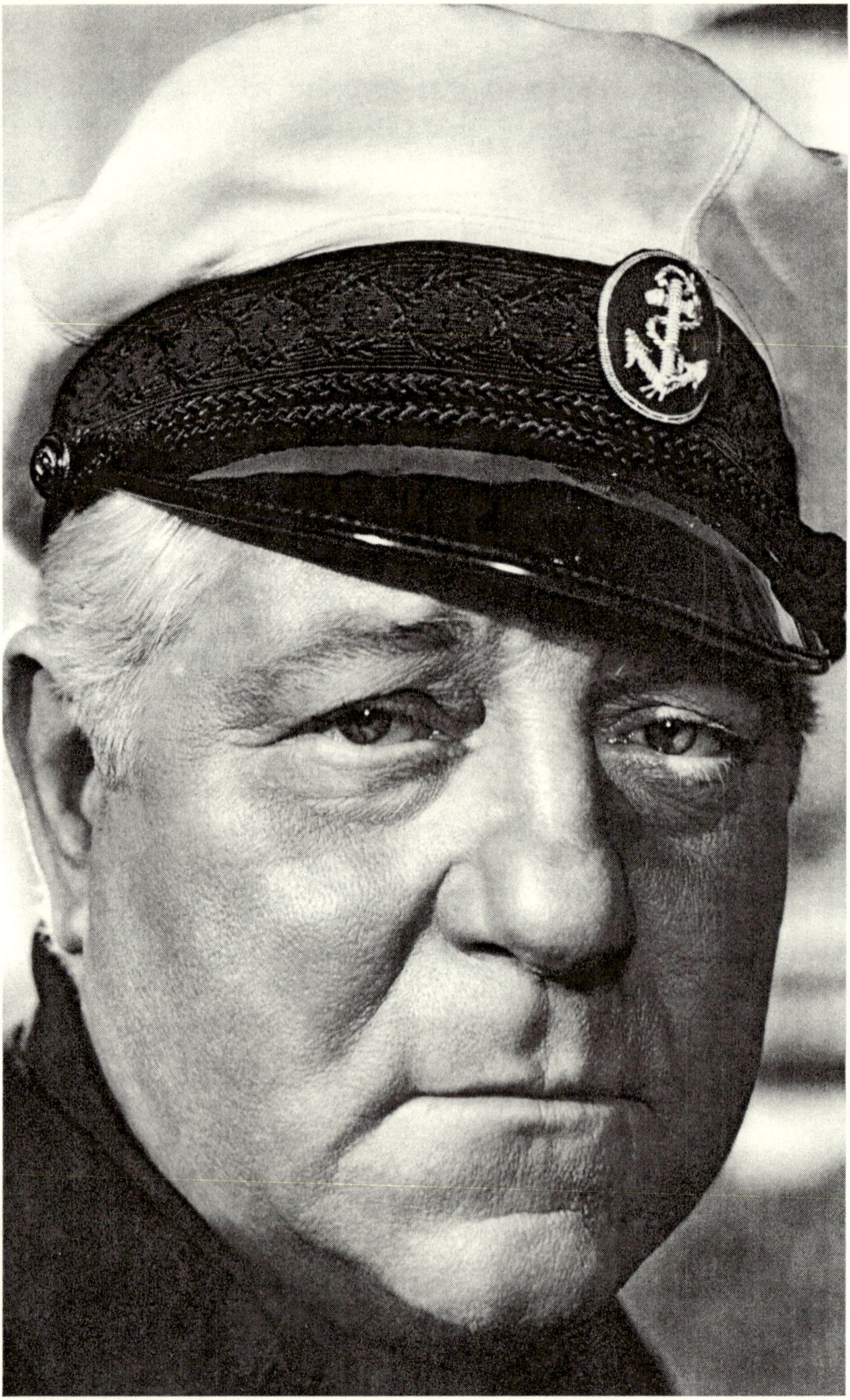

FILM 70

Le Baron de l'ecluse

France, 1960

(Literal English Translation, "BARON OF THE LOCKS") Directed by Jean Delannoy. Produced by Jean-Paul Guibert. Written by Michael Audiard and Jean Delannoy. Based Upon the Novel by Georges Simenon. Director of Photography (black and white), Louis Page. Music by Jean Prodromides. Editor, Henri Taverna. Production Designer, Rene Renoux. (GENRE: COMEDY) Running Time, 1 hour 32 minutes. Produced and Released in France by Cinetel/Filmsonor-SA/Intermondia Films, on April 13, 1960. Never Released Theatrically in the United States.

> "When you're young, girls like you 'just for you.' But as you get older, and the women get older, and they need to have a baby, they are really looking for a provider instead of a nice person. When I was younger, women liked me for my blue eyes. But then I got older, and I needed a car, and then a bigger car, and then a boat, to appeal to women."
> — *Jean Gabin, talking about 'what women really want,' in "Le Baron de l'ecluse"*

This joyous, life-affirming Gabin comedy, one of director Jean Delannoy's sweetest films since 1955's *Chiens perdus sans collier*, is a tribute to that special brand of people who live and love beyond their means, while all the time pretending to be somebody else—all hail the mighty con-artists! People love movies about con artists, these high-living low-lifes (or: those 'great impostors'), because all of us are starved for a bit of illusion in our humdrum lives. What's great about movie grifters is that, when a movie grifter's real life sucks, he or she just takes on the identity of someone whose life doesn't suck, and the 'free money' always follows…

Jean Gabin is Baron Jerome Napoleon Antoine (not his character's real name or title), who lives in the prestigious Normandy casino/beach town (pre-film festival) of Deauville, in northeastern France. The Baron dresses in the attire of a yachtsman, although he doesn't even have a yacht—well, not yet, anyway (read on!)—and he uses his charisma, and his 'honest-looking, Jean Gabinian mien' to con well-heeled folks, who should know better, out of their hard-earned bread. Whenever the Baron gets *un corniaud* ('a sucker') to give him money, he always uses it to place (mostly losing) casino bets, and even when he loses, which he does most of the time, the people he's grifted keep right on loving him, because he's so charming! When he's in grifter-mode, he even wears a monocle, *a la* Eric von Stroheim's Colonel von Rauffenstein in *La Grande illusion,* and whenever he passes French soldiers, who should know better, they always salute him.

On those rare occasions in which the Baron does deign to actually hold-down a real, salaried job, he works for the Deauville Airport as an amateur pilot and, as the film begins, he's flying an old, vacationing lady (Dominique Marcas)—an easy mark!—from Paris to Deauville, in a small prop plane. When he drops her off at her family's tony Deauville manse, the family members all look at him in awe, because he's so regal-looking. She wants to tip the Baron a few francs for flying her, but he cheerfully declines it: His whole 'bag,' as it were, involves taking big sums of cash from little people and, as he'll later admit in the picture, he can never be bothered with small amounts of cash, although (of course) he really needs any cash he can get. (Why else would he have this flying job?) "It's been my pleasure flying you," he tells the old lady, bowing to her courteously. "When you can't fly with your own wings, you have to fly with someone else's!" While the Baron is one of the most confident looking guys you'll ever see, he does look a bit worried that he's not going to be able to fly for much longer because, even though he feels healthy, he's getting older, and isn't sure that he'll continually be able to pass the rigorous annual medical exam which is required of all pilots. ("I'm the Methuselah of the skies," he brags to the old lady's family, very proudly.)

The Baron works alongside a lady con artist by the name of Perle, who's played by Micheline Presle (who played Hortense, the daughter of Michele Morgan's Josephine de Beauharnais, in *Napoleon*), and Gabin and Presle together recall, in a very favorable way, other great movie grifter-pairs: Redford and Newman, in *The Sting;* David Niven and Marlon Brando, in 1964's *Bedtime Story;* and even Annette Bening and John Cusack, in *The Grifters.* The Baron and Perle, as we're learning now, dated many years ago and remained friends, and *Le Baron d'ecluse* is just like lots of those other pictures which Jean Gabin would make in the '50s, '60s, and '70s, when he was a little bit older, and in which his characters would almost always remain friends with the women they had dated years before. Perle's still angry with the Baron though, because years ago, when she and the Baron were an item, he walked out on her. (Trying to spin his decades-earlier break-up with her in a positive light, the Baron, early in the picture, tells Perle that he knows he did the right thing by leaving her: "My walking out on you enabled you to meet that other man who ultimately became your husband." In fact, the guy whom Perle married after the Baron left her was a megamillionaire, who passed away shortly after she married him, and she went through the guy's money before the corpse was even cold, so that now, all the money she has in life, comes from running cons with the Baron.) While Perle and the Baron are only friends now, they both, clearly, still have the hots for each other, and flirt with each other whenever possible, although neither of the two actually ever 'does anything about it.'

When he's not flying people in and out of Deauville's airport, the Baron's always looking for a good mark, and today, he decides that he's going to try to sell an abandoned eighteen-foot fishing boat—one, by the way, which he doesn't even own—to a guy he sees lounging on the beach. The guy calls himself 'Prince Saddokan' (he's played by Jean Constantin), and he's one of those handsome 'dilettantes of indiscriminant national origin' which Western Europe is full of, and just like Gabin's character is a fake Baron—well, this guy, too, is a fake prince. ("See that sucker," the Baron tells Perle. "I'm going to sell him that boat!") Perle offers to help the Baron out, by seducing the guy, although the Baron pegs the guy immediately as being a total pushover, and so he tells her that, probably, she won't even have to bother.

The Baron is able to sell the vessel to Saddokan quite easily (for two million francs!), by telling Saddokan that it's twenty-five feet long instead of it's actual eighteen. The Baron and the rube *faux*-royal shake hands, and 'the grift-ee' tells the Baron that he'll meet him later that evening, with the cash.

The Baron's got a whole day ahead of him until he's going to be meeting-up with the guy again, and for right now, he's cash-poor, so to tide himself over, he borrows a few bucks from the Bartender (Bernard Musson) of the hotel in which he's staying, and of course, he's going to be using this money to play the ponies! "You know you have no chance of winning, Baron," the Bartender tells him, gleefully throwing money at him anyway, because the Baron is so cool and hard-to-resist. And right after he bestows the Baron with a big wad of 'play money,' the barkeep then gets second thoughts about what he's just done: "Hey, Baron, I'm sorry to bother you, sir, but—well, I just gave you that money and, *you know*, maybe I shouldn't have, because you really owe me—well, that is, you already owe the bar three hundred francs!" The Baron smiles, because for him, this problem is not insurmountable: He simply approaches an elderly couple whom he observes enjoying a late afternoon cocktail, creates a sob-story about how he's just lost his wallet, and the couple instantly hands him a stack of bills, which the Baron next brings over to the Bartender. (Now, at least, the Baron's bar tab has been settled!)

The Baron lives at the hotel permanently and, as he jauntily saunters out into the morning light, the hotel's Manager (Charles Lemontier) accosts him, and he does it very politely, because one never wants to offend a Baron! This guy is as nervous around the Baron, as the Bartender was: "Excuse me, Baron. I'm sorry to bother you, sir, but I'm just wondering if you'll be paying your hotel bill soon? You know, you owe us two thousand francs from this year, and another two thousand from last year, and while I don't really like to bother you with such trivia, sir—the hotel could really use it." The Baron is so 'Jean Gabin-Likeable,' that all of his creditors walk on eggshells around him, never getting mad at him, and never doubting for even a moment that he's a real Baron. (You've never seen such obsequious bowing and scraping in whole your life! It's great!) After the Baron leaves, telling this *Hotelier* that he'll soon (and of course, here, I'm referring to the non-existent 'royal soon') be paying the hotel all of the money which he owes, the *Hotelier* next brags to his underlings about how badly he feels over the fact that he's just had to ask the Baron for money: "I guess I really shouldn't ask him to pay. He's liable to get upset, and not come back to Deauville." Funnily, everybody is afraid of losing the Baron as a customer, even though the Baron has never actually paid for anything in his entire life!

Needless to say, it's not only the bar and the hotel, but also the hotel's casino which also keeps happily lending the Baron money to gamble with, even though he already owes them, too, and what he owes them is considerably more than what he owes the hotel—in fact, the Baron owes the casino three hundred thousand francs! Firmly ensconced at the casino's blackjack table, he starts playing and, within minutes, he has already won just enough to take his winnings back to the hotel, and he then pays the *Hotelier* the four thousand which he owes the hotel for his two past-due years of bed-and-board. Since the Baron's just pocketed sixteen grand at the craps table, he still has twelve thousand francs left for himself and, as he leaves the hotel with Perle, she asks him what he would have done if he had lost at blackjack. Without even batting an eye (and he's completely serious about this), he mutters, "I'd have just written them a bad check!"

Even though everybody thinks the Baron is confident and carefree, when he's by himself, we see, very bittersweetly, that this is very definitely not the case: Director Jean Delannoy gives us some tender close-ups of the Baron, who's alone in his hotel room (it's been a long time since those 1930s' movies which always showed Gabin brooding alone, in various dark rooms), and he looks afraid. (Of his mortality? Of wronging people? Probably, both. Featuring no dialogue whatsoever, this scene immediately shows us that the Baron feels guilty about his grifting; he has a conscience after all, and this one particular sequence has a lot to do with why we like Gabin's Baron-character so much: We understand, instinctively, how afraid he is, because—well… we're all afraid, too!)

After a little alone-time in his room, the Baron now enters the hotel restaurant, where he approaches a well-heeled looking family. The head of the clan is a businessman called Mr. Bonnetag (Emile Genevois), and the Baron greets him and his family very cheerfully: "Hello, folks! I won twelve-thousand francs today, and I'm inviting everyone at your table to have a drink on me." The Baron sits with the family and begins chowing-down with them at their invitation, and Bonnetag gets so immediately toasted, that he starts handing the Baron cash with which to pay the waiter—money which the Baron, instead, keeps shoveling into his own pocket! (Bonnetag doesn't even notice what the Baron is doing.) This 'diminished-capacity rich guy' is so impressed by the fact that he's associating with somebody whom he believes to be a Baron, that he also, very gleefully, allows the Baron to trip-the-light fantastic with his fetching wife, Gaby (Aimee Mortimer). The Baron seduces Madame Bonnetag with honeyed words, cooing to her that she's "The Princess of 1,001 Nights," and of course, she starts swooning right in his arms!

That night, the Baron plays high-stakes poker with the goofy 'Prince' Saddokan, the guy to whom he has sold 'his' boat, and the guy loses: So (get this!), now the guy is into the Baron for eleven million francs (two for the boat and an additional nine, which he lost in the card game)! The Prince tells the Baron that he lives, full-time, in Monte Carlo, and that, in order to retrieve the eleven million, the Baron's going to have to sail there in the boat which the Baron has just sold him. The Prince tells the Baron that, when he arrives in Monte Carlo, his

Breaking the bank.

(the Prince's) bank has been instructed to present him with a check for the eleven million. The Baron, like all Gabin characters, is an adventurer, and so, *of course*, he's eager to go. But Perle is less eager, making sure the Baron knows how nervous she always gets on water, but she reluctantly decides to go with him anyway, since she lives off of whatever money which they get, when they grift together. (Is this Prince going to be double-crossing the Baron? When the Baron arrives in Monte Carlo, will the money be there? We shall see…)

The Baron has hired a Skipper (Georges Lycan) to actually do the physical sailing for himself and for Perle; while the Baron can probably pilot the boat himself, he's trying to keep up appearances, and knows full well that it's a good idea to make it look like he's got 'people' doing all of the heavy-lifting for him. The next morning (it's now Monday), the boat is on the move and, after traveling for most of one day with the overly-demanding Baron and Perle, the Skipper quits! By his own admission, as he's now telling the Baron, he "hates working for fakes," and so he now leaves the two of them stranded out in what first appears to be the middle-of-nowhere; well, really, it's not the middle-of-nowhere: It's actually the Locks of Vernisy, outside of the small town of Chalon, in France's Champagne region (in the northeast of the country). High-maintenance Perle, who's used to being surrounded by fineries, detests being stuck on a boat, and she now starts freaking-out, telling the Baron that she'd rather travel on a fancy cruise ship, third-class, than to continue to be stuck with him out here, in the middle of nowhere. And to make them even testier than they already are, the Baron and Perle have forgotten to stock the boat with food, and she actually cries out: "If I don't get my paté, I'll die!" "If you're going to kill yourself over paté," he answers her, shaking his head, "you've got another thing coming!"

Even though they dress like nobility, the Baron and Perle are (at least, at the present moment) as penniless as John Steinbeck's sun-weathered Okies in *The Grapes of Wrath*; the Baron left the money, which he had recently won at the casino, back at the Deauville hotel, thinking that he wouldn't need it, because he'd soon be in the possession of a whole lot more. Anyway, at this point, they are very literally starving, and Perle tells the Baron that if they don't get some food, and soon, that she's going to have to sell her body! (Their bickering is very *proto-Sonny and Cher*.) "My dear," he responds, with the usual calm which Jean Gabin always exhibits (especially when all around him are in chaos), "you've never done anything differently. All that's left for you, are the sailors!"

Needing to come up with some food money, the Baron and Perle now try to find things on the boat which they can sell (not that there are any people around to sell anything to, because there aren't), and all they can muster up are some fancy cocktail dresses which belong to the boat's real owners, dresses which they've found hanging in a closet, but the Baron opines that they probably won't have any luck in selling them. "We can't sell anything to the people, here; they are poor, and would have no use for such fineries. It would be like trying to sell sweaters to sheep!"

Disembarking, against Perle's wishes (since she thinks that nature—a/k/a, 'the non-urban world'—is "dirty"), the two of them come across an apple orchard, and the Baron starts gallantly picking apples for her, and he even sings to her as he's picking them. Even though he's doing all of this for her, or mostly for her (because he's pretty hungry in his own right), she tells him that, in her considered opinion, apples aren't a meal, and she now asks him why they can't just find some locals whom they can con out of a little dinner money. The Baron tells her (we already know this, because he said it in an earlier sequence), "I never borrow small amounts. And never from little people." Even though the Baron looks hungry enough to eat shoelaces, as Laurel and Hardy once did in a hilarious 1940 comedy called *Saps at Sea*, he's still 'more proud than he is hungry,' and director Jean Delannoy now gives us a great shot: The two climb back onto the boat, and are now perched on the deck, staring into the quiet water, each one too physically *knackered* to offer-up any more frustrated verbiage. The Baron remains cheerful though, because in spite of their current setback, he knows, based upon his own past experiences, that life, after it brings bad times, almost always brings good times again: "A boat always goes up and down, just like life," he waxes pithily to his seasick-looking partner.

The Baron checks out some maps, and discovers, to his surprise, that he and Perle aren't too far from Chalon at all—in fact, they're only a couple of hours away. So he pilots the boat the rest of the way (and quite easily), by himself. Once he and Perle arrive in Chalon, and see a real city and actual people, they decide to split up, to see if each one, individually, can find a good mark who will give him (and her) some free money, or some food. So, Perle goes one way, and the Baron goes another.

After walking through Chalon for awhile, the Baron comes upon a street which has only two small, quaint eateries—La Café du Marine (it's the town's only bistro) and a pub called *L'Haricot vert de la chevre* (in English, it means, 'The Green Bean-of-the-Goat')! Needless to say, *La Café du Marine* sounds a bit more appetizing to the Baron's rarified tastes, and when the Baron enters the bistro, the first thing he sees, is a small group of local workingmen who are playing cards at a small table as they wolf down bread, cheese, and sausage. The Baron doesn't have any money to ante-up with though, so he tells them that he'd like to play against them, and not for cash, but for a bit of their food, and that if he loses, he'll be glad to subsidize their next course. The proprietress of the place is earthily-pretty Maria, played by Blanchette Brunoy, whose short haircut in this film gives her a more-than-passing resemblance to the American actress, Hope Lange. A kind and decent-looking person (we can see, just by looking at her face, that life has 'done her some dirt'), Maria is immediately impressed by the smooth, distinguished-looking Baron. Even though she's only-just meeting him, we can tell already, by the suspicious manner in which she's staring at him, that she's already figured out that he's not a real Baron, as he's claiming to be, but we can also tell, from the *hot glances* which she's sending him, that she also thinks he's a very *cool customer*. (He's Jean Gabin, so while his title might be 'fake,' his charisma is real.) He looks and *is* nice, and she can tell instantly that he's the kind of a guy who might lie to her, but would never hurt her.

While the Baron remains in the bistro, Perle, who of course walked-off in the opposite direction, has managed to find the town's only fancy restaurant! (Chicks not only have '*gaydar*,' but they also have '*fancy restaurant-dar*.') Although she's broke, she naturally orders the most expensive meal on the menu and, while she eats, she's, of course, busily scoping the joint out, trying to find a willing rube who'll pay for her meal, and of course, no sooner does she start looking, than one falls right into her line-of-sight: It's a real titled nobleman, the young and handsome Maurice Montbernon (Jean Desailly, who played Gabin's wimpy, child-man nemesis in 1957's *Maigret tend un piege*, and Gabin's wimpy child-man son, in 1958's *Les Grandes familles*), and she immediately heads over to his table with her plate, and asks to join him (and she looks to be older than him, by about twenty years—*but who doesn't dig MILFs?* [As Benny Hill famously once quipped on the subject of older ladies, "They don't yell, they don't swell, and they're grateful as hell!"]). Montbernon reveals to her that he's the son of the region's largest champagne-maker, and that his family's champagne happens to be the sole vintage which is served in this establishment. ("It is only available in this region," he brags, *re:* his family's sparkling beverage. "*We don't export.*") She now starts flattering Montbernon, telling him that she realizes the importance of champagne in all of our lives since, as she puts it, "Champagne is always served at big events, like funerals and weddings, and when you drink it, you're always in the company of great joy and great sadness." He asks her if she's come to Chalon alone, and she lies to him, telling him she's sailed here with her Uncle (!), whom she describes as being "an old aristocrat, who enjoys the water…" (!!)

Back at the bistro, the Baron is winning mightily for awhile ("I've been playing for twenty years, and *I've never lost my underwear*," he brags, goofily), and happily, he's snarfing-down the spoils of his victory—cheese, sausage, and bread. The Baron's a guy who knows (in fact, he's already said as much) that 'life is like a boat, [which is] sometimes up and sometimes down,' and just as we expected, his winning-streak doesn't last, and he loses the next five card games to the working guys. Thinking fast, he tells the other players that he's going to call up Prince Saddokan's bank in Monte Carlo, because they're holding some money for him, and that when he gets it, he'll hand over the money which he owes them. But the guys inform him that there might be a problem: Even though today is Monday, it also happens to be a holiday, and so all of the banks are closed; but these nice, card-playing guys very sweetly tell the Baron not to worry about what he owes them, because they can tell by his honest looks (!) that he's "good for the money." One really nice thing about this movie, is that none of the characters whom the Baron cons are stupid; all of them are portrayed by director Delannoy and screenwriter Michel Audiard as being smart people who are just inclined genetically, as we all are sometimes, to be fooled by Jean Gabin's intense charisma.

Back at that fancy restaurant on the other side of town, Perle is now entrancing Montbernon with a too-convincing sob-story about how she and her 'Uncle' were on their boat, when suddenly, the crew mutinied and stole their money, and that because of this, she and her Uncle will now never be able to reach their stated goal which is, she tells him, Monte Carlo. Montbernon, feeling sorry for her (and also because he's attracted to her), pays for her meal, just like she knew he would, and he tells her that if she'll still be in town the following day, he'd like very much to take her out, and maybe even to show her his wine cellar. (His invitation, as heartfelt as it is, is the 1960 equivalent of *'May I show you my etchings?'*) When Montbernon makes a pit-stop in the men's room, Perle very sweetly reaches for some of his leftover chicken, which she wraps up in napkins, and deposits into her handbag: Clearly, she means to bring it back to the boat, for the Baron to eat for dinner, but when the Waiter confronts her on the subject of her food-stealing (taking your left-overs 'to go' in a doggie-bag is *a big no-no* in food-worshipping France!), she tries to save face, by telling him that she's just taking the scraps for her dog. This scene humanizes Perle, just as that scene in the dark hotel room, in which we saw him brooding in silence, humanized the Baron: Before this moment, we thought that Perle was just a calculated shrew, but now, we really like her. Ultimately, according to the universe in which this film takes place, human nature is good—even, the human nature of con-artists.

Tuesday Morning: The Baron and Perle are back on the boat, and the Baron is definitely jealous that this young champagne-mogul is going to be calling on her today. When Montbernon arrives on board (he's even brought a few bottles of champagne with him, as 'a gift for Uncle'), the Baron welcomes him cheerfully, but he turns down the free bottles of bubbly, by lying modestly, and telling the guy that he never drinks in the afternoons. Montbernon tells the Baron that when Perle told him his [the Baron's] name, yesterday (the full-length version of the phony moniker—'Baron Jerome Napoleon Antoine'), he looked the Baron up in a *Who's Who* book and that, based upon his perusal of said book, he now believes that he and the Baron (and Perle!) might be distantly related. (Whoops! Guess the Gabin character borrowed his fake name from a real Baron—it's 'Identity Theft, 1960-Style.' [And if they're related—well, let's not even get into that whole issue!]) The Baron looks jealous when Perle heads off in Montbernon's car, to spend the day with him.

During their day-date, Montbernon sweetly asks Perle to marry him, and she tells him that it might not be such a great idea, since she's much older than he is. But when Perle returns back to the boat that night, the Baron is actually encouraging a wedded union between her and this young guy, because he (the Baron) knows that if she marries Montbernon, she'll be personally wealthy, and then, by extension, so will he! She gets offended, and lets the Baron know, in no uncertain terms, that she's not a whore: Perle deeply resents the idea that the Baron thinks she's the type of person who would marry for money, although, as we already know, she already did that, in the past. The Baron now sermonizes to her (and she already knows this, anyway [it's her *modus operandi!*]), about how it's always okay to marry for money, and to only pretend to be in love with one's rich spouse: "If truth were a prerequisite for marriage," the Baron waxes eloquently, "there wouldn't be too many people married!" And this is more true in Perle's case than we already know: Even before Perle married that rich guy—the one she talked about near the beginning of the movie (the guy whose money she went through like a sieve), she was married one time before, when she was nineteen, to a young army officer, a guy who wasn't exactly truthful with her, either: She didn't know, when she married 'Husband #1,' that he was gay.) The Baron next soliloquizes on The Eternal War Between the Sexes, reminding Perle that all male-female relationships are, in his opinion, based exclusively on money:

"When you're young, girls just like you for you. But as you get older, and the women get older, and they need to have a baby, they are really looking for a provider, instead of a nice person; when I was younger, women liked me for my blue eyes. But then I got older, and I needed a car, and then a bigger car, and then a boat, to appeal to women." The Baron says all of this with a smile though, and when he's saying it, he doesn't seem jaded or cynical—he's just telling the truth as he sees it, and he's also, without his even having to mention it directly, giving us his whole backstory pursuant to why he's needed to come up with a fake identity for himself. (As we say today, the Baron's a guy who's 'faking it, 'til he makes it.') And since he's never going to 'make it,' mostly because of his ever-increasing age, he's just going to keep right on faking it.

The Baron's taken some of the food which he won during the card games back to the boat (he brought some food back to the boat for her, just like she also brought some for him!), and when we next see him, he's cooking Perle some *cassoulle*, which is a French stew consisting of sausage, beans, and duck. (It's always been favored [even today] by French college students.)

The following evening (the Baron and Perle have decided to stay in friendly Chalon, and are sleeping on the boat), the Baron's back at the bistro, which is now closed for business, and Maria, the nice Hope Lange-looking proprietress, is telling him how much she would love to cook him dinner this evening—and hopefully, she'll cook him something which will be a bit more *chi-chi* than *cassoulle!* They genuinely like each other, and Maria is the only person in the movie for whom the Baron ever really lets down his guard, even though he still hasn't told her (and he probably won't) that he's not a real Baron. At first, he tells her that he can't dine with her, because he has to go back to his boat to make sure that his 'niece' is okay, but Maria breaks through his resistance in about three seconds: Even though it's unspoken in the movie, it's clear that the Baron, just like the characters whom Jean Gabin used to play back in the 1930s, doesn't want to open himself up too much to someone he really likes, because he's afraid of getting hurt, and he doesn't even have to say this, because it's *the baggage of the persona* which Jean Gabin carries with him, from film to film. He definitely wears his false 'Baron' identity like the impenetrable helmet of an astronaut, so that nobody can get through to him, and hurt him.

Dissolve to what probably must be a few hours later: Maria and the Baron are now dining alone in the bistro by candlelight, and she's telling him, as they munch-out on some *tres delicieux lapin* (rabbit), that she has a teen-aged son, who's away at boarding school in the Pyrenees. He tells her (he still has to lie a bit, because he's afraid that she won't like him if he doesn't spice-up his own life's story [even though she likes him, already]), that he spends his down-time attending both horse races and the *Grand Prix*. Since Maria is stuck in this small town, she thinks everything he's saying to her is exotic and romantic, and even though she's having fun with him, she's still grinning at him like she doesn't believe two-thirds of it—but she's swooning over him, anyway. He tells her that women used to compliment him on his blue eyes, but that now, as he's becoming older, his eyes have turned gray, and she replies that his eyes are beautiful, and also that, in her opinion, *they are still blue*. (The movie is full of genuinely heartwarming moments, of which this is only one.)

The next morning, the Baron finally makes it into a small local branch of Prince Saddokan's bank, and is able to retrieve a small percentage of the money which Saddokan owes him (so: the guy didn't try to double cross him, after all), and the first thing he does, is to go to Maria's bistro, where he pays off all of the guys to whom he lost at cards. While he's in the bank, the Baron even gives a few francs to the teller-lady's little boy, when he overhears the kid talking about the dream-kite that he wants to buy, but which his mom cannot afford.

The Baron tells Maria that, the first thing in the morning, he's going to be leaving Chalon for Monte Carlo—which, of course, is true. Maria tells the Baron she's unhappy that he's going to be leaving, because even though she knows he's full of shit (she doesn't say it out loud, but we know that she knows it, because she looks very wise), he still represents 'freedom' to her, and even more than that, he represents 'not being stuck in a small, rural town,' which is what she will always be; as she tells him, with zen-like acceptance, "I'm just a little person who owns a bistro. My lot in life isn't to travel, but only to stay right here." He tells her that she's brought him luck, and that leaving her is going to be the worst thing which he's ever had to do in his entire life and, at this point, he looks genuinely heartbroken, and even like he might start crying! As he walks out the door, he asks her when her birthday is, and tells her that, when he gets to the casinos in Monte Carlo, he'll place a bet on 'her birthday numbers,' and that when he wins big, he'll come back for her, and buy her "an apartment with a terrace." Maria's a realist, and knows he won't be doing anything of the kind, but she still really likes him anyway, and looks happy that he's just said this to her, even if it isn't true.

Perle does wind up with Montbernon though, and the Baron must now leave Chalon, on his own. In his old 1930s' movies, Jean Gabin always walked away alone, with a look of helpless frustration stretched across his face, but in this film, when he sails off alone, he's wearing a huge smile, and he's even singing just like he did when he was picking apples for Perle. So basically, this feel-good comedy is sending us away with a smile, and with a very sweet ending, to boot: The Baron is heading off to Monte Carlo, and Monte Carlo's a great town for a con man to wind up in anyway, because it's full of rich tourists whom, as we know, he'll definitely be able to bilk, quite easily. The Baron's brief acquaintance and flirtation with Maria, who was one of the few 'real' people he ever met in his life, has definitely replenished him, and we see that now, he's got lots of energy to dedicate to fun, new adventures in ripping people off—and being eminently loved for it!

Le Baron de l'ecluse is one of French cinema's all-time-great comedies-of-manners, because its theme is never out of date: It's a movie about how we all sometimes 'kiss up' to people who we think, because of their appearances) or because of their stations in life, whether those positions are real or only perceived), are better than us, whether they are, or not. There are definite parallels between Jean Delannoy's film, which was made in 1960, and our own, 21st- century culture of celebrity worship, a culture (to use the term in its loosest possible sense) in which even the smartest of us sometimes finds comfort and solace, living vicariously through the lives of all of the beautiful nobodies who the movie and music worlds are always pushing our noses into—people whose 'fancy' lives seem so much more special than our own. In an extremely underrated Woody Allen comedy which was made in 1992, *Shadows and Fog*, a magician-character, who is played by the great character actor and comedian, Kenneth Mars, explains this whole phenomenon very astutely, in the film's last spoken line of dialogue: "We need our illusions," he chimes. "We need them, like we need the air."

MGM released *Le Baron d'ecluse* in England, with English subtitles, as *Baron of the Locks*, but the picture was never released theatrically in the United States.

What a Critic Said at the Time: "Gabin is good. Story rests largely on Gabin's dexterity in playing a number of scenes calling for different moods." (*Variety*, 5-4-60 issue. Critic, "Mosk. [George Moskowitz.]" Reviewed in Paris.)

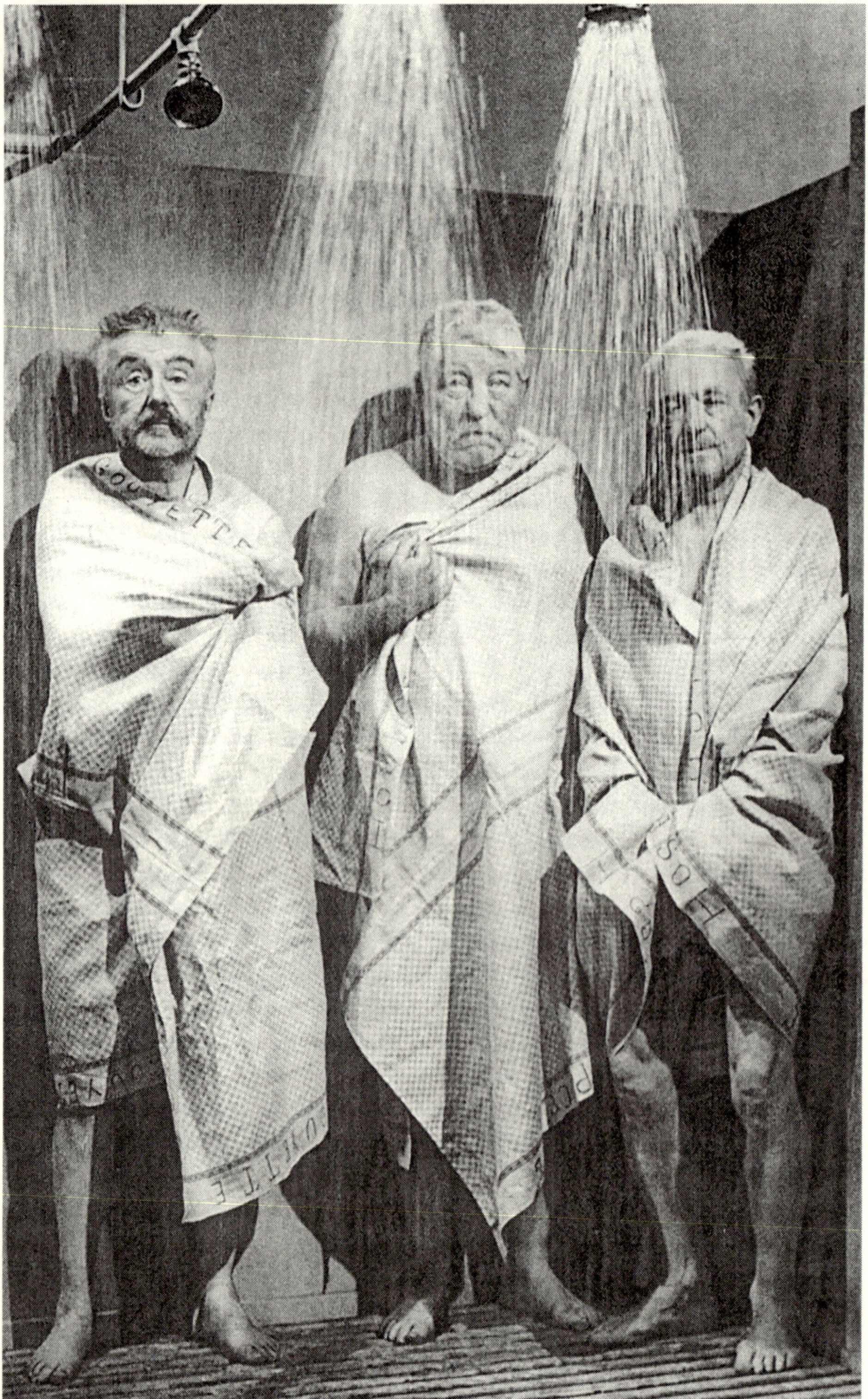

FILM 71

LES VIEUX DE LA VIEILLE

France/Italy, 1960

(Approximate English Translation, "THE OLD MEN OF THE OLD WOMEN") Directed by Gilles Grangier. Produced by Jacques Bar. Screenplay by Michel Audiard and Gilles Grangier. Based Upon the Novel by Rene Fallet. Director of Photography (black and white/scope), Louis Page. Editor, Paul Cayatte. Music by Paul Durand and Francis Lemarque. Production Designer, Robert Bouladoux. (GENRE: COMEDY) Running Time, 1 hour 30 minutes. A Production of Cinetel/Cite Films/Fides (France) and Silver Films/Terra Films/Titanus Film (Italy). Released in France on September 2, 1960, by Cinedis. Released in Great Britain with English Subtitles as "THE OLD GUARD," by Metro-Goldwyn-Mayer. Never Released Theatrically in the United States.

"I want to pinch your mustache! You're such a pig!"
— *Senior-citizen Gabin gets mad at one of his buddies, in "Les Vieux de la vieille"*

It's now 1960, and Jean Gabin will start the decade out, not with a movie, but with a record album: Walt Disney himself personally chose Jean Gabin to record the narration for the French-language record album tie-in with his internationally-popular Kirk Douglas-starring children's picture, *20,000 Leagues Under the Sea.*

Then, it was back to the movies, and this time, we've got another one of Gabin's wonderful comedies, a really first-rate picture which, just like the majority of Gabin's other great comedies, remains unknown in the United States.

Who doesn't love a good road-trip story in which people travel across huge geographical expanses, learning a little bit about the world, 'and themselves, in the bargain.' From Homer's *Odyssey* to Voltaire's *Candide* (and to Terry Southern and Mason Hoffenberg's free-wheeling satire of *Candide, Candy*); from Jack Kerouac's *On the Road* to Wim Wenders' astonishing road trip movies, *Kings of the Road* and *Paris, Texas,* the 'road-trip' story has always been one of (both) the literature and movie worlds' coolest, and most beloved genres.

Now: Imagine you've got a road-trip story in which the long-distance travelers are three curmudgeonly senior citizens? And what if the story was not just a comedy, but a really *hilarious* comedy, full to the brim with huge belly-laughs? Well, that's exactly what *Les Vieux de la vieille* is. It's directed by Gilles Grangier, from author Rene Fallet's very popular (in France) novel of the same name, and it teams Gabin up with two other great actors, Pierre Fresnay, with whom Gabin had not appeared since the two had played prisoners-of-war together twenty-one years earlier, in *La Grande illusion*, and Noel-Noel, another of France's best-loved movie stars. (In 2003, the world embraced a heartwarming French movie called *Les Choristes* [*The Chorus*], a film about a big-city teacher who instructs bad-apple boys in a rural reform school, on the art of singing, and *Les Choristes* is a remake of a 1949 film called *La Cage aux rossignols* [*Cage of the Nightingales*], in which Noel-Noel played the teacher.) Forget Larry, Moe, and Curly—*Les Vieux de la vieille* proves that the real Three Stooges are Jean Gabin, Pierre Fresnay, and Noel-Noel!

Welcome to the village of Tioune. (It's right, smack-dab, in the middle o' France.) This time out, Gabin is the semi-retired, working-class bicycle repairman, Jean-Marie Pejat, another one of those lovably-loudmouthed curmudgeons whom he always seemed to be playing in his 1950s, '60s, and '70s comedies, and when we first meet Jean-Marie, he is, of course, in the local bar, pontificating out loud to anybody who can hear him (just like Archimede) about all of the pretentiousness in the world which he just can't stand. Jean-Marie's gruff-but-amiable widower pal, Blaise Poulloissiere (Noel-Noel) shows up, and the two then sit around together, talking about *all the shit they hate,* as they anxiously await the arrival of their third curmudgeonly old pal, Baptiste Talon (Fresnay).

Patrons in the bar are bothered by noisy old codgers Jean-Marie and Blaise, both of whom are so deaf, they have no idea how loud they're talking. ("What's wrong with those two jerks," we'll hear more than one patron wondering.) Blaise doesn't take any *merde* off of anybody though, and he shakes his fist at the crowd: "My friend and I—we don't like it when strangers mess with us. It's not our fault that we're sixty-five!" (Gabin was only fifty-six when he made the movie, but he's a guy who always looked older than he was.) Of course, the other people in the bar aren't really strangers: Tioune's a small town, and everybody already knows these two 'curmudgeons-they-love-to-hate,' just as well as they know their own families. Blaise complains to Jean-Marie about how he hates the fact that, now that he's old, everybody treats him like a kid, and Jean-Marie hates that subject so much, that he changes it—"Back in 1912, we were quite a team together"—and here, he's referencing not only himself and Blaise, but also their third pal, Baptiste. Jean-Marie's never been married and he lives alone, usually sponging his meals off of Blaise's family since, very conveniently, Jean-Marie's house backs onto Blaise's house and farm.

It's not long before the mustachioed Baptiste (Fresnay) shows up and, within seconds, the three old friends are busily reminiscing about the glorious old days of World War I, which is (according to them, anyway) when they were all beloved. The perennially five-o'-clock-shadowed Baptiste tells his two friends that the railway retired him forcibly today, since he's just turned sixty-five, and that even though he saw it coming, he still can't believe it, nor can he accept it. ("After thirty-five years on the railroad, they've brought in educated kids from the Polytechnic school to replace me!") Gabin's Jean-Marie, always the level-headed (and sometimes, against his better judgment, even compassionate) one, tells his friend not to worry.

At this point, Blaise's eighteen-ish granddaughter Mariette (Yane Barry) enters the bar, and she's a girl who will soon be marrying her unnamed-in-the-film fiancé, who's played by the actor, Paul Bisciglia (in fact, at the time the movie was made, young actors Yane Barry and Paul Bisciglia were an item in real life, as well). Mariette's come to tell her Grandpa Blaise that it's time for him to come home, because dinner's almost on the table, but he tells her not to waste her breath, because he won't be coming, since his family always treats him like a little kid when he's around them, and he hates it. When Mariette leaves the bar, presumably to tell the family not to expect him, Blaise conspiratorially tells his pals that, in truth, he doesn't really care too much that people don't treat him with the same respect with which they used to treat him in his younger days: "Look, so what if people aren't so nice to me, anymore. Who cares? It's their fault—not mine." Jean-Marie, who's an expert at changing the subject, next starts in with a new topic: "Do you guys remember my friend Emile, the one who died last year? Well, get this: Right before Emile died, he told me there's an amazing old-age home in the south—in Gouyette [the real-life hometown of Rene Fallet, whose novel was the basis for this film]. Anyway, he told me that, not only does this 'home' serve excellent wine with every meal, but that they even have a giant swimming pool!" Blaise knows horsepucky when he gets a whiff, and he calls Jean-Marie on it, immediately: "Are you kidding me? There's no wine at an old age home. Anyway, you'd never catch me in one of those places. Old age homes are worse than prison—they're even worse than cemeteries!" Jean-Marie's mad that his friend has no faith in him: "You think I wouldn't investigate a place before I tell you about it? Well, *screw you guys!* Even if you aren't coming with me, I think I'll go, anyway!" The newly-arrived Baptiste, who's outwardly the most gruff of the three (Blaise and Jean-Marie occasionally exhibit a modicum of warmth, but Baptiste is 'all-grouch, all the time'), doesn't want to hear any more of Jean-Marie's rigamarole, either: "A home is for ninety-year-olds, not for strapping guys like us three—I mean, unless you're in some kind of a morbid hurry to die before your time. Are you?" Blaise seconds Bapiste's frosty sentiments: "I'm not going to any old age home, or anywhere at all with you guys. The only reason I'm here tonight at all, in fact, is because I just remembered that you [Jean-Marie] have owed me money for four years, and I've come to collect it." Now that he doesn't have a job anymore, Baptiste is calling-in all of his outstanding loans, but money's not the real reason he's come to visit his two friends: Just from looking at his face, we see that the real reason he's shown up, is because *he's the loneliest-old-man on earth*. Jean-Marie's reply, *re:* the whole money issue (which is calculated to disarm Baptiste, and he delivers this line with a giant, shit-eating grin) is, "I want to pinch your mustache. You're such a pig!" Then, Jean-Marie pours his buddies some more wine, and they all start updating each other on their lives, and laughing it up. The main thing that this scene is showing us is that, while these guys get on each others nerves a lot, they really, genuinely, love each other.

As I've already mentioned, Jean-Marie's home and garage, out of which he repairs people's bicycles, border Blaise's family's farm, which is now being run by Blaise's totally-dour fortyish son, Anselme (Andre Dalibert). Not only is Blaise mad at his always-defiant progeny for, in Blaise's opinion, not running the farm properly, but he's pissed-off at his son too, because Anselme rents out the family's prodigious lands, in between harvests, to a local soccer team, for its practices. Jean-Marie, because his property adjoins Blaise's, is just as much a prisoner of the constantly-noisy football mayhem as his friend is, and he tells Blaise, "You know, we've really got to try and get those football idiots off of your land!" Blaise hates that his grown son treats him like a child, just because of his old age: "I made the mistake of giving my son control of the farm, and now he doesn't want my advice on how to run it!" Jean-Marie tells Blaise that he should rebel against his son: "Look at me! I rebel all the time!" (We believe it, too. Gabin's been rebelling against authority, in his movies, for thirty years already, and he's going to continue doing it for sixteen more.)

In spite of the three guys' noise level, the bar's customers are happy because, two days from now (in fact, this coming Monday), Tioune is going to be celebrating its most-beloved holiday of all, *Snail Day*, which is exactly what it sounds like—a goofy rural holiday in honor of *les escargots!* (*Les Vieux de la vieille* is chock-full of great, slice-of-life local color, like this.) Blaise totally digs-on Snail Day, and he gloats that he's only missed five Snail Days in his entire life; and since Mariette has been unable to convince her Grandpa Blaise to come home for dinner, next up at bat is his son Anselme, who now barges into the bar, and demands that his dad come home: "Come on, Pop! Soup is on the table! *Now*, Dad!" Anselme's just as mean as Blaise said he was, and we're getting evidence of it right now because, directly after he commands his dad to come home for dinner, he lets-fly with a salvo of Evil Son Rhetoric: "If you weren't such an idiot, dad, I wouldn't have to be the leader of the family! Now get your ass home!" Blaise, who's scared to be alone with his family (it's no wonder!), invites his two friends to come home with him, no doubt to act as a protective barrier from his son's constant abuse, and Jean-Marie, who is a confirmed lifetime bachelor, accepts the offer without hesitation. But Baptiste (a guy so grumpy that he can't abide anybody outside of Jean and Blaise, and he can't really even abide them) does not.

Jean-Marie, the most good-natured of the three guys (he alternates his grumpiness with good, 'Archimede-like' cheerfulness), loves hanging around with Blaise's family ('the grass is always greener'), and can't see why Blaise is forever complaining about them: "They might get on your nerves," he tells Blaise sweetly, "but it's because they care. I'd take your whole set-up in a second." During dinner, Blaise asks Jean-Marie a question which he's probably never asked him before, even though the two have been best friends for a lifetime: "Hey, Jean-Marie: How come you never got married? I mean, you were always so nice to women, and women have always loved you." Jean-Marie's reply is as thoughtful as it is poignant: "First, I was too young. Then, I was too old..."

One subject at the dinner table, is Jean and Blaise's buddy Baptiste, who declined the dinner invitation: Blaise and his family, and Jean-Marie, now start gossiping about him, and it's turning out that not only did Baptiste just get fired, but also that, during the last few months, Baptiste's wife Adele has passed away, and rumor has it, that hot-tempered Baptiste may have pushed her into a river! Blaise regales his family and Jean-Marie with the gossip:

> BLAISE: She was by the river, I heard. Some say it was an accident. Others, that Baptiste pushed her. She cheated on him with a railway chief, you know...

The next day, the three oldies-but-not-moldies are together in Jean-Marie's garage-bicycle shop, and as they make pleasant conversation, soccer balls keep flying past their faces, from the direction of Blaise's field. Baptiste and Blaise think it's funny as hell to see balls continually 'almost-whacking' Jean-Marie's head over and over, but Jean-Marie doesn't think it's so funny: Now at the end of his tether, Jean-Marie catches one of the errant balls, dumps it into the well which he's got on his property, Gabin-Shrugs, and barks, "*C'est dommage*" ("Too bad") at the footballers.

The team's young Captain (Jean-Pierre Rambal) starts fighting with Jean-Marie, screaming, "I am the Captain of the team. You are not entitled to our ball!" Jean-Marie, not giving a shit (because what's the point of arguing with men with pasty legs who wear shorts and thigh-high white socks?) waves the young whippersnapper off: "What the hell do I care that you're the King of a Ball? I am not impressed!" The team-members, spurned-on by their Captain, start crawling over the fence onto Jean's property, to retrieve the ball themselves, but Jean-Marie's not worried about them: With a huge grin, he just aims his shotgun at them, and cries-out, mock-crazily, "Now, I'm going to kill you all like rabbits!" (And rabbits are exactly what these spindly little sports jerks scurry away like, too!)

If Blaise's only problem was that his family was loaning out his farmland for France's future World Cuppers, that would already be more than enough of a hassle for him to deal with, but Anselme has also enlisted Blaise and Jean-Marie, without asking their permission first, to turn the Poullosserie family fields into a temporary ballroom for the Snail Day extravaganza, a bifurcated-down-the-middle sunroom which, when it's finished, will be half-dining room and half-dance floor. Blaise tells his son that he refuses to lift a finger to help, and Jean-Marie's 'got his friend's back,' telling Ansleme, "I guess you want us to build it, because you can't do it yourself, and because you young people are lazy!" Blaise, feeling his oats, tells his son to "... watch your step. Or my two friends and I are leaving town, for good." Anselme just laughs, condescendingly, because he thinks his dad is bluffing.

Monday comes, and Blaise and Jean-Marie have, against their better judgment, constructed the little party pavilion which Anselme had demanded that they build; it's even got a bandshell, which has been strung with a goofy banner. ("It's party time, and the snails are dancing!") The fiesta seems to be progressing without a hitch, and the assembled guests (everybody in town) are really enjoying themselves, and that's when Jean-Marie himself shows up, and of course, he's three sheets (at least!) to the wind. Blaise and Baptiste are dining together in the eating area, and when Jean-Marie comes in to greet his two pals,

With Pierre Fresnay and Noel-Noel.

Blaise is already in the middle of bragging to Baptiste about how he once shot a bunch of raccoons which had made the mistake of trespassing on his property. (Blaise can't control his own son, but rodents *have* to listen to him! [Call him, 'the pie-eyed piper' of Tioune!]) Jean-Marie's entire role in life is, of course, to good-naturedly 'take the piss' out of every single, solitary syllable which comes out of his two friends' mouths. ("Did your raccoon talk before he died?! Heheheheh!") Blaise really wants to get mad at his pal, but he can't, because he's discovering, as we the audience are also discovering now (and for the first time) that Jean-Marie is so drunk, he's actually shown up at the shindig without putting on his pants, and best of all, he just doesn't care! "Give us three glasses of wine," Jean-Marie ('the original Captain Underpants') orders the open-mouthed waiter, who can't believe what he's seeing. When Jean starts feeling the breeze, and realizing for the first time that he's got a little 'wardrobe malfunction' going on, he plays it coolly, confidently shouting out as a brag, "I couldn't find my pants!"

    Jean-Marie next asks the other two guys if they'd like to join him in dancing with some women, but they think it might not be a capital idea for him to ask girls to dance, due to his lack of trousers. Baptiste thinks that he, himself, might ask somebody to dance, but Blaise reminds him, "Wait a minute. You're supposed to be mourning your wife! If Adele looks down from heaven and sees you, she'll think you're a bastard!" Baptiste answers that he's "finished with mourning," even though his wife died only several weeks ago, but he does admit that sometimes lately, he'll catch himself screaming-out during the night." With this one admission, we suddenly find ourselves genuinely liking, and feeling sorry for, crusty old Baptiste, for the very first time: Up until he said this, we just thought he was a right bastard—the only completely unsympathetic member of the Gabin/Fresnay/Noel-Noel triumvirate-of-terror, but as it turns out, he can actually be nice and human, when he wants to be. (Who knew?!) Jean-Marie, seeing an opportunity to take a dig at his newly-widowed pal, then offers up, "Well, of course you scream. Murderers scream!" Baptiste just shouts back at Jean-Marie, "How dare you! You told me you wouldn't say anything!" (Whoa! So: Baptiste really did kill his wife! [Or: At least, he wants his two friends to think he did, so they'll believe that he's still tough and cool!]) Loving every minute of Baptiste's humiliation, Jean-Marie chuckles, "Yeah, but swearing on the head of an assassin doesn't mean anything." Jean-Marie and Baptiste now start tearing each other new a-holes, and Blaise now shrugs, offering up a weak apology to the diners who look disturbed by Jean-Marie and Baptiste's fighting. The crowd starts yelling for the three old codgers to go home, and Jean-Marie tells his two pals, "Gee, if we knew how the young generation would be treating us, we would have lost the First World War. We won it for them—and all for nothing!" This is basically the same exact speech which Gabin made about 'the thankless younger generation,' in *Les Grandes familles*.

Jean-Marie, Baptiste, and Blaise agree to simmer down, and they now sit, listening quietly to the party's live jazz band, which they really seem to like. Jean-Marie nostalgically rhapsodizes, "Back in the day, we had real music. Now, it's just noise." A really wonderful moment, which we're now going to get in this scene, is that the always-angry Baptiste, even in spite of himself, looks genuinely happy to be with his two friends, even though they're always ribbing the shit out of him. Looking positively beatific, Baptiste smiles, "I think we're having fun, anyway!" (It's a very sweet moment.)

Fortunately for the other guests, old age is now dictating that these three are going to have to be leaving the party early. Jean-Marie, still without pants, heads over to the wall-mounted coat rack to retrieve his jacket (he brought a jacket, but forgot his pants!), and when he reaches for it, the whole temporary wall which he and Blaise constructed together comes crashing down—and right on top of his head! Jean-Marie, wanting to show the crowd that he's 'still got it,' tries to lift the whole thing up by himself (as Gabin's Jean Valjean-character did with the heavy horse-cart, in *Les Miserables*), but then—KLUNK—he's now completely buried under it! The partiers freak: "He's dead! Call a Doctor!" But nobody needs to worry because right then, Jean-Marie pops up from beneath the collapsed wall, like a cartoon character. He's a bit dizzy and worse-for-the-wear, but otherwise okay, and he looks embarrassed—not because he got hurt, but because he's no longer strong enough to lift up a temporary cork wall, and because everybody at the party has just witnessed his lack of strength. The party guests start making fun of Jean-Marie and Blaise for not even knowing how to erect a wall correctly, and Baptiste, who's now feeling a bit humiliated himself, suddenly changes his original negative view about Jean-Marie's old age home-plan: Suddenly, compared to the embarrassment which they're being forced to endure at the present moment, it no longer sounds like such a terrible idea: "You know, Jean-Marie, maybe I will go to that old age home with you, after all. We'll have a lot of fun there!" Blaise and Baptiste, who are tired of being treated like crap by The New Generation, are now both deciding to take Jean-Marie up on his plan; even if there's no 'free wine' and 'giant pool,' the old age home has simply got to be better than the massive disrespect-a-thon which is sometimes referred to as, 'The Golden Years.'

The next morning, Blaise and his son Anselme are inspecting their pigs, and Anselme is bitching his dad out for one thing or another, and Blaise is calling him a "dictator." Meanwhile, Anselme's daughter Mariette is getting fitted for her wedding dress, and Blaise tells her (and he does it gently, because he really loves his granddaughter) that he won't be able to attend her nuptials, because he's "running away from home." Anselme just laughs at him and, of course: This is the last straw.

Early the following day, without telling anybody, Jean-Marie, Baptiste, and Blaise sneak off, on what will be their Wizard of Oz-like odyssey/trek to the old age home in Gouyette, and it's now dawn as our Three French Stooges start their hilarious perambulation across the countryside, taking only one important piece of luggage with them—a basketful of wine! They're all happy to have made this somewhat startling decision to run away from home, and all three look revivified from the morning air: "Isn't life beautiful?" Jean-Marie smiles, breathing in deeply. "We're just like kings!" (These three kings now look as contented as George and Lenny looked at the beginning of Steinbeck's Of Mice and Men—that is, before Lenny 'squeezed the nice lady's neck too hard.') Since the three haven't started insulting each other yet this morning, and because they're getting a little bored with *not* insulting each other, Blaise gets the ball rolling, by calling Baptiste an assassin. Baptiste looks to Jean-Marie for support, but Jean-Marie just starts laughing and dancing around and backing Blaise up, and he, too, starts calling Baptiste a murderer. But the flow of harsh invective stops suddenly, when the three guys arrive at a country cemetery, and Jean-Marie reaches the grave of a woman, Marie, whom he had once dated when he was a young bachelor, and so he leaves his friends for a moment, to go and talk to her: It's a very poignant moment, as 'J-M' sits down at her grave-site, Gabin-Shrugs, and apologizes to her for not bringing her flowers: "Sorry, dearest! I didn't have time to go shopping. I couldn't even bring you a cabbage." When he gets back to his friends, they ask him what he was talking to 'Marie' about, and he gives them a quick summary: "I just told Marie that we're going to Gouyette."

As long as they're at the cemetery, the three guys now decide that they should find where Emile, the guy who told Jean-Marie about the old-age home, is buried, and Jean-Marie tells his friends, kind-of-cryptically, that Emile was quite the ladies' man in his day, a guy who was always getting into one kind of trouble or another: "Emile had an escapade with a 'fun girl,'" Jean-Marie tells his two pals, "and he got into a weird situation." (*'Weird Situation*' = 1960 Movie Code, no doubt, for 'unplanned, out-of-wedlock baby.') When the three guys reach Emile's grave, Jean-Marie pops a bottle of wine out of the guys' basket, telling his pals that he knows Emile would love it, if they were to drink a toast in his honor.

Meanwhile, back in Tioune, the citizenry is awakening this morning, to the news that everybody's three favorite curmudgeons have run away, and it causes an instant shit-storm: Even though everybody in town gives Jean-Marie, Baptiste, and Blaise non-stop guff, the three are completely beloved in their town, and the townspeople, who are now beginning to congregate in the middle of the town square, start talking about how they "just won't know what to do" without their three favorite old codgers around. The Mayor (Paul Mercey) tells the gathering crowd not to worry, because he's going to put search parties out on all of the roads which lead out of town.

Back at the cemetery, Blaise is now sitting on top of his own dead wife's headstone. (She's buried there, too.) At that point, a pissed-off Gravedigger (Robert Dalban, who's now appearing in his seventh Gabin picture) pops out from a freshly-dug plot, and starts shaking a fist at the three of them: "Hey, you clowns! What the hell do delinquents think you think you're doing?! It's not nice to sit on the dead and make noise! This is a cemetery. You have to be quiet!" (It's funny that he calls the three old guys 'delinquents,' just like they're teen-aged upstarts.) Blaise, Baptiste, and Jean-Marie start kicking dirt on the guy's head and laughing, and the guy then starts chasing them around the cemetery with a shovel, screaming, "You're next in my holes! I'll catch you *and* your bottles!" Our three pals bolt out of the cemetery, laughing hysterically (even sour old Baptiste!), but Jean-Marie has to go back: He's accidentally left one of his bottles of wine on Marie's headstone, and when he gets there, he finds that he's too late to retrieve it: The Gravedigger is already guzzling this suddenly-discovered Manna from Heaven, and when Jean-Marie sees him—well, is he ever pissed-off!

As Our Three Friends head out of the cemetery, three little boys walk by in the opposite direction, and they are little clones of Jean Gabin, Pierre Fresnay, and Noel-Noel, and this is a great sight gag. Right after this, a young newly-married couple pulls up in a car, and the husband asks Blaise for directions to a castle which is mentioned in his travel brochure; mischievously, however, instead of giving the couple directions, he instead offers them some homespun wisdom—wisdom which is filtered, of course, through his continuing anger at the French railway system. ("When the railroad used to be good, you didn't have to worry about getting lost!") He then continues, "I don't know about any castle. But would you like to see the crime scene where our friend Baptiste pushed his wife into the river? This is Baptiste, over here. Say hello to him! Sometimes he kills girls, and sometimes he drugs them, and other times—he even rapes them!" Baptiste's mouth drops, just like Spanky McFarland in a Little Rascals short, and he now starts threatening Blaise colorfully—"I'm going to render you into paté!" The three are so busy sniping at each other, that they've accidentally left their basketful of wine on the car's grill, and the couple drives away—but they're so nice that they drive back, and return the vino to our three heroes.

The three are now beginning to get on each other's nerves, and so much so, that they now finally decide it would be better if they were just to go their own, separate ways. A bus pulls up, and the driver chummily asks Jean, "Hey! Grandpa! You need a lift?" Jean-Marie climbs aboard, without even bothering to look back at his pals, and Blaise flags down an army transport truck, but Baptiste, who's mega ticked-off at his two pals, just decides to 'walk it.'

Soon tired of walking, Baptiste flags down a bus, and gets driven to the small nearby town of Trezelles. Meanwhile, a carful of nuns, which has been sent from the old-age home, is coming to look for them, because Anselme tipped them off: He knows that's where his dad, and his dad's pals, are headed, because he's heard Baptiste threatening to go there, on more than one occasion. But Baptiste doesn't want to be found, so he hides in a ditch. Eventually though, he becomes more thirsty than he is angry, so he heads into a local bar, just in time to see Jean-Marie, who's also wound up in Trezelles (since it's the only nearby berg which happens to have a pub), getting tossed-out on his ass for public drunkenness! Baptiste bypasses Jean-Marie, who's actually laying on the bar's front steps dead-drunk, and walks in, but nobody will serve him because he's too scary-looking, so he goes off on a giant tirade: "I just walked for hundreds of miles (!), and it's put me into a very weakened state, and if you don't give me a drink, I will complain to the Red Cross!" At that very moment, the military transport truck which has been carrying Blaise drops him off in front of the same bar: Lady Fate has now thrown the three bellicose buddies together again, which is very funny: They just can't escape from each other, no matter how hard they try.

After Blaise and Baptiste reunite, they pick their inert pal up off of the ground, and carry him through the countryside for hours, as day turns into night, and as some evocatively Arabic-sounding 'Ali Baba movie' music begins wafting gingerly over the soundtrack.

The three arrive at a farm, and just as Jean-Marie's starting to sober-up, he's suddenly attacked by vicious dogs! But he doesn't let the canine invasion of his ass stop him from his mission, which consists of finding himself and his friends a place to crash for the night, and suddenly, he even seems excited: "I've been to this farm before. They know me here! They'll be happy to see me!" Blaise and Baptiste don't believe that Jean-Marie really knows the owners, but when Jean-Marie greets the old Farmer (Alexandre Rignault), the guy greets Jean-Marie with a smile of recognition. Jean-Marie indicates his two pals, and whispers conspiratorially to the Farmer: "Hey, listen, friend: I was going to the old-age home… until these two bandits kidnapped me!" The Farmer takes Jean-Marie into his house, and gives him a bed for the night, but insists that the two 'bandits' (!) who came with him must sleep outside in the barn. Jean-Marie laughs and thumbs his nose at his incredulous pals, as he heads into the safety and warmth of the cozy house.

Baptiste and Blaise look uncomfortable out in the barn, and Baptiste tells Blaise that he wishes those dogs that hadn't just attacked Jean-Marie, but that they'd also *eaten* him! Blaise tells Baptiste that he just wants a *café-au-lait,* and that maybe they can find a bistro where some is served. The next morning, Jean-Marie enters the barn, completely refreshed from his comfortable night of restorative sleep. The other two guys slept very comfortably too, in the hay, but of course they want to make Jean-Marie feel badly about his having left them outside, so they pretend they couldn't sleep at all.

As *The Unholy Three* continue their walk, they soon come across a Cop (Jacques Marin)

Three French Stooges.

with a broken bicycle, and Good Samaritan-Jean-Marie fixes it for him *gratis,* feeling sorry for the bike, but not for its rider: "I don't like policeman very much. But whether you're a cop or not, you're still on a bicycle, so I'm duty-bound to help you." Jean-Marie fixes the bike, and then offers his official diagnosis about what was wrong with it: "Your bike is rotten! It must have been assembled by the Polish! Italians make better bicycles." Baptiste now whispers conspiratorially to the cop, "If my friends aren't respecting you, you can kill them like rabbits, if you feel like it. I won't try and stop you!" The whole 'Gabin-as-Bicycle-Repairman-bit' is no doubt director Grangier's winking reference to the one other movie which Jean Gabin and Pierre Fresnay made together twenty-two years earlier, Renoir's *La Grande illusion:* In *Illusion,* just like in *Les Vieux,* Gabin's character Lieutenant Marechal mentions to Fresnay's Captain de Boeldieu that, before the war, he was a bicycle repairman.

The three next begin marching military-style, just to kill time and to have fun, until they come to a second farm, where they crawl under a fence. Suddenly, they come face-to-face with a family of ducks—thousands of black and white ones! (It's the film's most beautiful image.) They all start whistling, *a la* Opie and Andy at the beginning of "The Andy Griffith Show," as they cross the fields, and very humorously, a sign now alerts them that it is 'Forbidden to Fish Here'—but ironically, there's no water, anywhere. (The guys are standing by a river which probably dried up twenty years ago.) Blaise guesses that they're lost, and Jean-Marie can't believe their collective misfortune: "I left my family to follow you idiots?" Baptiste, though, is resigned to whatever may happen to them, and he now exclaims, "Since there's nothing left to do, but to sleep and wait for death—I'll sleep." He then lays down in broad daylight, under the scorching sun, and tries to get a little shut-eye, but Blaise just insults him. ("You little jerk!") Baptiste's witty comeback: "Well, I might be a jerk, but in the War, I was a high-ranking jerk!" Each time one guy insults another, in this movie, all the other two can answer in self-defense, is something along the lines of, "Well, forty years ago, during the War, I was somebody!"

Sense and sensibility finally reign though, and the guys keep walking: They're lost, but they soon hear a train, and eventually, they come to a town which Blaise recognizes immediately: "Hey, Jean-Marie, we were here in 1920, remember? Do you remember the girls, and those great parties with all of that dancing?" Blaise then sees a familiar-looking milkmaid, Catherine (Mona Goya), whom they all know as 'Katie,' and all three of the guys start bragging to each other about how each one was the one who slept with her forty years ago. "I laid her in 1921," Blaise shouts, with delight. Then, to Catherine: "Don't you recognize me, Katie? It's me—but my mustache was smaller then!" Of course, she has no recollection of him, so Baptiste tries out his own luck, and she doesn't remember him, either. *Of course,* the only one of the three who she can remember clearly, is Gabin's Jean-Marie.

Katie prepares dinner for the three guys, and she gives Jean a pocket watch. As usual, Blaise and Baptiste have been made to sleep outside in the barn (again!), while Jean gets to go and sleep in the lady's quarters. (Yeah! Even as an older guy—Jean Gabin's still got it!)

Finally, our three heroes arrive in Gouyette, and at the infamous old-age home. Turns out, the place is no Paradise, as Emile had painted it to be in the embellished stories which he told to Jean-Marie: The ancient residents, who are languishing outside of the place on benches, all look like, if they have to stay at this place for one more second, they're going to start taking hostages—that is, if any of them can stand up.

The Mother Superior (Helen Dieudonne) sees the three 'newbies' loitering around aimlessly outside of the home's front gate, and leads them inside, informing them, "We've had a report from Tioune that there are three lost men who are trying to find us; you've been expected. Right this way, gentlemen." The 'Penguin' (*per* Dan Aykroyd, in *The Blues Brothers*) now takes Jean's wine bottle away, and he gives it up without a fight.

Even though the place looks a tad grotty, Jean-Marie decides to ask for some of that special treatment which Emile gushed to him about: "We're personal friends of Emile Gaspar," he winks at the Nun. "He recommended this place to us." She tells him he can talk to her more, after he and his two friends are freshly-showered, and next, we get a comical 'group shower scene,' reminiscent of how Moe, Larry, and Curly always used to shower together in Three Stooges shorts, and we get to see Jean Gabin, Pierre Fresnay, and Noel-Noel—three paunchy, former matinee idols—all standing under the shower together grimacing, as if they've never been under a nozzle before. (This priceless image, to this day, still 'sells' as a photo-poster in France.)

After the shower, it's chow-time, and the three are disgusted by the horrible cuisine: Baptiste yells out, "This soup is water! We still have teeth—where's our solid food?! And I thought you had wine! This is trust abuse!"

Back in Tioune, the Mayor's had some good news: "Guess what. I just got word from that old age home—the boys are there!" And when we cut back to what we would today call the Gouyette 'senior center,' Baptiste, Blaise, and Jean-Marie are all sleeping in the same bed, also *a la* the Three Stooges, pushing and shoving each other to get some room, and if this were a Stooges short, at this point, Moe would be tapping Curly on the forehead and nonsensically commanding him to, "Wake up and go to sleep!"

A bit later, the three pals try to sneak out of the home in the middle of the night, just like how they used to sneak out of P.O.W. camps in the old days, during the War, but they know they've got to be careful, since Nunzilla is patrolling the hallway. While they're trying to escape, and while some sinister, "Toccata and Fugue in D Minor"-sounding music is playing on the soundtrack, another resident, a seemingly ninetysomething senility-case who clearly has no idea where he is, is wandering around the kitchen, having no idea how he got there.

And just as our Three French Stooges are about to escape through the kitchen's back door, they take a pregnant pause, because suddenly, they've discovered that the kitchen houses an enormous wine cellar. (So: Emile was telling the truth… kind of!) In his effort to try and pinch some of the wine, Baptiste accidentally trips the 'center's' fire alarm, and the ensuing excitement doesn't scare our three heroes, but instead gets them joyously-amped, because it reminds them, favorably, of air-raid sirens. "It's been fifty years since we went on a secret mission," Blaise smiles, referencing their ancient wartime heroics (if, in fact, these heroics ever really happened)!

The next morning, after they've managed to sneak out successfully, Blaise and Baptiste are angrier-than-ever at Jean-Marie, and Blaise tells Jean-Marie that his stupid idea about escaping from Tioune has turned them all into migrants. Baptiste and Blaise blame Jean-Marie, squarely, for the fact that they're wandering again, even though all of them have escaped from the home, of their own free will and accord.

As the three wander the desolate roads of the small town, a bus pulls up before them, and the Driver asks them if they happen to be the three guys who got thrown out of the old age home, and he lets them know that he's been sent by their families to pick them up and take them back home to Tioune. Jean-Marie agrees reticently, and tells the driver, "Okay, we'll go back to Tioune with you, but only because we've been requested back." The three scramble to be first on the bus, and they then fight like spoiled little kindergarteners, all the way home.

Of course, they've returned home to Tioune just in time for Blaise's granddaughter Mariette's wedding, and *gendarmes* escort them into the service, otherwise—who knows? They may have become otherwise distracted, and not have shown up, at all. The Mayor is happy to see them, and so is Blaise's family, and even nasty Anselme looks happy and relieved, when he sees his father. And just as Jean-Marie, Blaise, and Baptiste are entering the proceedings, the Mayor addresses them: "You three have gone over the edge. From what I've heard, you've spent the last several days trespassing and drinking. Well, now you're going to stay here, with your families, all right? And just promise me that you won't act like kids anymore." Jean calmly tells his pals not to get angry: "Just let everybody say whatever they want about us. Let's be nice."

After the wedding, Mariette and her new husband kick out the first ball at the soccer game, which of course is taking place on the Poulloisserie family farmland that backs onto Jean-Marie's bicycle-repair garage. Anselme tells the three guys to be nice to the soccer players, and just as the three friends are now making this promise, we see them all lined up together, peeking over the fence at the game, and grinning cherubically—and hilariously, all three of them have animated halos superimposed over their heads.

Jean-Marie, Baptiste, and Blaise watch the soccer teams play, and we're starting to guess that their recent travels may have mellowed them: "Youth is nice," Blaise tells his pals, "It's the future of our country!" But when he's saying it, he looks really sarcastic, like he doesn't believe any of the treacly sentiments which are now issuing forth from his own maw. Now, once again (and as it's happened many times before), the ball sails over the fence into Jean-Marie's yard, and the Captain of the soccer team peeks over the fence which divides the two properties, to look for it: "Hey, our ball is at your place, again!" Jean-Marie tells the kid, cheerfully, that he and his two pals will find it for him, and Jean-Marie really *does* find the ball, but instead of returning it to the Captain's open arms, he just tosses it into his well, and the last shot of the film finds the lonely little soccer ball, bouncing up and down in Jean-Marie's well.

Like *La Traversee de Paris* and *Archimede, le clochard* before it, *Les Vieux de la vieille* is a great Gabin comedy, in which cinema's greatest silent stone-face is continuously loquacious and boisterous—and (decidedly) not quiet! At the time of this book's printing, the film is still not available in America, *which sucks,* because it's a brilliant picture and, truth be told, there are definitely two people who were (maybe) inspired by it: In 2006, the playwright Tom Stoppard won the Olivier Comedy Award, for his 'new' play "Heroes," an adaptation of Gerald Sibleyras's French 'original,' "Le Vent de Peupliers." Set in 1959, which is the year when *Les Vieux de la vieille* was in production, Stoppard's play concerns the misadventures of a trio of crusty, aging French World War I veterans who are planning to escape from their military hospital, so that they can be free.

What a Critic Said at the Time: "The three top French film character actors have a romp [and] raise some laughs under [director Gilles] Grangier's easy, sympathetic direction." (*Variety*, 9-28-60 issue. Critic: "Mosk. [George Moskowitz.]" Reviewed in Paris.)

FILM 72

LE PRESIDENT

France/Italy/Spain, 1961

Director Henri Verneuil. Produced by Jacques Bar. Screenplay by Michel Audiard and Henri Verneuil. Based Upon the Novel by Georges Simenon. Produced by Jacques Bar. Director of Photography (scope), Louis Page. Editor, Jacques Desagnaeaux. Music by Maurice Jarre. Production Designer, Jacques Colombier. (GENRE: DRAMA) A Production of Cite Films (France)/Terra Films (Italy)/S.I. Cinematografica (Spain). Running Time, 1 hour 50 minutes. Released in France on March 1, 1961, by Fides. Never Released Theatrically in the United States.

"You say you are a good Catholic—and yet you work with Israeli banks!"
—*A tinge of anti-Semitism rears its ugly head, in "Le President"*

In the chapter in which I discussed Jean Delannoy's comedy *Le Baron de l'ecluse*, I talked about the parallels between that film, which was made in 1960, and today's omnipresent culture of celebrity worship. Well, we've got more in store, ladies and gents, because director Henri Verneuil's 1961 Gabin effort, *Le President,* opens with a slew of near-psychotic journalists and paparazzi, who are stalking the home of France's retired ex-prime-minister, Emile Beaufort (Jean Gabin, replete with the hugest white mustache you've ever seen). An important British dignitary, who's identified in the film as being 'Sir Meryl' (Charles Cullum) is visiting him, and the media surrounds the place like vultures, with everybody trying to attain a snap—or, in the case of writers, a *snippet*—of this very important meeting. ('Sir Meryl' is probably the standing British Prime-Minister, although I'm just guessing this, because the film won't confirm it.) When Beaufort and Sir Meryl are together, Beaufort addresses his British contemporary in English, and Gabin's English-language delivery is really funny, because it's almost as if he had forgotten all of the English which he had learned for *Moontide,* eighteen years earlier. (He's reading it straight off of cue-cards: "Hello—my—friend—how—are—you?")

After Sir Meryl and all of the *photogs* and *journos* make themselves scarce, PM Beaufort grimaces through the vitamin shot which he's receiving at the hands of his Doctor, who's played by Robert Vattier. While Gabin was fifty-seven when he appeared in this film, his

Prime-Minister.

character is supposed to be seventy-three, and the 'good doctor' advises him that he should be taking it easy. ("You're not young anymore," *etc.*) Beaufort next retreats into his study where lately, he's been dictating his memoirs to his dutiful secretary, Miss Milleran (Renee Faure), most of which concern his tumultuous term-of-office, post-World War II. In the extended flashback which comprises ninety-five percent of the rest of the picture, Verneuil, who also directed 1956's *trucker-iffic* Gabin epic, *Des gens sans importance,* takes us back to post-WWII France (1946), and shows us, not *all* of Beaufort's career as Prime-Minister, but just the part in which Beaufort's in the chambers of the National Assembly (France's Parliament), fighting with the skeevy Assembly member, Chalamont. Chalamont is Beaufort's biggest *bete noir* in the Assembly, and you can't get a much better villain, in Gabin pictures, than chrome-domed Bernard Blier (Javert from *Les Miserables,* and the young-girl-loving nebbish in *Crime et chatiment*). The War has left France in ruins, physically and economically, and Prime Minister Beaufort's revolutionary plan, is to rebuild war-torn France, as well as all of war-torn Europe for that matter, by creating a 'One-Europe Economy.' (The idea that Prime Minister Beaufort suggests in this film actually pre-dates the implementation of the Euro, by almost forty years.) Chalamont is very adamantly against the concept of Europe's having only one kind of currency for the entire continent, and he tells Beaufort that, in his opinion, it is in France's best interest to remain economically-distinct from the other countries on the continent; as Chalamont reminds his fellow Assembly members, "France didn't lose 1.5 million people in World War II to lose our nationality, did we?" Beaufort tells the Assembly members that anybody in the room who opposes him, opposes freedom. (Sounds like something that a recent U.S. president may have said!)

More than 90 of this film's 110 minutes are given-over to the Gabin character's 1946 speeches to the Assembly, and Gabin's performance is electrifying. He talks and talks (and talks) for almost the entire film (there's no 'silent Gabin' on view, here), and he's utterly captivating, but the subject matter which he's lecturing about (it's all dry economic stuff) isn't too captivating. (It's so dry, in fact, that unless you have a Ph.D in pre-1950s' French Economic Theory, this film is going to lose you, and fast!) Apparently, Prime-Minister Beaufort's constituents—the 'regular people' whom we see in a number of crowd shots—*totally dig him,* but we can't figure out why (unless they just like him, because he's *super loud*)!

Another problem with *Le President* is that, besides being too leisurely-paced, it also earns a few demerits for its occasional outbursts of very plain-spoken anti-Semitism: In one scene, Prime-Minister Beaufort addresses the National Assembly, haranguing one member, thusly: "You say you are a good Catholic… and yet you work for *Israeli* banks? That is not possible, my friend!" (Whoops!)

I have to be careful in saying that I think *Le President* is slow (and ponderous, and talky), and saying, in short, that I don't believe it to be a good film, because lots of people think it is: It has remained a beloved film in France, where today, it's often transmitted over the television waves, and where it is also available as a popular DVD; indeed, there are a lot of good things in *Le President* (principally, Gabin's shimmering performance, as well as the great technical credits, which are as top notch in this picture as they are also, in almost every other Gabin picture). So, I'll just say this: As an American who's not conversant in a lot of the subject matter which the characters are talking about, I was hopelessly confused by the film, but if you're French, I guess—*c'est pour vous, mon ami!* (It's for you, my friend!) MGM released the film in Great Britain, but it never attained any kind of a theatrical release in the United States.

What a Critic Said at the Time: "Stolid and talky. Gabin's solid thesping, and the crusty, crotchety, sincere quality of the character weld well in this sketchy pic. Film is overlong and verbose, but director Henri Verneuil has subordinated all to Gabin's powerful presence. Interesting look at pre-War French politics." (*Variety*, 3-15-61 issue. Critic: "Mosk. [George Moskowitz.]" Reviewed in Paris.)

BONUS CHAPTER
(A live television play, starring Jean Gabin)

L'Homme qui ralait toujours

Synopsis of ("The Man Who Always Complained") an original, five minute television production written especially for Jean Gabin by Michel Audiard, and directed by Frederic Rossif. Broadcast over ORTF Television, France, on December 24, 1960.

A FIVE MINUTE AND FOURTEEN SECOND T.V. PLAY, BROADCAST LIVE, WHICH ALSO FUNCTIONS AS JEAN GABIN'S CHRISTMAS MESSAGE TO HIS FRENCH FANS.

On December 24, 1959, in connection with the release of *Le President*, Jean Gabin made an ultra-rare foray into television (and live television, to boot), appearing on France's national television network, ORTF, in a very amusing five minute and fourteen second, three-camera mini-play called *"L'Homme qui ralait toujours"* ("The Man Who Always Complained"). The title of this comedy, is a play on the fact that Gabin was notorious, in real life, for complaining a lot, whenever it would come time for him to do anything that he didn't really want to do. (Hence, of course, Gabin's extremely short film career in North America.)

As the presentation begins, the prominent French film director, Turkish born Frederic Rossif, with whom Gabin would never work outside of this one, short t.v. presentation (and who is 'playing himself'), is sitting around a meeting-table on a television set-stage, with a television producer. (Rossif famously portrayed Orson Welles for a French television documentary in 1968, while Welles was in France, directing his film of Isak Dinesen's *The Immortal Story*, starring Jeanne Moreau.) Gabin's frequent co-star and real-life buddy Bernard Blier enters, and the three men start discussing the possibility of getting the giant box-office kingpin Gabin to appear in his first television play. Rossif shrugs, "Oh… I don't think Gabin would do it. He's always complaining that he's tired. (Remember: At this point, Gabin was acting in three, four, and sometimes even five films per year.) Anyway, it's going to be hard for us to get *God* to do anything he doesn't want to do!"

Too terrified to approach Gabin with the idea himself, Rossif and his producer 'pass the buck' to Blier, asking him to do it, knowing that Gabin and Blier are real-life friends.

Hilariously, a look of terror crosses Blier's face: He runs off-camera in panic (in fact, he does everything except 'cross himself,' as in a *Dracula* movie), and we'll never see him again, in this piece.

The camera pans over to another part of the sound-stage, and we see Gabin, who's sitting on a throne adorned in jacket and ascot, looking super-surly and unapproachable, and definitely playing on his image of the cinema's ultimate, consummate 'quiet tough guy.' The remainder of the piece will consist solely of a medium close-up of Gabin in conversation with an unseen Michel Audiard, the legendary French screenwriter who had already either written, or co-written, thirteen movies (including *Le President*) for Gabin, and who would eventually, over the next several years, write several more.

Gabin immediately starts complaining to Audiard, in his most stentorian tones: "So! You want me to appear in a television play for Christmas? I can't believe it! My life has always been easy—well, that is, except for whenever the tax man comes around. But now, you're *really* asking too much of me, Audiard. I mean, first you asked me to star in one movie that you wrote, and then ten movies—and now, t.v.?! Don't you know that [after having already made 30 movies] I'm tired? And the worst thing, is that I didn't even hear about this play from you guys. I read about it a few days ago, in the press!"

Audiard is ready to raise the white flag of surrender: "Okay, Jean, okay. I'll go and tell Rossif that you're not interested. I'm sorry to have bothered you." But Gabin isn't done *chewing the scenarist out:* "You, Audiard: You write your little screenplay dialogue on the page. But who's the one that's always having to interpret your words? Me—a guy who suffers eight hours per day on movie sets. *Me: The Old Man*—I'm the one who has to suffer. Also, I can't believe that you've chosen Christmas Eve to propose this idea to me. Do you think I'm going to be improvising at my age? If you want, I *will* appear on television, and I might even write a poem and recite it, and I'll call the poem, "The Unfortunate People!" Anyway, just tell your friend Rossif that I forfeit!" ("*Je forfeit,*" he exclaims, and the word is exactly the same in French, as it is in English.)

Audiard tells Gabin that he's sorry to have bothered him, but Gabin's still got a whole lot of ranting, left to go: "Look: I'm a hundred miles from home [Normandy]. My Christmas tree is up. The logs are in the chimney. And I promised my three kids—Florence, Valerie, and Mathias—that daddy would be home on Christmas Eve."

Audiard now takes a 'kindler, gentler' approach, asking Gabin about what the actor bought his kids for Christmas. Gabin tells Audiard that his daughter Valerie asked for a race horse (and not a toy, wooden race horse either, but actually, a real live one!), and that his other daughter, Florence, asked him for a toy kitchenette. Gabin also mentions that, ever since his small son Mathias saw him playing a trucker in *Gas-Oil*, that the boy has been obsessed with *gas station pump jockeys,* and so, as a special surprise, Gabin has bought Mathias his very own filling-station uniform. Gabin adds, "The uniform of a gas station attendant is better than that of a soldier—and I was a soldier, so I know what I'm talking about. I can't believe those parents who buy their children war toys: Guns aren't for adults, so how on earth could

272 | THE FILMS CYCLE FIVE

they ever be for children? For me, you know, it's Christmas time, and you can't celebrate peace with a machine gun stuck in your chimney!" Gabin next turns the tables on Audiard, asking Audiard what the writer bought his own children for Christmas, and Audiard tells Gabin that he bought his own son a racing bike and a chemistry set. Gabin opines, "Great! Be careful of those chemistry sets. Your kid is liable to blow up your house!"

Gabin wraps the presentation up, by addressing not Audiard, but "us," the t.v. viewers, as the camera zooms-in for a close-up on his famous face: "For me, Christmas is like celebrating kids' birthdays. The best gift you can have at Christmas time, is when your children are around you. I don't think I'm too interested in doing a t.v. show for Christmas [of course, Gabin is being ironic here, because that's actually what this piece has been!], but if I did, I guess I would just want to wish everybody out there a nice Christmas. That's something I *can* do! After all—what have I got to lose?"

Gabin smiles, his famous surliness suddenly melting away, as our scene fades to black.

With Bernard Blier, Antoine Balpetre, and Franck Villard in "Le Cave se rebiffe" (Film 73, right).

FILM 73

LE CAVE SE REBIFFE

France, 1961

(Literal English Translation: "THE SUCKER REBELS") Directed by Gilles Grangier. Produced by Jacques Bar. Screenplay by Michel Audiard. Based Upon the Novel by Albert Simonin. Director of Photography (black and white, scope), Louis Page. Music by Michel Legrand and Francis Lemarques. Editor, Jacqueline Thiebot. Production Designer, Jacques Colombier. (GENRES: DRAMA/CRIME THRILLER) A Production of C.C.M./Cite Films. Running Time, 1 hour 38 minutes. Released in France, on August 26, 1961, by UFA-Comacio Films. Released in the United States (New York City) with English Subtitles, as "MONEY, MONEY, MONEY" by the Times Film Company on July 17, 1962, and in Los Angeles, as "THE COUNTERFEITERS OF PARIS" by MGM, on May 1, 1964.

"I like music… but not monkey music!"
— *Gabin tells us what he thinks, about this newfangled 'rock-and-roll fad,'*
in "Le Cave se rebiffe"

You know how they say that 'inside every Frenchman, there's an American waiting to get out?' Well, Gilles Grangier's smooth-as-silk Cinemascope crimeflick, *Le Cave se rebiffe* is the film that proves it, *especially* when you see the opening credit sequence, in which two small French hands are busily fashioning counterfeit currency plates in the amount of $100 (U.S.). Next, director Gilles Grangier cuts to a Paris car lot—it's called the 'Paradise of the Good Deal'—which is stocked, bumper-to-bumper, with huge American sedans. Eric (Franck Villard), a big, greasy, mustachioed-lug (he'll later be referred to in the film, by Jean Gabin's character, as 'goofy') is there buying a car, and he's trying a few out, happier than a pig in slop. When he finds the one, *per* Goldilocks, which is 'just right,' he pulls away without paying, after explaining to the aged car dealer that he just needs it for a few hours; obviously, the dealer knows Eric, because he lets him drive away, and doesn't even raise a fuss.

The first thing a man does when he gets a shiny new car, even if it's not really his own, is to find a *shiny babe* to take for a ride and, to that end, he speeds through Paris and picks up his main-squeeze, Solange, who's played by the short-cropped and mega-cute Martine Carol (whom Americans might know from her starring role in Max Ophuls' 1955 film, *Lola*

Montes.) Solange instantly proves the adage that, to most women, nice big cars are really nothing more than *nice, fulsome erections,* and when she sees the car for the first time, she actually looks like she's going to orgasm, right there one the spot: "Oooh, Ehhhhric, it's such a niiiiiice car! Ten cylinders? All automatic? Kiss me!" (Yup, she, really, said, "kiss me!" In the world of *Le Cave se rebiffe,* not just American cars, but 'America' itself, has intrinsic aphrodisiac-value!) Eric even offers Solange an American cigarette (a Kool!) to smoke in the American car, and this is (almost) more than she can handle.

Solange is having an affair with Eric, even though she's married to another man, Robert (Maurice Biraud), an up-and-coming, twentysomething counterfeiter, who's presented, in the film, as being very smart, even though he suspects that his wife is running around on him (although he doesn't know that Eric is the guy who's 'contaminating' her), and he won't do anything about it until very late in the film. (I guess it makes sense, because if you had a hot piece of ass like that, you'd let a few things slip by, too.) Eric, who's not that much more honest than Robert, is using today's 'alone-time' with Solange to make her an offer which she probably *can* refuse: "I'm offering you a better life than you have with your husband. I mean, he's nothing but an out-of-work forger." Eric's a small-time criminal, too, so Robert's not offering her that much better of a deal than the one which she's already got.

Next, Grangier shows us the opulent mansion which belongs to bald-pated Charles Lepicard (Bernard Blier, again), and we're not talking just your average mansion, either: Charles and his shrewish wife (every movie, no matter what country it's made in, has to have one of those!) Lea (Ginette Leclerc) live in a high-end whorehouse, a lusty fuckhouse for the very rich, which is replete with bizarre theme-rooms—rooms which are strangely reminiscent of San Luis Obispo, California's famously-kitschy Madonna Inn Hotel, which opened in 1958, three years before this film was made. (One of the filmmakers must have been acquainted with the place.) While the brothel is no longer operational, the house contains a 'jungle room,' an 'Oriental room,' and even a boudoir which has the requisite, heart-shaped bed.

Charles and Lea next start talking about Eric, who's been a longtime associate of theirs, in some of their other *not-very-legal* adventures. (As we'll soon be finding out, the Lepicards dabble in other crimes, besides just pandering.) As they discuss not-too-swift Eric's various merits and drawbacks, Grangier now cuts back to Eric and Solange, who continue motoring through Paris in Eric's borrowed American sedan, and while we're seeing them, we're also hearing, in voice-over narration which continues the dialogue from the previous sequence, Charles' voice, as he continues listing Eric's shortcomings: "Eric sure is 'half-a-guy.' He thinks he's a king, but he's all-show!" Lea replies, "Well, at least Kings arrive on time, and Eric is late." (The filmmakers sure are spending a lot of time making sure we know that this Eric guy is the most perfectly dumb cluck God ever made, and just from the sheer amount of time they're spending in talking about him, we can figure out already that, at the end of the film, whatever crime the film will be concerning itself with, won't be turning out as the criminals—who, as we already know, will include Charles and Eric—will intend it to, and that Eric will probably be the one who screws it all up for everybody. [*Maybe...*])

Next, the bearded and professorial-looking Lucas (Antoine Balpetre), a crooked attorney who also happens to be the third part of the Charles/Eric/Lucas crime triumvirate, arrives at Charles and Lea's *manse,* and he, too, is waiting for Eric to show up: Eric has borrowed huge sums of money from both Charles and Lucas in the past, and he owes a lot to both of them. Basically, Eric's been told to show up at Charles' place under the guise that Charles and Lucas are going to be telling him about a new criminal venture in which the three of them can be involved together—but instead, when he gets there, Charles and Lucas call Eric on the fact that he's in *bukku* arrears to them.

Charles reminds Eric that, over a year ago, he and Lucas lent him five hundred-thousand francs to open a General Motors plant in France (*told ya* that those Frenchies love American cars!), but that the enterprise never took off, and that Eric never paid the other two guys back, for the loan. Eric, showing a little backbone (he's not exclusively stupid, otherwise Charles and Lucas, who are pretty smart guys, would never keep bringing him into all of their schemes), tells Charles that he shouldn't talk, because they knew that 'the whole GM-thing' was risky, from the moment they went into it: The three guys opened the plant, intentionally, as a front for one of their counterfeiting operations, and that the fact that the cops shut it down (which they did, immediately) was, as Eric is now reminding the other two, just an occupational hazard, something which they all knew, even before they even opened the place, could be a possibility. Eric, further, explains to Charles and Lucas, that he didn't think anything would go wrong with that operation, because he hired France's most famous forger, Miguel de Monteresse, to head up the actual, physical money-making operation for them, and that Monteresse had always had a reputation for being the most careful guy around.

Eric knows that Charles and Lucas, even though they both look about as far away from being tough guys as you can possibly get, will probably *tear him a new a-hole,* if he doesn't remunerate them, and pronto (Eric's tall, but he doesn't look strong, physically); in fact, Eric knew already what the other two guys wanted to see him for today, even before he got there, so he's come to Charles' house to assuage them, by telling them that there's a new caper upon which they can work, together: "You guys want your money back, right? Okay, well, instead of my giving you guys back the measly five hundred-thousand francs I owe you, how would you like to make ten times that? Each! How about I let you guys in on a good counterfeiting opportunity that can't fail!" Ahh! So this is why Charles and Lucas keep letting 'dumb Eric' in on businesses with him, even when he keeps losing them their shirts: *They're dumber than he is,* and they believe everything he tells them! So, even though Charles and Lucas went into this encounter with their defenses up, ready to give Eric hell, this new idea of Eric's, in which they'll be making ten times five hundred thousand francs, sounds pretty great to them.

Charles' whorehouse-mansion is positively dripping with the requisite tacky paintings which the *nouveau riche* love to scoop up at those shitty sidewalk art galleries—the silliest of which, propped up in the house's entryway, is one in which a snarky-looking devil is holding a woman aloft, and instead of being a great and powerfully-moving demon, like the one in the famous Goya painting *Saturn Eats His Son*, to which it is intentionally similar, it looks like one of those cheesy black-velvet paintings which you can buy in Vegas. Charles doesn't know that his painting is kitschy, and he next starts pontificating emptily, about 'the nature of art,' even though nobody in the room is actually listening to him: "Isn't it wonderful? It's so naughty! Artists love to paint like this! Well, with artists, you know—*it's that way*." After a few moments, Charles and Lucas have very clearly decided to forget about the outstanding debts which Eric owes to them, and to start working with him on this great new counterfeiting plan of his.

It's now a few days later, and Charles, Eric, and Lucas meet again at Charles' place, and this time, Eric has brought Solange along with him. Charles takes Solange up into one of his fancy theme-bedrooms (one, in fact, which happens to feature a massive round bed), in which he grotesquely hits on her, with not only Eric, but also with Charles' own wife, Lea, downstairs, right below them. Lea knows that her hubby's probably putting the moves on Solange, but she doesn't get too rattled: No doubt, she's used to her husband's philandering (they run a whorehouse, for the love of mike!), and besides, in France, as we already know, a man is contractually-obligated to keep mistresses, as part of the marriage. (Yeah! Go, France!)

Later that day, Solange returns home to the dumpy apartment which she shares with Robert, her young engraver husband, and this is the first time we're seeing him in-person. Solange chastises Robert for never being able to get anything going on his own, telling him, "You had one chance to work under [the legendary counterfeiter] Monteresse years ago, but you never got your act together!"

Back at Charles' house, meanwhile, Charles, Eric, and Lucas are continuing to discuss their new counterfeiting venture, which is so secretive, that they're going to try and keep the exact nature of their operation from their women, although the women will be figuring it out soon enough, however, because their men have all counterfeited before in the past, and also because in this movie, the women are much smarter than the men. Charles and Lucas are excited about the new venture which Eric has brought to their attention, as it is going to be the first caper in which they'll be their own bosses, and in which they'll get to keep all of the profits for themselves, instead of having to share them with a 'big boss' (which is what they've always had to do, in all of their previous ventures). Charles tells Eric and Lucas that he knows a fourth guy who should 'come in' with them, and not as a boss, but just as a very knowledgeable consultant (someone to whom they'll pay only a flat fee, for his expertise)—a legendary, and now retired, super-counterfeiter who's been plying his trade for thirty years: Of course, Charles is referring to the greatest counterfeiter of all time, Ferdinand Marechal, only, nobody ever calls this mysterious figure 'Marechal,' or even 'Ferdinand:' If you're ever lucky enough to meet Marechal in your lifetime (and don't worry, you won't be), you have to call him by his nickname, *Le Dabe* (The Dude)! And who's the only actor on earth qualified to play a character called 'The Dude?' (I mean, other than Jeff Bridges in *The Big Lebowski!*) Why, of course, It's 'the star of our show,' Jean Gabin! Gabin's character, in this picture, is (sur)named 'Marechal,' in tribute, no doubt, to the 'Lieutenant Marechal' character whom he had played in one of his most famous movies, *La Grande illusion*.

Caracas, Venezuela: We're now at Le Dabe's very own ranch/race track, watching a carriage-horse derby, and at about a half-an-hour into the film, we're getting to meet Gabin's Venezuelan-living, French 'ex-pat' Le Dabe for the first time: Le Dabe's the smoothest of gentleman-criminals, just like Gabin's 'Max le Menteur' also was, in *Touchez pas au grisbi*, and when we first meet him, he's tricked-out in a white panama hat and sunglasses, and is addressing a group of his employees, in perfect Spanish. Le Dabe has invited breeders to his ranch today, so they can show him their new wares (or, I guess, '*mares*'), since he's looking to purchase a new racehorse.

Charles has just flown all the way to Venezuela to convince Le Dabe to come out of retirement, and to work with him and with his friends. Le Dabe has heard of Charles, as Charles is one of Paris's biggest brothel owners, but he knows also that Charles isn't very highly regarded for his other criminal enterprises—especially, his counterfeiting enterprises, most of which have failed.

Le Dabe doesn't want to spend one more minute with the buffoonish-looking Charles than he absolutely has to: "So, why do you want to get into counterfeiting with me? And more importantly, why do you think I'd want to work with you? I know that your last job [the GM fiasco which apparently made the headlines, even in Venezuela] didn't go well for you. If you're this hard-up for money, I guess I could loan you some. But other than my doing that, I have no interest." But Charles keeps on 'pitching' him anyway, telling Le Dabe that he's interested in producing more counterfeit money than anybody's ever made before in one operation; but Le Dabe just tells him how stupid the whole idea is: "You can make all the money you want, my friend, but your little miseries of today will mean nothing, when you go to jail! In jail, you will discover who is vicious. You're a lightweight!" Even after having been cut down to nothing like that, or perhaps maybe even because of it (because, as we all know, powerful people who shit on people for a living love it when other people shit on them, after hours), Charles now wants to work with the mythical Le Dabe more than ever!

Le Dabe continues the conversation with Charles at Le Dabe's home (Le Dabe is wealthier than Charles, and so naturally, his crib's décor is more subtle, and more tasteful, than the décor in Charles' house. [Charles has less money than Le Dabe, and he makes up for it, as we've already noticed, by living in a house which is fairly bursting with crude, tacky ostentatiousness.]) Le Dabe now tells Charles, for the last time, "Just forget about counterfeiting. You'll come up with another way to make money. Anyway, in my own career, I only engaged in currency-making operations five times over a period of thirty years, and only the first four times were successful." So, we're now learning that all of Le Dabe's giant fortune came from four mega-counterfeiting deals, which he perpetrated only very sporadically over the decades, and he now tells Charles that, outside of his breeding of race-horses, he is completely retired, and even offers-up this footnote: "Even I couldn't have told you that my fifth job wasn't working while I was doing it: I thought it was going well, and I hired the best people." In that botched job, as Le Dabe is now telling Charles, he was making guilders (Dutch money [yes, here's another French Jean Gabin movie which is goofing-on the Dutch!]), and the day the money he made was about to go on the market, the Dutch government switched over to a new currency, so that those 'old Dutch guilders' which Le Dabe had worked so hard to reproduce, were now unusable. Le Dabe says that The Big Screw-Up happened on June 17, 1945, which means, also, that it's been fifteen or sixteen years since his last counterfeiting job. Comically, Le Dabe reveals to Charles that he was able to get rid of the phony guilders before he got caught. ("I had the major bonfire of my life!")

Charles is no Einstein, but he does manage, finally, to intrigue Le Dabe a bit, by telling him the exact amount of the money he wants to make—one billion francs! Le Dabe, laughing at the sheer ridiculousness of that notion, can't conceal his laughter: "That's twenty years in prison, you know." Le Dabe, like every Jean Gabin character, even his criminal characters, is always pragmatic.

Le Dabe gives Charles a ride to the airport in his convertible which, as he tells Charles, is one of the few extravagances he allows himself, outside of his horses. "Your crazy ideas allowed us to meet," Le Dabe tells Charles. "We won't meet many more times in this life though, even if we do decide to work together—which probably won't happen, anyway, since I already have enough money to live to my hundredth birthday. And on the extreme outside chance that I *do* decide to help you, I'll deny everything about my participation."

Of course, as we expected, the next day, sufficiently intrigued by the idea which Charles has pitched him (even though he, of course, pretended he wasn't), Le Dabe is leaving Venezuela for Paris, for what is probably the first time in years. Charles and Le Dabe take two separate planes back to Paris, just to make sure that the police won't be able to link them together, and superimposed over Le Dabe's plane, which courses through the misty night skies, we see a teletype from the French police, just as it's printing itself out:

"DATELINE CARACAS: TO PARIS POLICE BUREAU, DEPT. OF FRAUD: LE DABE (FERDINAND MARECHAL) IS RETURNING TO FRANCE! KEEP YOUR EYES AND EARS OUT!"

The French authorities have been looking for Le Dabe for years, but because he's been in Venezuela, he's been far out of their reach—but not anymore! At the Paris airport, two cops—Remy (Albert Dinan) and Martin (Gerard Buhr. [Get it? *Remy-Martin!*]) are waiting for him, and they're practically smacking their lips, because they've been waiting for Le Dabe to return to Paris for fifteen years, and they know that catching him in the act of committing a new crime in Paris would be the career-making score of a lifetime. Le Dabe's unlike other guys," Remy says, and Martin remarks, "The last time he was in Paris, he had just arrived off of the *Queen Mary* from New York, and when I asked him what he was doing here, he told me that he was here to buy a Cezanne. And he wasn't lying, either: I followed him for three days, and he went from one gallery to another, and he really did buy a Cezanne! And then, he left."

As soon as Le Dabe gets off the plane, he recognizes his old nemeses, Remy and Martin, and they turn around, comically burying their heads in newspapers. Not only is Le Dabe not afraid of them, but he actually approaches them with a big, goofy smile: "Hey, guys! Waiting for someone?" Remy and Martin, even though they would love to take Le Dabe in, *can't*, because he hasn't yet done anything illegal (they're just there to keep an eye on him), and they actually respect the mega-cool Le Dabe, a guy who, for them, is a legend (one who is right up there with Jesse James, himself). Le Dabe even asks the two cops if they can drop him off somewhere in their car, and they're only too happy to do it. So, while the two cops have been sent to threaten him, and to make their presences known to him just in case he might think of committing any crimes during his stay in Paris, they instead wind up deferring to him, and giving him a ride! (It's exactly like the scene in Gabin's 1957 crime-pic *Razzia sur la chnouf,* in which smooth-criminal Gabin returned home to Paris, and the cops who had been stationed at the airport to arrest him, actually really liked him and, instead of taking him in, just wished him a good stay in France.) Meanwhile, in a separate terminal at the same airport, Charles has just arrived home as well at about the same time, and comically, he's trying to check twelve expensive leather suitcases, which he had purchased in Caracas, through customs—and of course, he's making a fine, Laurel and Hardy-like mess out of it.

Meanwhile, Remy and Martin, who are driving Le Dabe in their car, ask him why he's returned to Paris after so many years, and Le Dabe just Gabin-Shrugs, telling them that he's come back to buy a certain Van Gogh painting which he's had his eye on: "And I want to buy some mares, too; the ones in Caracas are anemic."

The first thing the Cops do, before dropping Le Dabe off at his hotel, is to accompany him, *per* his request, to a horse-ranch outside of Paris: Since Le Dabe's just told them that he's come all the way to France to buy horses, they want to actually see him buying one, and so, *buy one, he does*—a shaky little mare. ("She's a little nervous," Le Dabe smiles, patting the frightened-looking horse, and possibly referring to his own nervousness [which he's managing to cover up very well, in the best possible Gabin Fashion].) He even tests the horse out, carriage-riding it himself (because Jean Gabin's way too cool to use a jockey)!

After the cops drop Le Dabe off at the hotel where he's told them he'll be staying, he next cabs it over to where he's *really* going to be staying while he's in Paris—Charles' house—and since Le Dabe is 'the consummate good guest,' he's brought Charles' wife Lea a bouquet of beautiful flowers, although when he looks around the kitschy house, he's discovering, too late, that he probably didn't need to find something so classy to bring, because the first thing he sees, upon entering, is that stupid painting of the Devil holding up the lady, and he rolls his eyes when he sees it. Lea's proud of her ugly painting, and she brags to Le Dabe, "I don't mind that the painting is in the entryway. But if it was up to me instead of my husband, I'd put it in the living room, and make it the centerpiece of the whole house." Le Dabe retorts, and they're all too dumb to understand his put-down, "If it was my house, I'd put it in the basement!"

Lea shows Le Dabe to the bedroom in which he'll be staying, telling him that it's an exact copy of Napoleon's bedroom at Fontainebleu, and Jean Gabin is great in this scene, because you can totally tell that Le Dabe wants to burst out laughing at the goofy décor, but that he's totally restraining himself from doing so.

One thing we're beginning to wonder while we're watching this movie, is: If Le Dabe is so smart, what's he doing, knowingly working with this team of morons? Since we've seen dozens of caper pictures before, we know already that it's probably *because* they're morons that he's working with them: They're dumb, so he knows that he'll be able to control the whole operation, effortlessly.

After settling himself in, the first thing on Le Dabe's agenda is to immediately show Lea and Charles who the 'Big Boss' of their operation is going to be from now on (him!), and right away, he tells them the things that he's going to be needing from them, if he's going to continue to stay in their home—all 'things of real sophistication,' as opposed to the *kitschy* shit which Lea and Charles favor: He instructs Lea that each morning, she must run him a bath, utilizing some of the special salts which he's brought along with him, and also that he's going to be needing a crisp, unfolded copy of the New York *Herald Tribune*, each and every day. He has also brought along five containers of Venezuelan coffee which, as he's now instructing them, they must serve to him as soon as he wakes up. Lea tells Le Dabe that the coffee will be good for her husband, too ("My husband really needs coffee to clarify his brain!"), but Le Dabe cuts her short, making her understand that the coffee is solely for his own consumption. Meanwhile, a pair of looky-loo neighbors across the street (Helen Dieudonne, who played the Nun in *Les Vieux de la vieille*, and Paul Faivre) are now starting to wonder what Charles and Lea are doing with this guy, whose truckload of stuff is currently being unloaded onto the Lepicards' front lawn.

Eric arrives at Charles and Lea's mansion that morning, to meet Le Dabe for the first time, and he's excited, because this is probably the closest a guy like him will ever be to greatness. Eric asks Charles where Le Dabe is, and Charles tells him, "He's here, but he's informed us that we can't see him for two days. He's working upstairs." Indeed, Le Dabe is working in bed, and in total, abject splendor: First, we see him phoning up the New York *Herald Tribune* which, as we've already surmised, he's not just reading for the funny pages: He's placing a want-ad in secret code, so that a New York-living criminal friend of his, Tauchmann, his German-American 'fence,' will see it. The ad reads, "After a long absence in Europe, I'd like to exchange some big flowers for some modern engravings." Le Dabe tells the *Tribune's* classified-ad taker that he wants her to place the ad every day for one solid week, and that he'd like her to send the bill to 'Mr. Charles Lepicard,' in Paris.

After a few days of solitude, Le Dabe finally decides to favor the family with a visit downstairs, and as he heads down the staircase, Lea approaches him with a cup of his special coffee, but (Uh-oh!), it hasn't been prepared in the way that he likes it! He takes a big swig and spits it out all over the stairwell, bellowing out, in a side-splittingly funny Gabin-Outburst, "What's this poison?!" He continues to berate Charles, Lea, and their servants, at the top of his lungs, for "… conspiring to make me drink bad coffee! Are you all mad?" Lea offers to make him a fresh cup, but he can't be bothered: "If it's the coffee machine, go out and get a new one! If it's the maid, fire her immediately, unless you're trying to kill me! I brought you the finest coffee in the world, but this is SOCK JUICE! Are you all idiots?" (This is the only Gabin-Outburst which we're going to be seeing in the entire film, and it has nothing to do with any crimes which will be committed in the picture, although no doubt, sometimes, bad coffee is definitely a crime!)

Le Dabe heads into the library for his first meeting with his new 'Three Stooges'—Charles, Eric, and Lucas. This is the first time that Le Dabe is meeting Eric and Martin in person, and his expression tells us what his lack of words do not—namely, that it's too bad he's had to meet them at all. (Jean Gabin does not suffer fools!) "It's a pleasure," Eric gushes, and Le Dabe, who plainly hates all forms of brown-nosing, mumbles, "Me, too," believing what he's just said probably even less than anything else he's ever believed in his whole life. Lucas, while he's an attorney, is so dumb in his own right, that he doesn't even know how to be properly deferential to the kingly Le Dabe: "Mr. Le Dabe, I've heard that, for your efforts with us, you've asked for fifty percent of our take. Isn't that a bit excessive?" Le Dabe replies calmly, getting right up in the guy's face, past all known comfort-barriers, "I don't work for charity cases. Also: Never try to argue with me, ever! Do we agree? Because if you don't agree, I will be out of here in ten minutes." Le Dabe tells all-assembled that, in exchange for his receiving fifty percent of the total take (they didn't know he would ask for so much, so now we're getting this great, drawn-out moment in which Charles, Eric, and Lucas look like they're going to be having massive heart attacks), he will help them to make the one billion francs, which they need.

Eric next asks a completely avaricious question—"Why only one billion? Why can't we make more?" to which Le Dabe replies, curtly, that he has only one fence (Tauchmann) who would be able to take delivery of that much *faux*-cash. Le Dabe then asks the others if they've found a suitable location in which to print the currency, and of course, the concept hasn't even occurred to them.

Charles thinks they should be making the money right here, in his own home (in the basement), and when Le Dabe hears this, he throws his hands up like he's just been listening to a retarded six-year-old, and then snarks-back at the guy, "Hey! I've got an even better idea! Why don't we just make the money out on the sidewalk?" He tells them that the specific plate-making machine which he'd like to purchase is extremely noisy, and that they're going to have to do the job in a location which is very private, and that they might even have to buy a printing shop! (The other three guys' mouths drop.) Lea, at the point, brings Le Dabe some new, freshly-brewed coffee—coffee, which (finally) meets with his discerning approval, and he now tells the other guys that, earlier in the morning, when he was making phone calls, he discovered an available print shop (one that's been on the market for quite some time), and that he's already negotiated with the place's owner.

Later that morning, Le Dabe takes the three guys into their new print shop, and Eric and

Lucas then spend the rest of the day meeting different sellers of printing machines, asking them all if they carry a very specific machine, as dictated by their new 'managing partner,' and while they're doing that, Le Dabe himself has just entered a local trinket shop: The sign on the awning reads, '*Fleurs/Plumes*' ('Flowers/Pens'), and it's here that he comes upon a woman of his own age, Paulette (Francoise Rosay), who just like other old lady-characters in lots of other recent Gabin movies, is somebody whom Le Dabe dated, and probably decades ago. Paulette coyly pretends not to know Le Dabe when he first comes in, but when her young shop-girl assistant Georgette (Clara Gansard) heads out for lunch, leaving Paulette alone with him, she warms up immediately, telling him how fantastic it is to be seeing him again. After some small-talk about the good old days, Paulette asks Le Dabe if he's still doing the 'same thing' (counterfeiting, and she knows what he does, because she was always the person, during his former 'jobs,' who supplied him with all of the paper he needed.) She lives beneath her store in a small apartment and, as the two of them proceed downstairs, she tells him 'in code' that paper costs more than it used to: "Even the most common flowers are more expensive than usual," she winks. What she's letting him know here, and not-so-cryptically, is that if she's going to be involved with his fake-money operations again, her own price is going to be higher than it used to be.

Paulette and Le Dabe reminisce about old mutual acquaintances from their past business ventures ('this one was found dead;' 'that one killed himself'), and Le Dabe tells her that, for his current operation, he wants the exact same kind of paper which Monteresse, 'the world's greatest forger,' uses. She tells him that she *does* have the special paper he requires, but that it is under-seal, and so he then makes her an offer which she can't refuse: "Can the seal be broken for $1,000 [U.S.]?" She tells him that that amount is not enough, so he ups his initial offer to two. (That's more like it! The paper is now, officially, no longer under-seal.)

Paulette is now asking Le Dabe the name of the person who will be coming to her store and paying her for the paper, and he tells her to be on the lookout for Eric: "A big guy who looks like an idiot will come." She replies, amusedly, that in her opinion, "... a lot of big guys look like idiots," and as the two continue to make their small-talk, Le Dabe can't resist throwing in another line, pertaining to Eric's lack of smarts: "If idiocy was measured with a measuring stick—he'd be champion!"

Now, Solange is introducing Eric to her husband Robert for the very first time in the picture, and while Robert either doesn't know, or else, he doesn't want to know (it's possible that he's in denial) that Solange is diddling Eric, he immediately and accurately pegs Eric for being a major dork, and makes it very clear to Eric that he's only meeting with him because his wife has asked him to. Eric starts kissing Bob's ass, immediately (*it's what he does*): "I've heard that your work is impeccable…"

Later, all of our guys—Eric, Robert, Charles, Lucas, and Le Dabe—are setting-up-shop in that print store of which they've taken possession. Le Dabe sounds Robert out about which kinds of printing machines he's preferred to use in the past, and Robert, like all genuinely talented people, is modest, so naturally, he's the only person in the whole movie with whom

Le Dabe is going to be getting along (because Robert's not a big blowhard, like everybody else is); still at the same time, Robert *does* admit to Le Dabe that he considers himself to be a champion at counterfeiting, and Le Dabe likes Robert's confidence immediately, since it seems to be coming from a place of intelligence.

Next, Gilles Grangier cross-cuts between Le Dabe, who's luxuriating in bed at Charles and Lea's place, and Robert, who's toiling away in the print shop, expertly making an engraving of a one thousand-franc note. Le Dabe pays him a visit to see how everything is going, and he compliments Robert's fine, precision work, by comparing it to the great Renaissance paintings of Albrecht Durer, and the two men—one older, the other younger—continue to bond: Le Dabe thinks Robert is smart and cool, and he even tells Robert, "You remind me of me, when I was younger." Robert laughs, "Just call me 'Robert,' as you would call Michelangelo, 'Michelangelo!'" Le Dabe laughs, too, admiring the younger man's immodest wit.

The next day, at home, Robert complains to Solange that he's missing a button on his shirt, and that he can't do his work properly, unless he's dressed well. (He's in his underwear yelling at her, and it's exactly like how Le Dabe, too, expects 'the small things in life,' to be in order. [The scene very definitely calls to mind the similar, "I can't wear beige to a bank robbery" sequence in Woody Allen's hilarious 1969 crime comedy, *Take the Money and Run*.]) And while Robert's yelling at his wife, she's in bed, lying on her stomach, and Grangier now rewards us with a great, racy, 'cheesecake' shot of her ass, which sticks-up sumptuously, toward the camera. (A big high-five to director Gilles Grangier, for that!)

The next morning, Le Dabe is grumpy, because he's convinced that the maid is reading his morning newspaper before she's giving it to him, which means that the newspaper isn't coming to him 'crease-free,' as he had requested it. Downstairs, at the same time, Eric and Solange are quaffing-down some morning eye-openers, and Robert's there, too. (We still don't know if he knows that Eric is 'doing' his wife.) When Le Dabe descends down the staircase, he sees Robert drinking, and he warns them against imbibing on the job: "It would be a shame if your hands were damaged from drinking." (It's *L'Air de Paris*, all over again: Le Dabe is the 'coach,' or 'mentor,' and Robert is 'the shining star, who's on his way up.') Lea, at this point, decides to spin a rock-and-roll record on the family's hi-fi, and the music, instantly, makes Le Dabe wince; and here, now, is one of the very few times in any Jean Gabin movie, in which Gabin will directly reference rock-and-roll: "Turn that doggerel off! I like music… but not monkey music!"

Robert is feeling happy and buoyed-up from his new, 'father-and-son-esque' relationship with the mega-cool Le Dabe, and back at his own apartment, later that day, he's still buzzed from having just spent the day with this very cool older man, even telling his wife Solange, "I finally met a real man!" Solange naively asks, "You mean, Eric?" and this is the scene in which Robert, who kind of suspected that she was doing the guy the whole time (but who never said anything about it because he, like his mentor Le Dabe, is classy), gets to 'call her out' on it. ("You think that Eric guy is a real man?") Husband and wife now begin arguing vociferously, and he tells her that he can't kick her ass out onto the street, which is what he wants to do, because unfortunately, he's working with Eric, but that when this operation is complete, that she shouldn't let the door hit her ass on the way out. We're also getting the sense here that, after this whole counterfeiting scheme is over, the first thing Robert will do to Eric, even though he has to act civil to him for the time being, is to beat him to a bloody pulp.

Back at Charles' house, in Le Dabe's absence, Eric is now telling Lucas and Charles about his newest and most moronic idea of all, which is that they should all double-cross Le Dabe: "Let's make twice as much money as we said we would—two billion francs, instead of one—so that when Le Dabe gets his fifty percent, we'll still have our hundred percent, plus more! Is it fair that Le Dabe should get fifty percent? Remember: We hired him as a consultant, not as a partner." Now, we're really getting a sense about why some of Eric, Lucas, and Charles' past enterprises failed: For all of their big ideas, these guys really don't think too clearly.

Later that day, Eric hastens over to Paulette's trinket shop to deliver her the two grand for the printing paper, as Le Dabe promised her he would be doing, and comically, we hear Le Dabe in voice-over (it's a replay of what he had said about Eric during that earlier Le Dabe/Paulette reunion scene: "A big idiot will come and deliver the money to you")! Eric pays her, and of course, because Eric's a counterfeiter, she checks to make sure that the money he's giving her is *real*, and not only is it real, but he's just handed her twice as much as Le Dabe said he would—namely, four thousand francs, instead of two. She can't figure out why he's giving her so much money, and he (lamely) tries to explain 'the new situation' to her, as he sees it: "Well, you know, I thought that if I gave you twice as much money, you could give me twice as much paper!" "I don't sell this way," she barks at him, brushing off the extra 2K. Paulette, of course, has more allegiance to Le Dabe than she has to 'this big idiot,' and she's savvy enough to realize that the guy is requesting twice as much paper so that he can print twice as much currency, and all for his own benefit.

Meanwhile, Le Dabe finally gets an in-person meeting with the legendary counterfeiter Monteresse, who's ventured to Paris from New York. Monteresse tells Le Dabe that the American fence whom they both know, Tauchmann, will probably ask for twenty percent of Le Dabe's commission for unloading the counterfeit francs in the U.S., and Le Dabe remarks, "That's fine! As long as you pay me with American hundred-dollar bills." All of their dialogue in this scene is delivered in code:

LE DABE: 'Professor' Tauchmann will be teaching his 'navigation classes,' as usual.
MONTERESSE: What are the sizes of the tulips?

Le Dabe has figured out already, that the three guys mean to rip him off (obviously, Paulette, the lady paper-vendor called, and gave him a heads-up about what Eric tried to do at her shop, today), because the next time he's got Eric, Lucas, and Charles all together in one room, he tells them he's just decided that, for all of the troubles he's been going through, he would now like an additional fifteen-percent of what their take will be, as his payment—in other words, he now wants sixty-five percent, in lieu of the original fifty for which he had asked. The guys are all shocked, but they try to hide it, and at this point, Robert enters the room, and shows the guys the first completed samples—the first 'test printing' of his newly-minted francs. Le Dabe loves them ("Bravo! Perfect!"), and he tells the guys that it might be a good thing for them to not work on Sundays, because most shops are closed on the Sabbath day, and he doesn't want to arouse any suspicion. He next lets Charles, Eric, and Lucas know, in an extremely roundabout way, that he knows they might be trying to fuck him, although those guys are so dense, they have no idea just what he's referencing: "Everything that goes wrong is always based on trust," he lectures them. "In business, we never trust anybody." In private later, Le Dabe will confide to Robert about what he thinks (or rather, what he knows) the other three guys are doing.

Le Dabe isn't the only person who thinks that he and the guys shouldn't be working on Sundays, either: Solange, Robert's hot wife, even though she's not exactly in any kind of a position morally to be telling her husband what to do, doesn't like Robert working on Sundays either, because, as she's telling him now, in front of all of the other guys (including

Eric) it makes her feel ignored. (Chicks need lots of attention… as opposed to guys, who need almost none!) She tells the men, very seriously, that on Sunday, all they should be doing, is sitting around and listening to the accordion.

When we next see Robert and Le Dabe together later that day, they're walking around the docks of Paris, engaging in some more 'father-and-surrogate-son'-type bonding: "Last time I came here, I was twelve," Robert muses nostalgically. "Me, too," Le Dabe returns. Robert next assesses his friend Le Dabe, right to Le Dabe's face: "I notice you don't like people very much." Le Dabe, knowing it's true, just smiles a slow Gabin-Smile, and then proceeds to change the subject, telling Robert that, when Robert starts printing the actual money, he will have only three hours to produce the entire one billion. Robert asks Le Dabe for an extra half-hour because, as he's now explaining it to his older friend, after he prints out all of the money, he's going to have to break the equipment down all by himself.

That night, Solange eats dinner with Charles' wife Lea, and she tells Lea that Charles has been crassly hitting on her again, but Lea just laughs it off, because her husband is played by Bernard Blier, who's about as sexual-looking as a potted plant. The two women are clearly bonding here, and Lea tells Solange, "Maybe you and I can just go to Boulogne together and have a nice vacation—with no men!"

2:30 p.m rolls around: Le Dabe's at Charles and Lea's house with Eric, Martin, and Charles, and he tells them to meet him that afternoon at 5:50 p.m., on the fancy Place du Trocadero in Paris's 7th-district, and that he doesn't want to see any of them before that time. We're now in the film's final stretch, and director Grangier is setting up a whole 'ticking-clock' type of situation, in which Robert's got three hours to mint all one billion francs.

For his alibi (so that he won't get tied to the caper, in case the cops begin figuring anything out), Le Dabe checks himself into a hospital (pretending to have had a nervous breakdown!) but the joke, is that he's just as Gabin-Calm as ever, and he's even happy—probably, because he knows this whole *shmageggy* will soon be over. While Robert's producing the money physically, and while Le Dabe is hiding out in the hospital, Charles is dining with Lea and Lucas, and Eric's got a good alibi, as well: He's fucking Solange—and right on Solange and Robert's marriage bed!

Back at the hospital, the Doctor (Marcel Charvey) enters Le Dabe's room to check on him, but he's gone. It's now 5:50, and Charles, Lucas, and Eric, having finished all of their 'dinner-eating' (not to mention, all of their 'somebody-else's-wife-fucking') are all sitting in Charles' car, waiting for Le Dabe on La Place du Trocadero, right next to the statue of Field Marshall Foch (the man who commanded the Allied forces against Germany, in World War I). Le Dabe shows up a few minutes late on purpose, in case anybody should have accidentally heard about the 5:50 plan, and he now announces to his men that they are going to need another meeting: ("Tonight at 8:00!") He climbs into the car with them, and they speed off to the print shop, to check-up on how Robert is doing.

When they get there—Robert and the money are both gone! Robert, the only genuinely good guy in the movie (or so we thought!) has double-crossed them all. (Even steely old Le

Dabe didn't see it coming.) Le Dabe looks like he's going to tear Charles' throat out—"*You did this to me!*"—and he then slaps Eric's face hard, for having made Robert part of the team. (*So:* Robert didn't have to confront Eric physically about screwing his wife, at all; instead, to make Eric [not to mention the other guys] suffer even more, he's just decided, per 'Woody A.' again, to '*Take the Money and Run!*')

Le Dabe, Charles, Eric, and Lucas next barge into Solange's apartment, and she's crying, telling them that Robert has left her, and that Robert has also taken all of his clothes. Le Dabe, who's mortified, tells the remaining three guys that he's going to be leaving for Venezuela, and that he never ever wants to see any of them again. (Le Dabe now slaps Solange, for good measure.)

Okay, so who's ready for this movie's ultra-cool 'double-twist?:'

When we see Robert next, he's at the airport, boarding a plane (we're not sure where it's headed) with a carry-on suitcase. Le Dabe gets on, sits right down next to him, and wordlessly takes possession of the suitcase (which, of course, is full-to-the-brim with *faux* francs): Yes, folks, Robert and Le Dabe were really working together, double-crossing all of the other guys, the entire time! These two, a pair of grifters who, with this movie sequence, have just put all other movie grifters in history to amateurish shame, now head off to Caracas, together.

As we see a stock-footage 747 flying off into the wild, blue stock-footage horizon, a final credit crawl now tells us, with a touch of humor, "It goes without saying that the protagonists of this nasty little story were arrested the following week, according to Article 139 in the Penal Code." (This credit crawl doesn't tell us, however, exactly which of them was, or were, arrested. [All of them?]) Presumbably, Robert and Le Dabe were able to escape from the law, since they 'blew that pop-stand' (France) fairly quickly, and if these credits were meant to be taken seriously by audiences who saw the movie in the early 1960s (and not, in other words, as a joke), then it smacks of interference by Comacio, the company which distributed the film theatrically in France. This written admonishment is also reminiscent of those American movies which were made in the Hollywood of the 1940s, in which the censorious Hays Code demanded that American filmmakers made sure that criminals in their films always got caught because, as we all know, '*Crime Does Not Pay.*' (What? What's so funny about that?! Stop laughing!)

Jacques Bar's production of *Le Cave se rebiffe* was released in New York City in 1962, by the Times Corporation (yes, for one brief moment, the New York *Times* was actually in the film distribution business), under a new title, *Money, Money, Money,* and thereafter, it was also released, in Los Angeles by a somewhat-larger outfit (MGM!), in 1964, under a completely different title, *The Counterfeiters of Paris*. But no matter what name the film is known under, and no matter who distributed it, it continues to be missing in action under any title in the U.S. today, although in France, its country of its production, it is still considered to be one of the most fun caper movies of all time, and at one point, it was even (*yuck!*) colorized for home video. *Le Cave se rebiffe* is a superbly-entertaining piece of work, and its success is due to the fact that Michel Audiard, who was working from Albert Simonin's novel, has really whipped up a rogues'gallery of beautifully-drawn characters, all of whom are so realistic, that we even like the dumb ones! (The characters of Eric, Robert, and Lucas would definitely have done Damon Runyan proud.)

What a Critic Said at the Time: "Jean Gabin again plays a retired gangster who comes back for a last job. This [picture] has a sleek mounting and acceptable suspense, and a great surprise ending. All rests on the veteran shoulders of Gabin, who displays his usual[ly]-solid waspish and domineering presence." (*Variety*, 10-18-61 issue. Critic: [Mosk.] "George Moskowitz." Reviewed in Paris.)

What Another Critic Said at the Time: "A group of old pros, headed up by Jean Gabin, have a high old time, and a good deal of it rubs off on the spectator, [and the actors] prove that counterfeiting need not be sordid, but good, mild fun. The denouement is curious and is, in a sense, retribution for an unnatural love of money. As the brains of the outfit, Mr. Gabin is a truly polished professional—he's worldly and wise." (New York *Times*, 7-19-62 issue. Critic: A.H. Weiler.)

What a Third Critic Said at the Time: "A brisk and very amusing comedy has Jean Gabin in a part that is really worth playing. He is in splendid form as a master counterfeiter. He plays [the character] with a subtle, deadpan authority." (*New Yorker* Magazine, 7-18-62 issue.)

FILM 74

Le Gentleman d'Epsom

France, 1962

(Literal English Translation: "THE GENTLEMAN OF EPSOM") Directed by Gilles Grangier. Produced by Jacques Bar. Screenplay by Michel Audiard, Gilles Grangier, and Albert Simonin. Music by Michel Legrand and Francis Lemarque. (GENRE: COMEDY) Director of Photography, Louis Page (black and white, scope). Editor, Jacques Desagneaux. Production Designer, Jacques Colombier. Running Time, 1 hour 22 minutes. A Production of CCM/C.I.P.R.A. Released in France on October 3, 1962, by C.I.P.R.A. Released in the United States with English Subtitles by MGM on March 15, 1964, as "DUKE OF THE DERBY."

> "When he was a younger man, he came here to my restaurant. He ordered thirty pounds of caviar and dined with a topless woman. It was a spectacular night—a night which lasted an entire week."
> —*A very impressed waiter regales his customers with stories about Gabin, in "Le Gentleman d'Epsom"*

The second picture in which Jean Gabin (in the starring role) and comedian Louis de Funes (in a small role) would team-up, after *La Traversee de Paris* (in which de Funes played 'Jambier' the black marketer, opposite Gabin's 'Grandgil'), was producer Jacques Bar's production of director Gilles Grangier's fun, Damon Runyon-esque *Le Gentleman d'Epsom*, which charmed French audiences, and even French critics, back in 1962. In this *trés*-fun comedy, which was beautifully photographed, incidentally, by Louis Page (who shot many of Jean Gabin's 1960s' movies, including this one, in beautiful, widescreen Dyaliscope [a/k/a, 'the French Cinemascope']), we get to see England's renowned Epsom Downs Racetrack, in Surrey. Gabin's charming and jauntily-dressed (always, in a crisp white suit) Richard Briand-Charmeux, whom everyone calls 'the Commander,' is France's greatest handicapper of horse races, a man who uses his bottomless supply of charisma to tip rich people off about the winning horses which he feels they *should* be betting on, always grabbing himself a hefty commission, when the ponies which he picks out for them win—which they always do. The Commander's also a self-taught master of roulette, who tells fellow gamblers, in one of the

With Louis de Funes.

local casinos which he frequents, that he always depends on (and he's probably made this up, but it sure sounds good) *Rowbowski's Rule of Circular Motion!* Although he's a con artist, the Commander is also a true gentleman, and everyone with whom he comes into contact is always only too happy to help him out because, of course, everyone wants to get rich; the Commander is frequently even given secret 'inside' information about the horses from some of the racetrack's employees. (Is he really a 'Commander?' Well, only inasmuch as Gabin's Baron Napoleon Jerome Antoine, in *Le Baron de l'ecluse* was actually a 'Baron,' which is to say that he's *not*. [It's a made-up title, calculated to aide him in his grifting.])

    De Funes appears in a few sequences as Gaspar, owner of a local bistro, who entrusts the Commander with eight hundred fifty-thousand francs. He wants the Commander to bet on a horse on his behalf, a horse which the Commander has assured him is a sure thing. When the horse loses, and this is the very first time in his entire grifting career in which the Commander has ever picked the wrong horse, the Commander keeps his cool: He simply goes off to Gaspar's restaurant and lyingly assures the guy that the horse actually won, no matter what Gaspar may have heard, or even *read about in the Racing Form*, but that they won't be able to collect the money until the following day. (Gaspar is so dumb, he doesn't even think about checking up on the line of *bubbe meinses* which the Commander is handing him, since the Commander, just like Gabin's Baron-character in *Le Baron de*

With Madeleine Robinson.

l'ecluse, looks impeccably honest.) Until then, as the Commander now posits to Gaspar, how would he (Gaspar) like to bet the unseen eight hundred and fifty-grand which he's just 'won' (!) on another horse which will be running the following day, an animal which, as the Commander is now assuring him, is a sure favorite to win, and which will thereby make Gaspar four *million* francs, instead of a piddling eight hundred-and fifty thou. (The Commander, of course, knows full-well that this horse won't win.)

The next day at the track, the Commander pretends to place the bet for Gaspar, and he gives a knowing wink to the agent behind the counter, a guy who, like every other racetrack employee in the picture, is in the Commander's pocket. The horse loses, just as the Commander had planned, and now he doesn't owe Gaspar one red cent; the Commander has saved his own hide, and the next time we see restaurateur Gaspar, he's now impoverished, and is being carried away on a stretcher outside of his restaurant by paramedics, and as they throw him into the back of the ambulance, he goes through the whole repertoire of De Funes' signature funny faces. (Basically: He's rolling his eyes around in his head in pain, and popping his tongue in and out, just like a dyspeptic frog.)

Le Gentleman d'Epsom, which was released very briefly in a few U.S. art-houses as *The Duke of the Derby,* benefits not only from Louis Page's outstanding cinematography, but also from a sweeping score which was co-composed by Michel Legrand ("Windmills of

Your Mind," from 1968's *Thomas Crown Affair*), and *especially,* from its hilarious screenplay. While the Commander can effortlessly con everybody he meets, he's a guy who can be easily conned himself, by women, and most especially, by his ex-girlfriend Maud (Madeleine Robinson, with whom Gabin had already starred in the 1949 stage-play "*La Soif,*" as well as in the 1953 film, *Leur derniere jour*), a woman who left him years ago for the unseen 'Steve,' a miner of manganese and tungsten. Maud and the Commander enjoy a regal reunion dinner in this movie, and their scene together is wonderful because, while the two are *munching-out* at one table, the aging waiter, Charly (Jean Lefebvre), is off at a distant table, regaling other patrons, who are honored to be chowing-down in the presence of the infamous 'Commander,' with stories about the Commander's younger days. Charly's highlight story is the one he's now telling, in which one evening, thirty years earlier, when the Commander was at the restaurant, he ordered "thirty pounds of caviar" and "dined with a topless woman." ("It was a spectacular night," Charly now brags to his customers, "*one night that lasted an entire week!*") Best of all, the horses in the movie have really hilarious names, like 'Uranium,' 'Cumulus,' 'Ridoxine' (a French food additive), and (less funny, but this wouldn't be a proper French movie if it didn't have a quick burst of anti-Semitism), '*Holocaust.*' (*Whoops!*) In spite of this one unpleasant reference, the film still has much to recommend, if you ever get the chance to see it. (It's not yet available on North American DVD, but an out-of-print VHS version, with English subtitles, pops up from time-to-time on eBay.) *Le Gentleman d'Epsom* is perfect Saturday afternoon entertainment.

What a Critic Said at the Time: "Vet actor Jean Gabin again essays a type of role that has become familiar for him, of late. He is an old snob living off racetrack-touting and is not above [using] some clever, underhanded actions. He [plays] this role with the usual aplomb. Result is a breezy series of anecdotes…" (*Variety*, 10-17-62 issue. Critic: "Mosk. [George Moskowitz.]" Reviewed in Paris.)

FILM 75

Un singe en hiver

France, 1962

(Literal English Translation/U.S. Release Title: "*A MONKEY IN WINTER*") Directed by Henri Verneuil. Produced by Jacques Bar. Screenplay by Michel Audiard and Francois Boyer. From the Novel by Antoine Blondin. Director of Photography, (black and white, scope) Louis Page. Music by Michel Magne. Editor, Francoise Bonnot and Monique Bonnot. Production Designer, Robert Clavel. Assistant Directors, Costa-Gavras and Claude Pionteau. (GENRE: COMEDY). A Production of CIPRA/Cite Films. Running Time, 1 hour 42 minutes. Released in France on May 11, 1962, by 20th Century-Fox-Europe. Released in United States with English Subtitles on January 31, 1963, by MGM.

> "I haven't yet had my share of adventure! And I want it!"
> — *An older Gabin wishes for fun, in "Un singe en hiver"*

After the disastrously-boring *Le President*, director Henri Verneuil and master thespian Jean Gabin would re-team, for 1962's much better (in fact: this one's just *out-and-out great*) widescreen comedy, *Un Singe en hiver* (*A Monkey in Winter*), a full-of-feeling effort, which co-starred Gabin with one of France's up-and-coming young stars, Jean-Paul Belmondo, an actor who first came to international recognition in 1959, with Godard's *A bout de souffle* (a film which is better known in the U.S., as *Breathless*), and who continues to make movies in France, to this day.

The story, which takes place in 'Present Day, 1962,' begins with an extended World War II flashback, and very specifically, it's a flashback to D-Day—June 6th, 1944: As the small and temperate Normandy village of Tigrette (the locals call Tigrette, 'the California of Normandy') is getting bombed, so too is Jean Gabin's crusty-old 'Albert Quentin' character who, when we first see him, is lushing-it-up, re-enacting old War Stories which revolve, of course, around 'his heroic actions,' while he's also referring to himself, heroically, as '*Quartermaster Quentin!*' Albert, a *hotelier*, lyingly tells the two prostitutes who are drinking with him, Marie-Jo (Genevieve Fontanel) and Simone (Anne-Marie Coffinet), that ten years ago in the 1930s, he fought valiantly in Tonking, China, which is the exact same place where Gabin's deserting soldier fought, before he deserted, in Marcel Carne's *Quai des brumes*, although in this picture, as opposed to in that older one, Gabin's character is clearly making it all up; the prostitutes all love silly old Albert, and they all know that whenever the man is *soused*, he's prone to making-up all kinds of crazily-heroic stories about himself. While Albert is regaling the girls, we can hear, off-screen, the sounds of the town which is getting continually strafed by the German *Luftwaffe*, and the sounds of the bombing, instead of frightening the unshakable Albert, just pump him up with adrenaline, even causing him to sing, "It's a Long Way to Tipperary" (which, as we remember, Gabin's fellow WWI-P.O.W.s all sang together, in *La Grande illusion*), in very funny, broken-English. ("You know all that crap Albert always tells us about his military service in China," amused-looking Marie-Jo whispers knowingly, to Simone. "He got it all out of books!")

Director Verneuil now flashes-forward eighteen years later, to 'Present Day 1962:" A now-teetotaling (and resultantly much quieter) Albert, with his long-suffering wife Suzanne, who's played by Suzanne Flon, are still proprietors of Albert's small hotel which happens to be suffering through the rainy off-season, and he's bored out of his skull. He even confesses to her that, as he gets older, he realizes he hasn't had his share of adventure in life, and that he wants it. (The reason Albert is no longer drinking, is because, on that fateful night in 1944, he promised to stop if his hotel had not been destroyed by the bombs. As his hotel has been spared, he has stopped imbibing, to the relief of his wife.) Enter a young, twentysomething dandy, Gabriel Fouquet (Belmondo), a mysterious and impeccably-dressed stranger who shows up, takes a room, and immediately starts encouraging Albert to go off-the-wagon, and to get plastered with him. Albert is immediately intrigued by Gabriel, recognizing something of himself in the young man's brashness (both men make up stories about themselves, in order to make this boring life more bearable), and Gabriel takes a filial liking to the older man, even gently, at one point, calling him 'Dad,' which flatters the *progeny-less* Albert greatly. The two men, ultimately, go off together, to the town's friendly, *Cheers*-like watering hole, Esnault's Bar (it's crammed to the rafters with goofy regulars), but Gabriel is unable to get Albert to imbibe with him. Esnault, the owner, is played by Paul Frankeur, and this definitely wouldn't be a proper Gabin movie, if Paul Frankeur didn't show up as a bartender!

Esnault's convivial regulars now have two crazies among them—Albert, who continues to annoy everybody with his usual made-up stories, pursuant to his alleged 'combat' experiences, and now, in addition, Gabriel, who makes wild (and wildly-unsubstantiated) claims that he is 'the world's greatest French matador,' which he next, in the following scene, tries to prove, by taking everybody from the bar outside, where he stands in the middle of a busy, rush-hour intersection and waves a red cape over the speeding cars. Amused by young Gabriel's behavior, Quentin admiringly tells him, explaining (*kind of!*) the title of the picture, "You're like the monkeys I've seen in the east, who stray from their homes, and who get caught by the first winter chill," a line which screenwriter Michel Audiard has probably meant to be some kind of a pithy explanation of the film's theme (which has something to do with 'how some people are never able to find themselves'… or *'some deep crap,'* like that)!

Albert and Gabriel become such a crackerjack father-and-son-(esque) team, that they

With Jean-Paul Belmondo.

296 | **THE FILMS** CYCLE FIVE

finally stop b.s.'ing each other and, to paraphrase that irascible American t.v. shrink, Dr. Phil, "get real:" Gabriel, as we and as Albert already knew anyway, is not really a matador, just like Albert's not really a war hero: He's really just an advertising man who churns out unfunny t.v. commercials, some of which we hear him phoning in to his unseen boss, back in Paris. Gabriel admits to Albert that the reason he's actually come to Tigrette, has been to rescue his little daughter, Marie (Sylvaine Margolie) from the parochial boarding school in which she's enrolled: Marie's Spanish mom, Claire (Gabriel's ex-wife), deposited her in the place a couple of years ago, right after the free-spirited Gabriel ran out on the two of them.

Albert feels badly for Gabriel, and tells Gabriel that if he has any hope of getting his daughter back, that he'd better first lighten-up on all of his drinking; Albert paternally admonishes Gabriel that "All habits are bad. They're a kind of death, by stagnation." (Too bad Gabin's not here today, to give that advice to *all of those koo-koo-ka-joo Twelve-Steppers!*)

Gabriel drunkenly negotiates his way to Marie's school under cover of the night, but he is too embarrassed by his present, drunken behavior to admit to his paternity, so he just tells the English-speaking old Nun (Helen Dieudonne, who played the old-age home nun, in *Les Vieux de la vieille* [and she also played the neighbor-lady, in *Le Cave se rebiffe*]) who runs the school, that he's a distant relative of the little girl. The Nun tells Gabriel that he can't stay, unless he's immediate family and, nervously, he tells her that he's not, and leaves.

Albert, angry that Gabriel didn't have the courage to show up at the school sober, and that he didn't re-claim his daughter, decides to accompany him back to the school and, in the film's most rousing sequence, the two men now charge the gates of the parochial academy in the middle of the night, just like two drunken Trojan Horses. "I am Quarter-Master Quentin," Gabin hilariously erupts, as he nears the gates of the school. "Release this man's daughter at once!"

This gentle picture ends with Gabriel's daughter back in his arms, and we see the happily reunited father and daughter, as they pack for their train trip back to Paris. But before they leave Tigrette, and for young Marie's benefit, Gabriel and Albert buy a massive amount of fireworks, and put on a wondrous display for her, a display which is also enjoyed by the whole town; and because Albert's given his town this amazing treat, we see why everybody there has always adored him—even in spite of his constant, drunken weirdness.

Un singe en hiver's true success comes *via* its sharp and *non-smarmy* warmth, although, as he did in the previous year's *Le President*, director Verneuil can't resist throwing in a little good-natured French Anti-Semitism: In an early sequence, Gabin's 'Albert' character drunkenly warbles a tune about a "slimy Jewish pimp!" Anyway, in spite of this one awkward moment, it's a great comedy, which MGM once owned for the U.S. market, but sadly, not anymore.

In a 2004 interview with the French television presenter Philippe Labro, Jean-Paul Belmondo remembered that, on the set of *Un singe en hiver,* Gabin just couldn't abide anybody whom he perceived as being even *slightly* unprofessional, and in the interview, Belmondo relates to Labro a wonderful anecdote about how, during the making of film, the production's young sound recording engineer was straining, through his headphones, to hear what the famously soft-spoken Gabin was saying. The crazy-brave guy actually deigned to ask Gabin to "speak louder" (!), to which Gabin apparently replied, "I'm not going to speak louder, sonny. You have knobs on your tape recorder, don't you? *So, turn them the hell up!*" Belmondo also mentions to Labro, in the same interview, that Jean Gabin was one of the few actors who was able to be menacing, only with his (famously blue) eyes. In Jean-Paul Belmondo's estimation, Jean Gabin was a man of action, yet, as he put it, "… one, who never needed to throw a fist, in order to get his point across."

Fun-Fact: Who was *Un singe en hiver's* assistant director? It was none other than Costa-Gavras, who would soon give the world some of the best political thrillers ever made, including 1969's Z, and 1971's *Etat de siege* [*State of Siege*].

What a Critic Said at the Time: "This is a smooth vehicle for the acting talents of old-timer Jean Gabin and newcomer Jean-Paul Belmondo. Dialog[ue] is crisp, with a leavening of bite. The film is primarily an anecdote that is kept intact by the thespian know-how of the principals. Gabin manages to make his role sympathetic, while Belmondo holds his own with the shrewd, grizzled veteran. Might hit the spot for U.S. Gabin fans. (*Variety*, 5-23-62 issue. Critic: "Mosk. [George Moskowitz.]" Reviewed in Paris.)

What Another Critic Said at the Time: "A commendable chance to watch the deftness of Jean Gabin, in a nice, genial little comic exercise. [The film] works as entertainment, and has a sparklingly comical climax. [Gabin and Jean-Paul Belmondo] show their charm and dexterity as tosspots. A moodily-masculine story, [full of] robust humor." (New York *Times*, 1-31-63 issue. Critic: Bosley Crowther.)

A third and final go-around as Inspector Maigret in "Maigret voit rouge" (Film 76, right)..

FILM 76

MAIGRET VOIT ROUGE

France/Italy, 1963

(Literal English Translation, "MAIGRET SEES RED") Directed by Gilles Grangier. Produced by Georges Charlot. Screenplay by Jacques Robert and Gilles Grangier. Based Upon the Novel by Georges Simenon. Director of Photography (black and white), Louis Page. Music by Michel Legrand and Francis Lemarque. Editor, Marie-Sophie Dubus. (GENRES: DRAMA/POLICIER) A Production of Films Copernic (France) and Titanus Films (Italy). Running Time, 1 hour 25 minutes. Released in France on September 18, 1963. Never Released Theatrically in the United States.

> "American criminals, nine times out of ten, are complete professionals.
> And I always go totally to war with them."
> — *Gabin's French Police Inspector Jules Maigret warns Paris-based American bad guys to watch their steps, in "Maigret voit rouge"*

Four years after Jean Gabin played Georges Simenon's Inspector Jules Maigret for the second time, in *Maigret et l'affaire Saint-Fiacre*, he'd don the trenchcoat and pipe for one final go-around, in Gilles Grangier's French-Italian co-production (hence, the presence of so many Italian actors, this time out) of *Maigret voit rouge (Maigret Sees Red)*. This film is definitely the least exciting (and most confusing and hard-to-follow, plot-wise) of Gabin's three Maigret movies (the first 'Gabin-Maigret,' *Maigret tend un piege*, is the best), but it remains watchable, and this is mostly on account of Jean Gabin's completely solid performance, and also because this time out, Maigret's up against the *Mafia*. And who doesn't like a good, or even a not so good, Mafia movie?

As the film opens, three skeevy-looking American gangsters are cruising through Paris's prostitute-and-sex shop-themed Pigalle district in a white Citroen-DS, and they're clearly on the look-out for a little trouble. (As one of them will even be heard to comment, in a very lusty manner: "I like those girls in Pigalle!") Charlie Cinglia (Ricky Cooper) is the driver, and he's accompanied by his cohorts Bill Larner (Edward Meeks) and Tony Cicero (Michel Constantin), and when this triumvirate of terror finally finds what it's looking for, it's kicks all right, but kicks of a different kind: They see a frightened-looking older guy,

Curtis (Harry-Max), running down an alleyway, and he's wearing shades, *a la* the Blues Brothers, even though it's already dark outside! (Clearly, this is a guy who just doesn't want to be recognized.) The 'hood-sedan' follows the running Curtis through the alley, and the gangsters next gun him down, and just based on the fact that we've all already seen seventeen million other crime pictures in our lifetimes, we've already figured out that they've probably just 'whacked' him, because he bore witness to something they did—something which he shouldn't have seen (like, a murder). The Citroen zooms off, but a mustached, off-duty police Inspector, Lognon (Guy Decomble) just so happens to have been walking around nearby, and not only did Lognon see the shooting while it was happening, but he was also able to catch a glimpse of the car's license plate numbers—'34665.' Lognon goes to Curtis' aide, and finds that the man has been severely injured, but not killed. He radios for help.

Tipped-off by Lognon, a group of desk-bound area cops at the nearby 10th-District precinct house now begin running license plates. Turns out, the auto belongs to an American, Maurice Pozzo (Vittorio Sanipoli), who owns an American-style bar, in Paris, The Manhattan (!), a place which is so American, that it even has its own bowling alley: Just like *Le Cave se rebiffe* showed us how much the French love American cars, so *Maigret voit rouge* is a primer about how the French love everything American, no matter what they're always saying to the contrary.

Lognon enters The Manhattan to have-speaks with owner Maurice, and he asks Maurice why his Citroen was seen at the site of that drive-by shooting the previous night. ("You own a Citroen-DS, right, Mr. Pozzo? Where were you at 10:30 p.m.?") Maurice tells Lognon, truthfully, that he wasn't anywhere near his car last night, and that he uses it only on Sundays, which is the one day each week when he takes his family out "for a drive." The Inspector believes him, but adds, "Well, I saw your vehicle last night at ten-thirty. Some guys were using it, and they shot a man. Know who they are?" Maurice shrugs as though he doesn't know, but when Inspector Lognon leaves, Maurice *immediately* places a call to *the three thugs*, the guys who, as we already know, were in the car: Maurice is somehow in cahoots with them, and it's more than apparent that he might even be their boss. Right after Lognon leaves the bar and starts walking down the street, some different American thugs, obviously having been sent by Maurice, try to grab him and shove him into their own car, but the enterprising Inspector is able to break free, and to escape.

Now, fifteen minutes into the picture, we're going to be seeing Jean Gabin's pipe-smoking Inspector Jules Maigret for the first time, and he's introduced, iconically, with a close-up of the famous Maigret Pipe. Maigret is conversing with his colleague, Lognon, who's sporting a hideous shiner from his fracas outside the Manhattan, and Maigret wants Lognon to tell him everything that happened so far, and from beginning to end. Lognon tells Maigret that his 'almost-abductors' were American. ("They were speaking English, but I don't understand English—so I have no idea what they were saying!") Maigret decides that since the shooter was an American, maybe he (Maigret) should contact the FBI, and he tells Lognon that, since he (Lognon) is already, just by default, 'part of the whole thing,' that if he's interested, he can work with Maigret on solving the case: "We'll find out why the Americans in that car wanted to kill that guy, and we'll also have to figure out how to trace them back to the United States."

The great Marcel Bozzuffi, who had already appeared with Jean Gabin in *Gas-Oil*, *Razzia sur la chnouf*, and *Le Rouge est mis*, plays super-wiretapper-cop Torrence, whom we're now getting to meet, down at 10th District H.Q., and naturally, he's surrounded by the tools-of-his-trade (reel-to-reel tape recorders and phone-tapping equipment, his head engulfed between the *furry black* 'thighs' of an oversized headset). Maigret tells Torrence that he's on his way over to the Manhattan, and that he's going to need Torrence to wire him for sound for the trip over.

That evening, Maigret, with Torrence's wire hidden beneath his shirt, saunters into the Manhattan to interview Maurice Pozzo, and Maurice doesn't look too excited about the fact that he's now having to a meet a second meddlesome Inspector. Maigret notices immediately that the bar is constructed in such a way that the floor arches-up slightly, so that Maurice, who is behind the bar, can look taller and more intimidating than anyone who's standing opposite him—including, at this moment, Maigret. Maigret orders a beer, and Maurice tries to distract him, by asking him if he wants to bowl in the bar's bowling alley. (Unfortunately, we don't get to see Jean Gabin bowling, which would have definitely been worth the price of admission! Can't you just hear Jean Gabin shouting out, "*J'en ai marre*," when he gets a gutter-ball?) Maigret notices a framed picture of a boxer behind the bar, and while he doesn't know who the guy is, we, the film's audience, recognize the guy as being one of the American killers from the big alleyway gun-down—the ex-boxer, Charlie Cinglia. Maurice tells Maigret that he used to be Cinglia's manager, but Maigret doesn't have any more time to waste with small-talk: He points to the photo and tells Maurice, flat-out, "I already *know* this is the guy who was driving your car, and I also know that he and his buddies are Americans, because my men have been wire-tapping them. I couldn't hear their exact words, but I know they were American, because Americans speak through their noses!"

Maurice keeps his cool. Maigret asks him if he's an American citizen (he's not sure, since Maurice's spoken-French is Italian-accented), and Maurice replies that he's originally from Sicily, but that he became a naturalized American citizen in St. Louis. Maigret next turns on the heat, telling Maurice that he knows Maurice is hiding information from him, and that if he continues doing so, he (Maigret) will see that the French government revokes Maurice's liquor license. Tough-guy Maurice gets visibly scared so, for the very first time during this impromptu third-degree, Maigret now softens, changing his gruff tone to one which approaches near-David Carradinian/zen solitude: "Naah, don't worry, pal. Our government has more important things to do, than dealing with lemonade merchants like you." As Maigret leaves the establishment, Maurice asks him, "Do you always win, Maigret?" And before heading out of the bar's cowboy movie-looking wooden saloon doors, Maigret, very coolly, turns back to the guy on his heels. Director Gilles Grangier sticks his camera way down low on the floor, so that we're now looking up at Gabin, and now that Maigret's got the upper-hand on Maurice, Gabin is now physically higher-up in the frame than the other guy is. Maigret mutters, "Americans, nine out of ten times, are total professionals. And I always go totally to war with them." (*Wow*, that's even cooler than John Wayne biting down on that bridle, after yelling out, "Fill yer hand, you son of a bitch," in *Rooster Cogburn!*) Right after Maigret makes his Big Exit, a brunette, Lily (Francoise Fabian), pops out of the bar's kitchen, and like every woman who works in bars in every old French movie, she also happens to be *"une prostituee..."*

In the next sequence, Maigret re-caps his meeting with Maurice to his resident sound-genius, Torrence, who happens to have already made a stop-over of his own to the Manhattan, and Torrence is now showing Maigret how he's just figured out that Maurice has a set of numbers programmed into the keys of his cash register—'two, seven, three, zero'—which, as he's explaining to Maigret, might be some kind of code to the other guys in his gang (the 'drive-by shooting' guys), that police are around. Torrence believes that Maurice's cash register is hooked up to the other gang-members' phones, in whatever place, or places, in which they happen to be hiding-out, and since Torrence seems to be France's #1 Code Breaker, Maigret asks him to accumulate a list of all local addresses which feature the numbers 2, 7, 3, and 0.

Torrence and other cops who have been joined by Inspector Lognon (and his mustache), start rifling through phone books looking for addresses, as a very patient Maigret stands by, puffing calmly on his pipe. (Jean Gabin, maybe even more so than any other human being on earth, is a man who always looks like 'he's got all day.')

Director Gilles Grangier next makes with an optical dissolve, after which we see that the cops who work under Maigret have been looking for addresses for hours on end. Torrence informs Maigret that the only local street addresses which happen to have '2,7,3, and 0,' are 1.) a butcher shop, 2.) the home of an old, retired General, and 3.) a *convent!* But then, finally, he hits on one that seems like a pretty good bet: It's the Hotel Flanders, at 2730 Galvane Street in Paris's seedy Couderc section. (Inspector Maigret's creator, Georges Simeon must have had quite an affinity for Couderc, because he named another of his crime novels, *La Veuve Couderc* [*The Widow of Couderc*], after it.) And guess who lives at the Hotel: It's Lily, the Manhattan's favorite bar-maiden/prostie! Lognon tells Maigret that he'll be more than happy to go over to the hotel and question her, himself: Lognon's not admitting to it, but Maigret already knows that Lognon is most probably one of Lily's regular johns.

Lognon heads over to Lily's room, and not alone, but with Maigret accompanying him, and when the two inspectors arrive on the scene, the first thing they see on her dresser, is a framed photograph of the boxer, Charlie Cinglia. (She had tried to shove it away into a drawer, before they arrived, but didn't have enough time.) Maigret asks Lily if Cinglia's her boyfriend, but she's not exactly in a talking mood, so Maigret keeps looking around for more clues that Cinglia and/or any of his pals have been there, and sure enough, he then finds a packet of American cigarettes, the brand of which is called 'Miller.' According to the label, the smokes were manufactured in 'St. Louis, Missouri,' Maurice Pozzo's hometown, and more importantly, there's an address on the back of the packet, too—and it just so happens to be the address of the Manhattan bar! As Maigret pockets the evidence, he also finds Charlie Cinglia's expensive American leather jacket and Cinglia's pajamas (!) stashed away inside Lily's 'In-a-Door, Murphy-Bed.' Tossing away all of his usual Gabin-Eloquence, he then starts shouting at her: "Whore! Tell me everything you know about your American boyfriend—and right now!" Since Maigret's Gabinian intensity has worn her down, she now, naturally, begins singing like a bird: "Okay, okay. Charlie did sleep here, but he hasn't been here for a week. His friends Tony Cicero and Bill Larner were with him, and they slept on a couple of mattresses… and then I overheard them all saying that they were leaving for Cherbourg—but I honestly don't know where in Cherbourg they've gone off to." (The northern-French village of Cherbourg is best-known to American movie-viewers from Jacques Demy's sunny 1967 Catherine Deneuve-musical, *Les Parapluies de Cherbourg* [*The Umbrellas of Cherbourg*].) Maigret now informs Lily, "I don't know if you know this, but those friends you've been hiding out are being sought after for attempted murder, and if you don't tell me every single thing you know about them, you're going to be looking at a ten year stretch yourself—as their accomplice!" She swears up-and-down to Maigret that she doesn't know anything else, but she does reveal to him that Maurice always alerts her about Charlie and his pals' frequent visits to her room, by punching the numbers '2,7,3, and 0' into his cash register, and of course, it is this sequence of numbers which happens to be connected-up to Lily's telephone.

So: What's the significance of "2,7,3,0" in this film? Why was this sequence of numbers chosen, as opposed to any other numbers (say, for example, '867-5309?') Well, *here's why:* French cineastes have always deified the American action-movie director Don Siegel, who turned out lots of great action movies in the '50s, '60s, and '70s and the *Cinematheque Francaise* in Paris would often program Siegel festivals during each of those decades. Especially popular with French audiences, was the director's low-budget 1954 jailhouse epic, *Riot in Cellblock 11*. At the beginning of *Riot,* prisoners, who are languishing in their cells, are listening to a radio commercial (it's blaring throughout the jail, over a P.A. system) which is advertising a used car lot. The car dealer, who happens to be reading his own commercial, beckons potential customers to "hurry on down" to his lot, and the address which he gives, is none other than '2730.'

Maigret asks Lily if she knows how the guys got to France from the U.S. ("On a boat? A plane?"), and she tells him that she feels very uncomfortable finking on her friends, so he tries to make her feel better, by assuring her that she's doing the right thing. ("Love and justice are two different animals, young lady.") Maigret's happy that Lily has told him everything she knows, especially because everything she's telling him seems to be checking out. (*The Jean Gabin Bullshit Detector* is always chugging-along at 100%-capacity!) He now leaves the girl's apartment, but Inspector Lognon stays behind, obviously *to get laid,* and Lily (she's a regular Florence Nightingale!) is only too happy to oblige, even though the guy's just been complicit in shaking her down.

Maigret voit rouge wouldn't be a good-and-proper 1960s cop flick, if we didn't have at least one crooked cop in the story, and Georges Simenon and Gilles Grangier are only too happy to supply us with one: He's Officer Bonfils (Paul Frankeur), the dirty cop who operates out of Maigret's precinct house. Bonfils is currently working overtime, supplying Maurice and the bad guys with information about Maigret's investigation in return for cash, and when we first meet Bonfils (in English, his name, '*bon fils*,' means, 'good son'), he's phoning-up Maurice at the Manhattan, and letting him know that the Cops are keeping Curtis, the 'mystery witness' who got gunned-down at the beginning of the picture, under police protection, just in case anybody should be thinking about finishing him off.

Director Grangier now takes us to the countryside of Cherbourg: Maurice's Citroen pulls into the driveway of a plush country estate, and Maurice emerges with Charlie Cinglia and Bill Larner. The home belongs to an old surgeon, Dr. Fezin (Roland Armontel), who processes drugs for Maurice's gang in his basement, exactly like the scientist-character Birot did in *Razzia sur la chnouf*, and Fezin's the one who's currently hiding the gang out.

Back in Paris, meanwhile, Maigret is paying a visit to the American Embassy, where he's now meeting with his old FBI-agent friend and WWII buddy Harry MacDonald, who's played by a great Canadian character-actor named Paul Carpenter, a guy who appears in lots of French movies from the period, usually playing some kind of American spy or FBI man. The two old pals start making a little small-talk, and they speak in what the film's French-speaking screenwriters who adapted Simenon's novel (Jacques Robert and director Grangier) must, hysterically, have believed to be 'typically-conversational English:'

> MacDONALD: How ya doin', Jules? Haven't seen ya since Chicago, six years ago!
> MAIGRET: Hiya, Harry! Hey [he comically flexes his biceps]! Ya think they might want me out in Hollywood?!

The meat of their exposition-heavy conversation continues, next, in French: "Harry, I know you're just working for the American Embassy now, and that you've quit the FBI. But I also know that you've still got friends in the Company, and I need your expertise: I'm investigating these American guys who think Paris is prohibition-era Chicago. Can you get me some information on them?" MacDonald already knows about Pozzo, Cinglia, Cicero, and Larner, from having dealt with all of them in the past, when he was investigating mob-related crimes which they had committed on American soil, and he tells Maigret that the man for whom all of them work, is Walter Douglas, America's biggest drug czar who's based in St. Louis. MacDonald then, very gently, warns his Gabinian friend not to get involved with them: "Try to stay out of it, Jules. With your permission, I'll try to find out some more information about what they're doing here in France, okay?" (Red Flag to People Who Have Seen Lots of Movies Like This, Before: Why is MacDonald warning Maigret to stay off the case? Is MacDonald working with the gangsters? [We'll see, later!])

The next time Maigret makes an appearance at the Manhattan, the photo of Charlie Cinglia has been removed from the wall, and there's a new Bartender (Carlo Nell) behind the counter. Maigret asks the new guy where Maurice Pozzo is, and the guy feigns like he doesn't know—but just then, Maurice enters the bar, from the kitchen. Maigret asks Maurice, straight-up, about exactly *where* in Cherbourg his three hoods have gone, and he also lets Maurice know, in a not-so-indirect manner, that soon, the jig will be up: "Give me a beer, Pozzo. And I want you to charge me 27.30!"

Maurice now reveals to Maigret the exact Cherbourg location where his men are staying, and he doesn't seem to be fretting about handing this info over to Our Favorite Inspector, because he knows that Charlie and the other hoods are as tough as they come, and can take care of themselves, should Maigret be stupid enough to show up there. Maigret tells Maurice that he's just done the right thing by having given him this information because, otherwise, he would have had to arrest him.

Later that day, a low-rung cop brings Maigret, and some other cops who are helping him out on this case, cups of coffee, and once the men are all amped-up from the caffeine, Maigret gives everybody present his marching orders: "You three: I want you over at the Manhattan. But be discreet, because if the bad guys see cops going into the bar, they won't go in."

Meanwhile, in their Cherbourg hideout at Dr. Fezin's house, Charlie Cinglia confesses to Bill Larner that, in a moment of unguarded, post-coital lust, he told his girlfriend Lily, the Manhattan's barmaid/hooker, *he* was the one who shot Curtis, and that now that he's thinking more logically again, he's probably going to have to rub her out, too. (He has no idea that Maigret's already been to see Lily.) As Cinglia issues this proclamation, he also happens to be watching an ancient boxing match kinescope on t.v., and he suddenly perks up, discovering that he's one of the two boxers participating in the bout! ("Hey! Whaddya know! That's me, fighting Rocky Marciano in '54!") Bill Larner, a very all-American (and even 'JFK-looking') young guy, now leaves Fezin's house, heading for a nearby golf course.

In the next sequence, which takes place out on the links, Bill approaches Bonfils, the crooked cop, and tells him that Cinglia and Cicero mean to find Curtis, and to finish him off. In exchange for this information which he has just received, Bonfils next tells Bill that Maigret and a bunch of other cops are keeping Curtis and his wife sequestered at the Hotel des Flanders which is, of course, the same hotel in which Lily plies her pliant trade. Now, Charlie Cinglia arrives at the golf course too, to surprise his friend, and to play a few holes, and when he gets there, of course, he overhears the conversation between Larner and Bonflis. Very promptly, and without even thinking about it, he blows Bill to Kingdom Come. Bonfils, however, has come to the golf course unarmed, and now freaking, he jumps into his car, which is parked nearby, and makes his ultra-quick getaway, so that Cinglia won't be able to parcel out the same treatment to him.

Later that day, when Maigret arrives at the Hotel to check-up on Curtis, he discovers that Curtis' wife Lucy, whom we're now hearing about for the first time in the movie, is dead: Somebody, and most probably Tony Cicero (since he's the one member of the gang besides Maurice who *wasn't* at Dr. Fezin's place in Cherbourg), has shot her, and dumped her body into the bathtub. Maigret immediately phones the Chief-of-Police (Raymond Pierson), who's in a meeting, and reports to him about what's just gone down at the hotel, and following this, the hotel's Housekeeper (Paulette Dubost) tells Maigret what she knows: "These men you say you're looking for? Well, they were here in the hotel three weeks ago—in fact, they were in that woman Lily's room. Mr. Curtis was staying here too, but he left three days ago. Mrs. Curtis told me she was worried, because he left her suddenly without saying where he was going, and didn't come back. She was terrified that somebody from his old gang may have put a contract out on him."

As other investigating cops arrive and begin cleaning up the deceased bathtub-dweller, Mrs. Curtis, the Housekeeper (as well as another, younger maid, Lucienne [Laurence Badie]), continues to fill Maigret in on recent events: "Mr. and Mrs. Curtis weren't too friendly to each other; they didn't even stay in the same room." Lucienne reveals to Maigret that "two guys" came into the hotel this morning, that they were speaking English, and that "… one of them looked husky—that way boxers look." Maigret asks her if she thinks she might know why Mrs. Curtis was killed, and she confirms what we've already known since the beginning of the picture: "Maybe Mr. Curtis saw something that he wasn't supposed to see."

That night, as he tries to piece everything together with his steel-trap-of-a-mind, Maigret perambulates the streets near the Manhattan alone, and (uh-oh!) Charlie Cinglia and Tony Cicero are waiting for him, with their guns drawn! Maigret gets an eyeful of the two guys, and so he dashes into the bar, where he phones the Chief, and tells him that he's being followed. The Chief follows up, by placing literally *hundreds* of cops out on the streets near the bar, most of them in plainclothes so that 'bad guys' won't be able to identify them as cops.

Cinglia and Cicero have followed Maigret into the Manhattan, but when they see huge groups of cops walking toward the establishment, they quickly escape through the men's room window. Maigret enters the john, and all he finds is a packet of French cigarettes, and it's a rare brand—a brand which even Maigret has never heard of, called '*Algine.*'

Maigret and our old friend, Inspector Lognon, now head into a local pharmacist's shop, to find out what exactly 'Algine' is, and it is here they learn that it's not a tobacco cigarette at all, but actually *medicinal marijuana*, which can be dispensed only by prescription, and the Druggist (Charles Bouillaud) tells Maigret that the only person who's purchased any Algines, lately, has been Tony Cicero. ("I waited on the guy, myself!") Maigret asks the Pharmacist for the name of the doctor who wrote the prescription, and—*bingo!*—the guy hands Maigret Dr. Fezin's address in Cherbourg. Now, Maigret knows exactly where the hoods are hiding out, and to paraphrase a line from a great horror picture which John Carpenter made in 1987, *They Live!*, it's now time for mega-cool Jean Gabin "to chew bubble gum and kick ass—and he's all out of bubble gum!"

Later that day, Maigret and Torrence arrive at Dr. Fezin's country estate, with a phalanx of other cops, all of whom Maigret orders to wait outside. He then shoots through the window, blasting a large hole through Charlie Cinglia's right hand! Maigret and Torrence then burst into the living room, where they see Fezin, who's already started trying to remove the bullet from Cinglia's bloody lunch-hook, and Maigret gets right up in Charlie's face: "Okay, Cinglia. Listen, and listen good: I've got you, I've got your pal, and I've got Mario Pozzo, too. So now, tell me: Where the hell's your other partner, Tony Cicero?" Cinglia won't talk, so Maigret breaks out the handcuffs, and Dr. Fezin tries wimpily to intercede: "You can't arrest this man. I have to save him!" Maigret sputters, "You should really be a veterinarian, my friend, because you help animals, and you're headed straight to jail! Now *somebody* in this room had better tell me where Tony Cicero is!" Fezin says he has no idea, and Cinglia, who is completely unafraid of Maigret, defiantly yells out (this guy's obviously seen way too many Bogart movies!), "Shaddup, Flatfoot!"

Maigret's wondering if Mario's Citroen-DS is on or near the premises, and he now asks the Doctor if he's "got a car." Fezin tells him that he used to have a car, but that he sold it—of course, this medic is lying through his teeth, because when Maigret and Torrence enter the garage, the Citroen is right there, and double-crosser Bill's inert body is splayed across the back seat. Maigret interrogates the not-too-masculine-looking Fezin further, but Fezin, rather nervously, just tries to take himself out of the equation: "These guys are just acquaintances, okay? They don't tell me what they're doing. When I open my house to people who need help, sometimes they're in trouble, but it's none of my business. I have to nurse people, whoever they are, and no matter what they do. It's my job." (This guy is taking his Hippocratic Oath to dramatic new lows! Basically, the not-too-masculine Fezin likes hiding-out tough-looking gangsters because, even though the movie doesn't say it expressly, he's a repressed homosexual who gets his rocks off, ministering to 'rough trade.')

Maigret now asks Charlie what he and the other guys had against their partner, Bill Larner, and Charlie tells him that Larner was a stoolie for the cops. Fezin knows Larner's backstory, too, even though he's just said that the guys are only acquaintances, and that he never asks the people who come to 'crash' with him what lines of work they're in, and he now proceeds to give us some more background on the guy: "Larner had been in France for three years. He was forbidden to return to the United States, because he had skipped his own trial there, for some old crimes which he had committed. He wanted to be forgiven by the U.S. government, and so he became a pigeon for the French cops, thinking that if he helped them out, maybe they would help him get back to America." After his flow of verbiage has ended, Fezin stares at Maigret excitedly, like Maigret's a dominatrix, who's come there to whip the shit out of him, and that he (Fezin) can't wait for the whipping to start! "Will I have big troubles for telling you this, Inspector? Deep inside of me, I've always wished I could have troubles!" (He actually says this!)

At this point, back in Paris, Tony Cicero shows up outside the Hotel Flanders; he's come to shoot Lily, since she knows that his cohorts are the ones who blasted Curtis. Torrence and a bunch of other cops suddenly surround Cicero, who has remained *so* strong, even now, years after his boxing career has ended, that he actually starts karate-chopping the cops, and even shooting at them! (He's hopped-up on something-or-other, and if this movie were made fifteen years later, we'd swear it was PCP.) Finally, though, the cops are able to subdue Cicero, and they push him into a cop car.

Maigret shows up at the Flanders Hotel later that day, when all of the Cicero-inflicted damage has been cleared away, and when he enters the room in which Curtis was supposed to have been staying before he escaped, he's surprised to see Curtis sitting there, side-by-side with Harry MacDonald, Maigret's American pal: As it turns out, Curtis never left the hotel, and MacDonald was hiding him out the whole time, in a different suite. Maigret asks Curtis to tell him why it is that he came to France, and also why Pozzo's men wanted to kill him, but Curtis lets MacDonald answer for him. ("Now, tell me the truth, Harry," Maigret whispers to MacDonald, "I'm tired.") MacDonald reveals to Maigret that Curtis is actually a *Canadian* national whose real name is 'Polaire,' and that Polaire sought refuge in the U.S.—in St. Louis—because in his home-country of Canada, he witnessed a murder which was committed by drug-czar Walter Douglas' gang (as we already know). Curtis, the sole witness, was in danger of being killed, so he escaped to France, and then Douglas, very promptly, sent his best hit-men—Mario Pozzo, Tony Cicero, Charlie Cinglia, and Bill Larner—there, to wipe him out; and while in Paris, Mario opened the Manhattan Bar, as a front for the Douglas Organization's French drug operations.

Curtis tells Maigret and MacDonald that he'd be up for testifying about everything he knows about Walter Douglas, and he next tries to make a deal with MacDonald: "If I testify, you have to give me my freedom back and let me return to America." But MacDonald tells Maigret that Curtis can't testify, because the medical marijuana Maigret found was not Tony's—but his: "Curtis can't testify, because he's crocked!" (Curtis, an old pot-head of a *high* order, was in the Manhattan that night, taking his 'medicine!') Maigret tells Curtis, "If we don't keep you here in France, under police security, Douglas will keep looking for you, whether you testify against him or not." But MacDonald has a different idea: He wants to take Curtis back to the U.S. and place him into the government's Witness Protection Program.

Meanwhile, Tony and Charlie have been apprehended, and they're down at the 10th-District precinct. MacDonald tells Maigret that he's going to have to take the two guys back to the U.S., so that he can stand trial, but Maigret refuses to hand them over: "Forget it, Harry. I'm keeping these two here, in France. They killed someone here, not in the U.S." Even in spite of their bickering, or even because of it, and even though in the end they are still not sure exactly what the hell to do with Curtis, Charlie, and Tony, Maigret and MacDonald part on good terms, and we see that part of their enduring friendship, has always been related to the fact that they have always agreed to disagree.

At the end of *Maigret voit rouge*, Maigret walks away alone since, of course, Jean Gabin must almost always walk away alone, at the end of his films; but this time out, young Torrence

(Marcel Bozzuffi) runs after him, to see if the Inspector wants to join him for a drink at a good bar he knows of on Bayonet Street, but Maigret declines the offer: "Naahh. I'm tired. I'm going to bed." This time out, Maigret got into something too big for him, and nobody actually won.

Maigret voit rouge is the least satisfying of the three Gabin/Maigret efforts, not just because its complicated and hard to follow (like a number of Gabin's other, 1950s' pictures), but also because, in the end, Maigret was unable to solve the crimes which were perpetrated in the film, due to all of the international red tape which was involved. 'On paper,' you can see where the film's producer, Georges Charlot, thought that Simenon's novel of the same name would make a great movie: "Hey! Let's make a cop movie, where the cop can't solve the crime, because there's too much bureaucracy involved!" True, that happens a lot in real life (in fact, it happens most of the time), but *Maigret voit rouge* is a genre picture, and as with any good genre picture, audiences always demand an ending which will wrap the story up in a satisfactory way.

For any younger reader who watches *Maigret voit rouge* and starts wondering aloud, "St. Louis, Missouri, home of organized crime? Are you shitting me?" you might be interested in knowing that St. Louis, back in the 1950s and 1960s, was a Mafia hotbed, and in 1950, the Tennessee-born Senator Estes Kefauver even spearheaded a series of notorious hearings (informally, they were called the Kefauver Hearings), in which he attempted to rid the world of the *Cosa Nostra's* presence in St. Louis, as well as in thirteen other American cities. (Kefauver, additionally, tried to get rid of hot-and-sexy burlesque dancers, as well: Check out director Mary Harron's great 2005 movie, *The Notorious Bettie Page,* in which one of today's great 'everyman' movie stars, David Strathairn, plays the puritanical Tennessee Senator.) In fact, as long as I'm on the subject of crime in St. Louis: On October 30, 2006, a full forty-two years after *Maigret voit rouge* was made, the FBI released data suggesting that St. Louis remains, today in the 21st-century, the most dangerous city in America.

What a Critic Said at the Time: "Veteran actor Jean Gabin lends his implacable presence… some okay fight [scenes], but none of it takes on much life… Ordinary." (*Variety*, 10-2-63 issue. Critic: "Mosk. [George Moskowitz.]" Reviewed in Paris.)

Top and Above: With Alain Delon.

FILM 77

Melodie en sous-sol

France, 1963

(Approximate English Translation: "BASEMENT MELODY") Directed by Henri Verneuil. Produced by Jacques Bar and Jacques Juranville. Screenplay by Michel Audiard, Peter Fernandez, and Albert Simonin. Based Upon the Novel "The Big Grab," by John Trinian. Director of Photography (black and white, scope), Louis Page. Editor, Francois Bonnot. Production Designer, Robert Clavel. (GENRE: ACTION) A CCM/CIPRA/Cite Films Production. Running Time, 1 hour 58 minutes. Released in France by Cipra, on March 19, 1963. Released in United States (NYC) on October 8, 1963, as "ANY NUMBER CAN WIN," by MGM, at 1 hour 43 minutes. Re-released on video in the U.S. as "THE BIG GRAB" (long version) and as "ANY NUMBER CAN WIN" (short version).

"This isn't my world anymore."
— *Gabin's voice-over 'thoughts,' when he gets out of prison after a sixteen-year sentence and is released into a post-War Paris which he can hardly recognize, in "Melodie en sous-sol"*

1963 would bring the world a whiskey-smooth and razor-sharp (don't worry—I'm almost all out of clichés to describe how exciting Jean Gabin movies are) third team-up of Jean Gabin and director Henri Verneuil, *Melodie en sous-sol,* which MGM would release in the U.S., very briefly, as *Any Number Can Win.* In Jean Gabin's second heist flick after *Touchez pas au grisbi,* Gabin's wizened crime boss-character, Charles, has just been released from a sixteen-year jail stretch, and when we first meet him, he's walking through a Paris which he is unable to recognize, because it's teeming with those boxy, new(ish), apartment complexes which had started springing up in Paris after the Second World War. Charles' wife Ginette (Viviane Romance, appearing opposite Gabin, for the first time since they acted together almost thirty years earlier in Julien Duvivier's excellent lottery-ticket comedy, *La Belle equipe*), who's been dutifully awaiting his release for years, is excited to see him, and she's been entertaining a dream for years, as well—that the two of them will be able to buy a quaint little bed-and-breakfast, and retire to the coast. But such plans make no difference to Charles, a guy who, like all good movie gangsters past and present, is never really reformed, and who's much more interested in planning that one, big 'last heist' in which all caper movies must traffic.

This particular one-last-heist will take place at a casino in Cannes and, to that end, Charles hires a similarly-just-out-of-the-slammer 27-year-old, Francis (Alain Delon, the *au courant* French movie heartthrob), to be his partner. Charles tells Francis that, in order to rip off the casino, Francis will have to have to cozy-up to the hot dancers in the casino's burlesque show, since the casino's daily take is always left in the safe, behind the stage. Francis dutifully beds most of the hot dancers, including a blonde who's billed in the show as The Countess (Dora Doll). During the performance, Francis daringly sneaks down the heating vent, and grabs the loot, successfully.

Melodie en sous-sol, which would be released in Britain under the wistfully-charming title *The Big Snatch* (*Any Number Can Win*, as a title, pales by comparison), wouldn't be a proper heist film, if the thieves didn't lose the money directly after they've just acquired it, and knowing this, director Verneuil won't disappoint us: As the cops descend upon the hotel, Francis dumps a suitcase full of money (the loot) into the pool, as he and Charles sit by impassively, on beach chairs, hidden behind cool Ray-Bans, and pretending to be 'average hotel guests,' so as not to arouse any suspicion about themselves. As the suitcase opens up, thousands of franc-notes flower up to the surface, forming a kaleidoscopically-flowery tableau, and this scene is an amazing precursor of the unbridled, 'exploding household items'-climax, which would *turn-on* moviegoers, who saw Antonioni's psychedelic *Zabriskie Point*, seven years after *Melodie en sous-sol*.

Melodie en sous-sol has always been available on U.S. home video. Try to find the now out-of-print VHS version (sometimes, you can find a copy on eBay), in lieu of Image Entertainment's newer DVD version, because the VHS version is longer, by fifteen minutes.

What a Critic Said at the Time: "A slick and suspenseful tale, stunningly played by Jean Gabin and Alain Delon, it has the tangy flavor of the gaming halls [and] the true appearance of dazzling Cannes, [as well as] enough girls in brief bikinis to let you know you're in no other place. From the moment we see Mr. Gabin, we feel that the engineering of the robbery-to-be is in the best of hands, and that is execution will be performed like a symphony. Everybody [in the film's audience] can go home feeling richer for [having just had] such a tingling experience." (New York *Times*, 10-10-63 issue. Critic: Bosley Crowther.)

FILM 78

Monsieur

France/Germany/Italy, 1964

Directed by Jean-Paul Le Chanois. Produced by Raymond Danon. Screenplay by Georges Darrier and Pascal Jardin. Based Upon the Stage Play by Claude Gevel. Director of Photography (black and white), Louis Page. Music by Georges van Parys. Editor, Emma Le Chanois. Costumes by Marie Martine. (GENRE: COMEDY) A Production of Corona Filmproduktion (Germany)/Films Copernic (France)/Zebra Films (Italy)/Sancro Films (Italy)/Corona Films (Germany). Running Time, 1 hour 35 minutes. Released in France on April 2, 1964, by Comacico. Never Released Theatrically In the United States.

"You all thought I was dead, didn't you? Well, that was just the Old Testament.
I am the New Testament!'"
— *Jean Gabin re-emerges, after having faked his own death, in "Monsieur"*

In the 1980s and 1990s (and it still happens) American movie studios, with the emphasis being on Disney, were churning-out all manner of high-concept comedies which were remakes of successful French comedies (*Three Men and a Baby, La Cage Aux Folles, Blame it On the Bellboy, etc*), but not a single Hollywood studio ever entertained the idea of remaking one of movie history's very best mistaken identity farces, director Jean-Paul Le Chanois' fun and always-engaging Gabin comedy, *Monsieur*, which was adapted, in 1964, from Claude Gevil's popular (in France) play.

In 1959, the American counterculture author Terry Southern penned his novel *The Magic Christian*, in which a wealthy industrialist-character uses his wealth to deflate the pretensions of the rich, by playing *merry pranks* on other wealthy people, usually by causing huge, ultra-strange 'scenes,' out in public, and in the France of 1964, director Grangier gave movie screens another rich/fun old prankster, Jean Gabin's sixtysomething, richer-than-God bank owner, and Gabin's character in the film is called, very simply, 'Monsieur.' (Terry Southern was one of the 'ex-pat' American writers who lived, and had his first novels published, in France, in the 1950s, so it's more than likely that *Monsieur's* playwright, Gevil, may have read *The Magic Christian*, and you'll see why I believe that to be true, a few paragraphs down.)

When we first see lonely-looking Monsieur, he's just arrived home to his mansion, after

With Mireille Darc.

having walked his cat, and he tells his dutiful butler, Octave (Max Elder), to "go home and take it easy." Moments later, just as he's settling-in for the night, a striking young blonde, Suzanne (Mireille Darc) knocks on the door: "Don't you recognize me, Monsieur? It's me, Suzanne. I heard your wife died a few days ago, and I just wanted to come over and say how sorry I am." Suzanne is Monsieur's ex-housekeeper, who left his service months ago, for a new job.

Lonely Monsieur is excited to see his former maid, and he invites her in for coffee: "I'm glad you've come to visit, Suzanne, because I have something I'd like to give you." He presents her with an enormous pile of cash, and since he's never given her this much money before, she immediately presumes that he's suicidal: Maybe, now that his much younger wife has died, he doesn't want to live anymore (this is what she's now thinking, anyway), and so he's giving away all of his earthly possessions. "Don't do it, Monsieur," she cries out. "Your wife is not worth killing yourself over! In fact, if you really want to know, the whole time the two of you were married, and I was working for you in your house—she was cheating on you!"

Monsieur doesn't look too upset by Suzanne's sudden revelation, because probably, he knew all about his wife's indiscretions, anyway. When Suzanne worked for Monsieur, there was also a male secretary, Simon, in the household (we won't see him in the film), and Monsieur asks her if Simon knew about his wife's cheating, but she replies that he did not.

Tired of being all alone in his big house, he asks Suzanne if he can spend the night over at her apartment, which he does, although sweetly, it's all very father-daughter between them:

A rare smile.

She even gives him a goofy-looking pair of palm tree-print pajamas, and he never once hits on her. (Suzanne tells Monsieur that the pajamas belong to her sometime-boyfriend, Fernand.)

One thing that always cheers Monsieur up (when he's feelin' down), is when he can play a good prank on somebody, and he thinks that playing one right now will alleviate his boredom, and he knows *exactly* what kind of a prank he wants to play, too:

Monsieur knows that his wife's parents, who are lower-middle-class, and who are also loathsomely opportunistic, are complete money-grubbers. (They wanted their daughter to marry him, so that they could bask in her reflected glory. [Read: Maybe their daughter would share some of her hew husband's wealth with them.]) So he now decides that he's gong to plant a *faux* obituary in the newspaper, as a way of faking his own death. He knows that if his wife's parents think he's dead, they'll try to claim the inheritance which he has left for their daughter, and he just can't wait to get the ball rolling. (In France, just like in the U.S., if the husband has no other relatives, the wife's parents are legally permitted to collect the inheritance.) The obit appears the next day ("BANK OWNER COMMITS SUICIDE, AFTER DEATH OF WIFE"), and Monsieur grins at Suzanne: "You know, this whole 'faking-my-own-death-thing' is a pretty great idea: If I'm dead, there will be no more troubles. And, even better—*no more taxes!*"

Monsieur also slaps together a *faux* funeral for himself and, right on cue, his wife's parents—milquetoast Beau-Pere (in English, 'Father-In-Law') played by Henri Cremieux and Belle-Mere ('Mother-In-Law'), played by Gabrielle Dorziat—arrive at his house, and when they get there, Monsieur's lawyer, Flament (Jean-Paul Moulinot) tells them that, before Monsieur passed, he left his money to the local soccer team, and this news, of course, floors them; in fact, when Beau-Mere hears the news, she's practically on the floor!

Monsieur can't go back to his own house, since he's supposed to be dead, so he continues to hide out at Suzanne's, and this is when Suzanne decides to spring a little surprise on him. "You know my boyfriend, Fernand—the one I told you about? Well, he has two 'associates,' Antoine and Jose, and they're waiting for me downstairs. They think I work for you!" In the year since she's stopped working in Monsieur's household, Suzanne has become a high-end call girl, and Fernand is her pimp! Fernand thinks that Monsieur is a rival mack-daddy, for whom Elizabeth has left his 'stable!'

Monsieur playfully puts on a goofy tie with a picture of a naked lady on it (it's not one of his own [he's too genuinely classy to wear something like that]), relishing the idea of pretending to be a pimp, and he now tells Suzanne to send the two guys upstairs to see him. Antoine (who's played by one of those French actors who's too cool to use their first name, and so he just goes by his last, 'Andrex') and Jose (Jean-Pierre Darras) talk to Monsieur roughly, having no idea that he is really the famous zillionaire bank owner. "You cannot exploit Fernand's children [whores] without buying them from me," Antoine threatens Monsieur. Meanwhile, Jose is standing behind Antoine, pummeling an imaginary Monsieur-head with his fists!

Monsieur, who's now in full-on Pimp Mode, and who is loving every second of his charade, tells them, "Look you guys. I'm not going to do what you say. Suzanne's my bitch now, okay! But I do have this little project you might be interested in, and if you help me, I'll cut you in, fifty percent." The guys are intrigued, and Monsieur tells them to meet him at a local bar that night, at nine-o'-clock.

After the guys leave, Suzanne tells Monsieur that he's welcome to continue staying at her place, although she's going to be going away for a few days. (She doesn't say where but, most probably, some 'john' has purchased a few days worth of her time.) Naturally, Monsieur is sad about it: "I just pretended to be a pimp to get you out of trouble, and now you're leaving?" Monsieur's dedicated driver, Moncorbier (he's played by a character-actor called Pierre Moncorbier, who's using his own real-life surname) now arrives at Suzanne's apartment, and dutifully alerts his boss, "Monsieur, your mother-in-law and father-in-law arrived at your house yesterday. Not only have they moved in [lock, stock, and barrel], but I caught your mother-in-law actually trying to open up your safe!" Monsieur thanks Moncorbier, for giving him the 411.

Later that night, Monsieur meets up with Antoine and Jose at the local watering hole, exactly as planned, and tells them, "The job I want you to do for me has to take place tonight. You're going to help me break into my own house and get my money out of my safe. My in-laws think I'm dead, and they want my money. But if I have to share it, I guess I'd rather share it with you guys—that is, if you'll help me to [retrieve it]." Antoine and Jose ask Monsieur if anybody's living in the house right now, and Monsieur tells them that his in-laws have already moved in, of their own free will. (*Shit!* He can't even throw them out, since he's supposed to be dead!)

That night, Beau-Pere and Belle-Mere are sleeping in Monsieur's royally-appointed bedchamber, and they awaken to the sound of a disturbance which is emanating from somewhere downstairs, and figure that it must be Monsieur's cat: Well, screw cats! It's actually Monsieur himself, his head swathed in a hood (Gabin, in this scene, looks like 'The Original Gangsta Rapper!'), who is breaking into his own safe, and he's being aided and abetted by Antoine and Jose, who stand watch for him as he successfully extricates his cash.

After Belle-Mere hears some more noises, she sends her husband downstairs to see what's happening, and Monsieur and his two helpers hide behind the drapes, to avoid being spotted. Satisfied that there's nobody in the house (he wasn't actually looking that hard), Beau-Pere takes a swig of brandy, and he actually starts talking to the bottle, pretending that the bottle is a woman whom he'd rather be with, than with his shrewish wife! Monsieur replaces the money he's just removed from his safe with a rubber pig-head mask, which is basically a message to whoever opens the safe (especially, to his in-laws!) that they've just been, as we say today in our dumbed-down lexicon, 'punk'd.' (This bit is a direct steal from Terry Southern's 1959 novel, *The Magic Christian,* in which the prank-loving main character actually sends someone a pig head mask, in response to an unwanted party invitation.)

Monsieur now heads back to Suzanne's apartment, where she's sitting with Antoine and Jose. He tells them that, ultimately, his cash supply will be running out (all he has access to is what he had in the safe, which is just a few thousand) and that soon, he'll have to take a regular job, only he has no idea what kind of a position he'd be qualified for. (English teacher? Farmer?) Antoine and Jose are happy that Monsieur has cut them in on the money from the safe so, as a way of returning the favor, they decide to let him in on a little 'inside information' of their own: Antoine tells Monsieur that a rich Parisian family whom he knows about, the Bernadacs, are looking for a new butler, since a friend of Antoine's was the Bernadacs' previous one, but that the guy has just been *shit-canned* for stealing, and apparently, the Bernadacs have lots of expensive jewelry just laying around, all for the taking. Antoine tells Monsieur that the Bernadacs are probably in the market for a dependable (wink!) new butler, and that maybe, Monsieur could telephone the family, and request an interview. Antoine and Jose are all in favor of Monsieur's being in the Bernadacs' household because, if and when they ever choose to rob it, they'll already have an 'inside man' there! Monsieur thinks that this idea sounds even more fun than his other fun/*prank-tastic* ideas. (Weirdly, Antoine and Jose will never rob the Bernadac home at all in this movie, which suggests that either such a sequence was cut out of the finished film, or else it was never filmed at all.)

In the next scene, we finally get to meet the Bernadac family, which is headed-up by its hotel magnate patriarch Edmond, who's played by the fantastic Philippe Noiret. (Noiret, who passed away in November of 2006 was, of course, one of France's best, and most popular movie stars in his own right, and he's known in the United States, especially for his leading role in the Amazing French 1981 *neo-noir,* and Academy Award nominee for Best Foreign-

Language Film in '83, *Coup de torchon*, in which he co-starred alongside Isabelle Huppert, and in which he played a drunken, burned-out cop.) Edmond's wife, the always drunk and, correspondingly, always too-loud Nathalie, is played, and to the hilt, by Berthe Granval. (If this were an American movie, she'd be played by Granval's virtual *doppelganger*, Lee Grant...)

Edmond, when we first see him, is on the phone in his home office, talking to the caterers about what he wants them to prepare for the following week's major dinner party at his home. While he talks, Nathalie is trying to flirt with him, weaving all over the room as she does, but he ignores her, and not because she's obnoxious, but because he'd rather save his *sex chakras* for his hobby: He's always fooling around with his secretary-slash-mistress, Justine (Maryse Martin).

Monsieur now phones-up the Bernadac home, introduces himself (he's made-up a new name for himself—'Georges'), and sets up a meeting between himself and Edmond, and after he hangs up, he suggests to Suzanne that he'd like it a lot if she would consider taking a job at the Bernadacs too, pretending to be his daughter. In effect, Monsieur and Suzanne will be 'father-and-daughter' servants—a butler and a maid. Monsieur orders-up a butler's outfit from a costume shop, and Suzanne, who's tickled by seeing him in it, snuggles up behind him and (sweetly) calls him 'Papa,' which makes him laugh.

When Monsieur and Suzanne arrive at the Bernadacs address, Monsieur is shocked. ("I know this house! I almost bought it four years ago!") The Bernadacs immediately take to this friendly father-daughter team, especially after Monsieur (or 'Georges,' as he's now calling himself) tells the pretentious-acting Nathalie (he instantly pegs her as being the kind of *nouvelle-riche* freak, who loves name-dropping) that he used to be body-servant to the Duke of Westminster. Nathalie's already trying to bond with cute old Georges, telling him that before she was married to Edmond, that she, too, used to 'serve:' "I met my husband when I was a hostess for Air France!" Not only is Nathalie impressed by Georges, but the Bernadacs' teen-aged son, Alain (Heinz Blau), has taken quite the little hankering to Suzanne.

Monsieur and Suzanne take to their work immediately, and they go about their duties with the utmost amount of professionalism, but Edmond's aging mother, who's played grandly by another great 1930s icon of French cinema, Gaby Morlay (Gabin's love interest, 'Marie,' from 1937's *Le Messager*) is a bit suspicious of these new members of the household, and when we first see her, she's confronting her son about them: "This new butler—he's too good. He must be hiding something." Edmond waves his too-suspicious mother off.

A week passes, and it's now dusk: Tonight, the Bernadacs' Big Dinner Party (all mistaken identity comedies have to have one) is happening, and Edmond and Nathalie's teen-aged daughter (and Alain's sister), the relentlessly-sweet-looking Elizabeth (Liselotte Pulver) now enters the kitchen, where she finds Monsieur taking his evening meal alone, at a small card table. She starts flirting with him, and he blushes, "I can't eat while you're teasing me," to which she replies, "I can't help it. You're just so cute! You look like a little Yorkshire!" Right after Elizabeth leaves, and Monsieur lifts the fork to his mouth, Nathalie ('the Mom') next

Serving dinner to Marina Berti, Philippe Noiret, and Liselotte Pulver.

appears, and starts brazenly flirting with him, as well! She's probably been *nipping at the vermouth,* because *she's really turning it on,* but classy Monsieur, who is more hungry than he is horny, thinks that she's behaving inappropriately: "Look, ma'am, I'm hungry," he tells her, "and your presence is making me shy." Now getting a little too close to her butler, Nathalie confesses that she's been drinking too much today (how do you say "duh" in French?!), and mentions that she feels like she's an airplane, and that she's flying! She then stretches out her arms and starts zooming around the room, actually pretending to be a 747, while Gabin just sits there. (Jean Gabin's incredible non-reaction in this scene, which could be his best 'Movie Non-Reaction' ever, is alone worth the price of admission to this movie.) After *mama-san* leaves, sonny-boy Alain then enters the kitchen, to sound Monsieur out on the subject of Suzanne's romantic status. (Is she single? Available?) Alain, like everybody else in his family, is a huge lush, so Monsieur is able to manhandle him out of the kitchen, without breaking a sweat.

 Elizabeth's got a beau, too (kind of), a guy whom her parents have chosen for her, but with whom she's not overly impressed: It's nerdy, bearded Michel (Peter Vogel), a guy who, besides being France's Minister of Trade, is also in charge of many of his own private business ventures, many of which involve the buying and selling of Brazilian wheat, and tonight, Michel will be one of the family's dinner guests at the high-toned dinner party which Edmond had earlier been planning when we saw him on the phone with the caterers. Naturally (nerds have a lot of time on their hands, *especially* the rich ones), he's the first to arrive, and before even greeting Elizabeth, he immediately starts sucking up to Nathalie and

Edmond, his future (he hopes) in-laws, telling them that just today, he has purchased fifty locomotives. When Monsieur enters the room, Michele starts acting condescending toward the butler, telling the Bernadacs, right in front of Monsieur (like he's not even there), "I like your butler! He looks like a painting. He's very distinguished—not primitive, like 'the help' so often are." While Elizabeth may have zero interest in this greaseball (Michel is the spitting image of Michel Simon's Zabel character, from *Le Quai des brumes* [and, just maybe, the character has even been named Michel, in *homage* to Michel Simon]), Nathalie's not to proud to flirt with the guy herself, when her husband Edmond is out of earshot: "My husband treats me like a maid. Not like a woman…"

After the meal, which has gone smoothly, Michel instructs Elizabeth, "Your dad insists that you go up to your room, so that we men can have our cigars," and she's only to happy to oblige: In fact, she sneaks out of her bedroom window, and we know that she's on her way to an assignation with another guy, one whom she actually does like (and probably, one who's closer to her own age).

Back at Monsieur's own mansion, his wife's in-laws, Belle-Mere and Beau-Pere, continue to scheme, now working in collusion with a Private Detective (Jean Lefebvre) who they've hired to help, in investigating how they can secure all of Monsieur's fortune for themselves. "We have to pay a team of scuba-divers to go out and find his body," Belle-Mere opines coldly, "because if there's no body, we're not going to be able to get our daughter's inheritance for four years!" (She has no idea that a small amount of his cash used to be in the house, right in front of them, but that it was replaced by a pig mask. Belle-Mere and Beau-Pere haven't checked the safe yet, or maybe they did, but it was in a scene which was cut out of the finished movie.) "I've already contacted some divers," she continues, "and they want three hundred-thousand francs." Her hubby replies, "That's a lot of money, to pay divers," and the Detective tells them that the fastest way for them to get the money, will be if they can somehow obtain "… a replacement body. [Preferably, that] of a transient—someone who has no papers and no family. And forgive the visual, ma'am, but, it would also be very useful if we could find someone who's been in some kind of a terrible accident, so that nobody will be able to I.D. the face." As greedy Belle-Mere and Beau-Pere listen to this proposition, we can tell that they're taking it very seriously.

Back at the Bernadac residence, a still-tanked-up Nathalie is trying, as usual, to make her husband Edmond notice her ("Are you jealous of Michel? [Her daughter's fiancé.] He likes me, you know!") But Edmond, who learned to ignore his obnoxious wife years ago, doesn't give two shits! Meanwhile, Edmond's elderly Mother is growing even more suspicious of her family's always-too-calm-looking 'butler.'

Meanwhile, somewhere out in the woods, Elizabeth is out on her clandestine date, and she frantically phones Monsieur from a payphone: "Georges! I'm out with a friend, and my car broke down. I need you to come and get me!" She's calling from the local church, where she's sitting-around with her real boyfriend, Jose, who's played by Jean-Pierre Darras. (The two of them have obviously just been enjoying a surreptitious screw, and are now pretending that they've just been 'in church together, the whole time,' so that her parents won't get too mad.) Dutifully, Monsieur picks them up, and even (very quickly, and with little effort) fixes their car on the spot, telling them that "the starter was stuck." (Even though Monsieur is wealthy, this little scene clues us in to the fact that, before he made his millions, he was a working man, and that he isn't above getting his hands dirty. Little scenes like this, in many of the films which Gabin will make when he is older, will reinforce, to his French audience, that Gabin is still the consummate everyman.) Now, Elizabeth can drive home on her own, and nobody will ever know that she was missing. Monsieur smiles, and drives back to the Bernadacs' place alone, in his own vehicle, and it's a very modest car which the Bernadacs have loaned him. (Of course, Monsieur couldn't show up for his butler job driving one of his Rolls-Royces!)

A few days later, the Bernadacs are now having a second dinner party, and this time out, *Guess Who's Coming to Dinner:* It's a Mr. Danoni (Claudio Gora), the Vice President of the bank which Monsieur (whom Danoni believes to be dead) owns! When Monsieur finds out that one of his own underling-execs is coming, he feigns illness and takes to his bed upstairs, so that none of the guests will be able to find him. Very sweetly, however, the Bernadacs have come to love their new butler so much that, one-by-one, each family member comes up to Monsieur's bedroom, during the course of the dinner, to make sure he's feeling okay.

Edmond himself comes up, and talks to Monsieur gently: "Look, Georges, you're a great butler. But what's been going on in the house since you've come has been worrying me: I'm sure that you've noticed strange things going on in the house, as well." (He's referring to the fact that, since Monsieur and Suzanne have arrived, everybody in the Bernadac family is acting—well, for want of a better word—horny!) Monsieur placates his 'boss,' dutifully: "I'm just the butler, sir. I forget all that I see."

Edmond continues: "You know, Georges: My son Alain wants to marry your daughter. And even though I hold the two of you in the highest esteem, I simply can't allow her to marry the daughter of a butler. You know how it is." (Edmond has no idea that Monsieur is richer than he, himself, will ever be!) After Edmond leaves the room, Nathalie enters, because she thinks the two men have been gossiping about her, and after Nathalie leaves, Suzanne enters, and confesses to Monsieur that she's taken a shine to young Alain Bernadac, just as he also has, to her. Monsieur, who's as pragmatic as is any other Jean Gabin Movie Character, now ponders how a 'Suzanne-Alain relationship' could work: "As the daughter of a butler, you can't marry him. But as the daughter of a banker, you could. Maybe I can adopt you." (He's not kidding, either!) She gives him a great big bear-hug.

The next day, Monsieur's lawyer, Flament, arrives at the Bernadacs' residence, and Edmond's elderly Mom can't believe it: "The butler's lawyer is here? Why would a butler have a lawyer? What about the butler's banker—is he coming, too?" In front of the Bernadacs, Flament tells Monsieur, "Sir, your in-laws have discovered a body in the river. Tomorrow morning, they are going to claim it's you, and in the eyes of the world, you will be, officially, dead." Monsieur knows that he's now going to have to open up to this family that's been so nice to him, and to tell all of them the truth about who he really is. When he confesses his true identity to them, which is what he'll now do in this sequence, instead of getting mad at him, they naturally start loving him even more, especially because they're now finding out that he's one of the richest men in France, and so they welcome him with open arms. Alain Bernandac brightens too, because now he can marry Suzanne. Monsieur announces to the family that Suzanne isn't his real daughter, but that he's going to be adopting her effective immediately, so that she, too, will now be an official, card-carrying member of the upper class.

In the film's great final scene, Monsieur heads over to his own mansion with the entire Bernadac family in tow, and Beau-Pere and Belle-Mere freak-out, not believing that he's alive. "You thought I was dead, didn't you? Well, that was the Old Testament. *I am the New Testament!*" Lawyer Flament boots the skeevy in-laws out onto the street, making sure the door isn't hitting their asses on the way out, and now Monsieur, Suzanne, and the Bernadacs can live happily (not to mention, wealthily) ever after.

Monsieur is a very funny and extremely charming French comedy, and in its tone, it's even reminiscent of some of Blake Edwards' better movies. Even though this author totally loathes any and all movie remakes, one feels, while watching *Monsieur*, that it could definitely be remade today by an American studio, because Hollywood studios completely traffic in mistaken identity comedies, and *Monsieur* is not only a smart mistaken identity comedy, but one of the very highest order. Anyway, while we're all sitting back and waiting for the big American remake of *Monsieur*, which will no doubt star Anthony Hopkins or Morgan Freeman in Gabin's role of 'the aging banker, turned-butler,' it's definitely not a bad thing that we'll have to make do with the original, wonderful Jean Gabin version which, hopefully, one day, Americans will get to see for the first time. Presently, it's available on DVD in France, without any English subtitles or dubbing.

What a Critic Said at the Time: "Sleek comedy is tailored for the powerful presence of vet star Jean Gabin… Film is suavely directed, if it lacks the bite to remove its clichéd ring and patronizing air of class relations, and goody-goody aspects of the characters. May be needed family fare in France, but may not do well in the foreign market. It is technically good." (*Variety*, 6-3-64 issue. Critic: "Mosk. [George Moskowitz.]" Reviewed in Paris.)

What Another Critic Said at the Time: "This film is charming, because of Gabin himself. Old-school entertainment and comedy, and great social satire." (*Telerama* [France], 3/5/64 issue. Critic: C.M. Tremois.)

What a Third Critic Said at the Time: "Whether he's playing a banker or a servant, Jean Gabin is always believable…" (*L'Humanite* [France], 4/25/64 issue.)

FILM 79

L'Age ingrat

France, 1964

(Literal English Translation, "THE AWKWARD AGE") Directed by Gilles Grangier. Produced by Fernandel and Jean Gabin. Screenplay by Pascal Jardin. Based Upon a Story by Gilles Grangier (as 'G. Crougere') and Claude Sautet. Director of Photography (black and white, scope), Robert Lefebvre. Music by Georges Delerue. Editor, Jacqueline Sadoul. Production Designer, Jacques Colombier. A GAFER Production. (GENRE: COMEDY) Running Time: 2 hours. Released in France on December 23, 1964, by Comacico. Never Released Theatrically in the United States.

"They're so much alike, sometimes I think he made her himself!"
— *Gabin's wife thinks their daughter is just like him, in "L'Age ingrat"*

Just based on the title alone, you'd think that *L'Age ingrat (The Awkward Age)* might be one of those syrupy/maudlin Rock Hudson-Doris Day comedies, especially since it was made in 1964, which is around the same time that the studios were making all of their goofy Rock-and-Doris pictures. But that couldn't be further from the truth. In spite of the title, *L'Age ingrat* is a laser-sharp comedy about the trials of family-life, and one that's not so different from (although it's *much* smarter than) that big spate of criminally-insipid American comedies about big families which were being churned-out during the same decade (*With Six You Get Eggroll, Cheaper by the Dozen, Yours, Mine, and Ours*); in fact, I would compare *L'Age ingrat* very favorably to that great Peter Falk/Alan Arkin comedy, *The In-Laws* (1979), only *L'Age ingrat* adds those distinctively French elements of 'class' and 'class tolerance' into the mixture. This film would co-star Jean Gabin for the first time in thirty-years with his real life best friend Fernandel, France's all-time-greatest movie comedian. Gabin and the rubber-faced Fernandel had, of course, appeared together before, three decades earlier, in three other pictures—1931's *Paris-Beguin* and *Coeur de Lilas*, and 1932's *Gaietes de l'escadron*—but in those three pictures, both men were only supporting players. Gabin and Fernandel even co-produced *L'Age ingrat* together, as the inaugural effort of their new, jointly-owned film company, GAFER—'GA' for Gabin and 'FER' for Fernandel; GAFER also produced movies in which Gabin and Fernandel starred independently of each other, as well as movies which

With Fernandel, off camera.

featured other stars.

As *L'Age ingrat* opens, a handsome and idealistic young college student, Antoine Lartigue, who's played by Fernandel's real-life son, the 1960s' French singing sensation Frank Fernandel (who even today continues to be a popular vocalist, in his native France), is making a spirited speech to a teeming university crowd, and of course, he's so charismatic, that everybody present loves him to pieces. Antoine's scintillating blonde girlfriend, Marie Malhouin (Marie Dubois), runs up to him at the conclusion of his speech, to tell him that she's just passed her final examinations in science and 'rituals' (that's probably what they call 'comparative religions' courses, in mega-Catholic France), and that therefore, she, just like him, is ready to graduate. "Science and conscience will be the ruin of your soul," the revolutionary-minded Antoine reminds his lady-love, and we can see, from their tender exchange, that he loves her, in spite of how they sometimes agree to disagree. This weekend, Marie and her parents—Marie's dad is the wealthy captain-of-industry, Emile Malhouin (Jean Gabin)—will be taking a family car trip down to the little town of Luc, in the south (it's right on the Mediterranean), to meet fiancé Antoine's family, a family which is rich not in money, but (aww!) in love. Since there's always been a lot of North-*vs.*-South rivalry in France (the southerners think the northerners—the 'Paris People'—are rich, pompous, and pretentious, while the northerners regard the southerners as being hillbillies), we can tell already that the two families will have all manner of unpleasant fun, in insulting the heck out of each other. (And this insulting will be handled with great skill, because *L'Age ingrat* is no ludicrous *Meet the Fockers!*) Antoine now tells Marie excitedly, "I've told my father so much

With Fernandel, on camera.

about you, he feels like he already knows you!"

Jean Gabin's character, Emile Malhouin, is a powerful train magnate, and when we first see him, he's overseeing some business at northern Paris's famous, not to mention famously massive, Gare du Nord train station. Marie (she's the middle child, and Emile additionally has two other daughters: Sophie, the eldest of the three, is played by Nicole Courget, and there's also a younger daughter, Florence, who very obviously is named after Gabin's real-life daughter, and who is played by Christine Simon) comes to visit her dad, and he asks her if she's already received her degree. (Guess he didn't go to the graduation ceremony, or else, maybe there wasn't one.) She starts bringing the concept of marriage up, to him ("Now that I've finished school, I feel that I'm ready for…"), and he interrupts her gently, letting her know that, while he's agreed to go and meet Antoine's family in the south this coming weekend, that he still thinks she's too young to tie the knot: "You know, I waited three years to marry your mom, after we started dating."

Now, director Gilles Grangier cuts to the south, and we get to see the Lartigue family—the comedy relief of the film—which is headed up, of course, by patriarch Adolphe Lartigue (Fernandel). Just as Gabin's Emile Malhouin has a large family full of daughters, so does Adolphe, in the film, have a large family of his own, which is bursting at the seams with sons, and when we're watching the film, we'll see that Gabin's character represents 'reason,' while Fernandel's = 'emotion.' (Fernandel's Adolphe Lartigue-character, in this film, might be called, if you're a Freudian, an 'exploded id,' because, just as with many of Fernandel's other characters in movie comedies, he's a guy who has absolutely no filtering system between his brain and his mouth, and he always says exactly what's on his mind, even when what he's saying is unformed, or when it's 'double-talk,' and even when it just doesn't plain make sense.) Very wryly, all of the Lartigue sons have been directed, by Grangier, to be very 'Fernandel-like,' in that, they too are fast-talking, nonsense-spouting, and rubber-faced.

A portentous sign of things to come, will happen in the very next scene, which is the sequence in which the two future fathers-in-law are speaking on the phone for the first time: Grangier cuts back-and-forth between Gabin and Fernandel, and it's very funny when Fernandel talks in his trademark, mile-a-minute cadence to Gabin; in fact, Fernandel's one-sided conversation is zooming along so quickly, that whenever Grangier shows us Gabin's reaction shot, Gabin is just standing there, holding the receiver about half an inch away from his ear on purpose, because the sound which is coming from the other end is very clearly inducing a total tension headache, and all Gabin can do is to nod, completely stone-faced. (Jean Gabin is the perfect comedy straight-man because, as we'll be seeing throughout the film, he hardly ever reacts at all, no matter how silly Fernandel acts.) Although the Lartigues are not wealthy, as the Malhouins are (Adolphe Lartigue owns a small drug store, and he also rents out paddle boats), they're doing 'okay enough' to employ a housekeeper, a lady who runs around serving dinner to all of Adolphe's sons, who frenetically jockey for her attention, just like crazed brokers on a stock market trading floor.

When patriarch Adolphe joins his family at the table, his wife Eliane (Madeleine Sylvain) is pretty mad at him: "I can't believe you told Mr. Malhouin that we had a big house! Where are we going to fit his entire family?" The smallest son, Max (Georges Rostan), now, instinctively, starts defending his own territory: "They can't sleep in my room, that's for sure!" Adolphe tells his family, "Even though Mr. Malhouin is a technocrat [bad word, in France!], I still think he'll be up for whatever we plan for him."

Later that night, Antoine arrives home with Marie in tow, and here, Adolphe is meeting his future daughter-in-law for the first time. "She's so beautiful," he exclaims, opening his mouth Fernandel-wide. "She's as pretty as a virgin princess. Her skin is so white, but it won't be for long, with the amount of sun we get out here!" At this point, one of the paddle boats which Adolphe rents out to neighboring families (it's one of his side businesses) even starts sinking, with his uptight neighbors, Mr. and Mrs. Corbidas (Jean-Pierre Sardot and Riri Beuf) in it, because he forgot to put the stopper in it, before he rented it out to them. (*Whoops!*) Instead of freaking-out, he smiles and saves face, telling the Corbidases that the reason the little boat is sinking, is because they've rented the boat which he affectionately calls the *Titanic*, and that part of the fun of renting that particular boat, is that it's *supposed* to sink! But *The Sinking Corbidases* aren't buying this jibber-jabber for a second.

Gabin's Emile Malhouin and his wife Francoise (Paulette Dubost, the actress who played the owner of the Hotel Flanders, in *Maigret voit rouge*) are now making preparations for their long car trip, and the only thing Emile likes about the fact that he's going to have to go and meet his in-laws in the south, is that, at the very least, he'll be near the Mediterranean, which he really likes, and which he finds to be extremely relaxing. Emile's youngest daughter,

Florence, wants to take a net along for the trip, so they can all go shrimping, but Emile informs her, very sweetly, that there aren't any shrimp in the south of France.

Like all family road trips, and like all family road-trip movies, the Lartigues' 'Voyage to the Bottom of France' is fraught with all kinds of unexpected elements: For one thing, it takes them a whole day to go from the top of France to the bottom, due to execrable road conditions. (In 1964, there was only one long road which connected the northern part of France to the southern, just like how in the U.S., pre- the interstate highway system, only Route 66 was equipped to propel Americans directly across the length of The Upper 48.) "We could have taken the train from the Place de Concorde," Emile, who's getting sick of driving, mumbles tiredly at his family—plus, it's summertime, and this is before automobile air conditioning made it to France, and the Malhouins look like they're turning into summer sausages! Emile wishes that he could instead be taking his family to St. Tropez, the trendier part of the south.

Eventually, night falls (as it must), and Adolphe and his wife Eliane are waiting for the Malhouin family to show up, and it's starting to become very late. Eliane wonders if they got lost, and Adolphe decides he'll put up some signs, so that the Malhouins will know when they're getting close. ("Parisians are stupid," Eliane tells her husband. "They always need a lot of signs!")

Finally, after a whole day of driving, the Malhouin family arrives *chez* Lartigue: "Lartigue, it's me!" the overly-demonstrative Adolphe grins, running up to hug his exhausted future-brother-in-law. Adolphe helps Emile to park in his garage, and the space is so small that, in order to squeeze his car in, Emile must first back into the neighbor's garage, and of course (by mistake, because he's overtired), he runs over the neighbor's bicycle—and not just any neighbors either, but The Testy Corbidases, the family who sunk in Adolphe's boat, in that earlier sequence. "Your bicycle shouldn't have been there," Adolphe screams at Mr. Corbidas, shaking his fist; he knows he's totally in-the-wrong, but he's going by that old adage, which is, as we all know (especially if we live in Paris or New York), that 'the loudest person wins!' After the Corbidases beg-off, friendly Adolphe can't resist giving Emile another great big hug, and greeting him with a plaintive cry of, "Hello, my new step-brother!" "I'm not your step-brother," the dog-tired and bulldog-faced Emile reminds him, but Adolphe means to break down Emile's steely Gabin-Defenses, and as quickly as he can: "Of course we're brothers now. When your kids get married, the fathers become brothers!" (Emile looks like he'd rather be anywhere but here, and Jean Gabin's priceless non-expression in this scene is as on-the-money as usual.) Adolphe next pinches Emile's cheeks (Gabin's really doing a slow burn, now), and tries to compliment him: "Don't you like me? I am young, but even with your silver hair, you are younger than me." Finally, Emile bursts out laughing, in spite of himself. The two new fathers-in-law both like each other, in spite of the fact that one is a rubber-faced, too-demonstrative comedian, and the other is Jean Gabin.

The two families are soon sitting down to a very late dinner. Emile, who's exhausted from the long drive, mixes up the names of Adolphe's sons, and Adolphe gently corrects him:

"That's not Jules, that's Max. He looks like Jules, but he's not." Emile points out to Adolphe that in his opinion, his (Adolphe's) sons don't look like him, at all. (Adolphe's sons are all handsome, whereas Adolphe himself is... well, he's Fernandel!) "You're right," Adolphe tells his new best-buddy, nonsensically, "they don't look like me. It's because my uncle was a Swede." The two dads spend a few minutes learning all of their kids' names, but Adolphe isn't too worried about it, and he now claims, "By the time Antoine and Marie get married, we'll know who everybody is. Don't you worry!" Adolphe decides to start talking about when he was young, and about how he met Eliane, and he tells Emile, with his omnipresently-warming Fernandel Smile, that when it came time for him to ask Eliane's father for his daughter's hand in marriage, that Eliane's spendthrift dad told him, "You can marry my daughter, if you sell me some items cheaply!" Emile, trying to open up a bit (inasmuch as Jean Gabin ever can), says that when he asked his own wife Francoise to marry him, they were listening to a song with a girl's name in the title, but that he can't remember the name of the song. ("It's on the tip of my tongue, but I just can't remember what it was called.")

Adolphe next asks Emile what astrological sign he was born under, and he's happy when both men turn out to be Tauruses: "We were both born under the sign of the bull. We're going to be great friends!" (In real life, both Jean Gabin and Fernandel were strong-personalitied Tauruses, but anybody who's successful in the *uber-creepy* movie business has to have a strong personality!) After dinner, Emile gets up from the table and, very promptly, trips over a loose floorboard. Adolphe apologizes, and then changes the subject, by talking about what the weekend's sleeping situation will be. "I brought in a few cots for your family, which I bought from the American war surplus store. You will fall asleep fast, especially because we're so near to the ocean!"

After the evening meal, the young, 'almost-married' couple, Antoine and Marie, is sitting on the beach, holding hands, and this scene is shot 'day-for-night' (or '*nuit-americaine*'), meaning that it's supposed to take place at night, but was actually photographed during the day, so that we're seeing daytime shadows stretching across what is supposed to be the nightscape. Back at the Lartigue residence, meanwhile, the always silly and never-tired Adolphe wakes Emile from a deep sleep at 3:00 a.m., just to tell him the name of the girl from the song which Emile was unable to remember at dinner time! Pleased with himself, Adolphe innocently grins, "Now, you can sleep better, because I told you." (The name of the song, and the woman which it's about, are both "Germaine.") After Adolphe leaves the room, Emile is unable to fall back to sleep and, hilariously, he starts calling his wife Francoise 'Mommy' (Ronald Reagan's nickname for Nancy!), actually moaning, "*Mommy, I'm thirrrrsty,*" and it's hysterical to see Jean Gabin, in total deadpan, referring to his wife as 'mommy.' Adolphe goes back into his own bedroom and delusionally tells his own wife, "I really must have made Emile happy when I woke him up to tell him the name of that song!"

Since he can't fall back to sleep, Emile now decides to get a glass of water from the sink, but the sink's ancient pipes make some of the scariest sounds this side of any of your favorite 'Halloween Horror Sounds' record. When Emile finally climbs back into bed, of course (and right on cue), the not-so-whispering wind causes the shutters to open and close rather noisily, and just when Emile solves that problem and climbs back into bed, he suddenly hears a loud mosquito buzzing around his head. He grimaces as he tries to catch the little creature, and (*klunk!*), he tumbles right out of bed, and onto the floor.

In the morning, Emile awakens, having finally managed a bit of sleep (about five minutes worth), and he asks his dutiful wife Francoise to scratch his back. Meanwhile, Adolphe and his wife are in the kitchen, preparing breakfast for the two assembled families: "I should have told them 7:30 instead of 8:00, for breakfast," Adolphe muses. "Tomorrow, I'll tell them 7:30!" Eliane offers her husband coffee, and he replies, "No, thanks. If I start drinking coffee now, I'll be really nervous," which is hysterical because, next to the American comedian Sid Caesar, and the Mexican comic Cantinflas (and that mustached-guy from those American-made Federal Express commercials, back in the '80s), Fernandel was definitely the fastest-talking comedian in entertainment history. Meanwhile, Emile's smallest girl, little Florence, is now having a little freak-out of her own, because she can't find the bathroom, and a very funny sequence ensues next, in which two entire families are waiting in line for the use of the Lartigue home's sole 'W.C.'

After breakfast, the two families venture out onto Adolphe's paddle boats, and everybody starts chugging-down Pastis, France's great licorice-flavored aperitif. Adolphe and Emile start sharing their individual business philosophies, and Adolphe, who owns his one small store/pharmacy, and his equally small paddle-boat business, tells Emile, "I'd rather make a little money on a lot of little deals, than to make a lot of money on one big deal." Adolphe clearly doesn't have the stomach for high-finance, like his counterpart from the north, Emile, does, and he brags that, during the long hot summers, he does a booming business on suntan oils: "People get burned… and they need it!"

Adolphe drives Emile over to his store to show it off to him, but Emile would rather wait in the car expressionlessly, while Adolphe is conducting business with a rather gormless-looking client, a guy who's come to pick up some back-ordered sundries. "All of my merchandise comes with the Lartigue guarantee," Adolphe grins at the guy who, after additionally buying some long-playing records and a radio, marches happily down the street with his armful of exciting new purchases. After Emile checks out Adolphe's store, our two new brothers-in-law start their long drive back to the Lartigue residence in which, meanwhile, the wives are chirping away happily together, in the kitchen: Eliane Lartigue is telling Francoise Malhouin, "Your daughter Marie is so much like your husband." Malouin's wife agrees, delivering one of the funniest comedy lines in Gabin-Movie History: "He's so much like her, sometimes I think he made her himself!"

When we cut back to Emile and Adolphe, they've been driving for a couple of hours. Emile is sick and tired, and not only of the heat, but also of Adolphe's ever-flapping gums. (This freakin' guy never stops talking!) And then, suddenly (nightmare-of-nightmares, for Emile), the car runs out of gas. Emile isn't going to be quiet and respectful toward his host anymore, and we can definitely feel a Gabin-Outburst coming on. Adolphe tries to humor

Emile, with a shrugging (and smiling, and boyishly-coy) apology: "*Aaayy*, my car is difficult. What can I say? My son must have taken some gas out, to use in his motorcycle." Emile can't figure out why Adolphe doesn't keep a reserve in his trunk, and Adolphe replies that he'd never do that, because "… it might spill." (!) Well, this is the straw that breaks the camel's back: Emile can't take it anymore, and he now screams out, with a Mighty Jean Gabin Cry of "*J'en ai marre!*" ("I'm sick of it!")

> ADOLPHE: You're sick of me?
> EMILE: I'm sick of you running out of gas! And I didn't sleep all night!
> ADOLPHE: Why didn't you tell me? Anyway, you just relax. I'm going for a long [!] walk to get some gas. You just stay here—okay, brother?!

Great! Now, Emile's going to be stranded in a sweltering car for (possibly) hours, while this moron goes to scrounge up some petrol. As Adolphe is about to walk away, leaving Emile to fend for himself in the Hot, Hot, Heat (remember that Candian rock band?), a truck drives up, but the Driver, who's played by Andrex (one of the two pimps from Gabin's previous comedy, *Monsieur*) isn't coming to rescue the guys, but only to screw with them: "Hey, Lartigue," the guy chuckles, "Don't tell me you ran out of gas *again!* Hey, is that Parisian guy your brother?" The Driver can tell Emile is a snooty Parisian just by looking at him, even though Jean Gabin looks more dour than he does snooty, and when the truckdriver zooms away without even having offered them a lift, Emile finally blows his stack, calling Adolphe an idiot, right to his face.

Back at home, the two wives are now setting the dinner table and wondering aloud about what's taking their men so long to get back. "We're going to eat before daddy gets home," Eliane tells the kids of the two assembled families, who are so hungry, they look like a UNICEF commercial. (All that's missing, are flies buzzing around their heads.) But Emile and Adolphe forgot to come home, not because they're still fighting, but because they've buried the hatchet, and have gone off to get drunk together!

Emile and Adolphe are, when we next see them, in a local bar, boozing it up and taking the piss out of each other, and even the normally nice Adolphe is getting some good cracks in, at Emile's expense: "You Parisians had umbrellas instead of guns, during the War!" Emile's sleepy-eyed retort is, "Here, in the south, everything makes you sleepy. In the north, you can smell the ocean, but here, although you're closer to the ocean—nothing!" At that moment, Emile and Adolphe's two about-to-be-married kids enter the bar, needing to borrow the car keys from 'Big Daddy' Adolphe.

The two young lovers linger in the background, while their fathers continue to argue. Antoine turns on a jukebox to some rock-and-roll (which the French, in the sixties, used to call 'Ye-Ye Music,' since it sounded to them, like 'yeah, yeah, yeah'). Finally, the two older men take a hike, leaving the kids to do whatever kids do, when they're surrounded by jukeboxes and hard liquor. (Ask today's notorious independent filmmaker Larry Clark what kids do

"I know the name of that song!"

when they're all alone; oh, yeah, he knows!)

At that moment, another young guy enters the bar: It's Marie's old boyfriend, Charles-Edouard (Claude Mann), a preppy-looking guy with a serious chip on his shoulder, and he is of course completely jealous of, and angry about, Marie's new fiancé. When Marie tells Charles-Edouard that Antoine is the man she's going to marry, Charles-Edouard storms away, and since Antoine's never met, or even heard of, Charles-Edouard before, he has no idea that this guy is his fiancée's 'ex.' Marie then illuminates Antoine on the subject, and she does it more than a bit coquettishly: "That's Charles-Edouard. He was in love with me, once." Antoine now starts getting a bit mad and jealous himself, but Marie tells him not to be immature: "Oh, Antoine! You know there's never been any other boy! Just you!" At this point, other young guys start pouring into the bar too, and clearly, they too all know Marie, because they're Charlie's friends. One of Charles-Edouard's pals, Julien (Jean-Pierre Sardot) asks Marie to dance, and she does. Meanwhile, Charles-Edouard comes back and plops down right next to Antoine, in Marie's vacant chair, and he starts staring Antoine down, clearly looking to do a little Kung-Fu Fighting: "You took my Marie and you won't let me buy you a drink? That's very rude of you, you know." Antoine and Charles-Edouard then start going at it, *mano-a-mano,* and within seconds, of course, everyone in the bar has gotten sucked into the fight, which now resembles a whirling eddy of testosterone (and of course, the fight is underscored by more loud 'ye-ye' music, which surges forth from the juke, at top-levels).

Come the next morning, and director Grangier relaxes the narrative a bit, now treating us to a nice little slice-of-life moment: Emile is teaching Adolphe's smallest son Max how to fix something, and guess what Antoine is doing at the same time: Is he with Marie? *Nope!* Even though he's going to be marrying her soon, he's still got other girls interested in him and *vice-versa,* and since he's not married yet, he's already (presumably) sneaked off to spend the day with one of them—his ex-girlfriend, Juliette, who we won't see in the movie, but whom we will just hear about. (He's probably 'seeing' Juliette today, just to get back at Marie for throwing him to the lions the previous night, even if she didn't mean to do it.) Adolphe's little son Max (kids are like tape recorders—they hear something juicy, and they've just got to repeat it back) has overheard his big brother Antoine on the phone with Juliette, and now, when Adolphe joins Emile and Max in the room, the small boy reports the info he's heard to the two dads, because he's too young to figure out that both of them, upon hearing this news, will majorly freak. Upon hearing of this unplanned new development, Adolphe and Emile are suddenly at each other's throats—two *Grumpy Old Men* on a rampage! "If your bitch-of-a-daughter didn't come along," Adolphe, with a level of vitriol that is extremely uncharacteristic of the sweet-natured Fernandel, spits at Emile, "Antoine would have married his old girlfriend, Juliette. If my son has left your daughter, then she must have been horrible to him!" Emile counters that his daughter is 'sensitive,' and "… would never cheat—unlike how your son happens to be cheating right now!" During this *contretemps,* Marie enters the kitchen, and she now starts clearing-up the whole situation for the two dads, *vis-a-vis* what went down at the bar the previous night: "My ex-boyfriend Charles was there, and Antoine was mean to him." Adolphe is now taking his son's side, even though Antoine isn't present: "If my son went to Marseilles to see his old girlfriend, it was probably a good thing!" Now the fight escalates, and the two men are continuing to use their verbal Weapons of Mass Destruction on each other: "Your son is making my daughter unhappy, and I don't like it," Emile yells, continuing, "My daughter is too good for your son!" Adolphe is pissed: "Good? Good? Oh, no, your daughter's not 'good!' She's a bitch!" And while all of this fighting is going on, we're now about to get a nice surprise: We see that Adolphe didn't go off to be with Juliette, at all. (He thought about it, but didn't do it.) Turns out, he really just drove to Marseilles to be alone with his thoughts, since the whole bar incident made him feel really uncomfortable.

Wanting to get away from 'The Big Adolphe-*vs.*-Emile Blow-Out,' Emile's wife Francoise now decides to pack up her daughters, and to get the hell out of Dodge by train, and she's even found somewhere a little more relaxing for herself and her daughters to vacation for a few days—a small town which is due north of Luc, and which is also on the way back home to Paris. Marie, who's sick of her dad's fighting with Antoine's dad, even tries running away on her own, but she doesn't make it too far from the Lartigues' street, because Emile gets in his own car and tries to pick her up and calm her down, but she escapes from his car, and tries to catch a bus. Marie feels awful about what happened the previous night, and as she tells her dad tearfully, "It's my fault that Antoine is gone. I pushed him into going off with that other girl." In this movie, as in other French movies in which the guy in the relationship is cheating, the ever-faithful woman always believes that his straying was her own fault, because she is sexually inadequate! (That would never fly in an American movie. In American movies, just like in American Life, it's always 'the man's fault' when the relationship doesn't work out.) Anyway, Emile is finally successful in cajoling Marie back into his car.

Antoine has returned home now, and his dad Adolphe tells him that father-and-daughter Malhouin have already returned to Paris together, and Antoine just shakes his head: "We're a couple and we had a fight," he theorizes. "She shouldn't have taken it so seriously." Adolphe next imparts some paternal wisdom to Antoine: "In all of the years we've been married, your mother and I have never had a fight. You're young, so you haven't learned how to keep the peace in a relationship yet. Your mother and I respect each other." What Adolphe is telling Antoine here, runs directly counter to the whole 'Emile and Francoise Malhouin marriage:' Francoise told Eliane, earlier in the picture, when the two women were talking together in the kitchen, that she very often cowers in front of her controlling husband.

Adolphe now confesses that he's at fault, too, for the Malhouins' departure: "Mr. Malhouin and I got a little upset with each other. I called Marie a tramp—and so, I'm afraid to tell you, I guess your wedding is off." Antoine bursts out of the room, almost in tears and, later that same day, Adolphe rationalizes to his wife that Antoine will soon forget about Marie—that Antoine's only twenty-four, and that he will, no doubt, meet somebody else.

Now, Antoine has left the house as well, and we can guess that he's probably gone to Paris to reclaim his lady-love, and to apologize to her for his behavior (*a la*, when Dustin Hoffman's obnoxious character raced to Berkeley to re-claim his lady-love, Katharine Ross, in *The Graduate*, even though *L'Age ingrat* came first)! Eliane Lartigue is a very smart lady though, and she now tells her husband Adolphe that she'd like him to go to Paris to find their son, so that Adolphe can, as she puts it, "make Antoine feel better."

In the next scene, Emile and Marie arrive home, to the spectacular Malhouin mansion. Emile feels badly about how he's been acting toward his daughter, and tells her that the two of them should have a little 'father-daughter time,' just like they used to have, back when she was a little girl. She's a little mad (okay, she's more than a little mad) at her dad, but decides to help him cook dinner together, anyway. (Tonight's Menu: Lobster!)

Father and daughter, very sweetly, braise the crustacean together. (What's so funny? Sometimes, 'braise the crustacean' just means 'braise the crustacean!') "Remember," he smiles, "how we did this together once before, when you were little? When you had the mumps?" He picks this moment to tell her, too, very sweetly, that she's his "favorite kid," which is probably true anyway, because Marie's the only one of Emile's daughters with whom we'll see him interacting in the movie; but she still feels some residual resentment toward him, based upon the recent unpleasantness, telling him, "You're over fifty, dad. You'll never be able to understand me!" Emile knows that she'll get over whatever she's feeling, and so he does what any good father would do, in such a situation: Rather than stoking the coals of anger further by arguing back, he just nods silently.

And now, "Undercover of the Night" (per Messrs. Jagger and Richards), Fernandel's

334 | **THE FILMS** CYCLE FIVE

Adolphe, the consummate Southern Man (*per* Neil Young) arrives in Paris, and his first stop is a hotel, where he knows Antoine has sometimes stayed in the past with Marie. Adolphe asks the Desk Clerk (Max Amyl) if his son has been there lately, and the clerk, a friendly guy who knows Antoine but who hasn't seen him lately, gives him the old '*negatory, good buddy*' bit. Adolphe wants a room for himself, but the guy warns him against it: "You don't wanna stay here, pal. It's mostly young kids, and even worse—tourists!"

Back at the Malhouin home, dinner's ready, and Emile looks around for Marie ("Are you upstairs, my daughter?"), but she's sneaked out of the house, so Emile just Gabin-Shrugs resignedly, and sits down to eat alone. Simultaneously, in another part of the city, Adolphe Lartigue is now sitting on a bus bench, unable to locate his own (adult) kid, and then after director Gilles Grangier has given us this shot, he next cuts back to the Malhouin residence, where Emile is sitting alone, as well: It's now 9:25 p.m., and he's starting to get concerned about Marie, but he remains calm, first calling the cab company which he knows Marie sometimes uses. ("Hello, Beaujolais Cabs? Have you seen my daughter?") He also calls the shops which his daughter frequents, as well as a bakery which he knows she likes. ("Hello, it's Mr. Malhouin. Have you seen my daughter?") All of the shopkeepers in Paris know the prominent Emile Malhouin and his family very well, but none of them has seen Marie tonight.

And then, at the Malhouin house—*ring-a-ding-ding: It's the doorbell, baby!* Emile thinks it's going to be his daughter, but guess again! It's Adolphe Lartigue, and he's right there on Emile's doorstep! "Antoine has been gone for three days," Adolphe tells Emile, looking more than a bit distraught. "Marie is gone, too," Emile frowns. "She left a few hours ago." The two men pace around together, waiting for news of their kids, and surprise: We now cut to a local Paris hotel (to a different hotel) where Marie and Antoine are in bed together. *Yeppers*, while their fathers were worrying about them, the two young lovebirds have been away together, engaging in a soul-satisfying bout of 'make-up sex.'

Freshly-fucked, Marie now phones-up her dad. First, Emile screams at her ("Where are you?!"), but then, on a dime, he becomes gentle and understanding, not wanting to rock the boat any more than it's already been rocked: "Okay, my big girl. Whenever you want to come back, it's fine with me." Emile, who is relieved, tells Adolphe that he doesn't have to worry anymore, because he's just received confirmation that their kids are together. "I like this better," Adolphe smiles, his wide-mouthed Fernandel-Grin plastered all the way across his face. And when Adolphe sees the delicious 'lobster-for-two' which Emile has prepared, he mischievously inquires of his host, "Shouldn't we eat?" The two men dine together and now, for the first time, they're enjoying real camaraderie. "The only problem we might have now," Emile smiles (the wine they're drinking is helping immeasurably), "is that the kids might not want to get married right away." And it is in this sequence where we learn that Adolphe knows something that Emile doesn't: "Oh, I don't know about that, my friend. You know: We might even be grandparents really soon!"

At the end of the picture, now the best of friends, and probably now, also 'the best of fathers-in-law' (we didn't see it, but we can guess that the Marie/Antoine nuptials have already happened), Adolphe and Emile sit, side-by-side, in one of Adolphe's paddle-boats (don't worry—not the *'Titanic!'*), happily paddling away into the horizon, two legends of French cinema enjoying a lazy, sunny Sunday afternoon together. If the marriage between Marie and Antoine doesn't endure, we can tell that the great friendship between Emile Malhouin and Adolphe Lartigue will.

Yet another great Jean Gabin comedy, *L'Age ingrat* is based upon a story idea by the great film director Claude Sautet, who never directed Gabin, but who definitely remains one of France's greats: Sautet is known in the U.S. for five of his films—*Classe tous risques* (1959); *Borsalino* (1970); *Cesar et Rosalie* (1972); *Vincent, Francois, Paul et les autres* (1974); and *Nelly et Mr. Arnaud* (1995)—and he made great movies, in every conceivable genre, from gangster pictures, to Hitchcockian thrillers, to warm, romantic comedies. *L'Age ingrat* has never been seen in American cinemas or on American home video, and it's too bad, because in this author's opinion, Americans would take its very sweet story to heart, and would make it a perennial t.v. favorite, along the lines of Frank Capra's *It's a Wonderful Life*.

What a Critic Said at the Time: "Gabin gets his inevitable angry scene [and] Fernandel is his usual, big-talking self…" (*Variety*, 1-27-65 issue. Critic: "Mosk. [George Moskowitz.]" Reviewed in Paris.)

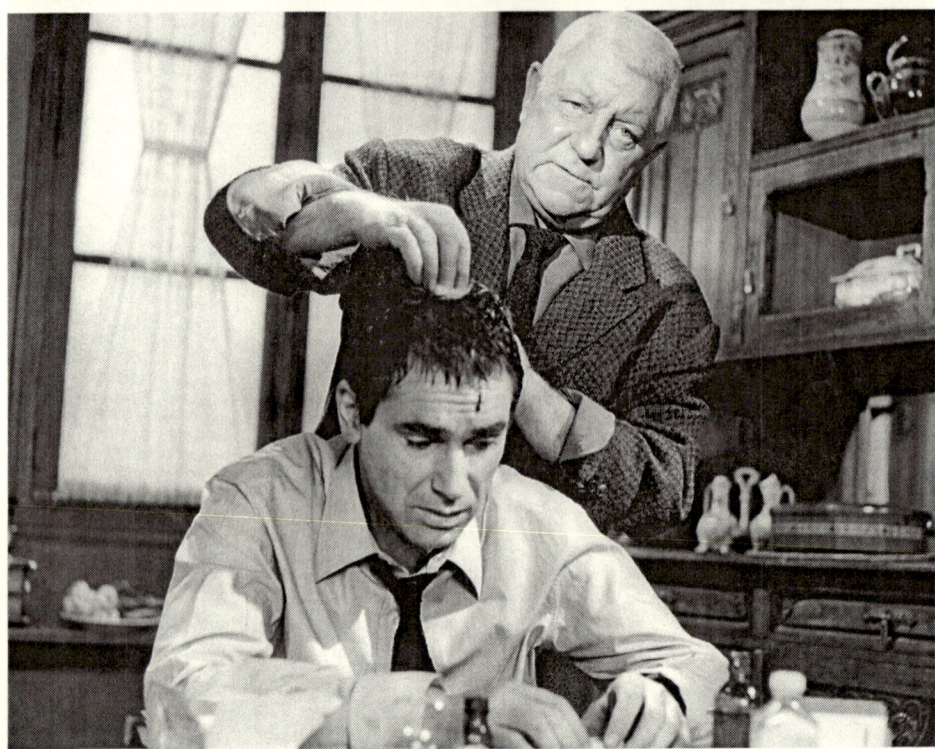

Top: With Lilli Palmer. *Above:* With Robert Hossein.

FILM 80

Le Tonnerre de Dieu

France/Germany/Italy, 1965

(Literal English Translation: "THE THUNDER OF GOD") Directed by Denys de La Patelliere. Produced by Raymond Danon and Maurice Jacquin. Screenplay by Denys de La Patelliere and Pascal Jardin. Based Upon the Novel "Qui m'emporte," by Bernard Clavel. Director of Photography (black and white, scope), Walter Wottitz. Editor, Claude Durand. Music by Georges Garaventz. Production Designer, Robert Clavel. (GENRE: COMEDY). A Production of Fida Cinematografica (Italy), Films Copernic (France) and Gloria-Film GmbH (Germany). Running Time, 1 hour 30 minutes. Released in France on September 8, 1965, by Films Copernic. Released in Great Britain with English subtitles as "GOD'S THUNDER." Never Released Theatrically in the United States.

"Why should I believe in God? I believe in people. Isn't that enough?"
— *Gabin tells a local Priest his feelings on religion, in "Le Tonnerre de Dieu"*

Le Tonnerre de Dieu is one of those excellent widescreen comedies which Jean Gabin made plenty of in the sixties, the kind in which the normally quiet, stonefaced Gabin, whom we know from his scores of serious dramatic films, has been replaced by a happy, smiling, and even *whimsical* Gabin. Shamefully never released in the United States (so what else is new?), this very memorable picture shares a plethora of very respectable similarities to that other great widescreen Gabin comedy which was made five years earlier, Henri Verneuil's *Un singe en hiver:* Just as in Verneuil's picture, here, too, 'Our J.G.' is a mega-likable drunk who becomes loud, boisterous and full of *faux*-heroic stories about himself, while under the influence of Daddy Liquor. Besides being a comedy, *Le Tonnerre de Dieu* also happens to be a Christ parable: While Gabin never played Jesus in any of his films (although he *did* play Pilate thirty years earlier, in Duvivier's *Golgotha*), his character here is a wealthy old eccentric who saves prostitutes, preaches the ultimate goodness of people, and is married to a strong older woman named Mary, who's more like his mother than his wife.

The picture sets its scene in a Frenchly-iconic local bar: Gabin's character, Leandre Brassac, is so toasty, that he's bragging very lustily about old taxes which he's never paid (he just didn't feel like paying them!) and about old wars which he claims to have fought in, even though he really didn't. In a moment of drunken surrealism, he even starts comparing himself to an old car that's still running smoothly, even though it might have a few miles on it.

Every bar in a French movie has *that one hot prostitute*—you know, the one in 'the room upstairs.' In this case, we've got cute-as-a-button Simone (Michele Mercier), whom we first meet when she floats downstairs, leaving her 'trick room,' with her schnauzer in tow. Oily Marcel (Robert Hossein, our favorite old-lady-killer from *Crime et chaitment*) is there, too; Marcel is Simone's pimp, and old, weather-beaten Leandre isn't afraid of him—he even calls the younger guy '*Le Petit Voyou*' ('Little No Good'), right to his face. While Leandre is sixty years old, he's still a man—he's still 'Le Gabin'—and so he buys a week's worth of Simone's time, from Marcel. The customers, of course, all stop what they're doing and marvel at the fact that this older guy is about to go to hog-heaven with a hot young thing, and ultra-confident Leandre cares not a whit about what they think of him: He confidently lifts up Simone's schnauzer and grimaces at the bar's besotted *looky-loos:* "What the hell is everybody staring at? I'm just taking the dog to the countryside to see flowers. Is that okay with everybody?!" As Leandre, Simone, and Schnauzer weave out of the bar, Marcel whispers to the Bartender (Nino Vingelli), *re:* Leandre, "The number of idiots in here is infinite," and after Leandre has left, the bar's assembled clientele all discuss him, giving us his backstory: Leandre's father was one of France's most prominent wine-grape growers as well as a horse-and-cow veterinarian, and Leandre, himself, although he inherited the family wealth and doesn't *have* to work, is a veterinarian in his own right (dogs only), and also a notary! He's more well-known, though, for picking up the occasional prostitute and taking her back to his home for a carefree weekend, to show her that she's a valuable person who really counts in this life. He never hits on any of these ladies, though: He just pampers them with good food, drink, rest, and sunshine, like a father (kind of!), giving them forty-eight-hour passes from the horror of their daily lives. (Leandre actually seems more interested in Simone's schnauzer, than he is in Simone.)

When we next see Leandre and Simone, the two of them are riding the public bus together. "I'm taking you to my place in the country," he brags sweetly to her, "to the country of Bluebeard." We can tell that she really likes him, because she tells him that he's "not so old," but he shrugs her compliment off, saying that, in fact, he's *so old,* that he was actually a friend of Joan of Arc's! Fun-loving Leandre now even decides to introduce Simone to his favorite game: Each time the bus makes one of its many extended stops, on its way to Leandre's estate, the two of them will have to get out, run into whatever local bar is around, and take a drink.

On their first stop of the evening, they head into a small bar, where they run into a brandy-sipping Priest (played by Louis Arbessier) who happens to be an old friend of Leandre's: "Hi, Priest!" Leandre grins cheerfully, hoisting the bottle of hard liquor that he's just purchased. "Want a drop?" The Priest, who's a very funny guy, is always ready to *give Leandre shit:* "Still angry with God, Leandre?" Leandre waves him off with a polite Gabin-Shrug: "God? Why should I believe in God? I believe in people! Isn't that enough?" Even though Leandre is seemingly making a very anti-religious statement, it's really a very affirmative thing for him to be saying (it's definitely in keeping with the tone of this consistently joyous and uplifting film), and Leandre really lives by his maxim, because he helps everybody he meets. Leandre continues, "Why should we talk about God? Let's talk about the Bomb! When I look in the Manger, I don't see Jesus. Do you know what I see? I see the thirty-five million who died in the Second World War! And I see the two hundred million who will die in the next war." In this nuclear-age/post-Hiroshima movie, Leandre's definitely anticipating (as we all are!) 'the big blast.' The Priest can't even argue with him, since he's got to tow the Vatican's 'company line,' so he just smiles at Andre and says, "You're not optimistic enough, my son."

Leandre, a polite and always happy-go-lucky guy, next apologizes to the cleric for bumming him-out: "Look, I say a lot of crazy stuff when I'm drunk. Don't pay any attention." This makes the Priest's day: "A few more drinks, and you'll believe in God!" Simone's taking this all in, with a smile: She definitely digs being around Leandre, and loves the fact that he's taking her seriously, and that, in other words, she's not just a piece of meat to him. On the way out of the bar, she tells him that she thinks it's "nice to hear people talk, and to have a genuine conversation about the world" because, no doubt, when she usually hears men, they're just grunting! Simone, in spite of her profession, is a genuine innocent with a good soul, and she really cherishes the times when she can just be around 'real' (read: non-horny) people.

A few stops later, the bus comes to a small village, where Leandre had parked his old Rolls-Royce earlier in the day; he and Simone pick the vehicle up and drive the rest of the way over to Leandre's opulent home, which doubles as a horse-and-cow farm.

Charmingly, when Leandre arrives home, all of his four-legged-friends (he owns a lot of dogs) are out in the barn, barking with excitement because he's home. When Simone and Leandre get to the front of the house, she sees only a tiny 'doggy door,' and he tells her, with a completely straight face, "My house has only small doors. You have to be on all fours to get in—and you'll need a tube of Vaseline to get out!" He's not saying this in a sexual way, though—he's just having her on. She actually believes, for a minute, that she's expected to enter the house through this tiny slot, but then figures out that good-natured kidding is a central part of his character.

Entering the house, which is just as opulent on the inside as it is on the outside, we see that Leandre has many dogs of his own, to go with the cows and the horses. He's also got a wife, Mary, who's played by (the late, great) Lilli Palmer, who sits at her desk, knitting and smoking cigarettes. This is clearly one of those marriages in which the romantic love burned-out a long time ago, but in which the couple still respects one another—at least, they respect each other enough to stay together (although, admittedly, the two are constantly walking on eggshells around each other).

Mary's seen Leandre bringing home 'ladies-of-the-evening' many times in the past, and she's not offended, since she knows that it's (mostly) not sexual. (Leandre Brassac rescues women, just like he also rescues injured animals.) Mary asks her husband about who the lady he's brought home tonight is, and suddenly, after being *only* nice so far, he blurts out (right in front of Simone), "Oh, she's not a lady. She's a slut!" After he says it, he blanches, because he doesn't really feel that way: He genuinely likes Simone, but it's just that sometimes, after a few drinks, as we already saw (when we watched him mouth-off to the Priest, back in the bar), he says mean-spirited things that he doesn't really mean because, as we've also already seen, when he's sober, *he's the nicest guy around.* (Leandre wrestles with himself, just like how Jesus himself was meant to have wrestled with himself, as well [if not in the Gospels then, at least, in the Nikos Kazantzakis version], and what makes the Leandre character seem real to us, is that even though he's a good person, he flies off the handle sometimes—just like we all do.) Simone looks really hurt, and he apologizes to her, which she accepts. Leandre shows Simone his backyard, and tells her that he and Mary have been married for twenty years, that he met her during World War II, and that his endearing nickname for her has always been '*The Kraut.*'

Back at the bar in Paris, Marcel's asking everybody in sight if *his prize piece-of-sirloin* Simone has returned yet, and when everyone tells him that she hasn't, we know that, at some point in the film, and sooner rather than later, he'll probably be venturing off to Leandre's farm, to find her and to bring her back.

When Simone wakes up in Leandre's house the next morning, she's (very humorously) sleeping under a giant crucifix. (Leandre, who's just inveighed against religion in the bar, when he was talking to the Priest, is actually way more religious than we've been led to believe: In reality, he's a God-fearing guy who was merely taking the piss out of a full-of-himself man of the cloth.) Simone goes outside and explores the grounds, discovering a beautiful lake, and returning to the house, she tells Mary that she's going to have to leave now, because, if she's not back in Paris soon, she knows she'll be in big trouble with Marcel. (You know how 'pimps' get when their 'ho's' leave!)

At the same time, Leandre is wandering through the woods alone, taking his morning constitutional. He sees two teen-aged boys who've just killed a mother hare, and while he's a nice-enough guy, he abhors the improper treatment of animals. ('G.E.T.A' = 'Gabin for the Ethical Treatment of Animals!') He beats all-hell out of the two boys with a sharp switch, and then, like the Lord himself, he "moves from his judgment seat to his mercy seat" (to quote from a great Bernard Malamud novel called *God's Grace*), and comes to the rescue of the baby hare. Returning home, completely out of breath, he tells 'his two women' that he "… just caught two kids. They killed a mother rabbit. She [had] just had little ones." He's completely distraught by the poor little animal's death.

Leandre asks Simone if it would be possible for her to stay for three more days, and she's touched by the invitation. ("That would be nice!") At that moment, Florence (Danielle Darou [not to be confused with another Gabin co-star, Danielle Darrieux]), a *glitzy-ritzy-titsy* lady socialite, pulls up to the Brassac residence in her Bentley, and she's brought her own aging poodle-dog with her: She knows Leandre is the best vet in this part of France, and she's been to the Brassacs' house before: While she's a rich socialite today, in her 'previous life,' she was yet another prostitute whom Leandre had rescued, and he's very happy to see her... *and her poodle*: "I remember the name of your poodle. It's Socrates!" He tells her that it's often easier for him to remember dogs' names than people's names, since people sometimes let him down, but dogs never do. (That's some very 'Gabinian' philosophy!)

Simultaneously, Marie's in the kitchen with Simone, whose long hair is now revealed to have been just a wig. (Her own real hair, underneath, is shorter and more natural.) The two women are now bonding like mother-and-daughter (Leandre and Mary have never had any kids of their own) as they prepare a meal together, and Marie is starting to lose her initial iciness toward the younger woman. Simone tells Marie how she could really get used to this bucolic country life.

Outside, Florence is getting Leandre up-to-speed about her poodle's problem: "My dog has eczema!" (It's like Dennis Potter's *The Singing Detective*, but instead of Bob Hoskins or Robert Downey, Jr. 'flaking away,' we've got a scruffy dog, which, some might say, is the same thing as Hoskins and Downey!) Socrates the Poodle runs around barking and, just like a proto-Rodney Dangerfield, Leandre now counters, "It's not only eczema that Socrates is suffering from. Your dog has another problem, too: He's also crazy!" Then, we can see what separates Leandre from other veterinarians: He can actually psychoanalyze animals—he's a 'horse-whisperer,' but for dogs! Leandre diagnoses little Socrates' problem, as follows: "Your dog is unhappy with you, and he's crystallizing his unhappiness into eczema." Leandre gives the dog some medicine—a powder—and tells Florence, "I'll bet you hang around with a lot of fancy men, in Switzerland and on the Cote d'Azur. Socrates is angry, because you hang around with jerky guys, and you don't give him enough time, so he's showing it by developing eczema."

Meanwhile, Simone is fascinatedly watching Leandre's friendly business dealings with Florence, and the tender way in which he's dealing with Florence's dog. Leandre asks Florence for two hundred and fifty francs, as payment for helping the dog, and she's so happy about the 'cure' which he's just provided, both physically and psychologically, that she happily gives him a thousand; no doubt, she's paying him not only for fixing her dog's skin condition, but also for (a long time ago) *fixing her*.

Just when the day seems to have started off well, a surly-looking guy fortyish Roger (Georges Geret) from the neighboring farm bolts up to the house, and he's really mad at Leandre: "You know those two boys you hit with sticks, for killing that hare? They're my cousins!" Leandre, who's now exuding tons of Gabin-Calm, tells the guy that that's what those kids should have expected: "That's what happens when people poach on my land!" Roger shakes a fist at his neighbor and calls him crazy and vicious, but Leandre sets him straight, right away: "A hare does not go to war, so nobody has a right to kill it." It's important to note that this film was made during the Vietnamese War, which is why it's so full of anti-Vietnamese War platitudes disguised as sentiment couched through animal metaphor, *a la* producer/director Stanley Kramer's hippy-dippy 1971 melodrama, *Bless the Beasts and Children*, in which a bunch of misfit summer camp kids, led by America's 1960s' t.v. favorite Billy Mumy (*Lost in Space*), saved a bunch of bison from hunters' rifles. "You'll die alone," Roger tells Leandre. "Everybody dies alone," Leandre Gabin-Shrugs, not seeing any problem with that.

While a bug exterminator is spraying Leandre's crops later that day, Marie summons Leandre and Simone, ringing the large bell which she tolls only in emergencies. Marcel the pimp has just arrived at the Leandre place: He's come to collect Simone, and doesn't look too happy about having to do it, either. Simone freaks, and hides behind Leandre's estimable frame: "I don't want to go back with Marcel. But if I tell him that—he'll kill me!" Marcel bursts through the front door uninvited, and informs Leandre that he's come to retrieve 'his woman.' Leandre, who's not at all flustered by this young and psychotic-looking guy, calmly invites Marcel inside, for a drink. "Look," he tells the pimp, pouring one out for him, "she doesn't want to work for you, anymore. So don't make her, okay?"

But Marcel isn't buying it, and he grabs Simone by the arm: "Let's go. Otherwise, I'll force you!" Leandre, who's remaining as calm as a river, next gets a great idea: "If you want Simone, you're going to have to buy her back from me!" He's goofily pretending to be her new pimp, which Marcel, of course, knows is utter bullshit. Marcel starts screaming at Leandre, "You look like a Saint Bernard, but you don't have a barrel of booze around your neck, so you can't be," and Leandre reminds him, "Here, in my home, we don't threaten and scream, like they do in your world. We just talk things out, calmly." But Marcel *does* threaten: "Careful, old man. I have friends, and you don't." Marcel leaves empty-handed, beyond-frustrated that he was unable to take his woman back. Leandre's Gabin-Calmness has won the day, over Marcel's potential violence, and Simone kisses his cheek for having protected her so grandly. At this point, Marie now enters the room toting a rifle, just like a French Annie Oakley, but of course Marcel's already gone, so she's not going to be needing it.

That night, Marie, Leandre, and Simone look like a real family: Marie knits by the fire as Leandre reads, and Simone sits happily at their feet, watching the fire crackle and pop, a contented smile plastered across her alabaster face.

The next day, just as we expected, Marcel returns to Leandre's house, accompanied by two psycho henchmen (Paul Pavel and Edouard Francomme). Marcel calls up to Leandre through the window and tells him that if he doesn't send Simone down, and *stat*, that he and his men will set fire to the barn. Leandre, though, even when he's seeing armed gunmen milling about his property, remains the soul of calm: He's not afraid of them, one iota.

The psychos have cut the phone lines, so Leandre is unable to call the police, and meanwhile, Marie is once again dutifully readying her shotgun. One of the henchmen starts threatening Leandre that he's going to shoot him in the stomach, and Leandre, without flinching, simply orders his benign-looking little lapdogs to attack the pimps, who now run away, freaked beyond belief by The Attack of the Four-Legged Friends. Leandre instructs Marie to reward the dogs with sugar, insisting that it won't hurt them.

Leandre accompanies Simone back to the Paris bar to pick up her things (she's afraid of going back, frightened that she'll run into Marcel), but since she's under Leandre's protective wing, she's feels o.k. about it. Marcel and his fellow-pimps are already, of course, in the bar, and as they stare Leandre down, Leandre calmly orders a white wine. "We don't want you here, old man," Marcel threatens, getting up in Our Gabin's face, with his chest puffed-out, and old Leandre, far from being scared, is actually gleeful, immediately chiming in with some of his favorite silly/nonsensical insults. ("Your mother smells of elderberry! Your father is a hamster.") "Your insults are stupid!" Marcel snarls, and within seconds, his henchmen are on their feet, and (look out!) one of them's got a knife. Jean Gabin, just like Clint Eastwood or Charles Bronson (the two American actors who happened to be coming to prominence internationally, at the same time during which *Le Tonnerre de Dieu* was being made, in a small group very successful, European-made/English-language westerns and cop flicks) now slaps Marcel, even breaking a bottle over his head. (Needless to say, the bar closes down for the night.) And because it's in Leandre's nature to be the kind of brawler who tempers his ass-beatings with 'nurturing,' in the next scene, hilariously, he's cleaning Marcel's wound, and reminding him to 'man-up:' "Stop screaming like a girl! And pull your pants down—I have to give you a tetanus shot." (It's just like the scene in *Desordre et la nuit*, in which Gabin's Inspector Vallois bashed in the creepy nightclub manager Blasco's head, and then brought the guy down to Danielle Darrieux's pharmacy, to get him cleaned up.)

Leandre tells Simone to take the bus back to his house, because he has things to do in town, and when she gets there, Marie's out in the shed, milking cows. She starts bonding with Simone further, telling her the story of how she and her husband met: During the war, Leandre and Marie would meet each night, exchanging German lessons for French lessons, and she then elucidates on the subject of Leandre's enduring kindness toward all creatures: "My husband hates injustice of any kind. Everybody hated me for loving him, because he was a Frenchman, but he saved me—just like he's always saving everybody else." (That's 'Our Jesus!' I mean, 'Our Leandre!')

The next day, Roger the neighbor—the guy whose young, rabbit-hating cousins got brained by Leandre—shows up again, while Marie and Simone are sitting in the living-room together, rolling a giant ball of yarn. Roger's not acting surly, like he was the last time we saw him, in fact this time, he looks positively sheepish. Exasperatedly, he tells the two ladies that he needs Leandre, and *stat*, because his mare is giving birth, but as Marie is now letting him know, Leandre's still not back from town. When Leandre does arrive home, he's drunk off his ass, and for the second time in the film, he's now going to be acting pitbull-mean, instead of nice (but 'hey, it's just the whiskey talking'): In lieu of just Ricky Ricardo-ing, "Honey, I'm home!" he picks up a chair and smashes it through a window, and then (retroactively and loudly), he cries out to the Heavens in agony about what he's just done, as if seeking instant forgiveness for it. ("Oh my Goddddd!!! I just broke a windowwwwww!") He then orders Marie to get off her ass and fix the damage which he, himself, has just perpetrated. Simone, who's freaked by the usually-sweet Leandre's angrily-drunken behavior, runs into the nearest possible bedroom to hide, and Marie joins her. Leandre starts banging on the door and insulting both of them, using the kind of nasty talk in which he only engages when Lady

Liquor has stripped him of his good sense: "Open up, Simone! Don't be a prude! So! The two of you are together—you little sluts! Put Simone in my bed, Marie—you owe me that!" Marie is now crying, and when Simone finally opens the door, Leandre even chastises her, right in front of the younger woman, about how she's never been able to bear him children, which is probably the reason for the couple's coldness toward each other. He now tells her, in what is surely one of the most evilly-wrought lines of dialogue in motion picture history (and definitely, this is the meanest movie-line ever spoken by Jean Gabin), *"Your belly is like a cemetery!"*

The next morning, Leandre's cooled off, again. He walks into the room where his wife and his new 'surrogate daughter' are and looks super-embarrassed about his behavior, the previous night. Simone tells her husband that he acted disgustingly, and that he should be ashamed. Leandre can't argue with what she's telling him and doesn't say a word, but whereas last night, he frightened Marie about the barrenness of her womb ("a rocky place," to paraphrase Nicolas Cage, in the Coen Brothers' *Raising Arizona,* "where [his] seed could find no purchase"), this morning, he's going to have the chance to make up for it: Neighbor Roger's mare has not yet given birth, and he goes over to Roger's own neighboring farm, to help out. ("Tell your mare not to worry! I'm coming!") Even though the two men sometimes fight, Leandre's dedicated friendship toward all mankind, always wins the day. Roger's mare, the one which is giving birth, used to belong to Leandre's grandfather: Twenty years ago, during the waning days of the Second World War, Leandre's grandfather drove the horse-drawn cart upon which the village people (not those disco guys) used to throw their war-dead relatives. (Can't you just hear Eric Idle calling out, *"Bring out your deeaaaadddddd!"*)

Later in the day, two *gendarmes* (Paul Frankeur and Andre Dalibert) make it over to Leandre's house, to question him about something: "We're here, *half* because we know you, and *half* officially." Leandre pours them some white wine, and they proceed to explain themselves: "We got a letter from one of your neighbors, saying that ugly things are happening here." Leandre thinks they must be referring to the rabbit-killing teen-agers, but they've really come about Simone: The first Cop (Frankeur) says, "It's not enough for you to bring home homeless people. Now you bring sluts? If this girl continues to work while she's here in the countryside, you can't keep her here." They obviously think, and they're utterly wrong about this, that Leandre is pimping Simone out. Maybe some neighbors saw her, and that's what they're thinking, *or else* maybe, Marcel called the cops and lied to them, telling them that's what's going on. Leandre asks them, meekly, what he can do to make things okay.

Leandre is next seen down at the offices of the small town's Mayor, who's played by Daniel Ceccaldi. The Mayor chastises Leandre gently, for fouling their beautiful countryside with a wanton woman: "We have to put this girl on the right track," Hizzoner tells Leandre, "which means that you have to send her back to Paris." But Leandre won't have it. He tells the Mayor, gently and truthfully, that the reason he's brought Simone to his home in the first place, has been to get her back on the right track, and that he has no intention of letting her prostitute herself again: "On the outside, I look old," Leandre tells the Mayor. "But inside,

I'm monstrously young. I like to have young people around me. I'm not her pimp, and she's not turning tricks. She's like a daughter to me." The Mayor throws up his hands, and sighs: "Well, we happen to live in the most beautiful countryside in the world. So don't mess up." The Cop's cynicism exposes the hypocrisy of all mankind: People always extol 'Jesus-like behavior' ('*do unto others*' and all that *horseshit*), but when somebody actually acts like Jesus, and really helps people, the world's hypocrites just aren't willing to listen!

Leandre then phones his wife Marie from the Mayor's office, and tells her that he's on his way home, and that she should get all dolled-up, because he's going to be taking her out to dinner. Needless to say, Marie, who feels more like a piece of lawn furniture than she does a wife, is beyond-excited: "He hasn't taken me to a restaurant in ten years!" she cries out cheerfully, to Simone. Marie, who is totally floored by her husband's unexpected offer of a night out (he realizes that he owes her big-time, for the horrible way he acted the other night), dresses herself to-the-nines, and the couple heads out to dinner, leaving Simone home alone with the dogs.

INT. RESTAURANT—NIGHT: Marie is so happy to be out with her husband on a date, just like they used to do a long, long time ago, that she gloats, "Tonight, I'm out of the house—I'm out of myself!" He takes this moment to apologize for his violently-angry alcoholic behavior: "Alcoholism is a bad habit. I started drinking over the last few years [he never drank that much when he was younger], because I've been bored, and because of all the things I never got to do in my life." (This is exactly what Gabin's other whiskey-marinated character, 'Quartermaster' Albert Quentin, told his wife in 1961's *Un singe en hiver*.) We see, in this tender scene, that Marie and Leandre really do love each other, and that their marriage is not loveless, as we originally thought it to be, and that Marie's been silently waiting, all of these years, for Leandre to start acting romantically toward her again. Taking her husband's hand, she poignantly tells him that she didn't make a mistake in marrying him: "I always followed you whenever you left me, but you never turned around and saw me." She then asks him if the feelings he feels for Simone are more than paternal, which is what he suggested during both of his two barely-remembered drunken rages: "Do you want to divorce me for Simone?" He sweetly takes his wife's hand: "Of course not. I need you, dear." (Thankfully, when he's sober, Leandre sees Simone as a daughter, and not as a lover!)

While Leandre and Marie are renewing their love for each other over *l'escargot au vin*, or whatever it is that *those Frenchies* like to chow-down on, Simone's now at the Brassac house alone, and it's a mega-stormy, rainswept evening. The weather is spooking Leandre's horses. Neighbor Roger, who's noticed this, comes over and helps Simone to quiet them, and at first, when Roger shows up at the door unexpectedly, and in the rain, we think he might do something unseemly, like try to rape her, since it's a dark night, and also because he's turned-up at the Brassacs' place wearing the kind of long, floor-length black leather coat which is usually favored by subway-dwelling perverts and Keanu Reeves in *The Matrix*. In the hands of a lesser filmmaker than Denys de La Patelliere, such a clichéd bit of business would probably happen, but it's to Patelliere's credit (the characters in his movies always act the way that people do, in real life), that Roger is simply genuinely nice and concerned, and has really shown up just to help her out with the horses. She invites him in to dry off, and because he was gentlemanly, she makes the first move on him! He lifts her shirt, carefully (and with her full-approval), and within seconds, the two of them are making out on the barn's muddy floor. Needless to say: She digs it, most heavily.

The next morning, both Simone and Marie are happy and freshly-fucked (we can tell from the beatific expression on Marie's face that hubby Leandre gave it to her good last night, for the first time in many-a-year, and that, concomitantly, Roger has rogered Simone): "He's nice, isn't he?" Simone asks Marie, *re:* Roger.

Then, the love between Roger and Simone grows. "I really like you," he admits to her, bashfully, in an endearingly sweet, 'aww-shucks'-manner. She's discovering that she loves Roger too, and that she wants to tell him everything about herself—even the not-so-good parts about her life. (He's probably the only person in the community who doesn't know what she does for a living, so this is where she has to break it to him): "I used to be a prostitute," she tells him, and obviously happy to be with any woman (it's lonely out there, with the horses), he doesn't care. She tells him that, during her young life, she was also a house-cleaner, and he then tells her his own story, which is that he fought in French Indochina, and that thereafter, he returned home and became a farmer since, in France, farmers are exempt from returning to military service, provided that they can prove they are cultivating land.

When Simone returns to Chateau Brassac, Leandre, who's not mad, asks her where she was all last night, even though he already knows and just wants to hear her say it, for herself. With a big smile, she asks him if he's jealous, even though she knows that his feelings for her are (mostly) paternal. He tells Marie later, when husband and wife are together, that he's glad Simone and Roger have found each other. ("That Roger really is a good guy. Not the smartest one in class, but good.") When the two young lovers are trysting behind the barn again, later that same day, Marie asks her husband mischievously, if he plans on going out and spying on them, and he smiles, white-lying, "If they kiss, I promise not to look!"

The next morning, Marie and Leandre wake up in bed together, after their second sex-filled night in a row. Having Simone in the house with them has definitely brought the older couple closer together and, of course, just as Marie and Leandre are waking up together, so, too, is Simone is waking up in Roger's bed. And today, a new woman emerges onto the scene: It's Francoise (Ellen Schwiers), Roger's type-A/ultra-high strung big sister, a woman who left the farm life for big-city life, years ago. She's heard (who hasn't?) that a hooker is *porking* her dopey little brother, and she's not happy about it at all: Francoise, even though she hasn't seen her brother in years, tells Simone to stop seeing Roger: "I'm sure you know [Simone *doesn't* know] that my brother's not just a small-time farmer, and that we're a rich family, and I know you're a gold-digger [Simone's not!], so don't start lying. You can't have him or his fortune." Simone, truly not knowing or caring that Roger is wealthy, stands up to the tough cookie: "What I get from Roger is something you can't get, because you're his sister." Then, Roger enters the room, gleefully unaware of the two ladies' topic of conversation. 'Toxic

Francoise' turns on a fake smile: "Oh, hi, Roger. We were just talking about family stuff, How are you?"

At the same time, Leandre and Marie are poring through the morning newspapers, giving each other little world-weary but bemused summaries of the world's typically-bleak news: "The dollar is going down... the whites don't like the blacks and the blacks don't like the whites... Blah, blah, blah!" Leandre shows the newspaper to his dogs and laughs, "You guys don't give a damn about this stuff, do you?"

That night, Roger meets Simone in the town's local bar. "My sister wants me to break up with you, and it wasn't just a conversation we were having—it was an ultimatum that she was giving me." And just when Simone's about to start thinking that her newly-beloved Roger is a henpecked (sisterpecked) girlyman, he proudly brags to her, "Guess what I did? I told my sister to leave, and that I can't live without you!" Simone feels unworthy of being with such a good man, and she tells him that even though he loves her now, that one day, he'll resent her for her past. ("One day, you'll be disgusted by me.") She now surprises him with the fact that she's pregnant, and they both look very happy, and he charmingly tells her, "Tomorrow, I'll talk with Leandre. I'll get dressed up in my suit and ask him if I can marry you!" Since Leandre has become Simone's surrogate dad, Roger, who's a genuine innocent, really feels like he needs to get Leandre's permission to wed her.

Francoise, the Evil Sister, has now returned to the Brassacs,' and she's now trying to spread some of her famous 'anti-sunshine' to Marie, who's not buying it for a second: Marie steadfastly defends Simone, who's become her new best friend and 'daughter.' Leandre, who's sitting in the background and poring over the newspaper as he listens to Francoise and Marie, now tells both women, "If they ask my permission to get married, I am going to give it." Even though Leandre's not related to Simone by blood, he really feels like he's her father and, because he's Jean Gabin, and because 'what he says, goes' in almost every one of his films, his 'will' even supercedes that of Roger's actual blood sister, and there's nothing anyone can do about it, because Jean Gabin Has Spoken! He even tells Francoise, "If your brother and Simone marry, I am going to give them my entire property, as my wedding present." But there's one catch to his offer: Leandre tells Marie and Francoise (who is now starting to calm herself down), "I know Simone is pregnant; I can tell from how she's behaving. It's fine, and I'm happy about it. But I want her to tell me about it, herself."

Roger tells Simone, *re:* his future father-in-law and long-time neighbor, Leandre, "He's a really nice guy, but he's totally crazy," and he means this in a good way. She tells Roger, "I don't want to lose you, but if Leandre says no to our getting married [which he won't; because, as we're about to find out, he's pretty freakin' excited about it], then I won't marry you, because Leandre's been kind of a father to me, lately, and I don't want to lose him. If he thinks we shouldn't get married, then I'll have to say no to you, even though I don't want to." "Having Leandre as a father-in-law would definitely be some kind of weird gift," Roger tells her, and Simone also brings up the issue of Roger's sister Francoise, again, because she's afraid that just like Francoise, everyone else in Roger's family will hate her too, because of, *per* Paul McCartney, '*her ever-present past.*' Roger doesn't care though, and he now shows some true intestinal fortitude (balls), declaring to her that he'll marry her no matter what anybody has to say about it.

While Leandre has admitted to his wife that he realizes he's a drunk, and that he hates the way he acts when he's been nipping at the bottle, he's soon back in the local bar anyway, swilling down booze with Paul Frankeur's Cop and the Priest. (Even in the world of this film, these great denizens of society are getting loaded!) Leandre is comically telling them about how horrible alcohol is while, at the same time, he's guzzling down Pastis like it's going out of style, and getting so tipsy, that he doesn't even get mad when the Cop confronts him about his latest 'hooker intervention:' "So, you think you can save prostitutes to save yourself?" (What's so wrong about trying to do that? Jesus Christ tried it, and so did the 20th-century Jesus—Robert DeNiro's Travis Bickle-character, in *Taxi Driver*. [And look what happened to 'Christ' and 'Bickle!' They both got deified at the end of their 'stories.']) Leandre is worried, because Simone hasn't talked to him about marrying Roger yet, and he's now thinking, erroneously, that she's decided not to go through with it.

Back at that big city Paris bar which Simone used to work out of, Marcel is present, and when we see him in the next sequence, he's holding forth to a tall, Eve Ardeny-looking lady, about how he originally met Simone: "I took her off of the streets, and I took care of her for six months, and now she's walked out and left me for an old man." Drunkenly, he adds, "Women aren't meant for real work, anyway: They should all just get married, or be prostitutes. All women are the same." With some pretty great comic timing—timing which is worthy of the real Eve Arden, herself—this matronly woman now asks Marcel if he's a homosexual!

Leandre apparently came home in the middle of the night, from his recent drunken escapade with the Cop and the Priest, and when Marie heads outside, she sees him passed-out in his barn, among his cows. Now, here comes Lilli Palmer's big dramatic moment (let's call it a 'Palmer-Outburst'), in which it's clear that, even though they're doing better now, she still hasn't forgiven her husband for a lot of the *mean shit* he's done, and she's now able to get it all out of her system in one juicily-written stream-of-consciousness soliloquy: "You should have told me you loved me more often. Every time you get drunk, you sleep out here with your dogs and your pigs. You're a drunk! You bring all the trash home. I don't even know if you want to make Simone your wife or your daughter! You're an idiot! It's better off that my belly is a cemetery, because there was never any room in it for anything of yours!" These are all things that you would only dare say to someone whom you truly love, because Marie really does love her husband and, as we've already seen, we also know that she loves Simone, 'the daughter-she-never-had,' as well.

At this point, the film's composer, George Garaventz, makes with the haunting theme music (a vinyl LP of the film's score pops up, on occasion, on eBay, and it's *maximum-beautiful*), as Roger and Leandre go for a walk in the forest, to talk about the marriage. Roger tells Leandre that Simone's *preggers,* and Leandre becomes more visibly excited than we've ever seen Jean Gabin getting in any other movie: Leandre summons all the joy in the world, shouting out, "We're going to have a little one!" Excitedly, he makes for the bar and treats everybody present to champagne, and he then heads to a local boutique, where he buys boxes and boxes of baby presents. He's so deliriously happy, that he even goes and tells Marcel, the pimp, about it, since Marcel definitely can't use a pregnant prostitute (so now, Simone has a very real 'out-clause,' which Marcel can't do anything about). Marcel asks Leandre if Leandre's "the father," and Leandre replies, "It's not me, you idiot! But I'm the honorary grandpa, if you want to know, and if it's a girl, we're going to call her Mary!" Weirdly, director Patelliere next smash-cuts to a quiet shot of an empty baby stroller, which is rolling around on a hilltop all by itself; this shot doesn't symbolize or suggest anything (except, maybe, that famously-eerie poster, for *Rosemary's Baby*), and it seems like it's an extra shot which was 'cut in' to the film by some moronic editing assistant, while Patelliere was out, having a *brioche*.

The last shot of the film is another shot of the same baby stroller: Grandpa Leandre has bought it, and tied it to the top of a new and mega-fancy Rolls-Royce, which he's also just purchased. Leandre is so excited about the pregnancy, that he even tells his dogs about it, as the film comes to its genuinely feel-good close. *Le Tonnerre de Dieu* is another great Jean Gabin comedy, and it's so great, you won't even notice that what you're really watching, is a wine-soaked and hilarious (and in the end, powerfully-moving) updating of The Gospels.

What a Critic Said at the Time: "This film appears tailored for Jean Gabin, but is also a rote trotting-out of his anarchic character, full of anger and tirades. Told solidly by director Denys de La Patelliere, Gabin is his usual stormy self." (*Variety*, 10-6-65 issue. Critic: "Mosk. [George Moskowitz.]" Reviewed in Paris.)

Top: Two icons, Jean Gabin and George Raft. Above: With Marcel Bozzuffi and Claudio Brook.

FILM 81

DU RIFIFI A PANAME

France/Germany/Italy, 1966

(Literal English Translation: "PARIS RIFF-RAFF") Directed by Denys de La Patelliere. Produced by Raymond Danon and Maurice Jacquin. Screenplay by Alphonse Boudard, Franco Dalcen, and Denys de La Patelliere. Based Upon the Novel by Auguste Le Breton. Director of Photography (color, scope), Walter Wottitz. Editors, Claude Durand and Vincenzo Tomasi. Music by Georges Garaventz. Production Designer, Robert Clavel. (GENRE: SPY THRILLER) A Production of FIDA Cinematografica (Italy)/Films Copernic (France)/Gloria Film (Germany). Running Time, 1 hour 38 minutes. Released in France on March 2, 1966, by Films Copernic. Released in United States by Paramount Pictures (English-Dubbed, at 1 hour 26 minutes) on July 26, 1967, as "THE UPPER HAND."

"Excuse me, where's the bathroom?"
— *Crime-boss Gabin excuses himself from a meeting of international drug czars, so he can set explosives and blow them all up, in "Du rififi a Paname"*

By 1966, movie screens across the globe were awash with giant, widescreen, Technicolor superspy pictures, which were inspired by Albert Broccoli and Harry Saltzman's immensely profitable James Bond franchise (Michael Caine as Harry Palmer; James Coburn as *Our Man Flint*; John-Philip Law adding cool to Mario Bava's *Danger: Diabolik*, and Marcello Mastroianni to Elio Petri's *The 10th Victim*). And so it was, that the French would come up with several offerings of their own in the 'Psychedelic Spy-Movie Cycle,' and even one which starred Jean Gabin: Fresh from directing Gabin in *Le Tonnerre de Dieu*, Denys de La Patelliere was now back with Gabin for the fourth of the six pictures which they would make together, the groovy-looking but soporific (that's why you've never heard it) *Du rififi a Paname*, an expensively-mounted production which would be released all-too-briefly in the U.S. by Paramount Pictures, as *The Upper Hand*, before disappearing from American shores forever. It's based, like *Le Rouge est mis* and *Razzia sur la chnouf*, on a novel by Auguste Le Breton, and it's one of the few Breton adaptations which doesn't really work, because Breton's cool 'David Mametian' writing style is nullified by some pretty lackluster direction. (Since Denys de La Patelliere is a great director, he mustn't have been too inspired by the material.)

When I (a/k/a, '*this author*'), with my limited French, sat down to watch the movie, I was fully expecting a movie which would take place in the city of Panama: Maybe, I thought, I'd be thrilling to a film in which Gabin has involved himself in some kind of criminal behavior, down by the Panama Canal—but that's when a French slang dictionary set me straight: The French word '*Paname*' has nothing at all to do with the country or Canal of Panama: '*Paname*,' with an 'e' on the end, is actually just antiquated French 'gangster slang' meaning, 'Paris.'

When we first meet the Parisian crime boss, Paulo 'The Gem' Bergere (Gabin), he's arriving at Paris-Orly airport, after having been away for quite awhile, having engaged in some international wheeling-and-dealing (just like Gabin's fellow smooth-criminal, Henri Le Nantais, at the beginning of *Razzia sur la chnouf*), and when an acolyte picks him up in his limo, he plops down in the back seat, right next to his bulldog, and this is a joke on the fact that, as Gabin got older, his face took on the appearance of a handsomely-jowly boxer! The driver drops Paulo off at the swank club he owns, 'The Voluptuous,' (!) a taxi-dancing establishment where nerdy businessmen *do the hang with* and buy expensive champagne for hot 'B-girls,' in little roped-off rooms, and two of the most popular women who work there, are the busty (dyed) blonde bombshell, Lily (Mireille Darc, who played Suzanne in *Monsieur*) and the hot, redheaded Irene (Nadja Tiller, who played another hooker, the strung-out Lucky, in *Desordre et la nuit*). It's a custom of The Voluptuous that the evening isn't over until all of the goofy-rube businessmen customers are totally broke, but one of the establishment's clients is decidedly un-nerdy: It's the guy who's the actual star/hero of the film, although he's billed sixth in the opening credits, the Italian actor Claudio Brook, who plays an intentionally 007-esque American Treasury Department agent by the name of Mike Cappellano. Cappellano, as we're learning here, has been working undercover in Paulo's crime operation (Brook has more scenes in the film than does the first-billed Gabin, who's really just a supporting player), in his attempt to chase the notoriously hard-to-catch Paulo all over the world, so that he can arrest Paulo for some major crimes which he committed on American soil, before the film began. We get the sense that Cappellano's not the greatest spy in the world because, throughout the film, some of the guys in Paulo's outfit, who've already figured out that Mike's really a Federal 'plant,' give him intentionally-false leads, which send him chasing Paulo all over the world, even though Paulo, throughout the picture, will continue to remain well-hidden, in Paris. One of Paulo's henchmen tells Cappellano that Paulo is hiding out in Japan, and we then follow Mike to Tokyo, where he enters what he's been told is Paulo's hotel room, and he is instead immediately surrounded by a phalanx of wily button-down Japanese Karate experts, who (naturally) Cappellano dispatches one at a time, and without even breaking a sweat, *a la* Sean Connery.

The film's weirdest and most unexplained moment: When Cappellano's on his way to the Tokyo hotel, director Patelliere sticks his camera in the car with Claudio Brook, and gives us a 'P.O.V.' shot of what Mike is presumably looking at out of the side window, as the car

With Marcel Bozzuffi.

zooms down the Tokyo freeway, and mostly, he's just looking at a bunch of billboards! This extended shot of 'nothing' goes on for three solid minutes, as if Patelliere went away to eat lunch and left his camera running. Conceptually, this bit is very similar to that similarly unnecessary bit in Gabin's *Mephisto,* thirty years earlier, in which (also for no good reason) co-directors Henri Debain and Nick Winter aimed their own camera out of a plane window and gave audiences a three minute look at the empty skies.

Paulo is the most respected and feared crime boss in Europe, which is bad news to the most respected and feared crime boss in America, Charles Binaggio, who's played in the film by a movie icon who's almost as famous as Jean Gabin—none other than Warner Bros.' coin-flipping depression-era legend, George Raft. Binaggio is *jonesing* to be Europe's Biggest Crime Czar as well, and that means that he's going to have to eliminate Gabin's Paulo. (Europe is Paulo's turf, and he ain't sharing. [Did somebody say "World Domination?" Yup, *Du Rififi a Paname* is an 007 rip-off, all the way!])

Twenty-five years prior to the making of this film, when Jean Gabin briefly lived in Los Angeles with Marlene Dietrich during the shooting of 20th Century-Fox's *Moontide* and Universal's *The Impostor,* Dietrich was actually cheating on her then-current boyfriend, Gabin, with George Raft, while Raft and Dietrich were filming Raoul Walsh's taut power lineman-epic, *Manpower,* at Universal, but with Gabin, in real life just like in his movies, the friendship between he and his male friends was always more enduring, and important, than the love between Gabin and women (even when the woman in question was Marlene Dietrich), and so Gabin was able to forgive Raft, even before he forgave Marlene.

Some of Binaggio's psychotic underbosses, especially the turtle-faced Marco the Milanese (super-cool Michel Bozzuffi, who would, with this film, be appearing in the fifth of his five Gabin movies), even threatens Paulo that, if he doesn't turn all of his operations over to Binaggio, he and Binaggio will make his life hell. But tough-as-nails Paulo doesn't scare easy, if at all, and he just won't budge, even when they kill his best friend Walter, who's played by Gert Froebe: That's right: In an effort to coin some 007-style scratch, and to gain the film some international visibility at the box-office (it didn't happen, but the producers tried), the filmmakers cast '*Goldfinger*' himself as a German antique dealer, who is also Paulo's occasional business associate (the two men sell drugs together, in Japan and Cuba). Paulo, in the best 'stoic Gabin sense,' doesn't even lift an eyebrow when the bad guys *ice* Walter. But when they kill Paulo's loyal bulldog—well that's when he really decides to 'Go Gabin' on their ass!

Paulo, under duress, telephones Binaggio and tells him that he'll agree to become just a tiny cog in Binaggio's operations, and that he's ready to turn all of his businesses over to his American competitor. He agrees to meet Binaggio, and all of Binaggio's international underbosses, in a lushly-appointed hotel conference room, where the two big muckimucks will have a big meeting to seal the deal. On the appointed day, Paulo enters the room with a group of his underlings, and Binaggio is there already, with a group of his own henchmen. And since nobody in the room trusts each other, director Patelliere now gives us an extended sequence in which everybody frisks everybody else for a really long time, and it's very funny—in fact, it's probably the most entertaining scene in what is mostly a lackluster movie. Paulo listens to Binaggio's whole *spiel* about how he (Paulo) now works for him, and Paulo next excuses himself to go to the bathroom.

Paulo and his underlings leave the room, run down the hallway, and (this is perfectly timed) the conference room blows up (Paulo snuck in the night before and set explosives), killing Charles Binaggio and all of Binaggio's men, now effectively making Gabin's Paulo the #1 crime boss in the entire world. This scene plays just like that big 'gangland massacre scene' (which, by the way, also featured George Raft) in Billy Wilder's *Some Like It Hot*, which was made seven years before this film.

Even though things are looking up after his 'explosive victory,' Paulo is immediately arrested by Mike Cappellano. While Paulo's arrest, at the end of the picture, is Mike's job, he still tells Paulo, truthfully, that he has a great deal of respect for him, and that he counts Paulo as one of the most intelligent men he's ever met. Paulo thanks Mike—and he then punches the younger man out, anyway!

The biggest problem with *Du rififi a Paname,* is that most of the interesting-sounding stuff I've just mentioned, like the big 'meeting' scene with all of the international crime bosses, doesn't happen until the second half of the film. The first half of the picture is mostly given over to *dull-as-dishwater* Claudio Brook, who the producers apparently believed had a chance of becoming 'the world's favorite new action hero.' (Whoops! Never happened!) Still, the picture remains watchably-colorful mid-1960s' eye candy, and it's the kind of a movie which you might sit back and *grok* on a slow Saturday night, just like you might also stare at one of those videos in which logs are sizzling in a fireplace. If you look fast, you'll even see the sexy German ingenue Christa Lang, who made a number of European films in the '60s and '70s, turning up as one of the bar-girls at the Voluptuous; of course, she's more known to movie aficionados for having been the real life wife of the late, great American film director/icon, Samuel Fuller.

And I just can't say enough about that interminable 'real-time' three-minute shot of the Tokyo freeway: I'd make fun of it more but I can't, because six years later, in his 1972 film *Solaris*, which is considered to be one of international cinema's greatest classics, the Russian director Andrei Tarkovsky actually stuck his camera out of the window of a car and (you guessed it) gave us three solid minutes of a Tokyo freeway! Did Tarkovsky steal *Solaris* from *Du rififi a Paname?* (Anyway, *yeah*, I'm just kidding about that, and I can pretty much promise you that those two films will never be mentioned in the same sentence, ever again!)

What a Critic Said at the Time: "A familiar tale of gang war. Gabin, again an aging lion of a gangster… is his usual anarchic self with [George] Raft fine in a cameo as an American gangleader. It is technically solid, with a helpful color envelope." (*Variety*, 4-6-66 issue. Critic: "Mosk. [George Moskowitz.]" Reviewed in Paris.)

What a Critic Says Today: "One of those latter-day vehicles in which portly and white-haired Gabin brushes importunate girls aside to lavish attentions on his pet boxer, meanwhile masterminding a series of unenterprising crimes which win him the usual admiring accolades ('He's a real man!') Thoroughly routine stuff, it mixes some passable action sequences with statutory travelogue footage, allows Gabin to coast through without exerting himself, and finds time for George Raft to do his coin-flipping act. But Claudio Brook, taking time off from Buñuel (he was the major-domo in *The Exterminating Angel* and the nutty saint in *Simon of the Desert*) makes a refreshingly unstereotyped hero, and Gert Froebe steals his scenes as a crook with leftist leanings." (From: *Time Out Film Guide* [website]. Critic: "TM." Year Reviewed in London, 2006.)

Top: With Curt Jurgens. Above: With Annie Savarin.

FILM 82

LE JARDINIER D'ARGENTEUIL

France/Germany, 1966

(Literal English Translation: "THE GARDENER OF ARGENTEUIL") Directed by Jean-Paul LeChanois. Produced by Roger de Broin. Screenplay by Alphonse Boudard. Based Upon the Novel "La Pere Tulipe" by Rene Jouglet. Director of Photography (color), Walter Wottitz. Edited by Emma Le Chanois. Production Designer, Jean-Paul Boutie. Music by Serge Gainsbourg. (GENRE: COMEDY) A Production of Films Vertried/GAFER/Les Films Copernic (France)/Roxy Film GmbH (Germany). Running Time, 1 hour 26 minutes. Released in France on October 17, 1966, by Les Films Copernic. Never Released Theatrically in the United States.

"It's people like you who burned Joan of Arc!"
— *Crotchety old Gabin berates a young woman who's stolen his umbrella, in "Le Jardinier d'Argenteuil"*

Director Jean-Paul Le Chanois directed four Jean Gabin movies—*Le Cas du docteur Laurent* (1956), *Les Miserables* (1957), *Monsieur* (1964), and this film, 1966's *Le Jardinier d'Argenteuil* (*The Gardener of Argenteuil*)—and they're all good, warm, fun (and ultimately uplifting) pictures, so it's too bad that Gabin and Chanois didn't make more movies together.

The film opens with a rich-voiced Narrator—director Chanois, himself—telling us that there's an old man in Argenteuil, an area of heavy industry and scattered farms eight miles north of Paris, who was happy spending each and every day painting landscape paintings and cultivating his vegetable garden (his specialty: asparagus!) and that this man is, according to our Narrator, "... not of this century. He does not watch t.v.—instead, he is helpful with people." (This film confirms it! 'Watching t.v.' and 'helping people,' are mutually exclusive!) He's also, as the Narrator is now telling us rather casually, a lifetime counterfeiter, who lives modestly on the small ten-franc (about $3.00 U.S., back in 1966) notes which he manufactures, down in his basement. (Since we didn't get enough of Gabin as a counterfeiter in *Le Cave se rebiffe*—here comes another very cool Gabin Counterfeiting Epic.)

The old man's (we still haven't seen Gabin's character, yet) garden and small house are located not too far from a housing project where, the Narrator adds, "... poor people live—people who can't pay much in the way of rent. And our man, Mr. Martin, whom the neighbors call *Monsieur Tulipe*, or in English, 'Mr. Tulip,' never leaves his property, except for when he makes his occasional day-trips to Paris, to buy those few things which he needs. Under his white hair, a lot of things are happening, things which Mr. Tulip never discusses with anybody." Just like the best of Jean Gabin's movie characters, and also just like Al Pacino's Michael Corleone in the *Godfather* movies, Tulip 'never tells anyone what he's thinking.'

Chanois, as director, next cuts to the offices of the French Internal Revenue Service, where we see one of those gigantic, old IBM-7094 computers (the kind of computer we remember from those old *Godzilla* pictures) which takes up the whole wall and spits out Fortran cards (remember those?), and as the Narrator now informs us, "One spring day, the computer became very interested in our gardener:" It seems that Mr. Tulip hasn't paid his taxes in about ten years, and in the following sequence, a dark-suited Tax Collector (Jean Berton) arrives at his house, asking for 'Mr. Martin,' but good-old Mr. Martin (a/k/a, Tulip) just Gabin-Shrugs, and replies, with a completely straight-face, "Never heard of him." The Tax Guy isn't fooled for a second, though: "Have you ever paid your taxes, Mr. Martin?" Tulip, who makes up his own logic and lives according to it, hilariously replies that he doesn't have any children and that, therefore, there's no reason for him to pay any. The Collector notices a few of Tulip's landscape paintings lying around and asks him if he ever sells any of them, and Tulip's answer is a very decisive, "no." (Just like in any number of other Gabin pictures which I've already described, whenever Jean Gabin is interrogated, he always denies everything!) "I will never retire from gardening," he tells the Taxman, "because I love having flowers and vegetables," and the guy now starts threatening Martin ("I could tax you as a farmer, for the past ten years"), but Tulip just takes it all in with a wry smile, and he then, suddenly, changes his mind: "Okay, okay. I'll pay off all of my back taxes now, so that my life will remain calm. I'll be right back." Tulip descends into his basement, grabs a bunch of stacks of newly-minted ten-franc bills... and pays off his decade's worth of back taxes. (There! That was easy!)

Martin's one friend in life is Albert (Jean Tissier), a guy of about his own age who owns the local produce store. Martin is godfather to Albert's twentysomething son, Noel (Pierre Vernier), who's just returned home from college and has just started his challenging new job, as a driving instructor! (Author's Note: With a fantastic career like that in front of him, Albert must have graduated from *film school!*) Martin tells Albert, "Your store had better sell two hundred pounds of my asparagus right away, because I've just paid off my back taxes, and I'm out of money!" Albert and his wife Dora (Mary Marquet) sell Martin's produce in their little general store, where they also sell *kitschy* (and 'not-so-fine') antiques. Dora now tells Martin that, since she and her husband are doing Martin a favor by stocking his asparagus, that they would like to keep fifty percent of the revenue from selling it, and he tells her that's fine, but that just for today, he'd like one hundred percent of the proceeds from their sales of all of his veggies which they purvey from their store. Dora's a shrew, like lots of the other wife-characters in lots of other Gabin movies, a woman who seems to spend most of her waking hours insulting her husband, Albert. (Very clearly, she's the one who wears the pants in the family.)

Besides being a general-store proprietor, Albert also happens to be a bookie who spends a lot of his time hanging out in the parking lot of Paris' famous horse-racing arena, Longchamp, taking bets. Of course, the bag-man for the local Mafia (Andre Dumas), who always takes a cut from what Albert gets, is pissed at him today because, in his estimation, Albert's hasn't given the mob what he's supposed to have given them. Dumas and his two Henchmen (Michel Charrell and Jo Dalat) push him into their truck (obviously they want to 'teach him some manners') but he's able, quite comically, to run away, and when Albert gets home from the track, and his son Noel, who doesn't know that his dad 'makes book' (merely believing that he just goes to the track and places his own bets, with his own money), asks his dad if he won today, Albert just shakes his head, non-committally.

While Gabin's Mr. Tulip makes only small ten-franc bills, because in his opinion (and he's right about it), the cops are less likely to look for a counterfeiter who only traffics in small notes, he always turns a huge profit anyway, and director Chanois will now show us exactly how he does it: On his frequent day-trips to Paris, Tulip always goes from one street corner flower vendor to another, buying up flowers—Lilies of the Valley—which, in France, happen to be good luck on 'May Day' (May 1st). When Tulip buys the flowers, using the ten-franc notes which he's made, he always asks to receive his change in coins (he gets back about eight francs from each two-franc flower purchase), and these coins are the real money, which he lives on. In a comical montage, we now get to see Tulip buying Lilies of the Valley from every single street vendor who's selling them, pocketing the change and then, very discreetly, dumping the unneeded flowers onto the pavement, as he walks away. At the end of each day of 'flower-buying/loose change-collecting,' he even weighs himself on a scale, and finds that on a good day of scamming, he always weighs twelve-pounds more than he did in the morning, since he's carrying twelve pounds of coins! Narrator Chanois tells us, in his voice-over that, on this particular day, "as Tulip got heavier and heavier, suddenly—it began to rain…"

Tulip, who is, like lots of Jean Gabin characters (at least, until the end of each film), a master of self-preservation, decides to duck into the entryway of a bank until the raging torrent lets up and then, by sheer happenstance, two hotties happen to be there—Hilda, a German nurse (she's played by Liselotte Pulver, who played Philippe Noiret's daughter Elizabeth Bernadac, in Le Chanois' previous Gabin effort, *Monsieur*), and her friend, Marguerite (Claude Nicot). But, of course, Hilda and Marguerite are hotties who forgot their umbrellas today, so Hilda and Marguerite grab Tulip's umbrella out of his hand (he's brought one along, for just such an eventuality), and start high-tailing it down the street. Tulip gives chase (Gabin runs pretty fast for a sixty-two year-old man, especially for a sixty-two-year-old man who walks slowly in all of his other pictures [even in the ones he made when he was young!]), and while he's not successful in catching them, and in retrieving his *parapluie*, he does, nonsensically, shout after them, "It's people like you who burned Joan of Arc! Now, bring me back my umbrella!" A couple of cops join him in chasing the girls, but it's too late: Hilda and Marguerite jump into Marguerite's car (like Batman and Robin!) and burn rubber, as they speed down the street.

Moments later, though (here comes our old frenemy, Lady Fate, again; we can't have too many Gabin movies where 'she' doesn't show up!), Marguerite's car smashes into Noel's driving school-car—which happens to have been coming right toward them, because Noel had just turned-off, from another street!

Hilda and Marguerite are soon down at the police station, and young Noel is there, too; and even though he's thinking about pressing charges against the women, Hilda thinks he's hot stuff anyway, in spite of the fact that she's just smashed his car into the shape of an accordion. And not only is Noel not going to be pressing charges, but he actually offers to take Hilda to dinner, an invitation which, of course, she gleefully accepts. (Marguerite's not chopped liver, but he forgets about her, in favor of Hilda.) He takes her to a weird/groovy African restaurant, the walls of which are decorated with colorful trinkets, most of which seem to come courtesy of the Serengeti. The dinner proceeds wonderfully, and now that Noel and Hilda know each other better, he invites her to use the familiar '*tu*' form of the word 'you' with him, instead of the formal '*vous*.' The good-humored Restaurateur (Noel Roquevert, whom we've already met during the final scenes of *Archimede, le clochard*) comically asks the couple if they've enjoyed the "lion" which he's just served them (it was actually veal), and Noel pays the check with some ten-franc notes which his godfather, Tulip, gave him. (Uh-oh!) When the Restaurateur returns to Noel and Hilda's table, he discreetly takes Noel into a corner, and concernedly asks the younger man if he knew that the currency with which he has just paid him happens to be counterfeit. (Noel didn't know it: I mean, he's always known that his godfather was a sometimes-counterfeiter, but he never suspected that Tulip would hand him fake bills, to use on his date.) Hilda's got some legitimate franc-notes on hand, though, and she saves the day, by paying for the meal herself. Noel feels embarrassed that she's had to settle the bill, so he tells her that he'd like to take her out to dinner on another evening in the future, to make up for it. Even though Noel's not a counterfeiter himself, we can tell, from the suddenly-excited look which her face took on when the Restaurateur asked Noel about the fake bills, that Hilda thinks he might be; although she's not saying it in words, we can tell she's really getting off on being with a man whom she considers to be a law-flouting badass, even though the button-down Noel is about as far from being a badass as a human being can possibly get. After dinner, Noel drops Hilda off at the mansion, where she toils as a housekeeper for wealthy Mr. and Mrs. Arnaud (Charles Blavette and Annie Savarin), and the couple immediately begins chastising her, because she was supposed to be home that evening to baby-sit their little boy (Jean-Francois Maurin); because of her absence, the couple has been unable to go out, and they're steamed beyond-belief.

Meanwhile, at Tulip's house, Noel is now confronting his godfather about the experience which he's just had in the restaurant: He's never broached the subject of counterfeiting with

Tulip ever—that is, until right now: "Why did you give me fake money to use on my date? Do you know how embarrassed I was?" Tulip gives his godson the only answer which can ever be completely appropriate for Jean Gabin: He just Gabin-Shrugs! ('nuff said!') Noel, next, asks his godfather why he doesn't have any real money socked away from selling his paintings, since in Noel's opinion, they're pretty good, and Tulip replies, "Listen, whether it's paintings or ten-franc bills, I'm an artist, and artists are always broke. I only make small bills, and as long as nobody looks carefully [here he's warning Noel gently, not to examine the situation too closely], I'm fine. If anybody asks me to pay my taxes, I just sit down and make more." Instead of apologizing for causing Noel problems at the restaurant, Tulip now decides to make Noel an offer: "If you want, I'll teach you the trade [counterfeiting]. I promise that you'll make more money than you'll ever make, teaching idiots how to drive. We'll be equal partners, and you'll get fifty percent of what we pull in. But if you're interested, I don't want you to expect that it will be easy, because it won't be."

It's now (probably, even though we don't know for sure) a few weeks later: Noel, who's now going steady with Hilda, brings her home, and Tulip instantly likes her, and isn't even mad that she happens to be the very same girl who swiped his umbrella—in fact, *he admires her balls,* and he asks Noel, "So, who is this enchanting thief you've brought home?" Hilda already knows about Tulip's secret job (Noel has apparently told her about his godfather's counterfeiting exploits, off-screen), and now, when she's meeting him formally, she smiles and says, "So, Mr. Martin. I understand that you're the famous Argenteuil counterfeiter!" Instead of getting mad, he's charmed by her, and even kisses her hand.

As it turns out, Hilda's not just an umbrella thief: In fact, the reason she feels so comfortable around crime, is because, she, too (independently of Tulip), is a counterfeiter in her own right (talk about kismet!), although when she counterfeits, she makes large bills. She threatens, half-jokingly, to turn Tulip in, unless he'll agree to make her part of his counterfeiting operation, of which Noel is now admitting to her that he's just become a part. Since Tulip likes Hilda's spunk, he readily agrees to her offer, and he now proudly offers her (and us) his whole Counterfeiting Backstory: "I've always counterfeited one thing or another. In elementary school, I made fake brownie points; in the regiment, I made fake holiday passes. During the War, I even made fake ID's for the Resistance." Hilda turns to Noel, and is impressed ("Why didn't you tell me your godfather was such a wonderful man?"), and then, since she doesn't have a family of her own, she promises Tulip that she would be honored to take care of him, as if he were her own father.

Soon, needless to say, Noel and Hilda are married, and they and Tulip are now in business together. (Tulip told Hilda that he wants to continue making small bills, in lieu of large ones because, at his age, he has no interest in going to jail, and she's fine with that.) Plus, Hilda is now, visibly, *very* pregnant. The young couple lives with Tulip now, too, and just like in *Le Cave se rebiffe,* Gabin's old counterfeiter-character absolutely abhors rock-and-roll, which in this film issues forth from the noisy records to which Hilda is always listening, and which he keeps shutting off every time she leaves the room. Then, director Chanois gives us a little primer on The Art of Counterfeiting: We see Hilda gleefully stomping on a barrelful of paper-pulp, just like Lucille Ball and Vivian Vance stomping grapes into wine. Tulip really enjoys having the young couple around, and loves that they're working with him, although he does tell the couple that it might be a good idea if, at some point, they might consider living on their own, and separately from him, so that the police won't become suspicious.

Noel and Hilda travel to Aix-en-Provence, in southern France (thirty kilometers north of Marseilles), for a weekend vacation, and Noel's parents, Albert and Dora, are there as well, selling their *kitschy* 'antiques' out of a friend's small shop. They love their new daughter-in-law ("You're Swiss—like chocolate!" a *kvelling* Dora proclaims), and now decide to help Noel and Hilda to buy their own home, although Dora is concerned, and correctly so, about 'her kids' being involved with Tulip: "You all are making money out of nowhere. And Noel, even though your godfather has never been caught, still, as you must know—this can't end well."

The next time we see Noel and Hilda, they're brand-new homeowners, in Nice, and Tulip's on his way to visit them; the kids even pick him up from the train station and, as they chauffeur him around town, Tulip starts holding-forth, majestically, on the state of the bouganvellia he sees all around them, and how, in his opinion, it's kept up abominably. "I could make it grow better in a week," he brags, and probably, he could! Tulip adores Noel and Hilda's new pad, and tells them that he knows he's going to love staying with them, and the next day, the young couple can't find him: Quite enchantingly, Tulip is outside on the beach, painting the morning's sweeping horizon on a canvas, which he's set up on an easel.

While Tulip is painting, a tuxedoed Baron (the international star Curt Jurgens, who's most famous to Americans for playing bad-guy Karl Stromberg, in the 1977 James Bond flick, *The Spy Who Loved Me*) and his young blonde wife happen by, and marvel at Tulip's beautiful painting, especially because, as we're now seeing, Tulip puts the same impeccable detail into creating his paintings that he does into counterfeiting. The Baron asks Tulip what his secret for looking so happy is, and Tulip replies, very simply, "For the last forty years, I've been going to bed at nine o'clock, and waking up at dawn." (It's just simple Gabinian working-man's logic: 'Early to bed, early to rise,' *etc.*)

Back at the kids' house, meanwhile, a Banker (Robert Rollis) is waiting for Tulip, who's offered to help Noel and Hilda with the second part of their two-part house payment. Tulip, who has a huge smile on his face, tells the guy that he doesn't have any cash at the present time, but that he knows he'll be getting some, soon. (And we know he will!) Hilda mentions to Noel and Tulip, later that day, that she's interested in opening a little campground near their new home, so that they'll be able to make some extra money (real money), adding that she doesn't want to be a counterfeiter forever, and this revelation causes the usually even-tempered Tulip to make with a window-rattling Gabin-Outburst: "I will not see people camping here on this beautiful land and ruining it! I will help you pay for the house, but not if you turn it into a camp. And as far as 'side businesses' go, forget about them. Let's just stick to the business we already have."

The next day, Tulip is fishing by the shore, and the smiley Baron and 'Mrs. Baron' show up for a second time, and the Baron, very politely, invites Tulip to spend the day on his yacht. (Tulip has no idea that this guy is a Baron; since Jurgens' character is always dressed in a tux, Martin thinks he's a croupier!) Later that afternoon, Tulip, who's accompanied by Noel and Hilda, arrives at the Baron's yacht, which happens to be crawling not only with bikini-clad women, but also with a groovy photographer, Patrick, who's played by none other than the legendary (even in his own time) counter-culture musician/icon, Serge Gainsbourg. Patrick is the Baron's official 'groovy party-cinematographer,' who seems to be present for the sole purpose of slinking around the boat, 'capturing' the hot babes on his eight-millimeter home-movie camera, while barking-out a whole range of *Blow-Up*-style 'direction,' at them. ("Yeah! That's right, baby! Give me more! YEAH!!!").

The yacht's bikini babes ask Tulip where he's from, and he tells them Argenteuil, but they've never heard of the place before (Argenteuil's very well-known in France, but remember—these are 'bikini babes!') Patrick tells Tulip that the reason the Baron has taken such a liking to him, is because the Baron finds Tulip to be 'whimsical.'

Anyone who's seen too many movies, and is waiting for a twist, will probably, at this point, think that the Baron knows Gabin is a counterfeiter, and means to blackmail him into joining his own criminal operation (whatever that may be), or else, to take over Tulip's 'outfit'—but refreshingly and charmingly, the movie will offer no such hackneyed plot twist. *Le Jardinier d'Argenteuil* is not a crime thriller, nor is the Baron a bad guy; he's just an old dilettante who's brought Tulip aboard, because he's genuinely charmed by Tulip's simplicity. Meanwhile, in one of the yacht's many finely-appointed staterooms, Noel and Hilda open the suitcase which Tulip has brought on board with him, and it's filled with all of the plates he uses to make his famous ten-franc notes; obviously, Tulip wasn't comfortable enough to have left his livelihood too far out of his purview.

Back on deck, the relentlessly-groovy Patrick, who's more than a little stoned, tells his captive audience of bikined beauties, in these exact words, "My camera is recording the truth, babies! This is a happening… and 'a happening' is the most important part of liberation!" (This is the French version of screenwriter Roger Ebert's great, iconic movie-line, "It's my happening… and it freaks me out," from director Russ Meyer's legendary 1969 head-trip flick, *Beyond the Valley of the Dolls*.) Everybody on board is dancing now, and partying (the film, during these boat scenes, resembles an episode of t.v.'s "The Monkees" gone terribly amuck), and it's grand good fun, to see that old and iconic warhorse Jean Gabin standing in the background, watching the kids groove-out. (One reveler, a guy who is, very obviously, tripping on LSD, is even crawls around the deck, screaming out, "I'm a rat! Where is my cheese," while, at the same time, one rather free-spirited woman dances around sensuously, and wields a gun in each hand, just like Juliette Lewis' free-wheeling *gangsta-cutey*, in *Natural Born Killers*.) Needless to say, this is all endlessly new and fascinating to Tulip: "I never thought anyone could live this way," he confesses to Patrick, amused by all of this weird behavior. The Baron tells Tulip that, in his own considered opinion, freedom is nice, but that in no way is it as nice as making money (something that all of us who are well past thirty figured out a long time ago)! The Baron still has no idea that Tulip is 'making' money too, although not in the same way that he, himself, 'makes it.'

The next day, the Banker returns to Noel and Hilda's house, to get the second payment from Tulip, but Tulip's not around, and the guy tells Hilda that if he doesn't get the balance of the money which the bank is owed, and today, that he's going to have to foreclose on the property. Director Chanois next dissolves to a few hours later, and we now see a happy Hilda, who looks to be as calm as Jean Gabin usually is himself, and she's drying some newly-minted counterfeit money on a clothesline. (The final payment to the bank now gets made, with no fuss and no mess.)

Hilda celebrates the finalization of her and Noel's purchase, by next driving way too fast through Nice, in her smooth-looking convertible. Two cops (Edmond Ardisson and Roland Malet) pull her over and issue her a speeding ticket, which she pays right on the spot, by handing them a handful of counterfeit ten-franc notes!

When she arrives home a few minutes later, Hilda freaks-out to Noel about the fact that she was just pulled-over, but he is utterly without sympathy: "Are you crazy? We came to Nice for sunshine, light, and fishing—not to give counterfeit money to cops!" (Giving the cops fake money is a weird thing for her to do, since her character is supposed to be smart—but maybe, on some sub-conscious-level, she's crying out for help: She already told Noel and Tulip that she'd like to get out of the counterfeiting game and so maybe, on some level which even she doesn't fully understand, 'getting herself caught' is the only way she can do it.)

Back at Noel's dad Albert's beachfront summer place in Nice, the same two Cops who pulled Hilda over have now shown up, and they're looking not for her, but for Tulip. (They've traced the fake banknotes, which Hilda gave them when they pulled her over, to him, and they believe, also, that, when Hilda gave them the bills, she didn't know they were fakes.) Dora, Albert's wife, doesn't care about any of that stuff, though: She's just trying to sell the cops some cheesy-looking urns!

When we next see Tulip and the kids, they're heading to a nearby casino in Cannes, as invited guests of the Baron, who's given Tulip a tux to wear; this is probably the first tuxedo Tulip's ever worn in his life, and he looks all kinds of uncomfortable, dressed in such finery, just like how Jean Gabin's characters always used to always feel out-of-place in some of those early films (especially *Gloria* and *Martin Roumagnac*), in those scenes in which Gabin was always portraying 'the lone poor guy, at the fancy-dress do.' "I'm going to teach you how to like money, friend," the Baron brags to Tulip, but the joke is, of course, that Tulip already likes money so much, that he actually manufactures it! Meanwhile, in the casino's VIP baccarat area, Hilda is about to gamble a few new counterfeit ten-franc notes which she's just made, in order to get the real money which she now needs to pay a couple of painters who are brightening up her and Noel's new digs.

Tulip plays high-stakes baccarat with the Baron (the Baron funds each 'hand' which Tulip plays) and, almost instantaneously (he's a quick study), he wins two hundred thousand francs. "I'm going to use this money to buy a horse and cart," the simple-living painter-gardener-

(counterfeiter) crows excitedly to the Baron. (The friendship between a Baron and a working-class guy is nothing new in a Gabin picture: Their relationship recalls working-class Gabin's similar relationship with Louis Jouvet's Baron-character, in director Jean Renoir's 1936 classic, *Les Bas-fonds*.) With his newfound winnings, Tulip is now obsessed with buying a horse and carriage, since he's never had one before, and in the movie's next (great) sequence, he buys a horse-and-carriage-combination right out from under the Farmer (Henri Rellys) who owns it, paying for it with ten thousand of the real francs which he's just won. "I want to drive it myself," Tulip announces, re: his new acquisition, and the Driver is so blown away by all the money he's just been given, that he even offers Tulip his complimentary services as Tulip's driver, forever! Tulip politely tells the guy "thanks, but no thanks," but he and Noel do take the Driver to Noel Roquevert's exotic, Serengeti-themed restaurant for a hearty meal. Since this is a 1960s' flick, *natch*, the requisite, bearded Hippie/Jesus Freak now sashays into the restaurant, and tries selling Tulip some 'groovy postcards:' "Hey, man, buy one of my groovy postcards for ten francs, so I can build a shrine in our Lord's honor!" While we've been conditioned to believe that Tulip is going to be giving the guy one of his *faux* ten-franc notes, the movie is, as usual, smarter than that: Instead of handing the guy some bread and shooing him away, Tulip brings the Hippie aboard the Baron's yacht, so that the guy can befriend all of the other long-hairs, since Tulip has determined, correctly, that he might just get along with them. (Jean Gabin: He brings 'dirty, hippie-freaks' together!)

Now, the film's director, Jean-Paul Le Chanois, re-emerges as the picture's voice-over narrator, to 'dot all of the I's' and 'cross all of the T's' in our story: "Later that day," Chanois tells us, "Mr. Tulip went home, to the Blue Lizard [it's the name the kids have given to their new abode], but Hilda and Noel were nowhere to be seen." Tulip, who was tired of waiting for them to come home, has left the house in his new horse and cart, having no idea that the kids are simultaneously returning home from wherever it is that they've been, using a different road. Tulip's moving out—and, in fact, he's moving back to his true home in Argenteuil, but before his departure, he's left the kids a present, the *real* ninety-thousand francs, minus the ten thousand which he used to pay for the horse and cart that he won, playing baccarat with the Baron.

The kids are amazed to find the money and, as they're staring at it, they suddenly hear a police siren wailing away from somewhere outside the house. The kids think that they're about to be busted, and that this real and legally-won money which Tulip has just left for them is counterfeit, so they throw it into the fireplace and burn it! As it turns out, the cops weren't really coming to their house at all: They were just driving past, searching for a lion which had apparently just escaped from the local zoo. (Hopefully, it's not the lion which Noel Roquevert claimed to have been serving at his restaurant.)

The film now ends with an invitation to us, the audience, from Narrator (and director) Jean-Paul Le Chanois: "Well, that's our story. If you ever go on vacation in Nice, maybe Hilda can be your nanny. Noel's a pretty great driving teacher too, if you ever need a lesson, and if you ever find yourself in Argenteuil, maybe, just maybe, you might even make a nice friend... like *Monsieur Tulipe!*"

Le Jardinier d'Argenteuil is one of those great Jean Gabin movies that has never been seen in the United States, even though it's a very popular DVD in France (without English subtitles, of course). And if you want to see a prominent prop from the movie, head over to the *Musee Gabin* (the Jean Gabin Museum), in Meriel: They've got a large painting of Gabin's *Monsieur Tulipe,* which Gabin's character is supposed to have painted of himself in the film, as a self-portrait.

Liselotte Pulver (a/k/a, 'Lilo' Pulver, who appeared in both this film, and in the previous Gabin/Patelliere collaboration, 1963's *Monsieur*) made mostly French and German films throughout her career, although she *would* also appear in two American films: She played a supporting role in Billy Wilder's great 1961 James Cagney comedy, *One, Two, Three,* and seven years before that, she was the leading lady in Douglas Sirk's World War II-romance, *A Time to Love and a Time to Die* (1954), which was filmed in Berlin, and in which she appeared opposite an actor whose name sounds a whole lot like Jean Gabin, the American actor, John Gavin.

What a Critic Said at the Time: "Gabin is his usual anarchic self. He stands around looking old, and is not even given the chance to do his 'stock anger scene...'" (*Variety*, 10-19-66 issue, Critic: "Mosk. [George Moskowitz.]" Reviewed in Paris.)

FILM 83

LE SOLEIL DES VOYOUS

France/Italy, 1967

(Literal English Translation: "SUN OVER THE NO-GOODS") Directed by Jean Delannoy. Produced by Raymond Danon. Screenplay by Jean Delannoy and Alphonse Boudard. Based Upon the Novel, The Action Man, by J.M. Flynn. Music by Francis Lai. Director of Photography (color), Walter Wottitz. Editor, Henri Taverna. Production Designer, Rene Renoux. (GENRES: ACTION/ THRILLER) A Production of FIDA-Cinematografica (Italy) and Les Films Copernic/Maurice Jacquin Films (France). Running Time, 1 hour 55 minutes. Released in France on May 31, 1967, by Les Films Copernic. Released in the United States directly to syndicated television in 1969, by Ben Barry and Associates (English-Dubbed) as "ACTION MAN," at 1 hour 40 minutes.

"Of course you've come to kill me. I know you're not here to give me a massage!"
— *Gabin's partner-in-crime (Robert Stack) finds a contract-killer waiting for him in his apartment, in "Le Soleil des voyous"*

The world is changing in 1967: The hair is getting longer, the skirts are getting shorter, and Jean Gabin is starting to look more like a gruff-but-cool white-haired bulldog than ever before. Gabin started the year off, *almost* starring in Michel Audiard's adaptation of the notoriously anti-Semitic author Louis-Ferdinand Celine's novel, *Mort a credit* (*Death on the Installment Plan*), but instead, wisely, he chose director Jean Delannoy's fun heist-a-palooza, *Le Soleil des voyous* (*Sun Over the No-Goods*), which was released in the United States under the title of the J.M. Flynn novel upon which it was based, *Action Man*, a title which makes it sound more like an Arnold Schwarzenegger picture than a Jean Gabin effort. *Soleil des voyous* teams Gabin up, for one of the few times in his career, with an American co-star, the legendary Robert Stack who, of course, played Eliot Ness on American t.v.'s iconic cult hit, "The Untouchables." According to Delannoy, who was interviewed in actress/director Nadia Gray's 1978 French television documentary, "Remembering Jean Gabin," Gabin was at first reluctant to work with Stack, whom he considered, as a t.v. actor, to be beneath him acting-wise, but apparently, when they met, and when Gabin got a taste of Stack's formidable acting chops, the two became fast friends and Gabin, a guy who was never famous for hanging

368 | **THE FILMS** CYCLE FIVE

One last heist.

around with his co-stars too much, even started accompanying Stack, on a nightly basis, to swingin' Left Bank nightclubs, during the shooting of the film; in fact, the whole 'Paris club scene' must have rubbed-off on Jean Gabin in a favorable way, because his next film after this one, *Le Pacha*, will feature an extended sequence in which the great white-haired icon sits stonefacedly in a trendy hippie bar, as turned-on young lovers gyrate to psychedelic music, all around him. Yes, sixty-three-year-old Jean Gabin was '*The Ultimate Club Kid!*'

Gabin's *Soleil des voyous* character, Dennis Farrand, is a Parisian bar-owner and, as in *Grisbi*, *Du rififi a Paname*, and *Melodie en sous-sol*, he's also a level-headed gentleman bandit/crime boss who, due to his extreme meticulousness, has been nicknamed The Perfectionist, and in this film, just as in *Melodie*, Gabin will spend a good deal of his screen time daydreaming of that obligatory 'one last job [heist]' which he'd like to pull before his retirement. Each night, Dennis and his *cutie-pie* young secretary/bartender Betty, who's played by the German actress Margaret Lee (who would also appear in innumerable Z-grade pictures, some of which would be churned-out by the Spanish exploitation-master, Jesus 'Jess' Franco), peek over at the bank across the street from the bar, where armored military vehicles regularly tote the weekly payroll, for U.S. soldiers who are stationed in France. Dennis has always dreamed of heisting the payroll, but for now his bar is successful, and so he's mostly content to let it remain a dream.

Of course, this wouldn't be a good Gabin Crime Picture without a rival crime boss whose sole job in life seems to be 'making Our Man's life hell,' and this time out, he appears in

Eliot Ness meets Pepe Le Moko: Robert Stack and Jean Gabin.

the person of Monsieur Henri (Jean Topart). Henri puts a contract out on Dennis, and pays the smooth, itinerant American mercenary Jim Beckley (Robert Stack) who, in Henri's own words, is just "out of the deep freeze" (a/k/a, six years in Sing-Sing), along with a trio of cauliflower-nosed thugs, to break into, and to bust-up, Dennis' place, as a warning that he (Henri) is not to be trifled-with. When Beckley begins tearing up the joint with his unsavory cohorts, he gets a big surprise, when he discovers that the joint belongs to Dennis, his old French war buddy who saved his bacon when the two were both parachutists in the wartorn Indochina of the 1950s. (Beckley was an American mercenary, and Dennis was a Legionnaire.) When Beckley sees that the bar belongs to his pal, he becomes so enraged, that he savagely kung-fu's (or, '*Stack-Fu's!*') the hell out of his own thugs, who are played by Bob Ingarao, Dominique Zardi, and Carlo Neil, all the while screaming at them, "You tell Henri that the contract is broken!"

After a liquor-filled reunion (Dennis doesn't hold it against Beckley that Beckley was sent to kill him [hell, a real man shouldn't expect anything less from a pal!]), Dennis enlists Beckley to be his partner in the big army payroll heist, and it's definitely good fun to watch these two cool actors utilizing ammo-filled household tools, including Hoover vacuum cleaners and sanitation trucks, to aide them in their crime, *a la* American television's inventive "MacGyver," twenty-some years later! The two hire their own team of misfits (shades of *The Dirty Dozen*) and blast their way into the bank by night, administering truth serum (!) to the ancient night watchman, played by Henri Coutet, who instantly reveals the combination to the bank's strong room to them. Dennis and Beckley rip-off the *grisbi* without too many problems, although the one mistake they do make, is when they accidentally trip the alarm system, which happens to be connected to the office of the Bank Manager (Yvon Sarray); anyway, Dennis and Beckley are able to knock the Watchman out cold, before he can give the two of them too much *tsurris*.

Stack is really on parade, in *Soleil*: His no-nonsense Beckley, who was obviously modeled on Sean Connery's 007, definitely holds his own against Jean Gabin; Stack plays Beckley borderline-psycho, and it's great, unpleasant fun to see t.v.'s Elliot Ness torturing one of Monsieur Henri's thugs, a greaseball called Ange Paracy (Pierre Koulak), who's been sent to kill Dennis and Beckley. (Beckley blowtorches Paracy's knees, threatens to heave a torch down his throat, and even shoves the guy's head into the teeth of a hungry skillsaw! [The skillsaw needs meat!]) Eventually, Beckley tosses Ange into the back of a garbage truck, where the guy gets ground-up into Alpo, sixteen years before James Woods would meet the same fate, at the finale of Sergio Leone's haunting *Once Upon a Time in America*. And while I'm on the subject of Sergio Leone: While Leone and Gabin never worked together, Jean Gabin, as I've already mentioned in this book, was Leone's all-time-favorite movie actor, so it's pretty certain that Leone must have seen *Soleil des voyous*.

Beckley next high-tails it over to Monsieur Henri's office, where he grabs the whimpering, and not-so-tough-in-the-presence-of-a-hardened-American-mercenary Henri, around the neck: "I know you sent Ange to kill me. I mean, I know he didn't come to give me a massage!" Beckley orders Henri to lift the contract on Dennis immediately, and Henri says that there's no way he can to do it, because the *capo* above him (Henri's only the under-boss), Ludwig Savigni (Mino Doro), would never agree to it.

Henri knows that Dennis has squirreled-away all of the U.S. Army payroll cash, and he wouldn't be a good gangster if he didn't make a few, furtive attempts to get his mitts on it, and so, to that nefarious end, he instructs his henchmen to kidnap Dennis' wife! Dennis goes to Henri, telling him that he is no longer in possession of the money, and this is true: The loot has disappeared from Dennis' bar, and he and Beckley have no idea where it is. "Now," Dennis continues, (SPOILER! ULTRA-FAB PLOT TWIST COMING!), "give me back my wife—and I'll give you back your mama!" Wily Dennis (in every picture, Gabin is always five zillion steps ahead of his rivals-in-crime) has already had the foresight to realize that Henri will try something stupid, like kidnapping his wife, so he has taken the pre-emptive strike, and he's kidnapped Henri's mother!

A truce is now necessarily called between the two sides, because Dennis wants his wife back, and Henri wants his aged mother returned, just as safely. And just as Steckley leaves Henri's mom's apartment (she's played by Lucienne Bogaert, the heroin-addicted old whore from *Voici le temps des assassins*), Henri's tough-as-nails old mother whips out a shotgun and blows Steckley to hell, in an eye-poppingly violent Bob Stack-*vs.*-Old Lady shootout! Wounded, Steckley staggers into his car, where he promptly expires, as he begins driving away! (Shades of the demise of the main gangster-character, 'Le Stephanois,' in director Jules

Dassin's Gabinless Auguste Le Breton-adaptation, *Rififi*. [Le Stephanois is, of course, another movie gangster who gets shot as he's steering his getaway car—almost!—to freedom.])

And now, before you can say "It's time for a double cross," well—it's time for a double cross! Betty, Dennis' sexy secretary, has stowed all of the stolen payroll money in the trunk of her car, having effortlessly ripped-off her boss, and as she makes her getaway and tries to skip town, fate, aided and abetted by frequent Gabin-movie screenwriter Michael Audiard, now issues her the major flat tire of all time. A couple of amiable Cops (Alain Janey and Antoine Baud) happen along to help her change the tire, and when they ask her what she's got in the trunk, which won't close completely, they become immediately suspicious. As they pop the hood open, their mouths drop, Tex Avery-style, when they discover the purloined army payroll, which they are able, very promptly, to tie to Betty's boss, Dennis. And so, as *Le Soleil des voyous* ends, we know that both Betty and 'Action-Man' Dennis, the boss whom she was trying to screw over, will probably now be settling for the relative 'in-action' of prison.

Le Soleil des voyous was released in the United States not theatrically, but directly to television, shorn of fifteen minutes, by Ben Barry and Associates, a small distributor which bought European movies, and sold them directly to syndicated American television (where the films would invariably appear at 3:00 a.m., interspersed, of course, with the obligatory used car ads—"Here's a 1969 Dodge Dart, for only $999.95")! Any American who was able to catch this flick at 3:00 a.m., back in '69, was very lucky indeed, because since then, the film has been missing in action in the U.S. As I mentioned, it's a very decent flick, and even if it weren't, it would still be important to movie history, because it's world cinema's one-and-only team-up of two of the world's coolest icons: *Pepe Le Moko* and *Elliot Ness!*

On December 4th, 1966, shortly after *Le Soleil des voyous* had completed production, Gabin's co-star Robert Stack sat down with Andre Leclerc, the host of the popular French t.v. show *"Au-dela l'ecran"* ("Beyond the Screen"), and spoke about how great it was to work with Gabin:

"I'm a huge fan of Jean Gabin. He's like Spencer Tracy. He was very nice to me on the set of the film, because he's worked in English a couple of times [on *Moontide* and *Impostor*], and so he understood how hard it was for me to work in a foreign language. I didn't learn a lot of French from Gabin, but I did learn a lot of great 'slang French' from him." [Author's Note: Stack delivers this t.v. interview in perfect, unaccented French, because he had lived in France for an extended period of time, when he was a young man.]

What a Critic Said at the Time: "A fairly slick gangster suspenser. Has good production dress. Gabin is his usual crusty self, and still wields a solid film presence." (*Variety*, 7-14-67 issue. Critic: "Mosk. [George Moskowitz.]" Reviewed in Paris.)

Top: **Investigating a murder with Robert Dalban.** *Above:* **With Dany Carrel.**

FILM 84

Le Pacha

France/Italy, 1968

(Literal English Translation: "THE BOSS") Directed by Georges Lautner. Based Upon the Novel by Albert Simonin. Screenplay by Michel Audiard, Jean Laborde, and Albert Simonin. Produced by Alan Poire. Director of Photography (color), Maurice Fellous. Production Designer, Jean D'Eaubonne. Editor, Michelle David. Music by Serge Gainsbourg. (GENRE: ACTION) A Production of Rizzoli Film S.P.A. (Italy) and Societe Nouvelle des Establissements Gaumont (SNEG)/GAFER (France). Running Time, 1 hour 30 minutes. Released in France by Gaumont-International, on March 14, 1968. Never Released Theatrically in the United States.

"If they could put jerks in orbit... you'd be a satellite!"
— Inspector Gabin interrogates a bad guy, in *"Le Pacha"*

French action specialist Georges Lautner's (he's kind of 'the John Frankenheimer of France') *Le Pacha* (*The Boss*), which was executive-produced by Jean Gabin and Fernandel's production company, GAFER, is our next Gabin heist film, and it was made right after Gabin's previous heist flick of the previous year, *Soleil des voyous*, although this time, Gabin is the hardass/warhorse cop who's in charge of putting the heisters away.

A van full of diamonds is ambushed by a sadistic/paranoid gang-boss called Quinquin (he's played by the actor Andre Pousse, and his name is pronounced 'can-can,' just like the dance), and the case is being investigated by Gabin's Inspector Joss. After Quinquin has the diamonds, he begins offing some of the associates who helped him in the crime, all of whom are people who pretend to be 'typical Parisians' (an old man, an art student, a husband and wife), all people whom the cops would never suspect. After giving his associates their promised cuts, he offs each of them, one-by-one, so that greedily, he'll be able to keep all of the loot for himself, and in one splashy (pun intended) sequence, Quinquin shoots away at the young art-student, blasting away at cans full of yellow, day-glow paint: In primo, Antonion/*Blow-Up* style, we get to marvel at the paint cans exploding, while the victim is splattered with what, very stylishly, appears to be yellow blood.

A 'rub,' is that the police inspector Gouvion (he is unseen in the film), who was Joss'

Quinquin has been responsible for the deaths of her boyfriend and her bother, Nathalie readily agrees to help Joss.

More determined than ever to get rid of Quinquin, Joss informs Quinquin's rival gang that a postal train full of money will be making an appearance at a local train station, and that it will be easy-pickings. He next asks Nathalie to inform Quinquin of the rival gang's dealings. She does, and she is then killed by Quinquin, who trusts her about as much as he trusts anybody else—which is, not at all.

The rival gang attacks the postal train, just as Joss knew they would, and its members then head over to a dilapidated old factory, to hide the loot. Of course, Quinquin and his gang are there, lying in wait, and the two gangs fight. The police arrive, and among them is Joss, who steps out of the shadows, Eastwood/Bronson-style. Joss blows Quinquin away, after uttering a few well-chosen words by scenarist Michel Audiard, and he has now avenged his old friend's death. Jean Gabin walks away alone, just like he's supposed to do.

While *Le Pacha* will never be confused with any of Gabin's best movies, because the pacing is frequently quite sluggish, it manages, nevertheless, to be 'medium exciting,' because it's one of those rare films which is driven not by the pull of its narrative, but by the turbo-charged engine of Serge Gainsbourg's jazz-inflected score, including *"Requiem pour un con,"* the movie's theme song, which became a big hit in France when the movie was released. In fact, Gainsbourg even makes a cameo in the film, playing himself: In high "Partridge Family" style, Gabin's Inspector Joss enters a recording studio, in which Gainsbourg just so happens to be playing the film's theme song, to interrogate Gainsbourg's drummer, a man who, apparently—at least in this movie—is a cohort of Quinquin's! As Gabin enters the studio, and as Gainsbourg leaves, the 1930s' film icon and the 1960s' rock icon share a knowing nod and wink.

Le Pacha scores some bonus points, as well, for featuring some of the best snow-chase footage this side of a James Bond picture, as well as one of Jean Gabin's very best movie lines, ever: Interrogating one of Quinquin's former henchmen, Jean Gabin's Inspector Joss really 'tears him a new one,' opining, "If they could put jerks in orbit, you'd be a satellite!"

What a Critic Said at the Time: "Slick and brutal cops and robbers pic. Gabin does his controlled anger scenes with his usual brio." (*Variety*, 4-3-68 issue. Critic: "Rick." Reviewed in Paris.)

Top: With Louis de Funes. Above: In the dojo.

FILM 85

LE TATOUE

France/Italy, 1968

(Literal English Translation: "THE TATTOOED ONE") Directed by Denys de La Patelliere. Produced by Raoul Baum and Maurice Jacquin. Written by Alphonse Boudard and Pascal Jardin. Director of Photography, (color/scope), Sacha Vierny. Music by Georges Garaventz. Editor, Claude Durand. Production Designer, Robert Clavel. (GENRE: MADCAP COMEDY) A Production of Ascot and Cineraid (Italy)/Les Films Copernic and Les Films Corona (France). Running Time, 1 hour 30 minutes. Released in France on September 18, 1968, by Cineraid. Never Released Theatrically in the United States. (English-Dubbed Version, entitled "MILLION DOLLAR TATTOO" was prepared, but never released theatrically.)

> "I don't eat and I don't imbibe. I don't take chances… Speed kills!"
> — *Elderly crackpot ex-Legionnaire Gabin tells a friend his secret to a long and happy life, in "Le Tatoue"*

1968: Vietnam. Russian tanks mowing down Czechs. And *weird, overproduced, 'mod' comedies* made on both sides of the Atlantic: *Le Tatoue (The Tattooed One)* is a French attempt at the lushly-Technicolored 'madcap' comedies which late-sixties Hollywood was churning-out in feverish droves, and it comes complete with the requisite psychedelic palate, lush anamorphic cinematography, and even its own jaunty Herb Alpert and the Tijuana Brass/*Casino Royale*-sounding soundtrack theme, which was composed by the prolific film composer, George Garaventz. The picture is notable not only for being Gabin's only out-and-out farce (it plays like a sporadically-funny Blake Edwards movie), but also because it's the only movie in which a completely un-silent Gabin goes way, way, way over the top, even by the standards of his other comedies, in which customarily, his characters talk a lot, instead of being silent: In *Tatoue*, and for the first and only time in his career, Jean Gabin actually 'acts silly' and, as we're watching the picture, we want him to 'pull it back' a bit. (Oh, well: "It was a choice!") The film teams Gabin up for the third time, after *La Traversee de Paris* and *Le Gentleman d'Epsom*, with the comedian Louis de Funes, although whereas in their other two pictures, Gabin starred and De Funes appeared only in a supporting role, in this picture, de Funes shares above-the-title billing with Gabin, and the two work as comedy team—a continental Abbott and Costello, in which Gabin plays boisterous straight man to De Funes' usual collection of goofy noises and grimaces, although as it will turn out by the end of the picture, Gabin's character is a lot wackier than is de Funes.'

Le Tatoue presents a skewed glimpse into what may have become of Gabin's 1930s' Legionnaire characters from *Gueule d'amour* and *La Bandera,* thirty years later: A retired Legionnaire who's living on his pension, Gabin's Albert, complete with a giant Kaiser-Wilhelm-looking mustache, spends his days haplessly posing for cheesily-patriotic Legionnaire paintings in a Paris art gallery. ('Legionnaire paintings' are, in the world of this film, the equivalent of those *kitschy* black-velvet Elvis paintings which get sold in Las Vegas gift shops.) One day, when Albert's removing his shirt and getting ready for 'the day's pose,' a visiting art broker and perennial schemer, Mezerey (De Funes), notices that the old Legionnaire has a large tattoo of a beautiful woman stretching the entire length of his back; when Mezerey questions Albert about the drawing, Albert informs him that the picture was actually painted, and then indelibly tattooed onto his back, by Modigliani himself, back in the 1930s! Of course, needless to say, Mezerey smells a gold mine.

It's not long before Mezerey is mentioning this incredible skin-art find to some visiting New York art dealers (they're played by Jo Warfield and Donald von Kurtz), who instruct him to offer Albert two million francs for the tattoo, but of course, they're going to have to skin Albert alive, in order to get it, and Mezerey's bizarre idea, such as it is, is to put Albert, who's a bit on the paunchy side, on a special diet, so that, as he puts it, "the skin will naturally loosen," and he'll be able to cut it away (or so he thinks) without causing too much pain for the aging Legionnaire! Amazingly, Gabin's bizarre Albert-character, whose (presumably, Alzheimer's-addled) motto in the picture is, "I don't eat and I don't imbibe. I don't take chances. Speed kills!" tells Mezerey that he may happily skin him, but only under the condition that Mezerey will help him to restore his magnificent sixteenth-century chateau! Since Albert and Mezerey are both certifiably loony, they quickly become fast friends.

What ensues, is a bunch of Keystone Cops-styled mayhem, in which various greedy art brokers are chasing Albert all over France, trying to skin his hide and, of course, crusty old Albert has a dungeon in his chateau, so that all of the *dermis-hungry* interlopers who make it over to the house to try and trap him, just like in most episodes of American t.v.'s 1960s hit, "The Munsters," wind up plummeting down a groovy slide, and into Albert's dungeon, where Albert and Mezerey gleefully taunt them with weirdly-nonsensical epithets. The occasionally-funny *Le Tatoue* is one of those movies which is definitely more fun to talk about than it is to watch, although one can't deny that it definitely *is* hysterical when Mezerey's bovine Wife, who's played by Dominique Davray, calls him 'Toodles,' and de Funes' angry rejoinder is, "I'm nobody's Toodles! Not even my own!" The film even attempts, if only momentarily, to touch upon the 'hot-button' 1960s' issue of race relations: Mezerey has a black Butler (Ibrahim Seck), who asks him, sounding, in the film's English-dubbed print, just like Stepin Fetchit, "Why is you mo' impo'tant than me, Mr. Boss?!"

If you want to see Jean Gabin acting really silly, this is the movie for you—otherwise, as the sign on the door of Legionnaire Albert's chateau says: "Keep out!" Director Denys de La Patelliere was always pretty hit-and-miss when it came to the movies which he made with Jean Gabin: Some were great (*Rue des Prairies, Le Tonnerre de Dieu*), and others not so great (*Du Rififi a Paname, Le Tatoue*, and an upcoming 1972 cop thriller which I'll soon be talking about, called *Le Tueur* [*The Killer*]), but I guess *Le Tatoue* is weird and funny and engaging *enough,* if you're in an undemanding mood. The picture was never released theatrically in any English-speaking territories but, as I've mentioned, an English-dubbed version was made, and if you pick up the French-release DVD of *Le Tatoue,* you can access the English-dialogue track. (Of course, other actors are dubbing Gabin and de Funes' voices.)

What a Critic Said at the Time: "A French *Odd Couple*. Gabin is still a top draw for older audiences… He holds his own as a rugged individualist who disdains the [present] times." (*Variety*, 10-2-68 issue. Critic: "Mosk. [George Moskowitz.]" Reviewed in Paris.)

FILM 86

SOUS LE SIGNE DU TAUREAU

France, 1969

(Literal English Translation: "UNDER THE SIGN OF THE BULL") Directed by Gilles Grangier. Produced by Roger De Broin and Robert Sussfeld. Screenplay by Michel Audiard, Francois Boyer, and Gilles Grangier (with uncredited script contributions by Claude Sautet and Pascal Jardin). Based Upon the Novel "Fin de journee," by Roger Vrigny. Director of Photography (COLOR), Walter Wottitz. Editor, Jacqueline Douarinou-Sadoul. Music by Jean Prodromides. Production Designer, Robert Clavel. (GENRE: DRAMA) A Gaumont Production. Running Time, 1 hour 21 minutes. Released in France by Gaumont-International, on March 28, 1969. Never Released Theatrically in the United States.

"I haven't told you anything for twenty years, and I'm not going to start now!"
— *Ultra-private Gabin doesn't like his wife knowing anything about him at all, in "Sous le signe du taureau"*

This genreless and meandering space-age Gabin movie is the most bewildering and impenetrable (and confusing, and unlikeable) movie in the entire Gabin canon, and worse—it doesn't make a lick of sense! Jean Gabin's twelfth and final movie to have been directed by Gilles Grangier, even gets off to a false start: The beginning credits are superimposed over some of those psychedelic-looking, late 1960s rocket ships, to which audiences were already getting accustomed from movies like *2001: A Space Odyssey*. Not knowing anything about this movie when I sat down to watch it, I thought, based exclusively on my viewing of the groovy opening sequence, that I was about to be treated to some kind of a 'mod, sci-fi epic'—Gabin in Space! But no such luck, because after the trippy opening credits complete themselves, it's time for seventy-nine minutes of talking heads (which talk... and talk... and talk...).

Bulldog-faced, sixty-six-year-old Jean Gabin (*he's* still cool in the movie, even though the movie itself sucks) plays rocket scientist (seriously!) Alain Raynal, top-dog of Raynal Industries, the French government's biggest contractor of war-armaments. (Raynal Industries mostly makes missiles. [Say that three times fast!]) As the film begins, tired-looking Raynal watches his men load some of his company's new, *per* Geo. W. Bush, 'W.M.D.'s' onto the back of a truck, and he looks like he doesn't even care; he's really more concerned, by his own admission, with heading over to the local 'rocket scientist bar' (I'm not making that up), and powering-down a few glasses of Pastis, in tried, but still-true, Gabinesque Silence. For the first time in a Jean Gabin movie, and this is due to the incredibly underwritten screenplay, which was co-authored by Michel Audiard, Francois Boyer, and the film's director, Gilles Grangier, the actor's stone-facedness doesn't suggest deep currents of thought or 'a reservoir of pent-up emotions' (or even 'a reservoir tip')! *Sous le signe du taureau* is the only Gabin picture in which, not only is he 'phoning in' his performance, but he looks like he's run out of change for the payphone. While in the bar, Raynal receives a phone call from a big muckimuck in the French government, informing him that France will no longer be keeping its contract with Raynal Industries.

Even though Raynal looks like he was ready to retire eons ago, he feels, still, that he needs to keep his company going, because of the allegiance which he feels toward his thousands of employees, people whom he just doesn't want to be out of work: The 'real' working-people, as in lots of other Jean Gabin films (going all the way back to 1933's *Le Tunnel*), are depending on him for their livelihoods, and he's not about to let them down.

Since his company won't be manufacturing weapons anymore, Raynal decides that, to stay afloat, he might have to start producing household goods instead, and he's more than a little upset about it: As he now bitches to another character, "I didn't work this hard all my life to make vacuum cleaners!" Now that the government won't be paying Raynal's overhead and operational expenses anymore, he knows he's going to have to go and glad-hand some investors, and just thinking about that is making him nauseous, because Jean Gabin is not a supplicant!

While Raynal is married to his long-time and long-suffering wife, Christine (Suzanne Flon, who also played Gabin's wife two years earlier, in *Soleil des voyous*) he, of course, has the requisite mistress which all French dudes get issued at birth. Her name is Rolande (Colette Dereal), and he's been seeing her behind, and even in front of, his wife's back for years, in fact, Rolande even owns the rocket scientist bar where all of the film's characters go to get loaded. Rolande tells Raynal, consolingly, not to worry about his company's sudden run of bad luck, because she knows a billionaire investor, a guy with deep-pockets who lives in Rouen, the bustling French port city on the Seine, between Le Havre and Paris (it's the place where Joan of Arc became a crispy-critter, back in 1431), by the name of Vacher ('*vache*' means 'cow' in French, and this is a great name for a wealthy, capitalist-pig!), who's played by Alfred Adam (he played the butcher, Barberot, in *Maigret tend un piege*), a guy whom, as she's now telling Raynal, he can meet, if he's interested. (It's more than implied, by the *moony-moony* way in which Rolande is gushing about Vacher, that she's probably *bumping uglies* with him, as well as with Raynal.)

Rolande drops Raynal off at the train station in Paris, and he is now off to Rouen for his meeting with Vacher. These two older guys, when they finally meet, get along well-enough, and Vacher tells Raynal that he'll be happy to supply him with cash, only asking that in return, Raynal should pay the loan back to him with only the smallest amount of interest, an amount which, by the way, is much less than a bank would be charging Raynal for the same exact loan. Even though the offer is too good to pass up, Raynal does pass it up, politely thanking Vacher for his time, and leaving. The offer, as it turns out, is completely honest, but Raynal has never borrowed money before, and in spite of the fact that he doesn't want his employees to be out of work, he's too proud of a man to accept help (even now, when he really needs it). Explaining his position gently to Vacher, Raynal tells him that he never works with partners, which is something we already knew about Gabin anyway, based on watching most of his other pictures. (Remember what happened in *Touchez pas au grisbi*, when Gabin had a partner—goofy old Riton? "Troubles, my friend!")

Shortly after meeting with Vacher, something really weird happens—Raynal disappears. Back in Paris, Raynal's wife Christine confronts Rolande, a/k/a, the 'other-woman,' asking her, "… where the hell [her] husband is;" of course, Christine holds Rolande responsible for her husband's disappearance, because Rolande is the one who insisted on Raynal's out-of-town business meeting with Vacher.

On the t.v. news that night, the top story is that France's legendary defense contractor Alain Raynal is missing, and the anchorwoman is now mentioning that, when Raynal was a young man, before he became a businessman, he was France's most legendary racecar driver (director Grangier chose not to incorporate any footage from *La Foule hurle*, Gabin's 1932 racecar picture, no doubt because, even in 1968, *La Foule hurle* was already considered to be a lost film), and that he met his wife Christine in Grenoble, during his biggest race, which occurred in 1948.

After a few days, Raynal phones home to tell his wife that he's okay, and that he just wanted to be alone for awhile. He doesn't have to say it, because we can see it in his face, but we know that he's beyond-exhausted from a lifetime of noise which has been supplied by racing cars, rockets, and people. He drives home in a sportscar which, presumably, he's just bought, during his lost weekend.

We now learn the exact reason that the French government has decided to ditch its contracts with Alain Raynal: Raynal Industries has apparently spent the last several years coming up with a new super-missile, the SR01, and not only did the missile not work but, when it was being tested, it actually exploded, a foul-up which wound up costing the government five million francs.

As Raynal drives back to Paris, he sees a beautiful young woman hitchhiking, but he doesn't pick her up, and we know from the resigned look on his face that he realizes his time has passed, at least when it comes to scoring with women who are one-third his age. Instead, he picks up a young male hitchhiker, a long-haired hippie who asks Raynal for a lift to Le Havre. (In director Marcel Carne's *Le Quai de Brumes*, which was made thirty years before *Sous le sign du taureau*, Jean Gabin himself was the young man who was hitchhiking, to Le Havre.) Raynal probably feels simpatico with the young guy, because hitchhikers don't have the problems and headaches which the heads of large corporations have and, in any case, Jean Gabin always responds positively to drifters.

Returning to Paris, and even before he goes home to his wife, Raynal stops off first at Rolande's bar. She's happy that he's returned, and she now makes him a new offer, telling him that if he doesn't want to borrow money from Vacher, that she will even be willing to sell her own bar and just flat-out give him the money which he needs to rejuvenate his company, with no payback necessary, but only on the condition that he'll agree to knock it off with his tiresome, 'too-much-pride'-routine, and just accept her help; Rolande has been intending to sell her bar anyway, and to buy a restaurant, but she'd much rather give the money to *her everlovin' Gabin-man,* and she tells Raynal that this is a very limited offer. She reminds him, also, about how generous it is for her to be making such an offer, especially in view of the fact that, over the years, he's dumped her ass, and not just once: As she's now reminding him, many years ago, he even took her on a trip to America, where he intentionally ditched her! (But Raynal is Jean Gabin, and so, of course, *naturally,* she still loves him, anyway!) He asks her if she'll give him some time to think about her new offer, but her answer remains a firm no. She tells him that he has to decide right now, so he passes.

If *Sous le signe du taureau* were a much better movie, it would almost be half as good as another movie (a really great one, by the way) on the theme of 'older men being phased out in a younger man's world,' director John G. Avildsen's tremendously emotional *Save the Tiger* (1974), in which Jack Lemmon plays a middle-aged New York garment district boss who's going to pieces, because the ageist world no longer needs him. We never feel as much for the Gabin character in *Taureau,* as we do for Lemmon's character in *Tiger* however, and this is mostly due to *Taureau's* severely underwritten screenplay. We have no idea what Raynal thinks about anything either, and the only thing we really know about him, outside of the fact that he used to be a racecar driver, is that he's just very, very tired.

Now, Raynal's about to learn that a lot of his old friends ('with friends like these...,' right?) are trying to buy his company out from under him: His wife Christine's brother, Jerome Laprade (Raymond Gerome), happens to be one of those guys (he's got grown kids who are starting their own families, and who need money), and another guy is his old friend Marchal (Jacques Monod), who happens to be one of France's biggest bank owners: Marchal actually has some ground to stand on, *vis-à-vis* taking over Raynal Industries, because the Raynal company owes Marchal's bank hundreds of thousands of francs worth of outstanding loans and, in this scene, Raynal's accountant Magnin (Michel Auclair) is telling Raynal that he's too cash-poor to pay Marchal back. Suffice it to say, Raynal's now had enough of every single person in the whole movie. (Alain Raynal is definitely the living embodiment of the famous Fred Neil-penned Harry Nilsson song which would be used in a classic American movie made the same year, *Midnight Cowboy:* "Everybody's talkin' at me/Don't hear a word they're sayin'/Only the echoes of my mind...")

Finally, Raynal has to admit that he's not even interested enough in keeping the company going even if only to provide for his employees. Christine thinks he's wishy-washy, because he had, of course, told her recently that he wanted to keep the company going, for his workers' sakes, and so, as you can imagine, she's now super ticked-off at him: "You never tell me what you're really thinking about anything. You've been keeping me in the dark for twenty years. But that bitch, Rolande—you tell her everything! I can't stand it anymore, and I'm divorcing you!" Raynal, in response to his wife's tirade, now wakes up (kind of), and begins defending his famous Jean Gabin Quietude, in the film's sole Gabin-Outburst: "You're right. I haven't told you anything in twenty years, and guess what: I'm not going to start now!" She tells him to expect a call from her lawyer, Fourchet (Fernand Ledoux), and she then walks out the door.

But as it turns out, these were all just harsh words, spoken out of anger because, as we'll now see, in the following tender scene, Raynal and Christine really aren't going to be getting a divorce. She re-enters the room and they now apologize to each other, and he even promises to take her away on a swanky vacation (just the two of them, together) in Cannes. In the film's final scene, Raynal even takes Christine into the actual factory where his missiles are made, and tells her that the government has changed his mind about him, and that France has just issued him a new contract to start building a brand new super-missile, the SR102, but that he's just not interested in making war toys anymore. He turns on a giant propeller-looking machine, and lets the sheets of his contract paper blow away into its crushing blades, as the end credits roll.

Sous le signe du taureau is probably the least interesting movie which Jean Gabin ever made, and since Gabin, by his own admission, was only interested in making quality movies, it's possible that it looked good on paper. Anyway, Gabin would have seven more movies to make, in his career (films #87—95) after this one, and six of them would be really great (the one which is not great is a crime picture called *Le Tueur*, which will be made in 1972), so if he wants to make the very occasional clinker—well, hell, Our Man deserves it!

What a Critic Said at the Time: "A thin tale… a talky little drama. Seems mainly designed to have Gabin grouse about the rich and bring off a few of his scenes of anger—a must in all of his pics. Pic drags." (*Variety*, 4-16-69 issue. Critic: "Mosk. [George Moskowitz.]" Reviewed in Paris.)

The 1970s have always been considered to be the 'Second Golden Age of Cinema' (the first one, being the 1930s), and it was a decade which was characterized by a few subgenres—including 'mafia pictures' (*The Godfather*, *The Valachi Papers*), 'revenge pictures' (*Dirty Harry*, *Death Wish*), 'small, character-driven art-house pictures' (John Sayles' *Return of the Secaucus Seven*), and 'issue pictures' (*Norma Rae*, *China Syndrome*). Over in France, Gabin, who was now in his seventies himself, would now star in at least one of each:

Top: With Lino Ventura and Alain Delon. Above: With Alain Delon.

FILM 87

Le Clan des Siciliens

France, 1969

(Literal English Translation/American Theatrical Release Title, "THE SICILIAN CLAN") Directed by Henri Verneuil. Produced by Jacques-Eric Strauss. Screenplay by Jose Giovanni, Pierre Pelegri, and Henri Verneuil. From the Novel by Auguste Le Breton. Director of Photography (color/scope), Henri Decae. Music by Ennio Morricone. Editor, Pierre Gillette. Production Designer, Jacques Saulnier. Art Director Jacques Saulnier. (GENRE: ACTION) A Production of 20th Century-Fox-France, Les Films du Siecle, and Europa Film. Running Time, 2 hours 2 minutes. Released in France by 20th Century-Fox, on December 1, 1969. Released in the United States, English-Dubbed (at 1 hour 58 minutes), by 20th Century-Fox, on March 29, 1970.

> "When you're done beating your eel, you can come over here, if you want to."
> — *Hot girl on beach tries to seduce Alain Delon, who tries to sublimate his desires by actually beating a giant live eel against a rock, in "Le Clan des Siciliens"*

Gabin's Mafia Picture, *Le Clan des Siciliens (The Sicilian Clan)*, represents the second of our *eminence-grise*'s three team-ups with Alain Delon, as well as his fifth heist picture, and it's also the second heist-a-palooza which he'd make for director Henri Verneuil, the man who put Gabin and Delon through their paces six years earlier in *Melodie en sous-sol*. Verneuil directs this rip-roaring (and for a Verneuil picture, surprisingly *anti-Semitism-free*) crowd-pleaser with style, and it's one of only three Gabin movies ever to have been financed (partially, in this case) by an American movie studio, 20th Century-Fox. Like *Razzia sur la chnouf*, *Le Rouge est mis*, and *Du rififi a Paname*, *Le Clan des Siciliens* is based upon a novel by France's mega-cool crime author, Auguste Le Breton.

As our story begins, smooth thirty-five-year-old Roger Sartet (Delon) is before his parole board: He was jailed several years ago, for *jacking* $150,000 (U.S.) worth of diamonds from a jewelry store, a crime in which he also, reportedly, fired upon the officers who surrounded the place, before he resisted his arrest, as well.

The police, who are led by Lino Ventura's crusty Inspector LeGoff (whose efforts in the film, to 'quit smoking' will be continually foiled by his job stress, a 'trope' which will be lampooned ten years later by Lloyd Bridges' cigarette-happy air-traffic-controller, in the great Zucker/Abrams comedy, *Airplane*) sticks Roger in the back of a heavily-armed truck, transporting him to a different penitentiary. Unbeknownst to the police, the Manalese crime family, of which Jean Gabin's Vittorio Manalese-character is the smooth, old *capo* (and Roger has labored for Vittorio on previous jobs), has arranged a little ruse, in order to get Roger sprung from the truck: They've arranged a Paris traffic jam, and one which is, in its execution, more genuinely exciting than the one which the picture's production studio, 20th Century-Fox, would be giving the world twenty years later, in its Keanu Reeves nail-biter, *Speed*: In *Siciliens*, While Vittorio's daughter-in-law Jeanne, who's betrothed to one of Vittorio Manalese's sons, is causing *l'emboutillage* (the traffic jam), Roger is busily cutting his way out of the back of the truck, and then stealthily escaping through a small hole in the bottom; Jeanne is played by the fiery-hot Irina Demick, a French actress of Czechoslovakian-descent who began making movies for 20th Century-Fox in 1960 (her first, was the WWII pic, *The Longest Day*), and she kept working for the studio, right up through this movie, in 1969, for the exclusive reason that, at least according to author Marlys J. Harris in her book, *The Zanucks of Hollywood: The Dark Legacy of a Movie Dynasty*, she was the longtime 'young, trophy girlfriend' of Fox's aging head, Daryl F. Zanuck.

Roger and his cohorts hasten away from the traffic jam in Jeanne's black sedan, arriving in the Batcave-esque underground parking garage of Manalese and Son Electronics, a storefront business which is legitimately (at least, according to the sign on its awning) a repairer of jukeboxes and pinball machines!

As Roger and his rescuers assemble themselves, a freight elevator descends into the bowels of the parking structure and, at about fifteen minutes into the picture, we're now getting to meet the authoritative Vittorio Manalese (Gabin) for the first time, and when he's first introduced to us, Vittorio is even accompanied, on the soundtrack, by his own sweeping Ennio Morricone theme, a majestic piece of music, which verily seems to proclaim that a myth is in the house. (In 1960s' European cinema, one true sign that an actor is truly a film icon, is when his presence on screen is accompanied by its own soul-and-testicle-stirring Morricone music; who, after all, can forget the eerie, 'Man-with-No-Name-theme' which Morricone composed for Clint Eastwood, in director Sergio Leone's *The Good the Bad and the Ugly*, or the haunting harmonica theme which Morricone wrote for Charles Bronson, in Leone's *Once Upon a Time in the West?*)

That evening, Vittorio and his family are dining with Roger, and Vittorio lets him know that, now that he's arranged Roger's escape, Roger owes *him* a favor: Namely, Vittorio needs Roger's expertise in helping him to plan an upcoming $150 million jewel robbery which, if it is successful, will go down in the record books as being the biggest jewel heist in history. If all goes according to plan, Vittorio, his sons, his daughters-in-law, and Roger Sartet, will heist some of the world's most expensive jewels, as they're being transported, *via* 747, from Rome to NYC, where the 'ice' will ostensibly be making its stateside debut at a New York City museum. Vittorio's wife, Maria (Elisa Cegani), just like the wife-character in Verneuil's earlier Gabin heist epic, *Melodie en sous-sol,* wishes that her aging husband would forego the heist, and retire with her to the Manalese family's native Sicily, so that they can finish out their days in peace but, of course, Vittorio tells her as per usual, in every heist picture you've ever seen, that he must first complete this "one last job."

The Manalese family bears many strikingly similarities to Mario Puzo's famous Corleone family, from author Mario Puzo's novel *The Godfather* which, while it was still two years away from becoming a movie, was a big international bestseller while *Le Clan des Siciliens* was in pre-production in early 1969: Vittorio (Gabin) is the steely patriarch; the Sonny Corleone-tough Aldo (Yves Lefebvre) is married to Irina Demick's hot, red-haired Jeanne, the girl who rescued Roger during that traffic jam; sensitive son Sergio (Marc Porel) is sagely-Michael Corleone-esque; and son Luigi (Philippe Baronnet), whose wife Teresa (she's played by Karen Blanguernon) has a six-year-old son named Roberto (Cesar Chauveau), is the film's legal-eagle/*consiglieri*/'Bob Duvall-Clone.'

Vittorio tells his assembled family members that he's going to let them know when the heist will be taking place soon, but until then, he informs them that he's going to need all of them to hole up in a house which he's rented for them on an Italian beach, where they will await his further instructions.

While lolling away on a Mediterranean beach a few days later, Alain Delon's smooth-as-silk Roger even begins a clandestine affair with Vittorio's daughter-in-law Jeanne, who is married to Aldo. At first, Roger tries to avoid this amazing, crimson-haired temptation (boffing the boss's married daughter is never good for one's health), but because Roger is played by testosterone-god Alain Delon, he just can't resist. As Jeanne sunbathes nude, Roger first tries to ignore her by going fishing, and (check this out, Sigmund Freud), he then pulls a giant eel out of the surf and, as he looks at her nude body, starts (symbolically) beating the eel frenetically against sharp rocks, even killing it! Within moments, however, his own, personal 'eel' has sprung back to life, and he and Jeanne are soon, in the lingo of 1960s' counter-culture scribes Terry Southern and Mason Hoffenberg, in their legendary novella, *Candy,* "going at it, like a couple of maddened warthogs." And meanwhile, as Roger is rogering Jeanne, little six-year-old Roberto, Teresa and Luigi's son happens to be spying on them from behind a rock. Jeanne, without getting flustered, since she thinks the kid is too young to figure out what's going on, tells Roberto that she and '*Monsieur* Roger' were just "wrestling" (!), and that he should "just forget about it." The small boy agrees to keep their secret.

On the day of the crime, Vittorio issues his family members and Roger Sartet fake passports, which have been fashioned by slimy nudie-photographer-*cum*-passport maker Malik (Andre Pousse, who played bad guy Quinquin, in *Le Pacha*), and the Manalese family boards the 747 to JFK Airport. Roger has even taken the extra step of disguising himself as the veddy-British insurance man who's supposed to be accompanying the jewels to NYC, and he's kidnapped the real insurance man (the guy is played by Bernard Musson), squiring the guy away at a secret locale, so that he won't be able to interfere with the family's operations, and the job proceeds so smoothly, that the Manaleses are able to get out of France, without

Inspector LeGoff and his men finding out. The family has been successfully (using guns, since airport security was nice and lax in 1969!) able to divert the jet from the N.Y. Airport, over to a highway in Queens, and the resulting freeway landing, in full rush-hour freeway traffic, is much more exciting than anything in a zillion Simpson-Bruckheimer noisefests put together. (Jean Gabin remained in France; he didn't travel to the U.S. for the American-lensed sequences, which didn't require his participation, anyway. [The film has a few close-ups of him getting out of a car on a New York freeway, but these shots were photographed in France.])

As the Manalese family and the jewels land on the freeway, Rolls-Royces are already in place, supplied by the family's American fence Tony Niciosa, a guy who also happens to be Vittorio's old World War II buddy. (Niciosa is played by Amedeo Nazzari who, like Gabin, was a matinee idol when he was younger, before he aged into one of Italy's most formidable character actors.) Niciosa immediately presents each Manalese family-member with a plane ticket to a different part of the world, so that it will be impossible for Inspector LeGoff and his men to track them all down, and he then instructs Roger to sit-tight in New York City. Roger dutifully takes a tiny room in a fleabag Times Square hotel, to await further instructions.

Director Verneuil now cuts to Paris, a few days later: The police have never been able to figure out how the Manalese family was able to abscond with the jewels so successfully. (In this movie, unlike how it usually happens in other heist pictures, *the Manaleses got away with it!*) That same night, Vittorio and his family are sitting around in his living-room, enjoying a television broadcast of an old, *From Here to Eternity*-esque movie, in which a couple happens to be making love on the beach, when suddenly Roberto, Vittorio's precocious little grandson, points to the couple and shouts out, "Look! Just like Auntie Jeanne and Mr. Sartet!" The family is now instantly horrified, learning in this innocently-offered manner that Jeanne has been cheating on her husband, Vittorio's son Aldo, with Roger Sartet! Jeanne runs out of the room, insisting that "it isn't true," but the whole family just sits there, glowering at her in disdain.

NYC: Roger Sartet remains in his hotel room and, at this point, Tony Niciosa pays him a visit. Roger believes that Niciosa has brought him his cut from the heist (Vittorio promised Roger that Niciosa would be delivering it), but Niciosa informs him that there's been a change of plans: "If you want the money, you have to go back to Paris and get it from Vittorio Manalese himself—he's holding it for you." Niciosa presents Roger with a plane ticket back to Orly Airport.

But Roger's whip-smart, and has already figured out that Vittorio is pissed off at him for *sexing-up* his daughter-in-law, and is just tricking him to get him back to Paris—and no doubt, to whack him.

The next day, Vittorio has his sons waiting at Paris-Orly Airport to nab Roger, and Inspector LeGoff and his men are also there, similarly awaiting Roger's arrival. (The French cops found out that Roger was returning when they interrogated Roger's sister Monique

[Danielle Volle], a *hottie* who works in a local snack-bar.) While the two separate factions (the good guys and the bad guys) are awaiting Roger's return in separate parts of the airport, Roger has tricked them all: He's savvy enough to have realized that everybody-and-his-brother will be showing up to apprehend him, so he took an earlier flight, foiling both the Manaleses *and* the police.

That night, Vittorio receives a phone call from Roger, who boldly orders the older man, "I want my cut of the money. Meet me tomorrow!" The next day, Vittorio and his errant daughter-in-law Jeanne drive up to a deserted beach with a suitcase full of greenbacks (Roger's cut) in tow. Roger himself turns up a few moments later in a second vehicle, and the two men emerge from their respective cars. Vittorio tosses a suitcaseful of money at Roger and, as Roger bends to pick it up, Vittorio shoots both Roger, as well as his own philandering daughter-in-law Jeanne, dead! Gabin, as usual, heads off alone, in his own car, although weirdly, he leaves the suitcaseful of cash on the dirt road, as the end credits roll. (Wouldn't *you* pick it up? [I would!])

Le Clan des Siciliens is one of the coolest and most riveting movies of Jean Gabin's later career, and it benefits greatly from co-scenarist Jose Giovanni's great adaptation of Auguste Le Breton's source material, as well as from Henri Decae's lush, widescreen, color cinematography, editor Pierre Gillette's rhythmically-crackerjack cutting, and one of Ennio Morricone's most jauntily-bizarre scores, ever (it's laced with Morricone's trademark 'twangy boing-boing' sound). The picture performed respectably at the U.S. box office, when 20th Century-Fox released it stateside in the spring of 1970. The version of the film which is currently available on DVD is the French-language version. Director Verneuil also shot English and Italian language versions of the film, featuring Gabin and the other actors speaking their dialogue in those languages. Because *Clan* exists in an English version, it is the third film in which Gabin spoke his lines in English, the other two being 1942's *Moontide* and 1944's *The Impostor*. In the canon of later-period Gabin movies, it's definitely one of the must-sees: It's a lot of fun.

What a Critic Said at the Time: "Vittorio Manalese (Jean Gabin) is a fine old gentleman *capo* who, from his appearance, seems to spend several hours a day caring for his beautiful white hair. A tired genre, but it has its occasional moments [and was] one of the most successful films ever released in France. [Co-star] Lino Ventura looks like Danny Thomas." (New York *Times*, 4-30-70 issue. Critic: Vincent Canby.)

FILM 88

LA HORSE

France/Italy/Germany, 1970

(Literal English Translation: "THE HORSE") Directed by Pierre Granier-Deferre. Produced by Gerard Beytout, Paul Cadeac, Cyril Grize, Rene Ignieres, and Luigi Waldeitner. Screenplay by Pierre Graniere-Deferre and Pascal Jardin. Based Upon the Novel by Pierre Lambesc. Director of Photography (color), Walter Wottitz. Editor, Jean Ravel. Music by Serge Gainsbourg. Production Designer, Jacques Saulnier. (GENRE: ACTION) A Production of GAFER, Imperia and PAC (France)/Romana Films (Italy)/Roxy Film-Munich GmbH (Germany). Running Time, 1 hour 30 minutes. Released in France on February 22, 1970, by Societe Nouvelle de Cinematographie (SNC). Never Released Theatrically in the United States.

"I knew somebody who used this shit. It blew his mind away!"
— *Concerned grandpa Gabin warns his grandson to stay off heroin, in "La Horse"*

This first-rate Gabin flick, his first released film of the 1970s, is a fast-paced, white-knuckle, *Death Wish*-style revenge picture, and it was adapted specifically for '*Le Gabin*' from a French novel by Michel Lambesc, and directed by Pierre Granier-Deferre. This is the first of two movies in a row which Granier-Deferre will direct with Gabin, although he *did* work with Gabin twice before: He was assistant director to Georges Lampin on 1956's *Crime et chatiment*, and he performed the same service for Denys de La Patelliere, on 1959's *Rue des Prairies*.

The Paris of 1970 has changed—but Jean Gabin, and his family farm, on the outskirts of Paris, has not. In *La Horse*, Gabin is the Charles Bronson-tough Auguste Marollieur, patriarch of a large, extended farm family, a family which includes his two adult daughters, Mathilde (Eleonore Hirt) and Louise (Danielle Ajoret), as well as Mathilde and Louise's *nebbishy* husbands, Leon and Maurice (played by Christian Barbier and Michel Barbey), whom Auguste spends most of the movie glowering at in disdain, only tolerating them because they are married to his daughters. (At one point in the picture, Gabin's character will even make a pronouncement about how "only blood is family.") Also living at the Marollieur farm, are Maurice and Louise's *groovy* college-age grandson, Henri (Marc Porel, who had just played Gabin's youngest son Sergio, in *Clan des Siciliens*), as well as Mathilde, and Leon's pretty, eighteen-ish daughter, Veronique (Oriane Paquin). Each night, the very large Marollieur family endures an uncomfortably silent dinner at a *looooong* table. (Think: Jimmy Stewart's large family, sitting around the dinner table in *Shenadoah,* only without the warmth [or also think: a world-weary "Waltons"].)

As *La Horse* begins, young Henri has just returned home to the family farm, on summer vacation from college in Paris, and he's brought home a mammoth foil-wrapped brick of heroin, which he happens to be hiding for a powerful drug lord. (Henri makes a little spending-cash working as the drug lord's go-between.)

Gabin's 'Farmer Auguste'-character has an underground storage shelter out in his fields, and when he goes down there one afternoon, he discovers the heroin, which is the only 'horse' we'll be seeing in the film, outside of the one which we'll see sprinting alongside Gabin's truck, during the opening credits. Knowing who put it there, he immediately brings Henri down into the cellar, letting him know, in no uncertain terms, that the young man has made a grave mistake:

"I knew someone who used this shit," tough-old Grandpa Auguste reprimands his errant grandson, brandishing the bag of white powder in front of the young man's nose, just like he's scolding a dog who's shit the house. It blew his mind away!" Auguste destroys the heroin by dumping it into a bucket of water, and then (there's nothin' like 'family values!'), he reprimands Henri, by actually whipping the shit out of him with his cane, while simultaneously Gabin-Outbursting at him, "You started out wanting to go to law school, or veterinarian school, or art school—and now, you're selling drugs?! Well, no drugs are sold on my land!" Then, after the tirade is through, it's time for more whipping! (Spare the rod, spoil the twentysomething college kid!) Henri's mom, Louise, Auguste's daughter, protests the severe beating, but it's eminently clear that Grandpa Auguste is the sole law in his extended family, ruling over all who live there with a firm hand (and cane).

> AUGUSTE: You didn't raise Henry right!
> LOUISE: I don't want him to be a farmer, with dirty hands.
> AUGUSTE: The earth is not dirty!
> LOUISE: The world changes!
> AUGUSTE: I haven't changed.

To keep Henri safe from the Parisian dope traffickers, who he knows will eventually be coming to the farm to retrieve their 'stuff,' Auguste locks him in the basement and, in short order, and just like we expected, Marc (Felix Marten), a henchman for the Parisian drug-syndicate for which college boy Henri is interning, arrives at Marollieur Farm to collect the foil-wrapped heroin brick. Marc threatens Auguste that if he refuses to hand over either the heroin, or its value in cash, and *stat,* that he'll kill everybody on the farm, and that he'll have Auguste's daughters raped! Auguste just listens, utterly Gabin-Stonefaced and

With Christian Barbier (left) and Michel Barbey (right).

expressionlessly—and then, wordlessly, he blows Marc away, Bronson/Eastwood-style, with his huge shotgun! Auguste and his loyal old farmhand, Bienphu (Andre Weber), a smilingly brain-damaged war buddy who fought in Indochina with him years ago, next dig a hole to rid themselves of Marc, after which they submerge his sedan in a nearby lake.

Paris-Orly Airport, Next Day: A 747 lands. Marc's brother, Tony (Dominique Zardi) has an appointment with Francis (Armando Francioli), the big drug czar for whom they all work, a guy who happens to run most of Paris' heroin trade. Tony tells Francis, "I sent my brother Marc to Le Havre to collect our merchandise, and some crazy old bastard farmer shot him to death!" Francis isn't too concerned about his missing foot-soldier though, which really roils Tony, and he just tells Tony that he has forty-hours to get his money back from "that crazy old bastard farmer," and that if he doesn't, that his ass is grass. Tony's not too interested in returning to the Marollieur farm himself, so he dispatches a new set of thugs to the property.

The following day, Auguste is confronted by a new group of gangsters, Mario (Bob Sissa) and Le Gros (Jean Cherlian), who are led by the psychotic Hans Rank (Reinhardt Koldehoff). Since Auguste tells them truthfully that he has no money to give them, they instantly, and wordlessly, burn down Auguste's barn! And then, in a jaw-droppingly-brutal sequence, the likes of which you'll never see in any American film (the American Humane Society would never allow it), the gangsters jump into the jeeps which they arrived in, and start graphically smashing them into Auguste's thirty cows, injuring our bovine friends in full close-up, and if you've never heard cows scream before—well, you will in this movie. (Well, shit, I guess it's okay, as long as the filmmakers ate 'em afterwards!)

After the cow-smashing, the 'gangstas' leave, and when they come back the following day for more fun, Auguste, without even thinking about it, whips out his trusty shotgun and blasts all of them to death, just like he did with Marc. Soon after, and right on cue, a coterie of big-city Paris cops, who are led by a humorless Inspector (Julien Guiomar), come to investigate, and Auguste informs them, 'Gabin-Expressionlessly,' that he doesn't know anything at all about any drug dealers, and that, in fact, no drug dealers have ever been to his farm!

> INSPECTOR: If there were no criminals here, who burned down your barn?
> AUGUSTE: I did.
> INSPECTOR: Why?
> AUGUSTE ('Gabin-Expressionlessly'): None of your business.

The Inspector knows Auguste is bullshitting him, and tells Auguste that if the drug dealers come back, he should report it, instead of taking the law into his own hands, lone-wolf style, and it's not long, of course, before Rank, Mario, and Le Gros *do* show up at the Marollieur farm (and naturally, Auguste doesn't report their arrival). Rank tells Auguste that he and his men will continue 'doing mayhem' on his property, until he gives them the money to pay for their lost heroin, and tough old Auguste just tells him to "fuck off!" (Go, Gabin!) Of course, thugs hate when people give them lip, so Mario hog-ties Louise, and Le Gros rapes Veronique. This is the part of the movie in which Auguste now gains instant respect for his sons-in-law (whom, previously, he just considered to be two big dopes), because Leon and Maurice hide in a drainpipe and shoot Mario and Le Gros, who are attempting to flee, post-rape. (These two thugs have had the right idea, too, as far as the fleeing goes: In any culture, it's never acceptable to stay and cuddle, after rape!) Auguste next ventilates Rank himself, and the farm is now refreshingly thug-free.

The Inspector orders an investigation and, once again, Auguste's family members, when sitting before a Judge (Pierre Dux) in his chambers, pretend they don't know anything about anything, but the disbelieving police squire Auguste down to the station, anyway. Many of Auguste's adoring neighbors from nearby farms, including one kindly old man who's played by Andre Rouyer, are now showing up to defend him. (It's just like all of the movies Jean Gabin made back in the 1930s, in which adoring neighbors always came to his aide, even in those pictures in which they knew that his characters had committed savage acts.) The neighbors tell the police, lyingly, that they have never seen any bad guys hanging around Auguste's farm and, surprisingly, even grandson Henri now defends his grandpa, Auguste, telling the cops that he locked himself in the cellar because, as an honored member of a farm family, he loves the earth, and enjoys being as close to it as possible! (He's so far down there in the cellar, he's practically in 'Middle-Earth!')

When *La Horse,* like everything else that's cool in life, comes to its necessary conclusion, all of the Marollieurs are back in fine form-and-fettle (although I can't really say the same thing for those cows), and Auguste and his family are back at their long, wooden dinner table, enjoying another tension-filled meal.

In playing Auguste Marollieur, Gabin would effortlessly inhabit the role of farmer, just like he did in real life, with his farm in Normandy. While Auguste is cold and distant with his family, we see that he genuinely loves the earth, and director Granier-Deferre presents those sequences in which Auguste is engaging in his farm labor, with a tenderness which we realize he should really be showering upon his family members. Besides being genuinely exciting, *La Horse* also benefits from another of Serge Gainsbourg's (*Le Pacha*) great, spare musical scores—some really great banjo stuff, which immediately (and by design) calls to mind Earl Scrugg's masterful contributions to *Bonnie and Clyde,* a film which Gainsbourg admired so much that, in 1968, the musician even recorded a song called "Bonnie and Clyde," which he performed as a duet, with Brigitte Bardot. (Gainsbourg's oft-printed [in France, anyway] quote about writing music for film is, "Film music should not be a pleonasm." For people who've been born without dictionaries, the definition of the word 'pleonasm' is, "redundancy in musical notes and lyrics;" in other words, according to Serge Gainsbourg, great movie music should always be simple. The music for this film, and the film in itself, are simple, direct, and very, very cool. When exploitation cinema meets art-house cinema, we get *La Horse,* a great and unfairly neglected (in the U.S., anyway) 1970s'-era revenge picture—a picture which was remade in 2006, for French television.

What a Critic Said at the Time: "Gabin still has a solid presence as the rugged head of [a farm] family, who solves his problems in an uncivilized way. [The] film makes drug pushers [into] less than human things [that can] be killed, *sans* any process of law, so it is reactionary." (*Variety,* 3-11-70 issue. Critic: "Mosk. [George Moskowitz.]" Reviewed in Paris.)

FILM 89

Le Chat

France/Italy, 1971

(Literal English Translation/American Release Title, "THE CAT") Directed by Pierre Granier-Deferre. Produced by Raymond Danon. Screenplay by Pierre Granier-Deferre and Pascal Jardin. Based Upon the Novel "The Implacable Cat of Saint Germain," by Georges Simenon. Director of Photography (color), Walter Wottitz. Music by Phillipe Sarde. Editors, Nino Baragli and Jean Ravel. Production Designer, Jacques Saulnier. (GENRE: DRAMA) A Production of Cinetel/Comacico/GAFER/Lira Films (France) and Unitas (Italy). Running Time, 1 hour 24 minutes. Released in France by Valoria Films, on April 24, 1971. Released in the United States on September 9, 1975, with English Subtitles, by Joseph Green Pictures, Inc.

> Gabin's Mistress: "Don't you love your wife?
> Don't you want to go home to her?"
> Gabin: "Yeah... I guess so."
> —marriage counseling, French-Style, in *"Le Chat"*

After churning out forty-years worth of plot-driven genre pictures, Jean Gabin would finally enter the art-house world in a small, but extremely powerful—and moving, and poignant—character-driven picture, *Le Chat (The Cat)*, in which he'd star, for the first and only time in his career, with another great icon of French cinema, Simone Signoret, and of course, Signoret was the real-life wife of another great French-entertainment icon, Yves Montand. Signoret is mostly known in the United States for her murderous role in Henri Georges Cluzot's classic 1955 suspenser *Diabolique* and, of course, she would also, seven years after appearing in *Le Chat*, win Best Actress at 1978's American Academy Awards ceremony for her role as a beloved old World War II-era Parisian brothel madame who takes a teen-aged boy under her wing, in director Moshe Mizrahi's film *La Vie devant soi* (*Your Life in Front of You*), a film which was retitled *Madame Rosa* for its U.S. theatrical release.

Le Chat is directed by Pierre Granier-Deferre, who had just directed Gabin in the previous year's *La Horse* (*Le Chat* and *La Horse*—two Granier-Deferre/Gabin collaborations with an animal in the title) and who, with this film, would demonstrate that he was just as adept at making small, quiet pictures, as he was with the big shoot-em-ups—and so, for that matter, was this film's author, George Simenon: *Le Chat* is based on Simenon's novel "*The Implacable Cat of St. Germain.*" and while it is a quietly contemplative piece, in which a husband and wife who stopped talking to each other years ago, have kept living together, anyway—possibly, because France is Catholic, and Catholicism frowns upon divorce (although it's never mentioned specifically in the film)—walking on eggshells around each other, and spending their days casting dirty looks at each other—that is, whenever they make the mistake of actually, Heaven forefend, making eye contact. (Gabin made some other movies where he was trapped in loveless marriages, as well: *Fille dangereuse, La Verite sur Bebe Donge, La Minute de verite*; and *Le Sang a la tete,* but his on-screen marriages were never as loveless as the one depicted in this film.)

As *Le Chat* opens, Gabin's retired typesetter Julien Bouin, and Signoret's Clemence Bouin, are in the kitchen, both preparing separate dinners, not talking to each other, and when we next see them, they're eating in silence, back-to-back—in fact, the first half-hour of the movie is absolutely crackling with tension between the couple, and yet features no dialogue. Later, after dinner, they sit opposite each other reading, in giant armchairs, still in complete and uncomfortable silence. Julien wants Clemence to tell him where his beloved cat Greffien is—his cat is the only thing in the whole house for which he feels even a modicum of affection—but because he won't actually talk to her, he just writes her little notes, which he crumples up and repeatedly pitches into her lap.

Clemence is jealous of the attention which her husband pays toward his cat, an animal which she absolutely abhors. When Julien leaves the house one evening, to sit, as he does each night, in stone-faced silence, at the kitchen table of Nelly (Annie Cordy), his caring, much younger mistress who is also a *hotelier*. Clemence berates the cat, really distressing the animal, and she also spends time perusing old photographs of her first meetings with Julien forty years ago, when they were both trapeze artists in the circus. (Gabin, of course, played a trapeze artist thirty-six years before *Le Chat*, in director Nicolas Farkas' 1935 melodrama, *Varietes,* but no footage from *Varietes* appears in *Le Chat*.) The Julien-Clemence marriage is one of those doomed marriages which, as Woody Allen's character remarked in 1992's *Husbands and Wives,* the couple 'just doesn't have the energy to end;' plus, for all of their mutual hatred, Julien and Clemence are clearly co-dependent on each other. At one point, Nelly asks Julien if he has any love at all for his wife and, after thinking about it for a moment, he monotonely offers up, "Yeah… I guess so." And then, very sweetly, he waddles home to Clemence.

While Julien has been out, vengeful Clemence hacks up his collection of old, historic newspapers with a pair of shears. (Both Julien and Clemence live firmly in the past, a past which is represented, in this film, by Julien's collection of old, yellowing newspapers.) She thinks this might rile Julien up, which is what she dearly wants (he never expresses any emotion at all, good or bad, and if Clemence had only seen a few other Jean Gabin movies, she'd already know that almost nothing ever gets Jean Gabin too excited—except, maybe, when people treat working-men badly! Indeed, Clemence gets so frustrated with Julien's inability to get angry at her, or to demonstrate any of humanity's known facial expressions, except for his constant, world-weary 'Gabin-frown,' that when he leaves the house yet again, the next night, to walk around the block, she does something worse—she shoots his cat, and it is this ultimate act of aggression, an act which will have dire consequences for both husband and wife, neither of whom will live beyond the end credits.

Of the ninety-five feature films which Jean Gabin made, *Le Chat* is unique, because it's his only 'non-genre' picture: It's driven completely by character, instead of by any kind of a big, complicated plot, and it's a heartbreakingly sad and compelling look into the existences of two people who are in the sunset of their lives; in fact, as the relationship between Julien and Clemence disintegrates, Granier-Deferre continually cross-cuts between them, and scenes of a giant wrecking-ball, which is smashing down old Parisian buildings. As symbolism, this is a bit heavy-handed and yet, it still manages to remain a somewhat effective metaphor for Julien and Clemence's crumbling non-marriage. *Le Chat* is a beautiful movie about 'real' old people, and few movies like that, have ever been made. It's not sugar-coated like *Coccoon* or *Grumpy Old Men* are, but it is instead bittersweet—like real life.

In 1975, four years after *Le Chat's* French theatrical release, it turned up at a few American art-houses, released by the exploitation master Joseph Green (a 'mini-mini-mogul' who, in 1975, also happened to be distributing XXX-rated Georgina Spelvin movies as well as double-features of Hopalong Cassidy westerns from the 1930), to great critical reception but, like many films in this book, it has since mostly forgotten in the U.S. In 2002, as part of its Jean Gabin Film Festival, the Los Angeles County Museum of Art screened *Le Chat* as a substitute for a print of *La Marie du port* which never showed up: The standing-room only audience thoroughly enjoyed *Le Chat*, applauding for three solid minutes after the film ended.

What a Critic Said at the Time: "*Le Chat* makes an impact. It is a remorseless, unrelieved study of death-in-life. As such, it is probably the best movie to see with someone you're not sure you love." (Los Angeles *Times*, 9-10-75 issue. Critic: Charles Champlin.)

What Another Critic Said at the Time: "Two heavyweight pro thesps are the main plusses in this downbeat drama of an aging couple living together in mutual hatred. Gabin and Miss Signoret are effective as the aging couple, and they build larger than life performances from these two, finally pathetic, people." (*Variety*, 6-16-71 issue. Critic: "Mosk. [George Moskowitz.]" Reviewed in Paris.)

What A Third Critic Said at the Time: "There is a good deal of excitement in watching these two marvelous professionals [Jean Gabin and Simone Signoret] having at each other with such passion and wit. Mr. Gabin and Miss Signoret are precise and perfect in their performances. This is a film that so minutely explores its limited territory that the territory becomes as large and varied as a new continent." (New York *Times*, 6-8-75 issue. Critic: Vincent Canby.)

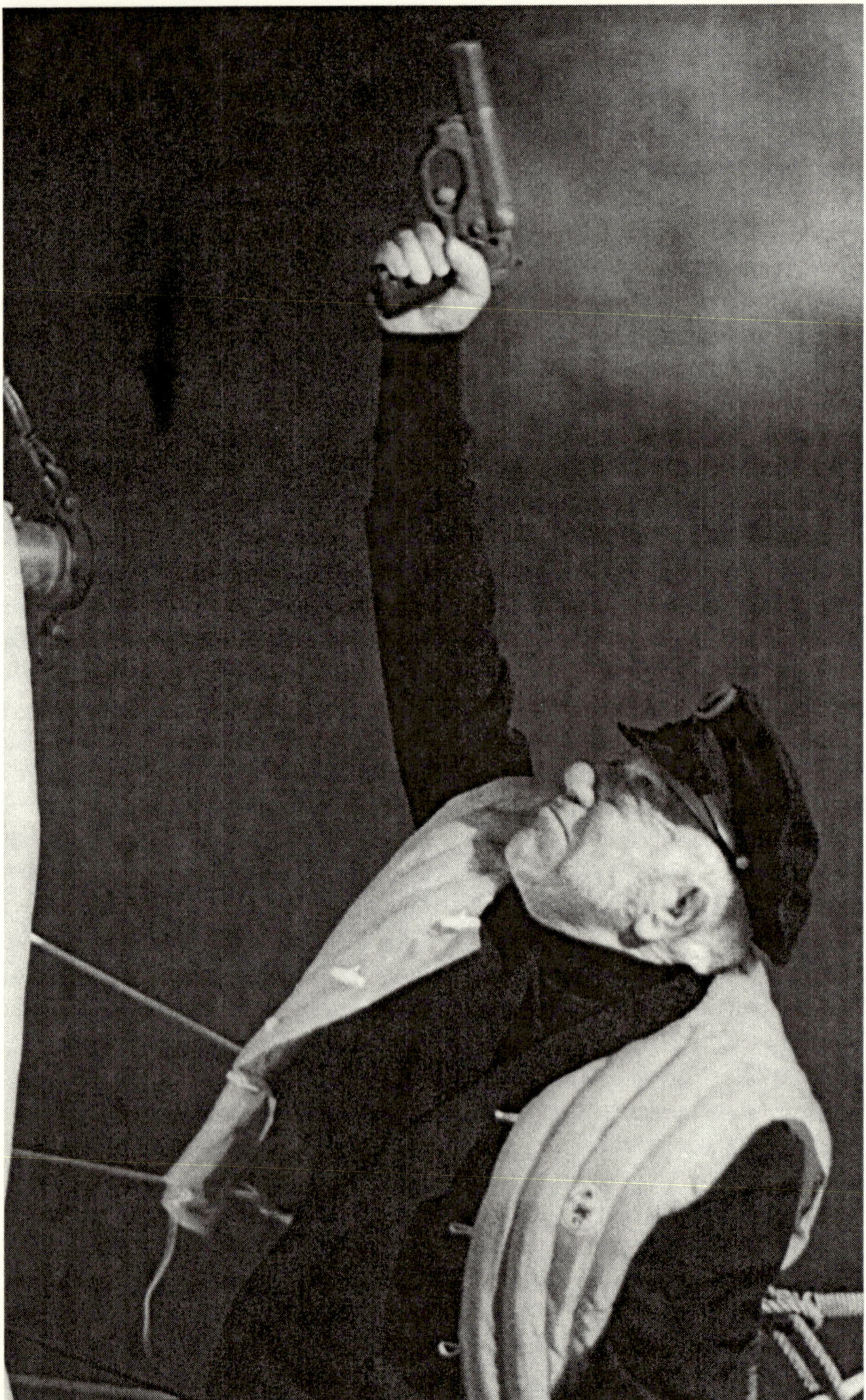

FILM 90

Le Drapeau noir flotte sur la marmite

France, 1971

(Literal English Translation, "THE BLACK FLAG FLIES OVER THE CAULDRON") Directed by Michel Audiard. Produced by J.P. Guibert. Screenplay by Michel Audiard, Rene Fallet, and Jean-Marie Poire. Based Upon the Novel "Il etait un petit navir," by Rene Fallet. Director of Photography (color), Robert Isnardon. Editors, Robert and Marie Isnardon. Music by Georges Brassens. Production Designer, Pierre Petit. (GENRE: COMEDY) A Production of Marianne Productions, S.A. Running Time, 1 hour 18 minutes. Released in France on October 13, 1971, by Profilm. Never Released Theatrically in the United States.

"My biggest weakness, is to believe in the goodness of people."
— Sailor Jean Gabin, in *"Le Drapeau noir flotte sur la marmite"*

In 1971, the legendary Michel Audiard, one of France's most prominent (not to mention prolific) screenwriters, who had already written nineteen of Jean Gabin's movies (beginning with *Gas-Oil*, in 1956), was handpicked by his friend Jean Gabin to make his big-screen directorial debut with the hilarious 78-minute comedy, *Le Drapeau noir flotte sur la marmite* (*The Black Flag Flies Over the Scow*), a film which was based upon the novel *Il etait un petit navir* (*There was a Little Navy Boy*) by Rene Fallet, whose other comedic novels, *Les Vieux de la vieille* and *Archimede, le clochard,* had already been turned into some pretty outstanding Jean Gabin comedies (in 1959 and 1960, respectively). This picture takes place in the small, seaside town of Villaneuve St. Georges-et-Pierre, about ten miles south of Paris, and instead of utilizing Fallet's original title, Audiard and Gabin decided on a new one, which was based upon a phrase that Jean Gabin had casually tossed off to Audiard twenty-one years earlier, in 1950: While Gabin was off in Italy making his Italian-French co-production, *Pour l'amour du ciel*, Audiard visited him on the set; apparently, Gabin complained to Audiard that, as far as his post-War career in France was concerned, there was a 'black flag over his (cooking) pot'—*meaning*, that Gabin was scared that he wouldn't be able to feed his family, because there was little film work to be had in France, at that point in time. The phrase reminded Audiard of something that a pirate might say, and when it came time for him to direct this movie years later, that's the title he gave to it.

The picture opens with a quick preview of our star Gabin, whom we won't be seeing again, properly, for a few minutes, as he's staring out of the top story window of his house (as though he's looking out of a ship's porthole), just like the real Jean Gabin famously stared out of his boyhood window, when he was a little boy in Meriel.

Audiard next cuts to a little makeshift art gallery which has been set-up in the café of a Boulogne train station. Judges walk around the room, examining model ships and nautical paintings, which have been painted by local residents. (These homespun folks, with their toothpick boat-sculptures and ships-in-bottles, definitely have no claim on being Van Goghs, in fact one resident has even fashioned a circa-1840 frigate, *La Belle poule* [in English, it means, 'The Pretty Prostitute'] entirely out of matches!) One of the town's richest fat-cats, Mr. Volabruque (Claude Pieplu), is the winner, but he's much too important a fellow to have crafted something like that by himself, and he's actually commissioned his dutiful employee/lackey Antoine Simonet (Jacques Marin) to create his model sailboat for him. (While it's not said in the film, no doubt this was very obviously a case of "build me a model boat or get fired!")

The judges kiss Volabruque's ass, asking him what 'his' next project will be. ("Mr. Volabruque, we see you as making nothing less than the *Titanic* for your next creation!") Full-of-himself, and equally full-of-shit, Volabruque brags, "Of course it will be the *Titanic*! And I will build it full-size!"

Modest Antoine doesn't care a whit about the fact that his boss hasn't asked him to share the glory, though; he's a simple worker bee with a simple life, a 'little man' who just wants to retire to the small coastal town of Dieppe, in Normandy, where his wife owns a small farm which was willed to her by her parents, where he'll be able to live (he hopes) off of the fishing trade: "I will catch twenty pounds of fish every day," Antoine brags to his wife, who just shakes her head because she knows that he always just 'talks' about doing great stuff, but that he never actually does any of the great stuff he's always talking about. Antoine's son Pierrot (Eric Damian), who's about ten, definitely has no feelings one way or another about his wimpy father, a *nebbishy* guy whom nobody would ever consider to be a strong male role model. The boy gravitates instead toward his dad's cool (to him, anyway) and powerful boss, Mr. Volabruque.

Volabruque's such an unmitigated asshole, that he sometimes walks in, quite unannounced, at his employee Antoine's modest house, and nobody even tries to stop him. On this particular Saturday morning, Volabruque has come to Antoine's to cajole his wimpy little employee into building him a real sailing boat (he wasn't joking, when he said he wanted to 'go *Titanic*' for his next project), but Antoine's not interested, and like a frightened little mouse, he meekly tells his boss, "Look, sir: This whole boat-building business simply wasn't in my job description. I'm just a trainsman and, besides that, I'm deathly afraid of being out on the water!" Still, he's fearful that if he doesn't build the real, life-sized boat that his boss wants, he'll get shit-canned, and since he's got a family to think about, that dog just won't hunt!

With Jacques Marin.

Antoine's wife Paulette (Micheline Luccioni), like her son, is more impressed with Volabruque than she is with her own husband. "I used to think your boss was a moron," she tells Antoine, "but he's not." Little Pierrot wants his dad to build the boat, and obviously, Antoine would do anything to impress his son, as a way of proving to the boy that he's 'a man' (as opposed to his being 'a mouse').

"I can't build you a real sailboat, sir," Antoine mumbles to Volabruque, cowering before his boss in worker-bee fright; so Volabruque next lightens his tone, deciding that it will be easier to catch a fly with honey: "You're not interested? But that little model boat you built me was so incredible! And anyway, if you won't build me the sailing ship of my dreams—who will?" It is then, that Antoine gets what probably amounts to the first good idea he's ever had, which he now blurts out, and just fast as he's probably thought it up: "My Uncle Victor will build it for you!" And this is where we'll now get to meet—or *re-meet,* since we saw him briefly at the very beginning of the picture—Antoine Simonet's irascible old Uncle Victor (Jean Gabin).

"Who the hell's your Uncle Victor?" Volabruque wants to know, and Antoine tells him that Victor's "… a man of the sea. A hero of circumnavigation, who's spent his life traveling around the globe. Once, he even built a sailboat, all by himself—and, I might add, he sailed it all the way from France to Canada!" (Needless to say, Volabruque is immediately impressed.)

Antoine hasn't seen his Uncle Victor for more than twenty years though, nor has his wife Paulette ever met or heard of him—in fact, she thinks that her husband has just invented the guy! And now that Volabruque is intrigued, Antoine looks confident (and no doubt, for the very first time, in his life): "It's possible that my Uncle might be able to build you the boat that you require, in two weeks." Volabruque tells Antoine that he's never heard of a real boat with the staggering specifications in which he's interested being built that quickly, but Antoine just replies, "Well, you don't know my Uncle Victor."

When we next see Jean Gabin's curmudgeonly Victor Ploubaz, he's disembarking from the train in the Simonet family's little town, but he's late, because he got lost along the way: There were two train stops with nearly the same name—'Villaneuve Prairie' and 'Villaneuve St. Georges-et-Pierre,' and Victor, apparently, got off at the wrong one ('Prairie,' instead of 'St. Georges-et-Pierre'), first. (While Victor's just been touted by his nephew as being the best of sailors, this guy can't even find the right train stop, which is a red flag to us, or should I say, *per* the film's title, a 'Black Flag,' that Uncle Victor might not be the fancy sailing man he claims to be, and that he might even be another 'Gabinian impostor,' *a la* J.G.'s characters in pictures like *The Impostor, Le Baron de l'ecluse,* and *Le Gentleman d'Epsom*.

When Victor arrives at the correct train station, he walks into town alone, his duffel slung over his shoulder, just like a forty-years-younger Gabin did, in director Jean Godard's 1931 picture, *Pour un soir..!* (Gabin looks really funny cosmetically in this picture, too: *Drapeau noir* marks the one and only time in Gabin's entire movie career, in which his character sports an intentionally silly-looking mutton-chop beard!)

When Victor first sees his nephew Antoine, he immediately starts giving him shit, just like Volabruqe always does, setting the scene for what their whole relationship will be in the picture. (Everybody else on earth uses mild-mannered Antoine as a whipping-post anyway, so why shouldn't his own Uncle?) "Why didn't you tell me the right stop to get off at?" Victor, yells at his nephew. (From the second Uncle Victor arrives in Villaneuve St. Georges-et-Pierre, he's in command, and he's not taking any guff off of anybody.)

Victor, Antoine, and assorted townspeople next repair to the local watering hole which we already visited at the beginning of the film (the one where the model boats were being judged), for Victor's 'welcome drink,' and Antoine, who wants to impress his Uncle Victor, now orders everybody in the place a glass of the region's famous vintage. But tough old Victor isn't interested, and more to take the piss out of his nephew than anything else, shouts out, "White wine? I'm a sailor! I want rum! White wine isn't a sailor's drink!" And not only does Victor want rum, but he wants a very specific rum which has been distilled in Kingston, Jamaica, and failing that, if none of that happens to be around then at least, he will require an equally-good brand he favors, which is made in Cuba! Volabruque waddles over to Victor and introduces himself, and Consummate Bullshit-Detector Victor immediately pegs the guy as being a pompous windbag/asshole/blowhard/freak. Volabruque next shows Victor a blueprint: "Take a look at this, Captain Ploubaz. It's a blueprint of the sailboat which your nephew said you will be building for me." Victor checks the blueprint out, gives the guy an oversized Gabin-Scowl, and very suddenly, starts exiting the bar without exchanging any further *unpleasantries* with anybody. And right before he heads out the door (he just got there, and already he wants to leave!), he whispers to his newly-discovered nephew, Antoine, "I accepted your apologies about the train station and the rum. But I will not accept this boat building proposition." Next, director and co-scenarist Audiard gives us this film's first of a three great Gabin-Outbursts, and one which is peppered by the salty language with which 'the new permissiveness' of the 1970s so generously gifted the world of international cinema: "I didn't travel all the way across the country to build a piece of shit!"

But Victor cools off immediately, suddenly rethinking his position (we're getting the idea that, in all actuality, he has nowhere to go), and in full-view of all of the bar's patrons, he now stands before a wall-mounted mirror and makes a chalk-drawing of the kind of sailboat which he would be interested in building, a boat which has nothing to do with the blueprint which Volabruque has just shoved in his face. He tells Volabruque, "This is the boat I'm going to be building for you—take it or leave it. It will be seven-and-a-half meters long. We'll make it my way. Or, you can make it your way, and without me. If you build the travesty which you've told me you want to build, you'll look like a gigolo from St. Tropez!" Victor has suddenly become Villaneuve-St. Georges-et-Pierre's new, resident Alpha-Male, replacing Volabruque (who used to be Alpha-Male until about five minutes ago) and Volabruque, probably for the first time in his natural life, immediately defers to him. Victor brags to Volabruqe, "I know people who have sailed the Atlantic with the kind of boat I am about to build for you—so shut the hell up with your shitty ideas, okay?!"

Victor's making fun of Volabruque in front of everybody, and he's the only guy in the room who properly can because, like all of Jean Gabin's great movie characters)and Victor Ploubaz is, indeed, one of the great ones), he's beholden to nobody, except to himself. He tells Volabruque, "When we finish your boat, you can take it out, and you can catch little sardines and marlins. But really, in the end, I don't care what you do with it. My business here will just be to build it for you, and then to leave." (Jean Gabin: Eternal Wanderer—even at the age of 67!) Next, we get a proto-Scorsese freeze frame of Victor, and over it, some voice-over narration which is provided by Antoine's son, little Pierrot, who will be narrating the rest of the picture. Pierrot is now telling us that he thinks his newfound 'Great-Uncle Victor' is a very cool cat, indeed!

Victor isn't going to physically build the sailboat himself, though: He's a consummate delegator, and so the next time we see him, he's in the family's gated front yard, luxuriating in a hammock, while Antoine's wife Paulette is bringing him sumptuous food and drink, serving her new guest on hand-and-foot, while all around, noisy trucks are dumping lumber all over the family's front lawn! What makes the scene even funnier, is that Victor persists in wearing goofy-looking pajamas during the daytime (they're striped, just like in *Touchez pas au grisbi!*), and he tells Paulette that he's used to hammocks like this one, and not beds, since he's been sleeping in hammocks for more than forty years! Victor tells Paulette that he's been long separated, but not legally divorced, from his own wife, whom he hasn't seen for years, since he is (in his own words) "… always away at sea. Two-thirds of the time that my wife Marie-Ange and I were together, she waited for me by the docks. But she never saw me."

The next morning, carpenters arrive at the Simonet residence and, *per* Victor's instructions, they're going to start building the boat right there, on the horrified family's front lawn. Victor emerges from the house, in his now-mandatory striped pajamas (he finally, on his second night, slept inside the house, and in an actual bed), and he traipses back and forth over the family's vegetable garden, totally crushing it underfoot, while taking measurements for the boat. (He's doing all of this crushing intentionally, and we can tell he's getting a mischievous charge out of screwing with this hopeless-looking little family.) Antoine tells Victor that the workers are going to have to be careful about how they're building the vessel because, if it stretches beyond the Simonet family's property, it will be touching the next door neighbor's land, and the neighbor in question, happens to be Mr. Ravasson (Yves Barsacq), Pierrot's tight-ass/Clifton Webb-esque schoolteacher, a guy who looks like, if he ever smiled before in his whole life, that it was probably by accident. Antoine's comment about 'being careful,' which was delivered innocently enough, now throws Victor into another, stellar Gabin-Outburst: With his arms flailing madly, Victor starts shouting at his nephew, that he's going to be building the boat as big as he wants to, and that there's nothing anybody can do about it. Then, as if Victor didn't squish the family's vegetables enough already, another giant lumber truck shows up now and, comically (to us, not to the Simonets) starts *shitting more giant cords of lumber* all over the garden. Little Pierrot now puts it all into perspective for us, actually referencing for us, in his voice-over narration (it's an in-joke, from director Michel Audiard), one of Gabin's most famous movie traits: "Every time we saw Uncle Victor, we knew there would be an outburst!" Pierrot is mightily impressed by his cool, new great-uncle, a man whom, as he's now telling us, he considers to be even cooler than Long John Silver, from his all-time favorite book, Robert Louis Stevenson's *L'Ile au tresor* (*Treasure Island*). Pierrot hops onto his bike and rides to school, looking miserable, because he won't be able to play hooky today and hang-out with Victor and the men who are building the boat. When Pierre arrives at school that day, Mr. Ravasson is mad at him, singling him out unfairly, just because his family is building the boat in such close proximity to his own home.

Meanwhile, 'back at the Ponderosa,' the workmen are *doing their thing*, while Victor, who is now adorned in a very cool-looking all-black captain's uniform, instead of those crazy striped pajamas, continues to laconically 'supervise'—which means that he's really just laying in the hammock, eating and drinking, and telling everybody in sight that he thinks the boat should be named the *Espagnola*, a name which nobody likes, except for him. Probably the funniest thing in the movie visually, is that the Simonets' tiny little house, with its little garden in front, exists *not* in tree-filled suburbia, but right in the middle of a teeming city! (It's one of only a few houses on a small residential street which is surrounded—and indeed, engulfed—by imposingly-monolithic buildings and factories, and the house's location is a truly-inspired sight gag, one which seems like it's emerged right out of one of those Terry Gilliam or Jacques Tati movies, films which always seem to be trafficking in 'the absurdity

With Eric Damian.

of modernization.') Meanwhile, Mr. Volabruque, who's commissioned the boat, is so excited about the project, that he's in the bathroom of the Simonets' house, where he's excitedly trying-on a multitude of different sailor hats!

Night falls, but there's no rest for Victor's construction crew: While Victor continues supervising from his hammock, his cadre of builders is weaving its magic. Pierrot heads into the front yard to visit with his cool Uncle, and man and boy definitely have a whole Mutual Appreciation Society going on: In fact, little Pierrot is the only person in the whole town whom Victor can truly stomach, since Pierrot isn't old enough to be crass and stupid yet! "In my estimation," Victor brags to the little boy, "the best place in the world to build a boat, is in Brisbane, Australia!" Victor is now telling Pierrot, just as he had earlier told Pierrot's mom, that he never sleeps, but he's obviously just lying to impress the little boy because, as we've already seen, he's now sleeping inside of the house—and on a bed, to boot! (Conversely, in Pierre Granier-Deferre's 1970 effort *La Horse,* Gabin's farmer-character, crusty old Auguste Marollieur, truly doesn't sleep, choosing instead to sit awake in a chair all night, every night!)

The next day, at work in the trainyard, Antoine is perched on a slow-moving little coal-car, eating lunch with his two buddies, Balloche (Andre Pousse) and Tartanville (Raymond Meunier), and telling them that he doesn't know what to do, because all of his neighbors are getting fed-up with him, due to the twenty-four-hour-a-day noisy boat building which is happening on his property.

Since Victor gets along with little Pierrot extremely well, we can tell, from Gabin's subtly-tender facial expression, that he feels badly about having lied to him about his majestic seafaring adventures, although he still has lots of fun telling the boy his little *bubbe meinses*, anyway! "Gosh! You're just like Long John Silver," Pierrot excitedly yells out, complimenting his Uncle, but Victor has no idea who Long John Silver is, another clue to the fact that he might not be a 'for-real sailor.' "I'm not a big reader," Victor replies, Gabin-Shrugging, and the boy can't believe that his savvy sailor-Uncle has never even read *Treasure Island*, but Victor worms his way out of this sudden 'book-club moment' quite gracefully: "I've never had too much time to read, son. I was in the Navy for five years, and I've been on ships since the age of fourteen. I've done everything, which is a whole lot better than just sitting around and reading about it." Victor now smiles, for the first and only time in the movie, and we now see that, besides the mutton-chops, he's also got bright yellow teeth! (*Yeah! Real men don't brush!*)

Later that day, Victor resumes his supervising, 'neath the cool of an umbrella, and Mr. Volabruque comes by to check up and see how everything's going, asking Victor if he doesn't think that the workmen, who look beyond-exhausted, should get a little break, and Victor replies that nobody will get a break until the boat is finished, which won't be, in his estimation, for at least two more weeks! (Clearly, Victor isn't running a union shop, here.) He tells Volabruque to get lost, and he then blows a whistle—and right on cue, Paulette emerges from the house, dutifully bringing Victor a bottle of good wine. Meanwhile, at school that day, Mr. Ravasson is back on Pierrot's case, and this time it's because the boy's grades have started slipping, ever since he started spending what used to be his homework time, sitting outside and watching the construction of the amazing boat.

Back at home, meanwhile, Paulette is telling Victor now that she and her husband are going to be gone until late, and that the family won't be having dinner until the two of them get home, but Victor eases her mind, telling her not to worry because he's going to be cooking for the family tonight, as a way of thanking them both for putting him up (or, more accurately, for 'putting up with him')! "I'm going to make you guys real sailor food: Chili con carne… with spare ribs!" (So, now, Victor's not only an expert seafarer, but he's also—at least, in his own grandly-inflated opinion of himself, a master chef!) When we see Uncle Victor next, he's in the kitchen, looking really out of place and trying to find some cayenne pepper. (Not only has this guy never been on a boat before, but he's probably never even been in a kitchen!) While the chili is cooking, Pierrot's up in his room, doing his homework for a change, and Victor comes in to visit him: When he opens the door to the boy's room, he's face-to-face with a poster of the Beatles—in fact, he's face-to-face with a poster for the band's 1970 movie, *Let It Be*—which he stares at, blankly. (Nothing in the picture is registering as familiar: Yes, here is cinema history's one-and-only historic convergence of Jean Gabin and the Beatles, and Gabin has no earthly idea who they are!) Victor notices that Pierrot's not doing his math homework, like he's supposed to be doing. (The boy is just reading *Treasure Island*, and staring dreamily out of his bedroom window.)

As Pierrot begins reading *Treasure Island* out loud to an impressed Uncle Victor, the chili is burning downstairs, and of course, this is the exact moment which Antoine and Paulette Simonet have chosen to arrive home. They're beyond-angry that their kitchen looks like Hiroshima, but Victor, who's as Gabin-Confident as always, turns the problem around onto them with a carefully-worded Gabin-Outburst, one which is totally calculated to make *them* feel guilty, instead of him: "You want me to build a ship, cook, help the boy with his algebra—and now you also want me to be a cleaning lady?" (That shuts them up, 'P.D.Q.!') Nobody can ever argue with Jean Gabin, because he has so much natural authority, even when his logic is 'all-over-the-place,' just as it is here.

It's now the next morning, and we're back on the Simonet family's front lawn. The film's cinematographer, Robert Isnardon (who additionally, with his wife, happens to have been the film's co-editor), opens the sequence with a very striking, fish-eye-lens-view of Victor's carpenters, who continue to hammer away on the boat. Antoine's out in the yard working too, and amusingly, the workmen are getting so bored, that they've now started hammering away musically, to a 'beat,' just like that French-favorite Jerry Lewis always does, in his own pictures, to alleviate their boredom (and by the way, it's a very charming little moment). The workmen look excited, believing that they're almost finished, but Victor, who's now staring at them from out of the kitchen window, sets them straight: "Finished? That's what you think. You've just started! You guys still have to paint, put up the mast, and do a whole lot more than that. Now, quit flapping those gums, and work, work, work!"

Back in school at the same time, Pierrot's staring out of the classroom window just as, back on the homefront, Uncle Victor is staring out the window, as well. Since his school is only about a block away from his house, Pierrot can see the boat's huge mast when he looks outside of his classroom window, and it's moving! The boat is now almost finished, and it's traveling down the street on the back of a large flatbed truck, as onlookers line the city streets, amazed at this incredible lunch-hour sight. (The boat is so big that onlookers are doing everything, except crossing themselves in horror, as in any Dracula movie!) At this point, Mr. Volabruque shows up again, and tells Antoine and Uncle Victor that he isn't interested in cutting a check for the finishing funds which will required to build a few parts of the boat which have still not been completed, so Antoine offers to do finance the project's completion himself, telling his boss that his wife owns a farm in Dieppe, and that if he asks her to, he knows she'll be willing to mortgage her farm, and pull out some of the capital. Of course, Paulette's just overheard her husband saying this (she's in the kitchen cooking, and can hear him as she's looking out of the window), and she yells out to him that she will be doing nothing of the sort.

At work the next day, Antoine has lunch with his two friends Balloche and Tartanville again, and he's telling them that his wife has denied him access to their joint checking account, and worse, to his cigarette money, because she doesn't want him spending all of the money for which the two of them have scrimped and saved. Balloche doesn't exactly back up his friend Antoine either, agreeing more with Paulette: "Antoine: As far as I'm concerned, you should just burn that eyesore-of-a-boat, and use it for heating wood." Balloche is now foreshadowing something which is going to be happening a bit later in the film (and you'll have to keep reading, to see what that is)! That night, when Antoine arrives home, he asks Victor about what he thinks they could do to get the rest of the money, and Victor smilingly offers to go off and blackmail some millionaires—and he says it in such a deadpan way, that we're not exactly sure if he's kidding or not. As we already know, from having seen *Le Baron de l'ecluse* and *Le Gentleman d'Epsom*, Gabin is second-to-none, when it comes to playing charming con artists, so we wouldn't put such larcenous behavior past him.

Victor, even though he would probably never admit it (Gabin rarely cops to any excess feelings, in most of his movies) is now starting to get attached to the little family, in spite of the fact that he's been trying hard as hell not to. He tells them that he's going to be taking a break for a few days, not that he's been doing all that much work in the first place, and they give him their blessings since, as they're now telling him, his workmen have been doing such a great job. He plans on paying his first visit, in many years, to his estranged wife, Marie-Ange, who owns her own grocery store in the port town of St. Malo, in Brittany: He doesn't have to say anything to the Simonets, but we know that the reason he's going to be visiting her, will be to try and charm her into parting with some of her cash (and maybe even *some of her thighs!*), so that the boat can be finished.

Victor arrives in St. Malo, which is one of France's most famous ports (most old French songs about sailors and adventurers are set in St. Malo), and soon after, he's arriving at his wife's grocery-and-fish tackle store, the eloquently-monickered *Maison Ploubaz* (or, 'House of Ploubaz'). Marie-Ange, who's played by Ginette Leclerc, has opted to keep Victor's last name, even though the two of them haven't seen each other for years, which is showing us, without anybody in the movie's having to say anything about it, that she still has feelings for her husband, even though she also knows, at the same time, that he's the biggest louse she's ever met. Even though Marie-Ange hasn't seen Victor since who-knows-when, the first thing she does when he arrives at her store, is to immediately call him on a lie which he had apparently told her years before: Once, when they were together, he told her that he grew up in an orphanage, when really, he did not, and what she's really letting him know, by bringing this matter up in their present conversation, is that he'd better tread lightly with whatever it is that he's come to tell her today, because she's got her *Bullshit Detector* turned on, and it's working just well as his own *Bullshit Detector* always seems to be working. He asks her right away if she can let him have some money, and he does it in a very funny, not to mention an exceedingly manipulative way, in case she should decide not to help him out: "I'd love it if you would give me some money, but I know you probably won't, because my biggest weakness is to believe in the goodness of people." Naturally, she turns him down, so he next tries a different approach: "I'm going to be naming the boat 'the *Marie-Ange*' in your honor, and I'm going to ditch the people whom I'm building it for. The two of us can sail away together forever, because I'm ready to take you out of your mediocre [he actually uses that very adjective] existence." But she's still not interested, especially because he's just called her 'mediocre.'

Pretending that he doesn't care that she's just turned him down, he tells her that he'll "just get the money somewhere else," and he now segues into a new topic: He tells her that he's recently been in Villaneuve St. Georges-et-Pierre visiting his nephew, and that he's also discovered, for the first time in his life, "the joy of being surrounded by family," and he's not kidding, either: This is the one thing in the whole movie which he's told the truth about. Even in spite of his own curmudgeonliness, he's genuinely beginning to love his goofy newfound family in Villaneuve-St.Georges-et-Pierre. As Victor now tells Marie-Ange, elaborating on this subject, "I've always been an adventurer—a Hidalgo, a *meteque* [it's a French word meaning, 'someone who's a foreigner everywhere he goes']. I've even been to *Caracas, in Brazil.* [!] But now, I've discovered the most wonderful thing in the world: Family!" Instead of being moved, Marie-Ange just starts laughing her ass off: "Considering that you're a sailor, it's pretty funny that you think Caracas is in Brazil, instead of Venezuela!" She ends this brief reunion by tossing his duffel out onto the street, and instructing him to follow it.

Director Audiard next shows us a fancy party-cruise ship which is docked in a nearby port, and it's a vessel which just so happens to have a smart dinner-dance in progress. There's a band-shell in the dining room, and a blonde with a cute, pageboy haircut is playing the violin and wearing a man's sailor suit: She's Marie-Ange's younger-by-ten-years sister Severine (Ginette Garcin), with whom Victor apparently had an affair thirty years before, and she, unlike Marie-Ange, is actually excited to see him. (Since he hasn't been able to prize any bread out of his wife, he'll now try his luck with his wife's sister.) Severine and Victor sit down together, and while they haven't seen each other in years, they've both always liked each other so much, that they're able to pick up effortlessly from where they left off, years ago. She tells him that she still has the same unfulfilled dream which she's always had, which is to live in Australia and to build a school there, and since Victor spends a lot of time talking about Australia himself, we can figure out that she probably caught her 'Australia addiction' years ago, by listening to Victor's made-up stories about how he used to travel there—which of course as we already know, he didn't. He starts buttering her up, a bit ("With your talent and my physicality, we could have had a great life together!"), and now that he's worn her down, he goes in for the kill, asking her if he can have some money for Volabruque's boat's mast, and when he asks her for a donation, the whole sweet tone of their conversation changes, and she looks, suddenly, like she's just been thrown to the lions. But guess what: Severine has always liked Victor more than Marie-Ange has, and so she finally decides, in spite of her better judgment, to give him the money for which he's just asked her. Ecstatically, because this isn't the answer which he thought she'd be giving him, he now blurts out that he "married the wrong sister." Like Marie-Ange, Severine, too, knows that Victor's a big talker, but she's still always loved him, anyway. When Victor leaves the party-boat and parts with Severine, it's a very poignant moment, because we know that the two of them will probably never see each other again, but that they'll always think about each other.

Back at the Simonets' house in Villaneuve, and probably one or two days later, the boat is now, finally, completely finished, and we're present at its dedication ceremony, which is attended by dozens of excited-looking neighbors and on-lookers. Some of the construction workers who built the boat are hoisting a French flag, Iwo Jima-style, onto the new mast, a mast which, of course, was purchased with the money which Victor had been able to procure from Severine. Mr. Volabruque, who's standing beneath the mighty vessel, now dedicates it, pompously: "As one adventure ends, so another begins!" The boat has been named *Le Cerf-volant* ('The Flying Kite'), which is a joke of author Rene Fallet's because, when you say *cerf-volant* fast, it becomes French slang, meaning, 'slow brain.' Volabruque then, ceremoniously (he doesn't have too much imagination), begins flying a kite. Antoine and Victor are up on the deck together, and because this is a festive occasion, Victor's *all duded-up* in his fancy black captain's uniform. "We can go around the world," Volabruque shouts, indicating his two preferred traveling buddies, Antoine and Victor, and while Victor looks excited about the proposition, *Antoine's shitting in his shoes!* In fact, Antoine is so nervous that Volabruque and Victor are going to insist that he'll accompany them on their maiden voyage to Port Arthur, in Victor's favorite country which he just *pretends* he's been to, Australia, that he locks himself up in the bathroom, and Victor tries to get him out, but the nerdy little guy just won't stop crying! ("It's Mr. Volabruque who wants the boat, not me! All I want, is to retire with my wife to her farm in Dieppe, to plant potatoes. Please, leave me alone.") Victor tries cajoling Antoine out of the john with tender words, but it just doesn't work: "Come on, pal!

Not only are you coming with us to Port Arthur, but I'll be honored if you'd be my first mate. I mean, if not you, who's going to help me watch out for cyclones?"

Anyway, it's possible that they're arguing for nothing, since the much-vaunted ocean voyage which they're all dreaming about might not happen at all, because just as the dedication ceremony is coming to an end, the boat breaks free from it's moorings in the Simonets' yard (the workers forgot to tie it down tightly enough), and it smashes right into the neighbor, tightly-wound Mr. Ravasson's, house! Ravasson, needless to say, looks pissed-off, but before he can say anything, Victor takes the pre-emptive strike, calling the teacher an idiot, to his face, for daring to have a house so near to a boat's construction site. Ravasson is so angry at the Simonets, we know that he'll definitely be taking it out on Pierrot at school.

In the classroom the next day, Ravasson sees Pierrot, who is dreamily drawing a black pirate's flag on his binder, and he suspends the boy for the remainder of the semester. But hours later, Ravisson is quaking in his boots, when Uncle Victor, and not the Simonets, comes to school for a little 'parent-teacher conference:' Ravisson, this effete little martinet/dictator, who's so powerful and controlling when he's in front of children now, instantly, just like everybody else in the picture, turns into a spineless jellyfish when faced with Real-Man, Jean Gabin! Antoine has some of the boat's carpenters fix Ravasson's broken window, and the teacher, who's now been placated (at least, temporarily) decides to allow Pierrot to return to the classroom.

That night, Victor promises Pierrot that when he gets a bit older, he'll take him on a voyage to the 'Island of the Turtles,' the not-for-real island mentioned in *Treasure Island*, and this is a very nice moment in the film, because it's showing us that Victor has just read the book, since it's really important to him to be able to score points with his great-nephew. Pierrot, however, calls him on this idea, gently letting him know that in real life, there's no such place. While Pierrot definitely looks up to Uncle Victor, even he, for the first time, is starting to figure out that the old man might not really be a professional sailor. (Crossing his arms and squinting, just like one of those thick-browed old cops who always seem to be interrogating Gabin's characters in some of the actor's other pictures [or like Laurel and Hardy's old nemesis, Jimmy Finlayson], little Pierrot now asks his mutton-chopped Uncle, "Are you sure you're telling me the truth?")

The next day, Uncle Victor is visiting the trainyard, and he comes across little Pierrot, who happens to be there, messing around on the old trains. He asks Pierrot why he isn't in school, and the boy replies, acting more like a tough little Dead End Kid, than the nice/smart kid he is, that he hates school. Victor, who doesn't want the kid to turn out to be a bum, which is what he, himself, basically is (even though he'd never cop to it), now tries to talk some sense into him:

> UNCLE VICTOR: Your father only has a junior high school diploma. I want you to study.
> PIERROT: But I don't want to study. I want to be like you, Uncle Victor,

and sail to Cape Horn and Nova Scotia.
UNCLE VICTOR: If you sail away with me and we get lost, what will your mom do? She'll worry!

Pierrot next tells Uncle Victor that he is going to run away from home, and that it will be fine because, in his opinion, his parents will never miss him, since they always seem to be too pre-occupied with their own lives. When Victor asks the boy where he got this idea, Pierrot tells him that it's because, earlier that morning, his parents refused to give him fifty cents to go to the movies, and to rectify the situation, Uncle Victor now takes Pierrot to see an American movie, *The King's Pirate* (starring the American actress/'Miss USA, 1959,' Mary Anne Mobley!), and as the two leave the theater, Victor tells Pierrot, "Promise me that you'll stay in school, and that you'll be better than your father, okay?" (Going to see a movie about sailing is probably the closest to being on water that Victor Ploubaz has ever come, save for, no doubt, the extremely occasional bath.)

Little Pierrot likes to hang out with old, seafaring Victor, because his parents are always ignoring him, and if this story sounds familiar, and like you've already seen it in another movie—well, you definitely have: *Le Drapeau noir flotte sur la marmite* was Michel Audiard and Jean Gabin's tribute to a movie which had always been a great favorite of both of theirs, director Victor Fleming's 1937 MGM classic *Captain's Courageous,* in which little Freddie Bartholomew's wealthy dad, Melvyn Douglas, was always too busy to spend time with him, so the boy, instead, began gravitating toward the nicer and more available Manuel, the Portugese sailor who was played by Spencer Tracy.

Back at home that night, Antoine excitedly shows Victor something that his boss Mr. Volabruque gave him as a present for having finishing the boat's construction: It's a metal sextant, the nautical device which sailors use to measure distance. It looks super-complicated, and too hard to actually 'use,' so Antoine hands it over to Victor, because he wants Victor to show him what to do with it. But Victor has no idea how to operate the otherworldly-looking device, and he tries to get out of explaining its uses, by confidently lying, "Well, to work a sextant, what we really need is a perfect horizon, and there isn't one right now... so I can't teach you, today."

The next morning, Victor, Pierrot, and Antoine are all hanging out at the trainyard together, and Victor's still trying to worm his way out of teaching Antoine and Pierrot two how to use the sextant; and while the 'men' are away from the house, Victor's estranged wife, Marie-Ange turns up at the Simonet house, and she's brought a St. Malo newspaper with her: The headline reads, "*UN MALOIN PREPARE LE RAID DU CHEMIN DE LA MER.*" (Translation: "A ST. MALO-IAN IS PREPARING A RAILROAD WORKER FOR AN OCEAN VOYAGE.") Marie-Ange Ploubaz and Paulette have never met each other before, and the first thing Marie-Ange wants to know from Paulette, is where she can find her (estranged) husband: "You've got to tell me where he is because, by wedding rights, I'm your Aunt, and you must know, just as well as I do, that *everything he does and says is bullshit!*"

At the trainyard, meanwhile, Victor is still unable to explain the proper use (or any use, for that matter) of a sextant, and he's really fumfering for words: "Well, you know, I guess you just have to look at a fixed point." Pierrot asks Uncle Victor what a fixed point is, and Victor stammers, "Well... it's like that house over there in the distance... yeah, I guess that house could be considered a fixed point." Even not-too-swift Antoine has by now figured out that something's not entirely kosher with Uncle Victor, and little Pierrot, who's not afraid to *call a spade a spade,* finally just calls his bluff: "Uncle Victor, you've never used a sextant, have you!"

Victor finally comes clean: "No, kid. You're right: I've never used a sextant before." Since the can of worms has been opened, Pierrot now feels comfortable enough to ask his Uncle, "Well, have you ever even really seen the ocean?" to which Victor replies that, yes, he really has: "Five years ago, I was on a ship, but... *I was the cook.*"

Back at the Simonets,' simultaneously, Marie-Ange is now telling Paulette that her husband Victor has always just been "a smooth-talking old gigolo," and that he recently came to see her, to ask her for money, "to buy some sails." Paulette tells Marie-Ange that Victor was able to come up with the money, and Marie-Ange, without knowing for sure, has a pretty good idea about who gave it to him. ("It was my idiotic sister, Severine, I'll bet. He's been after her for thirty years!") As the ladies continue talking, Victor, Pierrot, and Antoine walk in, and Victor now admits to his lifetime of untruths in front of everybody: "It's true. I'm not a sailor. I just wanted to impress Pierrot." Pierrot still loves his Uncle (in fact, he loves him even more now, because Victor is finally telling everybody the truth about himself), and he now asks Victor how come Victor knew how to build a ship so well, since he's not a real sailor, and Victor replies that once, a long time ago, a carpenter in St. Malo told him how to do it, and that he always remembered what the guy told him: This means that Victor, for all of his lying, must be a very intelligent man, and as we already know anyway, based on the fact that we've already seen *Le Baron de l'ecluse* and *Le Gentleman d'Epsom,* you can't be stupid if you're a successful con artist.

Antoine doesn't know what to say, and even though he's a *nebbish,* he now asserts himself: "So, you're just a cartoon hero, and you wanted to send me on a boat to Australia, where there's a possibility that we would have been killed?" Victor decides to take the high-road, responding not with anger, but with something which is pretty close to poetry: "Well... I guess I'll have to simply sail on in your son's dreams." Victor looks embarrassed, because he's disappointed the small boy, and he looks also like he wishes that this whole 'intervention' which has been suddenly foisted upon him would end, and as quickly as possible.

Next, we get a very sweet plot twist: Even though Victor doesn't know how to sail, Antoine is so touched by his honesty, that he decides, even in spite of his timidity about being on open water, to go sailing with the older man, anyway. (A quick little test-run around the harbor couldn't hurt anybody!)

So later that evening, it's time for the maiden voyage of *Le Cerf-volant,* which has now been moved to the trainyard, a place from whence it can't crash into people's houses. Victor and Antoine unmoor it and drag it down to the sea, and when we next see the two of them, they're alone on the boat, preparing 'her' (you've got to call a boat 'her!') for her maiden voyage, while singing what probably passes in Victor's mind, anyway, as a lusty/bawdy sea shanty. Meanwhile, Pierrot's at home, entranced by a Jules Verne novel, while his mom and the still-visiting Marie-Ange are busily preparing dinner together; the two ladies have no idea that Antoine and Victor are on the boat, because they told her that they were merely going out for a drink.

Of course, lots of fun (and unforeseen) third-act events transpire aboard *Le Cerf*, the most pressing of which, is that Victor has no freakin' idea how to steer the damned thing—he's completely clueless! Plus, the fact that a huge storm of black-clouds is nearing the boat isn't helping matters too much, either. (Real sailors would have checked the weather conditions, before sailing.) Completely unconversant in what he's supposed to do in case of emergency, Victor now starts panic-reciting some passages from *Treasure Island* which Pierrot taught him. (Charmingly, when Victor gets scared on the boat, all he can think of to stay calm, is little Pierrot, and it is the fact that Victor is thinking about the boy, which will ultimately save the two men.) Now making with a literary reference of his own, because he thinks that's what he's supposed to do (since that's what he's just seen Victor, doing), Antoine suddenly cries out, "Flaubert is screaming!" (Here, Antoine is referencing the famous, nineteenth-century author's storm-battered ocean-voyage saga, *A Simple Soul* [1872], and as he recites it, he and Victor are now changing into groovy, day-glow, orange life jackets!)

Back at the Simonet residence, meanwhile, it's almost midnight (in France, that's *almost* too late for families to start eating dinner), and Pierrot, Paulette, and Marie-Ange are all sitting around the living room, waiting for their men to come home. The women are really worried because of the storm, but Pierrot calms them: "I'm not scared for dad: He'll be okay, because Uncle Victor is there with him." Even though Pierrot knows his Uncle Victor has told him some pretty tall tales, he still respects him a lot, since Uncle Victor is basically the only adult in his life who's ever paid any attention to him, without also judging him.

Next, we're back on the scow, and—R-R-R-RIPPPPPPP!!! The sails have just torn, and the *Cerf-volant* now crashes, first into another boat, and then, right after that, into a bridge, and then suddenly, the whole mast splinters into pieces, as well. "Don't panic," Victor cries-out, goofily. "Panicking, is why the *Titanic* sank!" Victor is extremely Gabin-Calm at this moment, in fact he's the only 'calm' there is, in the eye of this frightening storm. Antoine fires off a flare from a flare gun which he's discovered on deck, but (and even Victor knows this, and he reprimands Antoine for it) it's the wrong-colored flare. "You idiot," Victor shouts at him (this is a total, 'Gilligan-and-the-Skipper'-moment), "You don't fire off a red flare for danger. Red means 'water disease!'" And groovily, since this film was made in *Swingin' 1971*, director Michel Audiard now proceeds to film the remainder of this sequence through a psychedelic red camera filter. "We just have to wait for the rescue team," Victor mutters, trying to calm his little buddy down.

Victor and Antoine next hitch a ride back to town from a truckdriver (Henri Cogan), and by now, it's got to be one or two o' clock in the morning. The driver has no idea that these two men have just been on a boat, and he asks them if they always wear orange vests when they're walking around at night. Victor flat-out lies to the guy, telling him that he and Antoine are Harbor Security, and that they've just spent the last three hours saving boats, which were in distress! (When the two guys get home, 'their women,' and little Pierrot, are already sound-asleep.)

The next morning, word has already started getting around Villaneuve St. Georges-et-Pierre, that the *Cerf* has disappeared from the train station. Victor wakes up in his bedroom at the Simonets, pretending to have been asleep all night, and feigning that he has no idea that the boat is no longer in the yards. (Outside of Pierrot, nobody knows that Victor and Antoine were out on the boat, last night.) Antoine then follows Victor's lead, and pretends that he, too, was in bed, sleeping all night, and he even starts crying out in mock horror, for dramatic effect ("The boat is gone?! Oh my God!"), and Victor pretends to be enraged, as well: "Who betrayed me and took the boat out? I demand to know! I've sailed around the world five times, and I've never had anything like this happen, ever. I'm totally screwed!"

The Simonets head into the local tavern with Victor, who's back in those striped pajamas, again, to commiserate about the boat's loss over morning eye-openers: The Bartender brings over some wine—the shit Victor wouldn't touch at the beginning of the movie—which Victor now quaffs down, as if the world is running out of it. "We did all that work for nothing," Victor moans, remaining in character. At that moment, Mr. Volabruque runs in, and announces to everybody present that the boat has been found. At that very moment, Victor and the Simonets all look out of the bar's front window, where they get a glimpse of the smashed-up *Cerf,* as it's getting towed back into town on the back of the Harbormaster's truck. Volabruque tells everybody that the Harbormaster discovered the 'ex-boat' in the mud, and he looks happy regardless, just because it's been found: "Now we'll just fix it up, and then—it's off to Port Arthur!" Once again, the boat gets moored in the Simonets' front yard, much to the consternation of Teacher Ravisson.

That night, Antoine and Paulette are asleep, and Victor's in bed too, in his own room—and guess what: Victor's wife Marie-Ange is asleep, right next to him! (Guess they're not so estranged, anymore.) Both men, independently of each other, and in their own bedrooms, start talking in their sleep, alerting their wives indirectly, that they are the ones who wrecked the boat. Antoine, in one of the cinema's very funniest 'talking-in-my-sleep' moments ever, now starts screaming out, "Crustaceans! They're coming to eat me up!"

Hearing his dad crying-out, Pierrot wakes up, and he's now too pre-occupied with his dad's mental state to be able to fall back to sleep. Soon, morning will come, and little Pierrot is afraid that once the townspeople start figuring out that Victor's the one who damaged the boat, they'll hate him, and so to save his beloved great-uncle's reputation, Pierrot, the youngest and the most clear-thinking of anybody in the whole movie, makes a fire, burning the vessel to cinders. Then, suddenly freaked-out about what he's just done, and afraid of dealing with the consequences (whatever they will be), the boy runs away from home. Victor guesses that the now-missing boy is most probably hiding out in the trainyards, and sure enough, when he gets there, that's exactly where Pierrot is. (The kid is hiding out behind some pilings, whimpering and shaking like a leaf.)

"Kid, what are you doing here?" Uncle Victor asks him, gently. "Don't you know the boat is burning?" Pierrot won't stop crying, so Victor tries to cheer him up by recounting a story about how he once, "… sailed to Mexico. And suddenly, I came upon the Zigomare, that amazing Mexican bird [Author's Note: The Zigomare is a 'Mayan Death Symbol!'], which actually has a furry body and two heads!" Pierrot, suddenly forgetting how sad he is, now starts laughing, from the sheer ridiculousness of the story:

> PIERROT: Oh, come on, Uncle Victor. You know you've never been to Mexico!
> VICTOR: Okay, kid. You're right. I can't lie to you, anymore. I didn't go to Mexico. I saw the Zigomare somewhere else.
> PIERROT (sarcastically, knowing he's hearing another lie): On a ghost ship?
> VICTOR: (not 'getting' the sarcasm) Yes! And when I saw it, suddenly, I saw dead people, and I heard their voices!

Pierrot knows that Uncle Victor is lying to him again, but this time out, he doesn't mind—in fact, the lie is so patently outrageous, that it just makes the boy giggle. (You've got to love an old codger who'll tell you a story as crazy as that.)

When we next see Antoine, Paulette, and Pierrot, they're all sitting around together on the deck of the smashed-up, burned-out *Cerf*, which is now back in the family's back yard, and Paulette is making an offer to her little boy: "Look, Pierrot: Instead of going to Grandma's house for the summer like you usually do, how about spending some time with Uncle Victor?" Even though Victor's full of shit, the family still loves (and even more importantly, forgives) him, because no matter what he says and does, he's also brought fun and adventure into the drudgery of their boring, suburban lives.

For the film's final moments, Michel Audiard cuts to Marie-Ange's grocery store in St. Malo: Summer's here and, not so surprisingly, Victor is now working behind the counter with Marie-Ange, as a happy Pierrot helps them out. It's a happy ending to a wonderful film, even in spite of the fact that Audiard has chosen to optically superimpose a written quote from the noted French novelist Louis-Ferdinand Celine, over the film's final shot: Celine who, as I already mentioned at the beginning of my chapter about 1967's *Soleil des voyous*, was one of France's most notoriously anti-Semitic authors, famously took some time out from Jew-hating, in 1932, to invent this quote: "*Voyager c'est bien utile. Ca fait travailler l'imagination.*" ("Traveling is good. But it is always better to travel in your imagination.") The quote is a line from Celine's darkly-comic novel of French colonials in Africa, *Voyage au bout de la nuit* (*Journey to the End of the Night*), a book which apparently inspired such authors as

Kurt Vonnegut, Jr. and Henry Miller.

In spite of the fact that *Drapeau noir flotte sur la marmite* ends with a quote from a proto-Nazi, everybody who loves great movies (and great comedies, and Jean Gabin) would really love this movie. Not only is *Drapeau* a great picture but, without any hyperbole, I would also like to state very firmly, that's it's just as great a movie as the movie which inspired it—*Captain's Courageous*. I saw *Drapeau noir* on an out-of-print French VHS cassette (with the obligatory 'no English subtitles').

In France, in the 1960s and 1970s, host Pierre Tchernia's "*Monsieur Cinema*" was the most popular Sunday afternoon program on France's ORTF television—it was a game show in which two panelists watched movie clips and answered questions about movies, each one vying for the title of "Monsieur Cinema." About halfway through each show, a different celebrity guest would appear and, on October 24, 1971, it was none other than Jean Gabin himself, who was making one of his ultra-rare television appearances. On the program, Gabin tells Tchernia that the sailor's cap he sports in the *Drapeau noir* was the actual cap which he wore in the Free French Navy during World War II, and that he had lost track of it for years, but had re-discovered it just a few years before, when he had found his young son Mathias playing with it. On the 'Gabin Episode' of the show, Gabin also tells Tchernia that *Drapeau noir flotte sur la marmite* was his second film playing a sailor, the first being 1940's *Remorques*. Clearly, Gabin wasn't concentrating when he said this, because *Drapeau* was actually the fourth movie in which he played a sailor. (The first, was his very early 1931 picture, *Pour un soir..!*, and the second, was 1934's *Zou Zou*.)

What a Critic Said at the Time: "Gabin is his usual cantankerous old self in this gentle, [and] even sentimental, tale…" (*Variety*, 11-17-71 issue. Critic: "Mosk. [George Moskowitz.]" Reviewed in Paris.)

Top: "Quelle heure est-il?" Above: Cult Italian action star Fabio Testi plays the heavy in "Le Tueur" (Film 91, right).

FILM 91

Le Tueur

France/Italy/Germany, 1972

(Literal English Translation: "THE KILLER") Directed by Denys de La Patelliere. Produced by Claude Giroux and Eric Rochat. Written by Pascal Jardin. Director of Photography (color), Claude Renoir. Editors, Clarissa Ambach and Claude Durand. Music by Ennio Morricone and Hubert Giraud. Production Designer, Michel de Broin. (GENRES: ACTION/POLICIER) A Production of C.O.F.C.I., Europa Films and GAFER (France), Mondial Te- Fi (Italy), and Rialto Film (Germany). Running Time, 1 hour 50 minutes. Released in France on March 1, 1972, by Prodis. Never Released Theatrically in the United States.

"These computers... they won't last!"
— *Sixty-something police inspector Gabin doesn't worry about this passing computer fad, in "Le Tueur"*

This late-career Jean Gabin effort is watchable but, at the same time, it represents, next to 1968's *Sous le signe du taureau,* what appears to be some of the least effort Jean Gabin ever put into a movie: Here's the one-and-only movie of his career, in which the actor actually looks just plain bored, as though he's shown up only for the paycheck (and that the check bounced). About half of Gabin's scenes, in fact, just find his character, crusty old police inspector Le Guen, sitting in his office chair with the camera focused in on an extreme close up of his face, just like in the late-career movies of Orson Welles and Marlon Brando (although, granted, Gabin didn't share those two other actors' sizable girths). Not dull like *Sous le sign du taureau,* but not overly-exciting either, director Denys de La Patelliere's *Le Tueur* feels like a direct precursor to those nail-the-camera-to-the-ground, Z-grade action movie shoot-'em-ups which Cannon Films' big muckimucks, Menahem Golan and Yoram Globus would begin churning out ten years later—those *Death Wish IV's* and *Missing in Action III's,* which would star the careerly-downswung Charles Bronson and Chuck Norris.

Le Tueur opens in a tiny jail cell, in which we're trapped with three hoods who are shooting dice together. When we meet them, two of the guys are telling the third guy (the toughest-looking *hombre* of the three), the Harry Reems-mustached Georges Gassot (he's played by the Italian '70s cop-movie icon, Fabio Testi), after he fails to roll a seven, that he has no luck line on his hand, and Georges is so psychotic, his immediate response, is to slice his own palm open with a piece of broken glass, and hold the bloody hand up to them, maniacally shouting, "Now I have a luck line!"

Next, Inspector Le Guen's (Jean Gabin's) young partner, who's played by Jean Barney, picks him up in front of his house for a hard day of sleuthing, and Le Guen mentions to Francois that, at his age (Gabin was sixty-seven, when he made this movie), he's more interested in the windy weather which Paris is having today, than he is in catching bad guys. (What a great movie character: A cop who's not interested in solving crimes anymore!) The news report which is coming-in over their car radio is telling them, and us, that the psychotic criminal Georges Gassot has just been transferred today from prison to a psychiatric hospital on the *Ville Juif* (Paris's eloquently named 'Jew Street.') Le Guen and his partner arrive at the 15th-District P.D. Headquarters, where they ride up the elevator, both ready for a little Monday-morning conference with Chief Tellier (Bernard Blier who, at this point, had been playing supporting roles in Gabin movies for seventeen years). Tellier, like Le Guen, is an older guy, and he, too, looks like he's not all that interested in catching criminals, anymore. (In fact, when we first see Tellier, he's just sitting in his office, reading the newspaper!)

Director Patelliere now brings us over to the mental hospital, Georges' new 'home away from home.' The Doctor (Emmano Casanova) who's been assigned his case happens to be a major sadist (and it's no wonder: this film is a French-*German* co-production!), and he starts trying to terrify his patient, psychologically: "I know you come from alcoholic heredity, Gassot. You've killed four times—and you like to kill! I will now give you electro-shock, because you are very sick, and you are bad. This will be very painful!"

Post-electro-shock, Georges' brother Francois comes to visit him. (Francois is played by Jacques Richard, a dead-ringer for the American t.v. actor, Robert Urich.) Georges asks his brother what time it is and, to illustrate that time is of no consequence in a mental hospital, where day and night are interchangeable, Francois shruggingly replies, "It's 11:00 Monday… it's Thursday at 3:00 a.m… Who knows?" After Francois leaves, an orderly tells Georges to go to sleep but, instead, Georges just head-butts the guy, *a la* World Wrestling Entertainment, and then quickly escapes through the hospital's sea of Star-of-David-shaped windows. (The hospital is on Jew Street, so, naturally, that's what the windows look like!) Georges is psycho, but he's not crazy, and yet he knew he had to act crazy in order to get transferred out of the heavily-secured jail in which he had been sequestered before, and into the (comparatively) laxly-secure mental hospital. Meanwhile, of course, Francois is outside, waiting for Georges in a getaway car.

Back at Police H.Q., Gabin's Inspector Le Guen is on the phone (it's another of the film's many extreme-close-ups of Gabin's head) and, as usual for Jean Gabin, he remains very calm, as he's now hearing from an associate that Georges Gassot has escaped from the loony bin. Chief Tellier tells Le Guen, "I know it took you eight months to arrest Gassot last time, but you did it. And I'm counting on you to do it again." Le Guen takes his time to solve cases, because he's 'old-school,' just like all of those older cop-characters in American movies (the ones whom the Chief-characters are always calling 'dinosaurs').

In the few days since he's escaped from the psychiatric hospital, Georges Gassot has now committed three more brutal murders (and all of them, mercifully, offscreen). Georges is a weird type of a personality because, as we've already seen, and as we're going to continue to be seeing throughout the film, he's kind of a masochist: He's one of these guys who really wants to get caught, and he thinks that the cops are morons, because they're not picking up on the too-easy clues which he's been leaving them. Down at H.Q., meanwhile, Chief Tellier is telling Le Guen that his fancy, new police computer will help them track Georges down, but Le Guen looks completely unimpressed by the giant machine; he just Gabin-Shrugs and tells his boss that computers are ridiculous: "The old ways are still the best. These computers—they won't last." Even though Le Guen has been working for Tellier for decades, they still call each other by the polite '*vous*,' instead of by the familiar '*tu*,' which shows (and this is very economical screenwriting) that the two men have always, basically, just tolerated each other. Tellier tells Le Guen, "I know you've had a lot of luck doing things your way in the past—but the world has changed." (Still, Tellier supports Le Guen enough to put him on the case.)

Le Guen and his young partner next high-tail it into the thrift store which is owned by Alfonse (Georges Staquet) who, as they happen to know, is an old crime partner of Georges.' "You helped Georges Gassot escape from the mental institution, didn't you?" Le Guen accuses Alphonse, not knowing that it was really Georges' brother, and not Alphonse, who aided in Georges' breakout. Le Guen and his partner then figure out that Georges must have gone off to Marseilles, since he has committed a lot of crimes there in the past, so they charter a plane to Marseilles, which is exactly what Gabin's young police detective-character Jacques Miral did forty-two years earlier, in 1931's *Mephisto*.

Next, we're in the offices of the Marseilles P.D. and, specifically, we're inside the *Groupe de Repression de Banditisme*, where the Marseilles Commissioner (he's played by Jacques Debary) pledges to Le Guen his own department's aide in helping Le Guen to track Georges down. The Marseilles Commissioner shows Le Guen his own office's brand-spanking new police computers (those freakin' things are popping up everywhere!), and Le Guen blanches. (He's followed around by these crappy new computers, wherever he goes! *Le Tueur* is what the Los Angeles *Times* critic Kevin Thomas once called, when he was writing about a low-budget Charles Bronson actioner from 1985, called *Messenger of Death*) 'an old man's movie;' in *Le Tueur*, computers are treated like the passing fad they are!

And meanwhile, while this has been transpiring, Georges has been hiding out in a Marseilles hotel room, where he reclines in bed, smoking a cigarette. Francois enters, and informs his brother that, three days from today, they're going to be perpetrating a new crime, in Marseilles, and that Alfonse is going to be helping them out. Francois tells Georges that he has already made an arrangement for Georges to get half of what Alfonse, who's going to be underwriting the crime, will be taking in, and Georges tells his brother that they're going to have to get their hands on some guns. (Georges really likes Marseilles, because fewer people know him there, than they do in Paris.)

Under cover of night, Georges next heads out into the skeeviest of neighborhoods, in search of a gun shop which he can easily rip off. The Paris P.D. has alerted Marseilles P.D. that Georges is in town so, unbeknownst to Georges, cops are now swarming all over the place, trying to catch him; one Cop even grabs a guy whom he thinks is Georges, but, as it turns out, it's a completely different mustached guy.

Since it's nighttime, and all of the good gun shops are closed, Georges steals a parked car, and smashes it through the window of what he considers to be the most well-stocked store in town and, after stealing all of the guns in sight, he celebrates by trying to fuck a hot, red-haired prostitute, Gerda (Uschi Glass), whom he's noticed walking down the street. The first thing she notices about him, is the scar on his recently-sliced up palm, and she tells him, just like his cohorts in jail also told him, that he has a "great luck line."

Georges brings Gerda home for a bout of hot monkey love, but it's *coitus interruptus*, because Francois now comes in, and informs them that Le Guen's in town, and looking for him. Georges likes Gerda so much, he tells her that after he commits his next crime, he wants to take her with him to South America. She tells him that she'd love to go with him, except for the fact that it would make her pimp, Lucien, very unhappy.

Georges, next, heads into a sleazy bar, a dive with a tacky Christmas nativity scene set up in the corner, where Lucien (Sady Reboot), Gerda's pimp, is present, shooting craps with a couple of cronies. Feeling his psychotic oats, Georges taps Lucien's shoulder and announces, "I am Georges Gassot. I want to buy your woman!" Lucien, wanting to prove that he's the tougher man of the two, just shrugs ("So?!") and Georges, hating the fact that he hasn't been recognized by a fellow lowlife, now whips out a gun and, without even giving it a thought, blows Lucien away. After Georges splits from the bar, Le Guen and his partner arrive on the scene, but they've just missed him.

Francois has commandeered a car (it looks like a milk truck) and Gerda, who's not as upset as she should be over the fact that her pimp has just been blown to Kingdom Come, now heads over to the dock, accompanied by the two Gassots. One of the Gassot brothers' friends, a guy with a yacht, has apparently offered to hide them out until such time as the police should stop their manhunt for Georges.

When Georges, Francois, and Gerda arrive at the yacht, they discover that the guy who was going to be hiding them out, is the major drug-biz player Toussaint Orsini, for whom Georges and Francois sometimes work. But our three fugitives have arrived too late, because Orsini has apparently just been killed, and his body is splayed out on the top deck of his own boat. The three now have to find somewhere else to hide and, after they leave, Le Guen shows up (late again, of course), with his partner and the Marseilles Commissioner, in tow.

Georges and Gerda next return to Paris, leaving Francois behind in Marseilles. Georges has already figured out that his brother is the one who keeps telling the cops where he is, because why else would Le Guen keep showing up? (Francois is a low-rent version of

The Godfather's Fredo Corleone-character, a guy who has no compunction about narcing on his own brother, in return for money.) Even though Georges knows what his brother is doing to him, he still has warm feelings toward him anyway, since Francois is family, and he accepts that his brother is simply a very weak character, just like Marcel Bozzuffi's character, Pierrot—Gabin's character's little brother, in 1957's *Le Rouge est mis*. Plus, as I've already mentioned, Georges Gassot is one of those criminals who, on some weird level, wants to get caught, and he hates every minute of his life in which policemen *aren't* catching him, and so, in some way, he truly (and not-so-subconsciously) likes that his brother is 'out there,' always trying to get him into trouble.

Next, we're back in Alfonse's Paris shop, which, as we're now seeing, is something more than just your average souvenir stand—in fact, it's a sex toy shop! Georges orders Alfonse to hide him out for awhile, and Alfonse agrees, but it's too late, because some cops have just seen Georges entering the store (they were obviously tipped-off, by Francois), and they now start chasing him through several buildings and alleys. Georges even shoots one of the cops who's pursuing him (which, in any country, is 'a major no-no') and, finally able to escape from the building, he hides under a parked sixteen-wheeler, and the cops lose track of him—at least, for awhile…

At the same time, Bernard Blier's Chief Tellier is organizing a crack-team of Supercops to help Le Guen catch Georges faster, and one of them happens to be a hippie (Philippe Valaruis) with (Heaven forefend!) long hair. Tellier, already knowing how the conservative-looking Le Guen will respond to being teamed-up with a greasy freak like this, asks Le Guen if he's happy with his new team, and Le Guen, keeping his cool (although we can tell that he'd really like to puke), just replies, "This new guy's kind of unkempt. Anyway, I don't care what people look like, I care about how they work." Le Guen does admit, though, that, to him, hippies are unclean. ("When I see young guys like this… I feel like I'm in Pigalle!") After Tellier and Le Guen rib each other a little bit more, about how it's a new world, and about how Le Guen prefers the old ways, Le Guen, for our benefit, now does a total Jack Webb, talking to Tellier, but really looking right into the camera, and addressing the movie's audience: "People complain about the police… but they need us!" Tellier opines that somebody should figure out "how to make cops more popular again:" Because of the Vietnam War, and also due to the American cops who had recently executed the college protestors at Kent State University in Ohio, in 1970, and also because of similar anti-war protests in France (where cops were similarly pummeling students, during in the riots of '68), being a cop, in the contemporary 1972 in which this movie is set, just wasn't cool anymore; in 1970s' movie vernacular, as Abbie Hoffman told us, cops aren't 'cops'—they're the fuzz and (worse than that)—they're pigs, too!

Le Guen knows, from having dealt with George Gassot in the past, that Georges smokes between two and three packs of cigarettes a day and, thusly armed with this knowledge, Le Guen and his new hippie partner decide to investigate all of the local tobacco shops, to see if anybody's seen him around.

Now, director Patelliere takes us back to Georges, who's currently hanging-out in his brother Francois' girlfriend, Lulu's (Ginette Garcin's) apartment. Lulu, a blonde with short hair, tells Georges that she realizes he's badly in need of money, and that she knows some people he can work for, who pay well: "Your friend, Toussaint Orsini, [the guy whom Georges, Gerda, and Francois found dead on his boat, in Marseilles] knew two guys, the Garcia Brothers. Like you, they worked for Orsini, in the past. They're drug peddlers and they don't know you were Orsini's friend. They think you're the one who killed him, so they're looking for you. Anyway, I know that some people from a rival drug organization want the Garcias dead, and if you want me to, I'll introduce you to them. They'll pay whoever kills the Garcias thirty-thousand dollars [U.S.], and after you wipe the Garcias out, you can go to Bogota [like you've told me you want to] and live like a king." She next tries to seal the deal, by mentioning that there's a lot of sunlight in Bogota, although she's not mentioning that Bogota now, if not then, is one of the most dangerous crime cities in the world. Inspector Le Guen knows, in the very next scene, that Gassot's planning on shooting the Garcias and getting $30K for doing it, which means, more than obviously, that Francois and Lulu have been working with Le Guen, in setting Georges up. (But what do Francois and Lulu stand to get out of it? Immunity? Cash? The chance to wipe out old criminal records? The movie never tells us.)

That night, in a Paris hotel room, Gerda's reading a paperback edition of Erich Segal's mega-popular early-'70s novel, *Love Story*. (Of course, Gerda's the consummate 'hooker with a heart of gold' who dreams of a better life so, naturally, she's going to be reading soppy old 'shite,' like that.) Georges enters, and tells her that they're going to have to take it on the hoof, and right now, because the Garcias are looking for him. Georges makes a frightened Gerda (she knows what's going to happen, if she's with him) accompany him to a countryside cabin in Argenteuil, which looks just like the country house in which Gabin and Lino Ventura were hiding out during the final moments of *Razzia sur la chnouf*, and the fact that Francois is the one who chose the place for them, is a huge red flag to Georges, and to us, that the place probably won't be too safe of a haven for him—but he goes there, anyway! Georges is no dummy: He knows the Garcias will be coming to this cabin to kill him and, most probably, he knows also, that Francois has already notified the Garcias, and probably Le Guen, too, that he'd be there. But he's not afraid of the Garcias or the cops, just like he wasn't afraid of Lucien, the pimp whom he had blasted, back at the Marseilles bar.

Of course, the Garcias show up at the cabin, right on cue; and also right on cue, Georges dispatches them to their Maker, courtesy of his mighty, scattering shotgun.

Director Patelliere now cuts to what is probably a few days later: Francois hasn't told the cops where his brother is (he hasn't told them about the cabin in Argenteuil because, obviously, he's starting to fear for his own safety; unlike the fatalistic Georges, Francois likes life, and he doesn't want his brother Georges to come and kill him), so, at the present moment, Le Guen has no clue as to Georges' present whereabouts. Chief Tellier tells Le Guen that they should lock Francois up until he decides to start 'singing,' again.

Fortunately, it's always much easier for the cops to find the moronic Francois Gassot than it is to find the smarter Georges Gassot: The police already know, based on past experiences, that Francois spends his nights in the basement of an office building, showing eight-millimeter stag movies to a small group of perverted businessmen who retreat into the building's dank depths, after telling their wives that they're going out for the evening "to watch educational movies about the Louvre!" Le Guen and some other cops stampede-in on the current screening and arrest Francois, and they also manage to snag a few horny businessmen, while they're at it. (As Ralph Kramden used to say to Ed Norton, on American t.v.'s great all-time-classic, "The Honeymooners," "Wait till the wives find out!")

Le Guen throws Francois in jail with a cellmate, a twentysomething, ex-con/police plant by the name of Fredo, who's played by a young Gerard Depardieu, in one of his very first movie roles. Fredo's a guy who looks very trusting, and Le Guen knows Francois will confess everything he knows about Georges' whereabouts to Fredo, in no time flat. Fredo tells Francois, whether this is true or not (and most probably, it is not), that he's an old friend of Georges,' and that he hasn't seen Georges in a long time, and wishes he knew where he might be able to find him. Right on cue, Francois gives him the location of the lodge in Argenteuil, in which Georges is hiding out, and—Bingo! Le Guen now has the information he needs to go and get Georges, but decides to keep Francois in jail, anyway. (Why take chances?)

Le Guen tells Chief Tellier, "Now, I know where Georges Gassot is, and I'm going to get him. But I want to warn you that I'm going to be using methods that you won't really like." (Author's Note: Old Man Methods!) Tellier gives Le Guen his blessings.

Georges and Gerda are still sequestered away in the Argenteuil cabin, and George tells her that, when all of this blows over, and after the cops are no longer looking for him, they'll be able to head off, to "the safety of Bogota!"

Gerda hears both cars and footsteps outside—the cavalry has arrived! Completely unafraid of the sheer numbers of cops who've come (a lot of law enforcement officers have shown up), Georges starts blowing them all away, and he even sends Le Guen's new, young partner to Hippie Heaven. Then, righteously amped-up with blood lust, and thinking (incorrectly) that he's killed all of the cops, Georges exits the house, and starts running triumphantly, like Rocky Balboa after he defeated Apollo Creed, through the fields. Gerda's chasing after him at a distance because, at this point, she's a little more grounded in reality than he is, and she realizes, correctly, that there are probably some cops who are still out there, waiting for him.

Cops with dogs are now on Georges' scent, and 'the ultimate dog'—Bulldog Jean Gabin—is now also on the scene, with Chief Tellier at his side. Le Guen announces to Georges, over his megaphone, that he should give himself up, and that he's "surrounded." Georges, knowing he doesn't have a Chinaman's Chance, simply—and without even thinking about it—places his shotgun in his mouth and kills himself.

As the end credits of this unsatisfying clinker roll, we leave the theater to the strains of a folky-sounding, rock-and-roll tribute-song to the movie's creepy, and ultra-unlikeable bad guy, George Gassot. Gassot's not an anti-hero who actually deserves his own theme-ballad, like those *actually great* 1960s and 1970s movie-bad guys and gals who actually earned their own ballads because they were so cool (and here, I'm thinking about Serge Gainsbourg and Brigitte Bardot's 1968 French song-tribute to 1967's American movie, *Bonnie and Clyde,* Nat King Cole's theme song from *Cat Ballou*, or Bob Dylan's songs for Peckinpah's *Pat Garrett and Billy the Kid*). Georges is just a creepy guy, whom the audience doesn't like at all, and whom we'd rather see, dead! The song is called "*C'etait un homme*" ("He Was a Man"), and it's 'co-sung' by Jean Barney, who played Le Guen's first young partner (the 'clean-cut' one) and the vocalist Pierre Delreaux. The song's tragically un-groovy lyrics were never destined for the Top 10—nor even, now that I'm thinking about it, for the 'Bottom 1,000:'

LYRICS:

"What do you think?
He was a man like you.
He thought he was a wolf.
He was a man who didn't understand.
The proof is that he loved and dreamed.
A bird that wasn't tamed, he was playing a dangerous game.
And killing men, solitarily.
He couldn't win anything but a toooooomb…"

Le Tueur is a film which proves that, back in the 1970s, the French could turn out shoddy exploitation actioners just like the Italians (who called their own B-grade cop movies '*giallos*') and the Americans. Fortunately, Jean Gabin's next four films—the final four films of his career—will all be very good, and Our Hero will finish his career on four (very) high notes.

What a Critic Said at the Time: "Plodding and telegraphed. Gabin appears listless, and is even deprived of his usual scene of rage and anger. Director Denys de La Patelliere does not get much dynamism, or deep insight into the judicial processes that help or hamper police work, in this generally rote offering." (*Variety*, 3-4-72 issue. Critic: "Mosk. [George Moskowitz.]" Reviewed in Paris.)

FILM 92

L'Affaire Dominici

France/Italy/Spain, 1973

(Literal English Translation: "THE DOMINCI AFFAIR") Directed by Claude Bernard-Aubert. Produced by Claude Giroux and Eric Rochat. Written by Claude Bernard-Aubert, Daniel Boulanger and Louis-Emile Galey. Director of Photography (color), Ricardo Aronovich. Editor, Louise Hautecoeur. Music by Alain Goraguer. (GENRE: DRAMA) A Bocaccio Films (Spain)/C.O.F.C.I. and GAFER (France)/Mondial Televisione-Film (Italy) Production. Running Time, 1 hour 40 minutes. Released in France on March 3, 1973, by Societe Nouvelle de Cinematographie (SNC). Never Released Theatrically in the United States.

"Well, just let me know if you're going to be executing me. In the meantime,
I need a nap. Do you have a bed here?"
— *Gabin, accused of committing a triple-murder, gets sleepy during his
police interrogation, in "L'Affaire Dominici"*

Everybody *thinks* the best movie of 1972 was *The Godfather*, and that's probably true, but it's only because director Claude Bernard-Aubert's mindbendingly-amazing *L'Affaire Dominici* (*The Dominici Affair*), a sweeping drama based on the true-life incidents of a French farm family in the 1950s was, *incredibly*, never released in the United States. It's not only one of the best films which Jean Gabin ever made during his forty-six year movie career (it's definitely up there with his all-time 1930s' classics, like *La Grande illusion* and *La Bete humaine*), but it's also, absolutely, one of the best movies of the entire 1970s, a big 'A-picture' with gorgeous, low-light cinematography by Ricardo Aronovitch (which recalls the naturalistic look that director-of-photography Gordon Willis gave to *The Godfather*, or which John Bailey gave to Kubrick's *Barry Lyndon*), and it's also got some of the best acting, writing, and directing you'll ever see. Truly, this movie is, at least (as far as distribution in America, goes) *the one that got away*. It's the kind of movie that movie awards were invented for, and it's also the only movie in which Jean Gabin would ever work for the young director, Claude Bernard-Aubert.

Dominici is a true story, based on events which took place in Lurs, France, in the 1950s:

One night, an English family on holiday, the Drummonds—father, Jack (Colin Drake); mother Anne (Jane Martel); and twelve-year-old daughter, Elizabeth (Nicole Giroux)—who are road-tripping-it through the French countryside, and who have been unable to secure lodging for the night, decide to camp-out on some farmland, which (and they have no idea about this) belongs to Gaston Dominici (Jean Gabin) and Gaston's large, extended family of sons, daughters-in-law, and grandchildren. At about 1:00 a.m., mysterious gunshots ring-out, from the Dominici property. All three members of the Drummond family—the mother, the father, and the daughter—are savagely killed.

When dawn comes, a police inspector (Paul Crauchet) is already on the scene, investigating with his men, and he decides immediately that the shooter, whoever he was, couldn't have been interested in money, because the bodies of the parents, and their money, haven't been disturbed. The bullet casings, which the Inspector and his men have found at close proximity to the bodies, match a rifle which, as he's now determining, belongs to Gaston's fortysomething son Gustave, who's played by the great, 1970s' French-movie-stalwart, Victor Lanoux.

When he sees the cops, Jean Gabin's Gaston heads over to where *the ex-Drummonds* are still splayed out on the ground, admits to the cops that it's his property, and tells them that it was he who telephoned them when he discovered the bodies. Gaston tells the cops that, in his opinion, it must have been "some traveling backpackers" who killed the family. The Inspector, however, doesn't buy it, and he notifies Gaston that Gaston and his family should now consider themselves to be "under suspicion"—and this is a *biiiig* family we're talking about!

A superimposed credit tells us that the next section of the film will comprise "The First Day of Investigation: August 5, 1952." Gaston, who is being interrogated at the police station, is now telling the Inspector, in greater detail, what he remembers from the fatal night: "I was asleep at the time, and I heard shots, at about 1:00 a.m., that woke me up." After the Inspector has finished questioning Gaston, he next talks to Gaston's son Gustave's young wife, Yvette (Genevieve Fontanel), who happens to be eight months pregnant. She's getting the third-degree as well, and she, too, claims to have no knowledge of who the murderer, or murderers, might be.

The cops are now learning that the deceased father, Jack Drummond, was one of Great Britain's most widely-respected dieticians, and the police are also making inquiries of all of the neighbors who live on outlying farms, but the neighbors claim to know nothing of the murders, either. (Just like in *lots* of Jean Gabin movies which were made over the years, 1935's *Les Bas-fonds*; 1949's *Au-dela des grilles*; 1970's *La Horse*—neighbors and friends always band together to protect Jean Gabin, whether his characters are guilty or innocent, just because, no matter what he's done or hasn't done, he's always nice and real, just like they are.) The Inspector now asks to see not only all of the Dominici family's guns but, also, all of the neighbors' guns as well, because he wants to check and see if any of the neighbors have any rifles which might take the same kind of bullets which were found near the bodies. Gaston makes a tactical mistake though, now drawing attention away from the neighbors and, accidentally, toward his own family, when he tells the cops, with great solemnity, "Usually,

Top: "J'accuse!" Above: With Paul Crauchet and Michel Bertau.

nobody ever comes to my land: Long ago, my father named it *The Big Fear*. Mostly, people don't come near my property because of the name, which I've posted on a sign. Even my favorite neighbors, [whom] I like very much, sometimes tell me that they're scared to come here." (Seems like he's trying to undo all of the good work which his neighbors have been doing on his, and his family's, behalf!) The neighbors have just been telling the cops that there's no way any of the Dominicis could be the murderer, but Gaston is telling the cops, in a very indirect way, that maybe he and/or members of his family is/are the killer(s)! Why on earth would he want to implicate himself and, even more weirdly, why would he want to implicate his own family? Is it that old 'fatalistic trope' again—that device which always pops up in both the early, and the not-so-early, Gabin pictures? (You know the drill: 'You're damned if you do, and you're damned if you don't.' [Maybe...])

Basically, what's happening, is that the Dominicis all know that it's one of their own who killed the Drummonds, and they're all protecting each other. (In most of his films, Jean Gabin's characters are quiet and cagey, never choosing to reveal too much, but in this film, his Gaston-character seems to have raised a whole family of 'Junior Gabins,' all of who share the famous Gabin characteristic of quiet caginess.)

The Dominicis dine in silence that night, and director Aubert now gifts us with a brief, tension-relaxing moment: Gaston holds a glass of wine up to his baby grandson's face, and tells him, "You're going to like this stuff a lot, one day!"

The Inspector believes Gaston's son, Gustave, to be the primary suspect in the killings, since the bullet casings match the bullets which go with Gustave's rifle, so he shows up the next day, to ask him some more questions. When the Inspector holds the rifle up to Gustave's face, Gustave (it's another wimpy son for strong Gabin, just like Jean Desailly's Francois character, in *Les Grandes familles*) immediately starts crying, and even throws himself down on his knees, telling the Inspector that this rifle hasn't been used for years and that, in fact, it's a family heirloom (this is true) which his father Gaston used during World War II, when he was part of the Resistance. Gustave adds that, whenever he sees the weapon he cries, because seeing it makes him think of all of the heroic things which his father went through during the War. (Note: When trying to get yourself and your family off the hook, always 'play the Resistance card!')

When Gaston arrives home later that day, having completed some errands in town, he sees that the Inspector has instructed his team of investigating cops to tear up the whole house. Gaston remains Gabin-Cool, not getting riled-up, at all—until, that is, he sees that the cops have smashed his beloved bust of Napoleon! (It's very funny that the family's steely ruler, Gaston Dominici, should empathize with his country's famously-steely ex-ruler.) He immediately launches into an amazing Gabin-Outburst, which he volleys right at the Inspector: "You go into people's houses? Why? What the hell are you looking for? You get paid by the month, so you should be happy enough. But instead, you and your men run around like sheep!" Gaston now throws the Inspector and the other cops out of his house, but not before issuing them a harsh warning: "You want to make it like it's my family at fault in the murders, but you can't. Now get the hell out!" Alone at the front door, having just thrown 'the law' out, Gaston, who's suddenly feeling the weight of the world, now mutters, as he tries to catch his breath, "It's starting again...just like in '44!" We're going to be finding out, a few scenes from now, that in 1944, when Gaston was fighting in the Resistance, the German army came very close to the Dominici family farmlands, and tried to attack Gaston and his compatriots, but that Gaston and his friends won the day, bravely killing all of their attackers.

Gaston also has a second wimpy son, besides Gustave: It's fortysomething Clovis (Gerard Darrieu), a fragile Anthony Perkins-clone: As weak as he is meek, Clovis has taken to bed, sick with fright from the recent unpleasantness, and a visiting physician, Dr. Dragon (Jean-Paul Moulinot), is telling him that he has to relax, because *all of this murder stuff* has turned him into a nervous wreck. As soon as Gaston and the Doctor leave, an Italian *paparazzo* (Alberto Farnese), who's been hiding in Clovis' bedroom closet for the whole time, pops out, and starts taking pictures of Clovis who, of course, begins smiling maniacally, truly excited about his fifteen-minutes of fame and, as it turns out, he's not really nervous at all. Clovis might be too addle-brained to answer the cops' questions, but he *is* smart enough to love being in a magazine!

According to one of the film's superimposed title cards which are going to be appearing at regular intervals throughout the film, it's now "August 15th, 1952: 11th Day of the Investigation:" Gustave's wife Yvette is trying to calm her anxious husband, assuring him that he's got nothing to fret about, especially since the town's annual carnival is coming up and that soon, they'll all be able to relax and just have fun. Simultaneously, down at local police headquarters, the Inspector is telling a few of his colleagues that he's been losing sleep lately, trying to figure out whether the Dominicis were responsible for the murders at all, because they're all so cagey and cryptic, that he honestly can't prove if any of them did it. Parallel to this, we're also finding out that Scotland Yard wants in on the investigation as well, since the family that was killed was British, although we won't be seeing any UK cops in the picture.

Against Gaston's wishes, the Inspector now interrogates Gaston's frail and long-suffering wife, Marie (Evi Maltagliati): He shows Marie Dominici the notorious 'Resistance rifle,' and she confirms for him that it's the armament which her husband used, during the War. He also asks her if it's true that, a few hours before the murders took place, Gaston had attended a nearby reunion of his old Resistance compatriots, some of who brought their own Resistance rifles along to the celebration—rifles which are similar to Gaston's—and she confirms that it's true.

"October 17, 1952—74th Day of Investigation:" A large inquest is now being held at the local courthouse. The Inspector has decided that he's not yet done ruling out the neighbors, since many of them (the ones who aren't scared of approaching 'The Big Fear') are all very friendly with the Dominicis, and so local Judges are now questioning the residents of every neighboring farm. Maillet (Jacques Raspail), a local shopkeeper who is also a long-time friend of the Dominici sons, is being questioned as well, since he owns a rifle which is similar to the one which was used in the murderers, and also because Maillet goes hunting regularly, with both Gustave and Clovis. The questioning of Maillet leads nowhere though, and now it's time for the Inspector to begin a new round of *Questioning Gustave*. (That's what the movie would be called if it were made today, since all movie titles, post-1990, have to begin with gerunds, right?!) Gustave now gives the Inspctor some new information about what he, himself, may or may not have seen and heard, on that fateful evening, in question:

> GUSTAVE: When I saw the little girl, her parents were dead. But she was still breathing.
> INSPECTOR: You saw her, but didn't help her? You let her die without bringing her water?
> GUSTAVE: My father called the police immediately… but they didn't show up for four hours.
> INSPECTOR: Had you immediately called for a doctor, I would let you go. But because you didn't call the Doctor you have, therefore, obstructed justice, and I am afraid that I have no choice, but to give you two months in jail.

Gaston is full of Gabinian-rage about his son Gustave's predicament, and admits as much, to his wife: "They're trying to condemn our son. But what about the person who was *actually* the killer? Yvette is about to have a baby, and Gustave will be in prison!"

That night, the whole Dominici family dines together, and Gaston sits, quietly and somberly, at the head of the table, just like Gabin's other, put-upon farmer-character, Auguste Marollieur, from 1970's more 'exploitation-y' *La Horse*. While the family in that other film looked and, in fact, *was*, innocent, here, in this picture, each family member is starting to look increasingly guilty, each one complicit (no doubt) in hiding the identity of the murderer who, very clearly, is one of their own.

A quick dissolve takes us to two months later and to a celebration dinner: Gustave has served his two months in jail and, during that time, the authorities were unable to find anything which would have connected him to the murders—so he's free! A group of neighbors are having dinner with the Dominicis, too, and it's Gaston's way of thanking them all, because the neighbors all helped to pay-off Gustave's legal bills, as well as his bail. The Inspector shows up during dinner and mentions, casually, that he's "just in the neighborhood," and that he thought he'd "stop over, for a drink." Tough-old Gaston, who is as unafraid of cops as Jean Gabin has ever been in any of his other movies, just shoos the pig out of the room.

The film next flashes forward by fifteen months, to what a superimposed title is now telling us, is "November 12, 1953: 465th Day of the Investigation:" It's been almost a year-and-a-half since the Inspector first started investigating the Domincis, and he still hasn't found anything solid upon which to incriminate any of them—plus, for a cop, this guy is really turning into a whiner: "Look, it's been over a year," he begs of Gaston. "Give me some information, if you know something. Anything!" Gaston definitely has the upper-hand over the Inspector, though, and so he even starts berating the public servant, right to his face: "I can only tell you one thing about the murderer, Inspector: Whoever it was, is a whole hell-of-a-lot smarter than you are!"

While most of the family members are stoic like Gaston, and never revealing of their thoughts through their facial expressions, Gaston's wife, Marie, is the sensitive member of the clan: She's taking this whole year-long (so far) investigation hard, and spends most of her time crying, and rightly so. Gaston wipes her tears away and tries to assuage her fears, telling her (and this is just making it worse, but he's trying), "If the cops are so eager to get a Dominici, they can have me." Gaston, like most of Jean Gabin's movie-characters, is resigned to his Shitty Fate: Whether he's the murderer or not, he's already deciding that he'll probably sacrifice himself by admitting to the murders, whether he committed them or not, just so the cops will leave his family alone. Since Gaston is an older man, we and he both understand that his time on earth is limited, and so it won't be such a big sacrifice for him to make.

Next, according to a brand new superimposed-title card, it's "December 11, 1953," and it's time now for what the card is also telling us, is "The New [Second] Arrest of Gustave Dominici:" While the cops had previously held Gustave for two months with no evidence, they've now found some, and it's rather compelling: After some more extensive testing of Gaston's WWII rifle, the cops have finally found Gustave's fingerprints on it! The Inspector brags to Gaston that he's got new evidence against Gustave, and so level-headed Gaston instantly decides to 'play the crazy card:' He tells the Inspector, straight-facedly and mischievously (and remember: the Inspector found the bodies on Dominci land!), "Yeah, well, maybe my son's fingerprints *were* on my rifle—but there was never any English family here! But if it brings you happiness to say there was, you can!" (The bodies have already been taken away by the police.) The Inspector thinks that Gaston is certifiably insane, and that he is just spouting out this *bubbe meinses* to obstruct justice, in order to string the investigation out for so long that it will go away. Yvette, Gustave's wife (their baby has already been born), next seconds what her father-in-law has just said, when she tells the Inspector that she has never seen any English family, either. When Gaston is telling the Inspector that the English family was never on the premises, it's just like that scene in *La Horse*, in which Gabin's farmer, Andre Marollieur, told the investigating cop (with the same kind of completely straight face) that there were never any drug dealers on his property, even though there were. Needless to say, the Inspector looks like his head his about to explode (just like the bald guy at the scientific conference, in David Cronenberg's 1979 horror classic, *Scanners*): "Come off it, Dominici. We *know* your son left your house three times on the murder night, and that it *had* to have been him, who killed the family." Gaston, next, really starts 'piling on the crazy,' defiantly changing his story, yet again: "Okay, well I actually *do* know *everything* about the murders. But I'm not going to tell you. What do you think of that?"

Having had more than enough of this bullshit, the Inspector now brings Gaston and

Gustave, as well as Clovis (for good measure), down to the station. Gaston is not only unafraid when he gets there, but he's actually excited, too, because he notices that the police station uses a lot of the handcrafted wooden chairs which the Dominici family has been making for them, over the years. With a mischievous glint in his eye, Gaston, next, tries to *escape* from the police station. Gabin is never afraid of walking out on his own interrogations in his movies, and even on his own arrests, but the cops quickly manhandle Gaston into a chair, which isn't too hard for them to do, because Gaston is in his seventies. (The spirit is willing to run away, even if the flesh no longer can!)

The Inspector then sits down opposite Gaston and starts questioning him again: "The English *were* camping on your land, no matter what you're telling us. I also know that they went toward your house, to ask for some water: Someone in your family has already confirmed that, and I want you to tell me who that person is." Gaston just Gabin-Shrugs non-committally, and tells the guy that that it can't be true, but the Inspector decides to end the suspense: "In fact, Mr. Dominci, your little eight-year-old grandson [Clovis' little boy] is the one who's confirmed it." Gaston starts laughing, hysterically: "Awww, that little kid? He's crazy!" Gaston's just made fun of his own, tiny grandson! Not only is he continuing to make a mockery out of the investigative process, but he's loving every single minute of it!

Then, the Inspector uses a devious new tactic, and we don't know if what he's saying is true or not, but he's not letting anything as abstract and as ephemeral as 'the truth' get in the way of his trying it out: "Your son Gustave recently told me that you were the murderer. Okay, so are you ready to make a full confession?" At this moment, the film's director, Claude Bernard-Aubert cross-cuts to another room in the precinct, in which Clovis and Gustave are being interrogated and, sure as shit, Gustave is continuing to finger his own father for the murders, and he doesn't even look guilty about doing it: "My father told my brother, Clovis, that he was the killer. He actually bragged about it, to Clovis—'I killed those English people.'" Clovis confirms what his brother has just said, adding that the reason Gustave fell on his knees in front of the rifle and began crying, when the Inspector had first interrogated him, wasn't because the rifle made him think of his father's heroic Resistance days, but because he was overwhelmed by the weapon, since the rifle made him think of the Drummond family murders, which his father had just committed. The Inspector then asks the two brothers, "Is it true that you two guys hate your father so much, that you'd even incriminate him, even if he isn't the murderer?"

So Gaston's own 'beloved' sons have just accused their father of triple murder and, weirdly, stone-faced Gaston doesn't even care. Looking especially drowsy, he just Gabin-Shrugs, and tells the Inspector, smugly, "Well, just let me know if you're going to execute me. In the meantime, I need a nap. You don't happen to have a bed here, do you?"

Now, Gaston changes his story, yet again! Only about three seconds after he told the Inspector that he didn't care that his sons had accused him, he's now ready to turn the tables on his sons, which he now does, in an amazing, stream-of-consciousness Gabin-Outburst—one which, by the way, happens to be one of Jean Gabin's all-time great movie moments:

"My sons are the ones who killed that British family," he exclaims. "I want to spit in their faces! Bring my spawn in front of me, and I will make them tell you they did it! I didn't know my own father, because he died when I was very young. But I know that he made me out of love, and I made my two sons out of love, as well. I would have gone to hell for my own father. But, as for me—I gave life to two pigs!"

The Young Cop, who's been interrogating Gustave and Clovis, now brings them into the room with their father, and then—the intra-family fireworks really begin!

>   CLOVIS: You told us that you were the killer, dad! You said you had a lot to drink, and you also told us that you would kill more people, if you could have.
>   GUSTAVE: I asked my father, 'What did you shoot at?' He said, 'The English!'
>   INSPECTOR (whispers in the Young Cop's ear): Told ya we'd nail that old jerk!
>   GASTON: I never shot anybody! I don't know why my sons are accusing me! *J'en ai marre!* [I've had enough!]

The Inspector ushers the two sons away, and Gaston is now left alone with the Young Cop, whom he really likes (he even calls him a "a nice boy," and he means it), since he thinks the kid is smart; he even gives the 'kid' some backstory about his own early days, while the genuinely intrigued Young Cop is serving him some coffee: "When I was a young man like you, I farmed other people's lands—I have always worked. Finally, I made enough money to buy my own land. My wife saw other men before she married me but ultimately, she loved me, because my land was the biggest!"

Gaston also admits now, for the first time, and to the young Cop (the Dominicis keep backpedaling so much, we don't even know what's true anymore—not that we ever did!), that he (Gaston), himself, really did murder the English family, but that it was just an accident: "I thought the English family was going to attack me, so I shot them!" The Young Cop tells Gaston that, if this is true, "... you should tell the Inspector what you're telling me," but Gaston replies in the negative: "I just can't. That man has been bugging me for too long. I'll never tell him what I'm telling you right now. It's true that I'm the killer, but he'll never know it from me. If you bring me to the Chief-of-Police, maybe I'll make a declaration in writing to him, and to him only—but otherwise, no." (Isn't French justice weird? Just like in Gabin's 1956 *Crime and Punishment* adaptation, *Crime et chatiment*, you can't get charged with a crime in France, unless you very specifically sign a written confession and yet, at the same time, you can serve several days in jail, just on the whim of a cop who might only have a reasonable suspicion.)

The Young Cop tries to get Gaston to talk about the murder at greater length: "What kind of a crime was it?" Gaston, who's now having more fun than ever with his ever-changing stories, goofily replies, with a rare Gabin-Smile, "The crime I committed… well, I guess I can say it… it was all about *ass!* I ran into the English woman, the mother, under my olive trees. She was with her young daughter; and this mother—well, she was getting dressed. I was behind the wall, watching her change clothes. I got closer. She didn't move. I touched her crotch! And then I fucked her! And guess what—she liked it! We made noise! The husband woke up, tried to take the gun from me, and it went off. Of course, I had to shoot the whole family, because they were all screaming! That's the truth, but I'm not going to sign any confession about it, because I'm innocent, since it was an accident." The Young Cop, thinking that Gaston is probably a total alky, based upon the way in which his stories just keep getting crazier and crazier, throws up his hands: "Look, Mr. Dominci: Just sign a confession, and maybe you'll be able to keep your dog and your wine, okay?"

The Young Cop next places a confession form in front of Gaston, and Gaston decides to sign it only moments after saying he wouldn't; and just as he starts scratching out his confession, he crosses out his words, retracting everything which he's just said about 'his accidental murder-spree:' "I'm the oldest person in my family. I have to sacrifice myself so that my family can keep the farm. Even though I might sign this, I didn't shoot anybody at all, I was just kidding, when I said I did!" The Cop now freaks-out, losing the tiny semblance of goodwill which he has been demonstrating toward the avuncular-looking Gaston, over the last several minutes: "Well, wait a minute, Mr. Dominici. If you're innocent, you'd better not sign anything!" Meanwhile, down the hall, in the second interrogation room, Gustave is now admitting to the Inspector that he, himself, was the killer, and not his father.

A group of cops brings Gaston home, and follows him into the shed in which the family keeps its guns. He excitedly shows them the famous rifle which he, as he's now saying, used personally, when he killed the whole Drummond family, all by himself. He even points to the ground, and grins, "Look! This is the spot where I fucked the lady, before I killed them all!" (You've got to love a movie, where Gabin drops 'the F-bomb!') Then, Gaston gives-chase for the second time in the picture: The cops (uproariously) start running after slow-moving old Gaston, who tries to jump into a ravine, but they're able to grab him, quite easily. "I fought you!" he proudly proclaims to the large group of cops who have chased him for the entire one-foot which he's just run! The cops throw him into their cruiser for a trip down to jail and, like an excited little kid, he starts manically shouting at them, "Drive fast! I like to go fast!" Meanwhile, down at P.D., the Inspector is getting a roomful of cops up-to-speed on recent developments in the case: "I'm not convinced that Gaston Dominici was the shooter: He made up the fact that he did it, and he also made up the fact that he had raped the wife, since the autopsy on Mrs. Drummond has proven that there was no sexual intercourse. [Note from the Author: I hope *my* autopsy never proves that!] Plus, Gustave's fingerprints are on the gun, not his father's." As the scene ends, the director now superimposes a title which reads, "End of Investigation: Monday, November 16, 1953," and then, immediately after, we get a second title card: "Wednesday, November 17, 1954: The Trial Begins."

We're now in the courthouse, with red-robed judges presiding and, surprisingly, it's Jean

No longer able to escape from his interrogations.

Gabin's patriarch, Gaston, who's on trial for the triple murder of the Drummond family, and not his son, Gustave: As it turns out, while Gustave's prints *were* on the rifle, so were Gaston's. (Well, it was Gaston's gun! That doesn't prove anything!) As in the 1946 film *Martin Roumagnac*, in which Gabin's character was similarly on trial for murder, here too, in this movie, Gabin's character, Gaston, is completely unfazed by the fact that he's on trial, and he remains as Gabin-Calm as ever. In a French courtroom, as we've already seen in *Martin Roumagnac*, and in other French films which feature courtroom trial sequences, anyone in the courtroom can chime in whenever one wants to (witnesses, the audience, or *whoever*), without any fear of repercussion. Judge Perier (Michel Bertay), who's in charge, asks Gaston, "How do you respond to the accusations of your sons that you are the killer?" Gaston quietly responds, "I am not the murderer of the Drummond family. When the shots were fired, I was in bed. What I really believe, is that poachers were the murderers. My son Gustave likes to go poaching, on occasion, with my grandson Zeze, and I really think that the two of them together may have been the murderers." Zeze, Clovis' twentysomething son, is present too, and he's played by Gerard Depardieu, who is now, following the previous year's *Le Tueur*, appearing in his second of three Jean Gabin movies.

The Judge isn't going to put up with this malarkey, though, just because everybody else has to. "Mr. Dominici, many times, you have told the police that you were the murderer of the whole family—including, [of] the little girl." Gaston replies, whimsically, that it would have been impossible for him to kill the little girl, because he *cared* about her! The Judge, who's sick of this lying, mutters, "You have a strange illness, Mr. Dominici," and Gaston just replies, "Illness? Nahhh... I feel fine!"

The Judge next questions Zeze: "Were you with your Uncle Gustave on the night of the murder?" Zeze, with that trademark Depardieu Smile, just shrugs, and oafishly giggles, "I don't know," and his reaction is so over-the-top, it makes everybody in the courtroom laugh. The Judge tells Zeze, sternly, that he's "using up the patience of the court," and he makes sure the records reflect that he doesn't believe Zeze was in on the killings, at all. The Judge tells Gaston, *re:* dopey-looking Zeze, "With a face like that, if he's guilty—I just don't believe in faces, anymore."

When the Judge calls Gustave to the stand, Gustave announces, very plaintively, that he's not the killer and that his father isn't the killer, either, and the Judge now snaps at Gustave that he (Gustave) is "the most vile witness I have ever met!" Anyway, this scene is confirming for us what the Domincis have been doing all along which I've already mentioned at the head of this chapter: Not only do the Dominici family members *not* hate each other, but it's also imminently clear that they've all been lying about their roles in the crime, to protect each other—just like Kennedys!—because they all love each other, and because the whole family is made up of anti-authoritarian rebels who love making a mockery out of French justice. Gaston and his sons, as we're about to find out, actually love each other very much, and are not as wimpy as they've been pretending to be, and the reason they've been acting wimpy in the first place is, as we're now figuring out, just a ruse, meant to deflect the cops' attentions away from them.

After a brief recess, the Judge addresses Gaston: "Mr. Dominici, you're very severe with your family. But the psychiatrist whom we've had examining you says that you're normal." In fact, Gaston is *so* normal, and so 'of-the-earth' that, as it's now being revealed, he even delivered three of his own children by himself: "We were far from a hospital. Could I let them die?" Then, out of the blue, Gaston blurts out that it's probably Clovis who convinced Gustave to help him in blaming his father for the murders since, in his opinion, "... my son Clovis doesn't know anything about family honor." Then, Gaston stands up and waves hello to Clovis, with a big, maniacal grin. (It's the 'classy Gabin-Version' of giving his son the finger!)

Finally, several days later, after the Judge has finished listening to all of the double-talking family testimony, during what a printed title is now telling us, is "The Ninth Hearing: November 28th, 1954," *hizzoner* now rules that it was Gaston alone who was guilty of the pre-mediated murder. Gaston doesn't deny having killed the parents, but he states flatly that he would never kill a little girl. ("It is unacceptable to me that you think I have may have committed such a horrible act.") The Judge sentences Gaston to death, by guillotine and, accepting of his Fate, in the usual Gabin Manner, he waves goodbye to his family, and exits the still-buzzing courtroom with his head down. According to a superimposed title, Gaston Dominici was "condemned without any direct proof at all."

The film-proper is now over, and we still have no idea which Dominici—or Dominicis, *plural*—killed the Drummonds, which makes *L'Affaire Dominici* one of those great movies that are open-ended in a good way, wherein you can discuss what you *think* happened, on the way home from the movie theater, weighing all of the evidence which the film both presented and didn't present, in your own mind. But before the final credits roll, director Bernard-Aubert tacks on a kind of oddball coda: The Dominci Family's real-life lawyer in the case, Emile Pollak, now makes a 'talking-head' appearance, as himself. Pollak looks directly into the camera, *a la* Rod Serling, and tells us, the audience, "It is the opinion of the producers and directors of the film which you have just seen, that Gaston Dominici was innocent. In 1957, the President of the Republic, Rene Coty, commuted Dominici's death penalty to hard labor for life. Dominici remained in prison for only six years before Charles de Gaulle, who had become the new President, pardoned him in 1960, and he was released in July of 1963. The pardon was for "humanitarian reasons"—because of Dominici's old age."

Pollak next goes on to describe another similar case, which happened to have been making its way through the French court system in 1972, during the film's production, then adding, "The sentencing of the innocent without proper evidence continues to be a major problem in France, today. Let what you have just witnessed in this film be a lesson to all people."

L'Affaire Dominici is one of the absolute best movies of the 1970s, period. Is the film a dig at the French judicial system? (Yes.) The film asks the question: "Does a family have a right to protect its members, even if one of its members has committed a crime, and even when, by doing so, the family is impeding justice?" (In other words: How far would *you* go, to protect your own family?)

While, to this day, nobody knows who really murdered Mommy, Daddy, and Baby Drummond, we might be able to surmise, just based on seeing how the filmmakers have lain the cards out for us, that it probably *was* Gaston, working in collusion with Gustave, but that's just this author's guess. And because the real-life Dominici family is still prospering in Argenteuil, to this day, and because also, to this day, no Dominici has ever revealed the secret of who among them was the actual killer or killers, *in a way*, the story will always continue—at least, for as long as there are Dominicis.

While Claude Bernard-Aubert's film has never existed in an English-subtitled or dubbed version, at least at the time of this book's printing, there *is* a way, at least for now, that non-French-speaking people can experience the Dominici saga for themselves: In 1955, as part of his weekly television series, "Around the World with Orson Welles" (which was produced in England for the BBC), the famous American filmmaker/actor presented a one-hour documentary-expose of the Dominicis which was, like the Gabin film, entitled "*The Dominici Affair.*" The Welles version features many of the story's real-life participants and, at present, it's even available on DVD in the U.S.

Based upon watching *L'Affaire Dominici*, a casual non-French viewer might guess that the film's brilliant, visionary director, Claude Bernard-Aubert might be 'the Scorsese or Coppola of France,' but you'd be surprised to know that Bernard-Aubert is actually one of France's legendary exploitation movie kings. Born in 1930, Bernard-Aubert very famously directed a fun, fast-paced, 1961 miscegenation-exploitationer called *Les Laches vivent d'espoir* (*The Cowardly Live on Hope*), which was dubbed into English, and released into American drive-in theatres in 1965, under the lurid title, *My Baby is Black!* (complete with that emphatic exclamation point, placed goofily at the end of the title). In the late 1970s, and up through 1990, which was the year of his most recent credit, Bernard-Aubert even directed several hard-core porn features, under the pseudonym of 'Burt Tranbaree,' many of which starred France's two major porn queens, Brigitte Lahaie and Karen Gambier. (Well…'work is work!') Even Bernard-Aubert's B-movies and *porn-chic* are excruciatingly well-made, though, and it's too bad that he never made more A-level fare like *L'Affaire Dominici*. The picture's producer, Eric Rochat also found his way into porn, producing (under the pseudonym of 'Ron Williams') a number of softcore features and television series'. (And maybe, for my next book, I'll write about "Why All of the Behind-the-Scenes People on *L'Affaire Dominici* Wound-Up in Porn…")

What a Critic Said at the Time: "Film is aided by the yeoman work of Jean Gabin, as the aging, irascible head of an inbred family of peasant stock. Gabin, more subdued than usual, gives a certain dignity and depth to the old patriarch [he plays]. Director Claude Bernard-Aubert has directed with a quiet, unforced drive which removes sensationalism. Actors are good down the line. Good production dress." (*Variety*, 3-28-73 issue. Critic: "Mosk. [George Moskowitz.]" Reviewed in Paris.)

FILM 93

Deux hommes dans la ville

France/Italy, 1973

(Literal English Translation: "TWO MEN IN TOWN") Directed and Written by Joseph Giovanni. Produced by Alain Delon. Executive Producer, Pierre Caro. Director of Photography (color), Jean-Jacques Tarbes. Editor, Francoise Javet. Music by Philippe Sarde. Production Designers, Jean-Jacques Caziot and Gianfranco Pucci. (GENRE: DRAMA) A Production of Adel Productions (France) and Medusa Produzione (Italy). Running Time, 1 hour 40 minutes. Released in France by Valoria Films, on October 25, 1973. Released in the United States in August, 1976 by Joseph Green Pictures, dubbed into English, as "TWO AGAINST THE LAW."

"My name is Cazeneuve. I deal with the torn fabric of men's lives."
— *Liberal social-worker Gabin's opening voice-over salvo, in "Deux hommes dans la ville"*

I saw this film first, when I began writing this book back in 2002, on a VHS tape which was supplied to me by an American eBay seller—it was an English-dubbed version of the movie, which had been duplicated from a Japanese laserdisc. Fortunately, if you're an English-speaker, you don't need to take such drastic measures to see *Deux hommes dans la ville* anymore, because in 2005, Kino Home Entertainment issued a great, English-subtitled version for the North American market. Dubbed or subtitled, director Jose Giovanni's *Deux hommes dans la ville* (*Two Men In Town*) is one of the best and grittiest 'issue films' of the 1970s, and it's definitely right up there with the other great issue-films (films which exist in order to call our attention to, and to rectify, society's wrongs) of the '70s and '80s—pictures like Martin Ritt's *Norma Rae*, or Mike Nichols' *Silkwood*. Jose Giovanni, who directed *Deux hommes*, had previously written the screenplay for another Gabin film, *Le Clan des Siciliens*, which he had adapted from Auguste Le Breton's novel of the same name.

This time around, Gabin is a gentle, seventy-year-old prison social worker, and the movie opens with his voice-over: "My name is Germain Cazeneuve. I deal with the torn fabric of men's lives." Cazeneuve has fostered a father-son relationship with Alain Delon's gentle Gino Strabliggi (this picture represents the third and final Gabin-Delon team-up, following *Melodie en sous-sol* and *Le Clan des Siciliens*), whom Cazeneuve believes to have fully reformed, after having a served twelve year-stint for a bank robbery. Cazeneuve makes an appearance at Gino's parole hearing, telling the board that, in his own considered opinion, Gino is now fully reformed, and is ready to become a productive member of society. The parole board members make fun of excessively-liberal old Cazeneuve, a guy who always gets on the prison system's case with a lot of The Trademark Gabin Bluster, because he feels that they don't use enough prevention and care with prisoners. Cazeneuve inveighs perpetually against the fact that the French penal system is too busy fighting crimes when instead, in his opinion, it should be more concerned with fighting the socio-economic problems which lead to the crimes. "If we let you social workers interpret the penal code," the tough-as-nails parole board-chief, who's played by Armand Mestral, tells Cazeneuve condescendingly, "you'd set it to music!"

Gino is paroled, and Cazeneuve accepts full responsibility for him, even lining the younger man up, immediately, with a nice job in a printing shop. Very quickly, everything starts going swimmingly for the younger man, with the exception of one slight setback: Gino's wife, Sophie (Illaria Occhini), a florist, is suddenly killed in a car accident only days after her husband's release from the pokey, and only hours after Gino and Sophie have been out, visiting kindly old Cazeneuve in the country (and right after the couple has run, hand-in-hand [in slow motion!] through a field of flowers). Gino is so pissed-off, that he locks himself up in his apartment for what we assume must be weeks, and begins a non-stop drinking-and-'loud-music-listening-to' binge, which is interrupted only when the neighbors come up to tell him to turn down the tunes: He even tries to beat up the most obnoxious neighbor, Mr. Vautier, who's played by Robert Castel.

But Gino won't be mourning for long, though: Soon—in fact, within a few, brief scenes—he's got a hot, new Swedish girlfriend, Lucie, who's played by the American actress Mimsy Farmer (the blonde, Joey Heatherton-coiffed libertine who's mostly known, in the U.S., for having appeared in director Barbet Schroeder's great, psychedelic 1971 head-trip movie, *More*, as well for starring in countless American B-movies and Italian-made detective thrillers), and the two new lovers dream of getting married, and starting a family of their own.

But fate, then, rears its ugly head and, in this picture, 'the Ugly Head' arrives in the person of the mega-crooked police Inspector, Goitreau (Michel Bouquet), a weaselly, vendetta-driven updating of *Les Miserables'* equally-loathsome Inspector Javert-character. Goitreau is the cop who put Gino away twelve years ago, and now, just when Gino is doing well (*a la Les Miz's* Jean Valjean), he pops back onto the scene, *Jason Voorhees-style*, to make Gino's life a living hell: Goitreau's whole purpose in life seems to be 'trying to put Gino away again,' in spite of the fact that Gino has committed no new crime, or crimes, since his release from prison. To this end, Goitreau tries to find incriminating evidence against Gino, and he becomes increasingly frustrated, when he learns that there isn't any. Gino's old gang includes Marcel (he's played by Victor Lanoux, who played Gabin's son, Gustave, in *L'Affaire Dominici*), as well a nameless gangster who's played by a young Gerard Depardieu who, with this film, and after *Le Tueur* and *L'Affaire Dominici*, is now appearing in the third of his three

Top and Above: Jean Gabin and Alain Delon, their third of three films.

Jean Gabin films). Marcel tries to re-enlist Gino, but Gino turns him down flat, because he's genuinely turned over a new leaf.

While Gino's at work, creepy Goitreau appears at Lucie's apartment, and harasses her into telling him about anything incriminating that her husband may have been doing recently, so that he can have something definite upon which to arrest him. Since Gino has committed no crime, Goitreau becomes so frustrated, that he's about to start beating the stuffing out of Lucie and, unluckily for him, Gino walks in right before he begins. Enraged beyond belief, Gino instinctively comes to his new lady's defense, and without giving it a thought, he strangles the unlawful lawman to death. Although we, the film's audience, have just observed firsthand that Gino's new crime was committed only in self-defense, Gino is guilty in the eyes of the law of having murdered a cop and, no matter what his motivation was, within a few scenes, he's now in the courtroom again, and the Judge (Maurice Barrier) is sentencing him to death, letting the young man know, in no uncertain terms, that he has an appointment with Madame Guillotine. In France, the Death Penalty was overturned in 1977, four years after this movie was made. (Too bad Gino didn't wait four more years to kill that shitty Inspector!)

Cazeneuve feels horribly about Gino's plight—after all, Gino has become more of a son to Cazeneuve, than Cazeneuve's real son, Frederick, has been. (Frederick, who's played by Bernard Giraudeau, is a cloying Mike Stivic-esque liberal, a guy who is, in fact, such a bleeding-heart, that his own liberal dad, Cazeneuve, always looks embarrassed to be around him!) But Cazeneuve is resigned (as per usual, for Jean Gabin) to Cruel Fate, and he tells his wife, Genevieve (Christine Fabrega) that there is nothing he can do, to save Gino: "Whatever happens, happens," Cazeneuve Gabin-Shrugs, adding that it's always impossible to beat the system. Gino is guillotined, and Cazeneuve remains stoic during the execution, although we know that he's holding-in his true, paternal feelings for his unfortunate young friend. At the end of this picture, as in so many of the others which he made over four decades, Jean Gabin walks away alone.

Deux hommes dans la ville is a great Gabin movie which is really worth seeing, because it's interesting to see Our Hero playing a soft-spoken liberal social worker who abhors violence of any kind, and who has just as many ideas about how to change the penal system as Gabin's 'Dr. Laurent'-character had about "how to make babies 'get born' in a more civilized manner," in *Le Cas du docteur Laurent*. While crimes are mentioned in the film, *Deux hommes* is not a crime picture at all, but is instead a warm drama about the healing power of family and one which is beautifully rendered, to boot.

The film's director, Jose Giovanni, who was interviewed for a Gabin documentary which appeared on French television in 2001, told his interviewer that "… Gabin was very aware of his silent power. I used to joke with him that he had such an imposing screen presence, I could even film him from the back, and he would still come across as being powerful and intimidating. Well, Jean just turned to me and said, 'I'll even let you film me from the front, if you pay me enough!'"

What a Critic Said at the Time: "[A] rather demonstrative film. Director-writer [Jose] Giovanni has kept it from becoming a didactic tract. Film is well done, and eschews action, for psychological suspense and social probing." (*Variety*, 11-21-73 issue. Critic: "Mosk. [George Moskowitz.]" Reviewed in Paris.)

FILM 94

VERDICT

France/Italy, 1974

(Literal English Translation: "VERDICT") Directed by Andre Cayatte. Produced by Carlo Ponti. Written by Paul Andreota, Andre Cayatte, Henri Coupon, and Pierre Dumayet. Director of Photography (color), Jean Badal. Production Designer, Robert Clavel. Editor, Paul Cayatte. Music by Louiguy. (GENRE: DRAMA) A Production of PECF and Les Films Concordia (France)/Compagnia Cinematografica Champion (Italy). Running Time, 1 hour 35 minutes. Released in France on September 11, 1974, by Warner Bros. and Columbia Pictures. Released in the United States, dubbed into English, by Avco-Embassy Pictures, as "A JURY OF ONE," in December, 1975.

"Keep her!"
—Jean Gabin responds to his wife's kidnappers in a way they didn't expect, in "Verdict"

In 1974, 70-year-old Gabin rang in his seventh decade on earth, appearing alongside Sophia Loren in his 94th feature film, (Loren's producer-husband) Carlo Ponti's French-Italian co-production of director André Cayatte's *Verdict*, a film which was released briefly in the U.S. by Avco-Embassy Pictures, at the tail-end of 1975, under the lurid, *Death Wish-y* sounding title, *A Jury of One*. (Director Cayatte had been one of the co-scenarists of Gabin's 1939/41 tugboat-classic, *Remorques*, and most of the films which Cayatte had directed, dealt with 'the moral issues of law.') While Gabin's character was liberal and anti-death penalty in his previous picture *Deux hommes dans la ville*, this time out, he's crossed over to the other side of the fence: In this picture, he plays the ultra-conservative Judge Leguen, and whenever we see him in his courtroom, he's very cool-looking indeed, in his red, judicial robes. Leguen's lobbying to get a Norman Bates-styled mama's boy, Andre Leoni (Michel Albertini), sentenced to death, for having murdered Annie Chartier (Muriel Catala), a nubile young girl who impugned his masculinity, simply because he was too shy to make a move on her when she was lolling around nude in his apartment (which is a scene that director Cayatte has had the common courtesy to show us)!

On the eve of the trial, Leguen is visited by the young man's hardened mom, Teresa Leone (Loren), the wife of a dead mobster whom, years ago, Leguen had similarly put away for murder. Teresa informs Leguen, coldly, that she has just kidnapped Leguen's diabetic wife, Nicole (Gisele Casadesus, of France's legendary Casadesus stage-and-screen acting family [they're the French Barrymores]), and that she'll return Mrs. Leguen to him, in exchange for Judge Leguen's offering-up of a not-guilty verdict for her son. This is the second movie in which thugs will kidnap Gabin's wife in order to get some leverage, the first one, of course, being *Soleil des voyous*, in 1967.

Leguen, his (Gabinian) expressionless mask-of-a-face belying how much he truly cares about his wife, and making him impossible for his foes to read, now throws Teresa for a loop, by telling her, re: his wife, "Keep her!" (This is exactly how Glenn Ford dealt with the kidnapping of his young son, in Richard Fleischer's outstanding 1956 *noir* thriller, *Ransom: He told the kidnappers, "Keep him!"*)

Eventually, Leguen caves to Teresa's demand, and in order to get his wife back, he upturns the boy's conviction on the murder charge. As agreed, Teresa sets out for the apartment in which she's sequestered Mrs. Leguen, but there's been one dramatic setback, and one which she never counted on: When Teresa enters the flat where she's been keeping Leguen's wife, she discovers that the old lady is dead! In an amazing act of martyrdom, not wanting to give Teresa the satisfaction of winning over her husband, Mrs. Leguen had apparently stopped injecting herself with insulin, her death representing the ultimate screw you to the shitty old criminals whose nefarious efforts Judge Leguen has been powerless to stop. Mrs. Leguen has made a (crazy, but in a way, true) statement with her death, which seems to be something along the lines of: If the legal system allows hardcore, cold-blooded killers loose on the streets, then none of us should be allowed to live. (What's the point?) The Judge misses his wife like crazy, but he's also satisfied, in his very quiet and Gabinian way, because she's given her life for him. He walks away alone, and Teresa Leone, unable to live with the events she has set in motion, drives her car into a wall.

Jean Gabin told everybody he knew that, after this film, he'd be retiring, but Sophia Loren didn't believe it, especially because the actor had been announcing his retirement, off-and-on, since 1959! Author Warren G. Harris, in his 1998 book, *Sophia Loren: A Biography*, has called Gabin, "… arguably, the greatest French cinema star ever" and, in the same book, the author quotes from an interview which Loren gave to a French newspaper, on the Paris set of *The Verdict:*

Sophia Loren: "Jean has got such energy, that I don't believe [he's going to retire]. He adores being an actor. He gets very excited and very nervous, and everything [else] that you can get when you adore your profession. If this was going to be his last film, he would not care—but he cares! He goes to see rushes. He looks at himself and says, 'I look good' or 'I look bad.' That man is a rock. He is a magnificent actor, one of the most expressive and charismatic in the [whole] history of cinema."

When *Verdict* was released in the United States as *A Jury of One*, by Avco-Embassy Pictures, the American advertising campaign was a bit different than the French one: The American movie poster depicted a giant Loren and a tiny Gabin while, in the French poster, both of the actors' legendary countenances loomed equally-large. To hardcore Jean Gabin fans though, the film will always be known under its original title, *Verdict* and, eight years later, when the iconoclastic American director Sidney Lumet would make his own legal-system-damning film, not only would he utilize the same title for his own film (*The Verdict*), but he'd also borrow for Paul Newman, the American film's star, Jean Gabin's hobby from Andre Cayatte's film: In both the Gabin *Verdict* and the Newman *Verdict*, the two great actors are seen to be playing pinball, while they're deep in thought. *Verdict* has not yet been issued on DVD in the U.S. (at least, not at the time of this book's printing), although New Star Home Video's out-of-print VHS version (which is Avco-Embassy's dubbed-into-English version) pops up on eBay from time-to-time, and is definitely worth checking out.

What a Critic Said at the Time: "Gabin is his usual leonine, shuffling self, as the gruff straight judge whose growing feelings for Loren make him a compassionate jurist. There is name value in Sophia Loren and Jean Gabin." (*Variety*, 9-18-74 issue. Critic, "Mosk. [George Moskowitz.]" Reviewed in Paris.)

1954 — 1976 | 455

FILM 95

L'Annee sainte

France/Italy, 1976

(*Literal English Translation, "THE SAINTED YEAR"*) Directed by Jean Girault. Produced by Gerard Beytout and Akaub Darbon. Written by Louis-Emile Galey and Jacques Vilfrid. Director of Photography (color), Guy Suzuki. Music by Claude Bolling. Editors, Michel and Marie-Christine Lewin. Production Designer, Sydney Bettex. Script Girl, Florence Moncorge-Gabin. (GENRE: COMEDY) A Production of Societe Nouvelle de Cinematographie (SNC) France, Tritone Cinematografica (Italy), and Imperia Films (Italy). Running Time, 1 hour 25 minutes. Released in France on April 23, 1976, by Societe Nouvelle de Cinematographie (SNC). Never Released Theatrically in the United States.

> "Oh, shit! I've already given!"
> — *Gabin's final line of dialogue in his final movie, which he utters when somebody asks him for a donation, in "L'Annee sainte"*

Gabin wasn't exactly right when he bragged that he'd be retiring after his previous and 94th film *Verdict*, because he still had one more movie left in him: On July 7, 1975, the *Hollywood Reporter* mentioned that Gabin would soon start shooting a thriller called *Ange noel* (*Black Angel*) for a thirty-year-old director called Michael Berny, who had just scored a big hit in France with a comedy called *Les Grands sentiments font les bons gueuletons* (*Big Sentiments Make Big Mouths*); but instead, Gabin would finish out his illustrious career with his ninety-fifth and final feature film, Jean Girault's *L'Annee sainte* (a/k/a, *The Holy Year Caper*, *The Holy Year*, and *Pilgrimage to Rome*), a fun caper-comedy that plays, in its tone and in its visual style, like one of the better Neil-Simon comedies which happened to be filling up those boxy, new American multiplexes back in the late seventies. (Remember those early '70s, multiplexes—those tiny little shoebox-rooms with the blue walls, the red chairs, and the shitty acoustics, where you could hear the movie you were watching, *plus* the movie that was playing in the adjoining room?) Gabin's Max Lambert is a 72-year-old convict who, when we first meet him, is serving his tenth year in prison, for what he claims was a "botched Lebanese bank job." ("How I was to know the vault had a leaky roof?" Max Gabin-Shrugs, to a friend.) Max and his younger cell-mate, Pierre (Jean Claude-Brialy), have already planned a prison break: It's been engineered by their boss, Paris's big crime-czar, Marcel (Maurice Teynac), who's promised to arrange their release in exchange for the two of them having to commit a crime for him: He wants Max and Pierre to fly to Rome, where they will steal millions of francs worth of gold—treasure which has been buried in the garden of an old cathedral, for decades. (The film is set during the Catholic 'Holy Year ceremonies,' which take place only once every twenty-five years.)

Max and Pierre escape from the hooscow, by emptying envelopes-full of bedbugs onto their cots—or, as Max will call the bedbugs in the North American DVD edition's scientifically-correct English subtitles, '*heteropteras.*' They get moved to cots in the prison infirmary, in which the windows are refreshingly barless, and as soon as they get there, the first thing they do, is to climb out of the window, where they meet their getaway car, which Marcel has already arranged for them and in which, in short order, they receive their disguises: For the trip to Rome, and to call attention away from themselves as being escaped cons, they're going to be dressed as priests: Max assumes the identity of 'Monsignor Lambrecht,' while Pierre becomes 'Vicar Roylant!' The escape-car driver issues them suitcases which have guns sewn into hidden compartments, as well as fake passports and two first-class Air Italia tickets to Rome. The two cons fool airport security quite easily when they head through the X-Ray machines, which only pick-up their canes. (Ahh, the bucolic/salad days, before 9-11!)

The first passengers to board the flight are an old, British Duke (Tommy Dugan), and his wife the Duchess, who's played by Danielle Darrieux (reunited here with Gabin for the first time in twenty years, since they played together in *Desordre et la nuit*). The Duchess immediately recognizes Max, with whom she had an affair many years before, and she excitedly goes along with his whole preacher ruse (the idle rich love their fun and games), when he winkingly tells her, "I don't think I've ever met you before!"

Then, a problem arises, and it's one which nobody could anticipate—except, of course, for screenwriters Louis-Emile Galley and Jacques Wilfrid: The plane is suddenly hijacked by a trio of young, hot-blooded, Spanish terrorists—two men and a woman, and it is this woman-terrorist, the sadistic Carla (Nicolette Macchiavelli), who insists that the pilots must now divert the plane to Tangiers. (Even though they are not identified as such in the film, the Spanish terrorists in *L'Annee sainte* must be a 'cell' of E.T.A., the organization which then [as now] was fighting for the independence of the more than two million Basques who continue to live today in the Pyrenees mountains south of France and north of Spain; the E.T.A., which has always cited the Basques' indigenous culture, language, and even DNA as part of a reason for their independence were, of course, most recently responsible for the Madrid subway bombings, of March 11, 2004.) The terrorists radio the control tower, where they instruct the air-traffic controllers that, as soon as the plane arrives in Tangiers, they will need to receive $1 million U.S. in cash, and to prove they're not to be trifled-with, Carla threatens to blow up the plane, if her demand is not met.

Since the remaining passengers (appropriately) begin freaking out, Max and Pierre, who

1954 — 1976 | 457

everyone on board believes to be authentic clergymen, start hilariously taking everybody's confessions! One passenger, a Tour de France bicyclist who's played by Andre Lawrence, believing that he'll very soon be meeting his Maker, even confesses to Max and Pierre that he's been cheating all of these years, by doping before his races!

Pierre tries to figure out how he and Max can capture the terrorists, and he now whispers to Max, conspiratorially, that they should go and grab their guns from their carry-on luggage, but Max doesn't seem all that interested: In spite of the imminent threat, he's having way too much fun, comically pretending to be a real monsignor, and calming everyone on the plane.

The terrorists have been civil enough to set all of the women and children free, except for the Duchess, as well as one incredibly butch-looking Women's Libber (Monique Tarbes), who earns Max's disdain by telling him she believes that women should be "treated equally to men." (Gabin, who is the last remaining vestige of the good old days, when men were men and women were women, just rolls his eyes!) The terrorists also offer the two 'clergymen' their freedom but, for obvious reasons, Max and Pierre don't want it (they've got that church job to pull in Rome), so they're going to have to remain on board.

Privately, Max lets down his guard in front of the Duchess. She tells him she remembers that decades ago, when they dated, he comported himself in the manner of a tough guy, and she asks him why he won't just 86 the priest-act right now, and start kicking some terrorist ass. She tries to goad Max into action by telling him, "I am a woman who appreciates your pre-War quality."

The jet lands in Tangiers (it's fun to see Jean Gabin back near Algiers again, forty years post-*Pepe Le Moko*), and the terrorists send Max into the office of the French Consulate, to act as their white-haired go-between. The head Consul, Giordano, who's played by Umberto Raho, hands Max the $1 million, and is relieved to be handing the money over to Max, whom he, just like everybody else, believes to be a real Monsignor.

Now that the terrorists have gotten their mitts on The Cool Million, they steal a car, hightailing it away from the plane with Max and Pierre in tow in the back seat for insurance, and of course, it's not long before *the local 5-0* are in hot pursuit. 'Father Gabin' instructs Carla, who's behind the wheel, to "Lose the cops in the alleys," and Carla's incredibly impressed response to his suggestion, is: "For a priest, you sure know a lot about weird parts of the city!"

Once Max, Pierre, and the terrorists are hidden away in an alley, and safe from the cops, Max dispenses with his holy-roller *shtick*, holding his own gun on the terrorists, and grabbing the million for himself and Pierre: "It's for my poor," he grins, with another Gabin-Shrug, and he then waves the terrorists away, screaming out, "The port's behind you. Now, get lost!" The Cops arrive at the scene, and Max lyingly tells them that the Spanish terrorists have fled with the money—money which, of course, as we've already just seen, is in Max's hands.

Now unexpectedly a million dollars richer, Max and Pierre re-board the plane, which will now continue-on to Rome as originally scheduled; after all, the two cons still need to rob the garden of the ancient church, for their boss, Marcel. When the plane arrives in Rome, a French inspector, Barbieri (Henri Virlojeux), and an Italian inspector, Mazzola (Gianpero

Albertini), both of whom are familiar with Max and Pierre's true identities, are lying in wait. Barbieri has instructed the pilots to keep Max and Pierre on board, because they're 'dangerous criminals,' and Barbieri now gets on the plane, to try and start negotiating with Max, but Max is now so revved-up, from having just spent the day with terrorists, that he humorously tells the Inspector, "If you trick me, I'll kill all of the passengers!"—which is comical because, even though Max is a notorious bank robber, he looks hopelessly benign.

Inspector Barbieri insists that Max should now hand over the $1 million and, after a pregnant pause, Max does it without a struggle, telling Barbieri, "In the old days, I would have kept it." (Barbieri is lenient with Max and Pierre because, although they're escaped criminals, they've also managed to recover the money which the terrorists had stolen, and they've also saved the passengers, the crew, and the plane.) Max is also thankful to Barbieri for, as he's now telling him, "… getting Interpol off my ass."

The picture ends with Max and Pierre's arrival in Rome: They cab-it-over to the old, ruined church which they're supposed to be robbing, and are surprised to find a brand new ultra-modern church, in its place. The resident Priest, who's played by Yves Wecker, informs Max and Pierre that several months ago, a huge cache of gold was indeed discovered, buried in the garden, and that it was used to build the new church on the old church's land. This is the surprising way in which Max and Pierre will learn that there isn't going to be any gold for them to steal on Marcel's behalf, but Max doesn't get upset: Remember, in his seventy-two years on earth, Jean Gabin has seen absolutely everything, and absolutely nothing surprises him anymore. He just Gabin-Shrugs expressionlessly, and he and Pierre leave, knowing that there's nothing they can do about it.

As Max and Pierre exit the sparkling new cathedral, a homeless man asks Max for a handout and, in one casually-offered line—a line which, by the way, seems to sum up his whole career—*Le Grand Gabin* just lifts his shoulders up, into the final big-screen Gabin-Shrug of his illustrious career, and utters his final line, of his final movie, a line which, in four brief words, will very concisely sum-up *the entire 'Jean Gabin Movie-Character Philosphy of Extreme Resignedness:'*

"Shit! I've already given!"

With these four words, Jean Gabin has now, effectively, spent everything he can give to us—his adoring audience.

Max and his buddy Pierre (buddies are better than women, because buddies can't hurt you) next walk off together in an extreme long-shot, through a Roman piazza. They pass a large group of marching, orange-garbed clergymen who are marching in formation, and all of these priests respectfully tip their hats to Max, at the same time. Jean Gabin is now walking off-screen for the last time, and right into the Pantheon of the Eternally Great Shining Movie-Superstars, where he will now assume his rightful position as *The World's Coolest Movie Star.*

(P.S.: Remember how I mentioned that other movie, which Gabin almost starred-in instead of this one, *Ange noel?* It was never made.)

L'Annee sainte, a great 1970s comedy, was a fitting end for Jean Gabin's movie career and, weirdly, his last movie also happens to be one of the earliest, commercially-produced feature films to deal with the subject of international terrorism, and with the blowing-up of planes. (Others from about the same time, include a 1975 Sean Connery thriller, which was [suitably] titled *The Terrorists,* and John Frankenhemier's terrorists-attacking-the-Super Bowl-classic from 1977, *Black Sunday,* starring Bruce Dern.) Even though Jean Gabin didn't know it, he was making a movie which, in its own small way, anticipated the tragedy of September 11, 2001, by twenty-five years.

L'Annee sainte was released on American home video in the 1990s, as *Pilgrimage to Rome* (on VHS), and for a second time, in 2003—this time, on a restored DVD, as *The Holy Year.*

When Jean Gabin passed away on November 15, 1976 at the age of 72, I'll bet that he just Gabin-Shrugged when the Reaper came, and I'll also bet that the Reaper was a hot brunette! The actor left behind three ex-wives, three adult kids, and a dazzling array of ninety-five films which will entrance moviegoers for years to come. I can guarantee that hundreds of years from now, audiences will still be jonesing for a world-weary but life-loving hero, thusly insuring that Jean Gabin's movies will continue to be both vital and relevant for all eternity.

What a Critic Said at the Time: "That venerable star, Jean Gabin, after a lot of lip service about retiring [from the screen], is now back in action, with this [fun] comedy actioner about human pettiness…" (*Variety,* 5-5-76 issue, Critic: "Mosk. [George Moskowitz.]" Reviewed in Paris.)

APPENDIX

IV

"SOLSTICE OF MARS"

A Poem About Jean Gabin, by Jacques Prevert (1954)

Le regard toujours bleu et encore enfantin
Sourit
Les levres minces accusent les blessures de la vie
On ne meurt qu'une fois
dit un dit-on
On meurt souvent
On meurt tout les temps
Repond Jean Gabin sur l'ecran
Jean Gabin
acteur tragique de Paris
gentleman du cinema elisabethain
dans la peripherie du film quotidien

Le cinema n'a jamais ete muet
Il avait tant des choses a dire
primitivement
qu'il le disait en se taisant
internationalement.

Plus tard on le paya pour parler
il ne put faire autrement.
Jean Gabin est l'un de ceux que l'ont le mieux aide
a dire ses pauvres reves
fasteux et vivants.

La voix de Jean Gabin est vraie
c'est la voix de son regard
la voix des gestes de ses mains
tout marche ensemble.

Jean Gabin est synchrone de la tete au pieds.
L'acteur le plus fragile et le plus solide.
en meme temps.

The look of blue in his childish eyes
Somehow smiles
His thin lips denounce life's miseries.
We only die once
One says, the other says
We die often
We die all the time,
Responds Jean Gabin, on the screen
Jean Gabin
dramatic actor of Paris
Gentleman of the Elizabethan Cinema
Within the cinema of the every day

Cinema was never mute:
It always had a lot to say,
Primitively
It spoke with its mouth shut
Internationally

Later, we paid, so it could speak
it didn't have a choice.
Jean Gabin is best helped
when talking about his poor dreams
which are fast, and which are living.

The voice of Jean Gabin is true
It's the voice of his gestures and
his hands,
all of them working together.

Jean Gabin is synchronized, from head to feet.
An actor so fragile, yet so solid.
at the same time.

Sobre comme le vin rouge
simple comme une tache de sang
et parfois gai comme le petit vin blanc
il joue "comme dans la vie"
comme dans la vie mysterieuse et revee.

Jean Gabin
c'est l'evidence meme
l'evidence meme d'un etre humain
qui joue son role publiquement
devant tant d'autres qui jouent le
leur secretement
et si mal la plupart du temps.

Acteur lyrique et peintre de talent
il reussit toujours le portrait
de ce qu'il a a faire
de ce qu'il a dire
a montrer
et sans meme y penser il ajoute
sa couleur a lui
et donne son avis sur l'amour
son avis sur la vie
ou sur la mort la faim l'ennui
simplement
en se jouant.

Une lueur de bonheur peut durer si longtemps
le malheur des uns ne fait pas le bonheur
des autres
il fait seulment semblant.
Jean Gabin
Toujours le meme, jamais pareil
Toujours Jean Gabin
Toujours quelqu'un.

As sober as a red wine
simple like a spot of blood
and sometimes joyful, like a white wine
he plays "life, like it really is"
that is the mystery and the dream.

Jean Gabin
is evidence
evidence of a human being
who 'acts' very well publicly
what others play
secretly and badly
most of the time.

Lyrical actor and a talented painter
He always manages to paint
what he needs to paint
to say what he needs to say
and show what he needs to show
Without even thinking about it
he adds his own color
and gives his advice on love
his advice on life
or on death, hunger, and boredom
simply
by playing 'himself.'

The subtle light of happiness can last a long time
the misfortune
of others
won't make anyone else happy.
Jean Gabin
Always the same, but never alike.
Always Jean Gabin.
Always somebody.

"MAINTENANT JE SAIS"

Jean Gabin's hit record in France, in the Summer of 1974.
Lyrics by Jean-Loup Dabadie; Published by D. Bourgeois-Bridget Music, CBS Records/France

In 1974, Jean Gabin recorded his first hit song since *"Quand on s'promene au bord de l'eau"* ("When You Walk By the Water") back in the early 1930s and, nearing 70 years old, he had a #1 hit on the French charts for the entire summer, with *"Maintenant je sais"* ("Now I Know"), a gentle ballad about aging and lost youth, which was written especially for him by the songwriting team of Philip Green and Jean-Loup Dabadie. *"Maintenant"* is a song about a man who thought he knew anything when he was young but, as it turns out, he didn't really know anything, until he aged. Gabin speak-sings the first few verses, *a la* Lou Rawls or Barry White, before bursting into actual song for the chorus, showing that almost forty years after *"Quand on s'promene,"* he still had his chops. Here are the lyrics to *"Maintenant je sais,"* in French, and in English.

Quand j'etais gosse, haut comme trois pommes,	When I was a kid, as tall as three apples,
J'parlais bien fort pour etre un homme	I tried to speak loudly, like I was a man
J'disais: "Je sais, je sais, je sais!!"	Always saying, "I know, I know, I know!!"
C'etat l'debut, c'etait l'printemps,	But it was just the beginning. It was spring,
Mais quand j'ai eu mes dix-huit ans,	But when I turned 18, I said,
J'ais dit: "Je sais, ca y'est, cette fois, je sais."	"I know! This time, I know."
Et auhourd'hui, les jours out je m'retourne,	And today, in these days where I'm looking back,
J'regarde la terre out j'ai quand meme fait les cent pas —	I'm looking at this world where I've walked a million steps —
Et je n'sais toujours pas comment elle tourne.	But still, I don't know how it turns.
Vers vingt-cinq ans,	When I was about twenty-five years old,
j'savais tout	I [thought I] knew everything about
l'amour, les roses, la vie, les sous.	love, roses, life, money.
Tienes, oui! L'amour! J'en avais fait tout l'tour.	Yes, love! [I told everybody that I had] done it all.
Mais heureusement, comme les copains,	But unfortunately [the truth is],
J'avais pas mange tout mon pain,	just like most of my friends

Au milieu d'ma vie, j'ai encore appris. C'que j'ai appris, ca tient en trois-quatre mots: Le jour ou quelqu'un vous aime, Il fait tres beau, J'peux pas mieux dire. Il fait tres beau.	I still haven't eaten all my bread, And at the middle of my life, I learned something, and what I learned, you can put it in three or four words: The day when somebody loves you, It's a very nice day, I cannot say it any better. It's a beautiful, shiny day.
C'est encore c'qui m'etonne dans la vie:, Moi qui suis a l'automne de ma vie. On oublie tant de soirs de tristesse, Mais jamais un matin de tendresse.	That's what still surprises me, in life: Me, who is at the autumn of my life. You forget the sad nights, But you never forget a tender morning.
Toute ma jeunesse, j'ai voulu dire, "Je sais." Seulement, plus j'cherchais et puis moins j'savais. Y'a soxiante coups qui ont sonne a l'horloge, J'suis encore a ma f'netre, j'regarde et j'm'interroge. Maintenant je sais, Je sais qu'on n'sait jamais, La vie, l'amour, l'argent, les amis et les roses, On n'sait jamais l'bruit, ni la couleur des choses, C'est tout c'que j'sais Mais ca, je'le sais	For my entire youth, I always said, "I know." Only, the more I sought, the less I knew. The clock has now turned more than sixty times, in my life. Today, I sit by my window, and I question myself. Now I know, I know that I know nothing. Life, love, friends, roses. You can never really know the noise, or the color, of things, This is all I know. That is all I know.

The B-Side of "*Maintenant je sais*" is a song called "*Madeline Corbeau et Juliette Renard,*" which is based on the old children's poem "*Le Corbeau et le renard*" ("The Crow and the Fox"). Gabin would also record an English language version of "*Maintenant je sais,*" which was called, "But Now I Know." The B-Side of the English version features a completely different song which Gabin also performs in English, "There's No Fool Like an Old Fool."

VI

ACKNOWLEDGEMENTS

About the worst movie experience I ever had in my life, was when I was forced, by acquaintances who wanted to go, to sit through the sickly-maudlin 1989 baseball movie, *Field of Dreams,* starring Kevin Costner. Everything about that movie was utterly false, although in its favor, the movie did feature the now-famous line, "If you build it they will come," and that's exactly what happened, when I decided to write this book: As soon as I decided that I was going to write the English-language's very first-ever book about Jean Gabin, and knew that I was going to have to track down dozens of films that have either never properly existed in the United States, or haven't existed in the U.S. for fifty or sixty years, I put out feelers, and met some of the nicest and most selfless people I have ever met, people who helped me with biographical research on Jean Gabin, with finding hard-to-find films, and with translating the films I found, from French (or, in the case of two films, German), into English. To all of the great people who made this book what it is (and if you didn't like the book, I guess, 'to all of the people who helped make this book what it isn't!') —to the people whom, collectively, I will now refer to, as my illustrious and exalted 'Team Gabin'—please accept my woefully inadequate and enduring thank you.

There is one, central figure without whom this book would not exist—the incomparable **Laurence Bardet.** Laurence (or 'Lolo') has completely bypassed the 'friend'-category: She and her family (husband Jean-Paul Danton, and their two amazing kids, Laetitia and Louis) have officially become a part of the extended and far-flung Zigman Family Empire. When I told Lolo, in Early 2004, that I would be coming to Paris for two weeks of extreme, Jean Gabin-oriented research, she and her family couldn't do enough to help out: Not only did Lolo organize my entire trip and make dozens of phone calls on my behalf, and not only did she set up all of my archival screenings of the rare Jean Gabin films, both in France and in Belgium, but she and her family also spent an entire Saturday hauling me back and forth to the *Musee Gabin* (Gabin Museum) in Meriel, and she even smoothed the way for me to snap a few photos in the museum, something which, up to that point, had always been strictly *verboten*. (The ladies who work in the Museum were so surprised by seeing an actual American in their midst, they even loaded me up with Gabin Swag!) Not only that, but

Lolo and Jean-Paul also invited me over for dinner just about every night that I was in Paris. (I came to Paris for the Gabin Movies, and stayed for Lolo and J.P.'s mouth-watering osso bucco and rabbit: Yes, I tried rabbit for the first time and, friends, I'd like to report to you: It really does taste like chicken!) And Lolo didn't just help me in 2004, either: During the entire five years it took me to write this book, between 2002 and 2007, she was always just an email away, answering all of my questions, making *French phone calls* for me, finding out information, and sending me every Jean Gabin article and television documentary she could get her hands on. My cousin, **Adriane Rothstein,** introduced me to Lolo and her family—so thanks, Adriane.

Now, here's a shout-out (I'm not in my twenties, anymore, but "I can still do the lingo") to my translators: When I was preparing this book, a lot of the research materials I needed—that is to say, many of the films, articles, and books—were in French. In fact, of the ninety-five films I saw for this book, fifty-eight of them didn't have English subtitles or dubbing, at all. Since I've forgotten most of the French which I learned in high school, I was in a huge rut, and the question which I began tossing around inside my noggin (and this riddle is as old as the sands), was: How will I be able to watch all of these French-language films, if I don't speak French? And then it dawned on me: I could hire translators! And so I did—people who sat with me and watched the movies, in effect acting as 'human subtitles,' and providing simultaneous translations, as I scribbled down everything they said. These are people whom I never would have met, were it not for this book:

Delphine Chabre: Not only was Delphine an incredible French-to-English translator who watched twenty-three Gabin films with me on video (and who never once got mad when I kept stopping and starting and reversing and fast-forwarding), but she's also an outstanding musician and composer of film music. I thank Delphine for her invaluable support.

Alexandrine Wiese: Alexandrine watched another twenty-some Gabin movies with me, and not only did she provide some amazingly accurate translations but, as we were watching the films, she'd always freeze the image and provide me with plenty of historical context for what was going on in certain scenes, or in certain lines of dialogue. Alex taught me a lot about what was happening in France when the films were made, between the 1930s and the 1970s, information which was beyond anything I could have learned from books, and her keen observations definitely sharpened this book, and have made it a thousand-times better than it ever would have been, without her contributions. Whenever I'm referencing a scene in a Gabin movie in which characters are talking about something obscure (at least, something that might be considered obscure to Americans), and by this I mean, anything about French poets, French politicians, French streets, or *French feelings*—much of this comes from Alex, so thanks, Alex. And thanks for not getting mad about the time when we were watching the movie *Les Grandes familles*, and you were translating some dialogue for me, and I fell asleep! (You're in good company: Once, I fell asleep during a job interview, as well.)

Edward Auslender: When I visited Paris, and watched some of the rarest Jean Gabin movies, Edward not only translated a few of the films for me, but he also, and completely of his own free will and accord, actually picked me up at my Paris hotel, and drove me to the *Cinematheque Francaise* archives in Montigny-le-Bretonneux, and didn't even want the gas money which I had offered him. For providing expert translations and a free ride—thank you, Edward.

Fred Goubet: Fred translated some films for me at the archives of the Royal Cinematheque of Belgium, in Brussels. (Talk about a movie's *not* playing at 'a theater near you.') When I was staying in Paris, and watching other films, Fred made the day-trip to Brussels with me by train, we saw three movies in one sitting, and we then returned to Paris, also by train, the same night. For his expert translations, and for introducing me to the simple joys of Belgian beer and gingerbread—thanks, Fred.

Philippe Bardet: The excellent Phillipe Bardet, brother of Laurence Bardet, went to the *Cinematheque Francaise* archives with me when I was in Paris, to provide translations for two Gabin movies. Not only did he translate, but he also pointed out all of one film's historical inaccuracies, 'first-hand' information, which I would have been unable to glean from books or articles. After the screenings, Philippe drove me to Fontainebleu, so that I could see where Napoleon lived and, additionally, he straightened me out about some of the intricacies of archaic French jurisprudence, information which I desperately needed, because some of the 'legalese' which the cop and lawyer-characters were spouting in a number of Gabin's 'cop' movies, was, to say the least, a bit odd-sounding to my American sensibilities.

Allen Sabiani: As I was finishing up the writing of this book, and adding the final whistles and bells, Allen helped me to translate a gigantic stack of articles about Gabin from old French magazines, and he also translated two French television documentaries about Jean Gabin, and some on-line video clips. He's a filmmaker/racecar driver/investor *par excellence,* and if you ever need any of those skills—Allen is the guy to call.

Trent zum Mallen: When it came time for me to watch the final two films for this book, *Die Schonen tage von Aranjuez* (the German-language, Gabinless-version of Gabin's missing film, *Adieu les beaux jours*) and *Der Stern von Valencia* (the German, Gabinless version of Gabin's *L'Etoile de Valencia*) at Berlin's Bundesarchiv Film Archives, Trent was an excellent German-to-English translator—all that, plus he's a real, live Baron!

Alain Carbuccia checked my photo-captions for accuracy.

Now, I'd like to thank the people who provided me with screenings of the rarest films:

Mark Quigley, at UCLA's Film Archives: The UCLA's Film and Television Archives in Los Angeles is home to a bunch of very rare English-subtitled prints of Gabin movies, many of which are unique—meaning, specifically, that there is only one print of each film in existence. Mark set up the screenings for me and made my life easy, and it was fun to go to UCLA and enjoy my own, personal showings of some of the more obscure (in the U.S., anyway) Gabin films, many of which, as he told me, hadn't been projected for thirty, forty, or even fifty years.

Gaelle Vidalie, Bernard Benoiliel, and **Emilie Cauquy** at the *Cinematheque Francaise* in Paris, and **Eric Le Roy** and **Daniel Fromont** at the CNC/French Ministry of Culture, in Paris: Through the combined efforts of these two organizations, I was able to screen a number of Gabin films, when I went to Paris. The CNC had a number of the films which I needed to see for this book, but they were unable to project them for me in their own facilities, so they sent their prints over to the people at the *Cinematheque Francaise* who, in turn, threaded them up for me. Thanks, everybody.

Hilda Delabie and **Anne Catteuw** at the Royal Cinematheque of Brussels: Just like the nice people at the Paris Cinematheque and the CNC, so too, were Ms. Delabie and Ms. Catteuw of the Royal Cinematheque of Brussels great, when it came to screening some of their rarest Gabin titles for me. They didn't even complain, when I went past their closing time of five o' clock—so my beret is off to them.

Wolfgang Schmidt of the Bundesarchiv Film Archives in Berlin arranged viewings for me of *Der Stern von Valencia* and *Die Schonen tage von Aranjuez* at his facilities, and he was also great about answering all of my questions relative to those movies, before, during, and after the screenings.

Besides translators and archivists, lots of other great people helped out with this book, as well:

Jacques Guillemin: Jacques, whom I've never met in person, is a great French journalist, who sent me DVD copies of two impossible-to-find Gabin pictures.

Marlene Pilaete: I discovered Marlene quite by accident, during the initial stages of this book, when I was first surfing the net, searching for hard-to-find Gabin films. One French movie-related website linked to another until, finally, I hit upon a site called Encinematheque.com. One of the Encinematheque's major contributors, Marlene is known by French-speaking movie lovers as *La Collectioneuse*, due to her amazing collection of movie memorabilia, including Jean Gabin memorabilia, which dates back to the beginnings of cinema. When I emailed Marlene and told her about my book, she found out that a few of the films which I simply could not locate, existed at the Royal Cinematheque of Belgium, and she very selflessly organized the screenings for me. Thank you, Marlene, for your fantastic help. Additionally, Marlene provided me with some great photographs which I have utilized in this book, as did **Christian Grenier** in Nimes, and **Isabelle Minard-Borde, Naima Zarouali** and **Andre Bernard** (all in Paris).

Tanya Sorkin provided the author's photo for the book jackets.

A great many of the photographs in this book were graciously supplied by **Daniel Bouteiller,** of France's TCD (Tele Cine Documentation) Archives.

Alex Berrier: I have never met Alex in person, but I hope to, someday: He's one of the most helpful and gracious people whom I've ever *not* met (!), and I first came into contact—or, I guess, I should say, 'e-contact'—with Alex, when I bought some Gabin-related memorabilia which he was selling on French eBay. Alex considers himself to be The World's #1, Super Gabin-Fan, and I really put him to the test: While I was proofreading this book, I discovered that I didn't know the names of a great many of the actors who played certain supporting characters in a number of the films, nor was this information available on the internet or in books, so I emailed him hundreds of times, and Alex answered every one of my ten zillion obscure questions ("Who played 'Thug #2' in *Le Rouge est mis?*" "Who played 'The Guy Standing Behind the Other Guy' in *Le Tatoué?*"), and he always had the answer. Thank you, so much, Alex, for helping me fill in the blanks (and also, for being so gracious about it).

Florence Moncorge-Gabin: When I was about three-quarters of the way through this book, I wrote Jean Gabin's daughter, Ms. Moncorge-Gabin, a letter, telling her that I had been spending the last few years writing of the very first English-language book about her father, and she wrote me back immediately, not only approving of my project, but also answering all of my questions about her father's films, and his life, in exquisite detail. Ms. Moncorge-Gabin, I hope this book honors you, your father, and your family.

Mary Moncorge who is the granddaughter of Jean Gabin and daughter of Gabin's son, Mathias, gave me a great deal of assistance as well, and she even made me a 'Gabin Family Tree,' so that I could write a bit about what the Gabin family is doing today.

Vanessa Z. Mills provided some stellar copy-editing for this book, and corrected my bizarre overuse of commas and exclamation marks. Thank you, Vanessa, for spinning my 'gonzo' punctuation into gold.

Historian. Film Buff. My friend since the age of six: **Lawrence Peck's** knowledge of 20th-century world history, and of rare, old movies, helped me immeasurably, when it came time for me to fine-tune this book.

When it came to locating old newspaper articles about Gabin, some stellar individuals helped to make my life easy: My excellent cousin **Andrew Rothstein**, a premiere documentary filmmaker, helped me find a lot of old articles about Jean Gabin from ancient issues of the New York *Times*, and some other people who were very nice about sharing articles and information with me, were—**Cheryl Kugler** of the CBS News Library in New York; **Elise Girard** at the *Bibliotheque du film* (in Paris); **Laura Repstad** of *Daily Variety*; **everybody** at the Margaret Herrick Library of the Academy of Motion Pictures Arts and Sciences, in Beverly Hills (particularly for supplying the Al Hirschfeld/*Pepe Le Moko* caricature, from the film's 1940 North American pressbook); everybody at the Beverly Hills Public Library; **Helene Lebas** in Paris; **David Cairns** in Edinburgh; and **everybody** at Francevision, the great French video-movie rental house, in Bethesda, Maryland. And before I forget, my computer crashed about fourteen thousand times while I was writing this book, and **Erik Ambro** was always there to fix it, as was my sister, **Felicia Zigman**.

Michael Kellner: If you like the way this book looks, this is the man who deserves the kudos. Thank you, Michael, for your outstanding book design, which has helped me to "re-present" Gabin to the world in the classiest way possible.

To everybody I've just mentioned, and to everybody whom I can't remember right now, thank you so much for everything. And one more time, before I vanish into the ether, I want to thank the late-great **Shirley Marilyn Zigman Rothstein,** my always-inspiring Aunt, for introducing me to the films of Jean Gabin. I would also like to throw in a special thank you to my fantastic, and always inspiring, high school French teacher (North Hollywood High School, 1980-'84) **Rachelle Berman,** who always expected a lot of her students.

To paraphrase Vito Corleone from *The Godfather,* 'a man is nothing, without his family,' so hello, and much love, to: **Eileen Zigman, Robert M. Zigman, Alyse Zigman, Felicia Zigman, Adriane Rothstein, Mark Billy, Harold Rothstein, Andrew Rothstein, Agatha Wirth, Andrea Zigman, Ted Scharf, Rob Scharf-Zigman, Eric Zigman, Julia Chiapella, Emma Zigman, Paul Zigman, Marcia Zigman,** the one-and-only **Anna Billy,** and 'some great family members who have passed on,' and who always gave me nothing but unconditional love and support—**Richard Carlin, Rose Carlin, Arthur Rothstein, Shirley Rothstein, Fernand Zigman, Rose Zigman, Esther Tropper, Joseph Tropper, Rose Horn,** and **Helen Horn.**

When I was growing up in the '70s and '80s, "Ben Hunter's Movie Matinee" on KTTV Channel 11 and "Tom Hatten's Family Film Festival" on KTLA Channel 5 (and channel 9's Saturday night "Million Dollar Movie," which always began with the announcer intoning, "Tonight's story is *Casablanca,*" or "Tonight's story is *Spartacus,*" while the show's theme—a Muzak version of Herman's Hermits' "No Milk Today"—played), were very instrumental in introducing me to old movies—so a very special thank you to **ancient Los Angeles television programming,** as well.

Before I go, I'd also like to remind the readers of this book that if you ever have any spare cash burning a hole in your pocket, please make a tax-deductible donation to one of the many great organizations around the world which restores old movies (UCLA, AFI, *etc.*). As I've already mentioned probably *two quintillion* times in this book, more than half of the movies which were made prior to 1950, all over the world, are gone forever, and we've got to save all of the films, before it's too late. Lastly, if you're ever in Hollywood, stop over and catch a flick at the American Cinematheque, at the Egyptian Theater on Hollywood Blvd, or at the Cinematheque's second house, the Aero Theatre, in Santa Monica. The Cinematheque's fantastic film presentations have added a lot of happiness to the last ten years of my life.

VII

HOW YOU CAN SEE JEAN GABIN MOVIES

Movies on video (and how I saw them).

Now that you've read the book from cover-to-cover (thank you!), I would imagine that, or I would *hope* that, you're ready to start watching the Jean Gabin movies you've just read about on your own, *without training wheels*. I mean, why listen to some bloated, pretentious author (me) telling you about these ultra-cool movies, when you can just hunt most of them down for yourself?

It took me five years to find Jean Gabin's ninety-five films, but you're going to be getting the benefit of my half-a-decade of steadfast film-sleuthing, right here. Many, but not all, of the films, are available on DVD or VHS somewhere in the world, if you know where to look (I didn't, at first), and I will now tell you exactly how you can see the films, and how I saw them.

• The following 34 Jean Gabin movies are, at the time of this book's printing, available on DVD and/or VHS, with either English subtitles or English dubbing. If I mention that a movie is available on VHS, that means it hasn't yet been released on DVD, but of course, new titles are being released in the DVD format each year, so by the time you read this, it's more than possible that some of the titles I mention as existing only on VHS may very well have been re-released on DVD, or Blu-ray, or Bluetooth, or the back of your eyelids, or on whatever creepy new technology is available when this book comes out. I have listed these titles in order of the years in which they were first theatrically released.

    Zou Zou (amazon.com, DVD, English subtitles)
    Maria Chapdelaine (moviesunlimited.com, VHS, English subtitles)
    Golgotha (sinistercinema.com, VHS, English subtitles)
    La Bandera (amazon.com, DVD, English subtitles)
    Les Bas-fonds (amazon.com, DVD, English subtitles)
    Pepe Le Moko (amazon.com, DVD, English subtitles)
    Le Grande illusion (amazon.com, DVD, English subtitles)
    Le Quai des brumes (amazon.com, DVD, English subtitles)

La Bete humaine (amazon.com, DVD, English subtitles)
Le Jour se leve (amazon.com, DVD, English subtitles)
Moontide (amazon.com, DVD, English-language film)
The Impostor (fnac.com, DVD, English subtitles)
Au-dela des grilles (moviesunlimited.com, VHS, English subtitles)
Le Plaisir (moviesunlimited.com, VHS, English-subtitles)
Touchez pas au grisbi (amazon.com, DVD, English subtitles)
L'Air de Paris (amazon.co.uk, DVD, English subtitles)
Gas-Oil (internet seller, Señor Noir, DVD, English subtitles)
Razzia sur la chnouf (notavailableondvd.com, DVD, English subtitles)
French Cancan (amazon.com, DVD, English subtitles)
La Traversee de Paris (moviesunlimited.com, VHS, English subtitles)
Les Miserables (amazon.com, DVD, English-dubbed)
En cas de malheur (eBay sellers, DVD and VHS, English-dubbed)
Un singe en hiver (eBay seller, VHS, English-subtitles)
Le Gentleman d'Epsom (eBay seller, VHS, English subtitles)
Melodie en sous-sol (amazon.com, DVD, English subtitles)
Du rififi a Paname (eBay sellers; English-dubbed)
Le Pacha (xploitedvideo.com, VHS, English-dubbed)
Le Tatoue (eBay sellers, DVD, English-dubbed)
Le Clan des Sicilens (Amazon.co.uk, DVD, English subtitles)
La Horse (Francevision.com, VHS, English subtitles)
Le Chat (moviesunlimited.com, VHS, English subtitles)
Deux hommes dans la ville (amazon.com, DVD, English subtitles)
Verdict (moviesunlimited.com, VHS, English-dubbed)
L'Annee sainte (amazon.com, DVD, English subtitles)

THERE ARE TWO WAYS TO WATCH THE FOLLOWING 46 JEAN GABIN MOVIES WHICH I WILL NOW MENTION.[*]

FIRST WAY: The following titles are, at the time of this book's printing, available on DVD, but the dialogue is only in French, and features neither English subtitles nor English dubbing. These DVDs have been recorded in the European, 'PAL' format, as opposed to the North American, 'NTSC' format, but you can play European-made DVDs in North America (or DVDs made anywhere in the world for that matter) if you buy an international, or 'codeless,' DVD player, which is basically just a basic DVD machine which has been doctored so that it has the ability to play both American/NTSC titles and European/PAL titles. You should be able to find a great international/codeless DVD player on-line, for under $200: Just go to your favorite search engine, and type-in 'codeless DVD player,' *et voila!* The best on-line merchants for all of the DVDs in this section, are—www.amazon.fr (French Amazon.com);

www.fnac.com; www.allocine.com; and www.ebay.fr (French eBay).

SECOND WAY: If you live in North America, Francevision (www.francevision.com), a mail order video rental house based in Bethesda, Maryland, will rent you U.S. format tapes and DVDs (NTSC-conversions) of all of these European Jean Gabin movies, so that you can see them without having to buy a special DVD player, and without having to order the films from Europe. (P.S.: I shouldn't really be telling you this, but any American DVD player can be converted to a codeless, or international, DVD player, which is capable of playing any DVD made anywhere in the world: Just ask your favorite twentysomething computer kid how to hack in to your American-system DVD player, and he should be able to do it without breaking a sweat.)

Chacun sa chance
Paris-Beguin
Les Gaietes de l'escadron
Coeur de Lilas
Le Tunnel
Pour un soir..!
La Belle equipe
Le Messager
Le Recif de corail
Martin Roumagnac
Miroir
La Marie du port
Pour l'amour du ciel
Victor
La Nuit est mon royaume
La Verite sur Bebe Donge
Le Minute de verite
Fille dangereuse
Leur derniere nuit
La Vierge du rhin
Napoleon
Le Port du desir
Chiens perdus sans collier

Des gens sans importance
Voici le temps des assassins
Le Sang a la tete
Crime et chatiment
Le Cas du docteur Laurent
Le Rouge est mis
Le Desordre et la nuit
Les Grandes familles
Archimede, le clochard
Maigret et l'affaire Saint-Fiacre
Rue des Prairies
Le Baron de l'ecluse
Les Vieux de la vieille
Le Cave se rebiffe
Maigret voit rouge
Monsieur
L'Age ingrat
Le Tonnerre de Dieu
Le Jardinier d'Argenteuil
Sous le signe du taureau
Le Drapeau noir flotte sur la marmite
Le Tueur
L'Affaire Dominici

*While the 46 movies I've mentioned in this category currently exist *only* in French-language versions, it bears mentioning that, back in the 1930s, '40s, '50s, and '60s, twenty-two of these forty-nine titles were, as I've already mentioned in this book, released in the U.S., usually in only one or two art-houses—generally, one in New York and, only occasionally, one more in Los Angeles—in either English-subtitled or English-dubbed versions, by small, 'mom-

and-pop' foreign film distribution companies. Unfortunately, when these small American companies went belly-up (which they all eventually did) they took the one or two English-language prints which they had struck, with them, into oblivion, although the UCLA Film and Television Archives, in Los Angeles, has managed to keep a small number of them. So to see these movies today, in the 21st century, you've got to be able to speak French, or you've got to hire some French-to-English translators to sit and watch the movies with you, like I did.

• The following 2 Jean Gabin movies showed-up on American cable television, while I was writing this book:

Maigret tend un piege (viewed by the author on the U.S. cable station TV5/French-Language TV, with English subtitles);
Le President (viewed by the author on the U.S. cable station TV5/French-Language TV, with English subtitles);

• Additionally: *Pepe Le Moko*, *La Grande illusion*, *Le Jour se leve*, and *Le Quai des brumes*, which are available on English-language NTSC-DVDs, often play on the American cable t.v. station, Turner Classic Movies (TCM).

• In February of 2007, Jean Gabin's American-made 1944 picture *The Impostor* was released on DVD in France (European, 'PAL' Format), by Universal Home Video, in its original English-language version, with removable French subtitles. Even though it is an American film, Universal has no plans to release the DVD in America.

• The following 7 Jean Gabin movies are not, at the time this book is going to press, available on home video or television anywhere in the world. I screened the actual 35mm film prints themselves, many of them one-of-a-kind, at various archives in the U.S., and in Europe. The following prints exist in the French language only, and do not have English subtitles or English dubbing:

Du haut en bas (viewed by the author as a 35mm print, at the Royal Cinematheque of Belgium, Brussels);
Mephisto (viewed by the author as a 35mm print, at the Royal Cinematheque of Belgium, Brussels);
Coeurs joyeux (viewed by the author as a 35mm print, courtesy of CNC [the French Ministry of Culture], at the archival screening facilities of the *Cinematheque Francaise*, in Montigny-le-Bretonneux, France);
Gloria (viewed by the author as a 35mm print, courtesy of CNC [the French Ministry of Culture], at the archival screening facilities of the *Cinematheque Francaise*, in Paris);
Tout ca ne vaut pas l'amour (viewed by the author as a 35mm print, courtesy of CNC [the

French Ministry of Culture], at the archival screening facilities of the *Cinematheque Francaise,* in Montigny-le-Bretonneux, France);

Varietes (viewed by the author as a 35mm print, courtesy of CNC [the French Ministry of Culture], at the archival screening facilities of the *Cinematheque Francaise,* in Montigny-le-Bretonneux, France);

La Belle Mariniere (viewed by the author as a 35mm print, at the facilities of the UCLA Film Archives, Los Angeles);

• The following 6 Jean Gabin movies are available on French language-only, PAL, or European format, DVDs, with no English subtitles or dubbing, however, I was able to view projected film prints of English-language versions (dubbed or subtitled) at archives, or public screenings, in Los Angeles:

Gueule d'amour (viewed by the author as a 35mm print, at the 2002 Jean Gabin Tribute Series, at the Los Angeles County Museum of Art, print supplied by the British Film Institute, with English subtitles). The currently available French DVD and Francevision transfers do not have English subtitles or dubbing;

Remorques (viewed by the author as a 35mm print, at Jean Gabin Tribute Series, at the Los Angeles County Museum of Art, print supplied by MGM-UA/Sony, with English subtitles). The currently available French DVD and Francevision transfers do not have English subtitles or dubbing;

Le Cas du docteur Laurent (viewed by the author as a 35mm print, the UCLA Film Archives, Los Angeles, with English subtitles). The currently available French DVD and Francevision transfers do not have English subtitles or dubbing;

La Nuit est mon royaume (viewed by the author as a 35mm print, at the UCLA Film Archives, Los Angeles, with English subtitles). The currently available French DVD and Francevision transfers do not have English subtitles or dubbing;

Le Port du desir (viewed by the author as a 35mm print, at the UCLA Film Archives, Los Angeles). The currently available French DVD and Francevision transfers do not have English subtitles or dubbing;

Le Soleil des voyous (viewed by the author as a transfers of a 16mm print, at the UCLA Film Archives, Los Angeles, English-dubbed). The currently available French DVD and Francevision transfers do not have English subtitles or dubbing.

...

• As it has already been mentioned in this book more than a zillion times, three of Jean Gabin's ninety-five feature films, *La Foule hurle, L'Etoile de Valencia,* and *Adieu le beaux jours,* no longer exist today, and each is considered to be a lost film. But thankfully, when the producers were making their French-language versions with Jean Gabin, they were also shooting simultaneous versions of the same films in other languages, for export to different countries. And mercifully, in the case of all three of these movies, the alternate, 'Gabinless' versions still exist. (You're not seeing Gabin, but you're seeing a movie, in each case, which is identical to the no-longer-existing Gabin-version, even though another actor is playing the role which Gabin played in the French version.)

The Crowd Roars: English-language version of Jean Gabin's missing film, *La Foule hurle*, viewed by the author on the U.S. cable station, Turner Classic Movies, and starring James Cagney in the role which Gabin would play in the French version;

Der Stern von Valencia: German-language version of Jean Gabin's missing film, *L'Etoile de Valencia*, viewed by the author, as a 35mm print, at the Bundsfilmarchiv, Berlin, starring Paul Westermeier, in the role played by Gabin in the French version;

Die Schonen Tage von Aranjuez: German-language version of *Adieu les beaux jours*, viewed by the author as a 35mm print, at the Bundesarchiv, in Berlin, starring Gustaf Grundgens in the role which was played by Gabin, in the French version.

• Additionally, a German-language version of the Gabin film *Gloria*, starring Gustave Froelich in the role which Gabin played in the simultaneously-filmed French version, can be purchased, on home video, from www.ihf.com. I saw the French Gabin-version in France, but if you can't go all the way to France to see it at an archive facility like I did, this might be the way to go...

VIII

GABIN'S MOVIES RATED ON A SCALE

From 1 (Bad) to 10 (Pure Genius)
(Most of them are great)

In answer to your probable (I hope) question, "Which Jean Gabin movies should I see first," my first inclination, since I'm the guy who's trying to introduce Jean Gabin to people who may not know him that well (because I want you to get excited about seeing his work) is to tell you to see all of them. But some of Gabin's movies are better than other ones, and even though Gabin made many more great movies than he made bad ones, there are definitely some that you should see first—and I guess that's most of them. So here's my numerical quality rating of all of the films.

• I'm rating the movies strictly on their entertainment value and, to qualify my rating system, which is not inflated (the reason for this book, as I've already mentioned over-and-over, is that most Jean Gabin movies are great), let me say that, 'in my regular life,' when I'm watching other (a/k/a, 'non-Gabin') movies, I very seldom give any movie a (perfect) 10-score, nor do I give too many movies (near-perfect) 9's and 8's.

• I am giving 66 out of Jean Gabin's 95 movies scores of 8, 9, and 10—these are the most entertaining and enjoyable films. The 7s and 6s are 'pretty good.' Maybe some of the pictures are a little slow, but Gabin is really great in each of them.

• There are only seven Gabin movies which I didn't like, the ones to which I've accorded scores of '5' or less, but as I said in the introduction to this book, most of Gabin's ninety-five movies are great, and Gabin has the highest good-movie-to-bad-movie ratio of any other movie star, anywhere in the world.

• Keep in mind, that my apportioning of scores to these films is entirely subjective. For example, I have given comparatively low scores to *Les Grandes familles* (6) and *Le President* (6), two movies which are beloved in France, but which bored me to tears. Gabin turns in fantastic performances in both of those movies—particularly, in *Le President*, in which he gives one of the finest performances of his career, but I just couldn't get into either one of them.

• Here are my scores, 'From Top to Bottom' (or, as I guess I should say, "*Du haut en bas*"):
Remember: 10 = Best, and 1= Worst.

10—*La Bandera*
10—*La Belle equipe*
10—*La Grande illusion*
10—*Pepe Le Moko*
10—*Le Quai des brumes*
10—*La Bete humaine*
10—*Le Jour se leve*
10—*Au-dela des grilles*
10—*Le Nuit est mon royaume*
10—*French Cancan*
10—*La Traversee de Paris*
10—*Le Cas du docteur Laurent*
10—*Archimede, le clochard*
10—*Les Vieux de la vieille*
10—*Un singe en hiver*
10—*Le Chat*
10—*L'Affaire Dominici*
9—*Du haut en bas*
9—*Le Tunnel*
9—*Zou Zou*
9—*Gueule d'amour*
9—*Les Bas-fonds*
9—*Remorques*
9—*Pour l'amour du ciel*
9—*Le Plaisir*
9—*Leur derniere nuit*
9—*Touchez pas au grisbi*
9—*L'Air de Paris*
9—*Razzia sur la chnouf*
9—*Chiens perdus sans collier*
9—*Le Port du desir*
9—*Le Baron de l'ecluse*
9—*Rue de Prairies*
9—*Le Cave se rebiffe*
9—*Melodie en sous-sol*
9—*Monsieur*
9—*L'Age ingrat*
9—*Le Tonnerre de Dieu*
9—*Le Jardinier d'Argenteuil*
9—*La Horse*

9—*Le Drapeau noir flotte sur la marmite*
9—*Deux hommes dans la ville*
9—*L'Annee sainte*
8—*Chacun sa chance*
8—*Mephisto*
8—*Paris-Beguin*
8—*Pour un soir..!*
8—*Coeurs joyeux*
8—*Gloria*
8—*Les Gaietes de l'escadron*
8—*La Belle Mariniere*
8—*The Crowd Roars* (U.S. version of *La foule hurle*)
8—*Die Schonen tage von Aranjuez* (German version of *Adieu les beaux jours*)
8—*Der Stern von Valencia* (German version of *L'Etoile de Valencia*)
8—*Maria Chapdelaine*
8—*Varietes*
8—*Le Messager*
8—*Le Recif de corail*
8—*Moontide*
8—*Martin Roumagnac*
8—*Gas-Oil*
8—*Maigret tend un piege*
8—*Les Miserables*
8—*En cas de malheur*
8—*Le Gentleman d'Epsom*
8—*Verdict*
7—*Tout ca ne vaut pas l'amour*
7—*Coeur de Lilas*
7—*Golgotha*
7—*The Impostor*
7—*La Verite sur Bebe Donge*
7—*La Minute de verite*
7—*Des gens sans importance*
7—*Voici le temps des assassins*
7—*Le Rouge est mis*
7—*Le Desordre et la nuit*
7—*Maigret et l'affaire Saint-Fiacre*
7—*Le Soleil des voyous*
7—*Le Tatoue*
7—*Le Pacha*

6—*Miroir*
6—*Fille Dangereuse (a/k/a, Bufere)*
6—*Les Grandes familles*
6—*Du Rififi a Paname*
6—*La Marie du port*
6—*Le President*
6—*Maigret voit rouge*
5—*Victor*
5—*La Vierge du Rhin*
5—*Crime et chatiment*
4—*Napoleon*
4—*Le Sang a la tete*
3—*Le Tueur*
2—*Sous le signe du taureau*

IX

BIBLIOGRAPHY

BOOKS

Arletty. *Les Mots d'Arletty.* Paris: VO Editions, 1993.

Bach, Steven. *Marlene Dietrich, Life and Legend.* New York, William Morrow, 1992.

Bazin, Andre. *Jean Renoir.* Paris: Editions Champ Libre, 1971.

Bernstein, Henri. *Le Soif: Piece en Trois Actes et Cinq Tableaux.* Paris: Theatre Opera, 1949.

Bloch, Marc. *Strange Defeat.* New York, WW Norton and Company, 1968.

Brand, Harry. *Moontide: 20th Century-Fox Press Book.* Los Angeles, 1942.

Brunelin, Andre. *Gabin.* Paris: Editions Robert Laffont, 1987.

Burroughs, William S. *Naked Lunch.* New York: Ace Books, 1964.

Buss, Robin. *French Film Noir.* New York: Marion Boyars, 2001.

Coward, Noel. *Future Indifferent.* New York: A&C Brown, 2004.

Cunningham, Ernest W. *The Ultimate Bogart.* Los Angeles: Renaissance Books, 1999.

Daidoji, Yuzan. *Code of the Samurai: A Modern Translation of the Bushido Shoshu of Taira Shigesuke.* Tokyo, 2000.

Demonpion, Denis. *Arletty.* Paris: Flamarrion, 1998.

Dietrich, Marlene. *Marlene.* New York: Grove Press, 1989.

Duroselle, J.B. *La Decadence.* Paris: Impr. Nationale, 1979.

Duncan, Paul and Faulkner, Christopher. *Jean Renoir.* Los Angeles: Taschen, 2007.

Faith, William Robert. *Bob Hope: A Life in Comedy.* Massachusetts: Da Capo Press, 1982/2003.

Forbes, Jill. *The Cinema of France After the New Wave.* London: Macmillan Press, 1992.

Fricke, Weddig. *The Court-Marshal of Jesus.* New York: Grove Press, 1990.

Fujiwara, Chris. *Jacques Tourneur: The Cinema of Nightfall.* Baltimore: Johns-Hopkins Press, 1998.

Gauter, Claude and Vincendeau, Ginette. *Jean Gabin: Anatomie d'un mythe.* Paris: Nouveau Monde, 2006.

Glatre, Patrick and Millot, Patrick. *Jean Gabin: La Traversee d'un siecle.* Paris: Creaphs, 2004.

Grangier, Gilles. *Passe la Loire, c'est la'aventure*. Paris: Terrain Vague Losfeld, 1971.
Guillaume, Andrew and Menant, Frederic. *Les Mots de Gabin*. Paris: Philippe Rey, 2005.
Harris, Marlys J. *The Zanucks of Hollywood: The Dark Legacy of a Movie Dynasty*. London: Virgin Books, 1989.
Harris, Warren G. Sophia *Loren: A Biography*. New York: Simon and Schuster, 1998.
Higham, Charles. *Marlene: The Life of Marlene Dietrich*. New York: WW Norton and Co., Inc., 1977.
Kael, Pauline. *For Keeps*. New York: Plume-Penguin, 1996.
Kolker, Robert. *A Cinema of Loneliness*. New York: Oxford University Press, 1988.
May, Ernest R. Strange *Victory: Hitler's Conquest of France*. New York: Farrar, Straus and Giroux, 2000.
Miller, Henry. *Time of the Assassins: A Study of Rimbaud*. New York: New Directions, 1962.
Moncorge-Gabin, Florence. *Quitte a avoir un pere, autant qu'il s'appelle Gabin*. Paris: Le Cherche-Midi, 2004.
Phillips, Alastair and Vincendeau, Ginette. *Journeys of Desire: European Actors in Hollywood: A Critical Companion*. London: BFI, 2006.
Powell, Michael. *A Life in Movies*. New York: Alfred A. Knopf, 1987.
Renoir, Jean. *My Life and My Films*. London: Collins, 1974.
Rioux, Jean-Pierre. *The Fourth Republic*, 1944-1958. Massachusetts: Cambridge University Press, 1987.
Servaes, Georges. *Au Pays de Gabin—Meriel-Val D'Oise—Gabin's Home Town*. Meriel val d'Oise: Society of the Friends of the Jean Gabin Museum, 1992.
Simmons, Sylvie. *Serge Gainsbourg: A Fistful of Gitanes*. Massachusetts: De Capo Press, 2001.
Southern, Terry. *The Magic Christian*. New York: Random House, 1960.
Spoto, Donald. *Blue Angel: The Life of Marlene Dietrich*. New York: Doubleday, 1992.
—————— *Variety Film Reviews, Volumes 4 to 14, 1930-1977*. New York: Garland Publishing, Inc. 1983. (Excerpts of Movie Reviews Written by Gene Moskowitz, Fred Hift, Nat Kahn, Robert F. Hawkins, Jerry Stein, Edwin 'Maxwell' MacSweeney, Wolfe Kaufman, *etc*.)
—————— *MGM Press Book: Stormy Waters* [*Remorques*]. Los Angeles, 1946.
—————— *Index de la Cinematographie Francaise 1947: Analyse Critique Complete de tous les Films Projects en France, de Juillet 1946 a Juillet 1947*. Paris: La Cinematographie Francaise, 1947. (Excerpted reviews by the critic, "L.O.")
Shirer, William, L. *Collapse of the Third Republic: An Inquiry into the Fall of France in 1940*. New York: Simon and Schuster, 1969.
Sichere, Bernard. *Gabin: Le Cinema, Le Peuple*. Paris: Maren Sell Editeurs, 2006.
Vincendeau, Ginette. *Companion to French Cinema*. London: BFI, 1996.
Waldman, Harry. *Missing Reels: Lost Films of American and European Cinema*. Jefferson, NC: McFarland & Co., 2000.

White, Susan M. *The Cinema of Max Ophuls*. New York: Columbia University Press, 1995.
Wolf, William Kramer and Wolf, Lillian Kramer. *Landmark Films*. New York: Paddington Press, 1979.
Youngkin, Stephen D. *The Lost One: A Life of Peter Lorre*. Lexington: University of Kentucky Press, 2005.
Wood, Ean. *Dietrich: A Biography*. Cornwall: MPG Books, 2002.

MAGAZINES/NEWSPAPERS/BROCHURES:

de Baroncelli, Jean. "Review of Film, *L'Air de Paris*," *Radio Cinema Television Magazine*, Paris, 5-8-1954.
Bazin, Andre. "Review of Film, *L'Air de Paris*," *Telerama Magazine*, 10-3-1954.
Birnie, Ian. *Le Grand Gabin*, program for Jean Gabin/Marlene Dietrich Film Festival. Los Angeles: Los Angeles County Museum of Art, 2002.
Bourdet, Maurice. "Review of Film, *Les Gaietes de l'escadron*," published in *Vu Magazine*, No. 236, 9-21-1932, pps, 1251-1254.
Bussot, Marguerite. "Review of Film *Gueule d'amour*," *Pour Vous* Magazine, 9-23-1937.
Bost, Pierre. "Review of the Film, *Du haut en bas*," *Les Annales Politiques et Litteraires* Magazine, 12-22-1932.
———. *Box Office Magazine*, Issues: 2-25-1939, 3-11-1939, 9-23-1939.
Champlin, Charles. "Review of Film, *Le Chat*," Los Angeles *Times*, 9-9-1975
Cowie, Peter. "Jean Gabin," *Films and Filming* Magazine, February 1964, London.
Chute, David. "Review of Film, *Le Chat*," Los Angeles *Herald-Examiner*, 9-9-1975.
De Baroncelli, Jean. "Review of Film *L'Air de Paris, Le Monde*, 5-8-1954."
Doringe. *Jean Gabin: Sa Vie/Ses Films* (a one-off fan magazine about Jean Gabin), Paris, Visages et Contes Du Cinema, 1938.
Gujonnet, Rene. "Review of Film, *Gas-Oil*," *L'Information Universitaire* Magazine, Paris, 11-12-1955.
Hogan, Nathan and Morehart, Phil. "Louise Brooks in *Prix de beaute*," *Facets Video Catalog*, Spring, 2006, page 27.
'H.T.S.' "A French Crook Romance (Review of Film, *Adieu les beaux jours*)," New York *Times*. 4-23-1934, page 20.
Huret, Marcel. "Review of Film, *Fille Dangereuse*," *Radio Cinema Television* Magzine, Paris. 6-14-1953.
Huret, Marcel. "Review of Film, *Leur derniere nuit*," *Radio Cinema Television Magazine*, Paris, 11-8-1953.
———. "Gabin's Next Movie: *Ange noel*," *Hollywood Reporter*, 7-7-1975.
King, Susan. "On DVD: Worthy of an Admiring Gaze," Los Angeles *Times*, February 12, 2006, page 32.
Klein, Andy. "French Twist: Melville's '*Le Doulous*' is Full of Dual Meanings,"

Los Angeles *City Beat*, September 6-12 2007 issue, p. 24. (Comparison of [*Fille dangereuse's* co-star] Serge Reggiani's resemblance to Rowan Atkinson.)

Labadie, Donald. "Jean Gabin: Gallic Grand Old Man," New York *Times*, 5-17-1964, Page X9.

Lachize, Samuel. "Review of Film, *Monsieur*," *L'Humanite* Magazine, Paris, 4-25-1964.

Lanwick, H. "Review of Film, *Fille Dangereuse*," *Noir et Blanc* Magazine, Paris, 6-24-1953 issue.

"Lucien." "Review of Film, *Gueule d'amour*," *Pour Vous* Magazine. 9-23-1937, p. 7.

——————-. *Cahiers du Cinema*, Winter 1975, page 11, "The Films of Serge de Poligny."

Mauriac, Claude. "Review of Film *L'Air de Paris*," *Le Figaro*, 10-2-1954.

"M.M.," "Review of Film, *Monsieur*," *Les Lettres Francaises* Magazine. Paris, 4-30-64.

——————. "Down to the Sea in Ships: Gabin's Next Film," New York *Times*, 2-13-1942, page 24.

——————. "Screen News, Here and in Hollywood," New York *Times*, 7-23-1943, page 21.

——————. "Jean Gabin Films Barred in France," New York *Times*, 5-8-1944, page 3.

——————. "Jean Gabin Out of Navy," New York *Times*, 12-10-1944, page 18.

——————. "New Bernstein Play ["*La Soif*"] Unveiled in Paris," New York *Times*, 2-9-1949, page 33.

——————. "Jean Gabin to Retire. Film Star Cites Health," New York *Times*, 9-17-1963, page 29.

——————. "Review of Film, *Monsieur*," *L'Humanite*, 4-25-1964.

——————. "Man at Work: Jean Gabin to Star in Film of Celine's *Mort a Credit*," New York *Times*, 10-29-1967.

——————. "Review of Film, *Gas-Oil*," *France-Soir* Magazine, 11-13-1955.

Reed, Rex. "Review of Film, *Le Chat*," *Vogue* Magazine, 9-1975.

Sovel, Etienne. "Review of Film, *Gas-Oil*," *Paris-Presse* Magazine, 11-11-1955.

Surowiec, Catherine Ann. "Programming Notes for Museum of Modern Art Screening of *La belle equipe*." New York, 12-17-1981.

Simenon, George. "*Mon Ami Jean Gabin*," *Cine-Revue* Magazine, No. 21, 5-24-1957, page 33.

Stein, Elliott, "Oedipus in Overalls—Jean Gabin: Everybody's Star," *Village Voice*, 6-26-2002.

Tremois, C.T. "Review of Film, *Monsieur*," *Telerama* Magazine, 3-5-64 issue.

——————. "Studio Searches for Gabin's Last Film [Remorques]," *20^b Century-Fox News* (the studio's in-house newsletter), 5-28-1941 issue.

Turan, Kenneth. "Review of Film, *Pepe Le Moko*," Los Angeles *Times*, Calendar section, 4-19-2002.

Various, "*Il etait comme ca Gabin*," *VSD* Magazine, No. 480. 11-11-1986.

——————. "Jean Gabin, West's Top Cinema Star in Russia; May Give Him a Horse,"

Weekly Variety, 4-24-1968.

Zendel, Jose. "Review of film, *Leur derniere nuit*," *Les Lettres Francaises* Magazine, Paris, 10-29-1953.

INTERNET SOURCES WITH INFORMATION ABOUT JEAN GABIN:

All Movie Guide.com (USA), including excerpts of reviews by Hal Erickson, Kristie Hassen, and Hans J. Wollstein;
Allocine.com (France);
Aubonticket.com (France);
Biosstars.com (France);
Cinedic.com (France);
CNN.com/2003/WORLD/meast/01/22/sproject.irq.schroeder.chirac/index.html (Jacques Chirac quote, "… war always means losing;"
Dvdcritiques.com/critiques/dvd-visu.aspx?dvd=4399 (DVD Review of film *Miroir*, Nov. 15, 2006. Author: Julien Sabatier);
DVDtoile.com (France);
Encinematheque.com (France);
Entertainment.timesonline.co.uk/tol/arts_and_entertainment/visual_arts/article1780174 ece. (London *Times* Online, "Surreal to Reel: Dali at the Movies" by Joanna Pitman [Pittman talks about problems on the set of *Moontide*, which were compounded by Japan's invasion of Pearl Harbor], 5-14-2007);
Filmsdefrance.com/FDF_Tout_ca_ne_vaut_pas_l_amour_1931_rev.html (Review of *Tout ca ne vaut pas l'amour*, by Chuck Leonard;
FNAC.com (France);
Francevision.com (USA);
Galichon.com (France)—"Gabin's Geneaology;"
Historia.fr (article about Gabin, "*Gabin sur l'honneur*" by Francois Quenin) (France);
Ifmagazine.com, Johnny Depp, interviewed by Emmanuel Itier (July 10, 2006) (USA);
Imdb.com (Internet Movie Database) (USA/France), *including excerpts of reviews and articles by* "D. B. DuMonteil" *and* Brian Raymond;
Jgana.club.fr (France)—*L'Encylopedie multimedia de la comedie musicale theatral en France, 1918-1940* (The Multimedia Encyclopedia of French Musical Comedy Theatre, 1918-1940);
Joeyy.free.fr/gabin_biographie.htm (France);
Meanderthal.typepad.com/meanderthal/2005/04/pater_noster.html. (Poem, "Pater-Noster," by Jacques Prevert);
Thelin.net (France);
Time Out London Film Guide (UK), Review of "*Du rififi a Paname*," Critic: "TR;"
Topcities.com;

TMZ.com/2006/11/23/brangelina-josephine-baker-wannabes/#continuedcontents.
  "Brangelina—Josephine Baker Wannabes?" by the TMZ Staff;
Wikipedia.org ("Jean Gabin");
Wikipedia.org ("Basques");
Xave.org (2003/01/22/226-souffrir-pour-la-cause). Arletty's Quote: *"Mon coeur est Francaise, mais mon cul est international."* ("My heart is French, but my ass is international.")

DOCUMENTARY FILMS, TELEVISION PROGRAMS, AND DVDS FEATURING BIOGRAPHICAL JEAN GABIN-RELATED MATERIAL:

1958 Jean Delannoy and Jean Gabin appear together on the television program *"La Joie de vivre"* (April 8, ORTF Television, France).

1959 Leon Zitrone (host) interviews Jean Gabin on the beginnings of his career (December 3, ORTF Television, France).

1963 Leon Zitrone (host) interviews Gabin about retirement (September 14, ORTF Television, France).

1966 Andre Leclerc (host) interviews Robert Stack about working with Jean Gabin on *Le Soleil des voyous*, on the program, *"Au-dela de l'ecran"* (December 4, ORTF Television, France).

1967 Leon Zitrone (host) interviews Jean Gabin about the movie *Le Pacha* (December 9, ORTF Television, France).

1971 Pierre Tchernia (host) interviews Jean Gabin about the film *Drapeau noir flotte sur la marmite*, on the program *"Monsieur Cinema"* (December 24, ORTF Television, France).

1978 *"Remembering Jean Gabin,"* a documentary for French television, directed by Nadia Gray. VHS-transfer, courtesy of Facets Home Video, Chicago, Ill.

1998 "Audio Commentary by Film Historian Peter Cowie, on *La Grande illusion*," issued as a Special Feature on The Criterion Collection's U.S. DVD release of, *La Grande illusion*.

1993 *"L'oeil de Vichy" ("Eyes of Vichy")*, a documentary directed and narrated by Claude Chabrol. A co-production of Canal +/FIT/ and TF1.

2001 *"Marlene Dietrich: Her Own Song,"* a Documentary Feature Film Directed by David Riva. A co-production of Turner Classic Movies and MGM/Sony (U.S.), APG, Apollo Media, Media ORB (France), and Gemini Film, GmBH (Germany).

2001 "*Gabin: Gueule d'amour*," a documentary directed by Michael Viotte. A co-production of Arte France/La Compagnie des Indes.

2004 "Bernard Montiel Interviews Florence Moncorge-Gabin, on the occasion of what would have been Jean Gabin's 100th birthday on Channel TMC, France (aired on November 17).

2005 "*Legende, Presentee par Philippe Labro: Jean Gabin.*" A television documentary directed by Jean-Marie Nizan and Robin Kaiser. A production of AIR Productions/PhL Communications for France Channel 3 (aired on November 17).

2005 Robert Osborne discusses the pre-production of *Le Jour se leve*, on Turner Classic Movies (aired on November 18). Peter Bogdanovich's On-Camera Interview about *La Bete humaine,"* issued as a Special Feature on the Criterion Collection DVD release of the film.

2007 David Mamet Discusses Jean Gabin and *Le Jour se leve*, on Turner Classic Movies (aired on March 22).

INTERVIEWS/CORRESPONDENCE:

Laurent Frau (grandson of the French vaudeville comedian, Raymond Dandy);
Florence Moncorge-Gabin (daughter of Jean Gabin);
Mary Moncorge (granddaughter of Jean Gabin);
Mark Gallagher, Ph.D, (Lecturer in Film Studies, University of Nottingham);
Annette Insdorf, Ph.D, (Professor of Film Studies, Columbia University);
Nate Nichols (film historian);
Lawrence Peck (historian/film historian);
David Sterritt (film critic, *Christian Science Monitor*);
Andrew J. Williamson (historian);
Michele Morgan;
Brigitte Bardot;
David Mamet.

MISCELLANEOUS:

JEAN GABIN, IN NEWSREELS: Besides his ninety-five feature films (and two shorts, and handful of television appearances), Jean Gabin also appeared as himself in eighty-seven French newsreels. Many of his appearances in these short films are only a few seconds long (Gabin walking into premiere screenings; Gabin disembarking from planes; Gabin waving at crowds), and I haven't listed them in this book, because these films have already been documented at two very fine on-line sources, and I don't want to duplicate information which you can already find, elsewhere. Check out information on forty-three Gabin newsreel clips at **http://data.gaumont.com**, and forty-five additional clips at **pathethearchives.com**. Most of these clips can be downloaded, for a fee.

HE SINGS, TOO, LADIES!: Check eBay; sellers usually have copies of some of the great Jean Gabin compilation CDs and vinyl albums. There are a lot of them, many of which repeat the same songs.

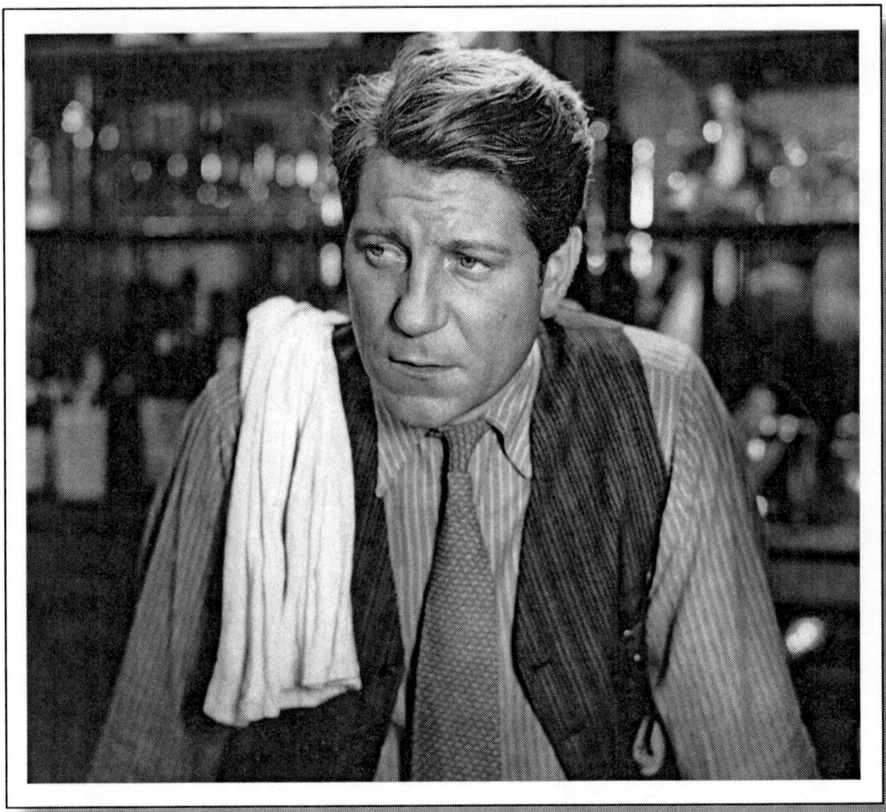

JEAN GABIN: THE DRINK

Now that you've read about Jean Gabin.... *Why not drink him?*
(I don't know if he ever drank this himself, but it sounds pretty tasty...)

"Jean Gabin" Recipe*

INGREDIENTS:

1 1/2 oz dark rum
3/4 oz Calvados © brandy
1 tbsp maple syrup
5 oz hot milk
1 pinch nutmeg

DIRECTIONS:

Heat rum, calvados and syrup in a heat-resistant glass or cup.
Fill with hot milk,
sprinkle with nutmeg, and serve.

* *Courtesy of Website:* www.drinksmixer.com